**The Age of Churchill and Eden, 1940–1957**

**A History of the Conservative Party**

# A History of the Conservative Party

This series, originally to have been published in four volumes, was established by an editorial board consisting of John Barnes, Lord Blake, the late Lord Boyle of Handsworth and Chris Cook. Those volumes marked with an asterisk have already been published. The three remaining volumes, by Richard Shannon (on 1881–1902) and John Ramsden (on 1940–1957 and 1957–1975) will be published in 1995–1996.

* The Foundation of the Conservative Party 1830–1867
Robert Stewart

* The Age of Disraeli, 1868–1881: the Rise of Tory Democracy
Richard Shannon

The Age of Salisbury, 1881–1902
Richard Shannon

* The Age of Balfour and Baldwin 1902–1940
John Ramsden

* The Age of Churchill and Eden, 1940–1957
John Ramsden

The Winds of Change: Macmillan to Heath, 1957–1975
John Ramsden

# The Age of Churchill and Eden, 1940–1957

John Ramsden

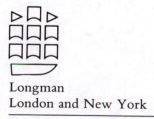

Longman
London and New York

**Longman Group Limited,**
Longman House, Burnt Mill, Harlow,
Essex CM20 2JE, England
*and Associated Companies throughout the world.*

*Published in the United States of America*
*by Longman Publishing, New York*

© Longman Group Limited 1995

First published 1995

ISBN 0 582 504635 CSD

**British Library Cataloguing-in-Publication Data**
A catalogue record for this book is available from the British Library

**Library of Congress Cataloging-in-Publication Data**

Ramsden, John, 1947–
     The age of Churchill and Eden, 1940–1957 / John Ramsden.
         p. cm. — (History of the Conservative Party)
     Includes bibliographical references and index.
     ISBN 0–582–50463–5
         1. Conservative Party (Great Britain)—History.
         2. Great Britain—Politics and government—1936–1945.
         3. Great Britain—Politics and government—1945–1964.
         I. Title.    II. Series.
JN1129.C7R22 1995                                          95–9778
324.24104′09′044—dc20                                         CIP

Set by 5EE in 10/12½ Bembo

Produced by Longman Singapore Publishers (Pte) Ltd.
Printed in Singapore

# Contents

*Acknowledgements*                                                    viii

*Abbreviations used in the text and footnotes*                           x

Introduction                                                           1

# Part I The War Years

| Chapter 1 | Conservatives at war, 1940–45 | 14 |
|---|---|---|
| | *Churchill and the collective leadership* | 14 |
| | *Managing the wartime Party* | 17 |
| | *The crises of 1941–42* | 28 |
| | *Post-war reconstruction* | 32 |
| | *America, India and the Soviet Union* | 34 |
| | *Debating post-war policy* | 38 |
| | *Experiencing the War* | 49 |
| | *Towards 1945* | 52 |
| | | |
| Chapter 2 | 'The Waterloo of the Conservative Party' – the General Election of 1945 | 55 |
| | *The electoral and political truce* | 55 |
| | *Conservatism under attack* | 58 |
| | *War and political change* | 63 |
| | *By-elections and opinion polls* | 66 |
| | *The run-down of the Party organisation* | 69 |
| | *The coming of the Election* | 73 |
| | *The 1945 campaign* | 76 |
| | *The results* | 86 |
| | *Explanations and expectations* | 88 |

# Part II The Fight-back, 1945–51

| | | |
|---|---|---|
| Chapter 3 | The organisational recovery, 1945–51 | 94 |
| | *Entering opposition* | 95 |
| | *The constituency agents* | 103 |
| | *Woolton, membership and money* | 109 |
| | *New departures* | 115 |
| | *Patterns of recovery* | 121 |
| | *The 'Maxwell Fyfe Report'* | 127 |
| | *The scale of recovery* | 136 |
| | | |
| Chapter 4 | Re-stating Conservatism – the Policy Review | 138 |
| | *Demands for a statement of policy* | 139 |
| | *Butler's 'backroom boys'* | 144 |
| | *The Industrial Charter* | 148 |
| | *After 1947* | 158 |
| | *Collectivism versus individualism* | 163 |
| | *Reactive policies: food and housing* | 168 |
| | | |
| Chapter 5 | 'The time of reaping' – winning back power | 177 |
| | *Tactics in parliament* | 177 |
| | *Responding to Labour's legislation* | 184 |
| | *Conservatives and foreign policy* | 194 |
| | *The quest for anti-socialist unity* | 197 |
| | *Local and by-elections* | 206 |
| | *The 1950 General Election* | 212 |
| | *Opposition again, 1950–51* | 218 |
| | *The 1951 General Election* | 226 |

# Part III Promise Postponed, 1951–57

| | | |
|---|---|---|
| Chapter 6 | Churchill's last term, 1951–55 | 234 |
| | *Settling into office* | 234 |
| | *The Churchill team* | 242 |
| | *'The march to freedom'* | 247 |
| | *Housing and industrial relations* | 255 |
| | *International policy* | 260 |
| | *Domestic policies* | 265 |
| | *Getting Churchill out* | 270 |
| | *Eden becomes Prime Minister* | 274 |
| | *The 1955 General Election* | 275 |

Chapter 7    The Eden Government, 1955–57              283
             *Eden as Prime Minister*                 284
             *Eden under attack*                      288
             *The middle class revolt*                294
             *Macmillan at the Treasury*              303
             *Suez – the crisis*                      305
             *Suez – the aftermath*                   315
             *Macmillan succeeds Eden*                320

*Bibliography*                                        329
*Index*                                               340

# Acknowledgements

This volume, and the following volume which will be published shortly, together take the Longman History of the Conservative Party through from the death of Neville Chamberlain to the beginning of the Thatcher period. They have been a long time in the making. Such a project comes to fruition only with the assistance of a very large number of friends and colleagues, and in this case with the assistance of institutions too. The Social Science Research Council, as it then was, made an exceptionally generous grant to allow the employment of a research assistant to collect constituency material that was dispersed all over Great Britain; without that financial assistance, and the remarkable assiduity of Chris Stevens who undertook that task for me, the essential local component in what aims to be a collective biography of a mass organisation would have been impossible. Through Chris Stevens' work, we were able to collect archival material from a sample of a hundred constituencies, balanced by region and social composition, and from all the Party Areas, so that the Party organisation as a whole can now be viewed from London, and Westminster from the provinces, an essential dual perspective. Our visits caused inconvenience to countless Party agents, Central Office Area staff and their secretaries, and I am most grateful for their forbearance. Other scholars have already used this resource and it continues to be available.

A different type of institutional input lay in the decision by the Conservative Party itself, more specifically by Sir Richard Webster and Sir John Taylor, to begin in the early 1970s the deposit of Central Office and National Union papers at the Bodleian Library in Oxford. This has now grown to be one of the largest and most important archives for the understanding of the political life of modern Britain, and I am especially grateful to Alastair Cooke in Central Office, to the Secretary of the 1922 Committee, and to the Government Chief Whip's Office, for granting me access to papers not yet generally available. The unfailing courtesy and helpfulness of Colin Harris and his staff in the Bodleian make work there a positive pleasure, and it is good to see that a new generation of scholars are now making such extensive use of this resource; my many footnote references to the unpublished theses of Harriet Jones and Michael Kandiah acknowledge two special debts in that direction. My own many references to the CPA, indicate how far my work has been underpinned by this Conservative Party Archive.

There are significant additional ranges of material to be derived from the private archives of Party politicians which are now available. I willingly acknowledge the assistance of patient staff in the various Colleges and record offices where these are housed. Several friends committed a good deal of their time to reading versions of the text and to making helpful suggestions; the final text owes much to Stuart Ball, John Barnes, Robert Blake, Michael Fraser, Peter Hennessy, Michael Pinto-Duschinsky and Chris Stevens. Any errors and omissions that remain are entirely my own.

I am most grateful to the following owners of copyright for permission to quote from various manuscript collections: The Avon Trustees (Papers of Sir Anthony Eden, 1st Earl of Avon); Mrs Elizabeth Crookshank (Diary of Harry, 1st Viscount Crookshank); Lady Harvie-Watt (Papers of Sir George Harvie-Watt); Captain J. Headlam and the Durham County Record Office (Papers of Sir Cuthbert Headlam); The Kilmuir Papers Trust and Lady Miranda Cormack (Papers of David Maxwell Fyfe, 1st Earl of Kilmuir); Mr H.P.R. Lloyd and the Carmarthen County Record Office (Papers of J.P.L. Thomas, 1st Viscount Cilcennin); Viscount Margesson (Papers of David, 1st Viscount Margesson); The Earl of Swinton (Papers of the 1st Earl of Swinton); The Master and Fellows of Trinity College, Cambridge (Papers of R.A. Butler, Lord Butler of Saffron Walden); Sir Nicholas Hedworth Williamson (Papers of Patrick Buchan-Hepburn, 1st Lord Hailes); Sir Charles Willink Bart., (Papers of Sir Henry Willink); The Earl of Woolton (Papers of the 1st Earl of Woolton).

Finally, I must thank Queen Mary and Westfield College for allowing me a full year of research leave in which to complete this volume and its successor, a rare privilege in these straitened times, and Corpus Christi College, Oxford, which made accommodation available to me to facilitate extensive work in the Bodleian, and thereby enabled me both to profit from the wise advice of Brian Harrison and to re-live just a little of my youth.

John Ramsden
July 1994.

# Abbreviations used in the text and footnotes

| | |
|---|---|
| ABCA | Army Bureau of Current Affairs |
| Aims | Aims of Industry |
| ACP | Advisory Committee on Policy (from 1950) |
| ACPPE | Advisory Committee on Policy and Political Education (to 1948) |
| AGM | Annual General Meeting |
| BMA | British Medical Association |
| BHL | British Housewives' League |
| CA | Conservative Association |
| *CAJ* | *Conservative Agents' Journal* |
| CBF | Conservative Board of Finance |
| CPA | Conservative Party Archive |
| CPC | Conservative Political Centre |
| CRD | Conservative Research Department |
| ILP | Independent Labour Party |
| LCC | Leader's Consultative Committee (shadow cabinet) |
| MCA | Middle Class Alliance |
| MOI | Ministry of Information |
| *NCP* | *Notes on Current Politics* |
| NHS | National Health Service |
| NJAC | National Joint Advisory Council |
| NUEC | National Union Executive Committee |
| PLDF | People's League for the Defence of Freedom |
| PWPCC | Post-War Problems Central Committee |
| TRG | Tory Reform Group |
| TUC | Trades Union Congress |
| UA | Unionist Association |
| UN | United Nations |
| WEA | Workers' Educational Association |
| YC | Young Conservative |

# Introduction

The Conservative Party entered the Second World War in 1939 full of a confidence that derived both from recent history and from its own self-image. The Party had so dominated British politics at the national level between the wars that it had won parliamentary majorities in five of the seven General Elections. No other party had secured a one-party majority since 1906; but in 1924, 1931 and 1935 Conservative MPs had taken two-thirds of the seats in the House of Commons, while in the two Elections of the 1930s the Party had also secured more than half of the popular vote – the last occasions on which any British party was to do so. There were certainly signs that at the local level this dominance was less secure: the London County Council, had been continuously under Labour control since 1934, several other industrial cities were also Labour dominated, and Labour was practically the only party in some coalfield urban districts. But pockets of urban resistance, even when so strong, did not seriously diminish the overall pattern. Conservative confidence was all the more marked by the folk memory that this inter-war dominance had arisen, phoenix-like, from the Conservative weakness of 1906–14, and in the first era in which Britain was a mass democracy with both manhood suffrage and women voting on equal terms. In this period of popular politics, in which (to quote Baldwin) democracy had arrived 'at the gallop', Conservatives had become used to success; the unpleasant Party crisis that beset Baldwin in opposition between 1929 and 1931 only confirmed just how high Conservatives now set their expectations.

After returning to office in 1931 with Baldwin and Neville Chamberlain yoked in partnership, the Conservatives' collective leadership was never again in danger either from the backbenches or from the press lords. There were battles over particular policies – unemployment pay, India and foreign policy – but these only temporarily disturbed the regime's stability and equipoise. The political generation that had been pitchforked into the Bonar Law/Baldwin Ministry of 1922–23 had steered the Party through the period to 1939, and the older men who had returned from coalitionist exile in 1924 had died, retired or (like Churchill) been sidelined again by 1939. When Chamberlain became Prime Minister in 1937 his Cabinet contained only men who owed their posts to Baldwin or himself. Conformists like R.A. Butler moved steadily up through the ranks, in his case as junior minister at the India and Labour departments and then as Commons spokesman for the Foreign Office, prior to what would have been an easy move into Cabinet in about 1940; rebels like Harold Macmillan still awaited their first post. From 1937, Chamberlain imposed a closer control over the Party and governmental team from Number Ten, to the extent even of using his press officer to brief Fleet Street against ministerial colleagues and of mobilising the Party machine to make life uncomfortable even for very senior rebels in their constituencies. It was a cohesive and assured group that governed Britain in the Summer of 1939.[1]

Nor was it a Party that was closed to new ideas and approaches; the Party machine was embarking on the reconstruction of its youth movement following the Fraser Report; was addressing the weakness of organisation in the big cities; was starting – albeit hesitantly – to tackle the question of candidates' financial contributions to local parties following the creation of the Standing Advisory Committee on Candidates in 1935 and allegations about the purchase of seats by rich candidates made by Ian Harvey in a press release that he issued on New Year's Day 1939; had developed a more active line in domestic reform when Chamberlain became Prime Minister and was in 1939 privately considering for inclusion in its next manifesto some items such as extensions to pensions that are often seen simply as reactions to the Beveridge Report of 1942. Since these developments came to fruition only after 1945, and were mainly carried by a new generation of Tory leaders who had only the haziest knowledge of what had been planned in 1938–39, there has been a tendency to assume that they happened only *because* of the War. But *post bellum* is not *propter bellum*.[2]

Nevertheless, Tory confidence owed as much to intangibles as to lessons of recent events and foreknowledge of future developments. The Party in the 1920s and 1930s set the agenda for domestic politics in Britain to a quite remarkable extent, notably through the considerable communicative skills of Stanley Baldwin. Its chief rival, the Labour Party, had found itself time and again arguing on Tory issues and when in Government found itself judged by a set of supposedly objective standards of behaviour that corresponded closely to the way in which Conservatives behaved when they – more usually – held the seals of office. The adherence to the Tory ranks of significant sections of the old Liberal Party, first as Liberal Unionists, then as Lloyd George Coalitionists and latterly as Liberal Nationals in the National

---

[1] John Ramsden, *The Age of Balfour and Baldwin, 1902–40* [all books cited were published in London unless stated otherwise] (1978); Richard Cockett, *Twilight of Truth: Chamberlain, Appeasement and the Manipulation of the Press* (1989), 85.

[2] John Ramsden, *The Making of Conservative Party Policy. The Conservative Research Department since 1929* (1980), 90–2; John Ramsden, 'A Party for Owners or a Party for Earners? How far did the Conservative Party really change since 1945?' in *Transactions of the Royal Historical Society*, 5th series vol. 37 (1987), 49–63; J.F.S. Ross, *Parliamentary Representation* (1943), 236–8.

Government, enabled the Party to claim to be something more than just another political grouping. Baldwin had in 1924 claimed a 'national' identity for his second premiership and had needed exactly that rallying cry to defend his Government against the General Strike in 1926; the claim to be something more than a political party was tarnished by Tory partisanship in the later 1920s but became even more important in shared government after 1931; for the rest of his career, Baldwin harped back to the crisis of 1931 as 'the acid test of democracy' when patriotic politicians combined to put their country first (hence the wound inflicted when in 1948 Churchill's war memoirs, *The Gathering Storm*, casually noted in an index reference that Baldwin had in 1936 admitted to putting party before country – which of course he had not, when the relevant speech was read in context). In effect, as Ross McKibbin has suggested, the Conservatives managed between the wars to define 'the public interest' in a way that suited them and then to claim it almost as their private preserve. They had an overwhelming predominance in the popular press for most of the inter-war period and also in the influential new medium of newsreel; the newly-arrived BBC was the most conformist of all the media and hardly likely to shatter the Establishment's easy assurance. With all the media sharing their broad approach to what was acceptable politics – at least until the *Daily Mirror* became a serious player in the mass market, and Victor Gollancz and Allen Lane recognised a new book market in radical politics, both of which developments came only late in the 1930s – it was almost impossible for Labour to contest the central position in national life to which the Conservatives assigned themselves.[3]

Chapter 1 below demonstrates how far between 1940 and 1945 this inherent strength was dissipated. Churchill might well have been asked in 1944–45, as the *Spectator* had demanded of Balfour in 1905, 'Varus, Varus, what have you done with my legions?' The collective leadership completely disappeared, to be replaced mainly by a court of favourites around Churchill, some of whom were anathema to the Party even when they used the 'Conservative' label. Churchill very reasonably devoted his entire attention to the War, and the Party occupied the foreground of his thoughts only when it had to be dragooned into the lobbies to show its confidence in his Government; even this could be problematic in 1941–42, but not at other times. Eden, as the only senior Conservative near the top of the political ladder who might have filled the political vacuum, was like Churchill too overburdened by his war responsibilities, and the attempt to give him a wider Party role as Leader of the Commons after 1942 created only the illusion that the problem was being dealt with. As a result of this, while the country and its war machine were being led very ably indeed under Churchill's administration, the Party that sustained the Churchill Government in office was not led at all.[4]

[3] Ross McKibbin, *Ideologies of Class* (Oxford, 1990), 259–93.
[4] Ramsden, *Balfour and Baldwin*, 16.

While Conservative ministers and MPs often fretted under these circumstances, they broadly accepted Churchill's view that the War must come first and that all else, including the Party's interests, must if necessary be sacrificed to that objective. It was for this reason that Conservatives consciously practised a form of self-denial, an abstention from party activity that went well beyond the terms of the wartime political truce, and, in the latter years at least, far beyond the view taken by Labour. In these circumstances, the Conservative Party's structure, finances and organisation virtually withered away, while its opponents continued carefully to tend theirs against the day when they would be needed. So for example, Labour's financial reserves increased steadily in the war years while Tory reserves disappeared; Labour therefore had plenty of money for the 1945 Election and spent twice as much as in 1935, while the Conservatives had available only a fraction of the sum that they had spent on that last pre-war Election. For an active fundraising organisation such as the Conservatives had been in the 1930s, this financial decline was both a disaster in itself and a mirror of the wider decline in activity; at the local level there was hardly any infantry campaign by Tories for the 1945 Election, because there was no infantry; there was no canvassing and no detailed scrutiny of voting from marked registers, which at least explains what has usually seemed to be a great paradox, how the Party could have still thought it had won, even after the votes for a Labour landslide had been cast.[5]

The extent of organisational decline in wartime also gives some advance explanation of the recovery of Party fortunes that took place between 1945 and 1950: even if the superiority of Conservative organisation and electioneering, a factor at every general election in this century *but* 1945, is valued conservatively as worth a mere 2 or 3 per cent of the vote, then the regaining of that organisational edge would on its own account for a third of the Tories' recovery by 1950. A major redistribution of constituencies and simultaneous changes of electoral law in 1948 produced a bonus that explains about another third of the regained seats of 1950. All of this puts both the defeat of 1945 and the subsequent electoral recovery in a very different contextual framework from that in which it is usually viewed.

This last point should not be over-stressed though, for in 1950 the Conservatives only drew level with Labour anyway, when the objective of their post-war recovery was to regain their inter-war hegemony in the nation's political life. Here the war years did more serious damage. The very fact of a prolonged 'People's War', which encouraged both wider aspirations of social betterment and hopes of a more egalitarian society, would have placed Conservative political forces on the defensive, whatever the other circumstances; in both Australia and Canada wartime elections were characterised by a similar swing to the left. The 'public interest' was

[5] Michael Pinto-Duschinsky, *British Political Finance, 1830–1980* (1981), 155–6, 279.

now re-defined in the popular debate, with the active encouragement of the Government's own propaganda machinery; collective action was the order of the day, high expenditure and high taxation were axiomatic, and the defence of individual property rights was easily castigated as mere selfishness at a time when willing sacrifice was needed in order to win the War. It would have taken a major effort to adjust the Conservative Party's political stance to this hurricane of changed attitudes. There certainly was a ferment of political thinking about the future from about 1942, in the Party as in the rest of the country. The Post-War Problems Central Committee (under Butler's guidance), the Tory Reform Group, the Progress Trust, the Imperial Group, and a host of lesser bodies, all sought to seize control of the Party for their own viewpoint. Churchill neither backed any of these attempts to formulate a new policy strategy nor authorised anyone else to do so, and the result was an almost total lack of policy coherence, and no official Party strategy at all. R.A. Butler, who was as close to Party policy activity as anyone, simply did not know in February 1945 what the Party's industrial policy was; a last-minute attempt to devise a Party policy on post-war health care was approved by Conservative ministers but then stopped in its tracks by Churchill and never published.

The final legacy of the War, alongside organisational decline and policy incoherence, was the postponing for six crucial years of all attempts at modernisation. It was a team of old men who faced the country in 1945, locally as well as nationally, and on both the voluntary and the professional wings of the Party there would need to be a handover to a new generation before the recovery could proceed. Talks about changing the financial relationships between constituencies and candidates, a trend under way in the 1930s but with a long way still to go, produced still more active talk in wartime, but little action, for a moribund and bankrupt Party machine could not embark on major practical reforms on that scale. The policy review also threw up a generational conflict, most apparent in both the supporters and the fiercest opponents of the Tory Reform Group. Churchill's instinctive alignment against the Party's young men in 1943–44 – the 'cheeky boys', as he called them – ensured that the Party's rejection of forward-looking ideas would be very visible.

For the 1945 Election then, the Party was unprepared with either a policy or an organisation, and well aware that its profile was not well-suited to the public mood of the time. Many Conservatives were all too conscious of the evidence of their weak position, for example from wartime by-elections, but satisfied from the analogies of 1900 and 1918 that some form of 'khaki' electioneering under the great war leader Churchill would see them safely home with a renewed majority. Since Churchill's hankering for coalition ensured that the type of election to be fought was not clear until a few weeks before the campaign started, they could make no other very active preparations anyway. As Chapter 2 shows, when the contest came, many of Churchill's Tory Ministers despaired of the tactics he chose to fight on, falling back as he did on a negative anti-socialism and on the abuse of his recent Labour team-mates, though, when the scale of defeat was revealed, few were disposed to lay the blame on the Leader. There were three reasons for this generosity to a defeated Leader, in itself rare in Conservative Party history: first, there was abundant evidence that other factors had contributed to the defeat, such as the low reputation of pre-war Conservatism, for which Churchill could not directly be blamed; secondly, there is no doubt that rank-and-file Conservatives in the constituencies did feel that gratitude to Churchill for his war service which the country seemed so conspicuously to lack; they would hardly have stood for any move to blame Churchill for the Party's defeat in order to remove him from command; thirdly, the Party's leaders in the main expected that the seventy-year old Churchill would have no stomach for the hard grind of opposition and would therefore bow out of his own accord. They could scarcely have been more wrong, for the next decade was to be a time in which successive attempts were made to prise Churchill out of the Leadership, to which he clung on with all his considerable tenacity whenever challenged.

The Election defeat did though change the balance of management in the Party. In effect, Conservatives regained control of their Party from Churchill on the morrow of defeat; such Churchillian confidants as Beaverbrook were never again to get their hands on the levers that operated the Party machine, and whenever Churchill himself tried to put trusted friends in key Party positions up to 1955 his efforts were faced down. Orthodox Conservatives like Eden, Butler, Stuart and Buchan-Hepburn therefore played the key roles in the recovery years, and not Churchill supporters like Lyttelton, Bracken, Macmillan or Sandys, while Churchill himself was present too intermittently to exercise detailed control in person. The one key appointment that on the face of it conformed to Churchill's desire to avoid employing those who had pursued conventional Party careers was that of Woolton as Party Chairman in 1946, for Woolton was a non-party minister until 1945, and had probably not been anyone's first choice for the post. In the event, Woolton at Central Office achieved a popularity with Party members that rivalled even Churchill's own (and made the great man more than a little jealous) and Woolton soon became a fierce and effective protector of the Party's interests against such Churchillian buccaneering as attempts to make electoral pacts with his Liberal friends. From 1945 to 1955, the Leader's role in purely Party matters was confined largely to the ceremonial – a role not to be underestimated in his capacity to inspire and enthuse – while 'the bucket-shop side of the business' (as Churchill had earlier put it in reference to the Treasury) was put into commission and run collectively by the rest of the front bench. Chapter 3 describes this organisational recovery, which was both less original and less substantial, compared to pre-war patterns, than has often been claimed.

The same was at least half true of the policy review between 1945 and 1951.

Churchill was convinced that it was tactically mistaken to become committed to any policies in detail while in opposition; any pledge would alienate support in one quarter while attracting it in another, and Conservative pledges would also complicate his wish to unite all anti-socialists behind his banner, so that he could return to office as more than just a party leader. His own chosen strategy, based on a serious underestimate of the Attlee team's capacity to govern effectively, was to allow Labour to make itself so unpopular that the country would turn to anti-socialism in despair. Lord Cranborne was not the only Conservative leader who pointed out that they were being reduced to hoping for economic disasters that were actually against the national interest in order for Churchill's strategy to succeed, and that even then an incoming Churchill Government would inherit a terrible legacy. All this was beyond the Party's control, but was anyway invalidated by the fact that the Party would simply not stand for the combination of masterly inactivity and generalised criticism which was the Churchillian recipe. The 1946 Blackpool Party Conference enforced a change of plan that Churchill's frontbench colleagues thoroughly welcomed. Thereafter, through the *Industrial Charter* of 1947, through a range of further 'charters' in 1948–49, and the full-scale policy-making in detail that took place in 1949, the 1940 halt to official policy-making was at last overcome. As the 1945 Parliament drew to a close, the Party's position and the Churchill position converged, for, with the possibility of an early return to government, Churchill was not prepared to have even the detailed wording of documents passed without stamping the texts both with his own input and his inimitable style.

It is no longer conventional to see this policy review as leading the Conservatives into a consensus of 'Butskellism', whereby it no longer mattered which Party governed in the early 1950s since the policy would be much the same. Such an analysis is anyway immensely complicated by the fact that Labour and Conservative parties had cooperated in office between 1940 and 1945, so that many post-war plans devised by joint ministerial groups continued to bear the imprint of their common origin; Labour also had in these years a *party* policy that was different from that of the Government, for under their party's rules, then as now, policy was decided by Conference (whatever a Labour administration might actually do); the Conservatives on the other hand, having no concept of an official Party policy other than in the actions of Tory ministers, and having in Churchill a Leader who banned any official policy statements that went beyond published coalition plans, even for by-election candidates struggling to answer the public's questions, had by 1945 established no policy identity that was separate from the all-party views of the Government. Since policy played little part in the Conservatives' 1945 campaign either, it is extraordinarily difficult to say what Conservative policy actually was when the post-war review started. In a number of areas, in industrial policy, for example, the plans that came out in 1947 related fairly closely to those proposed by Conservatives in wartime, with the crucial difference that from 1947 these were officially endorsed by both the Conference and the Leader, whereas in 1944–45 even the publications of the Post-War Problems Central Committee, though officially set up by the National Union and incorporating representation from MPs and peers, had received no *imprimatur* either from Churchill or from any representative Party gathering. In many ways then, the content of policy remained similar, but the unofficial became official, and it is no accident that the critical few months of the entire exercise came between March and October 1947, after the *Industrial Charter* had been drafted and while it was being 'sold' to the Party prior to its endorsement. This process is examined in Chapter 4.

Having stressed these continuities, it is only right to add two riders. First that, in order to counteract the widespread view that in 1945 Conservatism had been rejected by the electorate, the novelty element in the post-1947 policies was often over-stressed by the Party. It was necessary to seem to have new policies, especially where these were actually developments from wartime or pre-war models. Secondly, there were many policy areas in which decisions were made, and had to be made, in a reactive way, as both world events and Labour legislation impinged on the weekly debate in parliament. The increasingly anti-communist and anti-Russian tone of the Party's rhetoric, one of the few areas in which the Party caught up with Churchill rather than the other way round, is a case in point. This reactive strand in policy and strategy, together with the interim campaigns in local government and by-elections in which it was tested out, is analysed in Chapter 5.

With these provisos then, how far had Conservative and Labour policies converged by 1951? The answer depends, overwhelmingly, on which policies are being considered. In foreign affairs and defence there had been little to choose between the parties' actual policies even in 1945, despite Labour's exploitation of the Russian issue at the Election. It was, after all, a parliamentary joke in 1945 that when Bevin first answered questions as Foreign Secretary the word went round that Anthony Eden had put on weight. The transition from Bevin back to Eden via Morrison in 1950–51 was equally untroubled; in overseas affairs there was at least as much dissent within parties as between their frontbenchers, but not much even of that. On the methods of economic policy, which was the origin of *The Economist*'s invention of 'Mr. Butskell', there was again some convergence behind Keynesian methods, though it was the refusal of the Churchill Cabinet to back Butler's 'Robot' scheme for managing foreign exchange that kept that convergence in being, not the natural affinity of Butler for Gaitskell's methods at the Exchequer; Gaitskell was horrified at the idea of floating the pound, which Butler wanted to adopt. In industrial policy, the Conservatives had by 1951 shifted ground towards a more collectivist approach since 1939, if not so clearly since 1944–45, but it must be remembered that the ground had already been shifting before the War in this case; it was the Baldwin and Chamberlain Conservatives who helped to shape the 'Morrisonian' public corporation in such inter-war experiments as Imperial Airways, and the nationalisation of coal royalties indicated that even such a totem of free enterprise as the coal industry was not safe from Chamberlain's pragmatic interventionism. The 1940s did witness a further move towards an enlarged public sector, at least at a faster rate than Chamberlain would have envisaged or approved of, but the decade was also marked in the Steel debates by the first drawing of a *ne plus ultra* line beyond which the Conservative Party would not go. Road transport, steel and broadcasting were to be the contested no man's land between the public and private sectors for the next generation, and it was the Tories who had chosen the battleground; the decision to build motorways in the 1950s and the Beeching railway plan in the 1960s both had as much to do with that debate as a scheme to sell off the railways might have had. Whether this marked a zone of serious conflict that denied the existence of consensus, or merely a bogus form of warfare that concealed how much else was agreed, is largely a matter for the taste of the interpreter. It is notable though that when in the 1960s, the Conservatives finally (or so it seemed) conceded that steel might remain in the public sector, this opened the flood-gates for a new Labour agenda of industries for public ownership. The sheer ferocity of the steel debates of 1949–53, as the industry was first nationalised and then successfully sold back to the private sector, rather belies the idea of it being only a mock-contest, and in more general terms the private correspondence of Conservative leaders and MPs during the Attlee Government would suggest that they saw a real divide between the parties over public ownership and not just a matter of emphasis. On industrial relations there was indeed what a recent historian has called 'an industrial Butskellism', but on the Conservative side it owed more to fear than to conviction; Churchill's determination to avoid strikes at all costs was more pronounced than Attlee's, and this certainly led to unexpectedly harmonious relations with the trades unions, but its effect on inflation was less popular with the Party's supporters; solving the equation between industrial harmony and inflation was a problem bequeathed to the next generation of Tory MPs. Finally, on social policy, as Harriet Jones has shown, the Conservative response to Aneurin Bevan's legislation was always sharply differentiated from Labour policy; on both financial and ideological grounds the Conservatives approached the running of the NHS in a different way from Labour. These divergences of policy were to an extent disguised by the clear perception that the NHS was proving extremely popular with its customers and that the Party must not therefore run the risk of seeming to be hostile to it in any way. Where policy diverged, language was often misleadingly guarded.[6]

In the other areas of domestic policy, the Conservatives managed to differentiate themselves more clearly. As the climate of post-war opinion made the public increasingly critical of rationing and other manifestations of wartime

---

[6] Harriet Jones, 'The Conservative Party and Social Policy, 1942–1955', unpublished PhD thesis, University of London, 1992, 387–8.

controls, the terms of trade in the political debate moved in the Conservatives direction, into issues with which they felt more comfortable. It was relatively straightforward for Conservatives who favoured a less interventionist state to exploit the continuation of controls that were now 'unnecessary' and to make political capital out of the promise to remove them when returned to office; in turn, the Tory proclamation that such controls were no longer necessary must have contributed significantly to the public's demand for liberty; 'Set the People Free!' was both a natural Conservative stance and a popular one. This in itself concealed though a cleavage among Conservatives about the extent to which they really intended to roll back the state. The experience in office of the Churchill Government, described in Chapter 6, ensured that that question would be further postponed, as it was to be, in the event, until 1957–58. As it took time to denationalise a few industries, the Government did not yet have to decide how far to go. After the Korean War ended, it was possible to speed up the ending of controls, to reduce expenditure on defence and administration of a war economy, and thereby both to reduce taxes and raise social spending, so that it was once again unnecessary to fix new boundaries for state action. In a broader sense, the Churchill Government was marking time before the post-war generation took over in force and this also delayed the moment when the final course was set in post-war Conservative political economy. The Party's triumph in the 1955 General Election, which was the moment – not 1950 or 1951 – when the ghost of 1945 was finally laid, seemed to indicate clearly enough the success of the strategy pursued so far. The beginning of Tory affluence, especially in the southern half of Great Britain, Macmillan's housing policy, income tax reductions, and the explicit championing of the interests of the consumer in the creation of ITV, were all links back to the practice of Tory ministers in the 1930s. The continuities in policy delivery were striking.

Finally, the Eden Government, described in Chapter 7, proved to be a false dawn, first because the manner in which the Government was run and the disharmonious nature of Eden's team militated against the taking of long-term strategic policy decisions anyway; it was a reactive Government, the first in which the ability of Keynesian management methods to deliver risk-free, permanent affluence became suspect, so that Conservative supporters, for the first time since 1951, began to accuse their own Government of paying insufficient attention to their sectional interests; this was a pointer to things to come. And secondly, a critical decision was finally taken about Britain's future role in the world, but only because the failure of Eden's policy at Suez forced an unwilling Party and Cabinet to recognise the reality of British weakness on the world stage and the extent of dependence on the USA. The implications of this shocking discovery were still to be worked through when Eden fell in January 1957.

By the mid-1950s, the Party had recovered the confidence and the expectation of its own success that once again made it difficult to lead. Its organisation, membership and finances were unprecedentedly healthy, and the 1955 Election had shown how broadly based its recovery had been across the regions of England, the parts of the United Kingdom and the various sectors of society; the 'Maxwell Fyfe reforms' of 1949 were generally perceived to have achieved a broadening of the social base of the parliamentary party, typified by the talented 'Class of 1950' and the 'premier cru of that vintage', the One Nation Group; the broad political balance of post-war politics had been set. It was once again fashionable in university and intellectual circles to vote Conservative, and there was every reason to feel that the damage done to the Party by the War and by Churchill's idiosyncratic leadership was past. The first 'stop-go' crisis in 1955–56 indicated that the major new challenge would now be to modernise Britain's economy, so that the affluence to which Tory voters had now become accustomed could continue to be delivered in increasingly adverse economic circumstances. That too was a problem that Churchill and Eden bequeathed to their successors.

**Part I**

---

# The War Years

On the present form I have no doubt that the present Conservative Party, even if led by Mr. Churchill, will not accomplish enough of itself to govern again, unless the alternatives commit suicide . . . If any Tory wants shaking, go and see the new Ronnie Waldman film 'Guess What?' and hear what happens when Baldwin appears in the Coronation procession.

(from Tom Harrisson, 'Who'll Win?', *Political Quarterly*, January 1944)

I suppose that if one views the election from a historical standpoint one should not have been surprised at the outcome. Mr. Churchill joins the Elder Pitt and LL.G. as a great war minister who has been dispensed with as soon as the war situation permits and British politics reverts to colourless domesticity. I think the election is a vote for the people who are least likely to involve us in foreign adventures, or bring us up against Russia . . . It is a vote for domestic security; it results from the swing of the pendulum & the desire for a change and it is a vote against the 'brigands'.

(Cuthbert Alport to R.A. Butler, 29 July 1945)

**Chapter 1**

# Conservatives at war, 1940–45

By the time that Churchill so improbably replaced Chamberlain as Conservative Party Leader in October 1940, the strong position that the Party enjoyed on the declaration of war in 1939 had already changed beyond recognition. The events of the Summer of 1940 – the disastrous campaigns in Norway and Western Europe, the unpreparedness of the armed forces even after eight months of Phoney War, the crisis that brought about the formation of a real National Government under Churchill, the narrow survival in the Battle of Britain, and the *Guilty Men* attack on pre-war Conservatives in general and appeasers in particular – cumulatively transformed the political landscape between April and October. These factors were examined in the final pages of the previous volume in this series. After October, the corrosive influence of the War on Tory fortunes gathered pace.[1]

## Churchill and the collective leadership

Nature and the political arts first combined to destroy the collective Party leadership. Chamberlain himself died; Halifax was sent as ambassador to the United States and Hoare to Spain; Swinton (who had been out of office since 1938, but was still only fifty-six) had another non-political post in national security and later returned to government only in West Africa; Simon went to the Lords as Lord Chancellor. These arrangements removed from the central political scene the only Tory politicians of stature sufficient to challenge Churchill, or even to argue with him. The cohesive, loyalist leadership was wrecked beyond reconstruction, and Churchill had in any case other things to do than to worry about the fortunes of pre-war Tories who had treated him with scant courtesy in the 1930s.

By early 1941, the only Chamberlainite loyalist in the War Cabinet was Sir Kingsley Wood (until his own removal in 1942, though he remained in the Government until his death in 1943); the only other Conservatives at all in the War Cabinet were Eden (who had resigned in 1938), Beaverbrook (who had hated everything to do with Baldwin and Chamberlain, and now wrought his revenge by vindictively requisitioning Baldwin's ornamental

---

[1] John Ramsden, *The Age of Balfour and Baldwin, 1902–1940* (1978), 369–76.

gates for war salvage), and Oliver Lyttelton (who held no office at all until
Churchill appointed him in 1940); meanwhile, room was found for all of
Labour's senior men, Attlee, Morrison, Bevin, and Cripps, each of whom
emerged from the war as a proven administrator, competent broadcaster
and household name. The rest of the team at the top was made up of Sir
John Anderson (a former civil servant) and Lord Woolton (a businessman),
neither of whom belonged to any party. R.A. Butler in 1942 noted the
Conservative disaffection about this after even Wood was demoted: 'it was
said that there was now no orthodox Conservative in the War Cabinet.
Churchill was not orthodox; Eden was not liked; Anderson had never called
himelf a Tory; Lyttelton nobody knew & he was regarded as a city shark.'
A.J.P. Taylor later concluded that 'there was not a single reliable Conservative
in the Cabinet. It is not surprising that the Conservatives in the House of
Commons became restive.' Their hostility to maverick Conservatives could
be as great as hostility to Labour ministers; in July 1941 the 1922 Committee
even-handedly deplored the promotions of Ernest Thurtle (an 'atheist' as
well as a socialist), Duff Cooper ('a dangerous one') and Duncan Sandys,
Churchill's son–in–law.[2]

Lower down, the position was more mixed: Churchill did provide ministerial
posts for Conservative loyalists like Robert Hudson, R.A. Butler and
David Margesson, but they were matched by such rebels and mavericks
as Leo Amery, Brendan Bracken and Harold Macmillan among Conservative
ministers, and by another host of Labour MPs and independents. A snapshot
picture of the Churchill Government at mid-term, at the end of 1942,
demonstrates the transformation. Although Conservative MPs still made up
two-thirds of the Commons, they had only four seats in the War Cabinet (none
by then held by a Chamberlainite) alongside four Labour and two non-party
men. In the senior ministerial team as a whole, there were twenty-five
Conservatives out of forty but only five of these had sat in the peacetime
Chamberlain Cabinet, and two even of these five had chosen to resign in
1938. In the Government as a whole only the whips (ten Conservatives out
of thirteen) reflected the Tory predominance in both Houses. The suspension
of traditional Conservative politics was equally marked by the lack of peers
in the Government; only six of the twenty-eight government departments
even had a ministerial spokesman in the Lords, and of these six, one was not
a Conservative and at least two others had been critics of the Party hierarchy
before 1939. The route to preferment for Conservatives under Churchill then
was not a record of conformity but one of at least scepticism. Conversely,
Attlee was careful to ensure that the Labour portfolios were distributed on
conventional lines. The consequence of this approach to ministerial patronage

---

[2] Kevin Jefferys (ed.), *Labour and the Wartime Coalition, from the Diaries of James Chuter
Ede, 1941–1945*, (1987), 57; A.J.P. Taylor, '1932–1945', in *Coalitions in British Politics*, ed.
David Butler (1978), 90; Minutes of the 1922 Committee [hereafter 1922 Cttee.], 23 July
1941, CPA.

came in 1945 when Labour and the Liberals left office. Churchill had to create a Caretaker Government to run the country until the post-war General Election. The 1945 Churchill Ministry had sixteen Cabinet ministers and with an average age of fifty-seven was hardly a young team; four Cabinet Ministers were not Conservatives and about another eight, including Churchill himself, could not be considered Conservative loyalists. Of the sixteen, only four had had the sort of careers that would have secured preferment before 1939, and only one had been in Chamberlain's Cabinet when war broke out, less than six years earlier. There is one further significant characteristic of Churchill's ministerial patronage: whereas the whole drift of the Party's character and style, set by its collective leadership since Law became Leader in 1911, had been away from patrician, service and landed families and towards urban, provincial industry, in 1940 Churchill's team inaugurated a quarter-century move back in the reverse direction. In place of the thirty-year succession of Law, Chamberlain, Baldwin and Chamberlain – all owing their fortunes to the metal and engineering industries and rooted in Glasgow and the West Midlands – came the succession of a Churchill born at Blenheim, Eden from the Durham squirearchy, Macmillan related to the Devonshires, and the fourteenth Earl of Home. Oliver Lyttelton noted of the Churchill Cabinet of 1945 that 'tradition it certainly had':

> The Prime Minister was the son of a Chancellor of the Exchequer, Anthony Eden the son of a Governor-General and Viceroy of India [sic] . . . ; Lord Salisbury the son of a distinguished Minister and grandson of a Prime Minister; Lord Rosebery and Dick Law were both sons of a Prime Minister; James Stuart a descendant of James V of Scotland; Oliver Stanley the son of a Minister and descended from a Prime Minister; 'Rab' Butler the son of one of the most distinguished Colonial Governors; Harold Macmillan['s] . . . father-in-law had been a Minister and Governor-General of Canada; I was the son of a Secretary of State for the Colonies.[3]

Churchill's appointments were due as much to the need for effectiveness in office as to the protection of his personal position and the settling of old scores, but the actual allocation of portfolios certainly did the Conservative Party a further disservice. Labour Ministers held key posts on the home front – Morrison at the Home Office, or Bevin as Minister of Labour for example – and were able considerably to enhance their reputations and their familiarity to the public. R. A. Butler, able to capitalise on the unexpected prominence of the Board of Education in 1944, was a rare Tory who had similar opportunities – and he seized those opportunities against Churchill's advice. Most newly-promoted Conservatives like Macmillan were in war posts which left them almost invisible to the electorate. Even on the military

---

[3] Oliver Lyttelton, Viscount Chandos, *The Memoirs of Lord Chandos* (1962), 325; Lyttelton was presumably thinking of Eden's distant relative Lord Auckland who died in 1849, for Eden's actual father was an eccentric County Durham squire, but his basic point is valid.

front, where victory could have been a great boost to political careers, the only Conservative with a high profile was Churchill himself: during the second, victorious half of the war, the Air Ministry, the Admiralty and the War Office were held respectively by Liberal, Labour and non-party ministers.[4]

## Managing the wartime Party

It is not surprising then that Churchill's wartime relations with the Conservative Party were stormy. He had had reservations about taking on the Party Leadership in October 1940, reservations strengthened by Clementine Churchill who remained strongly Liberal in outlook. Back in May 1940, Churchill had begged Chamberlain to remain Party Leader when Churchill became Prime Minister: 'as Prime Minister of a National Government, formed on the widest basis, and comprising the three Parties, I feel that it would be better for me not to undertake the leadership of any one Political Party'. When Chamberlain's declining health demanded a new Leader in October, Churchill was urged to take the post and presumably did not dare allow it to go to a potential rival, which Chamberlain had not been. The Tory whip George Harvie-Watt, shortly to become Churchill's own PPS, was one of the persuaders: 'I said it would be fatal if he did not lead the Conservative Party . . . as the bulk of the party was anxious that he should be leader now we were at war.' Churchill's suspicions about the hostility of the Party to him (hardly justified since his inspirational role in the nation's war effort in the Summer of 1940 anyway) were brushed aside:

> I said it was only a small section of the party that took that line and the mass of the party was with him. My strongest argument . . . was that it was essential for the PM to have his own party – a strong one with allies attracted from the main groups, and especially from the Opposition parties. But essentially he must have a majority and I was sure that this majority could only come from the Conservative Party.

Churchill can hardly have forgotten the fate of Lloyd George after 1918, in Beaverbrook's famous phrase 'a Prime Minister without a Party', and in any case others reminded him of the comparison. After 1940, Churchill remained unsure as to whether he had made the right decision and others were ready to reinforce the doubt; Halifax described his assumption of the leadership as a mistake in 1943, and Bevin told Churchill the same thing to his face in 1945. Churchill himself continued to wonder whether he was hated by the majority of Conservatives because of his past, and occasionally the behaviour of Tory MPs gave credence to this; Jim Thomas, a Conservative junior minister, noted in 1942 that the 1922 Committee 'had decided to entertain Churchill to lunch

---

[4] D.E. Butler and G. Butler, *British Political Facts, 1900–1986* (1986), 26–31.

at 11/- a head although more than half of them didn't like him or his principal supporters in the Govt.'[5]

The speech given by Churchill at the meeting at which he was elected Leader can have done little to assuage initial Tory doubts. Knowing that the Party needed him, and his newly-enhanced prestige, even more than he needed the Party, he offered no apologies for past deeds and only made the flimsiest claim to Conservative principles. His secretary John Colville noted that in 'his apologia for Conservatism', he told the assembled MPs that all parties would need to make sacrifices in the national interest and 'the Conservative Party will not allow any party to excel it in the sacrifice of party interests and party feelings'. Not a reassuring message.[6]

It is hardly surprising that after this start Tory partisans continued to wonder about Churchill's position. In March 1942 a journalist at lunch with both the outgoing and the incoming Conservative Party Chairmen heard them agree that 'Winston is a difficult leader, and is not a Conservative at all, or even, perhaps, by normal standards, a statesman – being a creature of "Palace" favourites, of moods and whims and overriding egotism under his charm and geniality. Dugdale is fearful of what Max Beaverbrook may do. Him he described as a man utterly and completely untrustworthy.' In December 1944, the Conservative Ministers gave Churchill a presentation for his seventieth birthday; Harry Crookshank noted that 'he made a little speech, [saying] that he had always stood for the institutions (no one muttered House of Lords, 1910) & Liberty'. When in the same year Churchill made some graceful remarks about the French revolutionary tradition to mark De Gaulle's return in triumph to Paris, it was seized on by his critics; Rab Butler agreed with his Labour junior minister that all this showed that Churchill was still a Liberal, and added that 'Mrs. Churchill was aggressively, even offensively, a Liberal. If he dined with the Spanish Ambassador she always telephoned to know what he was doing in such company.' Asked by Woolton in 1944 'whether the PM was really a Conservative', Butler gave his 'view that the PM's fundamental idea of politics was a mixture of old Liberal doctrines of cheap food and free trade, combined with the Tory Democracy of his father.'[7]

In any case old antagonisms refused to die, and distrust came from both sides, from the Churchill side a deep sensitivity to the continued existence of 'Municheers' in the Tory ranks, from old loyalists that distrust of Churchill's 'cronies' epitomised by Dugdale's view of Beaverbrook quoted above. As a Churchill man, Harold Nicolson noted after the disastrous Malayan campaign

5  Martin Gilbert, *Finest Hour, Winston S. Churchill, 1939–1941* (1983), 347, 829, 835–7, 1003; Ben Pimlott (ed.), *The Second World War Diary of Hugh Dalton, 1940–45* (1986), 640; Jefferys, *Chuter Ede*, 63, 213.
6  Ramsden, *Balfour and Baldwin*, 375; John Colville, *The Fringes of Power, Downing Street Diaries, 1939–1955* (1985), 259.
7  Paul Addison, *Churchill on the Home Front, 1900–1955* (1992), 361; Crookshank diary, 13 Dec. 1944, Crookshank MSS; Jefferys, *Chuter Ede*, 189; Harriet Jones, 'The Conservative Party and Social Policy, 1942–1955', unpublished PhD thesis, University of London, 1992, 59.

of 1941 that 'all the good Tories are either in office or serving in the forces, and the dregs stink'; a Tory MP described this crisis as one in which 'the Municheers had raised the trouble in the House' but the resulting re-shuffle had been a victory for the 'anti-Municheers'. Angus Calder later described the 1942 political crisis as one in which 'the ghost of Neville Chamberlain was still master of the Commons'. Indeed, as the war crisis deepened in 1942, 'Chips' Channon noted that Churchill's strength relied on the fact that there was no serious alternative; 'if only Mr. Chamberlain was alive. Many a member who voted against him would now willingly withdraw his vote.' The Churchillian contempt for such critics was well known; a senior backbencher told the Chief Whip in 1942 that 'you yourself are well aware of what the PM thinks of the Tory rump; he may not say so himself, but R[andolph] C[hurchill] and B[rendan] B[racken] and his other satellites are not so careful of their tongues.'[8]

Churchill did not help matters by his unapproachability, due for the most part to the time taken up by the War, but resented nevertheless. When approached he was not famous for listening – Amery reported a meeting of Conservative Ministers in 1944 which was treated to 'a brisk and interesting monologue'. Others were less happy about such treatment: when Crookshank encountered it in March 1944, he noted angrily in his diary that 'Winston is becoming a garrulous and bibulous old man – the torrent of talk is fantastic & no one interferes'. They were made the more unhappy by the common knowledge of Churchill's actual dependence for advice on a few close friends, none of them popular with Tories: Bracken, Beaverbrook and Cherwell. Beaverbrook explained to Churchill's doctor in 1942 that 'the Prime Minister, Brendan and I met most evenings. We settled most things.' Earlier in the War, Churchill had been said to rely heavily on Sir Kingsley Wood precisely because he had in him a man who knew the Conservative partisans and what they would stand for; even that was not uncontentious, for Eden could not stand Wood. In February 1945, the Chief Whip's civil service advisers were urging the setting up of 'a really effective small unofficial committee of Conservative ministers whose duty it would be to examine legislative projects from a political point of view', for 'the late Sir Kingsley Wood used to keep an eye on these matters' and they were now being neglected; but the formal recommendation from James Stuart went to Churchill at the end of April when the coalition only had a month to go anyway.[9]

8  Nigel Nicolson (ed.), *The War Years, The Diaries and Letters of Harold Nicolson, 1939–1945* (1967), 198; Kevin Jefferys, *The Churchill Coalition and Wartime Politics, 1940–1945* (Manchester, 1991), 93, 97, 104; Philip Goodhart, *The 1922, the Story of the 1922 Committee* (1973), 124.

9  John Barnes and David Nicholson (eds), *The Empire at Bay: The Leo Amery Diaries, 1929–1945* (1988), 883; Crookshank diary, 1 March 1944, Crookshank MSS; Lord Moran, *Winston Churchill, The Struggle for Survival, 1940–1965* (Sphere edn, 1966), 95; John Harvey (ed.), *The Diplomatic Diaries of Oliver Harvey, 1941–1945* (1978), 139; Charles Harris to James Stuart, 24 Feb. 1945 and Stuart to Churchill, 27 Apr. 1945, Whip's papers, 'Coalition, miscellaneous', CPA.

After Wood moved from the inner group of trusted advisers in 1942, Beaverbrook was Churchill's closest adviser, and this brought even heavier criticism; when Beaverbrook was campaigning for a second front to aid Russia, his rhetoric was perfectly calculated to wound Tory susceptibilities; in April 1942, the 1922 Committee noted a Beaverbrook speech in the USA, 'in which he said that Communism had produced the best generals and the best fighting machine'. Channon noted in 1943 that 'there is serious unrest among the Conservatives at the growing influence and power of Beaverbrook; it is said that the new triumvirate of Bracken, Cherwell and Beaverbrook rule the country when the PM is abroad, and dominate and fascinate him when he is at home'. The problem was exacerbated by Beaverbrook's own failure to grasp how others saw him and his mistaken belief that he could be the Conservative channel to Churchill, while acknowleding that he was only 'a Conservative, but not of the Conservative Party'. Even the Labour Party could see how nonsensical this was. Hugh Dalton noted in 1944 that Beaverbrook 'always talks as though he were deeply embedded in the Tory Party machine, whereas in fact he is deeply distrusted by many of them and occupies a very detached position, exercising influence only through the PM on the one hand and his own press on the other'. Attlee was equally dismissive in writing to Churchill a few months later about delays in decision-making: 'the excuse is given that in [Beaverbrook] you have the mind of the Conservative Party. With some knowledge of opinion in the Conservative Party in the House as expressed to me . . . I suggest that this view would be indignantly repudiated by the vast majority.' Churchill replied loftily that 'you may be sure that I shall always endeavour to profit by your counsels', and was equally unmoved when Beaverbrook came under attack from nearer home, replying to Eden over the dinner table, 'Don't underrate Max. He is one of the most remarkable men, with all his faults, I've met in my long journey through this world.'[10]

The difficulty was heightened by criticism that Churchill's offhand method of conducting political business through unelected advisers was not only unrepresentative but also inefficient, a general impression that was dangerous to the regime only when the War went badly in 1941–42. A few examples must suffice. In 1943, Churchill was suddenly and briefly interested in the housing crisis brought on by the War and decided to get it solved while on one of his overseas trips: 'I have asked the Beaver, Brendan and Portal to prepare a plan by the time I get back.' Little came of this initiative, which ignored normal departmental channels and past practice in a field where pre-war Governments had been extremely successful. The same casually-urgent, appearance-of-'Action this Day', approach can be detected in the way in which individual appointments were made, neatly illustrated by the career

[10] 1922 Cttee., 29 Apr. 1942; Robert Rhodes James (ed.), Chips, The Diaries of Sir Henry Channon (1967), 380; Pimlott, Dalton War Diaries, 797; A.J.P. Taylor, Beaverbrook (1972), 555; Addison, Churchill, 237; Moran, Struggle, 260.

of Oliver Lyttelton. As a businessman of drive and experience he had been recruited to be Controller of Metals early in the War, but when Churchill moved to Number Ten he summoned Lyttelton, whom he had first met in the trenches in 1916, and 'greeted me smilingly. "I want you to stand for Parliament. I am now Leader of the Tory Party and I must have more old faces in the ranks, people I know and who know me".' After an interview with the Party Vice Chairman for candidates in the midst of an air raid, which established only that Lyttelton was neither a divorcee nor a bankrupt, various constituencies were mentioned. Churchill then offered him the War Office, only to withdraw the offer and suggest instead the Board of Trade, to which Lyttelton was duly appointed. The ever-helpful Chips Channon volunteered to give up Southend in return for a peerage, but this proved unnecessary; Lord Wolmer, already in the Government, was promoted to the House of Lords before his father died, and Lyttelton got Aldershot instead. He therefore joined 'the select club of those who made their maiden speeches from the Front Bench' – not all that select in fact since it included in 1940 alone four ministers in the Commons and three in the Lords. After nine months at Trade, he was shipped off to be Minister in the Middle East with a seat in the War Cabinet (which he could never attend since he was thousands of miles away, but the fact of his membership nonetheless caused consternation to the Foreign Office), and summoned home nine months later to take the Exchequer. On his return, Churchill told him that he had changed his mind; Sir John Anderson wanted to be Chancellor and he could not bear to disappoint him – a remarkable order of priorities when it is remembered that Anderson was non-party and Lyttelton a Conservative. Instead Lyttelton went to the Ministry of Production. Lyttelton was offered nine governmental posts by Churchill during the War, only three of which ever materialised. Other appointments were sometimes made in a similarly offhand way; it was the Chief Whip and not the Prime Minister who met and sacked the Secretary of State for War in 1942, and when Ernest Brown was moved from Minister of Health to Chancellor of the Duchy, with practically no responsibility and only half the salary, again he had no meeting with the Prime Minister.[11]

Of course, peacetime niceties could not be observed during a national struggle for survival, and no doubt some similarly casual appointments have been made under most governments, but surely not so continuously and with so little regard for appearance? This owed a great deal to the lack of any normal procedure or even of normal attitudes to party management. As Paul Addison has pointed out, between 1940 and 1945 the Conservative Party actually had no leader in the usual sense of the term. Nobody in authority regarded it as his duty to protect its interests as a central objective, to ensure that it was properly consulted, to devote time and energy to keeping

---

[11]  Chandos, *Memoirs*, 188, 192, 208, 317; Rhodes James, *Chips*, 271; Churchill to Margesson, 21 Feb. 1942, Margesson MSS; Willink unpublished autobiography, 78, Willink MSS.

it united, and to look to its future. Bonar Law had done all these things under equally trying circumstances between 1914 and 1918; Churchill never even seriously attempted the task until after his 1945 defeat. In March 1942, Cuthbert Headlam asked 'if our so called Conservative leaders take no interest in politics nowadays, what can one expect of the rank and file?'[12]

This emerges most clearly from a review of the wartime functioning of the usual system of party management through the Party Chairman and the Chief Whip. One pointer is given by the fact that these men hardly figure in accounts of wartime politics, or in the diaries of Churchill's intimate circle. Martin Gilbert's lengthy life of Churchill scarcely even mentions Douglas Hacking, Thomas Dugdale, Ralph Assheton or James Stuart, whose joint responsibility it was to run the Party for Churchill. The position of Chief Whip was one that Churchill understood well enough, having suffered under the rod of Margesson's tough whipping before 1939. For the sake of unity he retained Margesson, a leading 'Municheer', as Chief Whip until Chamberlain departed but then rapidly moved him aside. Much against his will, he was sent to the War Office, where, having never previously run a department at all, he was not a great success; in early 1942, he was sacked altogether with the consolation of a peerage, but the appointment of the civil servant Sir James Grigg in his place was not much more successful; George Harvie-Watt reported to Churchill that when Grigg met MPs he treated them all with great hostility, as if they were all hecklers, and then gave 'evasive and civil service replies to questions'. He did though provide a convenient figurehead who would not stand in the way of Churchill's wish to run the War himself, dealing directly with the generals.[13]

Margesson's departure from the Whip's Office created a problem in itself, for whipping required detailed and up-to-date experience of MPs, and Churchill had to have a reliable majority. He considered bringing in an outsider with earlier experience of the Whip's Office. Thomas Dugdale was therefore brought back from the army in the Middle East for that purpose, but Churchill then changed his mind and instead promoted Margesson's deputy James Stuart, apparently on the advice of Bracken and against that of Beaverbrook. Dugdale became Stuart's deputy, presumably with a view to ensuring one Churchill supporter in the office, but as old friends and Eton contemporaries Stuart and Dugdale got on better with each other than either did with the old Harrovian Churchill. Dugdale in due course combined the posts of Deputy Chief Whip and Deputy Party Chairman before becoming Party Chairman himself in 1942, while Stuart remained Chief Whip until 1948. Stuart's relationship with Churchill was loyal but far from subservient, and seems never to have been warm. Confronted by one proposed ministerial

---

[12]  Addison, *Churchill*, 358; Headlam diary, 30 Mar. 1942, Headlam MSS.
[13]  Gilbert, *Finest Hour*, 918; Harvie-Watt report, 20 Mar. 1942, Harvie-Watt MSS, 2/1.

appointment, he got up and prepared to leave the room, at which point the following dialogue ensued:

PM:      Stop. You're not going are you?
Stuart:  No. I'm only going to vomit. I'll be back in a minute.
PM:      Oh, so you don't like this?
Stuart:  Not much.

On another occasion, Stuart received from Churchill after a difficult debate a minute including the words, 'What does the great Conservative Party think it is doing? It is like a whale stuck in the mud and unable even to flap its own tail.' In 1943, on a visit to Chequers to discuss the problems in the House that had culminated in a Tory rebellion over Government proposals for wage-fixing in the catering industry, the busy Chief Whip was subjected first to one of Churchill's late dinners, then to a showing in full of a two-hour feature film, and finally to a harangue from Beaverbrook on the obstructiveness of the Tory whips; 'when calm prevailed I explained briefly where I stood' and explained that,

> my case was that my instructions on becoming Chief Whip were that no controversial legislation was to be introduced unless essential for the successful prosecution of the war. The only exception to this had been the Catering Wages Bill which had been agreed by the Cabinet and forced on me against my will. I added that if my original instructions were to be altered it would be quite simple to engineer the collapse of the National War Government within forty-eight hours. No more was said.

Such colourful exchanges were no doubt an effective way of dealing with Churchill, but they are not evidence of a harmonious team. Stuart was always at daggers drawn with Beaverbrook – 'Beaverbrook did not like me, and I regarded him as a political adventurer' – and was convinced that 'the Beaver' had instructed his papers to attack Conservative Party management in the Commons to undermine him. The effect of such corrosive advice on Churchill was obvious. In July 1944, Leo Amery was told by Stuart that 'Winston had spent an hour and a half with him arguing that James was trying to get rid of him by boosting his enemies, merely because James had recommended for some job or other that very able young man Henry Brooke, who, however, was at one time the director of some journal which before the war was critical of Winston'. The blockage of normal channels of party communication with the Leader was damaging, for backbenchers were now better organised in the 1922 Committee than they had been in the First World War. When backbenchers were collectively irritated, as for example by a dressing down given by Cripps as Leader of the House in 1942, it was to the Chief Whip that they complained, but his relationship with Churchill was not likely to ensure that their views were given much weight when received.[14]

---

[14] James Stuart, *Within the Fringe* (1967), 89, 92–3, 134; Barnes and Nicholson, *Empire at Bay*, 991; Jefferys, *Churchill Coalition*, 103.

The 1922 Committee tried to fill the vacuum of Party communications after Churchill became Leader; it resolved that the formal Party Meeting should contain no business but Churchill's election, but instructed its chairman to approach the new Leader, 'to express to him the hope . . . that there might be as close as possible a liaison between the Party and its Leader'. Initially Churchill intended not even to allow Ministers to address party committees, but this ran into 'strong opposition' early in 1941, and it was then agreed that ministers could address party meetings of MPs but that all-party meetings would also be held. The 1922 therefore continued to act as a sounding board of back-bench opinion, a safety valve at which ministers of all parties could hear what the majority party's MPs had to say. Later in 1941 a special liaison committee was set up to bring together Central Office and the 1922, in the hope that draft orders and regulations could be argued about before coming formally to the House and public clashes thereby avoided; this was never effective. Deputations, petitions and liaison meetings continued but relations remained bad, and there were constant complaints of the lack of Party activity in the Commons. In November 1942 this became dangerous, when Oliver Stanley, out of office since 1940 but now returned from the army, proposed a series of fundamental changes to the Party's relationship to the Government; in the event Stanley was back in office before anything came of this, and lesser men had to carry out the negotiation with Churchill. The 1922 therefore amended its rules so that ministers as well as backbenchers could be members, so in principle narrowing the divide between Party and Government. This was agreed early in 1943 but since, in practice, ministers were too busy to come to meetings unless they were themselves part of the agenda, this reform also failed to achieve its purpose. The more fundamental change that had been suggested, to allow a Party front bench in the Commons, separate from the Government but open to all Tory Privy Councillors who were not in office (and with priority speaking rights in debate), would have allowed the Party to enjoy something of the dual government *and* opposition status open to Labour; Churchill, who would have found that he would also have had to listen more to the Party in this eventuality, refused the change as one that would be 'impracticable and likely to create difficulties'. The reason for the lack of progress is again the lack of any Party identification at the top; at a celebratory lunch with the 1922 in 1941, Churchill repeated an old theme to 150 Tory MPs: 'we shall let no party surpass us in the great sacrifices we make'. This drew cheers on the day, but was an attitude that contributed signally to the underlying malaise.[15]

Party Chairmen had the same difficulty as the Chief Whip and the Chairman of the 1922. Douglas Hacking resigned in 1942 after six years

15  1922 Cttee., 9 Oct. 1940, 25 Mar. 1942, 21 Oct. 1942, 18 Nov. 1942, 2 Feb. 1943; Goodhart, *The 1922*, 103–7, 127–9; Jefferys, *Churchill Coalition*, 149; Colville, *Fringes of Power*, 410; Rhodes James, *Chips*, 395.

in the job, complaining that he was fed up of urging restraint on the Party. Darlington Conservatives in 1943 welcomed the fact that, with the appointment of Dugdale, the Party had again a Chairman devoted full-time to the job, but Dugdale experienced similar difficulties, as Headlam foresaw when he was appointed. He approved of the appointment because Dugdale was 'very popular, has great tact and charm of manner, and has guts which Hacking had not. He has, however, a very difficult job ahead of him as the Party is in a moribund condition and seems to have entirely lost confidence in itself – and of course Winston is a futile leader.' In June 1941 Dugdale was already, as Deputy Chairman, lamenting 'the first signs of a new class feeling in the House. The Tories, conscious of the great sacrifices they are making financially and of the exceedingly high wages being paid to war workers, are cantankerous about the many reports of slackness, absenteeism etc. in the factories.' He suffered from ill-health during his Chairmanship but at least he did not provoke Churchill, and neither did his successor Ralph Assheton, an ineffective speaker and a rather right-wing politician who attempted to use the position to press his own policy views.[16]

It is significant that the trio of wartime Party Chairmen were all men of lesser status than the 'cabinet rank' that had been attached to the post on its creation in 1911: Hacking and Assheton held junior posts but never sat in a Cabinet; Dugdale did reach the Cabinet, for a brief and unlucky few months in 1953; before honourably resigning over the notorious Crichel Down case for which he was constitutionally responsible, but hardly to blame; when desperately short of Conservatives for his 1945 Caretaker Government, Churchill did not offer a post to any of the three, which indicates clearly enough his own view of their abilities. In the half century after the War on the other hand, with the post of Party Chairman becoming a pivotal one, every Party Chairman but one (Oliver Poole in 1955–57) was to be a man who attended the Cabinet/shadow cabinet. It would be only fair to point out that Law, Baldwin and Chamberlain had also appointed Party Chairmen who were of less than Cabinet calibre, at least at the time, but they themselves had had a much surer grasp of the Party and what it would stand for than Churchill had. The low status attributed to this key post by Churchill in wartime, when he was so dependent on the Party, was indicative of his attitude both to party in general and to the Conservative Party in particular. The problem had been foreseen. On the morning of the Party Meeting to elect Churchill as Party Leader on 9 October 1940, the Conservative newspapers had all reported, as a whip's note put it, 'that some Conservatives intended to propose someone as Deputy Leader for the reason that in time of war the Prime Minister, with all his immense burdens, could not undertake effective Leadership of the Party'. It is not clear who scotched this plan or who were

---

16 Darlington Conservative Association minutes, 11 Jan. 1943; Headlam diary, 28 Apr. 1942.

the 'certain young Tories' who were pressing for it, but the 1922 Committee declined to support the idea and no formal proposal was ever made. Indeed, at the Party Meeting, the opposite view was taken. The only speaker other than Halifax, who exercised the beaten candidate's customary right to propose the election of the winner, and George Courthorpe who seconded the motion as a senior backbencher, was Sir Eugene Ramsden; although Ramsden was speaking as representative of voluntary workers in the country, he conceded, without even being asked, that 'it will be necessary for [Churchill] to take a more detached attitude and not one which is closely allied to the Party organisation'. This was a dangerous freedom to offer Churchill, and when the Leader then refused to lead, the vacuum could not be filled by any other Tory politician. Perhaps the only one with any opportunity to do so was Eden, a heavyweight figure who had held the Foreign Office and been seen as a future Leader as early as 1935, and was Churchill's own designated successor as Prime Minister from 1942; Eden was also the public's choice as successor to Churchill in poll after poll. No other Conservative minister even approached him in popularity with the public, and only Cripps, briefly in 1942, could challenge him from the Labour side.[17]

Unfortunately, Eden, like Churchill, had a love-hate relationship with the Party – and a considerably thinner skin than the Prime Minister. His rise was resented by the loyalists; in December 1940, Hugh Dalton clearly enjoyed needling Rab Butler on this point. '[Butler] himself is jealous of Eden . . . He says that Eden plays politics too much and does not make a success of his Departments . . . He is, I say, aiming a little obviously at the Leadership of the Conservative Party. Butler, bridling, says "He will never get that. The Party will never follow him." Later he says, "I have my own shop too, as well as Eden. I know that our Party is not behind him".' The antagonism was mutual: Eden told his diary only a fortnight later about a conversation with Richard Law: 'He talked much of the Tory party and my duty to lead it . . . I told him that I had little sympathy with it or the men that composed it.' He was constantly urging Churchill to 'clear out the Whips' Office' and complained that Stuart was intriguing against him by failing to find speakers to support his foreign policy in Commons debates. The whips 'were inefficient and nursed grievances about the past instead of being active for the future'. This was one of his few grounds for heartfelt agreement with Churchill: in 1943, 'we discussed Tory Party & both agreed how little we liked it & and how little it liked us. On which harmonious note we parted.' Such sentiments were reserved for private occasions. Usually Eden, as Harold Nicolson observed, 'hid behind his charm' and 'managed to create out of affability a smokescreen more impenetrable than any cloud of sullenness'.

---

[17] Note on Party Meeting, 9 Oct. 1940, Whip's papers, 'Party Meetings', CPA; Paul Addison, *The Road to 1945, British Politics and the Second World War* (1975), 200; Moran, *Struggle*, 261.

But on occasion the old Conservative right could puncture this mask and reveal the turbulence beneath the surface; confronted in 1944 by a potential Conservative candidate who did not want to join a party that included Sir Archibald Southby (a monied man of antediluvian opinions), Eden exploded 'But you do not imagine that I shall ever consent to lead a party of Southbys and Waterhouses? I will do no such thing. I will not represent the moneyed interests. There are young men who see clearer than we do the prospects of a new Toryism. It is them I wish to lead.' Butler, whose idea of the future of the Party was fairly close to this, cannot have been pleased to hear his own junior minister tell him in 1943 'that of the Tories [Eden] was the only one with pretensions at the moment. During this Parliament Hoare, Stanley, Elliott and W.S. Morrison had each, at one time or another, appeared to have the Tory succession in their hand. They had all faded out. Eden was the only candidate at the moment.' A year later, Beaverbrook reached the same conclusion: 'Eden, he thought, would have overwhelming support in the Party.'[18]

Churchill's advice to the King to send for Eden if the Prime Ministerial aeroplane were shot down in flames remained secret, but Eden's status as the Party's second-in-command was confirmed by his appointment as Leader of the Commons at the end of 1942, while retaining the Foreign Office. The appointment was not good for his relations with Churchill or for his standing in the Party, for an extremely overworked minister now found himself constantly under fire from both directions. Almost immediately Churchill attacked, as Eden's secretary recorded: the Prime Minister,

> rang up A.E. and raged at him about the King's Speech, the draft of which had been settled by a Committee including A.E. Why had he included all this about education? Had he not read what Cardinal Hinsley had said? Why had he allowed a reference to a Catering Bill to pass? Did he not know that 200 Conservative MPs would vote against it? A.E. replied that the Education proposals were those of R.A. Butler and the Caterers' Bill was recommended by Bevin. How should he know that there was opposition to them unless the Chief Whip came and told him so instead of sneaking direct to the P.M.? The exchanges were pretty hot . . . A.E. offered to leave the P.M. to govern with Kingsley Wood and James Stuart if he preferred it.

In 1944, the 1922 Committee considered that the combination of Leader of the House and Foreign Secretary was too much for any one man to cover, demanding that Eden come to a meeting to hear their critical views about 'the too abject appeasement of Russia' and the Government's apparent lack of interest in the rights of small countries; this line of dissent had been clear even at the height of the popularity of the Russian alliance, when in April 1942, Tory MPs complained to Harvie-Watt that the treaty with Russia

[18] Pimlott, *Dalton War Diaries*, 122, 797; Robert Rhodes James, *Anthony Eden* (1986), 245, 261, 275; Nicolson, *Harold Nicolson Diaries*, 335, 367; Jefferys, Chuter Ede, 131.

recognising Russian claims over the Baltic States was 'Munich again, but worse', a line of criticism about which Eden was understandably sensitive. It was also complained that Eden had lost sight of the value of exploiting Commons procedure, that there should be more Conservatives put up to move the adjournment, as Labour was doing – and thereby making useful news. By then Eden too had decided that the burden was too great and had told Oliver Harvey that 'he thought he had decided to give up the leadership of H. of C. to R.A. Butler after this session and do F.O. only'. Knowing Eden's jealousy of Butler, Harvey also noted 'I shan't believe it till I see it'. It never happened.[19]

## The crises of 1941–42

The unharmonious relationship between Party and Government deteriorated into a mood that could imperil the Government's survival only when the War itself went badly. Anti-Churchill feeling among the 'Municheers' was certainly a factor here, but there may also have been some feelings of guilt. R.A. Butler, a prime 'Municheer' as a Foreign Office minister in 1938, thought that the backbenchers 'began to search their consciences as to whether they had told the truth to Chamberlain. They came to the conclusion that they hadn't and that they must therefore tell the truth to Churchill.' There was little tendency among Conservative MPs to question Churchill's inspirational war leadership in 1940 and, if they thereafter carped continuously about his methods and his policies, they only rarely doubted his fitness for the job. As with medieval monarchs, bad news from the war front produced only demands for the changing of advisers and the improvement of decision-making. Although this recurred when reverses were suffered in the second half of the War, it only really mattered in 1941 and 1942 when it was possible to believe in the likelihood of British defeat. Reverses in north Africa and then in Greece and Crete in 1941 led to the first dangerous clashes. The 1922 Committee had discussed the crisis of war production, and its chairman Alec Erskine Hill had gone on to the offensive in Spring with public speeches in which he claimed that everyone except the Government now accepted that something needed to be done, but the Government received an overwhelming vote of confidence in the House. Defeats in the Mediterranean then caused damage to both Eden and Churchill. Channon noted in June that 'one hears increasing criticism of Churchill. He is undergoing a noticeable slump in popularity and many of his enemies, long silenced by his personal popularity, are once more vocal. Crete has been a great blow to him.' As in the weeks before Chamberlain's fall in 1940, Conservative MPs were encouraged in their criticisms by colleagues who had themselves returned from the fighting line: in June 1941, a Member

---

[19] Harvey, *Diplomatic Diaries*, 176, 347; Goodhart, *The 1922*, 131, 133; Harvie-Watt report, 24 Apr. 1942, Harvie-Watt MSS, 2/1.

reported to the 1922 Committee on his experiences in the naval campaign in the Mediterranean, and the minutes recorded that 'members were much impressed and shocked by the details he gave regarding the shortage of planes'. Eden also suffered a slump in support, since he had been personally associated on the spot with military decisions in the Balkans, but Churchill stood by him, and again the House backed the Government, this time by 447 votes to three. Although Churchill told his secretary that 'he didn't give a damn what the House of Commons thought as there was a bloody war on', he was in practice well aware that he had come to power as a result of a revolt by Conservative MPs and could be removed from office only in the same way; he made careful, well-prepared and persuasive speeches to the House when its support was needed. Unlike Chamberlain in 1940, he had no illusions that they would back him through any sentiments of friendship. Nonetheless, there was already a buzz of speculation in the lobbies about the need for ministerial heads to roll when Japan's entry into the War in December 1941 unleashed half a year of disasters.[20]

Between Pearl Harbor and Alamein the Government hardly had a week of political respite, and criticism now went much wider than just the embittered old guard who had never liked Churchill; Henry Willink, a very moderate Conservative who spent most of his time on social policy, was one who spoke in the House in 1942 against Churchill's management of the War. The collapse of British power in the Far East, the fall of Singapore and the sinking of two battleships, was followed by the 'Channel dash' in which three German warships steamed unmolested through the English Channel. This started the first great invasion scare since 1940, and was followed by continuous Allied defeats in Russia, Burma, the Pacific and north Africa, and in the Battle of the Atlantic. Channon, in February 1942, thought that the mood 'is not the post-Dunkirk feeling, but ANGER . . . The capital seethes with indignation and were Londoners latins there would be rioting . . . There is a flap on at 10 Downing Street and . . . Winston . . . is in a defiant, truculent mood.' A series of desperate ministerial reshuffles staved off an increasing tide of criticism, but by Autumn 1942, Bracken was convinced that only a British victory in the desert would save even Churchill's skin. Noël Coward decided in February that Churchill 'knows the temper of the people in crisis but I doubt if he really knows the people themselves. It may be heresy to say so, but I feel that if he goes on playing a lone hand, refusing to listen to younger and wiser men, he will fall.' A fortnight earlier, Cuthbert Headlam had decided that

> The truth of the matter is that we are still sadly lacking in war material and people, not unreasonably, are beginning to wonder why this should be so after 2½ years war. Winston is too cocksure of himself and thinks that he can go on

[20] Jefferys, *Churchill Coalition*, 74, 87–9; 1922 Cttee., 11 June 1941; Rhodes James, *Eden*, 253; Pimlott, *Dalton War Diaries*, 305.

carrying everything on his own back, and I don't think H of C will stand for this indefinitely.

Churchill himself, writing to Margesson in April, conceded that 'since I shouldered this burden, I feel its weight heavier now than at any time'.[21]

As early as 18 December 1941 things began to hot up. Amery was buttonholed by the Secretary of the 1922 Committee, and told of 'the feeling of restlessness about the Government in our party . . . not only about the conduct of war generally, but also because they did not feel that there was anyone inside the Cabinet who stood for the Conservative point of view at all. There was indeed considerable regret in many quarters that Winston had been made leader of the Party for it deprived the Party of someone who could speak on its behalf to Winston and stand up to him.' The following day a bitterly critical debate was launched by Lord Winterton, and Harry Crookshank warned that 'the temper of the House was not unlike what it was when Neville's government fell'. A week later Amery lunched with the Chief Whip and 'told him it was his duty to be really frank with Winston. We agreed that his best course would be to write a memorandum about it first which Winston is bound to read. Otherwise, if approached verbally, he might deliver a speech and prevent James getting a word in.' But Churchill was off to Washington to confer with Roosevelt.[22]

While Churchill was away matters deteriorated. Erskine Hill convened meetings of discontented MPs, at which it was agreed that Churchill should give up the Ministry of Defence and responsibility for running the War but remain Prime Minister, a proposal strikingly similar to the one that had levered Asquith out of office in 1916; Tory MPs also chafed when they heard that the Government would hold the debate on a confidence motion which would force them either to back Churchill uncritically or to damage the national leadership in a crisis; Churchill's PPS reported to him that many Tory MPs felt that confidence in the Prime Minister was not the same as confidence in his entire team and, a few weeks later, that there was 'an almost universal desire for a dramatic reorganisation of the Government'. Chips Channon thought that this time the problem would not be solved by 'the P.M. coming back and making one of his magical speeches'. A few days later he thought that 'the ineffectual whips are in a frenzy and a first class crisis, no doubt chuckled on by the Germans, is upon us'. Arriving back in the midst of this, Churchill raged liked a baited bear. He warned Eden that he was tempted to resign, but told Erskine Hill that it was 'disgraceful to come back to the scurvy treatment of a snarling House of Commons'. He also claimed that he alone stood between the Conservative Party and disaster, and made disparaging

---

[21] Willink unpublished autobiography, 71; Rhodes James, *Chips*, 321; Graham Payn and Sheridan Morley (eds), *The Noël Coward Diaries* (1982), 15; Headlam diary, 22 Jan. 1942; Churchill to Margesson, 27 Apr. 1942, Margesson MSS, 1/4/12.

[22] Barnes and Nicholson, *Empire at Bay*, 754–5.

remarks about Tory supporters of appeasement. But again he sought to deflect the criticisms with a more conciliatory tone in the Commons and some limited ministerial changes. When the unpopular Beaverbrook survived this reshuffle, Headlam noted sadly that 'he and Winston are boon companions – and there it is. So long as Winston continues, so long will the Beaver. But a few more votes of confidence like today – unless he can show some successes and a greater efficiency – will be the end of Winston.' Beaverbrook's subsequent resignation therefore seemed like further evidence that Churchill's premiership was mortally wounded.[23]

This reshuffle bought the Government only a few weeks respite before the fall of Singapore and the Channel dash re-started the clamour. Headlam was far from alone among Conservatives in feeling especially the shock of Singapore: 'one feels terribly depressed – more depressed, I think, than after Dunkirk – to be beaten and humiliated in this way by Asiatics is almost more than a Victorian Englishman can stand.' Much as he admired Churchill, he thought him 'an obstinate devil and full of hubris . . . I am coming to the conclusion that it would be better to have a β+ man who listens to good advisers . . .'. The 1922 Committee again demanded better decision-making but stopped short of demanding Churchill's surrender of the Defence portfolio; Amery noted that things had got 'tense'. The real reshuffle when it came was a surprise, for it involved the promotion of Sir Stafford Cripps, and the removal of Wood from the War Cabinet; a crisis provoked by Chamberlainites had led to their further exclusion from influence, and Churchill had placed himself instead in the hands of Labour. Amery felt that what 'the Conservative Party will not like [is] an extreme left winger leading the House and a War Cabinet containing not a single real Conservative, for they certainly don't class either Winston or Anthony as such'.[24]

Discontent rumbled on through the Spring, leading in July to the only parliamentary debate in which the Government might actually have fallen, on a critical motion put down by the Chairman of the National Expenditure Committee, Sir John Wardlaw Milne; Harvie-Watt advised that 'there was no need to worry about the solid mass of opinion in the House of Commons', and urged that this time the debate and the vote should be on the critics' own resolution, rather than on a confidence motion tabled by the Government. A meeting of the 1922 Commitee declined to support a critical motion at such a difficult moment of the War, and the proposer made a terrible hash of it in the House – by suggesting that the royal Duke of Gloucester be made Commander-in-Chief, which 'brought the house down'. This gaffe removed any chance of mustering a respectable vote against Churchill; Headlam reflected that Churchill had emerged from the debate as 'a giant amongst

[23] Jefferys, *Churchill Coalition*, 89–90; Harvie-Watt reports, 25 Jan. and 20 Feb. 1942, Harvie-Watt MSS, 2/1; 1922 Cttee., 21 Jan. 1942; Headlam diary, 29 Jan. 1942.
[24] Headlam diary, 8 and 10 Feb. 1942; Goodhart, *The 1922*, 112; Barnes and Nicholson, *Empire at Bay*, 776,

pigmies', but that he had had it easy because of the motion he had to defeat. In effect, throughout the first half of 1942, Churchill refused to step down from running the War personally and neither Labour nor Conservative MPs were prepared to take the leap into the unknown that would have been involved in trying to sack him. This whole attack was parliamentary; no Area or local Conservative association seems to have passed critical resolutions, and public support for Churchill hardly faltered; in Summer 1942 it reached its lowest ever point during the War, but even this was a 78 per cent approval rating. There was simply no other potential Prime Minister available. Cripps certainly saw himself as the Lloyd George to Churchill's Asquith, but this time it was the Prime Minister who had the better footwork and the aspirant who was misled by his own vanity; there was anyway never much chance that Conservative MPs would vote even an unorthodox Conservative out of office to replace him by a Labour left-winger. The Summer was therefore marked by further political tension, with Cripps effectively put on hold by Churchill in another reshuffle, until the Alamein victory in November (nearly synchronised with the turn of the tide on the Russian, Pacific and Atlantic fronts) put Churchill's position beyond attack for the rest of the War; Harvie-Watt noted with some satisfaction that Churchill's loudest critics earlier in the year were among those most pleased by the desert victory. After Christmas 1942, the question was *when* Churchill led Britain to victory and not *if*. He was never under serious political pressure again.[25]

## Post-war reconstruction

But Christmas 1942 was the Christmas of Beveridge as well as the Christmas of Alamein and Stalingrad. From 1943 onwards the emphasis of political debate shifted to the home front, and as a consequence the natural fault lines in the Conservative Party now reflected not pre-war foreign policy but post-war political economy. With Beveridge in mind, Harriet Jones concluded that 'the war caused deep disruption to policy-making in the Party, resulting in incoherence and uncertainty by 1945'. There had already been sharp clashes over the Churchill Government's domestic policy, inevitable when that policy was led by Labour ministers. In September 1941 the 1922 Committee and the National Union Executive reluctantly agreed to set up a Party group to meet the TUC, to discuss the trades unions' request for an amendment of the 1927 Trades Disputes Act. This had always been regarded by trades unions as vindictive legislation passed after the General Strike, but Conservatives naturally did not agree; nor could they see that wartime collaboration in government provided any reason for legalising

25 Harvie-Watt report, 26 June and 13 Nov. 1942, Harvie-Watt MSS, 2/1; Goodhart, *The 1922*, 120; Headlam diary, 27 July 1942; Jefferys, *Churchill Coalition*, 104–7; Harvey, *Diplomatic Diaries*, 136.

general strikes or mass picketing, or for boosting Labour Party finances; as early as October 1940, the 1922 Committee, urging the Government to abstain from controversial legislation, specifically mentioned the 1927 Act as something not to be touched. Warned by his PPS about hostility building up on the backbenches, Churchill minuted, 'a friendly talk cd. do no harm'. A meeting duly took place but it was not friendly; the Conservatives made no attempt to reach agreement and the whole matter had to be shelved. Since the official policy of the Government was the avoidance of controversial legislation unless needed for the war effort, it was not difficult to stall such initiatives when Conservatives spoke like this with a united voice. The same principle enabled the Party to ride out difficulties with Labour ministers over national service and creeping nationalisation in wartime, but irritation was caused; in December 1941, the 1922 Committee complained of 'undisguised attempts of the Labour Party to blackmail the Government into nationalising industry'.[26]

Things became more heated when another pre-war political chestnut, the coal industry, came up for discussion in 1942. Dalton, encouraged by Cripps, proposed a full-blown scheme of fuel rationing, but a hostile meeting with the 1922 Committee resulted in delay. The Committee then went on to the offensive, with the chairman telling *The Sunday Times* that they opposed the scheme. In Cabinet, Churchill, primed by the Party Chairman and backed by the Chief Whip, opposed Dalton's plans, and the original proposal was much modified; when his PPS told him that Tory MPs were opposing the plans of his own ministers, Churchill minuted 'good'. In response to a challenge from the *Daily Herald* to go down a mine during the recess and see working conditions for themselves, a show of hands at the 1922 indicated that 84 per cent of members present had already done so. Coal did though continue to raise hackles. A proposal to use pre-service military trainees down the mines to relieve the chronic labour shortage was strongly opposed: the London Area and several constituencies passed hostile resolutions.[27]

At this stage of the War though, local Conservatives were more exercised by the needs of agriculture than the other industries. The extent of Government intervention to encourage food production was welcomed in so far as it boosted farm incomes, but feared as a precedent for the future by an economic group of sturdy individualists; there was a strong Tory folk memory of wartime intervention leading to rural crisis after 1918. The South East Area Council, covering Kent, Surrey and Sussex, was constantly passing resolutions about the need to protect farmers' independence as well

26 Goodhart, *The 1922*, 109–10; National Union Executive Committee minutes [hereafter NUEC] 19 Sept. 1941, CPA; Jefferys, *Churchill Coalition*, 76; Harvie-Watt report, 11 Sept. 1942, Harvie-Watt MSS 2/1; 1922 Cttee., 10 Dec. 1941.

27 Jones, 'Conservative Party' thesis, 54; Goodhart, *The 1922*, 115–17; Harvie-Watt report, 17 Apr. 1942, Harvie-Watt MSS, 2/1; 1922 Cttee., 16 Oct. 1940; Addison, *Churchill*, 348–9; Pimlott, *Dalton War Diaries*, 433; East Islington CA minutes, 4 May 1944; Dulwich CA minutes, 11 May 1944.

as their incomes. The same was true of the agricultural Eastern Area. In Horncastle things became very contentious; in 1942 the Executive Council agreed to coopt two agricultural representatives from the National Farmers' Union because of increasing unrest; the Association Treasurer then moved an NFU motion that was fiercely critical of the Government; when the MP announced his impending retirement in 1944 there was a bitter row that led to the resignation of the Lincolnshire NFU chairman from the Association when it did not pick a local farmer as the new candidate; the candidate eventually selected had to give pledges to speak up for agriculture. In part this reflected simply the continuation of disputes from the 1930s, but with an added edge because of the increased flux of wartime policy. Speakers' notes provided statistics on 'the remarkable progress of agriculture under wartime administration' and dredged up quotations from ministers on the importance of farming to the war effort. At the end of the War the Northern Area hopefully resolved 'that our oldest and still greatest industry should be taken out of the realm of party politics'. The issue could become obsessive in some constituencies; the secretary was surely being a little ironical when he minuted Rab Butler's Annual General Meeting speech at Saffron Walden in May 1941, at the very height of the battle for Crete, as follows: [Butler] 'answered points on poultry rationing, cheese ration, milk etc. Mr. Butler concluded his address with a reference to International Affairs.'[28]

## America, India and the Soviet Union

On the other hand, Conservatives were not at this time happy with the extent of British dependence on the United States. Conservative MPs who wanted a secret session meeting in 1941, to discuss the Lend-Lease treaty before it was signed, were convinced that the United States was using Britain's weak position to extend its own influence; Churchill refused to allow such a debate even to take place. The Northern Area Council was unusually far-sighted in calling in 1943 for efforts to preserve a post-war spirit of friendship with the United States 'for the preservation of the peace of Europe and the safety of democracy'. More usually there were fears of American hostility to the re-establishment of British colonies after the War; the Central Office *Notes on Current Politics* found an unusual ally in Emmanuel Shinwell in 1944, quoting with approval a Shinwell speech saying that the colonies should not be thrown overboard just because Americans wanted it. The cost of the aid agreement with the United States signed in 1942, opening post-war British trading policy to considerable American influence, was a new source

---

[28] South East Area Council minutes, 21 and 24 Feb. 1941; East Midlands Area Council minutes, 25 Nov. 1944; Horncastle CA minutes, 18 May and 13 July 1942, 6 Mar. and 12 June 1944; Ramsden, *Balfour and Baldwin*, 363; Central Office, *Notes for Speakers* 3b, mid 1943, CPA; Northern Area Council, 21 Apr. 1943; Saffron Walden CA minutes, 17 May 1941.

of division. As a free trader at heart, Churchill was inclined to underestimate the significance that this held for old tariff reformers, notably for Amery and Beaverbrook. Amery was sufficiently concerned to plot with the Chief Whip against the Government policy on post-war economic relationships that was emerging by 1944: he noted that Stuart 'is naturally perturbed at the thought of a split in the Party and will do all he can to prevent it. His general sympathies are with us and he admits we are a majority of Conservative Ministers. The trouble is that there is no real constructive Conservative in the Cabinet since Kingsley [Wood] died. Winston is a die hard, mid Victorian Whig, Anthony is a sentimental internationalist . . .' On the following day, Ralph Assheton, Financial Secretary to the Treasury, entertained Conservative Ministers to dinner at the Dorchester to meet the Chancellor, and received a strong dose of the same views; the Party Chairman revealed 'that he had interviewed hundreds of would-be candidates lately who one and all were only out for one thing, to serve the Empire, and asked what would be the effect on them of a policy which clearly showed that we didn't care'. Hugh Dalton subsequently blamed the collapse of these commercial proposals on Conservative Party pressure, including a threat to resign by Amery.[29]

Curiously, the issue that might well have been expected to cause a rumpus in the Party, India, hardly even raised a murmur. The extreme peril of the Empire in Asia in 1942, and perhaps the recognition that of all people Churchill and Amery would not propose concessions to Indian nationalism unless it was entirely unavoidable, seem to have headed off trouble. In March 1942, two right-wing Conservative MPs visited Amery and actually urged him to go further than the Government intended, by handing over the whole power in India to Indians. There was some reservation in the 1922 about the inclusion of an apparent right to secede from the Commonwealth altogether in the new scheme of Indian government, but after the policy had been fully explained to them it was reported to Amery 'that the 1922 Committee and the House generally seemed very happy with the India solution'. The same was true in the constituencies. The South East Area Council resolved that 'India should attain as soon as possible to free and equal partnership in the British Commonwealth of Nations' (at a meeting at which an amendment to delete the words 'free and' from the resolution was overwhelmingly defeated). This was a resolution that would hardly even have attracted a seconder in the Tory heartlands before 1939.[30]

There was a similar revolution in attitudes to Russia when invaded by Germany in 1941. The East Midlands Area congratulated Churchill on bringing the help of the British Empire to Russia so speedily, and Central Council in October 1941 passed a resolution warmly supporting the Russian

[29] 1922 Cttee., 19 Mar. 1941; Northern Area Council, 18 Apr. 1943; *Notes on Current Politics* [hereafter *NCP*], June 1944; J.M. Lee, *The Churchill Coalition, 1940–1945* (1980), 149–50.
[30] Barnes and Nicholson, *Empire at Bay*, 169–70; Pimlott, *Dalton War Diaries*, 745.

alliance; in February 1942, Mrs. Tate MP was complaining that the local Labour Party in her constituency would not let her join an 'Aid for Russia' campaign. Supporting Russia was one thing, but the nature of the alliance was quite another; Conservatives could agree with Churchill's immediate offer of military assistance to Stalin as a way of diverting Germany's attention, but how far should it go? At Chequers in June 1941, 'Eden and Cranborne took the pure Tory standpoint that . . . it should be confined to the purely military aspect, as politically Russia was as bad as Germany and half the country would object to being associated with her too closely'. In this they were certainly reflecting the feelings of Conservative activists. The Party's ambivalence was expressed in September by the National Union Executive, when a meeting quixotically 'gave its blessing' to the formation of an Anglo-Soviet Public Relations Committee (exactly what it was soon to deplore) but refused to support 'the red Dean' of Canterbury's fundraising for medical help to Russia. More characteristic was the Eastern Area's November meeting which 'while advocating wholehearted support for the Russian war effort, view[ed] with alarm the growth in this country of propaganda, including an official film sponsored by the Ministry of Information called "Salute the Soviets", praising all aspects of the Russian social system'. Sir Robert Topping from Central Office wrote to reassure them that the MOI had received many protests on these lines and well understood that its material on Russia had not received 'anything like universal approval'. It was to be a recurrent theme, linked, as the war drew to a close, with protests about Russian intentions in Eastern Europe.[31]

For the sake of the Russian alliance, anti-Communists had, like Churchill himself, to turn a blind eye to what was actually happening in the Soviet Union, and few British newspaper editors who printed glowing correspondents' reports from Russia even knew that they were receiving censored copy from reporters who had been allowed nowhere near the battlefront. Churchill made ineffective attempts to restrict his Government's pro-soviet propaganda at home, for example banning for as long as he could the playing of the 'Internationale' on the BBC, but would not be drawn into any public dissociation from Soviet policy. Stalin enjoyed himself with the paradox that this created. He toasted the success of the Conservative Party at one of his first meetings with Churchill, and when a new Russian national anthem was adopted in 1944 he sent a message hoping that Churchill would 'set about learning the new tune and whistling it to members of the Conservative Party'. Tito had similar fun, allowing the traditionalist Croatian leader to take the place of honour at Churchill's right in a group photograph and saying that 'we mustn't get Mr. Churchill into trouble with the Conservative Party'. The Government tried to keep public enthusiasm for Russia within

---

31  East Midlands Area Council, 25 Oct. 1941; Central Council minutes, 2 Oct. 1941, CPA; 1922 Cttee., 18 Feb. 1941; Gilbert, *Finest Hour*, 1122; NUEC, 19 Sept. 1941; Eastern Area Council, 13 Nov. 1941 and 19 Feb. 1942.

bounds, and official sponsorship of demonstrations of support was intended to prevent them from being hi-jacked by Communists, but Conservatives were far from happy with the appearance this gave, or with the restraints that were imposed on them by the war situation. In October 1942, North Edinburgh Conservatives debated the agitation for a second front to help Russia but reluctantly resolved that they should pass no resolution because it would inevitably be open to misinterpretation. After the 1945 election, a Conservative candidate recalled how difficult it had been when 'at meeting after meeting questioners would get up and say: "Look what nationalisation has done for Russia and how strong and great she has become."' Central Office tried to brief Party speakers with prepared answers to such questions, arguing the difference of Russian conditions. They also sought to defend themselves by reminding the public of the Nazi–Soviet pact, but this cut little ice after years in which Britain's alliance with the heroic Russian people had been insisted on by the press, by politicians of all parties and by government propaganda.[32]

The Red Army's advance into Eastern Europe in 1944 and the Yalta Conference aroused Conservative feelings in a way that could not be suppressed, but this also brought Party feeling into collision with ministers and reignited Party divisions over appeasement. At the 1922 Committee in February 1945, the Government's acquiescence in Russian plans for Poland, undercutting the Polish Government in exile in London, came under strong attack. The critics this time received articulate leadership from Lord Dunglass, the future Sir Alec Douglas-Home, who had been Chamberlain's PPS at Munich and who had then been incapacitated by illness for most of the War: there was 'no doubt that the great majority of the Committee were opposed to the present settlement and would speak against it in the House'. The Chief Whip telegraphed Eden in Cairo to 'congratulate Prime Minister and you on your great success, but for your guidance must warn you of Conservative anxiety over Poland increased by active lobbying by Poles in progress here. Attlee and I have cabled Prime Minister advising against debate on motion of confidence which would inevitably be followed by some amendment . . . [any] open display of disunity among Conservatives would be deplorable.' Harvie-Watt advised that for many Tory MPs, this was 'the biggest event since the War began', and he successfully advised a long debate which would allow all the discontented a chance to speak, so that most would then vote the Party line. Churchill put in an unusual amount of time in the lobbies to reassure his supporters, and he agreed to a long debate, partly because a show of real Conservative doubts might impress Stalin. Despite any doubts that Eden and Churchill themselves entertained about Stalin's real intentions, in the debate on 27 February Churchill made one of his best set-piece speeches, though he only decided at the last minute to omit a claim

[32] Addison, *Road to 1945*, 134–41; Addison, *Churchill*, 346; Martin Gilbert, *Road to Victory, Winston S. Churchill, 1941–1945* (1986), 650, 894; Edinburgh North UA minutes, 5 Oct. 1942; *NCP*, Dec. 1944.

that Stalin sought 'peace with honour', a phrase with which the Municheers could have had a field day. All the same, twenty-five Conservative MPs voted against Government policy and many more abstained, mostly men who had been consistently anti-Russian and supported the Munich settlement partly for that reason; one resigned his junior ministerial post. Harold Nicolson was 'vastly amused that the warmongers of Munich have now become the appeasers, while the appeasers have become the warmongers'. He added that Churchill had performed well but confessed that he felt 'tired all through'. Cuthbert Headlam appreciated just how difficult the defence of the Yalta agreement was for Churchill, for

> nobody seems pleased with what Winston said, but I heard no one suggest what else he could have said in the circumstances – if he and Roosevelt could not persuade Stalin to be a gentleman and they were not prepared to quarrel with him, there was no alternative but to try and make the decent Poles acquiesce in the new partition and appreciate how nice it will be for them to have a semi-Russian Government in Poland . . . But it is a rotten business. One gets more and more fussed about Russian policy – God knows what will be the end of it.[33]

## Debating post-war policy

Churchill's sheer exhaustion at the War's end was matched by Eden's and by that of most ministers of all parties, but most were not also over seventy. Because he had concentrated leadership into his own hands, this was infinitely more important to the Conservatives than Attlee's corresponding weariness was to Labour. For five years, Churchill had given the Party no clear indication of its future, and when he had referred to the future at all it was in a negative way: in March 1943, he made what Woolton called 'a foolish broadcast' in which he said that it was still too early to think about post-war policy. In March 1941, he had told the activists at Central Council of the need for sacrifice:

> National unity requires sacrifices from all parties, and no party sacrificed more than the Conservative Party with its huge parliamentary majority. Many eminent men have had their careers interrupted, many Ministers of promise their prospects obscured, but none has thought of himself; all have made the sacrifice and we are proud that the Conservative Party has made the greatest sacrifice . . . I hope however that there will be national unity in making the peace (cheers). I hope also that there will be national unity in certain practical measures of reconstruction and social advance to enable this country to recover from the War and, like one great family, get into its stride again (cheers). If this hope is not realised, if no common ground can be found on post-war policy between the parties, it would be a misfortune because we would have to ask the nation to decide and party government would be the result. I may say however that some of the ties and

[33]  Gilbert, *Road to Victory*, 1223, 1234–6; Harvie-Watt report, 23 Feb. 1945, Harvie-Watt MSS, 5/1; Goodhart, *The 1922*, 135; Nicolson, *Harold Nicolson Diaries*, 437; Taylor, '1932–1945' coalition, 92; Headlam diary, 28 Feb. 1945.

friendships that are being forged between members of the administration of all parties will not be very easy to tear asunder . . .

As Paul Addison points out, it was strange for a Leader to tell a mass meeting of his party that it would be a misfortune if it had to form a Government, but the speech indicated in any case that Churchill still did not see this as likely. A year later, Churchill's equivalent speech was equally ambivalent, this time only half-heartedly defending his predecessor: 'I shall hope that when the whole story has been told it will be said of the Conservative Party in Parliament and throughout the land, "They strove for peace – too long – but when war came they proved themselves to be the main part of the rock on which the salvation of Britain was founded and the freedom of mankind regained."' Again there was no looking to the future. At the 1945 Conference, with an election imminent, Churchill's speech was even more sombre; he spoke again of Conservative sacrifices and the lack of respect for the political truce by politicians of the left, but continued to call for restraint and national unity; 'the Conservative Party had far better go down telling the truth and acting in accordance with the verities of our position than gain a span of shabbily-bought office', another odd stance for a Leader to adopt before his party.[34]

Labour's wartime position differed sharply from that of the Conservatives. Apart from ministers, Labour MPs sat on the opposition side of the House; a (Labour) Leader of the Opposition was retained to preserve constitutional niceties; individual Labour MPs such as Aneurin Bevan, Richard Stokes and Emmanuel Shinwell attacked Government policy with far more force and continuity than Conservatives allowed themselves. In effect, Labour was able to acquire the dual status of a partner in government with the resulting claim to have brought the country to victory *and* an opposition's freedom to dissociate itself from the bits of Government policy that it either did not support or believed were not being pursued energetically enough. Because there had then been a Liberal Prime Minister, the Conservatives had enjoyed a comparable advantage between 1915 and 1918. After 1940, Conservatives were in the Government but unable to control its policies, and under constant instruction to curb their oppositional tendencies. They were yoked to the other parties for the war effort – and had no great worries about that fact – but yoked too, so far as post-war planning went, because their Leader refused to contemplate anything other than a coalition after victory.[35]

Nothing indicated this more clearly than the Party's irresolution over the development of domestic policy for the post-war world. Education provided an exception, precisely because it was the one field in which an orthodox

---

34  Woolton diary, 21 Mar. 1943, Woolton MSS; Central Council minutes, 27 Mar. 1941 and 26 Mar. 1942, CPA; National Union Conference report, 15 Mar. 1945, CPA; Addison, *Churchill*, 361.

35  Stephen Brooke, *Labour's War, The Labour Party during the Second World War*, (Oxford, 1992), 76–8.

Conservative minister got a major issue in his hands, ignored or resisted Churchill's attempts to stop his proposals from coming forward, and worked closely enough with his Labour junior minister, as well as with the teachers and the churches, to ensure a broad basis of agreement for legislation, but also highlighted his own role sufficiently for it to be claimed as a Conservative initiative. Chris Patten, 'speaking both as a beneficiary of the '44 Act and a witness to its partial emasculation', has reminded us of,

> Rab's sheer, cussed courage in getting the Bill through. He received clear signals of Prime Ministerial disapproval for the whole project. His Permanent Secretary ran up the White Flag. But Rab refused to back down; it is extraordinary when one thinks about it – simply to ignore the opposition of a Prime Minister at the height of his formidable power and authority. He took on not only the Prime Minister triumphant, but the Church triumphant too.

It was a signal triumph whose passage into law as the 1944 'Butler' Education Act established Butler as a major figure for the future. The regularity of Conservative references to it in 1944–45 indicates both the reality of Butler's achievement and the paucity of comparable legislative material to plunder for evidence of Tory action.[36]

Butler's attempt to score the same triumph with the whole of post-war policy was far less successful. He had been approached as early as July 1940 to take on the chairmanship of a new committee of the National Union, which became the Post-War Problems Central Committee, though with the Party Chairman sceptical about meeting any of the costs involved when Butler initially sought to involve Labour members in its work as well as Conservatives; when the idea was revived in May 1941, the Chief Whip's first choice as chairman seems to have been Oliver Stanley (who was absent on war service), and even Baldwin's old confidant Lord Monsell was considered before Butler was appointed. The committee was set up 'with the object of collating and presenting to the Prime Minister the views of the Conservative and Unionist Party on post-war problems', which suggested a limited role only. The PWPCC began work in July 1941, with Butler in the chair and David Maxwell Fyfe as his deputy. They had an active two years of research work through sub-committees, though the impetus slackened somewhat when Butler handed over the chair to Maxwell Fyfe to concentrate on getting his Education Bill through; Maxwell Fyfe proved more interested in leafleting and propaganda (for which the Party had in any case little money and hardly any mechanism for distribution) than in policy development, which only seriously began again when Butler returned for the last year of the War. Throughout its life it had to fight a general Party feeling that all of this was too soon; as Lord Salisbury, a keen advocate of policy-making, wrote to Swinton in June

---

[36] Anthony Howard, *RAB, The Life of R.A. Butler* (1987), 107–38; Rhodes James, *Eden*, 281; Addison, *Road to 1945*, 172–4; Chris Patten, 'R.A. Butler – What We Missed', unpublished Inaugural R.A. Butler Lecture, delivered 25 May 1994.

1941, 'I expect you may say that in these days of anxiety it is impossible to give our minds effectively to post-war policy. If others would behave on those lines I should perhaps be content, but there are lots of committees and congresses hammering away at post-war policy and it seems that unless we do something moderate Conservatism will be left high and dry.' It is significant though that Salisbury was constantly having to badger Swinton – busy with the war – to send comments on various policy proposals being discussed by the Tory peers. The PWPCC's policy work is best linked with the analysis of post-war policy formulation. What is important here is to note the relatively low salience that its reports achieved in the political debate of 1943–45. There were exceptions to this; a report on industrial policy, from a sub-committee chaired by Henry Brooke, was fairly warmly reviewed in the press, even by the *Daily Herald*. Publications from the PWPCC formed the basis of attempts to get policy discussion going in Conservative constituency associations as 'Onlooker groups', but few constituencies had by 1943 an organisation that could be mobilised for that or any other purpose. Most seriously, there was no endorsement of PWPCC work by Churchill. Waldorf Astor looked back from beyond the 1945 defeat to bewail 'the lack of authoritative statements of party policy in the period previous to the election. I stress the word "authoritative". Before the Election, the Post-war Problems Committee's numerous reports, the "Signpost" booklets, the various pamphlets of the Tory Reform Committee, were all good, but they were not authoritative. They did not bear the *imprimatur* of the Prime Minister. There was no evidence that he had read them.' The reports are important for the long-term development of Conservative policy, but almost entirely unimportant in the short term; so far as the manifesto of 1945 is concerned, the PWPCC might as well not have existed. Eventually the collected work of the PWPCC was published as the book *Forty Years of Progress*, but not until June 1945, and then under a strangely backward-looking title than almost ensured that it would be disregarded. Butler later regretted 'that the work done by the Post-War Problems Committee played so little part in the formulation of our campaign'.[37]

Lack of impact by the PWPCC and the suspicion that the Party's parliamentary leadership was not sufficiently modern in outlook, led to the formation by a more determined team of modernisers of the Tory Reform Group. This arose from two sources, a widely-perceived need to promote younger men and their ideas in the Party, and a far less generally-agreed

[37] CCO file, 'R.A. Butler, 1940–1957', CCO 20/1/1, CPA; John Ramsden, *The Making of Conservative Party Policy, The Conservative Research Department since 1929* (1980), 97–9, 102; H.V. Armstrong to Chief Whip, 15 May 1941, Whip's papers, 'Political Truce', CPA; Salisbury to Swinton, 21 June 1941 and later correspondence between them, Swinton MSS 270/5/1; J.D. Hoffman, *The Conservative Party in Opposition, 1945–1951* (1964), 28–9, 38–9; NCP, March and May 1944; Lord Butler of Saffron Walden, *The Art of the Possible, The Memoirs of Lord Butler* (1971), 128.

belief that the Party must respond positively to the Beveridge Report. The parliamentary party was made up substantially of men who had gained or regained their seats in 1931, since there had been no Conservative seats gained since then and few wartime retirements; it was therefore an elderly team by the middle of the War. The same was true of the National Union and the constituency organisations, where a generation of office-holders had to soldier on in their posts because the potential younger replacements were in the forces. Constituency associations regularly noted the desperate need for younger office-holders but could do little about it, as for example in Leeds and in Bury St. Edmunds. A branch chairman, writing to the Kings Lynn agent after the selection of a new candidate in 1944, thought that 'looking round the room, I came to the conclusion that you, Cole, Leslie, Birbeck with myself, brought the average age down to about 75'. The problem was appreciated at the top too. In 1941 Churchill himself 'considered that the only hope for the Tory Party at the next election was to choose young candidates who had won their spurs in the war'. Amery perceived a different slant on this when he was told in 1942 that his son Julian had been seeing the Party Chairman: 'I understand they are now very keen on young Service candidates who, after the war, can disclaim any responsibility for the failures of the pre-war years.' Churchill had forgotten his earlier enthusiasm for the encouragement of youth when in 1945 he read in the press about Central Office's wish to avoid septuagenarian candidates; he minuted the Party Chairman to ask 'whether this ban applies to me'. He was told by Assheton that it did not, but that discreet words had indeed been had with some associations about the need for younger candidates. Some of the old and out of touch were forcibly removed before nomination stage in 1945, and Conservative candidates as a group then had a very similar age profile to the Labour team.[38]

This general search for younger men provided an opportunity for the Tory Reform Group. Harold Nicolson noted in his diary in March 1943 that people expected that Labour would sooner or later insist on leaving Churchill's government; 'this will give the Young Tory Group which is gathering around Quintin Hogg, Hinchingbrooke and Hugh Molson a great opportunity. As usual the Tory Party will be saved by its young men.' Woolton, meeting Hinchingbrooke, and 'a group of his Tory Reform friends', noted that 'they are the young Conservatives who see that the old Tory ideas have got to be modified'. In 1943, when the TRG was formed to press for a sympathetic Tory response to the Beveridge Report, which Lord Hinchingbrooke thought to be 'the very essence of Toryism', the first chairman, Hinchingbrooke, was thirty-seven, of the joint secretaries Hugh Molson was thirty-nine and Peter Thorneycroft just thirty-three; Quintin Hogg, the second chairman, was

38 Gilbert, *Finest Hour*, 1169; Kings Lynn CA minutes, 19 Feb. 1945; Barnes and Nicholson, *Empire at Bay*, 845; Gilbert, *Road to Victory*, 1316; R.B. McCallum and Alison Readman, *The British General Election of 1945* (Oxford, 1947), 75–7.

thirty-five. They attracted forty-one MPs into membership, met weekly to discuss parliamentary business, and became active publicists, much as Young England and the Fourth Party had been through a similar impatience with their elders in earlier times. Their pamphlets created an impression of action and enterprise, the content thereof rather less so. On the central economic issue of public ownership in industry, Hogg breezily wrote that it was an old-fashioned debate, and that the world of the technocrat was the world of the future, in which management rather than ownership was what would matter. Anthony Crosland would argue something very similar in *The Future of Socialism* in 1956, and to great effect, but only after the implementation of substantial nationalisation had sated the public appetite.[39]

In wartime, the TRG made little impact on the real political debate and came nowhere near capturing the Party, while Butler managed in 1944 to close down its research activities which were threatening to rival those of the official Party machine. It did though provoke opponents in the Party, older men who already feared that left-wing ideas were being too far advanced by the effects of the War and saw the TRG as an enemy within the gates. The TRG's readiness to accept what Tom Harrisson called 'permanent coalition' so as to pursue their social policy objectives also stemmed from their fears of the future, and Harrisson himself added in 1944 that 'such tendencies imply that the thoughtful Tories are far from sure of a sole success post-war', tendencies that other Conservatives saw as unduly defeatist. The Group's members were therefore careful to get the support of their constituency associations for each step that they took, as Molson did at High Peak, Simon Wingfield Digby in West Dorset and Thelma Cazalet Keir in Islington; E.E. Gates at Middleton and Prestwich and Christopher York in Ripon were less successful in mending fences locally, and their TRG work may have contributed in both cases to their early retirements. Meanwhile the enemies gathered, and these Party reactionaries were at least as influential as the TRG in influencing public perceptions of the Party. The ultra-conservative *National Review* dismissed the Beveridge Report (and implicitly its Conservative supporters) as the work of 'a well-known socialist bureaucrat'; in November, Spencer Summers formed the Progress Trust, with the support of some thirty Tory MPs and the direct aim of countering the influence in the Party of the TRG; with hindsight, the Progress Trust looks like an important precursor of the economic liberalism which captured the Party in the 1970s, but at the time it was not much noticed, and in any case was secretive about its activities and membership. Some went further and backed the diehard National Society for Freedom. The Wessex Area Council witnessed an unusually open battle in 1943 when Hogg announced that he would have to oppose the re-election of the Area President if

[39] Nicolson, *Harold Nicolson Diaries*, 286; Woolton diary, 15 Dec. 1943, Woolton MSS; Hoffman, *Conservative Party*, 41–2; Alan Beattie, *English Party Politics, Vol. II, 1906–1970* (1970), 495; Quintin Hogg, *One Year's Work* (1944), 126; Angus Calder, *The People's War, Britain 1939–1945* (1969), 532–4.

he did not stop making public attacks on the TRG; the President survived until 1945. Resolutions that were passed at Area meetings indicated greater support for traditional Conservative instincts than for the electoral calculations of the TRG, as for example in regular motions of support for individual rights against state interference. When in April 1944 the National Union Executive received from Sevenoaks a resolution calling for a full statement of Party policy based on the work of the TRG, it was decided to take no action, with only two dissentient votes. For all their undoubted talent, the progressives did not succeed in capturing the Party's public image from 'the old blunderbores', but they could prevent the reactionaries from taking control; at the 1945 Party Conference, a motion welcoming the creation of a National Health Service was passed, and Hogg and his allies succeeded in defeating a wrecking amendment. This was all contentious ground, and when asked for his advice by Assheton, Butler responded that in the Party 'my feeling is that you have a large pack of dogs – and indeed also of lady dogs! – and, if they fight one another, it is inadvisable for you to place any of your members in between their jaws'.[40]

When the War ended, neither side had won the internal battle of attrition. This wartime difference of approach between Tory interventionists and neo-liberal free marketeers, each claiming to root their philosophy in different strands of the Party's past practice, would continue through the policy-making in opposition. There were not though two mutually exclusive camps within the Party, even on the core elements of industrial policy, for the lack of definition of Party policy allowed a variety of middle positions. Hence, in February 1945, Butler (who would not figure on most people's lists of dogmatic economic liberals), wrote to Lyttelton (who was generally a stern critic of interventionism) to complain that the coalition's hybrid plan for electricity was unfair to private investors and 'seems to me to remove all incentive or responsibility':

> I am not going to say that one would not have to go further in regard to public control of a service like Electricity than one would desire to go with a productive industry. But I do not want to pledge myself to a hermaphrodite scheme at this stage without having the time and opportunity to try it out, not only on my own people in East Anglia, but on the country generally. We must in fact know where we are going in economic affairs.

If the various wartime policy discussions provided no real policy input by 1945, they did form some habits of association and make some reputations that would be of importance later; Hogg and Thorneycroft were both junior ministers in Churchill's 1945 Caretaker Government, largely on the basis of

40  Calder, *People's War*, 530; Addison, *Road to 1945*, 233; Jefferys, *Churchill Coalition*, 116, 133; Richard Cockett, *Thinking the Unthinkable, Think-Tanks and the Economic Counter-Revolution, 1931–1983* (1994), 68; Tom Harrisson, 'Who'll win?' in the *Political Quarterly*, vol. 15 (1944), 21; Wessex Area Council minutes, 19 May 1943; East Midlands Area Council, 25 Nov. 1944; NUEC, 20 Apr. 1944; Hoffman, *Conservative Party*, 38; Jones, 'Conservative Party' thesis, 22, 103.

their TRG activities, and Butler's emergence after 1945 as the impresario of post-war policy owed much to his work in the PWPCC. When such men became involved in official policy-making for the Party in and after 1947, they brought with them the ideas and attitudes that they had developed during the War.[41]

As a result of this stand-off between progressives and reactionaries, Conservatives were largely reactive in their attitude to social and economic policy in the second half of the War. Nowhere was this clearer than over the Beveridge Report, for the Party did not even submit evidence to Beveridge's enquiry. When the report appeared and scored its own public relations success, Conservatives were divided. At one extreme those like Sir Herbert Williams and the *National Review* were frankly aghast at the report's proposals. A second, more generous-minded group, like Churchill himself and the Conservative *Yorkshire Post*, welcomed the ideas but were worried about the potential cost, especially in wartime; Ralph Assheton, who disliked the report's emphasis on unselective benefits, told Butler that 'One of the chief troubles about the Beveridge Report is that whereas his diagnosis relates to Want, his proposals are very largely devoted to giving money to people who are not in Want'; this would handicap all other Government proposals because it would use up resources that could be better spent elsewhere. Men like Hogg both supported the ideas and argued that it would be electorally suicidal to do other than welcome the report.[42]

A committee was set up under Assheton, from which a Party strategy emerged which all but the Tory Reformers could accept; Harold Nicolson noted that this was 'to welcome the idea in principle, and then whittle it away by detailed criticism. They will say that it is all very splendid and Utopian, but we can only begin to know whether we can afford it once we have some idea what our foreign trade will be like after the war.' This was by no means so foolish a position as it has sometimes been made to sound, but it would never satisfy a public whose appetite for social betterment had been so whetted by Beveridge. Constituency parties and Area Councils, as at Leeds and in the Yorkshire and Eastern Areas, welcomed the report, as did Central Council on behalf of the whole Party, but always with reservations. Even months later, Butler found many Conservatives whose gut feeling was that Beveridge was 'a sinister old man who wants to give away a great deal of other people's money'. The redistributive elements in Beveridge's proposals were indeed the part which Conservatives most generally disliked, though the collectivist elements also failed to appeal, for reasons that Cuthbert Headlam put very effectively in his diary in February 1943: 'so many of our Party – more especially the younger members – are more "left" than the Labour

---

[41] Butler to Assheton 22 Jan. 1945, Butler MSS, G17 Butler to Lyttelton, 6 Feb. 1945, Butler MSS, G17.
[42] Addison, *Road to 1945*, 217–18, 224; Jones, 'Conservative Party' thesis, 74.

Party, terribly afraid of it being thought unprogressive – and nowadays to be thought progressive you must be all out for totalitarian methods of administration, no matter how much you may condemn such methods in Germany or in Italy.' Besides, it was all hopelessly unrealistic; as he noted two years later, 'Beveridge . . . knows as much about real men and women as I know about statistics'. Others, even those who supported Beveridge's actual proposals, resented the whole idea that social progress was the *quid pro quo* for war service: Henry Willink, who as Minister of Health strongly supported reform, nevertheless recalled that 'to me it was an article of faith that our fight was *against* Hitler and all his works, not "for" social reforms, however desirable'. For all these reasons, it was difficult for Conservative speakers to catch the right tone in debating Beveridge in 1943.[43]

As so often, the chief impression of the Party's response was given by the parliamentary debate and its reporting. Kingsley Wood briefed Churchill strongly against anything other than a guarded response because of the cost, and although some Tory Ministers like Amery tried to get a more balanced Government policy, Churchill was happy to be persuaded that it would all have to wait until the end of the War. In Churchill's absence through illness, the Government's spokesmen, Anderson and Wood, concentrated far more on the Report's costs than on its opportunities, while backbenchers like Williams gave a clear impression that they would not stand for any implementation of the Report before the end of the War, and probably not afterwards either. Labour meanwhile put down a reasoned amendment which made clear its wish for quicker progress, and nearly all Labour MPs who were not actually ministers voted for it. In 1944, Central Office found itself indignantly defending the voting records of its MPs in the Beveridge debate, pointing out that they could not be fairly criticised from the left for voting for a motion that Labour ministers had actually proposed. The Party had been put firmly on to the defensive.[44]

Similar impressions of Conservative foot-dragging and Labour enthusiasm for change were created in other debates on post-war policy. The biggest Conservative rebellion came in February 1943 when Bevin persuaded Churchill to allow 'uncontroversial' wages increases in the Catering Industry; Douglas Hacking, only just retired from the Party Chairmanship, led more than a hundred Conservative MPs into the lobbies against Bevin's bill, while the 'indignant' Tory Reformers vociferously backed the Government; on the way out of the House Hacking asked Eden if the Government still thought the issue was uncontroversial.[45]

---

[43] Nicolson, *Harold Nicolson Diaries*, 264; Leeds CA minutes, 2 Feb. 1943; Eastern Area Council, 24 Mar. 1943; NUEC, 14 Apr. 1943; Jefferys, *Churchill Coalition*, 122; Headlam diary, 11 Feb. 1943 and 17 Jan. 1945; Willink unpublished autobiography, 74, Willink MSS.

[44] Addison, *Churchill*, 365–7; Jefferys, *Churchill Coalition*, 120; Nicolson, *Harold Nicolson Diaries*, 181–2; *NCP*, Dec. 1944.

[45] Addison, *Road to 1945*, 232; Jefferys, *Chuter Ede*, 118–19.

The push for a more progressive policy on Town and Country Planning had largely emerged from non-political sources, but the implementation of the land valuation clauses of the Uthwatt Report became highly partisan. The Labour minister James Chuter Ede observed that 'a small gang of landowning Tories are giving considerable trouble & are lectured & hectored by the Tory Reformers'. A few days later he noted that the Bill had been 'nearly wrecked yesterday by the diehard Tories. The P.M. had to intervene and suggest the postponement of the compensation clauses.' But any effective system of Party management would have foreseen that a Party whose supporters included so many property-owners would find it extemely hard to swallow new rules allowing the public acquisition of private property at less than current market values. Lord Selborne had threatened resignation from the Government and the Chief Whip had told Churchill that Conservative MPs as a whole were so hostile that the Government's best hope was that they would abstain rather than vote against; Churchill's riposte to such threats was to say that if a majority did vote against he would resign the Party Leadership. Revision of compensation levels resulted in the Bill going through, but with more than fifty Conservative MPs still voting against. Again Labour had made clear its public support for a more egalitarian policy. Churchill's official biographer writes of this incident that it 'forced him to intervene, as he so seldom did, in an entirely Party political matter'; you would scarcely know from this that he was Conservative Party Leader, a position that implied some obligations as well as conferring the right to be Prime Minister.[46]

The 1944 White Paper on Employment, committing all the coalition partners to the pursuit of 'a high and stable level of employment' in post-war policy caused less visible friction but much private heart-searching. On this issue, after the experience of the 1930s, most Conservatives could see clearly enough that they had to give the same pledge as Labour, though even here Herbert Williams was on hand to denounce the policy as 'this miserable document'. Some were indeed eager to tailor it to local needs, as when the Northern Area asked for special consideration to be given to shipbuilding and to policy on the location of industry. But while Sir Kingsley Wood can be claimed to have presented Britain's first Keynesian budget, many senior Conservatives remained dubious about the Keynesian employment pledge in terms of its attainability and the strains it might impose on other policies. The Party Chairman, Ralph Assheton, privately described the full employment pledge as 'a series of empty shams' and feared that 'the public has been promised more than can possibly be performed'. The real problem in this policy area was not only that Labour could manage more enthusiasm for a popular idea than the Conservatives could, but that any pledge to promote high employment levels cast a sinister retrospective light on the pre-war governments that had argued

[46] Jefferys, *Chuter Ede*, 190–1; Jefferys, *Churchill Coalition*, 178–9; Gilbert, *Road to Victory*, 1037.

that unemployment was a natural disaster entirely beyond the wit of man to control – much as the praise for Russia's military power cast an equally sinister light on the politicians who had underestimated Russian strength in 1938–39.[47]

However, the bitterest public division came over a minor aspect of the Party's one domestic policy success, Butler's Education Bill. Flexing their muscles and determining that the Party must be given a progressive appearance for its own good, even if it did not want one, the TRG ambushed the whips in March 1944 with a proposal that men and women teachers should receive equal pay. The principle was one that had little to do with the Bill and was not in any case a matter for the Board of Education alone, so Butler opposed the amendment, only to find that the TRG and Labour backbenchers could together defeat the Government – its only defeat on a policy vote during the War. Butler hastened to Churchill and offered to resign, but Churchill decided instead to fight back, to pay off accumulated scores and frustrations, and to get a useful expression of parliamentary support just before D-Day. The House – in effect the rebel Conservative MPs – were told that there would be a further vote on the following day which the Government would treat as a motion of confidence; Chips Channon exulted that 'the rebels looked foolish, dreading the prospect of having to eat their words'. To his son, Churchill wrote merrily that he had been 'molested by a number of cheeky boys' but that 'the Mother of Parliaments' had 'chased them out of the backyard with her mop'. To MPs in the smoking room who thought his reaction excessive, Churchill countered, 'Not at all. I am not going to tumble round my cage like a wounded canary. You knocked me off my perch. You have got to put me back on my perch. Otherwise I won't sing.' Others were less sure: *The Economist* felt that 'the advice the Prime Minister is getting is bad advice. If it goes on it will finish by doing the impossible – that is by alienating him from a large section of the country . . . The leadership of the war is not in question but for every elector who, two months ago, suspected that the Government was needlessly obstructing reform or who doubted whether Mr. Churchill was the man to head the country in peace as well as in war, there must now be three or four.' Quintin Hogg wrote 'an open letter to the Party' for *Picture Post* after the debate, arguing that 'as a party we are heading for political suicide'. Such impressions there certainly were, but they did not rest on one debate, more on the cumulative impression given by the whole series of public statements about the post-war world on which politicians had to take a stand. Labour seemed open-minded and forward-looking; Churchill seemed hostile and far more interested in the fighting side of things which would soon be over; the Conservative Party had established no position separate from Churchill's. In August 1943, Eden met with a troublesome deputation of TRG members, who had 'stressed the question of the necessity of definite pronouncements

47  Addison, *Road to 1945*, 246; Jefferys, *Churchill Coalition*, 172; Northern Area Council, 15 Apr. 1944.

by the Government on post-war matters', especially about 'arrangements arising out of the Beveridge Report'; Eden wearily reported to the Chief Whip that, without going into details, 'I tried to make them understand that the Government had also thought about these matters'; he seemed unaware that it was precisely in the distances between generalities and details, and between thought and decision, that the problem lay. It is characteristic that the Party was outmanoeuvred on the issue of the future government of Greece, when Conservative ministers backed a highly interventionist policy to counter Communist subversion, but managed to be portrayed in parliament and the press as the supporters of a backward monarchy against popular government. By the 1945 Election, Eden was desperately having to argue that Labour as well as Conservative ministers had backed his Greek policy, but the public perception was different.[48]

## Experiencing the War

It needs to be remembered that Conservatives as a body of people and the Party as an organisation took a full part in the Second World War *as a war*, and at least in their own estimation had 'a good war'. Like any other group of Britons in the early 1940s, Conservatives were affected by the War's destructive and disruptive force, by its cost, and by its domination of ordinary life. The Party had its heroes and its sacrifices. Early in the War, the Tory agents claimed one of the first naval war heroes, Captain Kennedy of the armed merchantman *Rawalpindi*, sunk by German battleships when defending a convoy. Kennedy had been agent for Aylesbury since 1930 and returned to the Navy in 1939. The *Conservative Agents Journal* enthused over the example set by 'the immortal Kennedy of the Rawalpindi', reported a memorial to him unveiled in Aylesbury – ironically by a socialist First Lord of the Admiralty, and even had a correspondent in India who took part in a collection to raise a further memorial in Rawalpindi itself. By the start of 1941, 184 agents and organisers were in the armed forces and another 159 were employed on other war work outside the Party; as the 1945 General Election approached, twenty-three Central Office and Area staff and 292 agents and organisers were still employed in war work. The parliamentary party also joined up, as in 1914–18 a natural consequence both of innate patriotism and of including many Members who were retired career officers. One hundred and fifty-five Conservative MPs served in the armed forces, more than a third of the parliamentary party and a very high proportion of those who were of military age. (This compares to fourteen Labour MPs, about one in ten of the party and four Liberals.) Fourteen Tory MPs were killed in action, and seventeen

---

48 Rhodes James, *Chips*, 390–1; Gilbert, *Road to Victory*, 722; Addison, *Churchill*, 376; Addison, *Road to 1945*, 251; Tom Hopkinson (ed.), *Picture Post 1938–1950* (1990), 134; Eden memorandum, 5 Aug. 1943, Whip's papers, 'Coalition, miscellaneous', CPA; Anthony Eden, *Freedom and Order, Selected Speeches, 1939–1946* (1947), 350.

were decorated, and this does not include Patrick Munro, who collapsed and died in the House itself in May 1942, due to 'overstrain training with the H of C H[ome] G[uard]'; Headlam mournfully supposed 'that he was too old to run about like a boy playing at soldiers'. The 1943 by-election at Bury St. Edmunds, which produced a stiff contest, was just one of those occasioned by the death of the sitting Member on active service; the adopted candidate at Lewes withdrew in 1945 when his son was killed, and Eden's own son was posted missing by the RAF at the very end of the War. Sometimes the War's impact was more indirect; the North Camberwell Conservatives, meeting in July 1941 could not read and approve the minutes of their previous meeting which had been lost in an air raid, and most of Central Office's files for the pre-1939 period went as paper salvage for the war effort; the incidence of flying bombs and the impossibility of transport in Southern England after D-Day necessitated the cancellation of the proposed Party Conference in 1944; East Islington Conservatives congratulated Thelma Keir on the time she had spent visiting Party members and other constituents during and after bombing raids; Nancy Astor in Plymouth went rather further, performing cartwheels on the Hoe to entertain the sailors.[49]

More often the War's impact was more mundane. The crushing impact of war taxation on middle-class incomes, which led Churchill to tell a journalist in 1941 that 'some of the poor wretches were already taxed up to 18s.6d. in the pound', had an equally crushing impact on constituency association incomes. Many treasurers reported that they were simply too embarrassed to 'bother' people with demands for money for the Party. Guildford, where the subscription income halved, had one of the best financial positions; Kings Lynn and Hexham, where it fell by three-quarters, were more typical; in Denbigh subscriptions fell by more than 90 per cent. The position was often worse than it looked, for some of the remaining income, half of it in East Edinburgh, came from payment for use of Association offices requisitioned by a government department. Sharing or loss of offices was not only a temporary form of financial relief, it was also a constant source of friction; the Tynemouth Women found on reoccupying their premises not only that most of the chairs needed repairing, but that 139 cups had gone missing, and Guildford had considerable trouble in getting the Ministry of Food to return the office typewriter; there could be some compensations, as when Galloway Unionists found that the RAF had installed electric lighting in their committee rooms.[50]

It was not easy to get agents back once they had gone; those in the armed forces could not be demobilised until the War ended, but considerable

49  *Conservative Agents' Journal* [hereafter *CAJ*], Jan., Apr. and July 1941, CPA; Central Office file, 'Agents release from the forces, 1944–45', CCO 4/2/2, CPA; Quintin Hogg, *The Left Were Never Right* (1945), 11–14; Headlam diary, 3 May 1942; North Camberwell CA minutes, 31 July 1941; NUEC, 8 June 1944; East Islington CA minutes, 31 May 1945; Tom Harrisson, *Living Through the Blitz* (1976), 233.
50  Addison, *Churchill*, 360; Area and constituency records, various.

moral pressure could be applied to those on voluntary home service too –
running, say, the ARP in Darlington or the Food Office in Totnes, and
frequently as local organisers for the Ministry of Information or the War
Savings Movement. In many places, the functioning of the Conservative
associations was simply suspended for the duration; no meeting at all was
held between 1940 and early 1945 in Kettering or in Walsall or in North
Hampshire; in North Cornwall, the only wartime meeting, in 1941, produced
such a small attendance that 'the meeting then adjourned indefinitely'; South
East Cardiff met three times between December 1939 and March 1940 but
not again until September 1945; despite the constant Central Office urgings at
least to keep organisations in being, there was scarcely any activity in Eden's
constituency of Warwick and Leamington; the North West Area Council
seems to have closed down altogether (since it held no meeting at all), and
Central Office itself closed its Area Office in Cambridge.[51]

Where activity continued, it was usually in women's branches, and
was non-political. The *Durham City Advertiser* reported the October 1940
meeting of the Northern Area Council with the headline 'No time for
politics. Northern Conservatives engaged in war work.' The Tory Women's
formidable powers of social organisation and fundraising, which had served the
Party so well after women's mass entry into the Party in the 1920s, were turned
over to the war effort. In Glasgow, the Unionist women kept the Citizen's
Advice Bureau going throughout the War and the Pollok association collected
for the Shipwrecked Mariners' Fund; in Ilford the Tory women knitted
some 5,000 'garments for Ilford men serving in HM Forces', ran a servicemen's
canteen, and raised money for the Forces Welfare Association and the Lord
Mayor's Empire Air Raid Fund; in Gravesend the favoured war charity was
the Spitfire Fund and again the women knitted thousands of comforts for the
troops. But the prize should have been awarded to the women of Sheffield
Central; in 1940 alone, they provided 8,000 knitted comforts, ran whist drives
to buy the wool through the Mistress Cutler's Wool Fund, and had an array of
flag days and other events for the St John's Ambulance; in 1941, they raised
£350 for war weapons week (noting that it would buy thirty-five rifles), ran
further flag days and affiliated to the Army, Navy and Air Forces Association
in order to coordinate their work for servicemen's dependents; over the war
period as a whole, they raised £9,800 for war savings, £1,143 for war charities
and a further £1,536 for medical causes, and ran numberless canteens and
social amenities for war workers and servicemen. In the great outpouring of
voluntarism that the War prompted, Conservative organisations pulled their
weight.[52]

[51] *Ibid.*
[52] Constituency Association records, various.

## Towards 1945

All of this contributed no doubt to the Party members' feeling that they were playing their part, and must have helped significantly in aspects of the real war on the home front. The combination of its men fighting and its women keeping the home fires burning certainly bolstered the Party's self-image as an important contributor to the War. It could do little though to help in what was to come when the War ended. That task could only fall to the Leader, and when the War ended the Leader was still undecided about the policy of the Party and the future of his Government. In part this reflected an entirely understandable determination that military matters, which he knew that he did best, should not be hampered by his wasting time on issues that could be deferred; in part though it reflected a personal determination that nobody else should commit the Party in areas he had not the time to master. Of his own Government's plans for a National Health Service he told Eden in 1944, 'it is absolutely impossible for me even to read the papers let alone pass such a vast scheme of social change through my mind under present conditions'. How then did Churchill envisage the political future? Early in his administration he had foreseen that the War would be followed by 'a short lull during which we had the opportunity to establish a few basic principles . . . But all this talk about war aims was absurd at the present time: the Cabinet Committee to consider the question had produced a vague paper, four-fifths of which was from the Sermon on the Mount and the remainder an election address.' In 1942–43, pressure from within the Government forced him to allow more active consideration of post-war policy, hence the policy arguments of the later war years, but he seems never to have abandoned the assumption that there would be a transition phase between the end of the fighting and the start of peacetime politics. That is the way in which he defined the policy future in his 1943 radio broadcast, and he was harping on the same theme to the March 1945 Conservative Conference when he explained that the key jobs were to finish the War and bring the troops home, and that making decisions for the future could wait until all that had been done.[53]

All this presupposed that an immediate post-war election could be avoided, which was possible only on the assumption that coalition government would continue, and on this Churchill's personal hopes were always at odds with the likely outcome. In December 1940, just after becoming Leader, Churchill was already saying that he 'did not wish to lead a party struggle or a class struggle against the Labour leaders who were now serving him so well. He would retire to Chartwell and write a book on the war . . .' A month later he 'hoped Coalition Government would continue for two or three years after the war'. By 1943, with the prospect receding of Labour agreeing to

---

53  Addison, *Churchill*, 368–9, 374; Colville, *Fringes of Power*, 346; Central Council Minutes, 15 Mar. 1945, CPA.

continue in partnership after the end of the War, his PPS was reported as saying that Churchill 'wishes the National Government to go on, not only till the war is won, but also to make the Peace and shape the first post-war years. But at other times [Harvie-Watt] has heard him say, "If the Socialists won't cooperate, then I should like to lead the Conservative Party to victory." He thinks the P.M. has not really thought it out.' Unlike 1918, there was no practical basis on which an electoral deal could be done, since Conservatives would hardly give up a hundred seats that they held, and Labour could not accept a huge Tory majority for another five years. With a new electoral register and Parliament ten years old by 1945, an election could not be long delayed either. Labour was in fact consistently telling Churchill that coalition would end with the European war, and the Liberals were telling him that they would not stay in if Labour left. In October 1944 Churchill reluctantly conceded the likelihood of this outcome in a Commons speech, but this was not followed by any ringing appeal to his Party, or indeed in any changed attitude to the Party at all; in the early months of 1945 Churchill was still trying to get Labour and the Liberals to change their minds and to stay in office, at least until Japan was defeated.[54]

For the Conservatives' real partners, this uncertainty was even worse than it was for Conservatives. National Labour MPs, for example, could expect no quarter from the Labour Party and were themselves refusing to support a peacetime government that included Labour; the MP for Lichfield refused to stand again, since he could not back 'a Churchill election on a Con-Lab ticket', only to change his mind at the very last moment in 1945 when it transpired that that would not happen. The Liberal Nationals, led by Ernest Brown since Simon's elevation to the Woolsack, entered into discussions with the independent Liberals about Liberal reunion because of their uncertainty about their own prospects if Churchill did a deal with Sir Archibald Sinclair; in the end these discussions foundered because Brown, like Churchill, favoured continued coalition while Sinclair did not, and so he committed his Party to an uncertain future with the Conservatives rather than rejoin its older Liberal allies. Conservatives too were given no clear guidance of what to expect; in January 1942, Hacking's New Year message to the agents speculated inconclusively about the sort of election they should be preparing for. Dugdale was in much the same position in January 1944 and had to whistle in the dark to produce an encouraging message. He told them that the War should end in 1944 and would be followed by an immediate general election, but 'we shall probably not know, until late in the day, what will be the alignment of parties, how much assistance, voluntary or otherwise, will be available . . . [but] the Conservative Party is in high fettle today . . . Mr. Butler's universally welcomed Education Bill, the speeches of our leaders, the reports published

---

54 Colville, *Fringes of Power*, 310, 333; Pimlott, *Dalton War Diaries*, 595; Jefferys, *Churchill Coalition*, 174.

by the Post War Problems Committee [sic] and other publications have all contributed to impressing on the minds of the public that Conservatism is very much alive and looking ahead.' Rather more significantly, the General Director announced in the same issue that he was conducting a survey to find out where in the world the qualified agents who had been in post in 1939 now were. Assheton's message in January 1945 spoke more prosaically of plans being made for a 'simplified plan of campaign' which could be run with limited personnel and resources. It was to be a utility campaign or – as the agents returning from the forces might well have termed it – a 'tactical exercise without troops'.[55]

Man is not on oath when composing political New Year messages, and the truth was very different from Dugdale's rosy picture of 1944; it had not much improved by the start of 1945. The Party was pleased enough with its contribution to the War, and the rank and file had an admiration for Churchill that far exceeded that of Conservative ministers and MPs. But team spirit had been notably absent from the Party at Westminster for five years, the current Leader had no intention of defending his predecesors in a campaign that was bound to pivot on their record, and the battle between Tory Reformers and reactionaries had been fought out in public for two years. The attempts to give a fresh face to Conservatism in a time of rapid social change had scarcely touched the real problem because, above all, they had been *unofficial*. For more than four years the Party had been nailed to the Churchill Government without being in control of it, and without having anyone at the top willing and able to protect its collective self-interest. Churchill was the one man in a position to do this but had decided that he would really rather not, and he had failed to appoint anyone else to do it for him. Worse, he had made it clear that he would really rather not run a Conservative Government at all, and that he had no distinctive policy to impart through one. He told the 1945 Party Conference, by now expecting a party election, that his team would still include 'men of goodwill of any party or no party' and even added that he might, after winning an election, further broaden the base of his Government. What was the Party to make of the suggestion that after winning a tough contest he would find jobs for party opponents who had beaten Conservative candidates, at the expense of Conservatives who had fought on his own side? When that mighty Churchillian trumpet gave forth such an uncertain note, is it surprising that his Party was unready for the battle?[56]

55  Lichfield CA minutes, 20 Mar. 1942 and 21 Dec. 1944; Gerard de Groot, *Sir Archibald Sinclair* (1993), 212–15; *CAJ*, Jan. 1942, Jan. 1944 and Jan. 1945.
56  Addison, *Churchill*, 381.

# Chapter 2

# 'The Waterloo of the Conservative Party' – the General Election of 1945

An opinion poll taken at the outset of the 1945 General Election campaign but almost entirely ignored at the time, indicated that 84 per cent of the electorate had already made up their minds how to vote. The evidence of other polls and of wartime by-elections lends credence to this view. The origins of the Conservatives' crushing 1945 defeat must be sought much earlier in the War, during the years of political truce between the parties.

## The electoral and political truce

There never actually was a political truce. An *electoral* truce was agreed in September 1939; the three Chief Whips agreed on behalf of their parties 'not to nominate candidates for parliamentary vacancies that now exist, or may occur, against the candidate nominated by the Party holding the seat at the time of the vacancy occurring', an agreement that was to last for the duration or until one of the participants formally terminated it. Minor parties and independents broke this electoral peace with some regularity, and often to great effect, but at first at least the major parties observed it scrupulously; Labour expelled party members and disaffiliated local parties when they stepped out of line. But that was as far as it went. Even after 1940, when the parties were all serving together in government, there was no formal obligation on them to suspend political activity, only a moral imperative to respect national unity and a practical objective of minimising disharmony within the coalition. Yet the Conservatives always felt that the truce meant, or ought to mean, more than it actually did. Writing in 1946, McCallum and Readman concluded that 'the Conservatives interpreted the electoral truce as a political truce, while the Labour party, on the contrary, drew a sharp distinction between the two and held itself bound only by the electoral truce'. James Stuart explained in 1942, to Colonel Blair in Scotland, that this was indeed a conscious sacrifice of Tory interests: 'the Party Truce in letter only states that the Parties supporting the Government will not fight each other at by-elections. In spirit, I think Unionists naturally took it to go beyond this, as it is difficult to avoid by-election contests if the Parties indulge in heated warfare at all other times. It was also obvious that, in the interests of national unity, it was better to avoid such Party controversy.' The Conservatives therefore held no wartime

Party Conference until 1943, and then no other until March 1945; Labour held a Conference every year, a difference of approach that carried on down through the respective organisations. When Labour's 1942 Conference was reported in detail by the BBC, the 1922 Committee complained about bias; the BBC responded that they would give equal billing to Tory meetings, but since they were hardly ever held this did not help much. Hence also the Conservative insistence that the Government should avoid 'controversy' and their extreme irritation when it did not.[1]

Central Office advice was that local parties should not respond to provocation, as Sir Robert Topping argued in 1940 when partisan Labour activity in Poplar was reported to him. There was therefore embarrassment when occasionally local Tory activists broke the pact as Conservatives imagined it to be, as in 1944 Conservative councillors in Gateshead took advantage of the death of Labour Aldermen to take control of the Borough, something that would have been permissible under Labour's idea of the truce anyway. In 1943, Dulwich Conservatives noted that they had taken the truce too literally, by closing down altogether; Central Office advised them that the intention was to keep formal activities going but to be non-partisan. Guildford decided in 1941 to keep a skeleton organisation going 'to counteract socialist tactics', but to keep it very low key. In Penryn and Falmouth it was agreed in 1942 'that future political activity should remain in abeyance'. The Yorkshire Area received a resolution from Bradford in 1943 calling for political organisation to be strengthened despite the truce, but it was left to lie on the table. Complaints were more often about the lack of activity than about Conservatives breaking the truce; the Petersfield Association complained about this to Central Office in 1941 'but gained the impression that Party Headquarters were not very concerned about it'.[2]

With their elevated but imaginary idea of the nature of the truce, Conservatives frequently cried foul about Labour's more robust attitude. The Whip's office were complaining to Churchill in 1942 that Labour in Cardiff were doing nothing to help get the new War minister elected to the Commons at a by-election; in January 1944, Stuart was again complaining to Churchill, reporting that at ten by-elections so far the local Labour and Liberal parties had given near-overt help to anti-Conservative candidates; the imminent candidacy of Charlie White as an independent in West Derbyshire,

[1] Agreement of 21 Sept. 1939, Whip's papers, 'Party Truce', CPA; Paul Addison, *The Road to 1945, British Politics and the Second World War* (1975), 163; R.B. McCallum and Alison Readman, *The British General Election of 1945* (Oxford, 1947), 4; Stuart to Blair, 21 July 1942, Whip's Papers, 'Political Truce', CPA; Kevin Jefferys, *The Churchill Coalition and Wartime Politics, 1940–45* (Manchester, 1991), 142; 1922 Committee minutes [hereafter 1922 Cttee.], 3 June 1942, CPA.

[2] *Conservative Agents' Journal* [hereafter *CAJ*], Oct. 1940 and July 1944, CPA; Dulwich CA minutes, 9 Dec. 1943; Guildford CA minutes, 12 Sept. 1942; Penryn and Falmouth CA minutes, 29 Apr. 1942; Yorkshire Area AGM, 20 Feb. 1943; Wessex Area Council, 26 Nov. 1941.

where he had previously been the official Labour candidate, was a case in point – whatever he actually said, it was well known in Derbyshire to which party White belonged and who were his workers. It was not enough for the Labour and Liberal parties to abstain from official opposition; they should, argued Stuart, tell their supporters to vote Conservative, which was no doubt rather hopeful. The Party tried to respond to the erosion of the truce in a number of ways, for example by allowing ministers to go and speak at by-elections. Ministerial electioneering, which had been against constitutional practice since a Commons resolution of 1779 had warned the King's ministers off from interfering in elections, had already been authorised in exceptional circumstances by Chamberlain in 1938, but Churchill positively refused to allow any but the most junior members of his team to go to the hustings. In January 1944, Topping went much further in complaining of 'the difficulties of our candidates fighting by-elections'. There had been a revival of party feeling in the past few months, so that while there was still strong support for Churchill, a general appeal for national unity, 'so effective in the early days of the war' did not now 'secure much response outside the ranks of the Conservative Party'. He deplored the way in which independents who were known Labour sympathisers would make statements of loyalty to Churchill and then attack everything he and his Party stood for; these opponents would promise anything for votes, while the Tory candidate 'is handicapped too by the lack of a positive policy on home affairs', and 'has to fall back on requests to the electors to "Trust the Government" and "First win the War", which the by-election results indicate are falling on deaf ears'. Topping's suggested remedy for this was to allow the Tory candidate 'to take the offensive', which 'he cannot do without effective ammunition'; where there was no published coalition policy in detail, Tory candidates should be allowed (as Labour candidates already were) to use material from their Party, specifically from reports of the PWPCC. He concluded prophetically that 'here, it would appear, is the next General Election casting a shadow before, with the growing apprehension of an electorate which, seeing the end of the war in sight, is beginning to wonder what lies beyond'. Despite his desire to protect the Party's interests, Stuart felt bound to warn Churchill that, if Topping's suggestions were implemented, the Party truce would probably end altogether. Unsurprisingly, since he was preparing for the great national effort of D-Day, Churchill refused the request and the one-sided truce remained in force.[3]

In April 1941 the National Union Executive noted 'the wartime activities of Socialists, Communists and certain subversive societies, often of a political character' and urged local Conservatives to keep their guard up; in October

[3] Stuart to Churchill, 2 Oct. 1941, 10 Apr. 1942, 28 Jan. and 31 Apr. 1944, Whip's papers, 'Party Truce', CPA; Topping memorandum, 12 Jan. 1944, Whip's papers, 'Coalition, miscellaneous', CPA.

the 1922 Committee deplored 'socialist propaganda all over the country'. The following year, West Midlands Tories urged the Central Council to demand a response to 'those who were not sincerely supporting the war effort. There were indications in the Black Country of a deal of quiet working for a political revolution.' Churchill acknowledged both the Conservative restraint and the Labour foul play in March 1945: 'We have held in abeyance all party activities, and have allowed our organisations, both local and national, to be devoted entirely to the prosecution of the War. In doing this we have endured patiently, and almost silently, many provocations from that happily limited class of left-wing politicians to whom party strife is the breath of their nostrils.' The rhetoric may have been exaggerated and the sense of injured innocence a politically convenient position to adopt, but there was a real point here. Birmingham's historians have shown how trades union membership soared in the war years, and the City's Labour Party 'extended its canvassing, public meetings and membership drives as soon as the worst raids were over'. Then, 'from 1943 Labour began to campaign openly on issues which seemed likely to dominate the next general election, and the Labour group in the City Council began to raise issues of policy (many of which did not concern the Council) in order to publicise Labour policies, and to force the Unionists to take an opposing stand'. Looking back from November 1945, the Birmingham Chief Agent argued that 'the socialists . . . reaped advantage from the fact that during the War thousands of people entered factories and came under the sway of shop stewards. Whilst our agents were in the Forces, the trades union officials and Co-op Socialist officers remained at home and continued their political work.' Birmingham was not an isolated case. Hugh Dalton told Jock Colville in July 1945 'that while the Tories had left the constituencies untended, their agents being for the most part away fighting, he, like Herbert Morrison, had spent much time and effort in ensuring that the Labour electoral machinery was in good order'.[4]

## Conservatism under attack

More often, Conservative complaints were not of the silent burrowings of Labour and trades union organisers, but of the audible left-wing voices in the mass media. After defeat in 1945, Ralph Assheton argued that 'throughout the War the Socialists have never ceased to preach their materialistic gospel in season and out . . . This theme (with variations) was plugged in the popular Press, in yellow-backed books and pamphlets, on platforms and at street corners, and, above all, by ardent disciples in the guard rooms and

---

[4] National Union Executive minutes [hereafter NUEC], 14 May 1941, CPA; 1922 Cttee., 1 Oct. 1941; Central Council minutes, 26 Mar. 1942 and 15 Mar. 1945, CPA; A. Sutcliffe and R. Smith, *Birmingham, 1939–1970* (1974), 81; Birmingham UA minutes, 12 Nov. 1945; John Colville, *The Fringes of Power, Downing Street Diaries, 1939–1955* (1985), 611.

wardens' posts, on fire watches and at factory benches.' J.B. Priestley was a favourite target after his 1940 radio 'Postscripts'. A deputation from the 1922 Committee protested to the BBC about his broadcasts, and this was one of the factors that finally removed him from the air waves – another being his own ego and the large fee he demanded before he would broadcast his egalitarian message. Disturbingly though, 80 per cent of letters received and an even higher proportion of listeners surveyed, were found to agree with Priestley. Removing him from the air did not therefore settle the BBC, and Conservatives continued to complain to the War's end about its alleged left-wing bias. The National Union resolved in 1942 to deplore 'the continued tendency of the BBC to give undue publicity to the spokesmen of left wing opinions', to complain about the free publicity given to Labour's Party Conference, and to petition Churchill to take action. In November 1943, the Party Chairman arranged to have BBC overseas transmissions monitored to collect evidence for further complaints. The 1922 Committee was, if anything, even more vociferous.[5]

In the dock with the BBC were the Workers' Educational Association and the Army Bureau of Current Affairs. The Eastern Area Council was just one of many Tory organisations that complained that the WEA was putting out propaganda at the taxpayer's expense. But it was ABCA that really raised temperatures, and in this case there certainly were some active socialists like George Wigg who did try to use the machinery for political purposes. Churchill had a running battle with the War Office over ABCA, and in 1943 the Party Chairman interviewed the Director of Army Education to express the Party's deep concern. A Conservative backbencher writing to Churchill's PPS urged him 'for the love of Mike do something about it, unless you want the creatures coming back all pansy-pink'. Even the Labour Party's Ernest Bevin felt that ABCA went too far, sparking off another row by showing Churchill an ABCA poster which depicted pre-war slum conditions.[6]

Conservatives also had a far from an easy ride in the press. There is no provable correlation between newspaper readership and voting, but an interesting coincidence remains even after scepticism is given its due: the only period in which Labour has won a consistently high share of the popular vote, between the 1940s and the 1960s, was also the only time in which leftish newspapers approached half of total daily sales. The continuing rise of the *Daily Mirror* tilted the balance towards Labour during the war years, and by 1945 the papers backing Labour and the Liberals had almost half the circulation of the national daily papers. This left the Conservatives heavily dependent on the *Daily Express*, with easily the biggest circulation on the

---

[5] Addison, *Road to 1945*, 128, 145; Angus Calder, *The Myth of the Blitz* (1991), 197–8; NUEC, 8 July 1942 and 11 Nov. 1943; Philip Goodhart, *The 1922, The Story of the 1922 Committee* (1973), 105.
[6] Eastern Area Council, 18 Apr. 1945; NUEC, 11 Nov. 1943; Addison, *Road to 1945*, 145–9; Paul Addison, *Churchill on the Home Front, 1900–1955* (1992), 355.

right, but a dubious asset in the contexts of Beaverbrook's tendency to use it as a personal mouthpiece and of his equivocal relationship with the Tories. When the Party was defeated in 1945, many Conservatives heaped the blame on Beaverbrook, not for his part in the campaign, but for the role of his newspapers over the years. Assheton told him that 'the view was that if you have employed a brilliant propagandist such as Low, an amusing (but not the less deadly) propagandist in Nat Gubbins, a vitriolic propagandist such as Michael Foot, or a subtle propagandist such as J.B. Priestley (to mention but a few) over a period of years, no whirlwind campaign of a few weeks can undo the long-term anti-Conservative work of these men'. When Churchill complained to Eden after the defeat that Conservatives were being unfair to Beaverbrook, Eden replied that 'tho' to you he is the bottle imp, to most of world he is Satan'. The same partisanship in a popular press outlet was true of the photographic magazine *Picture Post*, which in June 1945 welcomed Labour's ability to offer 'a programme to give the world a stability which the anti-Russian, anti-Irish, anti-French, anti-American, anti-Resistance section of the Tory Party is working so hard to prevent'.[7]

Michael Foot was also a target in the context of the 'yellow-backed books' of which Assheton complained. From *Guilty Men* (by 'Cato', 1940) onwards, the Conservatives were subjected to a torrent of destructive writing from the Gollancz publishing house and from Penguin, regular doses of hatred in dangerously large quantities; when Oliver Stanley called for more Party activity in the Commons in 1942, he complained that through Foot and his friends, 'the pre-war record of the Party had been hung like a millstone round its neck by its critics. This must be got rid of,' *Guilty Men* went through twenty-two printings in its first four months, and had sold a quarter of a million copies by the end of the war; it was in all public and circulating libraries. Its basic message was unrelentingly hostile to all pre-war Conservatives who had backed Chamberlain, but warily supportive of Churchill and Eden. Geoffrey Mander's *We Were Not All Wrong* more modestly went through seven wartime editions, arguing in great detail that many MPs of all parties (but few Conservatives) had warned early and often about the rise of Nazi power. *Your MP*, by 'Gracchus', was so eagerly awaited in 1944 that it reprinted twice even before publication; it claimed that no Conservative who had backed Chamberlain could now be trusted, whatever his war record since, for 'he is still, in spite of any changes, the sort of person who could believe what he did believe in 1935 or in 1938, and the sort of person who could in May 1940, the month of defeat, vote to keep Mr. Chamberlain in power'. The bulk of the book consisted of analytical tables of the voting records of MPs in eight crucial debates since 1935, from which some tendentious conclusions

---

[7] Addison, *Road to 1945*, 152; McCallum and Readman, *General Election of 1945*, 181; A.J.P. Taylor, *Beaverbrook* (1972), 566; Eden diary, 1 Aug. 1945, Avon MSS, 20/1/25; Tom Hopkinson (ed.), *Picture Post, 1938–1950* (1970), 185.

were drawn. Churchill and Eden for example had voted on the 'wrong' side in the 1940 debate that put them into power, and Attlee and other Labour ministers had voted for a motion which the book said 'means a vote *against* Beveridge'. Neither of these facts was highlighted, and when Conservatives sought to do so, they were arguing from a beleaguered position and on their opponents' agenda. The most vicious of all these slim volumes was that by 'Celticus', (though in his case the pseudonym was rather spoiled by a postscript over Aneurin Bevan's own signature), *Why Not Trust the Tories?* This told a highly slanted tale of the history of Britain between the wars, warned electors to beware of Conservative electoral stunts, and argued that as in 1918 so in 1945, 'the problem of the Tories is the same – how to ride the crisis, how to lie, deceive, cajole and buy time so as once more to snatch a reprieve for wealth and privilege'.[8]

The combination of venom and effective writing in these best-selling texts was highly effective. In 1945, Conservative candidates around the constituencies found themselves having to explain away votes they had cast years ago, in response to questions that took no account of the contexts in which the votes had been taken. Quintin Hogg was characteristically direct, in the introduction to his *The Left Were Never Right*, a rare Conservative attempt to enter this pamphleteering war: he had written because it was being too widely believed that the Conservatives had no answers to the slanders that were being put about. Hogg promised to eschew 'the weary muck-raking indulged by the gloomy trinity of Roman pseudonyms', but could not resist the temptation: 'I make no complaint that only one of them, so far as I can ascertain, has served in this war, although more than one is of military age. There are doubtless good reasons for this. But I am entitled to observe that whilst some of the poor derided Tories were fighting the enemy, these egregious pamphleteers were sowing discord in the ranks at home behind our backs and attacking our personal honour.' The rest of the book was a highly defensive account of the same parliamentary votes and debates from the Conservative viewpoint, useful ammunition for candidates beset by hecklers, but on issues that they would not have wished to argue about in the first place. In response to the Gollancz books, the Party's publications could only provide the facts, for example on the large number of housing completions in the 1930s in contradiction of Bevan's arguments, and leave Conservative speakers to get on with it. The value to Labour of all this argumentative ammunition stored up over the war years can be seen in a Central Office account of the 1945 General Election published in the following October. There had been

> calculated misrepresentation of Conservative policy between the wars. The general socialist line was to paint a picture of Britain in grinding poverty, misery and

---

[8] 'Cato', *Guilty Men* (1940), 21; A.H. Booth, *British Hustings, 1924–1950* (1956), 218; Harvie-Watt report, 23 Oct. 1942, Harvie-Watt MSS, 2/1; Geoffrey Mander, *We Were Not All Wrong* (1944); 'Gracchus', *Your MP* (1944), 8, 94; 'Celticus', *Why Not Trust the Tories* (1944), 13.

unemployment before the War. No misrepresentation or abuse was too mean or shabby for them to use. No insult to the enterprise and commercial ability of their fellow countrymen too gross for them to offer. No wilful disregard of the facts of the foreign situation too irresponsible or shameless for them to indulge in . . . British Governments before the War were accused of deliberately 'sabotaging' the League of Nations, of nourishing Hitler and encouraging the growth of fascism. Every effort to maintain peace was misconstrued or distorted.'[9]

The Birmingham Chief Agent regretted in 1943 that there were 'lots of sevenpenny Penguins but no Tory books', and urged Central Office to take counter action against the left. Hogg's book was one response to such complaints, another being a series from Hutchinson, with red, white and blue rather than yellow covers, that included *Labour's Great Lie* by 'Candidus'. These pulled no punches; he argued in 1945 that 'the war against Germany was an ideological war. It was our libertarian ideology fighting against the Nazi totalitarian ideology. We won on the battlefield. We are in imminent peril of losing at home.' But these books were published only at the very end of the War, were frequently about future defence and foreign issues that were out of the mainstream of domestic concern, and rarely sold well. Nevertheless the homing-in by 'Candidus' on the supposed threat to democracy from socialist controls was characteristic, and the same instinct no doubt guided Conservatives in welcoming Friedrich von Hayek's *The Road to Serfdom* when published in 1944. The Party Chairman ordered several copies of Hayek's book to send to leading colleagues, so that it was probably through Assheton that what Harriet Jones called 'Hayekian rhetoric' entered Churchill's language in 1945; Central Office's *Notes on Current Politics* called it 'an important book', and the editor of *Conservative Agents' Journal* urged agents to get hold of a copy; but this would have been difficult, for despite reprints the book was almost unobtainable. For the 1945 Election, Central Office released part of its own jealously-guarded stock of paper to allow another reprint, but this did not arrive in time for the campaign. Hayek's time was not to come for another thirty years, but he was in any case hardly a propagandist of the type of 'Cato' or 'Gracchus'. The anti-interventionist idea was though a seam worth mining at the time, and would certainly be so in the later 1940s; the Bradford Chief Agent foresaw in 1944 that the British people would in due course resent interference with their rights and liberties, for 'even under the present abnormal conditions the country grumble about bureaucracy'.[10]

9  Nigel Nicolson (ed.), *The War Years, The Diaries and Letters of Harold Nicolson 1939–1945* (1967), 471; McCallum and Readman, *General Election of 1945*, 152; Quintin Hogg, *The Left Were Never Right* (1945), 7, 15; Central Office, *Notes on Current Politics* [hereafter *NCP*], Dec. 1944, June and Oct. 1945.
10 Birmingham UA minutes, 16 Oct. 1943; 'Candidus', *Labour's Great Lie* (1945), 57; Harriet Jones, 'The Conservative Party and Social Policy, 1942–1955', unpublished PhD thesis, University of London, 1992, 105–8; Richard Cockett, *Thinking the Unthinkable, Think-Tanks and the Economic Counter-Revolution, 1931–1983* (1994), 85; Addison, *Road to 1945*, 265; *CAJ*, Apr. 1944.

## War and political change

In part this Conservative demand for a fight back reflected the lack of any obvious Conservative participation in the media battle of ideas, in part it reflected the deep feeling that all this mattered enormously, and that a deep-seated change in popular attitudes was taking place. The Newcastle under Lyme Conservatives demanded in 1942 that Conservative ministers should visit the provinces to make speeches, as Attlee and Bevin were doing, and later in the same year the West Midlands Conservatives urged 'the Party authorities to make available to the general public writings, articles and pamphlets with a Conservative viewpoint'. In deference to the truce, Central Office literature continued to report favourably the speeches of Labour and Liberal as well as Conservative ministers, and allowed no negative copy about Labour to appear. This resolutely 'governmental' approach did not provide an answer to the attacks from the left, for the Government's own public relations were devoted almost entirely to the war effort. Where the Government did move into more political areas, through the WEA, ABCA and the Ministry of Information for example, its agencies were overwhelmingly staffed by left-of-centre intellectuals – for there was no obvious right-wing pool from which similar talent might have been drawn. As Paul Addison concluded, 'although the Coalition was predominantly Tory in composition, Government propaganda owed more to the Fabians or the Workers' Educational Association than to Conservative Central Office'. Anthony Eden, for example, the most popular Conservative minister and one of the few both trusted by Churchill and likely to appear as sensible and forward-looking to the public, did not broadcast on the BBC at all between 1941 and the end of the War.[11]

A groundswell of anti-Conservative opinion was forming, and Conservatives were well aware of the changes in attitudes that war had brought in its train. Elton Halliley, agent for Bury St. Edmunds and a key figure in the National Society of Agents, wrote an editorial in the *Conservative Agents' Journal* on this theme in late 1941: 'the course of the war has brought about a great change in our way of life; there has been increasing state intervention in practically every phase of activity; and the necessities and conditions of total war have swept away all kinds of conditions which were held sacred before the war'. Conservatives recognised and accepted for example that war required appointments and promotions to be made on grounds of talent rather than education, background and experience; this led to the changed social composition of the officer corps with the introduction of scientific recruitment testing, and the same approach was then extended to the civil service. Churchill and the more traditional Conservatives did not welcome

[11] NUEC, 14 Jan. 1942; West Midlands Area Council, 4 Dec. 1942; Central Office *Notes for Speakers*, 2c [early 1943], CPA; Addison, *Churchill*, 344; Anthony Eden, *Freedom and Order, Selected Speeches, 1939–1946* (1947), 346.

such moves, but they did not resist the idea that they were needed to fight a modern war more effectively. Their reservations stemmed from a view that such changes eroded tradition itself and the authority that derived from it. As the historian Denis Brogan put it in 1943, discussing the demand for such changes, 'in their silent, unrhetorical, undramatic way, the English people seem to be registering a vote of no confidence in their recent rulers'.[12]

Churchill himself acknowedged the great change, addressing the boys of Harrow in 1944: 'I can assure you that during this war great changes have taken place in the minds of men, and there is no change which is more marked in our country than the continual and rapid effacement of class differences.' Mass Observation found in 1944 that popular opinion had moved away from 'selfish', individual ideas to a more community-based acceptance of collective action. Harold Nicolson recognised the same swing of opinion, but unlike Churchill he saw it as leading to more rather than less class feeling:

> People feel, in a vague and muddled way, that all the sacrifices to which they have been exposed . . . are all the fault of 'them' – namely the authorities or the Government. By a totally illogical process of reasoning, they believe that 'they' mean the upper classes or the Conservatives . . . Class feeling and class resentment are very strong. I should be surprised therefore if there were not a marked swing to the left.

Others picked up the same sense that the interests which Conservatism had stood for were now resented by the mass of the population, and that a different approach would be needed. An activist in Kings Lynn in 1945 asked 'is it realised that the day has long gone when a bloke like Lord Fermoy could collar fifty per cent of the West Walton votes simply by standing on the platform and saying, "Ladies and Gents, I want you to vote for me. I'm in favour of the Prime Minister, agriculture and all that sort of thing."' An agent writing in July 1944 thought that alongside housing, employment and industry, the public's great concern was with 'the removal of vested interests', and Baldwin's old agent in Bewdley was saying something very similar in April 1945 when he predicted that the election would turn on 'demobilisation, gratuities, jobs, housing and social security, all subjects so readily adaptable to the wild promises of our opponents'. The drift of opinion was marked even in the Church of England, a direction from which Conservatives had not often had to face flanking fire in the past. Archbishop Temple's Penguin Special *Christianity and the Social Order* (1942) sold 150,000 copies for its exposition of the redistribution of wealth; Karl Marx, said Temple, 'was not far wrong'. The Bishop of Durham was more reliably Tory, but the Bishop of Birmingham intervened directly on Labour's side in the 1945 campaign;

---

12  *CAJ*, Oct. 1941; Angus Calder, *The People's War, Britain 1939–1945* (1969), 472; Addison, *Churchill*, 351; R.A. Chapman, *Leadership in the British Civil Service* (1984); T.E.B. Howarth, *Prospect and Reality, Britain 1945–1955* (1985), 14.

'Bishop denounces free enterprise' was the *Daily Mirror*'s headline. The danger that these ideas represented is shown by the fact that, when the Central Office speakers' notes began to offer subscribers ready-made answers to popular hecklers' questions in 1943, the very first of the series was an answer to the question 'why do six per cent of the population own eighty-six per cent of the national wealth?'[13]

However, these concerns related to the whole population, while the sharpest fears were about the changing views of servicemen. Such fears may be summarised, along the lines of a song from the previous war, as 'how you're going to keep them down on the farm, now that they've seen Paree?' War service, shared experience and travel all combined to raise the horizons of conscript soldiers; Paul Addison quotes one such example from a natural conservative who was transformed by the army: 'when I came out I was an entirely different person, I wasn't going to be pushed around, I realised that the people above me were no better than me . . .'; he also quotes David Niven recalling from his own time in the army that 'the vast majority of men who had been called up to fight for their country held the Conservative Party entirely responsible for the disruption of their lives and in no circumstances would they vote for it next time there was an election – Churchill or no Churchill'. The problem here was that Churchill seemed to be very popular with the troops when he met them on his forays to bases and war fronts; but as Harold Watkinson noted, 'from inside the Services the Conservative chances looked much less bright . . . cheers for Winston were not the same as votes for the Conservative candidate'. And at the end of the War Jock Colville saw that, when ministers visited Berlin, Attlee, who had played no direct role in military matters, got an even bigger cheer than Churchill from the assembled British troops. The Barnsley Agent, on duty in Africa, wrote back home to tell his colleagues what the troops were thinking in 1944: 'one of the things that has most struck me . . . has been the deep thought that has been given by the men themselves to the kind of Government they want after the war . . . There is a general feeling that must be taken into account, however ill founded it may be in fact, that the domestic policies of the governments preceding the war were time-serving to a degree, whilst their foreign affairs were accompanied by a series of humiliating reverses that could have been avoided had stronger men been ruling.' In the Mediterranean, Harold Macmillan was ruminating on the same theme,

> The more I see of the army the more I wonder what they will make of England after the War. Will they be soothed in the syrup of Beveridge? Will they be victims of that Pied Piper Morrison? Will Dick Acland and Priestley be able to cash in on

[13] Addison, *Churchill*, 381; Peter Hennessy, *Never Again, Britain 1945–1951* (1992), 78; Brian Gardner, *Churchill in his Time, a Study in a Reputation 1939–45* (1968), 297; Kings Lynn CA minutes, 19 Feb. 1945; *CAJ*, July 1944 and Apr. 1945, CPA; Howarth, *Prospect and Reality*, 9; McCallum and Readman, *General Election of 1945*, 173; *NCP*, Mar. 1944.

their vague aspirations and sentiments? Or will they be able (as we failed to do 25 years ago) to construct a virile creed, firmly based on the glories of the past, but looking avidly to the new duties and ambitions of the future Empire?

Futher down the ranks, another Conservative MP who was a company officer closely in touch with his soldiers' views (and a future chairman of the 1922 Committee), Bill Anstruther-Gray, finished his war in May 1945 with the observation, 'I'm going back to be a pot-bellied politician. We shall get kicked out, but we'll be back.'[14]

## By-elections and opinion polls

The problem with predicting soldiers' opinions was that they were not able to cast votes in any serious test of opinion until the post-war election that most mattered. Civilians were not necessarily so disadvantaged, and here the result of the many wartime by-elections could be studied for evidence. If so studied, the lessons were not hopeful, and it is surprising that the Conservative Party managers were so sanguine about the 1945 election in the light of their previous fears of defeat.

The first half of the War presented no such difficulty. The truce held firm and the contests provoked by independents and freak candidates were easily beaten off. The most common themes of these early contests were the need to wage the War more effectively, the wish to back up Churchill against alleged lack of support, and a flavour of patriotic populism more reminiscent of 1914–18 than predictive of 1942–45. Interest and turnout were both low; when only 17.3 per cent of the electorate voted in Hampstead in November 1941, and this at a time when the House of Commons was in an uproar over the War, the Conservative agent reported that 'the view was fairly widespread that the by-election was a waste of time, money and paper'. Earlier in the year, the Birmingham Chief Agent reported on 'a by-election in a blitzed city', when Kings Norton went to the polls after the death in action of Ronald Cartland; with virtually no workers, no paper, no rooms for meetings and hardly any cars, it was hard to predict how 'even a Birmingham constituency' would respond. The by-election of this period that caused the most Party concern was an entirely domestic affair in June 1940 in Newcastle-upon-Tyne North. When the sitting Member, Sir Nicholas Grattan-Doyle, died, his supporters immediately selected his son; there were in fact several selections of widows, relatives and constituency chairmen for by-elections in the cosy wartime world of non-functioning constituency organisations; it was no doubt a safe way of retaining the large subscription on which organisations now depended.

---

[14]   Paul Addison, *Now the War is Over* (1985), 5, 14; Harold Watkinson, *Turning Points, a Record of Our Times* (1986), 19; *CAJ*, Jan. 1944; Alistair Horne, *Macmillan, 1894–1956* (1988), 213; Hennessy, *Never Again*, 85.

Other prominent citizens objected though to this apparent nepotism and found an alternative candidate in Cuthbert Headlam, a former MP who was currently Area Chairman; Headlam defeated the younger Grattan-Doyle at the subsequent by-election and was immediately accepted by the Conservative whips, but the local association remained bitterly divided over the affair for more than a decade. However, no Conservative seat was lost in a wartime by-election up to the end of 1941 and in nearly every case the independents contesting the seats were easily seen off.[15]

Things were less cosy in and after 1942. The West Dorset Agent noted the change in mood in May 1943: 'the anti-political mood of the pub, which was so noticeable in the first years of the war is, however, changing, and this is largely due to the consideration of post-war problems and the publication of various reports'. A strong anti-Tory mood developed, rallying first around another collection of adventurers and independents, but increasingly around the distinctively left-wing candidates of the Common Wealth Party. These were often backed informally by local Labour and Liberal activists, and were in effect surrogate candidates for Labour. Churchill's PPS reported to him in May 1942 that 'the electorate favours independents, who tend to be Leftists, largely as a result of the Socialist and pro-Russian propaganda, together with the talk of Colonel Blimp and the Old School Tie which have been much in evidence in the Daily Mirror and other papers'. The first outburst came in 1942 as the war situation deteriorated; four Conservative seats were lost at Grantham, Wallasey, Rugby and Maldon, and there were poor results almost everywhere. 1943 was a better year, with no Conservative seat lost – though Eddisbury was lost by the Liberal Nationals. Party literature made great play with this fact to claim a Conservative recovery, though in fact several of the seats held had been close shaves, as for example at Chippenham when David Eccles hung on by just 195 votes. In any case, the last period of the War again produced bad results, though few of them; ten Tory-held seats that fell vacant were contested between January 1944 and May 1945 but three of these were lost, at Skipton, West Derbyshire and Chelmsford, and again others were held by only the narrowest of margins. When William Teeling of the RAF was selected for a vacancy at Brighton in 1944 he faced an anti-Catholic backlash added to the mounting anti-Conservative feeling, and the near impossibility of fighting a campaign when you could not even enter a south coast town without a permit, when half the electorate had been evacuated and many of the rest had moved with trace, and when Churchill's intemperate letter of support to the candidate could not be used for fear of a libel action. The majority fell from 41,437 to 1,959 and Teeling was popularly – if somewhat

---

[15] *CAJ*, July 1941 and Jan. 1942; National Union General Purposes Committee papers, NUA 6/2/8, CPA.

unfairly – known in the Party for some years after as 'the man who made Brighton marginal'.[16]

The message seems clear enough: all of the seven Tory losses had been safe seats which had returned Conservative MPs for the previous twenty years, and Eddisbury was a solidly agricultural seat that had not even seen a Labour candidate before. Conservatives were certainly anxious about these adverse results, but at a loss to explain them, frequently attributing defeat to poor candidates. Lichfield's MP, G.B. Craddock, complained in 1942 that 'in nearly all the by-elections recently the seat has been given to the person who has promised the biggest amount to the local association. For example I have it on the best authority that Harrow was "sold" for £600 per annum to Bower.' The West Midlands Area Agent reported of Rugby in May 1942 that, even despite the feebleness of the Conservative candidate (the association chairman), the defeat 'was a surprise to everyone', including the Labour candidate and the local pressmen; it was certainly a shock to the Tory candidate himself, who had written a press article in advance under the headline, 'Why I won'. The Area Agent went on to report that 'the public are restive about the conduct of the war and they attribute many of our difficulties to the mismanagement of public affairs, both during the pre-war period and since the outbreak of war, . . . to what is termed "the old gang" . . . Nor does the name of Churchill carry the same weight as an appeal for support as it did a year ago.' When he added that there was strong feeling against running the War through 'staff colonels with Great War reputations', Topping minuted 'I agree'. By the time that Skipton was lost in January 1944, there was a readiness to blame Labour and the Liberals for breaking the truce; Central Office was reminded that the Party lacked 'a positive policy on home affairs' and urged to take the gloves off. Churchill refused to authorise a partisan approach, but he did finally relax the rule that forbade Cabinet ministers from speaking at by-elections when the Duke of Devonshire demanded it. The loss of the rock-solid, neo-feudal West Derbyshire constituency a month later really set alarm bells ringing. Chips Channon attended 'a crowded Conservative meeting which seemed in a panic over the recent by-election'. Churchill called in the Chief Whip to urge the tightening up of the local organisations, and the release of agents from the forces was considered – but not done. Significantly, it was noted by the Common Wealth Agent in West Derbyshire that the anti-Conservative speakers 'would make reference to Churchill's war record and the debt owed him by the people of this country. Great and enthusiastic applause always greeted this. Then they would go on to say that despite his services to the nation no man, Churchill nor any other, had the right to dictate

---

16    Paul Addison, 'By-Elections of the Second World War', in *By-Elections in British Politics*, eds Chris Cook and John Ramsden (1973), 165–90; *CAJ*, Jan. 1944; West Dorset CA minutes, 15 May 1943; Harvie-Watt report, 7 May 1942, Harvie-Watt MSS, 2/1; *NCP*, Mar. 1944; William Teeling, *Corridors of Frustration* (1970), 73–7.

to the people of the country how they should vote. Invariably this brought even louder applause.'[17]

The opinion polls of the war years produced an equally bleak picture. Between June 1943 and the end of the year, the Conservative share of the vote in Gallup polls fell from 31 per cent to 23 per cent and remained at that low level through 1944; Labour had a double-figure lead in every poll. Such polls were of course in their infancy. No British general election had been held since Gallup began polling in 1938, and the polls' record in the United States had been distinctly patchy; the polls published in the *News Chronicle* were therefore neither noticed much by the other newspapers nor discussed by politicians and party organisers. The public had though formed their own impression about the likely outcome of the next general election, in a way that confirmed the trend of both by-elections and opinion polls. In March 1942 Mass Observation asked respondents in three areas which party they expected to win the next general election; in all three areas those expecting a Labour win outnumbered those expecting a Tory win by a large margin. A Gallup poll in February 1945 found three voters expecting Labour to win for every two who expected a Conservative victory. Indeed, the polls suggest that the Conservatives would actually have been defeated even more heavily than in the Summer if an election had been held three months earlier.[18]

## The run-down of the Party organisation

The by-elections pointed clearly enough to the weakness of Conservative organisation, without administering enough of a continuous shock to ensure that attention was given to repairing deficiencies, even if this could have been done. Central Office advice to keep local organisations in being was not much observed in practice, and organisation ran down continuously from 1940 onwards. The 1943 and 1945 Party Conferences must have been attended almost exclusively by men and women selected in 1938 and 1939, because hardly any meetings were held to select new representatives. Elton Halliley felt of 1943 that 'this was no "half a loaf is better than no bread" Conference. This was the real thing', but it did not lead to a Party renewal. In 1944, the Party Chairman was seeking invalided-out officers who might be seconded to agents in post for training, but finding few available, and was explaining that Central Office was still seeking 'a first rate public relations officer', a vacancy that was not to be filled until 1946. At the 1945 Conference, Chips Channon was 'impressed by the large attendance and great enthusiasm of the

[17] Central Office file, 'Rugby by-election', CCO 1/3/312, CPA; Lichfield CA minutes, 20 Mar. 1942; Addison, 'By-Elections', 174, 177, 184; Jefferys, *Churchill Coalition*, 155, 157; Robert Rhodes James (ed.), *Chips, The Diaries of Sir Henry Channon* (1967), 387; Addison, *Road to 1945*, 252.

[18] Addison, *Road to 1945*, 163, 248; D.E. Butler and G. Butler, *British Political Facts, 1900–1986* (1986), 254.

audience'; it passed resolutions in a contradictory way, welcoming plans for a National Health Service but passing others in a more reactionary mood; a visiting journalist felt that 'although the 1945 Tory Conference had a naturally exultant mood which came from having Winston Churchill as the leader, among the rank-and-file there was a traditionalist carry-over which seemed to me completely out of tune with the times'. There was still no great sense of urgency; the National Union Executive, when it met on 12 April 1945, decided that of the nine resolutions passed at Conference only three should be endorsed for action; when a further resolution was received from the Wessex Area calling for the urgent production of one-page leaflets in bulk, the Area was told that 'the question of leaflets is receiving the attention of the Chairman of the Party'.[19]

The gradual resumption of partisanship certainly did lead to some revival of activity in the constituencies in the last year of the War. Accrington Tories in November 1944 began to collect subscriptions again and started registration work; Bradford, Cambridgeshire and Hemel Hempstead had all re-started in the previous Summer; Shrewsbury did so in October. Many others though did not even meet to make such a decision, and those that did made only slow and limited progress. In some cases, subscriptions began to recover from the low point of 1943–44, but nowhere did they approach peacetime levels of income; at Denbigh for instance, where income had been £506 in 1939, it fell to £55 in 1944 and even with an election appeal recovered only to £273 in 1945. Bath's attempt to re-start activity foundered when over 2,000 appeal letters brought in only £149. North Edinburgh only found out in April 1945 whether their agent would be demobilised for the campaign and only on 28 May, when the campaign had almost started, did they set up a committee to consider organisation for the General Election.[20]

Not only was money short, but so was time with which to raise it and staff on which to spend it. Local minute books are full of the resigned recognition that even the reduced number of party members were too pressed to do much, for 'the various war activities of members takes up an increasing amount of their time'. Office accommodation could not be found and there was no paper available for printing increased numbers of political leaflets and magazines. There were no agents applying for jobs even when they were advertised; those on war service could not be brought back from the forces while the War continued, and many of them would never actually return anyway, but in the meantime Central Office's training programme

---

[19]  *CAJ*, July 1943; NUEC, 27 July 1944 and 12 Apr. 1945; Rhodes James, *Chips*, 399; J.D. Hoffman, *The Conservative Party in Opposition, 1945–1951* (1964), 38; Alan Thompson, *The Day Before Yesterday* (1971), 14.

[20]  Accrington CA minutes, 11 Nov. 1944; Bradford CA minutes, 18 Aug. 1944; Cambridgeshire CA minutes, 12 Aug. 1944; Hemel Hempstead CA minutes, 9 Sept. 1944; Shrewsbury CA minutes, 24 Oct. 1944; Denbigh CA minutes, various dates; Bath CA minutes, 19 Oct. 1944; North Edinburgh UA minutes, 28 May 1945.

had been suspended with the rest of the Party's activities and there were no new entrants to the profession for seven years. Since the whole Conservative approach to organisation had relied on agents with fully-staffed offices, as the other parties had not, there was never going to be any real organisational recovery until this problem could be solved. A sign of how desperate things had become was the acceptance by the National Society of Agents in 1944 of Topping's plan for a Guild of Party Workers which would include both qualified agents and volunteers given a crash course in electoral law; it is inconceivable that the agents would have accepted this threat to dilute their professional status in anything but an extreme situation. Some constituencies that had managed to keep in touch with their pre-war agents by paying retaining fees, or had tracked down and appointed an officer agent when a vacancy arose, could look forward to at least having a professional for the election, but only at the very last minute and in trying circumstances, as one wrote early in 1945: 'the time is probably not very far distant when many of us will be suddenly and hurriedly released from the military to – what? (a) a constituency organisation stagnant for nearly six years, which will need a very thorough and extensive overhaul, (b) revolutionary changes in election law and, above all, (c) the prospects of an immediate General Election. In addition we shall have to (d) readjust ourselves to civilian life . . . househunting, children's schooling etc.' All-party talks on the release of agents from the forces began in December 1944 and reached agreement in February 1945; eventually 187 Conservative Agents were temporarily released from the forces or the public service, but by 12 May, a week before the election was announced, only eighty of them had yet been demobilised.[21]

The reference to electoral law is significant, for the War years were, as in 1914–18, a time in which important reforms were proposed. There was a Home Office enquiry in 1942 which recommended sweeping changes to the electoral registration system, using the wartime national register run by food offices instead of a local authority canvass for names as in peacetime. It also recommended a redistribution of seats, but it was not till 1944 that the Government decided whether this should involve the whole country or be an interim measure to deal only with the greatest anomalies. Parliamentary pressure from MPs who wanted immediate reforms then led to the setting up a Speaker's Conference in 1944. Within the Conference, Liberal proposals for proportional representation were heavily defeated, but other changes that were contrary to Conservative interests were let through, despite there being a Conservative majority reflecting the Commons as a whole. Maximum levels of electoral expenses were reduced; there would be only a limited redistribution of seats; the local government and parliamentary franchise would be assimilated into a single electoral register for civilians, with a

---

21 West Dorset CA minutes, 29 Apr. 1944; *CAJ*, Oct. 1944; Central Office file, 'Agents' release from the forces, 1944–45', CCO 4/2/2, CPA; NUEC, 12 May 1945.

separate register for servicemen; business voters would have to claim their rights personally, for there would be no local canvass and there would be no business votes for spouses. But at least business votes would survive in some form, as would university constituencies which Labour had also wished to abolish. This seems to have been the compromise reached in the Conference and then enacted, and worried agents were told by Topping that it could not be challenged in parliament precisely because it reflected all-party agreement. This makes a sharp contrast with the way in which Conservative MPs were able to shape electoral changes to protect the Party's interests in 1917–18, when they did not even have a Commons majority, but did have effective leadership and confidence in themselves.[22] As it turned out, having swallowed half of their opponents' plans in 1944–45, the Conservatives were to find the rest of Labour's proposals were in any case forced on them in 1948. The wartime changes became law only in January 1945. They cannot be said to have had a major effect on most constituencies in the 1945 Election, but they did greatly affect some areas where Conservatives did especially badly. The changed rules on business voting, for example, led to a reduction of the business voters' register by 86 per cent; 2,000 Conservative voters disappeared from the Bradford register and 9,000 went in Glasgow. In the country as a whole there were now only ten constituencies where business votes totalled over 1,000; the two-member City of London constituency was saved, but since its electorate was down from 40,000 to 10,000 its days were clearly numbered. On the other hand, the limited redistribution of seats might have helped the Party if the 1945 Election had been a close one, for all that was done was to split suburban constituencies that had become grossly under-represented, by increasing the total number of seats by twenty-five; since nearly all of these were in traditionally Conservative areas, especially those on the London fringe like Churchill's Epping constituency, this seemed a positive move. Coping with the redistribution and reconstructing local associations was a further organisational problem to be dealt with at the gallop in the Spring of 1945.[23]

A whips' survey had found the local structures to be run down, compared to Labour's in 1944. After many years of not contesting the constituency, and then six years of wartime abstention from Party activity, the Middlesbrough Conservatives decided reluctantly not to fight the Middlesbrough West constituency at all in 1945. An extreme case was the Western Isles: when the 1945 Election began, there was no Tory association in being so a meeting was called to set one up, attended by only two people; Iain Macleod proposed

22   D.E. Butler, *The Electoral System in Britain since 1918* (2nd edn, Oxford, 1963), 87–101, 114; F.W.S. Craig (ed.), *British Parliamentary Election Statistics, 1918–1970* (Chichester, 1971), 49; John Ramsden, *The Age of Balfour and Baldwin, 1902–1940* (1978), 119–25; *CAJ*, Oct. 1944; Bradford CA minutes, 28 Aug. 1944.
23   Glasgow UA minutes, 26 Mar. 1945; McCallum and Readman, *General Election of 1945*, 275.

his father for the chairmanship, and his father returned the compliment by selecting Iain as the candidate; Central Office, knowing nothing of this, duly obliged by sending Macleod Churchill's letter endorsing him as the official candidate. Party finances were so stretched that Central Office was able to spend on the 1945 campaign, according to Sir Joseph Ball, only about a tenth of the sum available in 1935; recent research suggests that the fall was not as great as that, but confirms that there was far less money to spend than in 1935. By May 1942, Central Office had already reduced its staff by four-fifths, at which level it seems to have remained, and for the Election, the Conservative Research Department consisted of just two staff members and two secretaries. A meeting of Area Agents warned the Party Chairman in May that the Conservatives could not win in the Summer of 1945, and after totalling up their local predictions Assheton came to the same conclusion. All in all, as Butler told Chuter Ede at about the same time, 'the Tory Party's organisation was by no means good'.[24]

## The coming of the Election

How then, amidst so much evidence of their Party's weakness and its lack of appeal did Conservatives manage to discount their real fears and come to expect to win in 1945? There were some plausible, technical reasons that could be produced. First, all wartime by-elections until Chelmsford in April 1945 were based on the 1939 electoral register, which was so seriously out of date by 1942 as to make the contests almost meaningless as a test of current opinions. Mass evacuation, especially of middle-class voters who could stay with relations in the country, as from Brighton and from Wallasey, could render those entitled to vote at a by-election highly unrepresentative of the electorate as a whole, and low turnouts – at about half of peacetime levels – were a further pointer in the same direction; even with Chelmsford using a fresh register, as Harvie-Watt reported to Churchill, the absence of thousands of evacuees and the presence of 16,000 temporary war workers still made it a hopelessly abnormal contest from which to draw general conclusions. Finally, while the last three wartime by-elections, fought on new electoral registers and with some evacuees now returning home as the threat of bombing and rocket attacks receded, included the dramatic Conservative defeat at Chelmsford, they also included a Conservative victory in marginal Newport – since 1922 a talisman seat for the Party – in which the Conservative share

24  Nigel Fisher, *Iain Macleod* (1973), 55; Michael Pinto-Duschinsky, *British Political Finance, 1830–1980* (1981), 127, and I am grateful to Dr Pinto-Duschinsky for sharing his more recent findings with me; Harvie-Watt report, 21 May 1942, Harvie-Watt MSS, 2/1; Lord Egremont, *Wyndham and Children First* (1968), 137; Henry Pelling, *Winston Churchill* (1974), 558; Hoffman, *Conservative Party*, 22; Kevin Jefferys (ed.), *Labour and the Wartime Coalition, from the Diaries of James Chuter Ede, 1941–1945* (1987), 219.

of the vote against an ILP candidate actually rose above the 1935 level. But such calculating was largely beside the point. Conservatives, and most politicians of other parties too, discounted the electoral and organisational evidence of 1942–45 because they believed that victory would transform the electoral landscape anyway, that Churchill would, like Lloyd George in 1918, sweep to victory with the Conservative Party on his coat tails. In 1943, Mass Observation, while finding strong Labour support, had also found among electors an overwhelming view that 'whatever Party or Group Winston Churchill heads will win'. Early in 1944, Tom Harrisson reported a press consensus to the same effect, right across the political spectrum from *The Spectator* to the *New Statesman*, and including Michael Foot in the *Evening Standard*. Both Churchill and the Labour Party prepared their campaigning thoughts for that scenario; half the 1945 Tory candidates had pictures of Churchill in their election addresses and nearly all referred glowingly to him in the text. Most Conservatives only returned to look at the pre-election evidence after they had lost. That shrewd old campaigner Cuthbert Headlam was more sceptical much earlier; in March he lunched with the Chief Whip and was surprised

> to find how many of our younger leaders appear to be convinced that we shall win the election – a reduced majority very likely – but defeat, no. They base their confidence very largely on Winston's popularity and also on the futility of the opposition. I much doubt whether Winston will retain his popularity very many months after the war, and futile though the opposition may be, it does, I think, represent the futility of the electorate. So many people fail to appreciate how much they would dislike Socialism.[25]

Much was expected to depend on the circumstances in which the election was called, for it was acknowledged even by politicians who wanted an end to coalition politics that the public rather liked the idea of cooperation in government and would not look favourably on those who broke it up. The final real chance of continuing coalition in peacetime probably faded when in October 1944 Churchill publicly accepted that it was unlikely. Party activity increased, and there was a sharp flurry of partisan speeches from Assheton and Bracken in February and March 1945; Assheton drew on Hayek to open up the case against economic interventionism and its relationship to totalitarianism; Butler's contribution to the debate was a speech that aimed to remind the political world (and perhaps Churchill in particular?) that there was nothing particularly democratic about government by independents; the *Manchester Guardian* headed its report 'No democracy without parties', and the *Telegraph* summary was 'Party system necessary'. While diverging from

25  Addison, 'By-Elections', 167; McCallum and Readman, *General Election of 1945*, 92, 101; Harvie-Watt report, 4 May 1945, Harvie Watt MSS, 5/1; Hoffman, *Conservative Party*, 21; Tom Harrisson, 'Who'll win?' in the *Political Quarterly*, vol. 15 (1944), 21; Cuthbert Headlam diary, 14 Mar. 1945, Headlam MSS.

this view, Churchill was also starting to make his return to the fray of normal politics, in April attending his first lunch with the parliamentary press corps since 1926; following representations from Stuart about the dangers of a clothing shortage coinciding with an early election, in April Churchill personally directed the switch of clothing workers from war work to the production of civilian clothes. At the Party Conference in March, Sir Herbert Williams welcomed the fact that 'before very long, the Conservative Party, for the first time since 1931, will be free of its chains. That will make all the difference in the world. Then we will have a cause to fight for.' The sort of freedom that Williams stood for was indicated when in the previous month he opposed a new requirement that cyclists must show a rear light when riding after dark; Harvie-Watt recorded that the libertarian Williams thought this to be 'reactionary', which was 'an odd word for Herbert to use'. Churchill's Conference speech indicated that he was still unsure of the future, and he made a final attempt to secure post-war cooperation with Labour when the European War ended in May – or perhaps just an attempt to throw the onus for national disunity on to them? Nearly half of all Conservative candidates blamed Labour's desertion of the National Government for the fact of a party election in their election addresses.[26]

When the Labour Party Conference rejected Attlee's advice and called for an immediate end to the Coalition, Labour and Liberal ministers withdrew and on 23 May Churchill formed his Caretaker Government to administer the country until there could be a General Election on 5 July. The decision for an immediate election was taken against Labour and Liberal urgings to delay until the Autumn, a further cause of a bad-tempered campaign, but it could hardly be considered to be a snap election when six weeks passed between its announcement and polling day. In this decision Churchill was supported by Eden and nearly all the other Conservative ministers consulted, and by both the Party Chairman and the chief Scottish organiser. Only Butler warned insistently that a Summer election would be a lost election. He was reprimanded by Beaverbrook, '"Young man, if you speak to the Prime Minister like that, you will not be offered a place in the next Conservative government." [Butler] replied, "That really doesn't affect me, for if we have an early election, there is not going to be a Conservative government".' For his part, Beaverbrook told the Chief Whip that 'the great war leader, Churchill, was an obvious odds-on favourite, . . . pointing to the rest of us as a collection of gutless oafs with perpetual cold feet'. Beaverbrook announced that 'we will have a great Conservative majority in the country' and looked forward to its being led by the 'triumvirate' of Churchill, Eden and Bracken.

[26]  McCallum and Readman, *General Election of 1945*, 8, 102; cuttings on Butler speech in Butler MSS, G17/101; Stuart to Churchill, 5 Apr. 1945, Whip's papers, 'Coalition, miscellaneous', CPA; Cockett, *Thinking the Unthinkable*, 93; Harvie-Watt report, 2 Feb. and 28 Apr. 1945, Harvie-Watt MSS, 5/1; Hoffman, *Conservative Party*, 15.

Colville, more soberly, felt that 'on the whole, I think the people are on the P.M.'s side in this preliminary skirmish and it is generally supposed that many will vote for the Conservatives merely out of personal loyalty to W.S.C'.[27]

## The 1945 campaign

If the campaign was to depend so heavily on the Conservative leader, then much would depend on who had his ear and could guide his campaign. Lord Moran, Churchill's doctor, wrote that 'Max and Brendan are his advisers, and he will not learn from anyone else'. This was exaggerated, for Churchill was certainly in touch with the Chief Whip, and to a lesser extent with the Party Chairman. But it is correct to say that the advisers who gave him the most influential, because the most palatable, advice were Beaverbook and Bracken; they alone were also ready to bully Churchill to get their way. Broadly their view was that Churchill was the Party's only real asset and that he should campaign in what McCallum and Readman called his 'pugilistic mood'. So for example, he tried to allow service candidates to campaign in uniform to emphasise the Conservatives' war record, a blatant attempt to fight another 'khaki election' like the one he had himself fought in 1900, but this plan was thwarted by the War Office. As recently as March, Churchill had told the Party that the election should be conducted 'with British fair play, and, I trust, with a minimum of personal and party rancour, and above all with the least possible injury to the underlying unity of the nation'. Now in June he threw himelf into the fray without restraint, and his sudden shift of gear deeply offended many opinion formers in the country. The literary critic Raymond Mortimer felt that 'Churchill more than anyone else was responsible for the squalid lies in these elections'; Stephen King-Hall, a popular writer and broadcaster, argued that the election 'might have been a dignified and serious exercise in the arts of citizenship and an example to the world. It was a tawdry affair, a cheapjack business, a stunt redolent with the odour of the *Daily Express*. For this deplorable state of affairs the Prime Minister must shoulder the chief blame. He set the tone.' Noël Coward, who idolised Churchill, told his diary that the campaign was 'almost too squalid to be borne. To read of Mr. Churchill's eager repartees after his great phrases during the war is discouraging. How right I was to say to him "Don't descend to the arena".' The *Manchester Guardian*, influential among the Liberal voters that Churchill hoped to attract, said that 'probably never in our political history has a party leader exhibited such a shameless determination to subvert the constitutional process of an election to his own ends'. And Arthur

[27] Pelling, *Churchill*, 550–1; McCallum and Readman, *General Election of 1945*, 19–21; Martin Gilbert, *Never Despair, Winston S. Churchill, 1945–1965* (1988), 10; Lord Butler of Saffron Walden, *The Art of the Possible, The Memoirs of Lord Butler* (1971), 127, confirmed by contemporary evidence; James Stuart, *Within the Fringe* (1967), 136; Tom Driberg, *Beaverbrook* (1956), 300; Colville, *Fringes of Power*, 601.

Booth, who covered the campaign for the Press Association, concluded that 'many electors, perhaps millions, rapidly became dismayed by Mr. Churchill's campaigning methods'.[28]

Beaverbrook also attracted attention personally as the campaign progressed, partly by making such outrageous claims in his speeches and partly by getting reported so prominently in the *Express*. His former employee Tom Driberg had Beaverbrook much in mind when he wrote of 'the Prime Minister and his yahoo friends'. Sometimes Beaverbrook's partisanship and loyalty to his friends led him from the exaggerated to the absurd, as when at Chatham he lauded Bracken as 'the best First Lord of Admiralty since Churchill', when Bracken had been in the post for just a fortnight; it is probably not true, as legend long had it, that he actually said 'the greatest First Lord since Nelson', but it may well be correct that a heckler shouted 'why not since Noah?' Colville noted simply that 'Brendan and the Beaver are firing vast salvoes which mostly, I think, miss the mark'. There was an extensive programme of speeches by other Party leaders, but they were hardly reported.[29]

Less visibly, a conventional election campaign was going on. There were 543 Conservative candidates, fighting alongside thirteen Ulster Unionists, fifty-one Liberal Nationals, and seventeen 'Nationals' , none of whom were opposed by a Conservative – a total of 614 Government candidates for 640 seats. These allies were taken largely under the Conservative wing for literature and speakers' notes, but there could be touchy local negotiations about the exact relationship between the parties, as in Bradford, in Dumfries and in Totnes. About half of these Conservative candidates had served in the forces in the recent war, another quarter in the First World War, mostly as officers of the rank of Major or above. They were an inexperienced team of candidates, most of them fighting for the first time, and to back them up the Party devised a new mechanism that remained in effect at each subsequent election; a small committee under Swinton met daily to deal with policy questions and questionnaires put to candidates (mainly by pressure groups), so avoiding probable gaffes and public divisions under the intensive scrutiny of campaigning.[30]

The campaign that they ran locally was a quiet one, mainly for lack of active Conservative workers, though it could get very heated where Labour was attacking a noted 'appeaser' in a marginal seat, as Alec Dunglass found at Lanark. John Boyd-Carpenter had only one supporter prepared to speak

[28] Lord Moran, *Churchill, The Struggle for Survival, 1940–1965* (Sphere edn, 1966), 276; Taylor, *Beaverbrook*, 564; Addison, *Road to 1945*, 260–1; McCallum and Readman, *General Election of 1945*, 142; *NCP*, Apr. 1945; Gardner, *Churchill in his Time*, 300; Graham Payn and Sheridan Morley (eds), *The Noël Coward Diaries* (1982), 34; Booth, *British Hustings*, 201, 216.

[29] Tom Driberg, *Colonnade* (1949), 285; Taylor, *Beaverbrook*, 565; Driberg, *Beaverbrook*, 301; Colville, *Fringes of Power*, 607; Gilbert, *Never Despair*, 38; McCallum and Readman, *General Election of 1945*, 136.

[30] McCallum and Readman, *General Election of 1945*, 64, 69, 75, 80; Bradford National Liberal Association minutes, 23 Apr. 1945; Totnes CA minutes, 16 Feb. 1946; J.A. Cross. *Lord Swinton* (Oxford, 1982), 257.

on his behalf in his first contest at Kingston, the young Geoffrey Rippon. In Chislehurst, the candidate found that there were 'only sixteen voluntary workers, most of them elderly'. Across London at Heston and Isleworth it was much the same: the candidate 'could not help being angered from time to time by superior people who were doing nothing themselves to help, but who approached one saying, "Young man, where are all your canvassers? They have not called on me yet".' Both of these Tory seats were lost. In North Croydon, Willink found that 'after nearly six years of war there was not much of an organisation . . . Most people assumed that I should get in again quite easily', but his majority fell to 607 votes. Macmillan found the contest at Stockton an eerily quiet one in which nobody seemed to want to know his views, and concluded correctly that he would lose. Amery had 'no organisation and a pretty defective distribution of my election literature'. It was observed that in Edinburgh 'the local Conservative parties showed strangely few signs of activity on polling day'. And in Birmingham Sparkbrook, in a city that was traditionally a by-word for organisational efficiency, 'most of the [Conservative] committee rooms were "manned" by dear old ladies of 80 or thereabouts and I don't think I saw a man anywhere except at the three main ones. Several [polling stations] had no tellers at all. In the end a few seemed to have polled well but for most of them there were no returns at all.' Such a pattern – no recently marked-up register, little canvassing, and ineffective polling day organisation – explains one of the great mysteries of 1945, why the Party believed that it had won even after the votes had been cast. This was foreshadowed by the Party Chairman's message to Eden at the outset of the campaign, optimism already struggling for the upper hand against evidence: 'I am just off to my constituency and though I shall be in constant touch with the office I shall not be in London very much. I think things are in pretty good trim. We have got a fine field of candidates and some excellent literature and posters. The real difficulty is manpower to distribute them.' Assheton was to be one of the casualties, and Rushcliffe one of Labour's less likely gains. Surveying the scene in his Northern Area in mid-campaign, Headlam noted the poor attendance at meetings and concluded that 'the people have made up their minds one way or the other – which way I don't know – I am still convinced that this hurried election is a mistake. Elections cannot be won without organisation – and our organisation has been in cold storage for too long while the Left Wing people have been busy all the time . . .'[31]

31  Kenneth Young, *Sir Alec Douglas-Home* (1970), 70; John Boyd-Carpenter, *Way of Life* (1980), 74; Fisher, *Macleod*, 59; Reginald Maudling, *Memoirs* (1978), 37; Willink unpublished autobiography, 86, Willink MSS; Harold Macmillan, *Tides of Fortune, 1945–1955* (1969), 31; John Barnes and David Nicholson (eds), *The Empire at Bay: The Leo Amery Diaries, 1929–1945* (1988), 1047; McCallum and Readman, *General Election of 1945*, 171; Assheton to Eden, 15 June 1945, Avon MSS 11/4/68; Headlam diary, 21 June 1945.

With a poor showing in the infantry battle, reliance had to be placed on the national artillery, and once again this emphasised Churchill's centrality to the Conservative effort. The main Party poster, what Tom Driberg called 'the face', was simply a picture of Churchill with the three-decker slogan 'HELP HIM/finish the job/VOTE NATIONAL'. The word 'Conservative' did not appear, convenient perhaps for a piece of literature used by four different party groups, but not encouraging for Tory partisans. Eden's constituency canvassing card was much the same, with the legend printed in purple: 'Your vote and interest are solicited on behalf of Sir Anthony Eden MC (Secretary of State for Foreign Affairs) who stands for support of the National Government'. Henry Willink's Croydon election address used a quarter of its space to print Churchill's picture and his letter of support – 'Mr. Willink is pledged to support me. I ask you to give him your vote.' – in a document that did not anywhere contain the word 'Conservative', or even the word 'National' in this case. Similarly, while Labour's manifesto was explicitly a party document, the Conservative one was titled *Mr. Churchill's Declaration of Policy to the Electorate* and again played down the Conservative link. Historians who have commented on the personalised title have rather missed the point, for this was the traditional form of Conservative manifesto rather than an example of Churchillian egotism; the real contrast was in the opening words which set the tone for the respective documents: Labour's text began with the words 'Victory is assured for us' while Churchill began 'Britain is still at war'. The actual pledges in the manifestoes were not very dissimilar since much of both texts derived from coalition plans, but the tone and nuances of the Conservative document considerably scaled down the optimism that Labour put into similar proposals on the home front. The Conservative manifesto was written personally by Churchill, but with the assistance of Assheton, Bracken and Beaverbrook.[32]

No wording of the manifesto could in any case disguise the deficiency in authoritative Conservative policy work over years past. To some extent this was even deliberate: Henry Willink had as Minister of Health prepared a Conservative model for a National Health Service, approved by the Caretaker Cabinet and ready for the election, only to be told by Churchill not to announce it, for 'he decided that it would lose rather than gain votes' and as Churchill told him, 'Beaverbrook thought it inexpedient'. This health white paper was printed but never published; it emphasised that it differed from earlier coalition plans only as to 'means not ends': 'where they differ, the changes from earlier proposals are mainly to strengthen the protection of individual freedom in using or providing part of the service, to

---

[32] McCallum and Readman, *General Election of 1945*, facing page 82, 87; Eden canvassing card, Avon MSS 11.4.9; Willink election address, Box 2, IV, Willink MSS; Pelling, *Churchill*, 553; Gilbert, *Never Despair*, 37.

eliminate any possible excess of standardisation and to encourage variety and individuality in the services provided'. Even if some of the freedom rhetoric is discounted, the fact that this draft had been approved by the Caretaker Cabinet before Churchill cancelled its publication confirms both the likely difference in character of a Health Service that a Tory Government would have sought to introduce if in office after 1945, and the continuities of Party policy through into the 1950s. Others were equally keen to plug the gaps; Harvie-Watt reported in the final week of the European War that the Party's fuel and power committee were urging a definite policy statement on coal; 'there is a considerable feeling that Conservative ministers ought to be meeting now to consider policies of this kind'. Under the searching scrutiny of the campaign, other policy holes appeared too. Persuaded to adopt a more positive stance for the second half of the campaign, Churchill reverted to the idea of a four-year plan of domestic reform such as he had prefigured in his 1943 broadcast, but since no real work had been done on this the plan could not be produced; Labour commented tartly on this, and the election's first historians reported that 'Mr. Churchill assured the electors that "this plan has now been shaped", but so far no one had seen it in writing'. Polling evidence suggested that housing was the electorate's most pressing policy concern, and also that Labour was strongly preferred as the Party likely to build more houses – an astonishing public relations failure by the Conservatives, given their pre-war record. Ninety-four per cent of Tory candidates mentioned housing in election addresses, but could not point to actual plans to prepare for a housing drive. More damagingly, Conservatives found themselves having to defend their Party's other pre-war policies, against a Labour onslaught, in some cases rather carefully. Churchill did not exactly help this process when he said in a broadcast, 'I have given you my warnings in the past, and they were not listened to', but Labour was in any case able to dig up plenty of anti-Conservative Churchill speeches from his Liberal days and reprint them as leaflets. Labour candidates wrote and spoke about 1918 in terms of 'hard-faced men who look as if they have done well out of the war', presumably without knowing that they were quoting Baldwin rather than Keynes. Conservatives on the other hand deliberately ignored Baldwin: local party supporters in Worcestershire retained control of the county newspapers and were able to conduct through them a spirited defence of both pre-war policy and Churchill as war leader, but even in Worcestershire Baldwin did not now merit a single mention in the Tory press. On the general issue of the future of industry, again seen by the electorate as a key issue, Labour both had a clear view that public ownership ought to be extended and a shopping list of industries to be taken over, while the Conservatives stressed the virtues of free enterprise without ever quite ruling out state intervention as well. Eden, broadcasting on 27 June, said that he 'would draw no rigid line. I would judge each on its merits.' It was unclear whether that committed the

Party, and in any case he did not say which industries fell on which side of his invisible line.[33]

Perhaps the one issue that had not been foreseen but which damaged the Party a great deal was the future of relations with Russia. Churchill's war-leader stance and his anti-communist past allowed Labour to argue that Churchill might irresponsibly involve the country in a new war, while, because 'left can speak to left', Labour would build bridges to the Soviet Union and ensure peace. This was given credence by Churchill's insistence on priority for the Japanese War over domestic reform, and by the extent to which all Conservatives but few Labour candidates harped on the need to keep up strong defence forces after the War. Conservatives were indeed outraged by Labour's foreign policy claims, believing as they did that left-wing pacifism had contributed to the weakness of British policy in the 1930s. Eden also reversed the argument by suggesting that the British people should choose their own government, and not just one that Stalin could get on with. Nevertheless, the Labour advantage remained, for as Arthur Booth recalled, 'there was much optimism'; in the end, 'events were to prove, beyond cavil of party, that Mr. Churchill could hardly have been less successful than was Labour in trying to reach tolerable terms of co-existence with the Russia of Mr. Stalin, but . . . as mistakenly seen by millions of optimistic electors in 1945, the Russian factor could be described as little more than a mirage of the hustings, but it had palpable impact on the polling nevertheless'. The writer George Beardmore noted in his diary, two days before polling day, a teashop conversation between two workmen in Harrow, on exactly these lines:

> 'Don't want him again.' A long look at the other man . . . He replied: 'Enough battles for one lifetime'. After a long pause and a sip of tea, the first man said: 'Bloody Russia' . . . The second man said: 'The old cock's just aching to wave us up an' at 'em again', to which the first man replied, having waited to see if the other was of the same mind, 'Catch me.' They had been talking about Churchill, and had just agreed not to vote for him. Now multiply their little chat by tens of thousands and one gets the result of the election. Those men weren't *for* Attlee, they were *against* Churchill, who in other circles is known as the Happy Warrior.[34]

These perceptions were of course largely shaped by the way in which the media reported the campaign, and the way in which the Party leaders used the media. As anticipated, the Party had a rough ride in the press. The *Daily*

[33]  Jefferys, *Churchill Coalition*, 192, 198; Willink unpublished autobiography, 81–2, and Box 2, IV, 'Scraps', Willink MSS; Harvie-Watt report, 28 Apr. 1945, Harvie-Watt MSS, 5/1; Gilbert, *Never Despair*, 47; McCallum and Readman, *General Election of 1945*, 52, facing page 83, 96, 102, 242; Central Office file, Worcester, CCO 1/4/316, CPA; Eden, *Freedom and Order*, 354.

[34]  McCallum and Readman, *General Election of 1945*, 98; Eden, *Freedom and Order*, 348; Booth, *British Hustings*, 214; George Beardmore, *Civilians at War: Journals, 1938–1946* (Oxford, 1984), 197.

*Herald* and the *Daily Mirror* were both consistently and skilfully marshalled behind the Labour programme, to particularly good effect with the *Mirror*'s 'Vote for Him' campaign, which urged parents to think of their servicemen-sons' future interests in casting their own votes. The *Manchester Guardian* was especially hostile to Churchill: 'when Winston Churchill calls up the nation's vast reserves of affection towards him for the benefit of a reactionary party which only lately despised and rejected him, when he divides the candidates at the election into his friends and his opponents, when, in short, he asks for a personal plebiscite, he is straining loyalty too far'. Unusually, *The Times*, which had hoped to see coalition continue, could not bring itself to endorse the Conservative campaign either; 'how', asked the editor, 'can I throw up my hat for Winston in his present temper or encourage people to vote for his Govt without the assurance that they are going to do as well as the late coalition or better, in fulfilment of its policy and pledges?' The loyal *Daily Telegraph* continued to back Churchill and the Party, but frequently found that it had to explain away his words rather than endorse them; like the Party the *Telegraph* was largely on the defensive. Much therefore continued to hang on the *Express*. It was not in fact personally directed by Beaverbrook throughout the campaign as was alleged, but, as A.J.P. Taylor suggests, it did not need to be, for by 1945 his editorial staff knew how to give him what he wanted anyway. The *Express* campaigned with as few inhibitions as Beaverbrook displayed in his speeches: Labour were proclaimed to be 'THE NATIONAL SOCIALISTS' by a banner headline over a report of an Attlee speech. The left-wing cartoonist David Low was quietly removed from the paper and sent on holiday, and without the faintest justification from any Party spokesman, the *Express* announced that the Conservatives would reduce income tax by half-a-crown in the pound. Charles Fenby wrote that 'the tactics employed by Lord Beaverbrook seem to be based on one idea – that, by marshalling all that is ignorant, prejudiced, and irrational in this country, it is possible to sail to victory on a stream of impenetrable muddiness'.[35]

However, the main events of the campaign, more discussed than manifestoes, policy debates or press coverage, were party broadcasts, far more important than in 1935 because of the enhanced prominence of radio during the War; on average almost half the adult population listened to each election broadcast, slightly more for Churchill than for other speakers. A difference of strategy between the parties was clear enough. Whereas Labour had a different speaker for each of its ten broadcasts, four of the Government's were by Churchill, one was by Bracken and three by

---

[35] McCallum and Readman, *General Election of 1945*, 182–4, 190, 209; Gardner, *Churchill in his Time*, 297; Donald McLachlan, *Barrington-Ward of The Times, 1927–1948* (1971), 208; Taylor, *Beaverbrook*, 566; Driberg, *Beaverbrook*, 301–2.

non-Conservatives; Butler and Eden had one broadcast each. Eden, laid up at home ill throughout the campaign, was advised on his broadcast by the former editor of the *Yorkshire Post* and veteran election-watcher Arthur Mann, who told him discouragingly that 'your Party is losing'. On the air, Eden spoke calmly and persuasively. Butler was also thought to have done well, though he later felt that his moderate tone had completely missed the mark with an electorate seeking sweeping changes. None of this mattered much compared to Churchill's efforts, particularly the broadcast which launched the Conservative campaign. It has become a popular myth that Churchill was a good radio communicator, no doubt because of the undoubted impact of his war speeches, though these were for the most part written for the House of Commons and were less effective when delivered to a microphone. Colville noted that when he spoke on the BBC on 4 June, he was speaking against the clock and sounded hurried; 'his gestures to the microphone were as emphatic as those he uses in a political speech to a large audience, and far more pronounced than he employs in ordinary conversation'. More seriously, his argument was equally exaggerated: socialism, was a threat to freedom in Britain, and would be driven to introduce some form of Gestapo (pronounced, inimitably, to make it sound truly foreign) in order to enforce its interventionist policies. The text was not the work of Beaverbrook, as was immediately claimed by Attlee, but Churchill's own; Attlee also identified the source of Churchill's freedom rhetoric as being 'the Austrian Professor Friedrich August von Hayek', which, since Austrians were not exactly popular in Britain in 1945, was as shrewd a hit below the belt as Churchill's later attack on the equally foreign-sounding Harold Laski as the sinister influence behind Attlee. If Beaverbrook did not write it, the first broadcast did though match exactly the campaign that he was advising and was himself fighting. Whoever was responsible, it was soon clear that it had been a bad mistake. Moran noted that 'for the first time the thought entered my head that he may lose the election'; Amery likewise,

> was greatly depressed by it. The whole strategy of the campaign I should have thought would have been to lay stress on the external situation and urgent measures of demobilisation and housing etc. and to have insisted on putting the issue of socialism versus individualism in the background and so far as possible side-tracking it by indicating an alternative constructive policy. Instead of that Winston jumped straight off his pedestal as world statesman to deliver a fantastical exaggerated onslaught on Socialism . . . I fear Max and Brendan have completely collared him.

Crookshank thought it 'very poor. Much talk of a National Government, in sorrow rather than in anger about the Liberals & very cheap anti-socialism.' James Stuart telephoned angrily to say 'if that is the way he wants to conduct the campaign he must decide. He is the Leader of the Party. But it is not my idea of how to win an election.' Churchill's daughter, Mary, gently urged him to change tack, and Harold Nicolson's wife wrote to him to say she was 'dreadfully distressed by the badness of [Churchill's] broadcast Election speeches. What has gone wrong with him?' Later broadcasts continued the uninhibited tone though.[36]

Churchill had hated the thought of sinking from a national to a party leader: 'people who have grown to love me will grow to hate me and that will hurt me'. Now, briefly, in mid campaign, his own morale faltered under the storm of abuse that he had provoked. He told Moran on 22 June that 'I am worried about this damned election. I have no message for them now,' and one of his staff members felt that 'his heart isn't in this election'; his daughter reported that 'he thinks he has lost his "touch" and grieves about it'. Morale was quickly restored by the reception he received on his extensive election tour: on 26 June he spoke in eleven cities and on the next few days ten more, a punishing schedule that he kept up for much of the remainder of the campaign. The Conservative candidate at Jarrow (of all places!) wired to beg Churchill to include his constituency in the tour, so that Tyneside could 'touch the hem of your garment'. Everywhere there were huge, cheering crowds, flags, banners, and the singing of patriotic songs. The *Glasgow Herald* reported that 'the carnival appearance of the streets through which the Premier passed was reminiscent of VE Day. Overnight they had become aisles of flags and bunting . . . Mr. Churchill's car slowly wove its way through miles of densely packed, cheering crowds. Glasgow has had little opportunity of hailing the Prime Minister during his five years of office, and the crowds were bent on giving way to their pent-up feelings.' It was this joyful reception in Scotland that led Churchill to tell Colville that 'nobody who had seen the enthusiasm of the crowds could be doubtful of the result of the election'. Despite Colville's warning that this would be true only if it were a presidential election, Churchill was convinced that he had popular support and only needed to transfer it to his Party; part of his final broadcast was devoted to thanking people for their cheers and to reminding them that he could not stay on as Prime Minister unless his candidates were elected. He would have been less confident had he known what happened when the parade had gone by; Margaret Cole frequently told the story of how, once Churchill's Walthamstow motorcade had passed through one such flag-waving street demonstration, a group of Fabians persuaded the same crowd to cheer for Labour's programme; a perplexed Labour speaker was reassured when told by a local man that 'just because we cheered the old bugger, it doesn't mean we're going to vote for him'. The support for Churchill's tour could even work against his Party. Alison Readman noted down a conversation between a group of dockers in Merseyside:

---

36   McCallum and Readman, *General Election of 1945*, 140, 154; Eden, *Freedom and Order*, 346; Anthony Eden, *The Reckoning, The Eden Memoirs, vol. 2* (1965), 544; Gerald Sparrow, *RAB, a Study of a Statesman* (1965), 94; Butler, *Art of the Possible*, 129; Colville, *Fringes of Power*, 606; Driberg, *Beaverbrook*, 303; Cockett, *Thinking the Unthinkable*, 94; Moran, *Struggle*, 377; Barnes and Nicholson, *Empire at Bay*, 1046; Crookshank diary, 4 June 1945, Crookshank MSS; John Colville, *Footprints in Time* (1976), 207; Gilbert, *Never Despair*, 49.

One man said that if Mr. Churchill were standing in that Division he would vote for him, but he was not going to vote Tory just for his sake. Another said he thought the Tories had used him for their own ends. A third expressed indignation that they had dragged him all round the country on their behalf, wearing himself out for them, when they would throw him over whenever it suited them.[37]

Gallup continued its polling during the campaign and its final prediction was 42 per cent for the Conservatives against 47 per cent for Labour, very close to the actual result. By then though, Gallup also found that 54 per cent of the public thought the Conservatives would win. Churchill seemed to have it in the bag, and during the three weeks between polling day and the declaration of the results on 26 July, an intermission needed to allow the collection of service votes from all round the world, Conservatives remained mainly confident and Labour gloomy; Hugh Dalton felt at this time that 'but for the personality of the PM, we should undoubtedly have trampled the Tories underfoot and got a large majority'. In the expectation of a Conservative win the stock market was buoyant too. Conservatives did expect that there would be seats lost and victory by a smaller margin than the 1935 landslide, but no change in the overall predicted outcome. Central Office, having consulted its Area Agents, at first expected to hold 337 seats in Great Britain, to which Ulster Unionist seats would need to be added, giving an estimated majority of about fifty even if all the 'doubtful' seats went to Labour. In the final prediction, compiled on the day *after* the votes had been cast, the Area Agents put more of these doubtful seats into the Conservative column, and suggested more optimistically that the majority would be as high as 211 if the remaining 'doubtful' seats stayed Conservative; their considered view now was that the Party would definitely hold 346 seats (plus Ulster), with 193 going to other parties and seventy-one still 'doubtful'. These forecasts were hugely wide of the mark: in London, where the Party actually held only twelve seats, twenty-five had been thought to be safe and twelve more to be winnable; in Wales only three seats were held of the nine considered to be secure. This degree of inaccuracy takes some explaining, particularly when the optimistic figures are contrasted with more sceptical prose in the same reports. From the West Midlands it was reported that agents seemed quietly confident even where the prediction was of a Labour win, and Smethwick (eventual Labour majority over 10,000) and Nuneaton (over 18,000) were considered to be possible Tory wins; but 'on the other hand it cannot be anything but guesswork as there was no canvass on which to base results'; the Area Agent added that there had been plenty of cars available on polling day but that agents had 'wisely' not used them much as 'owing to the lack of canvass' they could well have been giving free lifts

[37] Addison, *Churchill*, 381; Moran, *Struggle*, 276–7; Anthony Howard, 'We are the masters now', in *The Age of Austerity, 1945–1951*, eds Michael Sissons and Philip French (Harmondsworth, 1964), 18; McCallum and Readman, *General Election of 1945*, 157–9, 170; Gilbert, *Never Despair*, 47, 50–1; Margaret Cole's account of the Walthamstow meeting was given at a lecture in Poplar Town Hall in about 1975.

to socialist voters. The South East reported on 'the excellent organisation the socialists have built up'. From Scotland, Colonel Blair's ambivalence was typical of all the reports; lack of information rendered a 'forecast with any pretence of confidence with regard to its accuracy' as 'quite impossible', but he sent in, 'for what it is worth (in my opinion nothing)', a prediction that Conservatives would hold between forty-one and fifty-two Scottish seats (they had had forty-two in 1935, and would hold only twenty-seven in 1945); but even Blair then added that 'I think nevertheless that taken all over the result will be quite satisfactory'. The Party so wanted Churchill to win, and had so little evidence on which to base any real prediction, that its agents and Area staffs saw what they expected to see. The only consistently warning note came from the East Midlands, and that was in a late report on 17 July, indicating that Conservative optimism had waned, but only after polling day. East Edinburgh on the other hand, reviewing their own campaign on 16 July, felt that all had gone fairly well. Beaverbrook, tapping local *Express* sources, told Churchill to anticipate a majority of a hundred, but his confidence faltered as the three-week intermission went on, saying first that the figure of a hundred was 'not sacrosanct' and then that something nearer thirty might be a safe bet, but this can only have been based more on nerves than on new information. The same jitteriness probably explains the gloom that Crookshank found at the Carlton Club between the voting and the count, and the uncertainty that was reported from contacts all over the country by Headlam on 11 July; two days later he found that 'people are now talking of a "bare majority" or even of a Labour win'. Churchill told the King to expect a Conservative majority of thirty–eighty seats, and in view of the professional advice he had received he must have thought he was erring well on the side of caution.[38]

## The results

The results when they came out on 26 July were therefore a terrific shock; for Crookshank it was 'bad, and worse and worse, with the result that there is a complete landslide and we are out for years'. James Stuart 'felt that my entrails had been pulled right out of me'. Declarations began at ten that morning, and by 10.03 Labour had its first gain; a few minutes later Harold Macmillan had lost Stockton and within another half hour Labour had taken ten of the thirteen Birmingham seats, including Leo Amery's. The day continued as a relentless tide of Party disaster, and Churchill resigned by the end of the afternoon. In maudlin mood, he told a meeting of junior

[38] McCallum and Readman, *General Election of 1945*, 242–3; Ben Pimlott (ed.), *The Second World War Diary of Hugh Dalton, 1940–1945* (1986), 357; Central Office file, General Election, 1945, CCO 4/2/61, CPA; East Edinburgh Unionist Association minutes, 16 July 1945; Jeffreys, *Churchill Coalition*, 198; Gilbert, *Never Despair*, 93, 105; Crookshank diary, 9 and 10 July 1945, Crookshank MSS; Headlam diary, 11 and 13 July 1945; Hennessy, *Never Again*, 85.

ministers that 'this is a feckless vote, but I do not blame the people; they were crying aloud for relief, for food and for some easing of all the hard things we have had to do for them'. Sharing in Churchill's sense of rejection, Lord Baldwin told Butler that 1945 'will go down to History as the classic example of democratic ingratitude'. When all the results had been declared, there were shock waves throughout the Party; Chips Channon, who had held his own Southend seat, was 'stunned and shocked by the country's treachery, and extremely surprised at my own survival'. Headlam noted that

> Winston has resigned and little Mr. Attlee reigns in his stead – it is a sorry business and one feels ashamed of one's countrymen. But there it is – this is democracy – the people wanted a change and, no longer being afraid, voted Labour. The Left Wing propaganda has had its effect and it would seem that the vast majority of the new generation has gone Socialist for the time being. What a H of C it is going to be – filled with half-baked, young men mainly from the RAF so far as I can make out.[39]

Conservatives and Unionists had held only 197 seats, and their National Liberal and National allies only thirteen, though this latter figure increased by three after the Election with the adherence of three independent MPs, making a total of 213 – only half of the seats held before the Election and only three-fifths of those considered 'safe' even after polling day. Five Cabinet ministers (Amery, Bracken, Grigg, Macmillan and Somervell) had lost their seats, as had eight departmental ministers, nineteen junior ministers and the Party Chairman. Churchill himself, offered an unopposed return by Labour and the Liberals, had had to fight an independent almost unknown in the constituency but who now turned out to have scored more than 10,000 votes without even running a campaign. It was clearly an anti-Conservative *and* an anti-Churchill as well as a pro-Labour movement of opinion, and easily the worst Conservative defeat since 1906. This was confirmed by the fact that seventy-nine of the Labour gains were in places that had never had a Labour MP before, and these included such unlikely rural and suburban constituencies as Winchester, Dover, Hitchin and Wimbledon. Conservatives lost three of the four seats in Buckinghamshire, and seven out of eight in Norfolk. In the Labour stronghold of the north, there were only three Conservative MPs, though one of them had cheered up local Tories by unseating Beveridge. McCallum and Readman, witnessing the shock waves caused by the declaration of a tiny Tory majority at Henley, commented that 'such things had never happened before in South Oxfordshire'. It was no more traditional in middle-class Enfield, where Labour won the parliamentary seat and the young Norman Tebbit lost his first election in form IIIS of

---

[39] Crookshank diary, 26 July 1945, Crookshank MSS; Jones, 'Conservative Party' thesis, 114; Booth, *British Hustings*, 219; Willink, unpublished autobiography, 87, Willink MSS; Baldwin to Butler, 12 Aug. 1945, Butler MSS, G17; Rhodes James, *Chips*, 409; Headlam diary, 26 July 1945.

Enfield Grammar School. Conservative candidates did particularly badly in the outer London region, with its extra seats added by the 1945 redistribution, where the anti–Tory swing since 1935 averaged 20 per cent, and did best of all in Glasgow where there was hardly any swing at all. But the regional pattern of swings is not very instructive in this case, for it reflected the patchiness of the parties' performance in 1935 (when Conservatives had done very well in the London area and relatively badly on Clydeside) and the massive migrations in the ten years since, as well as wartime changes of party support.[40]

Compared to 1929, the only previous election that Labour had come near to winning, the Conservative performance seems less catastrophic. In 1945, the Party and its allies polled nearly ten million votes, a larger number of votes (despite a lower turnout) and a larger share of the vote than had been achieved in 1929. The really significant difference was the way in which the anti-Conservative vote now aligned: with the collapse of Liberal voting, a Conservative share of about 40 per cent now brought not a hung parliament as in 1929 but a landslide to Labour. Looked at regionally, the Conservatives had in 1945 twelve fewer London seats than in 1929, twelve fewer in the Midlands and eleven fewer in northern England, while they had won more seats than in 1929 both in Wales and in Scotland, but the biggest shift came in southern England outside London, where the inter-war Liberal vote had persisted most strongly, and where its collapse now left the Conservatives with twenty-three seats less than in 1929. 1945 was the only election after 1906 at which Conservatives failed to hold a majority of the seats in that area.[41]

## Explanations and expectations

How then had this come about? Professor W.L. Burn thought it 'odd that Mr. Churchill should have made the mistake of declaring war on his opponents who were at least half mobilised when the mobilisation of his own party was scarcely begun . . . The Conservatives lacked a doctrine. It was fatal that they should have lacked a method as well'. *The Times* concluded that the result should be attributed entirely to Churchill's mismanagement of the campaign, but the deputy editor of the *Telegraph*, Colin Coote, spread the blame more widely: 'this has been a vote against the Tory party and their records from 1920 to 1939. Moreover, I have seen ten elections, but never one conducted with more phenomenal imbecility than this. I am told Winston has at last parted brass rags with Beaverbrook: and high time too. He (B) cost the party *millions* of votes. He has already done his best to ruin my profession and now has ruined the Tory party.' *The Economist* pointed out, cuttingly but surely

---

40    Craig, *Election Statistics*, 73; Norman Tebbit, *Upwardly Mobile* (Futura edn, 1989), 12; McCallum and Readman, *General Election of 1945*, 163, 292–5.
41    Butler and Butler, *Political Facts*, 230–1.

fairly, that for all Churchill's reputation as a world statesman, he could still take lessons in party management from Baldwin. Robert Boothby 'maintained that the Brendan–Max methods had cost the Tories a hundred seats'. Macmillan on the other hand, exonerated both Churchill and his advisers, arguing in his memoirs that

> at the end of the war the people, who felt a deep sense of gratitude to him, would have done anything for him except return him to power as a Tory Prime Minister. They would have acclaimed him as a duke; they would have contributed to build him another Blenheim. But in the post-war mood they did not want him, and still less his political friends. It was clear to an unbiassed observer that it was not Churchill who had brought the Conservative Party so low. On the contrary it was the recent history of the Party, with its pre-war record of unemployment and its failure to preserve peace.

More equivocally, Eden noted on 'this staggering day' on which the results came in that 'before Campaign opened I thought Labour would quite likely win . . . but I never expected such a landslide as this. Nor do I think it need have been. We fought the campaign badly. Beaverbrook was no help. It was foolish to try to win on W's personality alone instead of on a programme. Modern electorate is too intelligent for that, and they don't like being talked down to. Finally, while there is much gratitude to W. as war leader, there is not the same enthusiasm for him as PM of the peace. And who shall say that the British people were wrong in this? We should, I think, have probably been beaten anyway, but the Labour majority should have been smaller.' This seems a fair and balanced verdict. Defeat probably was inescapable in 1945, even with the recovery that the Party had made from its 1943–44 nadir of support in the opinion polls, but the recovery was in spite of rather than because of the Party's national election campaign. Only the scale of – and not the fact of – the defeat is to be explained by the events of June 1945. As to what sort of voters actually switched and for what reason, the evidence is now almost impossible to pull together. The most plausible view may well be that given by Mass Observation at the time, from their own survey: among electors old enough to have been on the register in 1935, very few actually switched from Conservative to Labour and these were anyway cancelled out by voters moving in the opposite direction, but there was an increased intention to vote among Labour voters and an increased abstention by Conservatives; new voters (of whom there were an unprecedentedly large number, since the last election was ten years earlier), were going overwhelmingly to Labour, as were former Liberals.[42]

---

[42] Hoffman, *Conservative Party*, 24, 28; Gardner, *Churchill in his Time*, 309; Robert Rhodes James, *Bob Boothby, a Portrait* (1991), 333; Eden diary, 26 July 1945, Avon MSS, 20/1/25; Macmillan, *Tides of Fortune*, 287; John Ramsden, 'From Churchill to Heath' in *The Conservatives, a History from their Origins to 1965*, ed. Lord Butler (1977), 413; Eden, *The Reckoning*, 551.

Butler, in a paper entitled 'Reflections on the Recent Election (based on communications received)', found that while a few attributed the result variously to the women's vote, the soldiers, Labour's promises, and the collectivist influence of wartime factory work, four-fifths of his correspondents agreed that there had been three real causes. The first of these, left blank on the carbon retained on file to save the blushes of the typist, was presumably the tactics of the leadership; the second was 'six years of left wing propaganda accompanied by a virtual cessation of right wing propaganda', and the third was run-down of organisation, which had again happened only on the right. These matters should all be addressed, and the crucial need was to restore the Party's local organisation, which would need to raise far more money under the changing National Union rules, and on which recovery would have to rest. His Party contacts reassured him that the Central Office work for the Election had been excellent, but started nine months too late.[43]

Most contemporary Party opinion took the Eden line, that defeat was more or less inevitable and that it was therefore not useful to enquire into the management of the campaign; it was indeed a rare Conservative defeat in not being followed by a search for scapegoats among either the organisers or the leaders. In Rugby, 'it was the unanimous opinion of the meeting that in the existing temper of the electorate, no organisation or committee work, however perfect, would have won the election'. North Cornwall resolved that 'in view of the results throughout the country there was no need for recrimination'. Elton Halliley wrote that 'the general trend of thought was against us . . . "the winds blew and we were scattered"'. The Birmingham Chief Agent reported that 'the majorities against us at the general election were so emphatic that it would seem that local influences like the personality of the candidate, the strength of the organisation or the capacity of the agent counted for little. The public were in the mood for a change.' Sheffield Central happily reassured themselves that 'in normal conditions we would easily have retained the seat'.[44]

Another favourite explanation was the service vote. General Slim had told Churchill that most of his soldiers would vote Labour and the rest would probably not vote, and it seems likely that this is what happened. Since votes deriving from the service register had to be verified separately on the day before the main count, it was easy enough to observe that they went heavily to Labour. So, when the results were declared, and with memories of their earlier complaints about ABCA, it was tempting for Tories to conclude that the Army vote had been decisive. This cannot be true. First, it must be remembered that had it been possible to identify separately the votes of

---

43   Butler Memorandum, undated [Summer, 1945], Butler MSS, G17/216.
44   Rugby CA minutes, 20 Nov. 1945; North Cornwall CA minutes, 15 Sept. 1945; *CAJ*, Oct. 1945; Birmingham UA minutes, 12 Dec. 1945; Sheffield Central Women's Association, 1945 Annual Report.

young, mainly single and mainly working–class men at any other post–war election, they would also have been seen to have gone mainly to Labour, so there may be very little to explain anyway. Second, the numbers will not add up to an explanation. The total number of service votes cast was far less than Labour's lead in the national popular vote, and since some of these anyway went to Conservative and Liberal candidates, the votes of servicemen may contribute to an explanation of the result, but they cannot explain it on their own. Moreover, if Mass Observation was correct in its finding that most 'new' voters went to Labour, then voters in uniform, who were mainly aged under thirty and cannot therefore have voted before, may well not have behaved any differently from their contemporaries in mufti.[45]

The Party's conclusions were comforting without being dangerously escapist; they were unlikely to encourage complacency after such a crushing defeat. They also enabled the Party to unite after some years of division; despite his disastrous conduct of the campaign, Churchill's leadership was not challenged with any determination. On the other hand, neither Beaverbrook nor Bracken ever exercised much influence again; the majority of the new shadow cabinet that gathered in October 1945 was more orthodoxly Conservative than any Churchill Cabinet had been, and of its members only Lord Cherwell could be thought of as being there simply as a Churchill 'crony'. This renewed unity was reinforced by finding an external alibi. Conservatives told each other that they had fought the War and had then been defeated by a Party that had seized an unfair advantage while they had been away. Lichfield Conservatives decided that 'six years in which the Conservative Party made no effort to combat the continuous Socialist propaganda had had its effect, and the apathy which was prevalent among many of our supporters proved to be an almost impossible obstacle to surmount'. Ralph Assheton, more brutally, told the agents that 'the Party could not make up in a few months for its six years of neglect of its organisation and propaganda. We need not be ashamed of that neglect. Our Party went to the War.' The Conservative Party therefore settled into the period of opposition stunned, but looking outwards rather than inwards for scapegoats, a bonus that would not have been available if a different campaign had produced only a narrow defeat. And prospects for the future justified some optimism: a solid bedrock of Conservative voting strength remained, and when organisation was restored and apathy removed by the existence of a government of the left, that core strength would naturally increase, at least to some extent. Life would be difficult enough for the post-war Labour Government and would provide many attractive opportunities for the Opposition. Noël Coward, horrified by Churchill's rejection, nevertheless felt that 'it may not be a bad idea for the Labour boys to hold the baby. I always felt that England would be bloody

45   McCallum and Readman, *General Election of 1945*, 30, 47.

uncomfortable during the immediate post-war period, and it is now almost a certainty that it will be so.'[46]

The Party embarked on its first period out of office since 1931 extremely conscious of the size of the task ahead of it if it was to win back power. In 1945 for the only time in recent British history, Conservative organisation had been no better than, and possibly worse than, that of its major rival. Its policy apparatus had withered and the content of policy had become out of touch with current preoccupations. And finally, while maintaining a perfectly respectable vote – only Labour in 1945 and the Conservatives themselves in 1931 and 1935 had ever polled more votes than Conservatives did in 1945 – the Party's strategy and political stance had lost it the support of middle opinion, lower middle class, former Liberals and merely moderate voters, who – or whose parents – had backed Baldwin in 1924 and the National Government's Conservative candidates in 1931 and 1935. The tasks now were to restore the organisation, to bring policy back to an appearance of relevance, and to adjust the Tory stance to win back the voters lost during the War. When McCallum and Readman called 1945 'the Waterloo of the Conservative Party' in 1947, they quite understandably picked the wrong battle for their comparator. Napoleon's bloody defeat at Aspern-Essling in 1809, followed as it was by an extensive organisational build-up, a slow recovery of morale, and a narrow victory in the subsequent hard-fought battle of Wagram would have been the better analogy. Unlike Napoleon at Waterloo, the Conservative Party did come back.[47]

---

[46] Lichfield CA minutes, March 1946; *CAJ*, Jan. 1946; Payn and Morley, *Coward Diaries*, 36.
[47] McCallum and Readman, *General Election of 1945*, 243.

# Part II

# The Fight-back, 1945–51

One of the most interesting things [in the election results] is the list of high level leaders who have been defeated. Almost without exception we are well rid of them all. So, the field is clear, and we can start building a leadership and a party for the next twenty years. What an opportunity, my dear Rab, particularly for you . . . The result is a bad one in some ways. It is rather like a man standing on the edge of an icy river who knows that sooner or later he has got to swim across it. As he stands putting off the evil moment, a friend pushes him in and off he goes in his effort to reach the other side. We will have some swimming to do now and I've no doubt the passage while in opposition will be bitter, but I'm glad we haven't had to put it off any longer in some ways.

(Cuthbert Alport to R.A. Butler, 29 July 1945)

I know that you, like I, never shared the optimistic views of some of our friends that the old gentleman would be willing to retire gracefully into the background. He has had too much of the limelight for that . . . Anthony might very well be able to restore the position, for he is a progressive Conservative. Winston, in his old age is neither a Conservative nor progressive. He is an old-fashioned reactionary.

(Lord Cranborne to J.P.L. Thomas, 27 March 1946)

The power of an idea had persisted right from 1947 onwards through the Churchill régime, based upon what he would simply call in the terms of his father Randolph a 'Tory Democracy'; what I would call 'the rendering of the traditionalist régime respectable in the eyes of the prosperous working class which it had begotten'.

(R.A. Butler's note on 'Events since 1951', 18 May 1957)

## Chapter 3

# The organisational recovery, 1945–51

The years between defeat in 1945 and the return to power in 1951 have acquired a legendary significance in the Party's history, a period in which the Party was modernised, its appeal and its social constituency broadened, and its readiness for power demonstrated in policy-making that laid the foundations for the thirteen years of Tory rule that followed. In 1963, when inviting Selwyn Lloyd to take charge of another modernisation review for the next generation, Iain Macleod, who almost personified this modern Tory approach, harked back to the 1940s:

> I expect you remember the Maxwell Fyfe Report in about 1948. I have always thought this had a profound effect on the changed image of the Tory Party, and it certainly made it possible for many people to join our ranks who could not otherwise have become Members of Parliament. Indeed, last year when I made my first speech to the Conference as Chairman, I said that Maxwell Fyfe ranked with Woolton and Butler as the architects of the post-war change.

That account, which was confirmed in memoirs and biographies and in most accounts of the Party's post-war history, contained much truth. But those truths were so embroidered after 1951 that it is far from easy to disentangle myth from reality. Most subsequent accounts derived from the same limited range of flawed witnesses, notably on the organisational side from the inaccurate memoirs of Maxwell Fyfe and Woolton. For the policy review, Butler's memoirs presented a more accurate account, but were deliberately imprecise and understandably foregrounded his own role.[1]

Neither organisational nor policy developments were as original as has usually been proclaimed, but it is easy to see why those responsible tended systematically to overstate their case. In the first place, war and defeat cleared out an entire generation of managers and organisers. Their successors had no detailed knowledge – in Woolton's case no knowledge at all – of how things had been before 1939. When Central Office staff, for example, proclaimed the importance of film as a new electioneering weapon in 1949, they cannot have known how extensive had been the Party's use of film in the 1930s. When Woolton found on his arrival in 1946 that Central Office was so hopelessly

---

[1] Central Office, General Director's file, 'Selwyn Lloyd Enquiry', CCO 120/4/1, CPA.

unbusinesslike that he considered winding it up and starting all over again, he was reacting to the war-ravaged structure he inherited from Assheton and not to the formidable machine that had existed under Davidson, Blain and Topping in the 1920s. At constituency level, agents and officers rediscovered how valuable fêtes could be for fundraising, something long known to their predecessors. Having never seen a wheel in action, it was easy to believe that they were inventing one. There was also a more subtle reason for the systematic claim of novelty, and this lay in the Party's reaction to defeat. If, as was generally believed, the Party had seemed old-fashioned and out of touch in 1945, then it would hardly do merely to restore the structures of 1939; if the Party seemed to lack a relevant policy and to be linked in the public mind with appeasement and unemployment, then it would hardly be appropriate to stress continuities with the inter-war years. Whatever the reality, it suited those in the know as well as the newcomers to proclaim a brave new world of modern Conservatism.

## Entering opposition

But the first reaction of the Party to defeat was not a move towards modernisation so much as deep, numbed shock. There was no Party Conference in Autumn 1945 and the National Union Executive like most constituency parties reacted to defeat by not even meeting until well into the Autumn; its review of June's Election campaign did not take place until 11 October. Indeed, over the first year of peacetime, the clear-out initiated by the War and the 1945 Election continued remorselessly; Headlam, who had watched Central Office at work in the war years from a position on the National Union Executive, thought that 'the only hope is a clean sweep at the Central Office'. Topping, who was sixty-eight in 1945 and had stayed on only because of the War, retired in August after seventeen years as General Director. At the same time, the Vice Chairman responsible for candidates also left; his successor was J.P.L. (Jim) Thomas, a confidant of Eden whose PPS he had been, and a whip for most of the war years. The new General Director, Stephen Pierssené, had been Area Agent for Yorkshire until 1935, but had then left for industry and subsequent war service. By April 1946, Pierssené had appointed seven new Area Agents to cover most of England. Lower down things were much the same; many agents appointed early in 1945 did not stay in post, and it was soon clear that most of the qualified agents in the forces would never return either; those released for the 1945 Election had to return by 7 September, and desperate efforts were then made to get them out again for the local elections in November. In Summer 1946 the National Society of Agents formally terminated the membership of all those who were not by then back in a Party post, and only 156 qualified agents then attended the first post-war Conference in October. With this degree of flux, it was hardly surprising that even simple organisational tasks could not be performed. For a year after the Election there was no such basic data as lists of Central Office staff and departments, no handbook of agents and their addresses, no Party telephone directory. Most Party publications that had been monthly before 1939, like the *Conservative Agents' Journal*, remained quarterly throughout 1946 for lack of paper. These elementary procedures were back to normal only by early 1947, but by then the Party also had a new head office and a new Chairman. The requisitioning of the Party's Palace Chambers offices for war work did not terminate with the ending of hostilities, and Central Office was therefore one of many organisations trying to find office space in Westminster in 1945; by late 1945 Central Office had expanded to fill nearly seventy rooms, but its staff were divided between six different buildings; in January 1946, a brief for Eden argued the need for about 20,000 square feet of space, which must be within half a mile of Parliament Square; Churchill and Eden offered their assistance in pressing Attlee directly to release space, pointing out that Labour was satisfactorily accommodated in Transport House. Assheton's efforts to find suitable accommodation were fraught with difficulties, but eventually bore fruit when Abbey House, a former hotel in Victoria Street, was de-requisitioned in June 1946. The Party leased the whole building, itself occupied ninety rooms on the three upper floors and sub-let the lower floors. Central Office moved into the building in August; 24 Old Queen Street was returned to the Research Department, but most of the other central units were now located together.[2]

Assheton had indicated that he wanted to retire from the Chairmanship as soon as the organisation had been re-started, and was keen to go in Summer 1946. Churchill had initially wanted a full organisational enquiry under Oliver Lyttelton and then to replace Assheton with Harold Macmillan, but this had been blocked by Eden; Eden's own candidate was Jim Thomas who was not acceptable to Churchill, but he remained Vice Chairman. Instead, the choice fell on Woolton, who had only joined the Party on the day *after* the 1945 defeat, in a fit of gratitude to Churchill and because of his opposition to Labour's nationalisation plans, but had been included in the shadow cabinet straightaway. The name of Woolton had been widely discussed before he agreed to accept the post, those pressing for him including Sir Joseph Ball and the Vice Chairman; Thomas told Churchill that Central Office was 'handicapped by the tradition of many years that we are inefficient! Only a name that gives real confidence to Conservative MPs and to our workers in the country can banish that general feeling'; even if Woolton could do it only

2  National Union Executive minutes [hereafter NUEC], 23 Aug. and 11 Oct. 1945, CPA; Headlam diary, 27 July 1945, Headlam MSS; Central Office file, Agents' release from the forces, 1944–45', CCO 4/2/2, CPA; Thomas to Eden, 7 Feb. 1946, Eden to Assheton, 6 Jan. 1946, Assheton to Eden, 19 Jan. 1946, Avon MSS, 11/12/27–29; Central Office file, 'Central Office Accommodation', CCO 4/12/136, CPA.

part-time, he would be 'of the greatest psychological value'. At first Woolton resisted, pleading business commitments, but after meeting Churchill in June 1946 he agreed to try to clear these other commitments out of the way so as to be able to accept, 'much against both my will and my own interests'. Woolton was formally appointed in July 1946, but needed time to settle his business affairs, and did not take up the reins fully until September. On 8 July, Thomas wrote that 'we are horribly overworked at Central Office, but good Lord Woolton is arriving to help us bear the burden . . . In August we go to a larger but much more unpleasant office at the end of Victoria Street where we can expand still further . . .'[3]

The parliamentary party was if anything in a state of even greater disarray. The reduction of its size by half was not random, for all the marginals had been lost, as well as many seats thought to be safe. The MPs elected were predominantly rural and southern, and their social character was therefore rather traditional. Walter Elliot, who had lost his own Glasgow seat in the deluge, noted that 'it is now a Front Bench of gentlemen – Oliver Stanley, Rab Butler, Anthony Eden . . . The century of domination by the industrial North is over. We have now to reckon with the rule of the Home Counties again.' The Tory gentlemen on the backbenches did not take kindly to the changed social character of the House, one complaining that many of the new Labour MPs were 'just like a crowd of damned constituents'. Cuthbert Headlam thought 'the new Labour MPs are a strange looking lot . . . this rabble of youthful, ignorant young men'. The new MPs did not necessarily respect the traditions that determined which parties occupied each area of the Commons dining room, and because they did not for the most part belong to West End clubs they were always about the place; Crookshank noted glumly in October, 'House and precincts again packed. It is to be hoped this will soon end.' About half of all Conservative MPs had no previous parliamentary experience and some had difficulty in finding their feet. William Teeling was not alone in noting the relatively low calibre of the 1945 Conservative intake; only Selwyn Lloyd and Derick Heathcoat Amory went on to hold high Cabinet office, though the new boys also included such reliable workhorses of future administrations as Ernest Marples, John Boyd-Carpenter and Freddie Erroll. What was lacking in experience was to

---

[3] *Conservative Agents' Journal* [hereafter *CAJ*], Oct. 1945, Apr. and Oct. 1946, CPA; J.D. Hoffman, *The Conservative Party in Opposition, 1945–1951* (1964), 77; Martin Gilbert, *Never Despair, Winston S. Churchill, 1945–1965* (1988), 227; Michael Kandiah, 'Lord Woolton's Chairmanship of the Conservative Party, 1945–1951', unpublished PhD thesis, University of Exeter, 1992, 33, 48, 56; Churchill to Woolton, enclosing copy of Thomas letter, 21 May 1946, Churchill to Woolton, enclosing Ball memorandum, 21 May 1946, Woolton to Churchill, 6 June 1946, Woolton to Churchill, 28 June 1946, Woolton MSS, box 21; Earl of Woolton, *The Memoirs of the Rt. Hon. Earl of Woolton* (1959), 304, 328; Thomas to Geoffrey Fry, 8 July 1946, Cilcennin MSS.

some extent made up in team spirit, some of it inherited from staff work in the Army; on 3 August 1945, seven new Tory MPs who had been Brigadiers were all sworn in together. Some of the new arrivals also had a burning desire to be active as an Opposition, which was difficult in the disorganised early days of the 1945 Parliament; in October 1945, Eden found Churchill on the front bench supported only by the acting Chief Whip, Buchan-Hepburn, 'whom he scarcely knows', and two former under secretaries. The backbenchers pressed for guerrilla campaigns to disrupt Labour's business, a tactic which was in any case rather distasteful to older colleagues; Sir William Darling asked plaintively in the House why MPs were so determined to *do* things, and was sharply reminded that most of them felt that was what they had been elected for. The 1922 Committee, which had lost most of its senior members in the rout, also took time to recover its role.[4]

Gradually though, normality was restored; special induction arrangements on Party tactics were organised for new Members, coordinated by Crookshank, and a series of ten lectures for them on the rules of the Commons were laid on by the officers of the House. The whips found that they had to eschew all previous practice and actually encourage backbenchers to speak as much as possible, and the backbench policy committees were revived to provide coordination, fully operational and with a proper briefing system by March 1946. Late in the 1945 campaign, Churchill had been personally attacked by Herbert Morrison, and he now forbade his whips to talk to Morrison as Leader of the House. James Stuart had to wait his moment and then explain that Conservatives in the House would be put at a serious disadvantage by refusing to discuss Commons business with the majority party; the Leader graciously agreed that 'while the firing will continue between the opposing forces, this does not mean that messengers may not pass between the lines'. Stuart needed all the help available to him, for there were neither whips nor policy advisers who had any experience at all of opposition. Early in the opposition period, as Michael Fraser of the Conservative Research Department later recalled, the Party 'dropped a lot of catches'. Here too time and experience ensured that operations began to come to order; in late 1945, when the Parliamentary Secretariat first got going, its three staff had to service twenty-three parliamentary committees. Even in 1947, the Secretariat had to produce 319 separate policy briefs, but the number of new briefs required then fell steadily as Members became more experienced, and as less policy areas remained to be covered. As Michael Kandiah has shown, the work of

---

[4] Colin Coote, *A Companion of Honour, The Story of Walter Elliot* (1965), 248; Headlam diary, 15 Aug. 1945; Crookshank diary, 19 Oct. 1945, Crookshank MSS; Earl of Kilmuir, *Political Adventure, The Memoirs of the Earl of Kilmuir* (1964), 137; William Teeling, *Corridors of Frustration* (1970), 122–3; Eden diary, 9 Oct. 1945, Avon MSS, 20/1/25; Philip Goodhart, *The 1922, The Story of the 1922 Committee* (1973), 140–1.

Assheton in reviving basic structures in the the first year of peacetime deserves more credit than he has usually been given.[5]

The most serious catch dropped in the first session was undoubtedly the Party's disarray in the debate over American loans for post-war reconstruction, and the Keynesian mechanisms agreed at Bretton Woods for post-war international finance. Already in 1944 such proposals had upset Tories who felt that the long-term trading position of the Empire had been sacrificed to the anti-colonial USA. In December 1945, Churchill tried to limit these divisions by calling on the Party to abstain in the debate; 118 Conservatives followed his lead, but eight backed the Government and seventy-one voted against, a humiliating three-way split. The tone of the debate was as bad as the vote; Robert Boothby accused America of extracting terms worse than those imposed on defeated enemies, and said that the Government and its Conservative supporters had agreed 'to sell the British Empire for a packet of cigarettes'; Oliver Stanley did not help much with the jibe that when Boothby died he would be found to have 'Bretton Woods' engraved on his heart (nor with the rider that it needed Boothby's portly figure to encompass a phrase so much longer than 'Calais'). The issue was also being emotively discussed in the Party outside parliament; West Midlands Conservatives pledged themselves 'to oppose the Bretton Woods proposals and the adoption of a world trading or currency system' as likely to lead to domination by American companies and American finance; in 1947, this Chamberlainite homeland of tariffs was still opposing 'with deep dismay' new trading arrangements with their 'breaches made in the Imperial Preference system'. In the Lords, Beaverbrook delivered a stinging speech against wreckers of the Empire and then never attended the House again when it refused to vote against the American loan. He spent much of the rest of his life out of Britain, and away from Churchill. This final withdrawal from British politics was a considerable blessing to the Conservatives, though one not immediately obvious since the *Daily Express* continued to follow Beaverbrook's personal politics. In 1949, under pressure from Party colleagues who were enraged by the *Express*, Churchill had to cancel a trip to Beaverbrook's Jamaican home, so as not to be seen associating with him. As he told Moran, Beaverbrook 'wants the jockey to win, but he hates the horse. The Tories, Winston added sadly, hate [Beaverbrook] and he hates them.' How strong that hatred was came out when in 1949 Beaverbrook did not renew his subscription to his local Epsom Conservative Association – though for old times sake he did continue to

5 D.R. Thorpe, *Selwyn Lloyd* (1989), 102; John Boyd-Carpenter, *Way of Life* (1980), 77–8; T.F. Lindsay and M. Harrington, *The Conservative Party, 1918–1970* (1974), 149; James Stuart, *Within the Fringe* (1967), 150; Geoffrey Hodgson, 'The Steel Debates', in *The Age of Austerity, 1945–1951*, eds Michael Sissons and Philip French (Harmondsworth, 1964), 328; John Ramsden, *The Making of Conservative Party Policy, The Conservative Research Department since 1929* (1980), 104, 141; Kandiah, 'Lord Woolton' thesis, 48.

give £100 a year to Ashton-under-Lyne; Central Office promptly leaked
to the press that Beaverbrook was no longer a Conservative, so anxious
were they that he should not be able to claim to speak for the Party; his
only remaining Conservative intimate, Bracken, wrote 'what fools Central
Office are'. Bracken himself had returned to the Commons via a by-election
in Bournemouth, and rejoined the shadow cabinet, but was in poor health
and giving priority to his business interests.[6]

The American loan fiasco was a frontbench rather than a backbench crisis,
for there was no coordination of the debate; Crookshank wrote that 'Winston
is very upset, talks of giving up etc'. The defeat of so many major figures
in 1945 contributed to the delay in getting together an effective opposition,
and to something of a crisis of confidence. It was recognised that by-elections
would have to be risked to strengthen the debating team in the House, but
the choice of those to return was not easy. Eden, called in by Churchill to
discuss the matter with Assheton, was 'annoyed to find worst by-election
proposed for Dick Law and young Thorneycroft at bottom of the list for
later attempts. Exploded. Told A. in front of W. that if he & his friends
continue to regard our party as close corporation for extreme right it had
no future. This treatment was typical. Remained glowering all the evening,
thought it necessary.' The same problem arose over initial membership of
the shadow cabinet. Eden was shocked to find that Hoare was proposed:
'There is no hope for the Tory party unless we can clear these disastrous
old men out, and some of the middle-aged ones too!' In the event, 1945
by-elections allowed the return of Macmillan – who now followed Walter
Elliot's prescription by abandoning the industrial north for the home counties
– Bracken, Law, and Thorneycroft, with Elliot himself reappearing in 1946.
Not all the defeated were so lucky. Alec Dunglass, left high and dry by his
defeat in Lanark, was out of parliament until he won the seat back in 1950;
his being away when so much of the Party was 'renewed' after 1945 was one
reason why his emergence as Leader in 1963 was so profoundly shocking to
such modern Conservatives as Macleod.[7]

With these returning ex-ministers, the front bench once again had a
respectable look, but confidence was less easy to restore. Eden had been
contemplating the post of Secretary General of the United Nations and
would probably have taken it if offered; Lyttelton, like Bracken, retreated
into the City for much of the next few years, just as Maxwell Fyfe and

6  Paul Addison, *Churchill on the Home Front, 1900–1955* (1992), 389; J.E.D. Hall, *Labour's
   First Year* (Harmondsworth, 1947), 83; West Midlands Area Council, 25 Dec. 1945 and
   6 Dec. 1947; A.J.P. Taylor, *Beaverbrook* (1972), 572; Gilbert, *Never Despair*, 462; Lord
   Moran, *Winston Churchill, The Struggle for Survival, 1940–1965* (Sphere edn., 1966), 372;
   Tom Driberg, *Beaverbrook* (1956), 311; Richard Cockett (ed.), *My Dear Max: The Letters
   of Brendan Bracken to Lord Beaverbrook, 1925–1958* (1990), 62, 101.
7  Crookshank diary, 13 Dec. 1945, Crookshank MSS; Eden diary, 27 July 1945, Avon MSS,
   20/1/25; Kenneth Young, *Sir Alec Douglas-Home* (1970), 75; Alistair Horne, *Macmillan,
   1894–1956* (1988), 287.

Hogg spent more time at the Bar; Macmillan was more active in the family firm and considered giving up politics for a full-time career as a publisher. Butler though, remembering Baldwin's advice to him that he should always cultivate the Commons, accepted only a single directorship in the family firm Courtaulds, and continued to devote nearly all his time to political life; Baldwin also advised that 'it doesn't look well if our people rush into jobs which in practice are not open to our opponents'. In avoiding this temptation and remaining available full-time, Butler undoubtedly increased his practical influence over the events that followed.[8]

In all these calculations though, and especially in Eden's, loomed the question of Churchill's personal future. In the black despair that followed his defeat, Churchill considered throwing in the towel, recognising that, as he was now over seventy, he could probably only lower his reputation by going on. Throughout 1945 he was hinting to Eden that he might soon have to take over, but as the shock of defeat and the exhaustion wore off, his depression was replaced by a burning desire to avenge himself for the 1945 defeat and a wish to retire as a winner. The Australian premier Robert Menzies later recalled Churchill often saying at this time '"they dismissed me, they dismissed me". You see this had really bitten into him. It wasn't a question of how long he might be Prime Minister again, but that he should be elected Prime Minister for whatever the period might be. That really assumed a magnitude in his mind.' As Bracken put it in 1946, 'Winston is determined to continue to lead the Tory Party until he becomes Prime Minister on earth or Minister of Defence in Heaven.' In the end it was only his own view that mattered. Moran heard many 'whispers . . . in the inner circle of the Tory hierarchy that Winston needed a long rest. He ought to get on with his book . . . Prefaced by elaborate protestations of admiration and respect, his colleagues cautiously advanced the same theme to me, though in all kinds of circuitous ways . . . They would have liked to have got rid of him, I fancy, if they had known how.' But Moran declined to recommend Churchill to step down on health grounds and the mutterings of colleagues in 1945 seem never to have reached the stage of formal suggestions that he should retire. Indeed, when he entered the Commons on 1 August, Conservative MPs treated him to a spirited rendering of 'For he's a jolly good fellow'. He responded to a 'tumultuous' reception at the Central Council in November with the complacent words, 'You give a generous welcome to one who has led you through one of the greatest defeats in the history of the Tory Party . . . It may perhaps be that you give me some indulgence for leading you in some other matters which have not turned out so badly.'[9]

[8] Anthony Eden, *The Reckoning, The Eden Memoirs*, vol. 2 (1965), 554; Horne, *Macmillan*, 295; Baldwin to Butler, 12 Aug. 1945, Butler MSS, G17.
[9] Alan Thompson, *The Day Before Yesterday* (1971), 84; Cockett, *My Dear Max*, 60; Moran, *Struggle*, 334; Henry Pelling, *Winston Churchill* (1974), 563; Gilbert, *Never Despair*, 173.

Churchill continued to hint that he might shortly hand over to Eden, as in Summer 1946 when Thomas, on Eden's behalf, was investigating how Baldwin had financed his office as Leader of the Opposition before 1931; Eden would feel obliged to give up his directorships if he became Leader, but did not know how he would then be able to pay the staff. But it is difficult to avoid the conclusion that these hints were just cases of Churchill expertly playing Eden along, without ever seriously intending to step down, much as he was to do when back in power between 1951 and 1955. Cranborne, speculating in April 1946 on the possibility of forcing the issue, realised how little chance there would be for Eden to outwit Churchill: 'He clearly cannot act alone. Either he would invite a bitter quarrel with W., or the latter would adopt a pained and grieved attitude which would make A. feel like an utter cad. In either case, he wld. probably have to give way.' Butler's later view was that 'in active politics as in the hunting pack, the strongest wolf will retain leadership while his fangs are still firmly bedded in his jaw. It became clear after endless armchair exchanges that Churchill was fitter than for several years and was prepared to fight.' In December 1945, he reported in similar terms the view of a dinner attended by Cranborne, Crookshank, Macmillan, Stuart and other frontbenchers: 'there was a surprising degree of calm, i.e. a general agreement that the older man could not be "shoved", & that either he goes early if he wants to, or that we just see things through.' From the backbenches, later in the Parliament, Headlam reached a similar conclusion, though remaining very critical of Churchill, who 'has always been too much interested in himself to run a party': in 1948 he concluded that 'the Tory Party cannot give Winston his congé, especially at a time when he is the only really big noise it possesses. The only way of getting rid of Winston is for him to retire of his own accord and this he will never do. The mistake was ever to make him Leader, and at the time when Neville died it was almost impossible not to do so . . .'[10]

Churchill's decision to stay on as Leader did not though mark any great change in his view of the duties of the post. His irregular presence in the House and the lethargic Opposition performance of the first year led to criticism of his leadership that had to be headed off with a staged no–confidence motion. The fiasco over the American loan produced more criticism and a stormy meeting with the 1922 Committee. MPs were not pleased to read in the press that he was devoting himself to the organisation of his war memoirs with exactly the military staffwork that they felt to be missing in the Commons. Calm of a sort was restored by Churchill's decision to spend several months abroad in early 1946; in his absence, Eden led in the Commons (and effectively in the

---

10  Thomas to Geoffrey Fry, 8 July 1946, and Cranborne to Thomas, 26 Apr. 1946, Cilcennin MSS; Lord Butler of Saffron Walden, *The Art of the Possible, The Memoirs of Lord Butler* (1971), 132–3; Butler to Buchan-Hepburn, 4 Dec. 1945, Hailes MSS, 4/12; Headlam diary, 19 Feb. 1948 and 23 Feb. 1949.

country too), and things were brought under control; before he left Churchill 'confirmed' for the shadow cabinet that Eden had full authority to run things in his absence. The transition was over and the real work of opposition rebuilding could begin in 1947.[11]

Even in the immediate aftermath of defeat, sparks of recovery had spontaneously appeared. The municipal elections in November 1945 had been even worse for the Party than the General Election, perhaps not surprising when it is considered how low Tory morale was and how high was that of Labour. But in November 1946, with organisation still at a low ebb, the Conservative vote began to recover; 262 local government seats were won back from Labour by Conservatives and another 165 by Independents who were Conservatives in disguise. Membership also began to recover where local activists in middle-class areas took their own initiatives; in Uxbridge, a 'Conservative week' in 1946 nearly doubled the association's size by adding 2,174 new members to the list.[12]

## The constituency agents

Nevertheless, in their New Year messages for 1947, Woolton and Pierssené were careful to remind the Party that a recovery on the required scale would not happen by leaving spontaneous events and local initiatives to take their course; there was no reliance to be placed on 'the swing of the pendulum'. The General Director reported that they had now restored the basic structures but had not yet got back the supporters lost in 1945, and 1947 would be the year to begin that task. Given the traditional nature of the organisational structure and the particular weaknesses of 1945, a major priority was the reconstruction of the professional arm at the local level – the agents. Training programmes were re-started in 1946 and then on an increasing scale. Much of the training was effectively done on the job, but this placed additional pressures on the few experienced constituency agents who could give such training; other trainees, already appointed to existing vacancies, learned on the job. From 1947 the *Conservative Agents' Journal* regularly listed new groups of about thirty trainees who had passed the examinations, nearly all of whom were already in post. All in all, 278 agents gained full qualification during the 1945–50 Parliament, and many more were given intermediate certificates. If the calibre of new Tory MPs was thought to be low in 1945 and to be unusually high in the 'class of 1950', then the generation of constituency agents who joined the profession in the later 1940s was probably the best of all time. A high proportion were wartime officers, 'characters' with RAF nicknames who were

11 Addison, *Churchill*, 286–9; Robert Rhodes James, *Anthony Eden* (1986), 315; Anthony Eden, *Freedom and Order, Selected Speeches, 1939–1946* (1947), 388; Leader's Consultative Committee minutes [hereafter LCC], 20 Nov. 1945, CPA.
12 *CAJ*, Oct. 1946 and Mar. 1947.

at a loose end in 1946, strong anti-socialists who welcomed a job that was important in their own estimation and gave them a chance to run their own show; many were only in their thirties when appointed and remained with the Party until retirement in the 1960s and 1970s. These new agents would though be relatively inexperienced until they had been in post for a few years. By 1948, when there were 440 qualified agents in post, only a third had taken part in more than one parliamentary election, and more than a third had not fought one at all. Week-end schools and teams of agents brought together for by-elections were ways of blooding the new boys, but were no substitute for running a campaign with full responsibility. In the meantime one thing that could be done through in-service training was to weld the new men together into a team, and week-end courses and the like were probably as important socially and for the anecdotal exchange of experience as for anything learned from instructors. By Summer 1948, all the branches of the National Society of Agents were flourishing again, even in Scotland where its existence before 1939 had been exiguous; there was a full programme of inter-branch cricket matches, and branches were playing MPs' elevens as well (which must in some regions have been rather testing for the MPs). On occasion the social aspect could get out of hand; the *Journal* received complaints from those who felt that the status of the profession was being let down when some members were so much more interested in the bar than the Annual General Meeting that speeches became inaudible. Council wisely decided to take no action, 'it being felt that we were in danger of being too censorious of our lighter moments'.[13]

Retaining agents was as important as training them. Area Agents worked as in the 1920s to encourage constituencies to pay good salaries and to include all appointees in the superannuation scheme, but after 1945 the scarcity of trained and experienced agents was probably the main factor that drove up remuneration and conditions. The range of salaries advertised in 1948 ranged from Chief Agents for Nottingham (£800) and Bristol (£1,000), through Rutland and Stamford and an unidentified Middlesex borough constituency (each £600), to a Yorkshire urban constituency (£400 to £600, depending on experience). These advertised salaries were well up on the equivalent figures for the 1930s and by a margin that indicates that they were at least keeping pace with general salary levels. Pensions were also improved, another traditional feature of the agents' efforts to raise their professional status. Part of the proceeds of Woolton's fundraising was devoted to enhancing the capital of the Agents' Superannuation Fund, and when this was done in 1947 the pensions payable were increased by a third. In 1949 a futher step was made by discussing a move to the more usual system in superannuation whereby

[13] *CAJ*, Jan. 1947, Apr. and Aug. 1948, Apr. 1949; Arthur Fawcett, *Conservative Agent: A Study of the National Society of Conservative Agents* (Driffield, Yorkshire, 1967), 41; Hodgson, 'Steel Debates', 326.

final pensions were related by formula to final salary as well as to years of contributions.[14]

Central Office under Woolton and Pierssené was therefore an important influence in the agents' favour, but there was nevertheless a continuous undercurrent of suspicion by the more senior members of the profession. This went back to plans hatched in wartime for a complete rearrangement of agents' employment. In 1941, there were serious worries that heavy wartime taxation would generate a reluctance by MPs and candidates to subsidise their local parties as in the past; one reaction was to review the question of candidates' contributions as such, but another was to consider taking off the shoulders of the local associations their largest single financial burden, the salary of the agent. Topping was authorised by the National Union Executive to draw up a scheme, for discussion with the National Society, whereby agents would henceforth be employed by the Party rather than by local associations, on a single agreed salary scale. The Party nationally was thought better able to raise the money needed, and there would be other advantages: there would be a proper system of promotion on merit; the best agents would be put in the most marginal constituencies; agents on war service would be guaranteed a job on their return. It was all very rational, but when presented to the National Society for discussion in early 1942 it produced uproar. Opposition to the proposals was led by three key men, Frederick Walker of Bolton who had been elected to the chairmanship of the National Society for the duration as a strong man who would fight for agents in a difficult time, Captain Edwards, the formidable Chief Agent for Birmingham, and Elton Halliley, still editing the *Journal* and a veteran of earlier fights on similar issues. They welcomed anything that offered job security for their absent colleagues, but had 'grave doubts' about a scheme 'so radically opposite to the system and methods which have hitherto applied'. They were sceptical about the possibility of raising enough money centrally to fund the scheme, they disliked any system of dual responsibility that would leave agents paid centrally but working with locally-elected association officers, they rejected the proposed national supervisory board as inadequate and, most crucially, they opposed the proposed limitation on agents' freedom to decide where to work and for whom. Through the *Journal*, these negative views received a wide circulation, not least to agents abroad who could not get to meetings to hear Topping explain his scheme in person. It would not be fair to suggest that the *Journal* rigged the debate, for Halliley's invitation to contributors to send in contrary views did not apparently produce many, and those that did come in were not effectively argued. The branches that met voted half in favour and half against the scheme, but all were poorly attended. The Society's Council then voted to reject the scheme and, after complaints, also to reject a motion of

---

[14] *CAJ*, Apr. 1948 and Feb. 1949; John Ramsden, *The Age of Balfour and Baldwin, 1902–1940* (1978), 240; NUEC, 16 Oct. 1947.

censure on Walker, Edwards and Halliley. The Society offered the compromise of an acceptance of central employment for the poorest constituencies only, but this was worth nothing, for few agents would want to go there to fight against hopeless odds if they were free to take a safe seat at a higher salary. It was not likely that Topping, who was himself a former agent and still opened his addresses to their meetings with the invocation 'fellow agents', would try to force his plans through against such opposition. Cuthbert Headlam was a National Union representative in these talks, about what he dubiously called a scheme 'for instituting a board to administer a Central fund (provided by the better off constituencies!) for supplying agents to the less well-to-do constituences'. Before the first meeting he thought that 'it is all rather hopeless', and after several sessions had concluded that it was 'the old, old, hopeless story'. Topping's face was saved by a statement that no final decision could be made while so many agents were abroad. It was all deferred until after the War, and then in 1946–47 the Party had more urgent priorities to consider; a few experiments were tried, as when Belper was persuaded to employ a qualified agent in July 1946, two-thirds of the cost falling on Central Office and one third on the Area; later in the year Area funds were also injected into paying for agents for Loughborough, Grantham and Bosworth, but even then the constituency association seems to have remained the employer.[15]

When discussions about central employment re-started in 1948, many of Topping's premises had become invalid: job security for wartime service was now irrelevant; and although personal taxation remained high and candidates were, as anticipated, reluctant to find such large sums as hitherto for the Party, the constituencies had not only made up the deficit but were now being cajoled into paying towards Central Office costs as well. Most constituencies now had agents and were meeting their salaries. The rational part of Topping's case remained, but not the part that had derived from expediency, and the agents' profession had in the meantime acquired a new generation of sturdy individualists who had not the faintest wish to be moved around the country at the whim of a supervisory committee in London. Walker wrote in the *Journal* to explain what had been opposed in 1942 and why the same view should now prevail, and was forthright; good agents could get jobs anyway, so why overthrow a good system for the benefit of poor ones? Dual control would lead to divided loyalties, and 'in any friction with London, a "Central Office man" will always be suspect by his Constituency Association'. This time the correspondence columns were more evenly divided, but the Council again rejected the scheme, this time without even taking a vote. The National Union Executive pressed on, and their sub-committee recommended a scheme for

15  *CAJ*, Jan., Apr., July and Aug. 1947; National Union General Purposes Committee papers, Discussions with NSA, 1941–42, NUA 6/2/1, CPA; NUEC minutes, 12 Nov. 1941 and 11 Nov. 1942; Headlam diary, 14 Jan. and 24 Feb. 1942; East Midlands Area Council, 1 July and 2 Nov. 1946.

central employment in June 1948, though the report recognised that since there was no consensus any scheme could only be voluntary. Even this generated hostility from those who saw it as an attack on all local autonomy, and not just that of the agents; since the Party was just then campaigning for freedom against alleged socialist centralisation, this was embarrassing for the scheme's supporters. Thomas Dugdale, now Yorkshire Area Chairman, moved that the report be not proceeded with, saying tellingly that 'distinguished people came from all sides in Yorkshire to ask one question, "are they going to nationalise our agents in London?"' Woolton begged the Executive not to forget that other items about agents' employment were also in the report and on this basis it was allowed to go forward for further discussion, but central employment was quietly buried. It was eventually decided that this part of the report 'might well form a useful basis for future enquiry'. The issue recurred with dreadful regularity but no progress was ever made.[16]

In this atmosphere, it is not surprising that other Central Office initiatives towards agents should have been greeted with doubt. When Halliley retired in 1946, it was not easy to find an agent to edit the *Journal*, but a suggestion that it be taken over by Central Office was turned down flat; copy on technical matters would be welcome, but it would remain the organ of the agents and not of the Party. Something similar happened over appointments. Complaints were made when an uncertificated agent was appointed with Central Office recognition, in Birkenhead; since 1926, a joint examination board representing Central Office, the National Union and the agents' National Society ensured that professional qualifications after training were properly validated. Woolton offered a soothing reply to the effect that it was necessary to train more applicants before insisting on certificates before appointment, and the Society in effect accepted his argument. But when Central Office itself promoted uncertificated agents to more senior posts, they were very hostile indeed; this arose from the decision to make a woman either the Area Agent or the deputy in every Area, at a time when there were few women organisers with full qualifications. The National Society refused to admit these appointees to membership, though it did insultingly allow them to attend branch meetings for the part of the agenda when purely organisational matters were being discussed; the situation had to be regularised by the Party examination board giving out certificates to such appointees even though they had not taken the examination. This gave them automatic qualification for membership, but in return a promise was given by Pierssené that the experiment would not be repeated. Even an administrative matter could be difficult. The *Journal* continued to advertise some vacant posts, but the official notification was now through the weekly mailing sent out by Central Office to constituencies. This

---

[16] *CAJ*, Apr., May and June 1948; National Union General Purposes Committee papers, 'Sub-Committee on Employment of Agents, 1948', NUA 6/2/4, CPA; *Interim and Final Reports of the Committee on Party Organisation* (1949), 7.

was in itself uncontroversial, but when Central Office added the proviso that all applications for a constituency vacancy must go through Central Office (which would send them on to the constituency chairman), agents were again suspicious of creeping centralisation; it was feared that applications would not just be forwarded but would also be subject to blocking and to the addition of confidential advice that would prejudice a fair contest – that in effect central employment would be introduced by the back door. There is no evidence of blocking; pointed advice was certainly given to constituencies through Area Agents, and this may have contributed to decisions but it did not determine them, for constituency associations were just as jealous of their freedom as were agents themselves. The *Journal*, reporting a National Society AGM that had got 'distinctly liverish – to be blunt, dignity was lacking', reminded agents that it was foolish to talk of other agents being 'caught in the webb of Central Office'. After all, most Area and Central Office staff were themselves trained agents first. 'Certainly (so far as we have been able to discover) Abbey House is not a Kremlin. It does not house a sinister force or evil genius, manipulating through a network of Vishinkys or Sokolovskys seated in Area cells, a network of conspiracy to the disadvantage of Agents, collective or individual.' Sarcasm was all very well, but the appointment of an uncertificated agent at Ormskirk in 1950 led to a public row; the local association complained, in a circular letter to Conservative MPs that found its way into the press, that the agents were attempting to dictate to the Party and operating a closed shop; Central Office and the National Union both took the agents' side in the dispute, and Ormskirk had to give way, or risk expulsion from the National Union itself. In 1950, when the Northern Area tried to delete the word 'certificated' from all references to 'agent' in its rules, to recognise that poorer constituencies in the North East could not always afford the best, it was sternly told by the National Union itself that Areas had to conform to the national rules and that only certificated agents could be recognised. Already in 1947, 90 per cent of agents in post held a certificate, and these arguments were very much at the margin, but no less contentious for that. This acceptance by the voluntary side of the Party of the agents' professional aspirations showed that the convergence of interests in making the organisation more efficient at every level was widely recognised. Area Agents had to tread warily in seeking to encourage, warn and guide the constituency associations into action, and some of their frustrations can be deduced from the scathing way which they often referred to agents and association officers in their confidential reports, but they nonetheless exerted a continuous pull in the direction of more businesslike financial and electioneering methods. The extremely detailed annual reports submitted by Area Agents on every constituency ensured that no dark corners of the land would be overlooked in the drive to modernise the machinery.[17]

---

[17] Ramsden, *Balfour and Baldwin*, 238–9; *CAJ*, Apr., July and Nov. 1947, Nov. 1949, Jan. 1951; NUEC, 14 Dec. 1950; Fawcett, *Conservative Agent*, 43–4; Northern Area Council, 11 Nov. 1950.

## Woolton, membership and money

The *Journal* reminded agents that it was especially foolish for them to forget that Woolton was running Central Office, and that Woolton had done an immense amount personally for the agents; when Kettering in 1954 resolved at last to appoint an agent at the recommended national rate, this was minuted as agreeing to the 'Woolton scale'. Nor did such reminders fall on deaf ears. Agents were not simply paid officials who jealously guarded their corner: they were also dedicated enthusiasts who put in immensely long hours and who, despite a surface cynicism that went with the job, for the most part cared deeply about the Party and its success – and sincerely hated socialism and wanted to do it down. When Woolton appealed for funds in 1947, at least one agents' branch sent in its own donation from its benevolent fund. It is not easy to assess Woolton's personal contribution to the Party revival, for he took over at such a low ebb that the only way forward was up; when he retired in 1955, Robert Hudson joked that it was typical of Woolton to have bought only at the bottom of the market, a remark that Woolton took as a compliment. The press at that time paid him less ambiguous compliments though, setting him alongside Salisbury and Disraeli as a maker of modern Conservatism, wildly wide of the mark as an assessment of his contribution to the recovery. The press was always cultivated by Woolton, and invited to see and report his Central Office work, sometimes literally; the *Yorkshire Post* in 1949 described the layout of his office, down to the details of the coloured constituency charts on his walls, a story that signally indicated (and was meant to) a man in full command of his task. In judging that his capacity to inspire was his greatest asset, we must rely on his colleagues' testimony. Macmillan, who after all might have had the job himself, felt that 'no more suitable choice could have been made for this post. Woolton was not only a great organiser, but he was also the best salesman that I have ever known.' And Butler, no personal friend to Woolton, thought he had been 'one of the principal restorers of Conservatism during this period – financially, administratively and, perhaps above all, psychologically'. Woolton's own later perception was that 'the primary need of the Conservative Party, but in particular of the Central Office, was that it should believe in itself and in its capacity to convert the electorate to Conservatism'. His own personality was a useful start here; a Somerset delegate told the 1946 Conference that 'we are so grateful that we have someone who has qualifications other than that he is a well-informed gentleman of outstanding respectability'. The Sheffield Tory women reported in 1946 that when 'in July [1946] it was announced that Lord Woolton was to be the new Chairman of the Party, this was received with great satisfaction by all members'. A self-made man as Party Chairman was in itself a statement about the Party's future, but each time Woolton spoke there was confirmation of the fact of his origins from his accent. Workington Conservatives, having had the relevant paragraph of his 1946 Conference speech read to them, immediately agreed to contest every local council seat in their area, because that was what he had asked for. The easy bonhomie of 'Uncle Fred' went with a sharp sense of how truths could be communicated to inspire Party workers, a talent derived both from instinct and from previous experience in the retail trade and as wartime Minister of Food. Much evidence could be piled up as to how far this inspirational effect worked on the Party activists, and especially on those in Central Office. Reporting Woolton at his first Conference in 1946, Elton Halliley enthused, 'what an inspiration and a will to win came from the very personality of Lord Woolton'. His editorial successor reported of a dinner in 1948, ' "Be a militant army!" said his Lordship, and who among us could help (or dare) being otherwise?' At the same dinner, Pierssené remarked that 'five minutes in the presence of Lord Woolton made the hardest job seem easy', and the National Union President paid a more backhanded compliment when he said that 'Abbey House is the grimiest and grimmest place I've ever seen. The Party must be good employers or the folk would never stick it.' Bradford Conservative Association was just one of many local parties that by 1949 had named their headquarters 'Woolton House'; many others, as in Derby, called theirs 'Churchill House'. Huddersfield Tories united the two by using the neat, punning slogan 'Winston to lead us, Woolton to feed us'.[18]

Feeding the troops with optimism was one thing, it was quite another to plan the actual process of organisational reform – or 'restoration', as Butler was always careful to call it. In this, Woolton was left very much to his own devices, for Churchill still had only the most limited interest in such matters. Much credit is therefore due to Woolton and his advisers in Central Office for taking initiatives that transformed the Party's finances and membership. In this, membership came first in time, though since the members provided much of the money the two were inseparable. In April 1947, the National Union Executive was told that 320 constituencies had taken part in Woolton's first recruiting campaign over the previous winter, and had recruited 233,000 new members. Fifty-five associations had entered a recruiting competition, for which the first prize and a cup was won by Harrow West; the runners up were Hartlepool, Honiton and Houghton-le-Spring, an alliteratively exact cross-section of the country, but no doubt a source of general encouragement. The 438 associations in England and Wales who had so far made returns had 905,663 paid up members, suggesting a Party total of perhaps 1.2 million. This was probably not much above – if at all – pre-war levels of activity, and there is some sense from the local records that this phase was not very taxing, as irritated middle-class people already wanted to express their opposition to Labour. A ward branch in East Croydon got 152 recruits in a single day,

<hr />

18  *CAJ*, Oct. 1946, Nov. 1947, Nov. 1948; Kettering CA minutes, 29 June 1954; Harold Macmillan, *Tides of Fortune, 1945–1955* (1969), 292; Butler, *Art of the Possible*, 149; Woolton, *Memoirs*, 334; Kandiah, 'Lord Woolton' thesis, 4, 65–6; Sheffield Central Women's Advisory Council minutes, 5 Mar. 1947; Workington CA minutes, 11 Oct. 1946; Central Office file, Bradford South by-election, CCO 1/7/136; B.J. Evans and A.J. Taylor, 'The Rise and Fall of Two-Party Electoral Co-operation', in *Political Studies*, vol. 32 (1984), 260.

and more than doubled its membership to 1,100 in two months; Bracken reported that

> in Bournemouth, without any great effort on our part, the Tory Association has trebled its membership in the space of twelve months, and in comparison with our past balance sheets we now have loads of money. In this respect Bournemouth is not exceptional. I understand that all over the country many middle-class people are joining the Tory Party because of the losses they have incurred through the nationalization of railway, electricity and other shares.

Not everywhere was as easy as Bournemouth. In the East Midlands it was reported in April 1947 only that there had been 'notable increases in membership' with few constituencies quoting numbers, though by the end of the year the news from the stronger constituencies at least was better, for Grantham was 'doing well', Belper 'now really alive' and Harborough 'really going ahead'; even industrial Clay Cross was 'greatly improved', but still relying on Area for financial support to keep an agent; average constituency membership in the Area at the end of 1947 was still only about 3,000. Despite the doubling of the number of members in 1947, Bradford still had an average of only 2,700 per constituency at the end of of the year. Central Office was disappointed by these early overall results.[19]

The second stage though was both more ambitious and more significant; it was also given much more of an impetus from the centre: Woolton took on over 150 paid 'missioners' who worked mainly in the marginals at Central Office's expense, and visited in 1948 over a million homes; at the peak in late 1949, there were 246 paid missioners covering 70,000 homes a week; their contracts were terminated for the 1950 campaign to conform to election law (though many were temporarily put on to a different payroll as collectors of local political intelligence for Central Office) but they were then sent back to the constituencies for the period between the 1950 and 1951 Elections; only when the Conservatives returned to office was this scheme wound down. Eden launched the official recruiting campaign with a mass rally in Manchester in April 1948. West Woolwich was by the following month reporting that a canvass of the whole constituency had recruited 4,500 new members – but only £300 in new subscriptions, suggesting that at an average of 1/4d each, they were not committing themselves very far. The following month, South Croydon reported recruiting 1,533 new members in a day. Between the end of 1947 and Summer 1948, overall membership rose by a million to two and a quarter million, the winning constituencies this time being Uxbridge, West Woolwich and Wembley North – a regional concentration of success that perhaps indicated how far the impetus was by this stage pointing towards the Party's strong performance in outer London in the 1950 General Election, but

19 Woolton, *Memoirs*, 348; NUEC, 17 Apr. 1947; *CAJ*, June 1947; Cockett, *My Dear Max*, 72; Kandiah, 'Lord Woolton' thesis, 83–4; East Midlands Area Council, 26 Apr. and 24 Oct. 1947; Bradford CA minutes, 5 Nov. 1948.

surely indicating too that the new members were still coming heavily from the middle class. That view should be qualified by the large figures declared all over the country, including the industrial north; Bradford had doubled its total to more than 20,000 members by early 1949, a figure that was nearly a third of the size of the total Conservative vote in the city in the following year; in Darlington, the 1,413 members at the end of 1947 were doubled in 1948, and by 1952 there were 4,367. In the Welsh marginal, Barry, there were by 1951 an astonishing 11,000 ordinary members (mainly women) and 6,000 more in Conservative clubs (probably all men); even if a lot of club members were not really Conservatives and if some Tory clubmen had been counted in the other totals as well, this still adds up to a huge proportion of the 1951 Conservative vote (24,715); this strength may explain how the seat was held on to so tenaciously when once it had been gained. There remained though some constituencies with hardly any middle-class vote, where even the greatest efforts did not produce encouraging results; in the heavy industrial constituency of Pontefract, the Conservative Association still had only 480 senior members and about a hundred YCs in late 1949, though Conservative clubs in the division had a further 800; in the Durham mining constituency of Easington the 1950 figure was 360 seniors and forty YCs. The official campaign ended at the Party Conference in October 1948, but local recruiting continued, in part a desperate attempt to hold on to these high figures. The evidence suggests that overall numbers rose a little further during the rest of the Parliament to about 2.5 million, and after another campaign in 1952 peaked at 2.8 million; since these figures included only the constituencies of England and Wales for which Central Office was directly responsible, the addition of Scotland and Northern Ireland would produce a peak national figure of well over three million members. Scotland remained entirely outside Woolton's remit, the organisation there being controlled by the 'Scottish Whip', James Stuart (appointed Party Chairman for Scotland in 1950), but run in practice by the long-serving Colonel Blair, who was Political Secretary to the Scottish Whip/Chairman from 1922 to 1960; there is no doubt though that organisation in Scotland also improved considerably after 1945 in parallel with the recovery in England and Wales, and up to 1955 the Party enjoyed outstandingly good election results in Scotland too. The peak membership figure was spectacular, easily the biggest individual paying membership that any British voluntary organisation has ever achieved, and if very small subscriptions indicated only a limited level of commitment, three million of them did nevertheless bring in a great deal of money.[20]

---

[20]  Stuart Ball, 'The National and Regional Party Structure', in *The Conservative Century: The Conservative Party since 1900*, eds A. Seldon and S. Ball (Oxford, 1994), 193, 205; National Union Executive minutes, 16 Oct. 1947; *CAJ*, May and June 1948; Central Council report for 1949, NUA 2/2/15, CPA; Central Office constituency files, CCO 1/7/163, 1/8/148, 1/7/182, 1/8/61, 1/8/528, CPA; Central Office, *Notes on Current Politics* [hereafter *NCP*], 1 Nov. 1948; Central Office file, 'Recruiting', 4/5/89; J.T. Ward, *The First Century, A History of Scottish Tory Organisation* (Edinburgh, 1982), 36–7.

The financial recovery followed similar lines. In 1945 the Party's finances had run down badly, and little could be afforded for the 1945 campaign, even if mechanisms had existed by which to spend it. It also became clear that informal systems of raising large contributions to the central funds were no longer adequate to the task, and a 'Special Finance Committee' was set up to consider a whole range of future financial issues. Following a decision of 1944, a Central Board of Finance was created in 1946 to supervise the work of the Treasurer's Department, but mainly to help raise money. The CBF included not only the Party Treasurer(s), but also Area Treasurers and a few coopted members; the CBF then appointed at least one collector in each Area who, because he worked with the Area Treasurer, did not get lines crossed with local fundraising from industry or from individuals who could afford large contributions. These procedures were shrouded in secrecy; a debate in the National Union Executive late in 1945 led to a question about the Special Finance Committee and when it would report; the Chairman undertook to make enquiries but never seems to have reported back, and neither did the Special Finance Committee. At first money remained short. When in 1947 there was pressure for a re-starting of the Young Britons organisation, the Party Treasurer offered £1,500 as pump-priming money and when criticised for lack of generosity 'he asked the [Executive] Committee to dispel the idea that the Party had a big reserve fund. No such fund existed and if members would make this known, more might be forthcoming.' In April 1947, Crookshank noted a lunch with Woolton and Macmillan to discuss Party finance, where it had emerged that Central Office's annual income at about £75,000 was barely a quarter of annual expenditure. Woolton famously decided to break out of this dilemma by asking the 1947 Conference for a million pound fundraising effort, much as he asked for a million more members. His own view, derived from his business experience and charity work, was that it was psychologically easier to motivate people to go after a large target than a small one, and the wisdom of the approach seemed to be clear even on the day of the appeal, for Woolton had hardly sat down before a representative from Kettering had handed him the first cheque; £12,000 seems to have been raised at that first Conference session, and it was rumoured that a quarter of a million was already pledged; whether true or not, such rumours were extremely helpful. In November 1947, Woolton reported 'astonishing support' for the fighting fund; 'money was being subscribed in half crowns, five shillings and guineas. Old age pensioners had sent a few pence in stamps, saying that their present living conditions were intolerable. The response in the larger amounts had been rather disappointing and . . . he had just been telling that to a meeting of Peers. The constituencies were doing magnificently.' Reporting similar news from Woolton, Headlam reflected that 'it is infinitely better that there should be thousands of small subscribers of £1/1/- to £10/10/- but it takes a lot of these to make a million £'. It was actually a great deal more organised than all this makes it seem; each constituency had a negotiated target which was regularly monitored, but which only made up a third of the million pounds in total; Conservative clubs displayed 'And one for Lord Woolton!' posters behind the bar; there was a huge sorting job for volunteers from the Ladies Carlton Club in mailing appeal letters to every railway stockholder in the country, the Party hoping to cash in on its anti-nationalisation stance; the CBF worked hard on industry, but since it would have done so anyway in 1947 it is not clear how far these efforts should fall within the appeal anyway. Care was taken to ensure that it was on the constituencies that the spotlight fell: Cambridgeshire was a rare constituency that decided that local needs should take priority over Woolton's appeal; most of them explicitly decided the opposite. When Hexham easily exceeded its target of £500, it promptly raised the target to £1,000 and then exceeded that as well. In many places the raising of money from safe Tory areas was explicitly linked to the need to win marginals; Farnham in Surrey, which already had a strong association and a large parliamentary majority, had a 'win the seats' appeal. The difficult constituency of South East Cardiff was given a target only of £50 but raised £286. In less good areas, some of the money was quietly creamed off locally in the first place; Derby decided to split the proceeds of the Woolton appeal between Central Office and local funds; Newark were anxious that the appeal should not imperil their local efforts, but in the end easily raised their appeal target and also put as much again into their election fighting fund.[21]

Woolton's tactic thus proved to be sound, as he reported to the 1948 Conference: 'I asked you to put me in a position financially to run the Party, and since I never thought it worthwhile making a fuss about small things, I asked for a million pounds. That was in October 1947. You gave it before the end of the year.' (It is in fact clear from the files that if a million pounds was pledged by the end of 1947, then it was months later before much of it actually arrived – but that did not make so good a story.) The million-pound fighting fund was indeed a great deal of money – far more than a whole year's central expenditure, and about four times Labour's annual central expenditure. It bought time, and allowed the launching of several new organisational efforts, but it could not be repeated annually without loss of momentum. The constituency contributions were far from being the whole story. The CBF raised a good deal of money directly, and the United Industrialists Association, formed in 1947 to provide a channel through which companies could provide funds without directly supporting a party, had raised more than three million pounds by 1955. Area funds, most of the money raised from companies on a regional basis, also climbed steeply; the North West

21 Michael Pinto-Duschinsky, *British Political Finance, 1830–1980* (1981), 128–9; NUEC, 23 Aug. 1945, 12 June and 13 Nov. 1947; Crookshank diary, 25 Apr. 1947, Crookshank MSS; *CAJ*, Nov. 1947; *NCP*, 11 Nov. 1948; Headlam diary, 7 Nov. 1947; Central Office files, 'Fighting Fund', CCO 4/1/94–97, CPA; Woolton, *Memoirs*, 336–7; Derby CA minutes, 4 Dec. 1947; Newark CA minutes, 21 Jan. 1948.

had raised only £492 in 1945, but £11,360 in 1948. Nevertheless, the demands of expenditure were insatiable, and what would be needed to sustain the new level of spending would be a permanent change in the pattern of Party finance, a regular flow of resources from the constituencies towards the central funds. Party managers now began to argue for this and with Woolton's advocacy the case received a surprisingly warm hearing. The 1947 Party Conference received and endorsed a motion from Hitchin calling for just such a system, and the National Union Executive promptly set up a sub-committee to devise a suitable mechanism.[22]

On occasion the drive for financial recovery produced some belated changes. Liverpool, in an earlier period a by-word for modern Tory organisation, had been very backward; in the war years, two-thirds of its income was raised from the subscriptions and donations of its MPs, Aldermen and councillors. Only in 1953 did the city party make ordinary membership dependent on the payment of a subscription, 'in addition to political conviction'. The relevant resolution noted sadly that 'the days have long passed when the Party could depend on the goodwill of a few wealthy supporters. The future lies in the hands of our many thousands of voters throughout the City from whom the necessary finance must be raised.' This debate in itself sheds an interesting light on the meaningfulness of earlier claimed membership totals in such places. In 1956, the city party was still calling special meetings of large subscribers to raise money for much of the city's basic organisation, and still allowed those subscribers to elect their own representatives to help run the city party; meanwhile, as the Area Agent reported in 1956 of the Edge Hill, Exchange, Garston, Scotland and Walton divisions, 'there is no actual subscribing membership at the present time'; the other divisions were just beginning to recruit members but none could yet quote figures. This failure to modernise the Party in a city that at that time still had six Conservative MPs (one of them Maxwell Fyfe) in turn sheds much light on the spectacular collapse of Liverpool Conservatism in the 1960s. Barry and Liverpool were opposite poles in the extent to which the organisation was entrenched in the community – and in the success that the Party would enjoy in the next generation.[23]

## New departures

The money raised was partly spent on an expanded Central Office, partly on support for poorer constituencies through Area funds, partly on Area staff

---

[22] Kandiah, 'Lord Woolton' thesis, 76, 116; Cambridgeshire CA minutes, 6 Dec. 1947; Hexham CA minutes, 1 Dec. 1947 and 2 Feb. 1948; South East Cardiff CA minutes, 14 Oct. 1947 and 28 Mar. 1948; North West Area Executive Committee, 28 May 1949; Central Council reports for 1947 and 1948, NUA 2/2/13 and 14, CPA.

[23] Ramsden, *Balfour and Baldwin*, 48; Liverpool CA, AGM minutes, 20 Feb. 1953 and 12 Mar. 1956, and Finance Committee minutes, 23 Feb. 1944; Central Office constituency files, CCO 1/11/107–115.

who could themselves assist the constituencies. A common theme was a much more outgoing approach to public relations and political communication. For example, press officers were appointed in each Area so that the local as well as the national press could be cultivated. At Central Office, Woolton was determined to have a permanent public relations staff who would not themselves be seeking election, and for that reason he parted company with the existing publicity officer. The new appointee, Mark Chapman-Walker, had to train on the job since he was inexperienced in the field, calling on Woolton's own personal experience in the early months, but becoming in due course a skilled media operator who later had a successful career in broadcasting; he was largely responsible for introducing the Party to television when broadcasting resumed after the War. Central Office tried to train Party spokesmen in microphone and camera techniques, primitive efforts by later standards but an important start. In considering television, the enthusiasts had a tough time persuading Party leaders to take the new medium seriously. Churchill was horrified to find that his 1947 Conference speech would have to be delivered under television lights, and noted that 'Mr. Maudling is finding out if the things are as beastly as they sound'. Maudling reported that the lights would not shine into his eyes, and the event went off well enough, but did not persuade Churchill of the virtues of 'teevee'. As broadcasting officer, John Profumo hoped to get Churchill to do a party political broadcast on television early in 1950, to upstage the Labour Party's jubilee celebrations on the eve of the Election, but Churchill was having none of it. Profumo was also reporting that parliamentary candidates, of which he was one, were pressing for more ordinary people to be included on Party radio broadcasts, suggesting one whose 'democratic Yorkshire voice' would be proof of the sort of people who now got on in the Tory Party; his advice was again not heeded, or not until Marcus Fox joined the broadcasting team for October 1974. Woolton asked himself whether it was worth a major effort to 'get ahead' of the other parties with regard to television, and decided it was not. When plans were drawn up for broadcasting at the 1950 General Election, Conservatives joined Labour in rejecting the BBC's advice that party political broadcasts should now be on television as well as on radio. The Conservative and Unionist Films Association was re-started though in 1948, with the first films including a version of Churchill's speech to an Albert Hall rally. By March 1949, there were again thirteen daylight cinema vans out in the constituencies showing mixed programmes of Party films, cartoons and such patriotic material as the royal wedding; this activity alone cost nearly £100,000 a year, roughly what all the constituencies were asked to pay in quota. For the 1951 Election, the Northern Area had two such vans, and during the campaign 193 meetings were arranged to make use of them.[24]

[24] Lindsay and Harrington, *Conservative Party*, 159; Woolton, *Memoirs*, 343–5, 361; Gilbert, *Never Despair*, 353; Central Office file, 'Party funds', CCO 4/4/229, CPA; Northern Area, General Purposes Committee, 3 Dec. 1951.

In other ways too, the approach was traditional; the Party's trades union organisation was revived along the lines of the pre-war 'labour committees' and constituencies urged to join in; as before the response was patchy. The Party College at Ashridge had gradually drifted out of politics altogether during the War, and although the National Union continued to nominate some members of its governing body, they could not bring it back under control. In 1947, thanks to the generosity of Lord Swinton who gave part of his own house to the Party, a 'Conservative College of the North' was opened at Masham in north Yorkshire. This played an important role in educating the new activists, training agents and constituency leaders, and adding too a dimension to the Party's social life, with its all-year programme of courses and week-end schools, organised in collaboration with the Conservative Political Centre; in the first half of 1949, there were forty-two courses at Swinton, attended by about 2,000 people; in the same period 10,000 had attended CPC courses elsewhere in the country and 54,000 had been to single lectures that it had organised. The eventual failure to reclaim Ashridge left the Party with only Swinton, then known as Swinton Conservative College. One Woolton initiative that never got off the ground was his idea for a Party song: he was offered the free use of lyrics and music from a popular review song of 1947, 'I want to see the people happy' by A.P. Herbert and Vivian Ellis (in the style of Ellis's 'Spread a Little Happiness'). Herbert even agreed to write a new version of the words for a more political effect. Woolton duly arranged for this to be published in a Party magazine, hoping that it could be sung at constituency meetings – 'it would rouse them up' – but for once he miscalculated; Gracie Fields refused to record the song, and Malcolm Sargent wanted nothing to do with the idea of his conducting a choral version; with the Party the idea never caught on.[25]

In part these media activities were another example of the renewal of old approaches, with the Party now slowly adapting to television as it had earlier adapted to film. Other organisational developments were undeniably new, notably the Young Conservatives and the Conservative Political Centre. The CPC had a hybrid existence as a Butler initiative that was housed at Central Office, reporting until 1948 to an Advisory Committee on Policy and Political Education under Butler's chairmanship. The staff recruited by 'Cub' Alport, its Director, were not intended to have the intellectual calibre of the Research Department, but were undeniably involved in policy content as well as pure presentation. Alport was, like Macmillan, a pre-war progressive Tory who had now come into his own: 'we had the opportunity, which would never come again in our lifetime, of remoulding the party along

---

[25] Central Office, General Director's file, 'Broadcasting', CCO 120/1/1; Central Office file, 'CUFA', CCO 4/2/25, CPA; J.A. Cross, *Lord Swinton* (Oxford, 1982), 262; Central Council report for 1950, NUA 2/2/16, CPA; Advisory Committee on Policy papers, ACP 1/1, CPA; Central Office file, 'Songs', CCO 4/2/87, CPA.

our lines, which we'd had aspirations for in those years before 1939.' He was a believer in policy discussion being diffused throughout the Party, hence the preparation of Party literature that had a serious policy content but which nonetheless remained accessible for discussion at ordinary branch meetings, and the encouragement of constituencies to set up discussion panels of their own. By Autumn 1947, there were 557 local discussion groups, usually meeting informally in a member's house, with about 6,000 members taking part. By the following Spring, two-thirds of constituencies had a CPC group meeting regularly. The most important use of this structure was Butler's suggested 'two-way contact programme', whereby coordinated discussions on specific policy questions could be held all round the country at about the same time. The National Union Executive was told in November 1946 that 'the experiment had two objectives: first to encourage the study, by as large a number as possible of the rank and file of the Party, of present day political problems, and secondly to keep the leaders of the Party informed of the views of the members'. By then too, ten of the Party's twelve Areas had a Political Education Officer on the staff to foster such activities. The CPC was also an active publisher in its own right, producing forty-six books and pamphlets in its first thirty months. Its one serious failure lay in its attempts to run a chain of bookshops which would stock books sympathetic to the Party's viewpoint – another bow to the memory of *Guilty Men*. A first shop was opened in Abbey House itself in November 1947, and others followed in Leeds, Cardiff and Newcastle, but it proved impossible to get Party members to use these rather than their nearest ordinary shop, and presumably political opponents refused to use them anyway. The Conservatives were not much better at running bookshops than the Labour Government was at growing groundnuts. By 1948, Woolton was urging Party members to buy their copies of Churchill's *War Memoirs* from a CPC shop since they needed the trade, and in the early 1950s the other shops were closed and only the London branch remained, generally losing money but accepted as service to the Party.[26]

The Young Conservative organisation was not entirely new, since the Party had had in the Junior Imperial League a youth wing for most of the century, and had intended to re-launch it in 1939 when the War intervened. In scale and vitality though, the YCs easily outgunned their predecessors, and this in itself gave the new structure a different weight and significance in the Party. It was one of the first sectors of the Party to enjoy a full revival, with the formal re-launch decided on during the War, and its growth and subsequent consolidation coming rather earlier than that of the main Party branches. A few Party youth branches staggered on through the War but only fifty were known to exist in Summer 1945. By the end of 1946, there

[26] Thompson, *Day Before Yesterday*, 84; Central Council report for 1947, NUA 2/2/13, CPA; Patrick Cosgrave, *R.A. Butler, An English life* (1981), 84; NUEC, 14 Nov. 1947, 9 Jan. and 6 May 1948; Butler, *Art of the Possible*, 137.

were 1,062 YC branches and only fifty constituencies did not have at least one; every constituency in Birmingham had long had a 'Young Unionist' branch by then, but the pre-war total of thirty-one youth branches was only reached in the city in 1947. At the end of that year there were 1,546 branches nationally, and in mid-1948 there were 2,129 branches with a total of 148,988 members. Only a handful of constituencies in safe Labour seats, almost all in Wales or inner London, did not have at least one YC branch and many safe seats had half a dozen. From this point, the publication of figures even in confidential minutes more or less came to a halt; there were claims of further advances but no figures were cited and it seems likely that here too the expansion came to an end. Each Area had its own YC Committee and by late 1946, with these regional structures in place, the first meeting of the YC National Committee could be held. The mushrooming size of the YC organisation led some traditionally-minded National Union stalwarts to detect a rival, and when it was proposed to hold a separate national YC Conference in 1947, this was overruled by the Executive as an example of undesirable separatism. Further discussions followed though and in September 1948 it was agreed to hold a YC Conference, something that immediately caught on as an annual event. The YCs always had a distinctly social character, attracting and retaining members as much by the local programmes of events as by politics as such; in 1949, a Butlin's holiday camp at Filey was taken over by the Party for a YC 'holiday week' attended by 1,281 members; in addition to a programme offering a choice of twenty social activities a day, there was a political rally, and a YC mock parliament each morning with visiting MPs taking turns as Mr. Speaker. This became a regular event with a different camp used each year. Relations at constituency level were sometimes fraught with difficulty, and in 1951 the Northern Area Chairman was writing round to constituencies to urge them to give their YC branches more encouragement, but most associations welcomed the advent of young, enthusiastic members and were quick to use them for canvassing and delivery at election times; the High Peak Conservatives were, by 1947, typical in reserving places for YCs on their Executive and always had a YC as one of the Association Vice Chairmen. The YC organisation itself became a route to the top for the politically ambitious. In 1950, forty YCs stood as Conservative parliamentary candidates; all had to be under thirty-one to be YCs and many of these were therefore in hopeless constituencies, but eight were elected, as was John Hay, a former national YC chairman.[27]

The general expansion of membership and the YC increase in particular led to a change in the character of many National Union activities, notably

[27] NUEC, 14 Nov. 1946, 13 Feb. and 12 June 1947; Central Council reports for 1947, 1948, 1950 and 1951, NUA 2/2/13, 14, 17 and 18, CPA; Birmingham UA minutes, 6 Mar. 1946; Central Office file, 'YCs', CCO 4/5/389; Northern Area, General Purposes Committee, 13 Mar. 1951; High Peak CA minutes, 11 Apr. 1947; Woolton, *Memoirs*, 338.

of the Conference. Motions of a democratic character were now passed on a regular basis; the National Union Executive resolved at the end of 1945 that elections to all posts in the Party should be by ballot, and that merit alone should determine the choice (the motion did not indicate what other criteria had previously applied, but seniority was almost certainly in mind). By 1950, elections to choose the chairman of the Executive or National Union representatives on outside committees were conducted by postal ballot. A year later it resolved that women should be entitled to a fair share of places on all Area and National Committees; this decision was never policed very rigorously, but women did come to play a more significant role in the National Union, which itself elected a woman chairman in five years out of the next ten. Conferences generally remained as stage-managed as before 1939, though both in 1946 and in 1950 the Conference exerted an influence on policy, in the first place by insisting that the Party should have one, and in the second by deciding what part of it should be. From 1950, Conference agendas allowed time for debate on the final morning on motions chosen by ballot. The gathering of large numbers of activists took on a new significance in such a revivalist mood; a Sheffield delegate reported back in 1947 'how impressed she had been by the enthusiasm of the three thousand people present'. John Biffen, an active Conservative student at this time, felt that it had been one of Woolton's major achievements to turn the annual Conference week into such a focus of activity, as it had never really been before the War. From 1947 the whole Conference was recorded and gramophone records sold of individual speeches; from 1947, a verbatim transcript was published too, selling 4,000 copies on the first occasion. On an initiative of Walter Elliot, a special session was held for Conservative councillors, developing into a full Local Government Conference. The arrangement of Conference week in 1947 reflected the diversity of activities; on Tuesday evening there were agents' meetings and dinners for special interest groups; on Wednesday there was a Local Government Conference and YC meetings; Thursday, Friday and Saturday morning were for the Conference proper, and Saturday afternoon for the mass rally addressed by Churchill. All of this made for a new problem that was to plague the Party through to the mid-1950s: with so many activists wanting to come, with now 200 press places reserved (compared to thirty-five in the 1930s), and with the need to include significant numbers of places for YCs, Conservative women and councillors, the total rose alarmingly. At Blackpool in 1947, more than twice as many Conservatives turned up as had attended the Conferences of 1936 or 1937. In 1949 there were 3,992 accredited representatives and over a thousand visitors on day tickets. With a potential attendance of around 5,000, the traditional rotation of Conferences around the Areas was dropped, for hardly any town had either a hall that was big enough or enough hotel rooms. Even in Brighton, the Dome would hold only half the Conference and the other half had to hear proceedings relayed to the Pavilion. In 1948 it was decided that only Scarborough and Llandudno could now accommodate a Party Conference at the size required, but it was decided to play safe in 1949 for what was expected to be the last pre-election Conference and hold it at Olympia in London; here there was a hall big enough for Conference business, but the social aspect was undermined by the fact that representatives' hotels were spread all over the capital – and London offered so many alternative attractions that it was not easy to get the huge hall full for any session but Churchill's rally speech. The experiment of a London Conference was never to be repeated.[28]

## Patterns of recovery

The flourishing of the Party Conference both encouraged and demonstrated the real growth in the Party's vitality at the grass roots. Churchill's own constituency gives one such example; in 1946, the Woodford Conservatives raised £781 in regular income, and this at the end of a year of what the annual report called 'sustained progress'; by the end of 1949, membership was up to 12,898, including 1,172 YCs, about one in six of the electorate in the constituency and a third of the Conservative vote in 1950, producing an annual income of £2,584 and a bank balance equivalent to a full year's expenditure. In Butler's Saffron Walden constituency the steady improvement of numbers meant that by 1952 there were over 9,000 members, equivalent to nearly half the Tory vote; both the figure and the proportion were much the same at Barkston Ash in the West Riding. A few other examples indicate the same upward trends: membership at Shrewsbury rose from 3,510 in 1946 to 7,075 in 1950; in Gravesend it rose from 1,110 to over 3,000 in the same period; in 1951 there were over 5,000 members in the safe Labour mining seat of Newton, about a quarter of all Tory voters. Direct comparisons of numbers over the length of the Parliament are vitiated for many constituencies by the redrawing of boundaries in 1948, but the overall totals of the new associations set up in 1948–49 tell their own tale: Ashford – 8,358 members, Heston and Isleworth – 8,100, Harrow West – 10,859, Ilford (two constituencies) – 15,000, West Dorset – 9,000. The Home Counties South East Area, comprising just three counties had 437,407 members in 1950 (a third of the Conservative vote in the whole Area in that year), but the pattern was almost as favourable in city areas as in the suburbs and the country: there were 20,000 Party members in Bristol, about the same in Leeds, and nearly 60,000 in Birmingham – two-thirds of the latter being women, but almost all recruited by paid missioners. These private figures from minute books and from Central Office reports bear out the scale of the published

---

28 NUEC, 13 Dec. 1945, 13 Dec. 1946, 17 Apr. 1947, 8 July 1948; Sheffield Central CA minutes, 9 Oct. 1947; John Biffen, 'Party Conference and Party Policy', in the *Political Quarterly*, vol. 32 (1961), 257; Central Council reports for 1947, 1948 and 1950, NUA 2/2/13, 14 and 16, CPA; Coote, *Walter Elliot*, 256.

national figures, but in any case the pattern had to be nearly universal to explain attendances at regional and local rallies organised to provide both fundraising opportunities and audiences for political speeches. The Eastern Area, for example, turned out 50,000 people to hear Churchill speak at a fête at Luton Hoo in 1948; a joint constituency event run by Monmouth, Newport and Pontypool later in the year raised £1,749 in a single afternoon but also allowed Oliver Stanley to address a crowd of 12,000. In Twickenham the size of the increase meant that members could no longer be automatically entitled to attend the Association AGM for there was no hall within miles that would accommodate them if they all chose to come, and similar rule changes were adopted in Guildford.[29]

In East Edinburgh there was a typical Scottish pattern, rather different from that in England and Wales; a long-term campaign with paid canvassing for subscriptions raised membership much more slowly; from 509 in Autumn 1945, it rose only to 912 (already the largest number ever) in 1948, but it then passed 2,000 in 1951 and 3,000 in 1956; in South Aberdeen there was a similar story, with the collector in 1947 retaining 15 per cent of any new subscription, and a smaller proportion on renewals; the number of members returned to pre-war levels in 1947, but by 1950 was three times the 1939 figure and continued to rise steadily until 1953; in Glasgow Scotstoun there was a mixed system, with in 1953 about 600 members in conventional branches and four times that number retained on the books only through visits from paid collectors, but these Scottish numbers did at least hold up, even if in 1953 in Forfar the Party's collectors were being described as 'hawkers'. By 1950 in England though, there were already signs of a struggle to hold on to the earlier increases in membership and income. Kings Lynn had done exceptionally well in recruitment by employing a missioner; initially paid for by Central Office, the cost was later taken over by the local association; he recruited 838 members in 1949, bringing in only £111 against a salary cost of £250, and although he was kept on until after the 1951 Election, the system was then discontinued and the membership fell. Hampstead had to decide in December 1950 to strike off 432 members who had not paid anything since 1947, probably new members in the initial recruiting drive who had not renewed their subscriptions even once; with a minimum subscription as low as 1/- it was not too difficult to get a contribution once, if only to get the canvasser to go away, but obtaining renewals year after year was a different matter. At Brentford and Chiswick, there were in theory 5,152 members at the end of 1950, but 2,249 had not paid a subscription for over a year; Central Office was advised that the apparent strength on paper was illusory, for there were actually only 300 'active members' and very few 'workers'. For the by-election held in Bradford South in 1951, it was found that the

29  Woodford CA, annual reports, 1946 and 1949; *CAJ*, June, July and Oct. 1948, Jan. 1949.

City's large membership could produce very few canvassers and that most of the real campaign had to be run by people drafted in from outside.[30]

Despite these troubles at the margin, the membership recovery brought a big improvement in local finances; Gravesend noted proudly as early as 1946 that the association now had income exceeding expenditure for the first time ever; an expansion of activities created further problems, but by May 1947 the treasurer reported a slow advance 'into the sunlight of solvency'; in 1949, the association debated the need for more money with an election looming, but decided not to make a special appeal to industry, which 'raised the old bogey of the Tory Party being tied up with big business'. West Derbyshire, on the other hand, decided frankly that the Labour Government's plans made road hauliers good people to approach for money. Except in industrial areas like Birmingham or Sheffield, such local appeals rarely brought in much money, for industrial subscriptions mainly went to the CBF, and benefited the local parties only as credits set against their quotas when that system was introduced in 1949. The great bulk of local money continued to come from members, both in subscriptions and in the much-enhanced income from social events that a renewed mass membership allowed – just as it had in the 1920s. Harrow West's 13,339 subscribers in 1950 paid a minimum 2/6d, reflecting the relative affluence of the constituency, which guaranteed a healthy income even if all had paid the minimum, which they certainly did not. The Eastern Area found in 1950 that only one constituency in its seven counties needed financial help for the General Election. Nearly all Conservative candidates in winnable seats spent right up to the legal limit, and over the country as a whole they spent 93 per cent of the maximum.[31]

Hemel Hempstead was one of many constituencies in which the end of the War was marked by the retirement or resignation of most of the old guard of constituency officers who had run affairs for many years past; in this case the chairman and treasurer specifically stepped down to make way for younger men. By 1951 Hemel Hempstead (which because of the Davidsons as its MP had always been rather advanced and active) was regarded as a model constituency – with a large membership, thriving social life, strong finances and a working democratic structure; it was the local association in which two future Party Chairmen, Cecil Parkinson and Norman Tebbit, were to learn the ropes. The Eastern Area actually recommended the retirement of all local officers who were seventy and where this did not happen immediately, it did usually take place when the new boundaries enforced the reconstitution of associations in 1948. Harold Watkinson thought that the 1948 redistribution had ended generations of continuous influence, 'severed old allegiances and

---

[30] Constituency records and Central Office constituency files (CCO 1 series), various.

[31] Gravesend CA minutes, 10 May 1946, 2 May 1947, 9 Sept. 1949; West Derbyshire CA minutes, 3 May 1946; Harrow West CA accounts; Eastern Area, 1950 Election report; H.G. Nicholas, *The British General Election of 1950* (1951), 17.

broke the old Tory political patronage system'. However, he also noted that in his (new) Woking constituency, 'my first president was the Duke of Sutherland who lived in state at Sutton Place, later to be owned by Paul Getty. My first chairman, General Haining, was also Lord Lieutenant of Surrey. His successors included the one-time editor of the *Times of India*, Sir Francis Low, two brigadiers, and the last British head of the Indian Civil Service.' Democratic change was all rather relative in Surrey, but the advent of a new generation of local leaders and a bigger membership did generally bring new approaches. Totnes agreed to hold meetings on Saturdays rather than on weekdays so that members who worked for a living would be able to attend; Ruislip likewise decided to go over to evening canvassing. Newbury adopted a new branch structure with more elected representatives on the Executive Council, on the advice of the Area Agent, so that more of the rank and file would be in direct touch with the MP; a similar reform took place at Uxbridge. Where separate women's and men's branches had persisted through the inter-war years they were now often combined, with women members holding additional daytime social meetings; in rural areas like Barkston Ash in Yorkshire though, separate men's and women's branches remained in existence into the 1960s, and all over the country Conservative clubs tended to remain male preserves until about the same time. Even the acceptance of women on an equal basis remained problematical in other ways; in Brentford, the women's chairman still sat on the association's main committee only by cooption; in Walsall, women seem to have done most of the work, certainly in raising money, but still had only limited representation and the association firmly decided not to appoint a woman agent; North Cornwall on the other hand had a fully integrated structure in which the women's chairman was automatically also association vice chairman. Whatever their rights, the women were usually important to the financial structure; in St Marylebone in 1951, the women raised over £2,200 from a programme of Derby Draw, bazaar, Christmas Ball, and whist drives. In many constituencies women were clearly the mainstay of the Party's voluntary work.[32]

The central focus of local organisation inevitably remained the agent and the candidate. The problem of agents had been largely dealt with by the Central Office training programme and by careful placement. Candidates were also selected under the watchful guidance of Jim Thomas, the Party Vice Chairman, who was keen to see finance removed from the procedure of selection. His task could be trying, as for example when a by-election occurred in Jarrow in 1947; Thomas wrote wearily that 'the North East coast

---

[32] Hemel Hempstead CA minutes, 9 Aug. 1945; Eastern Area Council, 8 Nov. 1945; Harold Watkinson, *Turning Points, A Record of Our Times* (Salisbury, 1986), 22, 27; Totnes CA minutes, 20 Jan. 1949; Ruislip CA minutes, 26 July 1949; Newbury CA minutes, 27 Nov. 1945; Uxbridge CA minutes, 7 Sept. 1945; Brentford and Isleworth CA minutes, 28 June 1950; Walsall CA minutes, various dates; North Cornwall CA, 4 June 1946; St Marylebone CA minutes, 1951 report.

is not prolific in Conservative candidates', but he was eventually able to offer them a list that included one past and two future Cabinet ministers – none of whom were selected, though the Area Agent then found that the one who was chosen turned out to be 'a complete wash-out – lost his nerve completely – and could hardly be induced to go on a platform in the later stages of the campaign'. When he went there to speak, Headlam, himself a Tyneside MP and former Area Chairman, found that 'no-one offered me a bite or a drink in Jarrow – but there is no-one to do so in that God forsaken hole – surely one of the most depressing places in England?' Thomas cooperated closely with the Area Agents, who filed reports on all candidates who were interviewed, and these provided the evidence from which Thomas's own advice to constituency chairmen was drawn; after the 1945 Election, the Area Agents produced a list of fifty defeated candidates 'who had done really well in the general election', and nearly all of these were in winnable seats by 1950. There were though strict limits to the influence that could be wielded from the centre; when the Chief Whip's Liverpool constituency was adversely affected by boundary changes in 1948, Churchill himself weighed in with a peremptory instruction that he be given the safer Garston seat; the Liverpool Tories ignored this, indeed probably resented it to the extent that made the instruction counter-productive, and Buchan-Hepburn had to migrate instead to Beckenham. Thomas exercised more tact to secure the removal of an unsuitable candidate, or one of whom the local association had simply grown tired. Hampstead had adopted Charles Challen back in 1941 when the Association had had very few to choose from and only 166 members to take part in the choice. By 1947 the association had 4,887 members and decided to have an open selection. This became almost like a primary; a shortlist of thirteen was narrowed to four, and the Executive Council selected Henry Brooke, but decided to put the names of Challen and Brooke to a meeting of all members – and even to allow postal votes; Brooke won by 714 to 449 and when Woolton and Thomas made it clear that they now regarded Brooke as the official candidate, Challen dropped his threat to stand at the 1950 Election. At Bexley, there was once again local concern about the calibre of the prospective candidate, who was said in 1947 to have the 'dual capacity of candidate and largest individual subscriber'. In these circumstances, even after nearly winning the seat in the 1946 by-election, the association did not flourish. A row between the agent and the candidate, over the candidate's reluctance to canvass personally and his dictatorial methods, led to a resolution of confidence in the agent, which effectively forced the candidate to resign. Seeking a replacement, the association resolved that 'the qualifications they want for their new candidate are that he must be primarily a good speaker, an ex-service professional or business man, under 40'. Under Thomas's guidance they selected Edward Heath, a remarkably close fit with their specifications, and one whose active leadership rapidly put the association on a sound footing. In 1951, the Area Agent reported that

Mr. Heath is without doubt one of the hardest working Members of Parliament in this Area. He is also one of the most able. He gives up his time to assisting constituencies outside – within and without the Area – but does not neglect to maintain the personal touch with the electors in his own constituency.

Reginald Maudling was also guided into a safe haven by Thomas, after seeking his advice on whether to try for Uxbridge or to stick out for the safer Barnet seat, which he duly won in a selection contest with Ian Orr-Ewing and Robert Carr. It is indeed striking how high was the calibre of final shortlists for the winnable seats. Harold Watkinson, already constituency chairman for Dorking where he lived, was urged to try the various new Surrey seats created in 1948; he just missed selection for Reigate but got Woking. The same principle of horses for courses got Enoch Powell selected for West Wolverhampton in 1948, after a tactful procedure had been followed to get rid of the previous candidate, the association President's son-in-law. Iain Macleod, selected as a fighting candidate who might reduce the Labour majority at Enfield, found himelf in possession of a safe seat when Enfield was divided into two constituencies in 1948. There were though severe limits to Thomas's influence, particularly where the 1948 redistribution of boundaries set up competing claims; he could only write resignedly in February of that year that 'the jockeying for the new North Cardiff seat has apparently to be seen in order to be believed'; the three contenders were unenthusiastically described as, first, a 'crop of grey, military hair, glass eye and sweet peas or chrysanthemum in the buttonhole', second, one who 'leaves much to be desired' and third, the one who eventually won, but whom Thomas dare not be seen to support as 'he is known to be my personal friend'.[33]

All in all, led by these younger and more energetic agents and candidates, the associations were remarkably confident and outgoing; any audience seemed a legitimate target; the Bath YCs decided to infiltrate the local Boy Scouts in 1950, while the Accrington Tories attempted the more difficult task of infiltrating local trades unions and subsequently claimed success in persuading a significant number of their new comrades to contract out of the political levy; a member in Birmingham had in 1948 joined two branches of the British Legion and three other veterans' organisations, solely to provide himself with opportunities to make conversational propaganda opportunities for the Party; the East Grinstead agent proudly reported that he had managed to get a foothold in Christ's Hospital, where twenty-eight of the boys had become YCs and the authorities were allowing a Conservative display at the forthcoming parents' day (somewhat superflously, it might be felt). Confidence was also

33  NUEC, 9 Jan. 1947; Central Office constituency files, CCO 1/4/382, 1/5/63, 1/7/16, 1/5/39, 1/8/306, 1/7/519; Headlam diary, 25 Apr. and 12 May 1947; Churchill to Liverpool CA, Aug. 1948, Hailes MSS, 4/2; Central Office file, 'SACC', CCO 4/2/8, CPA; Watkinson, *Turning Points* 25–6; Andrew Roth, *Enoch Powell, Tory Tribune* (1970), 57; Nigel Fisher, *Iain Macleod* (1973), 67.

shown by the reaction to attacks from the outside; when Aneurin Bevan mischievously called Conservatives 'lower than vermin', many in the Party sensed an opportunity: 'vermin clubs' were founded in several constituencies and 'I'm a vermin' badges were sold for Party funds and proudly sported at the subsequent Party Conference; Churchill though, never so good at taking abuse as he was at dishing it out, reported to the shadow cabinet that he was taking advice as to 'whether Mr. Bevan's speech calling all Tories spivs etc. was libellous'; it wasn't. One of the few nasty scenes at the 1950 Election was when Attlee was shouted down with cries of 'Vermin!' at a meeting in Leicester; this heckling was not by rowdly urchins but by well-dressed young men and women who sound from the reports to have been a band of local YCs.[34]

## The 'Maxwell Fyfe Report'

The various manifestations of organisational recovery were brought together in the 'Maxwell Fyfe Report', more accurately the *Interim and Final Reports of the Committee on Party Organisation*, 1948 and 1949. This is more accurate not only because the published reports bear those titles, but because Maxwell Fyfe had very little to do either with their gestation or with most of the content. Three organisational resolutions carried at the 1947 Party Conference respectively supported new limits on financial contributions by candidates and MPs to constituency associations, the financial support of Central Office by the local parties, and an investigation into agents' employment and remuneration. In response to this, the National Union Executive set up the following week three sub-committees, one for each of the three resolutions, and a fourth one to consider constitutional relationships within the National Union itself. The reconsideration of agents' central employment, which ran into the sand, has been considered above, but the financial and constitutional questions remained significantly on the Party's agenda. Membership of the groups was left to the initiative of their chairmen, Henry Brooke for the finance committee and William Robson Brown MP for the committee on candidates' contributions; they were made up of National Union worthies with a few backbenchers and candidates. No Party frontbencher sat on any of these committees which did the real work; between October 1947 and May 1948 the committees met regularly, interviewed people with experience in their fields and drafted reports. On 10 June 1948, the Executive set up, as had always been intended, a coordinating 'special committee' to pull the reports together and it was this that Maxwell Fyfe took under his wing, presumably to give the authority of a frontbencher to what were clearly controversial matters; all but two of the

---

[34] *CAJ*, July and Oct. 1948; Bath CA minutes, 13 Dec. 1950; Accrington CA minutes, 20 Jan. 1948 and 18 Jan. 1949; Birmingham UA minutes, 14 June 1948; Robert Blake, *The Conservative Party from Peel to Thatcher* (1985), 263; LCC, 7 July 1948.

members of Maxwell Fyfe's committee had already sat on one or more of the earlier sub-committees. But before the new, over-arching group even met, the Executive had full dress debates on each report and passed on verbatim minutes to guide Maxwell Fyfe in his future work. The Maxwell Fyfe Committee only had time to meet a couple of times and to interview one witness (Pierssené, who must already have known and approved of what was being proposed) before sending their interim report to the printers for the October 1948 Party Conference, and it does not seem to have worked all that energetically before the final report was published for approval by Central Council in 1949. Very little that appeared in Maxwell's Fyfe's interim or final report was not already in the earlier National Union reports of June 1948.[35]

The sub-committee on Party finance recommended a quota system whereby a published formula would identify the target contribution of each constituency association to central funds, 'flexibly related to Conservative strength in the immediately preceding General Election'. It was acknowledged that such contributions would be forthcoming only if there was 'full trust and goodwill' throughout the Party, and 'evidence, plain to everyone, of first rate business efficiency at the top'. Brooke explained that his report had unanimous support, 'even from some tough and strong-minded realists', and that a survey of constituency views had come out eight to one in favour of a quota system. The three big issues were therefore the method of calculating constituency contributions, the downward flow of financial information to build local confidence, and the total to be aimed at. In considering the form of the quota, a capitation fee was rejected because it would discourage the recruitment of new members, and a fixed percentage of constituency income was rejected as being too unpredictable as a basis for serious budgeting. Instead, quotas would be based on the number and proportion of Conservative votes in the constituency in 1945, so compensating automatically for levels of support and differences in constituency size. In return the CBF would automatically credit the first £10 of any direct donations from a constituency against its quota target, and more if the donor wished. The total to be aimed at was to be £200,000 a year, which was explained to be the 'gap' between what the Party could afford from regular central income and what it needed to spend to pursue existing organisational objectives, though it was recognised that there would need to be a phasing in of such a large annual target over about ten years. Brooke added that 'the most crucial part of our report' was a greater openness about the Party's financial position. 'We have recommended, and the Treasurers did not flinch when we told them, that an annual statement of accounts should be issued.' At the Executive meeting, the Party Treasurers agreed to accept the main principles of the report, but made no reference to publication of accounts, and the Executive warmly endorsed the report. It was

---

[35]  Central Council report for 1948, NUA, 2/2/14, CPA; NUEC, 16 Oct. 1947 and 10 June 1948.

noted that some careful bargaining might be needed over the actual fixing of targets; the East Midlands Area Treasurer argued that 'if you are expecting to get from my Area £12,000 I want to have at least a £15,000 figure when I go to my constituency chairmen'. The later discussions on this issue concentrated in the main on technical issues – how was the quota actually to work? – and an important objective gradually dropped from view. The interim Maxwell Fyfe report, endorsed by the 1948 Party Conference, agreed that annual accounts be published; the final report, approved by Central Council, asked rather 'what machinery, if any, should be set up which will keep the Party as a whole, aware of the broad facts concerning party expenditure?' It then proceeded to ignore the decision already taken, and to suggest instead an administrative reorganisation of the CBF and the creation of a Consultative Committee on Party Finance; this would be chaired by the Party Chairman and consist mainly of Area Treasurers, with representatives from the 1922 Committee and the National Union Executive. Its deliberations might be the subject of informal reports to its constituent bodies, but nothing would be published. No Conservative Party accounts were in fact published until the law changed in 1967, and only long after that did Michael Pinto-Duschinsky persuade the Treasurers to release balance sheets for the period since 1945. The reasons given for this – largely to the outside world rather than to the Party – were that publication would offend donors who had the right for their affairs to remain confidential, and that published accounts would be 'misleading' since they would make the Party look much better off than it actually was.[36]

Some changes did occur as a result of these reforms; there was an annual budget for discussion with the CBF and the Consultative Committee, whereas previously the Party Treasurers had simply made bilateral deals with each Area. But the Consultative Committee never played a serious role; it met once a year in July between 1950 and 1954, with only about half the members turning up, and was then replaced by an annual cocktail party, which improved the attendance but was hardly the right type of meeting for analysis of detailed financial figures. The theoretical obligation to report to the National Union Executive was never honoured, and the Executive never called for a report either. The result was that financial quotas for constituencies were introduced, and over the next decade the constituencies paid up over a million pounds, but got no real information as to how it was spent. When he was Party Chairman between 1959 and 1961, Butler tried to unlock the doors of secrecy, but without effect. Briefing Selwyn Lloyd in 1963, the Party Treasurers listed nine reasons why accounts had still not been published, noting for example that 'it would become apparent that quota income is small compared to industrial', which would be embarrassing, but concluding with the clinching point that 'there

---

[36] National Union General Purposes Committee papers, Sub-Committee on Constituency quotas, NUA 6/2/2, CPA; *Interim and Final Report*, 15, 34–5; Pinto-Duschinsky, *Political Finance*, 135–8.

is no demand from our friends. The demand for publication comes only from our enemies.' They must also have known that the elaborate network of private companies, each named after a river, set up in 1949 to channel funds to the Party but remaining entirely secret until revealed by *The Independent* in 1988, would not have been easily understood by the ordinary half-crown subscribers.[37]

In 1948–49 though, there *was* a demand from 'our friends'; one agent wrote of quota that 'we shall try to find it, but the shrewd heads controlling our finances will not only want to know what happened to the money, but they will *indeed* be asking for a voice in saying how the money will be spent before it is actually disbursed'. The West Derbyshire Tories agreed to 'honour' their quota of £250 only if they were given full details of Central Office's expenditure, and they had a running battle over this with their Area Treasurer over the next several years, but never got the figures they asked for. Next-door High Peak took the same stand but with the same effect. Burton upon Trent took no immediate action in 1948, but the Area Agent urged them to make sure that their treasurer attended the next Conference; when he came back, they then agreed to pay. Guildford tried to make payments after the first year conditional on the receipt of financial information, but always succumbed to the urgings to contribute, and in 1952 accepted an assurance from the Area Treasurer that their money was in fact carefully scrutinised and stopped asking questions; Truro was very dubious about the idea, but usually paid; Saffron Walden rejected the idea of quota outright, but agreed to make a 'donation' of an equivalent size, thereby retaining their theoretical independence but not much else; the West Dorset treasurer craftily called quota the 'Central Office quota for marginal constituencies', so exerting moral pressure for it to be 'honoured'. Whatever the varied processes of persuasion, the majority of constituencies paid their share; the Wessex Area Treasurer reported for 1949 that £7,625 had been paid out of £9,397 due, with thirty-one associations paying in full, three in part, and only four refusing; in 1950, the Area reached 97 per cent of its target, with by then only Swindon refusing to join in; in the East Midlands, £4,827 was received out of £6,124 due in the first year, but the total was up to 95 per cent in 1950 with nearly all constituencies contributing at least something, and 96 per cent in 1951. In the West Midlands in 1951, fifty-six of the fifty-eight constituencies paid up in full. By 1955, only twelve constituencies in the whole country had not paid some form of quota, though a further twelve had not paid any since 1951. William Teeling claimed in 1970 that constituency associations' quota payments were one of the criteria used to determine the distribution of honours to their officers, an unlikely link, but a claim that indicates that suspicion of the quota system remained; MPs certainly felt though that a

---

[37]  Central Office, Chairman's file, 'Publication of Accounts, 1959–61', CCO 20/22/1, CPA; Central Office, General Director's file, 'Selwyn Lloyd Enquiry', CCO 120/4/9, CPA.

long record of successful payments was good evidence in the case for giving their chairman or treasurer an honour, so any discrimination may well have been positive rather than negative. The quota flowed in and the demand for reciprocal information gradually died away; it proved indeed not that 'our friends' did not want the accounts to be published but that they were not prepared to make a big enough fuss to get it. Indeed, even before the argument came to a head, Central Council had overwhelmingly rejected a motion from Cambridge which demanded that constituencies should have a formal say in Central Office appointments and expenditure; the active rank and file were not accustomed to making such demands.[38]

The financial contributions of candidates raised even more of a stir, but this was a much less new debate since the war years had already produced important shifts of policy. In May 1941, the 1922 Committee discussed proposals from a Member which called for 'cheaper seats for better candidates'; in the following year, Butler told the 1922 that 'the party in the future had to depend on ideas and not on money, and that the selection of candidates was of vital importance'. Worries about the danger of relying on such contributions with existing taxation, and a defensive attitude to the issue after J.F.S. Ross drew attention to it in his *Parliamentary Representation* in 1943, led to a sharp debate in which the progressives called trenchantly for action; Hogg, reviewing Ross in *The Spectator*, deplored 'the virtual sale of safe seats' as 'a festering sore in the Conservative Party for years. At Conference after Conference the system has been pilloried and condemned, but, although the bottom has dropped out of the market since the war, no radical reform has been attempted.' His own agent was valiantly attempting to rouse the Oxford members to end the practice locally by raising a subscription to pay for the next election. In fact Central Council had in 1941 endorsed the Standing Advisory Committee on Candidates' view that no financial questions should be asked during selection meetings, and had authorised the Party Vice Chairman to deny recognition to any candidate selected in defiance of that rule, an amendment to delete this provision being heavily defeated. It was difficult to enforce such rules in wartime, but the will was now there. In December 1944, after the issue had been embarrassingly aired again in a Commons debate on electoral reform, the National Union Executive agreed to fix a maximum contribution of £100 a year, plus half of the election expenses, for all candidates selected in future, on pain once again of non-recognition of candidates selected against the rule. It seems clear that this was generally accepted, though occasional deviations

[38] Kandiah, 'Lord Woolton' thesis, 119; *CAJ*, Mar. 1949; West Derbyshire CA minutes, 16 Oct. 1950, 19 Feb. 1951, 23 Mar. 1953; High Peak CA, 1949 report; Burton on Trent CA minutes, various dates; Guildford CA minutes, 14 Nov. 1952; Truro CA minutes, 29 Oct. 1948; Saffron Walden CA minutes, 24 Nov. 1948; West Dorset CA minutes, various dates; East Midlands Area Council, 22 Apr. 1950 and 2 June 1951; West Midlands Area AGM, 17 May 1952; Teeling, *Corridors of Frustration*, 145; National Union Central Council minutes, 18 Mar. 1948, CPA.

persisted; the candidate for Swindon paid his large subscription through the Area (which promptly subsidised the constituency by the same sum) so as to observe the letter of the rule, if hardly its spirit; in other cases, candidates' wives could be surprisingly generous. The 1948 National Union report concluded though that a major change had already happened over the previous few years, and that what was needed was a tightening up of procedures now generally observed; after extensive research by Central Office, the 1948 position was said to be that no candidate selected since 1945 had broken the new rules and that half of *all* MPs and adopted candidates were actually paying less than the 1944 rule allowed. Big changes had already been claimed in the 1947 Conference debate; Woolton argued that 'we are a democratic party. We come from all classes of society and so must our candidates.' Jim Thomas went much further: 'the old school tie has appeared on the Socialist benches, but the trades unionist, the tenant farmer, the working man, and the son and daughter of the working man, can all be found in very encouraging numbers on our list of candidates.' (Apart from the quite valid second-generation claim, if this was true then it must have related mainly to the part of the list from which candidates did not actually get selected by winnable constituencies.) In fact, as Pierssené told Eden in 1947, the collection of information by Central Office was in itself a form of persuasion, for it was recognised that constituencies were becoming increasingly embarrassed to reveal dependence on their candidate. The National Union Committee therefore saw its job as completing a process well in train rather than launching a new reform, and the reasons given for going further were both pragmatic and democratic: on the one hand, with a 95 per cent top rate of income tax there were now very few people with 4,000 a year of disposable income, so even a rich man's contribution could only be raised by disposing of capital; and on the other hand, the Party had had an influx of middle-class members and 'it is expected too that in the future a larger proportion of Conservative candidates will be drawn from their ranks'.[39]

One fortuitous occurrence was the Labour Government's decision to reduce maximum election expenses, to a much lower level even than the reduced figure of 1945; if the local associations took on the full cost of election expenses they would now have to find little more money than the half share many had paid in 1945. It was therefore proposed that no candidate should pay any election expenses at all, not even the personal expenses allowed by election law, and should make no personal payment to an agent either; all of this would be met by the association. For annual subscriptions, there would be a new limit of £25 for candidates and £50 for MPs; financial questions must

[39] 1922 Committee minutes, 21 May 1941, CPA; J.F.S. Ross, *Parliamentary Representation* (1943); Quintin Hogg, *One Year's Work* (1944), 124; Harvie-Watt report, 6 Mar. 1942; Harvie-Watt MSS, 2/1; Oxford CA minutes, 7 Dec. 1943; Wessex Area Council, 10 July 1946; *NCP*, 27 Nov. 1947; Pierssené to Eden, 6 June 1947, and attached letters, Avon MSS, 11/12/59; National Union Central Council minutes, 2 Oct. 1941.

not be asked until after selection was completed, and candidates must not be invited to subscribe 'on a great scale' to local charities either. Introducing his report, Robson Brown announced that 'right throughout the deliberations there was a clear-cut intention that financial restriction of no kind should exist which would preclude any man or woman of capacity, integrity, courage and good record from being selected'. The Executive were not unanimous this time; Woolton welcomed the report and urged the selection of more working-class candidates – as Party Chairmen had been doing since the office was created in 1911 – but others were not so sure. Charles Waterhouse talked of 'swinging too far in a dangerous direction', Herbert Williams deplored the danger that the change might bring in 'a breed of professional politicians' (as indeed it did help to do), and Mrs Elliot wondered if MPs might lose their independence to the control of local activists. On the other hand, John Hay for the YCs gave strong support, as did Lady Davidson and Arthur Colegate (though both felt the proposals were too rigid and went too far). Nevertheless, the report was formally adopted and commended to Maxwell Fyfe's committee, and on this issue he may have been influential, for he had at the 1941 Central Council debate seconded the motion calling for tighter restrictions. There was to be no going back; the Maxwell Fyfe Committee adopted the National Union proposals *en bloc* and recommended them to the 1948 Party Conference as part of its *Interim Report*. The formal motion was simply that the report be considered, but on Brooke's proposal it was overwhelmingly agreed to approve it instead. The new rules therefore became obligatory on constituencies and on *all* candidates, not just newly-adopted ones, from 31 December 1948.[40]

How much difference did this make to the complexion of Conservative candidates and the parliamentary party? In the short term very little, for hardly any constituency was still to select a candidate in 1949; already by June 1947, before the original National Union committee was even set up, only forty-two of the 517 English constituencies had no candidate. The 'class of 1950' who were taken to demonstrate the new, more broadly-based Conservatism, had almost to a man been selected before the Maxwell Fyfe rules were even debated, and some of the most prominent, like Macleod and Maudling, were among the two-thirds of Conservative MPs in 1951 who had first fought seats in or before 1945 anyway. In the longer term, big claims were made; Woolton argued in his *Memoirs* that 'the change was revolutionary, and in my view did more than any other single factor to save the Conservative Party'. This was nonsense on both counts: it was neither particularly revolutionary at the time nor greatly effective later. The social composition and educational background of the parliamentary party did not

---

[40] National Union General Purposes Committee papers, Sub-Committee on the Financial Arrangements of Candidates, NUA 6/2/3, CPA; *Interim and Final Report*, 13–14, 26; Hoffman, *Conservative Party*, 101–3.

change quickly and the majority did not change at all, at least for a generation, but the lack of progress produced no demonstrable disadvantage, perhaps because of what was perceived to have happened. After 1948 there were no barriers in the rules or the system of selection to prevent the advancement of men and women of talent from whatever background they came. There was even a new opportunity to cry foul against Labour: in 1955, the Party quoted with pride from a *Fabian Journal* article that 'the purchase of seats in Britain nowadays is almost entirely confined to the Labour Party', and from 1959 the presence of Robert Maxwell as a Labour candidate provided similar openings. To understand why men and women from less privileged backgrounds rarely actually got selected for winnable Tory seats would have required a good deal of inside information from selection committees and association files. That was not generally available until Michael Rush's researches were published in 1969.[41]

Over time, the quota system and the requirement that constituencies receive no large subscription from their candidate tended to be self-compensating in the finance of the local associations; the Ripon association created after the 1948 redistribution had a struggle to pay a £750 quota to Central Office and to buy itself new offices, and was pleased to receive £1,830 in a 1950 election appeal for a campaign that cost only £708; Eden's Warwick and Leamington constituency had to raid its election reserves in December 1954 in order to make its annual quota payment to Central Office; when the General Election came five months later, a special appeal raised £1,550 but the election itself only cost £834, so the equivalent of two years of quota payment could be returned to the reserves; in 1955, Barry Conservatives raised £2,133 in an appeal for a campaign on which they were allowed to spend only half that much, and this enabled them to pay off a deficit incurred in purchasing a new headquarters. That pattern could be replicated with countless examples: now that rich men were not paying the bills, most associations could raise more than was needed for each general election, and this helped to cushion their other activities – and especially the obligation to pay quota. The exact sources of the increased local incomes varied widely from association to association, but two clear patterns emerged; first, with more paying members, the subscription list itself contributed more to the total (and in the best-organised wards the assiduous use of the book scheme for collecting the money also gave organisers at street level a great deal of contact with and information about supporters); second, less seems to have depended on the big annual events – bazaars, fêtes or garden parties – which depended on

41  NUEC, 12 June 1947; John Ramsden, 'The Conservative Party since 1945', in *UK Political Parties since 1945*, ed. Anthony Seldon, (1990), 23–6; D.E. Butler and Michael Pinto-Duschinsky, 'The Conservative élite 1918–1970. Does unrepresentativeness matter?', in *Conservative Party Politics*, ed. Z. Layton-Henry (1980), 186–209; D.E. Butler, *The British General Election of 1951* (1952), 36; Michael Rush, *The Selection of Parliamentary Candidates* (1969); *NCP*, 23 Sept. 1957.

drawing in the public at large, and more on the multiplication of smaller social events attended mainly by those same members, especially the YCs' wine and cheese parties and the women's equally regular teas.[42]

The rest of the *Interim and Final Reports* of 1949 were devoted to structural matters, predominantly relating to the National Union, but also defining by cross-representation its relationship to other bodies, by for example putting MPs from the 1922 Committee on the Executive. In part it was a matter of deciding *not* to make changes; asked about the role of the Party Chairman, Woolton advised that it would not be sensible to increase the Chairman's powers over constituencies, since it would be unpopular, and sufficient powers already existed, 'but these are powers of persuasion'. Pierssené had written in 1947, in a comparison that sounds as if it might have derived from one of Woolton's retailing analogies, that the Conservative Party was 'not a chain of multiple stores, but an association of voluntary and independent bodies with an intense dislike of domination from the centre. The strength of this structure is derived not from methods or systems, nor from any driving force from above, but from personal relationships built on "goodwill".' Woolton also opposed decentralisation of the professional structure, preferring to work through a small number of large Areas rather than through many county offices (as had existed after 1906, and been found to be unworkable then). These discussions involved few issues of principle, much of the business being the tidying up of changes that had come by accretion as organisation was re-built after 1945. The 1949 *Final Report* delineated the structural working of the Party in a way that no previous document had done, and was almost the equivalent of a constitution for this phase of Party history. The Leader was certainly aware that it might be interpreted as such, and took a personal hand in drafting the section on policy-making, lest it might seem that he was surrendering his independence. 'It is essential for our Party, in sharp contrast to the socialists, to preserve the principle that, when we are in office, the integrity of Cabinet responsibility to Crown and Parliament cannot be impaired. Nothing must be done when we are in opposition which would offer the slightest grounds for such wrong ideas.' Specifically, he refused to nominate half the members of the new Advisory Committee on Policy, presumably because that would appear to commit him too far to its decisions, but agreed to nominate the chairman and deputy, and surrender the rest of 'his' half of the committee to direct representatives of MPs and Peers. The Advisory Committee on Policy remained what it had been intended to be, a consultative body only, and with value in that role, but with no opportunity to advance to a different station.[43]

---

[42] Ripon CA minutes, 24 Mar. 1953; Warwick and Leamington CA minutes, 16 Dec. 1954 and 9 June 1955; Barry CA minutes, 21 July 1955.

[43] *Interim and Final Reports*, 28–46; Kandiah, 'Lord Woolton' thesis, 109; Ball, 'National and Regional Structure', 215; National Union General Purposes Committee papers, Committee on Party Organisation, NUA 6/1/6; Ramsden, *Conservative Party Policy*, 131–2.

# The scale of recovery

By 1950–51 then, the organisational deficiencies of 1945 had been more than repaired. H.G. Nicholas recorded in 1950 the state of the organisation that he found in existence in Birmingham. 'Each of the 13 Birmingham divisions has its own full time certificated agent with secretarial assistance. Similarly, all but one or two of the 38 wards of the city has its organiser, generally certificated; these work under the divisional agents. At a similar level there are 30 or more full-time "missioners" or paid canvassers or subscription collectors.' (Compared to these dozens of professional Party employees, there had been just seven trained agents in Birmingham for the 1945 campaign.) He noted though that Birmingham was untypical: under the guidance of Geoffrey Lloyd it was once again the Cook County of British politics, as it had been in the heyday of the Chamberlains. More typically, in the East Midlands, there were forty-two constituencies broadly representative of the country as a whole; every Conservative Association there had a full-time agent and fourteen also had a second paid professional; there was in addition a chief agent for Nottingham, and an Area team of seven professionals and five secretaries; the North West, with more hopeless constituencies, had fifty certificated agents and thirteen organisers or trainees in its seventy-two constituencies. Central Office had in 1951 a staff of just over two hundred working at what David Butler called its 'surprisingly dingy' Abbey House headquarters, and in the more elegant CRD office in Old Queen Street, with a further forty-one in Areas; in 1928 the corresponding total figure had been 243. Overall 'peacetime' expenditure in the early 1950s was a little over half a million pounds a year, compared to about a quarter of a million pounds in the late 1920s, but when allowance is made for inflation, the Party's central expenditure in real terms was probably as high in 1927–28 as in 1952–53. (The actual *pattern* of expenditure was different of course, with more going on research in the 1940s and far more on paid speakers and on printing literature in the 1920s, but the overall totals were comparable.) Despite all the much-boosted advances of Woolton's reforms, his Party machine was just about the same size and just about as well-financed as Davidson's had been when the Party had last been flush with money before the 1929 crash. This entire professional structure represented the restoration of a pre-war scale of activity, just as some pre-war practices were also rediscovered. The advances of membership, money and activity in the localities both reflected the renewed professional input and were needed to keep it going; their assumption of financial responsibility meant that constituency associations *did* have to perform more strongly than before 1939 – or rather that all now had to do as only the liveliest had done before the War; here real advances had been made. By 1950, a Conservative Association following recommended organisational practices needed a turnover of some £3,000 a year if it was to pay for its qualified agent, secretary, office and office expenses, car, missioner, quota to Central Office and election expenses. It had become a very large operation indeed, and the period after 1950 would see a constant battle to retain the organisational recovery that had been made. In the intangibles, the Party machine both centrally and in the localities was clearly in better trim than it had been for years, and for this part of the recovery Woolton deserves credit for his inspirational efforts. There is not the slightest doubt that these various organisational recoveries, and the sense of momentum that they generated, had given the Party a major boost to its morale, nor that they provided some part of the explanation of the recovery of Conservative seats in the elections of the 1950s.[44]

---

[44] Nicholas, *General Election of 1950*, 26–7; North West Area Executive, 21 Oct. 1949; Butler, *General Election of 1951*, 25; Ramsden, *Balfour and Baldwin*, 221, 229; Ball, 'National and Regional Structure', 191; Pinto–Duschinsky, *Political Finance*, 138; *CAJ*, July 1948.

# Chapter 4

# Re-stating Conservatism – the Policy Review

In the Party's historiography, policy renewal has had a parallel place with the modernisation of organisation in explaining Conservative recovery from the 1945 defeat. In 1945, as was shown above, some Conservatives were already fretting that the Party did not have a clear (and preferably constructive) policy to put before the electorate, and these demands became more vocal when the initial shock of defeat had worn off.

Churchill, on the other hand, was determinedly opposed to policy-making in opposition on several grounds. Strategically, he believed that an opposition should manoeuvre in covered ground, not exposing its policies to the counter-fire of the Government until the next Election approached. If an Opposition did otherwise, he told Butler, 'having failed to win the sweets of office, it fails equally to enjoy the benefits of being out of office'. Tactically, Churchill intended to occupy the central ground of consensus, while portraying the Labour Government, and especially its nationalisation measures, as partisan and divisive. In the House of Commons in December 1945, he argued that,

> if I had obtained a substantial majority at the last election, my first thoughts would have been to seek the cooperation of the minority and gather together the widest possible measure of agreement over the largest possible areas. I charge the Government with deliberately trying to exalt their partisan and faction interests at the cost not only of national unity but also of our national recovery.

This claim was not only a tactical convenience that the Party adopted for public occasions; in the great freeze-up of 1947, Cuthbert Headlam, in his diary, was contemptuous of appeals for national unity from 'Attlee and Co.', for 'while they scream for help from us all and the "Dunkirk spirit", they persist in forcing through Parliament their silly policy of Nationalisation which so many of us believe is wholly wrong and against the National interest. It is a hopeless business.' Churchill also stressed, to emphasise Labour's partisanship in economic matters, that other parts of Labour's programme derived from the wartime consensus or could be claimed as policies arising out of the pre-1914 welfare reforms for which he could claim paternity rights. His tactical stance depended on the Conservatives not obviously widening the gap between the parties by defining too clearly their own policy, which would also be separate from that of the wartime coalition. But he had two personal reasons for wanting to delay policy-making anyway; on the one hand, he was conscious of the indignity of seeming to want a return to office too obviously after his rejection in 1945, of being 'an old man in a hurry'; and on the other, he did not intend to spend his own time on policy matters, needing to achieve financial security through his *War Memoirs* and lecture tours in the United States, but he was not willing to allow anyone else to make policy commitments for him either.[1]

## Demands for a statement of policy

Churchill's first post-war speeches were therefore a disappointment to Conservatives, even when they cheered him to the echo – from motives deriving equally from gratitude for his war leadership and from consolation for his 1945 defeat. Even the right were impatient; in December 1945, Sir Waldron Smithers was inviting the South East Area to agree to a resolution urging 'the leaders to issue immediately a restatement of policy, modified to meet present-day conditions, and in simple terms'. The Eastern Area Council rejected a resolution stating that constituency revival was being held back by 'lack of policy', but passed one calling for more propaganda work on policy. Quintin Hogg wrote in January 1946 of the need for a clear policy, and Macmillan did the same in a whole series of speeches in May, stressing though that these policies should be only broadly defined; intriguingly, Macmillan went on in July to call for 'a new industrial charter' to reassure workers, apparently the first appearance of the phrase, and one that was well ahead of any Party decision. Brendan Bracken complained at the end of the year that 'many of the Tories are becoming restive about the industrial policy which is being sedulously advocated by Macmillan and his friends. Speaking for the Party . . . [he] said that the State should have greater powers to intervene and to manage industry. He also said that discipline in factories should be left to the workers. I think the latter thought is even too ambitious for the TUC, though it will certainly meet with the hearty approval of the [Communists].' The Guildford Tories, receiving a branch resolution calling for a policy statement, drew attention to the recent Macmillan speeches, noting that ' "policy" must not be confused with "programme". If we stated a programme now, Labour would use it against us.' Rab Butler was saying much the same as Macmillan, arguing not for detailed policy, but 'to lay the foundations and to start erecting the pillars on which a platform can ultimately be built'. But John Hare, addressing the East Islington AGM in May, simply 'suggested the need for a standard or policy on which our own party could work'. The Walsall Chairman urged his association in April to back an Area resolution on the need for a policy statement, suggesting that

[1] Lord Butler of Saffron Walden, *The Art of the Possible, The Memoirs of Lord Butler* (1971), 133–5; Central Office, *Notes on Current Politics* [hereafter *NCP*], 10 Jan. 1946, 11 Feb. 1947, 3 May 1948; Headlam diary, 4 Mar. 1947, Headlam MSS.

there was some coordination of this grassroots pressure. Leo Amery actually had a pamphlet published by the CPC in which he called for 'a clear and comprehensive restatement in the light of present-day conditions' of all Conservative principles. In April, the National Union Executive received five strong motions calling for a policy statement, from Brigg, Reading, Yarmouth, and the Wessex and North Western Areas; these five local bodies effectively represented the country as a whole, and all the motions had been unanimously passed at meetings attended by almost a thousand activists. The Executive passed them on to Churchill for his comments. Churchill then made a big speech to Scottish Conservatives in May in which he spoke again on 'the failure of the Government's "doctrinaire socialism"'. Characteristically, much of the speech was devoted to foreign policy, but he did also set out eight fundamental Conservative principles as a reply to critics in the Party. He then told the Executive, with some asperity, that

> I have been aware for some time of the concern within and without the Party at the supposed lack of Conservative policy. It is for that reason that I stated in general terms, and thus brought to the notice of the public, the cause and aims for which the Conservative Party stands, when I addressed the Annual Conference of the Scottish Unionist Association on Monday. Meanwhile, apart from this, it would be a great help if those who are pressing for a more detailed programme would kindly state precisely what they have in mind in the light of the statement I made on Monday.

But in fact his eight principles were so bland as to be almost useless; the *Scotsman* pointed out that his speech 'would describe Conservative economic policy at any time in the past 30 or 40 years, if not further back than that'. Critical resolutions from the constituencies and the Area Councils continued to flow in, notably a trenchant one from Workington that demanded 'the early announcement of a policy'.[2]

   To be fair to Churchill, it was a bit much to expect a comprehensive restatement of domestic policy in that first year of opposition, when the supporting machinery was not yet in place, and when the front bench were struggling to mount an even half-effective opposition in the House. Eden was among those pressing for work to be done on policy, but his own speeches were little better than Churchill's in putting flesh on the bones of traditional principle. For example, he made four major speeches on domestic

---

[2] South East Area Executive, 4 Dec. 1945; Eastern Area Council, 8 May 1945; *NCP*, 29 July 1946; Richard Cockett (ed.), *My Dear Max: The Letters of Brendan Bracken to Lord Beaverbrook, 1925–1958* (1990), 68; Guildford CA minutes, 10 May 1946; Harriet Jones, 'The Conservative Party and Social Policy, 1942–1955', unpublished PhD thesis, University of London, 1992, 116; Islington East CA minutes, 23 May 1946; Walsall CA minutes, 29 Apr. 1946; Martin Gilbert, *Never Despair, Winston S. Churchill, 1945–1965* (1988), 229; T.F. Lindsay and Michael Harrington, *The Conservative Party, 1918–1970* (1974), 150; National Union Executive minutes [hereafter NUEC], 11 Apr., 9 May and 11 July 1946; Robert Blake, *The Conservative Party from Peel to Thatcher* (1985), 258; Workington CA minutes, 25 May 1946.

policy in 1946, in addition to speeches on legislative proposals, and achieved a good deal of publicity for his Conference speech calling for 'a Nationwide Property-Owning Democracy'. This phrase, often attributed to Eden as a key statement of modern Conservatism, had originated from Noel Skelton, one of Macmillan's 'YMCA' allies in the 1920s, and was already fairly widely in use among progressively-minded Tories by 1946. Two days later, Churchill picked up the phrase in his speech to the Conference, having already used it for a Scottish Tory meeting in April (at the suggestion of the Scottish Whip's political secretary), and he added it personally to a draft letter of support for Enoch Powell as a by-election candidate in the following January. A previously unorthodox statement from the Conservative left had thus achieved the stamp of official approval, but no actual work had been done to define its meaning; in the early 1950s the phrase had progressed to the point in which it was often printed in the Party Conference handbook entirely in capitals, an honour otherwise reserved in Party publications for such Disraelian *obiter dicta* as 'the elevation of the condition of the people'. What did it mean? A fortnight after the 1946 Conference, James Stuart reported that 'from conversations overheard among not unintelligent citizens, it would appear that there is some confusion as to the exact meaning . . . Some are misled into thinking that the ownership of the Mines, Bank of England and so on by the nation is a step in the direction of a "property-owning democracy"'; he suggested to frontbench colleagues in a shadow cabinet paper that Eden's intention to stress *individual* ownership had failed to get across, had in fact achieved the exact opposite of its original purpose. The Central Office publicity director, while glad that Eden was taking up a popular theme, warned him in October that 'it takes an immense amount of reiteration to get a thing of this sort across to the public. The position at the moment is that they have become aware of the phrase and are asking "What is this 'Property-owning democracy' idea that Anthony Eden is talking about?" The next stage is to get them to understand it!' Something similar seems to have happened with another catchphrase; Cranborne, writing to Macmillan early in 1946, observed that 'the fault of the Capitalist system seems to me to be not that there are too many capitalists but too few'. The same phrase appeared shortly afterwards in a speech by Eden, but again no real work had been done to explore its implications. Eden himself was well aware of the problem: he wrote to Assheton in April, returning a draft for a pamphlet, and arguing the need to be more specific on industrial matters:

> This is after all the biggest political issue of the day and I do not think it is enough just to say we believe in freedom and free enterprise. What is our conception of the function of the state in relation to industry? I tried to set this out – not very well I frankly admit – in my Hull speech. What is our industrial policy?

The policy draft that he was commenting on as being so inadequate was precisely the doctrine of economic liberalism in which Assheton himself implicitly believed, but not Eden: it offered balanced budgets, repayment of international debts as quickly as possible, rapid reopening of foreign exchanges, an end to tariffs whatever other countries might do, and a reliance on market forces to create employment. Without the Industrial Policy Committee of 1947, this was the direction in which things might have moved.[3]

In the course of the Summer, Churchill became more isolated; Eden told Thomas in August – 'Policy: Bobbety [Cranborne] and I are agreed that something must be said'. Cranborne was in fact very dismissive of 'the old gentleman' and his wish just to allow the Government to discredit itself, while avoiding saying anything definite in case it offended someone;

> The truth is that he lives in a past world, where there were two parties but only one political philosophy. Today, there are two political philosophies, almost two political religions. To imagine that a man can be converted from socialism to individualism merely by boredom with socialism is like imagining that a Mohammedan can be converted to Christianity by becoming bored with Allah. If our creed is to prevail, it must be preached, and not only the broad principles but their practical application. And we must not be afraid of antagonising someone . . . The socialists do not make this mistake. They are not constantly apprehensive of losing the St. George's, Hanover Square, vote. In this we ought to take a leaf out of their book. But I am afraid we shan't. There will be a woolly statement at Brighton which will satisfy no one . . .

Things came to a head at the Party Conference in October. Eden was urged by Reginald Maudling to devote his speech to a big policy theme:

> I think there is no doubt that people expect a statement of the first importance on our domestic policy to be made at Blackpool, and there is widespread hope that this statement will contain some broad but definite general principle on which Conservatives throughout the country can work in explaining what our policy is. If I may say so, I think that such a principle is contained in your expression 'a nationwide property-owning democracy'. In the principle of the diffusion of ownership rather than its concentration we have something wholly opposed to Socialist principles, which we can develop and which can be made understandable to the average elector.

Churchill had also been urged, by Eden, Maxwell Fyfe and others on the the front bench, to devote more of his own Conference speech to Conservative policy, advice he did not heed. He explained that he opposed systematic policy-making as un-English and typical more of Socialism than Conservatism: 'I do not believe in looking about for some panacea or cure-all on which we should stake our credit and fortunes, and which we should try to sell in a hurry like a patent medicine to all and sundry . . . We ought not to seek after some rigid symmetrical formula of doctrine such as delights

[3] Anthony Eden, *Freedom and Order, Selected Speeches, 1939–1946* (1947), 394–5, 418–19; Gilbert, *Never Despair*, 312; Jones, 'Conservative Party' thesis, 177; Geoffrey McDermott, *The Eden Legacy and the Decline of British Diplomacy* (1969), 86; Leader's Consultative Committee minutes [hereafter LCC], 21 Oct. 1946; Harold Macmillan, *Tides of Fortune, 1945–1955* (1969), 301; Toby O'Brien to Eden, 31 Oct. 1946, and Eden to Assheton, 25 Apr. 1946, Avon MSS, 11/12/46 and 36.

the mind of Socialists or Communists.' In fact, by the time that he spoke at Blackpool, it was already too late for him to stem the tide. There were fears even of a secession of younger Tory reformers like Thorneycroft if something was not done. On the first morning, the YC Chairman John Hay caused a stir by moving the reference back of the annual report of Central Council on the grounds that it did not say what had happened to the policy resolutions passed at the 1945 Conference; Hay also got a round of applause for his complaint that all the constituency resolutions calling for a policy statement had been put in an omnibus 'additional resolutions' section at the back of the handbook, and none of them selected for debate. Under fire, the Conference Chairman agreed that one of these resolutions could be debated, and next day the Conference was therefore able to pass almost without dissent a resolution demanding a statement of Party policy; speakers for the motion included Harry Crookshank, Geoffrey Rippon, and Quintin Hogg, who argued that is was absolutely essential to prove the fallacy of Labour's claim that Tories had no policy but *laissez-faire*. The National Union Executive appointed a deputation led by Woolton to take the resolutions to Churchill in person. Several shadow ministers told Churchill that this pressure could not now be resisted, and Woolton in any case raised it at the shadow cabinet himself on 9 October. It was then announced that Churchill had set up an Industrial Policy Committee under Butler's chairmanship, and explained that this was a matter that the Leader had had in mind for some considerable time; but the claim that the new committee would be 'following the lead given by Mr. Churchill and Mr. Eden at the Blackpool Conference' was hardly very credible. As Aubrey Jones MP remarked a year later, the demand at Blackpool was for action – any action – 'a cry that the party should march somewhere, though few could suggest where'. This was precisely what opened up the way for the policy model that men such as Butler had wanted since at least 1943.[4]

The shadow cabinet did not set the new committee any exact terms of reference, but there were heads for discussion approved on 16 October, apparently presented by Butler, and worth reproducing *in extenso*:

1. *Future of Controls*
   How is it possible to reconcile our claims that controls should go with the admission of the necessity of some controls in these days?
2. *Treatment of Monopolies*
   Sometimes the situation demands these, sometimes not.
3. *Attitude to 'Keynesian Theory'*
   How far can we use Government credit and works to even out a slump?
4. *Partnership in Industry*, of which profit-sharing only *one* aspect.
5. *Reform of Taxation*

[4] Maudling to Eden, 16 Aug. 1946, and Eden to Thomas, 14 Aug. 1946, Avon MSS, 11/12/39 and 13; Cranborne to Thomas, 16 Sept. 1946, Cilcennin MSS; Jones, 'Conservative Party' thesis, 19, 118; Paul Addison, *Churchill on the Home Front, 1900–1955* (1992), 393; NUEC, 15 Oct. and 14 Nov. 1946; LCC, 9 Oct. 1946; Butler, *Art of the Possible*, 145.

6.   *Treatment of Nationalised Industries*
(7.   *Wages Policy?*)

This was a formidable agenda, and the final item in parenthesis was highly significant – it may be said to have remained in parenthesis in Conservative policy-making for the next thirty years. The vagueness of the first two is some indication of how wide was the gap that the new committee had to fill.[5]

## Butler's 'backroom boys'

The choice of Butler to chair the committee was itself one of long-term significance, but at the time followed logically from the centrality of his existing involvement in the Party's policy machinery. In November 1945, the Central Council resolved that the Post-War Problems Central Committee should be put on a peacetime footing as an Advisory Committee on Policy and Political Education, and Butler simply continued as chairman; he also retained the right to nominate its members, and used that right to ensure that, until the structures were reformed on a representative basis in 1949, the ACPPE was filled with like minds; an addendum to the motion, moved by Hugh Molson and also passed, provided for 'the necessary Secretarial and Research organisation'. There were clearly critics to appease, those who had never approved of Butler or the PWPCC, and the first annual report of the new body was very guarded; a Central Office official remarked that it was 'not so much a report to the Conference as an apology for the life and purpose of the committee'. Alport, the Director of the new Conservative Political Centre, which was the executive arm of the ACPPE in its 'political education' side, was a contact of Butler's from pre-war days; the announcement of the CPC stressed just this point in explaining that it would 'revive and extend the educational work which between the wars had been undertaken by the Central Education Department'. When the Conservative Research Department was re-started, Butler became chairman, though Churchill's own preference had been for his son-in-law Duncan Sandys. The Shadow Cabinet had quite a fight to stop this idea going through, but it was Sandys' proposals for initial staffing of the Secretariat that the shadow cabinet accepted in October 1945; while resigned to having Churchill as Leader, his Conservative colleagues were determined to prevent him from putting people close to him into key Party posts. In April 1946, by which time the Sandys proposal had been stopped, Butler asked Assheton if he could assume that as chairman of the ACPPE he was automatically also chairman of the CRD. Assheton's reply urged him to take it on, as 'you are so much the right man for the job and you have been so long connected with this side of our policy'. This was a post previously occupied, apart from wartime expedients, only by

5   Paper with LCC minutes, 16 Oct. 1946.

Neville Chamberlain. It took time to prise the records and finances of the CRD from the jealous hands of Joseph Ball, but Butler managed this and got the Department re-launched in 1946. As chairman both of the ACPPE and the CRD, Butler therefore combined the direction of the Party's policy civil service with the coordination of its consultation processes. This was a brilliantly successful choice; Butler's background in a Cambridge academic family, and his personal experience as a history tutor at the start of his career, gave him an understanding of the processes of research that was available to few of his senior contemporaries, and a recognition of the necessary tolerance that would be required if very bright minds were to be used effectively in the Party's service. He also had by 1946 sufficient weight and experience in the higher reaches of the Party to protect his proteges from a suspicious Central Office, which under Woolton was unhappy about having to pay the Research Department's bills without controlling its activities in any way (since the Chairman of the CRD was directly responsible to the Leader of the Party alone). Woolton's *Memoirs* praise the work of the Industrial Policy Committee and laud several of its members for their contributions, but fail to mention that Butler was even a member. Under Butler's leadership, the CRD and the Parliamentary Secretariat, with which it was formally merged in 1948, blossomed with a staff that rose to over fifty, half of them graduates, by the next Election – compared to a dozen at most before 1939 and just four in 1945. The staff were also of extraordinarily high calibre; by 1948, the team under David Clarke as Director (the only survivor from before 1939) included Iain Macleod, Reginald Maudling and Enoch Powell, all on their way to ministerial careers, and another group headed by Michael Fraser and Peter Goldman who were embarking on a long-term career of Party service behind the scenes.[6]

It is possible to exaggerate Butler's role; Eden in his *Memoirs*, in one of his few comments on the opposition period, sensitively suggested that Butler and his backroom boys had indeed been given too much credit. It can also be shown that Butler did not personally assemble this array of talent; Macleod and Maudling for example were both recruited by Clarke and Assheton. But there is no doubt that Butler's role as a facilitator and impresario of policy work was crucial: asked by the BBC in 1983 what had been Butler's significance, Michael Fraser concluded that 'the answer to that is that without him it probably wouldn't have happened', and he later argued that Butler 'was the only person at the top level who really put drive and coherence into the policy exercise, recreated the Research Department and got

6  National Union Central Council minutes, 28 Nov. 1945, CPA; Crookshank diary, 16 and 30 Oct. 1945, Crookshank MSS; Central Office, Chairman's file, 'Correspondence with R.A. Butler, 1940–1958', CCO 20/1/1, CPA; Anthony Howard, *RAB, The Life of R.A. Butler* (1987), 151–3; John Ramsden, *The Making of Conservative Party Policy, The Conservative Research Department since 1929* (1980), 104–9, 131; Earl of Woolton, *The Memoirs of the Rt. Hon. Lord Woolton* (1959), 347.

the show on the road. Macmillan was the next greatest influence but at that time relatively limited, since he had not got an army and Butler had.' It may be worth adding a more sceptical contemporary comment on Butler, at the pivotal moment in his career when the *Industrial Charter* was being produced. Headlam thought that

> he is quite certain that he is one of our leading lights and has been successful, so far, in making other people think the same of him. He is ambitious and means to be leader sooner or later. He may be – everything is possible in politics – but he never strikes me as having much personality or go – he is a don and an intellectual – not, I fancy, the type of man who could inspire a crowd – and so long as 'safety first' is his guiding principle it is difficult to see him leading a party effectively.

The character traits that were to deny Butler the top job – however unfair the assessment – were already evident to the resolutely unintellectual majority of the Party.[7]

John Wyndham described the atmosphere in the CRD's Old Queen Street offices as being akin to a graduate common room; the staff put in long hours and enjoyed the intellectual cut and thrust of each other's company, but after a busy week and a series of late nights they might be late in in the mornings for the week following. Maudling recalled it as an exciting time for a young man, constantly in close touch with major public figures and exercising an important influence while he was still only about thirty. Macleod and Powell shared an office and became firm friends, Powell devouring textbooks on town planning as if they were light fiction, Macleod silently self-absorbed and then dictating complex letters from memory. Macleod was largely responsible for the Party's policy in Scotland, and Powell, made responsible somewhat reluctantly for Wales, had to devise a policy for the Principality at very short notice. Butler felt that Fraser was 'the best adjutant the party had ever had', and that the loss of Goldman 'would be as important as the resignation of any Cabinet Minister'. This high-calibre team also owed much to the talents of David Clarke, who shared Butler's determination that one aspect of the CRD's work should be real research on long-term issues that would help to win back the vital support of intellectual opinion. As it turned out, devoting time to truly long-term issues was a chimera that the CRD was always to chase but could never quite find time to catch up with. But Clarke's publication of the work of Conservative philosophers, the commissioning of Quintin Hogg's *The Case for Conservatism*, his own *The Conservative Faith in the Modern Age*, and other such 'Third Programme efforts', undoubtedly helped the CPC campaign to win back important ground among intellectual opinion-formers. A high standard was insisted on in literary presentation,

---

7 Anthony Eden, *The Reckoning, The Eden Memoirs, vol. 2* (1965), 554; Michael Fraser quotation from BBC television programme 'Reputations', broadcast, 13 July 1983; John Ramsden, 'Churchill to Heath', in *The Conservatives, A History from their Origins to 1965*, ed. Lord Butler (1977), 422; Headlam diary, 12 Feb. 1947.

and in other ways too; in 1947, when *Conservative Industrial and Social Reform* was produced, a successor to the 'What the Conservatives have done for the British People' series of pamphlets that had been almost continuously in print since 1880, it was agreed to pay twenty guineas to a distinguished Cambridge historian who would check it for accuracy.[8]

In 1947, motions favourable to the Conservatives were passed in both the Oxford and Cambridge Unions, and in 1948 Swinton reported from Cambridge where 'in a packed house we beat the Government by 423 votes to 209'. In Scotland, Walter Elliot was elected Lord Rector of the University of Glasgow where a socialist pacifist had won in the last pre-war poll. Woolton also took to this onslaught on the universities and proved a highly successful speaker at undergraduate political societies. In 1948, there were 3,458 undergraduate members of Conservative societies in English universities, more than half of them in Oxford and Cambridge. All of this laid the foundations for a period of ten years or so in which it was fashionable to be Conservative in British universities. The same was true of graduates: the university constituencies, mostly Tory in the 1920s as a reflection of the social composition of the graduate body, had drifted during the 1930s into the preserve of independents, and in 1945 Conservatives won only three of the sixteen university seats, worse than their share of seats in the rest of the country. But in subsequent by-elections for both Combined English Universities and for Combined Scottish Universities, Conservative candidates were elected. This proved to be a mixed blessing, for in 1948 the Labour Government abolished university constituencies altogether, and one reason given for this was that they were said to have become once again Conservative fiefs. Their graduates would though continue to exist in their thousands, to vote in ordinary constituencies, and to influence opinion well beyond their own numbers, so the quest for intellectual backing went on. All this was far from uncontroversial. In April 1948, the Worthing agent complained about the time and money being wasted on an *Industrial Charter* that was of no interest to anyone but the 'intelligentsia'. For the CPC, Alport was quick to respond:

> The Conservative Party have always underestimated the sort of people known as the intelligentsia, yet it is these people who in the past have been singled out by the Liberals, Socialists and Communists as being a most important element in the struggle to mould public opinion. They are the professional classes, school and university teachers, writers, scientists, economists . . . It was these people who were captured by the Fabian Society and who today dominate the Socialist

---

[8] Lord Egremont, *Wyndham and Children First* (1968), 139–41; Reginald Maudling, *Memoirs* (1978), 43; Ramsden, *Conservative Party Policy*, 105, 120–7, 141; T.E. Howarth, *Prospect and Reality, Britain 1945–1955* (1985), 130.

Party . . . If the Conservative Party ignores them, they will have no alternative but to gravitate towards the left as they did between the wars.[9]

## The *Industrial Charter*

The fact that the policy-making machinery was effectively in place by the time of the 1946 Conference united motive with opportunity for the serious policy review to begin, but it was significant that the 1948 dispute outlined above should have involved the *Industrial Charter*. Alport also rather scathingly pointed out that the *Industrial Charter* had never been intended to excite the populace of Worthing, but that elsewhere things were different. He was supported in the next issue of the *Conservative Agents' Journal* by the Cannock agent, the redoubtable Fred Hardman, who reminded his Worthing colleague that if he had to fight a Labour majority of 19,000 in an industrial seat (rather than just defend a Tory majority of the same size in Worthing), he would see things rather differently; for the industrial Midlands, a Conservative industrial policy was crucial. From the start, the Industrial Policy Committee approached its work in this latter mood, seeing their work as of historic importance to the Party. The composition of the Committee was the first indication of this, since as well as Butler it included Macmillan, Maxwell Fyfe, Stanley and Lyttelton from the front bench, and four backbenchers with industrial experience – a committee including three future Chancellors of the Exchequer and two more who were widely tipped for the job. Thorneycroft was also on the original list but decided not to join the Committee, lest it inhibit his privateering attempts to negotiate a new policy settlement between Conservatives and Liberals; the Chief Whip advised Eden that this would be an excellent opportunity to 'show him up' to backbenchers for disloyalty, and Eden had already decided, according to his diary, that he 'should not like to go tiger-shooting with that man'. David Clarke acted as the Committee's secretary, with Maudling and Fraser assisting; initially Churchill decided that membership was not to be announced, but Butler sought and got his permission to tell the National Union who was involved, in order to build confidence in its work. The members approached the meetings with a consciousness of their task: Quintin Hogg had suggested to Butler, and Butler concurred, that what was needed was a new Tamworth Manifesto, and Macmillan had already floated the idea of a 'Charter', a vocabulary that indicated in both cases something less like a regular review of policy than a contract with the people.[10]

[9]  Swinton to Salisbury, 18 Oct. 1948, Swinton MSS, 174/4/1; Colin Coote, *A Companion of Honour, The Story of Walter Elliott* (1965), 151, 252; Advisory Committee on Policy and Political Education minutes, 4/6/47, ACP 1/1, CPA; Woolton, *Memoirs*, 337–8; NUEC, 9 Jan. 1948; Blake, *Conservative Party*, 262; D.E. Butler, *The Electoral System in Great Britain since 1918* (2nd edn, 1963), 151; *Conservative Agents' Journal* [hereafter *CAJ*], Apr. and May 1948, CPA.
[10]  *CAJ*, May and June 1948; Ramsden, *Conservative Party Policy*, 109–10; Stuart to Eden, 23 Oct. 1946, Avon MSS, 11/12/14; Eden diary, 2 Oct. 1946, Avon MSS, 20/1/25.

The same seriousness characterised the Committee's working; regular meetings were held throughout the terrible winter of 1946–47, evidence was taken from many industrial witnesses, and voluminous papers were circulated by the secretaries. In early Spring 1947, the Committee broke up into smaller groups to visit the provinces to hear more evidence; for example, Fraser went with Macmillan and James Hutchinson to Newcastle and Leeds, with Lyttelton and Derick Heathcoat Amory to Liverpool and Manchester, and with Maxwell Fyfe, David Eccles and Peter Bennett to Cardiff; Maudling and Clarke serviced groups visiting among other places Edinburgh, Glasgow, Birmingham and Leicester. The Committee worked like the most conscientious of Royal Commissions and was certainly more thorough in its work than any Conservative Party policy group before or since. But the methodical nature of the work indicates not only the seriousness of the task of policy review as such, but the extent to which the members realised that they also had an educational job to do in selling their report to the Party and its industrial supporters. It was therefore vital to listen, and to be seen to listen, before producing proposals. Eccles, defending the report in the Commons on 8 July placed great emphasis on the consultation that had preceded it:

> The consensus of opinion from Scotland, Wales and England was that business wants firm government at the centre with maximum freedom at the circumference. Employers, technicians and wage-earners all described to us how, under the Labour Government, they were checked and bewildered by the muddled and conflicting policy at the centre, combined with the maximum interference at the circumference.

There is no reason to doubt in any case that some at least of the industrialists who gave evidence were themselves very persuasive; Anthony Howard may well be right in detecting the influence of Butler's father-in-law, Samuel Courtauld, in the report's idealistic references to industrial partnership, though Heathcoat Amory's own industrial experience pointed the same way.[11]

The instinctive economic views of the Committee members ranged from Eccles, who was well on the interventionist wing of the Party and described by Bracken in 1948 as 'that semi-socialist', to Heathcoat Amory and Lyttelton who were more inclined to stress the virtues of free enterprise. It was remarkable in these circumstances, and says much of Butler's skills as chairman, that the committee agreed to a report without dissentients, and then all loyally supported it in the Party debates that followed. This agreement was perhaps made easier by the fact that the report was deliberately phrased in the most sober language. Butler recalled that 'rarely in the field of political pamphleteering can a document so radical in effect have been written with such flatness of language or blandness of tone. This was not wholly unintentional. We were out-Peeling Peel in giving the Party a painless but permanent face-lift;

---

11  *NCP*, 28 July 1946; NUEC, 14 Nov. 1946; Howard, *RAB*, 155.

the more unflamboyant the changes, the less likely were the features to sag again.' In fact though, a close reading of the text indicates how far, as Robert Eccleshall puts it, 'the language advocating an enlarged state was deliberately bland, yet there were sparkling passages defending individual initiative and entrepreneurial rewards'. For the many who did not study the text in detail, such a pattern in the draftsmanship no doubt helped to carry them along. Only at the very last moment was the high-profile word *Charter* attached as a title, for as late as 20 March, Clarke and Alport were still suggesting titles of a more routine type.[12]

The report was eagerly awaited. Asking to see a copy of the draft report, and as yet having no real idea what was in it, Woolton wrote that 'this document may be one that will determine the party allegiance of many men. I believe it will have an immense effect on the intellectual vote and, unless some crisis situation intervenes, it will be a vital factor in the next election.' When Peter Thorneycroft circulated MPs with his own thoughts on economic policy in February 1947, apparently attempting to pre-empt the coming debate, the shadow cabinet reminded them not to sign anything to indicate their support, since policy 'could only come from the Leader himself'. There was some embarrassment caused in what Heathcoat Amory called 'l'affaire Thorneycroft', which led Crookshank to tell his diary that 'that young man wants kicking'. The shadow cabinet considered the proposed report at two meetings in March and April, and on 16 April formally authorised Butler to proceed with the revised proofs; the minutes do not indicate that its contents had been approved, but that was the implication of publishing it. There had certainly been some problem in getting it past frontbenchers who had not been on the Committee; Assheton denounced a very late draft as likely to require the actual intensification of controls, and 'that would be socialism of the worst kind'; Lyttelton, who approved the drafts at committee, then seems to have changed his mind several times; he was reported in May to have 'come right round' and to be 'now' in favour of the *Charter*; Bracken, who might well have been a severe critic, offered Butler only minor verbal suggestions on the text. The *Industrial Charter*, was published on 12 May 1947, and then had five months in a curious state of limbo, the report of an officially-appointed policy committee that did not yet have any official approval as the policy of the Party. Churchill gave a dinner at the Savoy and placed Butler at his right hand, 'plied me with cognac and said several agreeable and no disagreeable things about my work', but from this his agreement with the *Charter* had to be deduced, since it was not stated. The Committee's members now went out to sell their proposals to the Party. Butler's full statement of the *Charter* in the May edition of the Party's *Notes on Current Politics* was entitled simply 'Conservative Industrial Policy' and the whole issue was devoted to it. It was, said Butler, not 'a detailed programme' but 'a broad policy for industry as a whole'. The theme was 'realism, free opportunity, incentive and justice'. The detailed proposals were as follows: (1) there would be better 'machinery at headquarters' to run economic policy, centring on 'a strong committee' of government, industrialists and trades unionists, chaired by the same minister who chaired the Cabinet's economic committee; (2) free collective bargaining but better information to be made available to both sides of industry about the economic effects of their bargains; (3) 'a high and stable level of employment' to be produced by the Government; (4) an end to rationing as soon as possible, especially for food; (5) reduced public expenditure to allow reduced taxation; (6) encouragement of savings as a contribution to industrial investment; (7) trades unions were said to 'have a great and vital part to play in industry', but individual workers must be free not to join if they wanted; (8) monopolies and restrictive practices to be attacked; (9) further nationalisation to be opposed, and there would be a 'rigorous examination' of existing schemes to ensure parliamentary accountability and protection of the interests of consumers; (10) a workers' charter would give security of employment, incentives and status; (11) encouragement to be given to equal pay, and payment by results; (12) more emphasis on training; (13) joint production councils to be retained in industries where they already existed; (14) co-partnership schemes in industry to be encouraged but not imposed.[13]

This was, as Butler said, 'impressionism', and we need indeed to examine it from a distance to appreciate its bold juxtaposition of colours, rather than to analyse each brush-stroke. When his constituency chairman asked him at a public meeting in 1948, 'how much of the provisions of the Charter do [you] envisage making the subject of immediate legislation, and how much is simply an expression of Conservative principles?', Heathcoat Amory replied that 'comparatively little of it is a prospective Act of Parliament. It is mostly a rule of conduct rather than a programme of legislation.' In January 1949, Birmingham Conservatives were complaining that too few of the employers who had welcomed the *Industrial Charter* had actually implemented such ideas as joint production committees in their own works, suggesting that they saw the *Charter* as a menu for voluntary action at least as much as a programme for the next Tory government. In this context, did it deserve to be called 'radical'? Some parts of the *Charter* were unexceptional; items 4, 5 and 6 above were obvious Conservative responses to the problems bequeathed

---

[13] Woolton to Butler, 24 Mar. 1947 and Heathcoat Amory to Butler, 17 Feb. 1947, Butler MSS, H92; Crookshank diary, 13 Feb. 1947, Crookshank MSS; LCC, 4 Feb., 26 Mar., 2 and 16 Apr. 1947, CPA; Assheton to Butler, 22 Apr. 1947; Bracken to Butler, 22 Apr. 1947, Frank Owen to Butler, 12 May 1947, Butler MSS, H92; Alan Thompson, *The Day Before Yesterday* (1971), 85; *NCP*, 19 May 1947; David Clarke (ed.), *Conservatism 1945–50* (1950), 49–76; Ramsden, *Conservative Party Policy*, 112.

by the War, and 3 re-stated a commitment given in 1944 and 1945. But even relatively straightforward proposals had implications of significance; for example, proposal 9 not only opposed nationalisation but also stopped well short of promising to denationalise any industries already in public ownership, and this implied that the future Conservative government would learn to live with a far bigger public sector than Chamberlain had envisaged in the 1930s. Proposals 1, 2, 8, and 10 implied a greater degree of economic intervention by government than had been customary in Conservative thinking; proposal 7 was more generous in spirit to the trades unions than any Conservative policy had been since the 1870s; and proposal 11 explicitly accepted a principle that the Tory Reform Group had fought for against the Party whip as recently as 1943.[14]

It is not difficult to find the roots of the *Industrial Charter* in earlier Tory thinking: Macmillan's speeches and writings between the wars made much the same case for more government intervention, and the industrial policy report of the Post-War Problems Central Committee, produced by Henry Brooke in 1944, closely prefigured the 1947 proposals in respect of trades unionism, joint production councils, monopolies and co-partnership. But there was certainly no precedent for a group of frontbench Conservatives producing such a package as a comprehensive Party policy, and in that sense it was radical. Baldwin had told Butler in the 1930s that the art of leading the Party lay in steering a middle course between Harold Macmillan and Henry Page Croft. By 1947, Page Croft's old-fashioned imperial and tariff reform Toryism had almost vanished off the end of the Party's political spectrum, and Macmillan truly represented *The Middle Way* and not the left. When the Party's right wing jibed that the *Industrial Charter* 'tried to amalgamate the Tory Party and the YMCA', they were mocking its earnest idealism, but they were also not far wrong, for Macmillan's 'YMCA' ideas of the 1920s had now become the Party's idea too. He can surely be forgiven the summary in his memoirs: 'all of this was a source of great satisfaction and some little pride to me. For the leaders of my party and its members as a whole had now broadly accepted the policies for which I had striven in the past.' If Macmillan pressed for ideas with which he was already associated (and, if Butler is to be believed, bored its members by reading to them at length extracts from his own past works), Butler's own role in the Committee's work is more difficult to pin down. He had always been known as a Conservative progressive, though one who had managed to combine that ideological stance with loyalty and conformism. He no doubt welcomed the progressive thrust of policy in 1947, as he had done in his educational reforms and through the abortive work of the PWPCC. Perhaps that combination of loyalism and progressiveness

---

[14] *NCP*, Mar. 1944, 19 May 1947; Butler, *Art of the Possible*, 30, 144; W. Gore Allen, *The Reluctant Politician, Derick Heathcoat Amory* (1958), 89; Birmingham UA minutes, 28 Jan. 1949.

was the secret of his successful chairmanship in 1947? Macmillan generously wrote to him that 'without you, it would have been quite impossible to have reached any conclusion at all', and Oliver Stanley, more sceptically, observed that 'if any credit comes out of all this, it belongs to you'. It is clear that Macmillan and Butler were perceived from the outside as the two key figures in the Industrial Policy Committee, and that they did indeed get the credit – but together. *The Observer's* political correspondent shrewdly noted in June 1948 that 'the really solid work of plotting the Party's future course has been largely done by two men – Mr. Butler and Mr. Harold Macmillan. While the immediate succession would fall automatically to Mr. Eden, the influence of Mr. Butler and Mr. Macmillan will remain a highly important factor.'[15]

What motives produced this shift? In part the social and economic facts of life outlined by Keynes and Beveridge in the aftermath of total war were just too strong to be denied; in part, the Conservatives' political weakness after the 1945 defeat dictated an appeasing attitude to trades unionism and a greater attention than hitherto to the material interests of industrial workers who had to be wooed back to the Party, as had middle-class voters with promises of tax cuts and an early end to rationing. Idealism and calculation therefore went hand in hand, but this was only possible with a group of men from a new generation at the helm. The oldest of these had, like Macmillan and Eden, shared in the trench experience of 1914–18, and the youngest of them had grown up in a modern world of militant trades unionism and a strong but moderate Labour Party. Churchill apart, the Victorians had passed on the torch to the next two generations. Macmillan had astutely seized on this point when in his 1946 speeches he called for a policy relevant to 'modern problems'. Introducing as National Union President Churchill's 1947 Conference speech, he spoke of the 1930s as a dead period for Conservative policy in all fields, linking his own rebellion on domestic policy to Churchill's opposition to appeasement, both rebellions now validated by the War. When the *Industrial Charter* was published, 'Crossbencher' in the *Daily Express* reminded his readers that Macmillan 'once wrote a political treatise called *The Middle Way*. This is the second edition.' The *Industrial Charter* was therefore more important for its very existence, and for the recognition that a younger generation had produced it, than for any actual proposal that it contained. Butler later summarised its intention as being 'to give the impression that you could be in favour of free enterprise without trying to do in your neighbour'. At the time, *The Spectator* warmly concluded that the Charter removed 'the last excuse for labelling the Conservative Party as at present constituted as reactionary'.[16]

However, before such panegyrics could be delivered, the Party itself had to be persuaded to accept the *Charter*, for either rejection or half-hearted

[15] Macmillan, *Tides of Fortune*, 312; Howard, *RAB*, 158; Ramsden, *Conservative Party Policy*, 115.
[16] Ramsden, 'Churchill to Heath', 425, 476; Macmillan, *Tides of Fortune*, 291, 303, 307; Thompson, *Day Before Yesterday*, 85.

acceptance would leave exactly the wrong impression in the minds of voters. The knowledge of the Committee's work had created an expectancy before the *Charter* was even published. In April 1947 the National Union Executive received a resolution from the South East Area which pointed out that recruiting was being inhibited because 'the majority of the electorate is still not convinced of the sincerity of Conservative industrial principles', and called for 'an Industrial Policy which takes care of the welfare and the interests of employees, and explains the functions and problems of management'. The same meeting received from Rushcliffe a resolution calling for any new policy statement to be debated in the constituencies before adoption; the constituency association was sternly reminded that 'in our Party, policy is decided by the Leader who consults anyone he thinks proper'; but it was also pointed out that Conference and Central Council represented the constituencies anyway, and that it would be impractical to have each local party taking up different positions. At the next meeting, Butler gave the Executive details of the *Charter*, shortly before it was published; since a quarter of a million copies were being printed for distribution, to sell at only one shilling each, there would be opportunity for a full debate at every level. When published, the press gave the *Charter* a great deal of attention and, apart from the Beaverbrook papers which were hostile to policies that they saw as too left wing, the Conservative-leaning papers were favourable. The old right, led by Sir Waldron Smithers and Sir Herbert Williams, began to mobilise resistance, and there seemed to be a chance that they might be widely backed. After all, most of those who had demanded a clear policy in 1946 had certainly not anticipated the emergence of anything like this. At Blackpool, Reginald Bevins had attacked the ACPPE report for being too 'weak, vacillating and compromising, particularly in its reference to the nationalisation of British industry', and William Robson Brown, moving the crucial resolution that demanded a policy statement, had asked the Party to make it clear that they would 'denationalise all nationalised industries'. A well-attended meeting of the 1922 Committee on 22 May 1947 endorsed the *Charter*, 'pending the party conference'; some present had doubts, but mainly as to whether the policies could be delivered rather than whether they were desirable.[17]

The right's campaign quickly ran out of steam. A thirty-page memorandum by Smithers, entitled 'Save England', made little impact, despite its copious biblical cross-referencing; the title page bore the legend 'For when the time comes that ye ought to be teachers, Ye have need that one teach ye again which be the first principles of the oracles of God', from the Book of Hebrews; Butler insouciantly replied that 'if I may, I will reply in the vein of Christian Charity which the quotations in your document, rather than its

17 NUEC, 17 Apr. and 8 May 1947; J.D. Hoffman, *The Conservative Party in Opposition, 1945–1951* (1964), 154–5, 158.

text, inspire'. Under Eden's chairmanship, the shadow cabinet had finally given approval to what Crookshank called 'the great policy report' on 24 April. Butler was now inhibited by his consultative position as chairman of the ACPPE and, writing in the *Telegraph*, was keen to point out that the new policies were not final, merely proposals that could be amended after the full debate now starting in the Party. But others could be mobilised for the public campaign of persuasion; Oliver Poole was busy working on backbenchers, 'giving his fellow Conservative Members', as Michael Fraser has put it, 'a general feeling that they were being consulted and in the secret, by taking around a pre-publication copy and showing it them individually and secretly'. Eden launched the *Charter* at a rally attended by 17,000 Welsh Tories at Cardiff Castle, and thereafter spoke up for the policy in speeches throughout the Summer, while all the committee members campaigned for it around the country, with organised support from the Speakers' Department at Central Office. Macmillan was especially active; on 21 May he gently mocked the *Charter*'s opponents, pointing out that 'the socialists are afraid of it; Lord Beaverbrook dislikes it; and the Liberals say it is too liberal to be fair; What more could one want? Was ever a child born under such a lucky star?' Williams and Smithers, he said, were 'gentlemen for whom time does not merely stand still but, if anything, runs backwards . . . So all the forces of reaction in the country, the *Daily Herald*, Lord Beaverbrook, Sir Waldron Smithers and Co., are united in saying that this *Industrial Charter* is not Tory policy. What they really mean, all of them, is that they wish it were not Tory policy. Fortunately their wishes cannot be granted.' And on 14 June he robustly rejected the right's claim that the *Charter* was just 'pink socialism': 'the *Industrial Charter* is merely a restatement in the light of modern conditions of the fundamental and lasting principles of our party'. Increasingly, the *Charter*'s defenders drew the distinction between limited planning (which was seen as well within the Tory tradition of a responsible state) and unnecessary interference (which was seen as typically socialist); Butler proclaimed in a CPC pamphlet in September that 'Conservatives were planning before the word entered the vocabulary of political jargon'. A CPC pamphlet argued that *laissez-faire* 'was an interlude which ended long before the end of the Nineteenth Century . . . and that the central tradition of British industry is to be found in forms of positive guidance by the State which allow for the utmost diversity of individual effort'. On state intervention then, as those carefully chosen words show, the *Industrial Charter* represented what John Boyd-Carpenter called 'a central position between Manchester and Moscow'.[18]

18  Smithers to Butler, July 1947, and Butler to Smithers, 8 Aug. 1947, Butler MSS, H92; Crookshank diary, 22 Apr. 1947, Crookshank MSS; Philip Goodhart, *The 1922, The Story of the 1922 Committee* (1973), 142; Anthony Eden, *Days for Decision, Selected Speeches, 1947–1949* (1949), 10–13; Lord Fraser of Kilmorack, letter to the author, 30 June 1994; Lindsay and Harrington, *Conservative Party*, 153; Macmillan, *Tides of Fortune*, 306; Butler, *Art of the Possible*, 145, 149; Clarke, *Conservatism*, 48; Eccleshall, *English Conservatism*, 186; Jones, 'Conservative Party' thesis, 30.

Constituencies that debated the *Charter* over the Summer gave firm support, for example in Denbigh and in the West Midlands and Eastern Areas; the Northern Area Council, generally rather right wing in its opinions, actually endorsed the *Charter* unanimously, but at its next meeting approved only by forty-two votes to thirty-four the industrial co-partnership idea that was central to it; Guildford Conservatives specifically told their Conference representatives to vote for it when a member 'feared that it might be sidetracked'. In June, on the proposition of the Young Unionists, the Birmingham Central Council unanimously 'welcome[d] the Industrial Charter as the first instalment of a policy which will show the country that the Unionist Party have a positive alternative to Socialism'. The Sheffield Chief Agent reported in June that 'the Industrial Charter was having a far-reaching effect', partly at least because 'there was little in it with which a Liberal could disagree'; in the city, all of the divisional Executives and both of the sitting MPs had by then agreed to support the *Charter*. But despite the barrage of support, from a united front bench and from much of the Party machine, the National Union was nervous about its reception at the Conference to be held in Brighton. The agenda included thirty-three motions on the *Charter*; those in support came from the Northern and Yorkshire Areas, but also from an array of constituencies such as Barnet (where Maudling was candidate), Cambridge, Clitheroe, Enfield (Macleod), High Peak (Molson), Mitcham (Robert Carr), Paddington, Southampton, Wallasey and Sheffield. On the other hand, there were critical motions from the London Area (where Williams was chairman) and Spelthorne; there were nine others which, while not attacking the *Charter*, called for denationalisation to be the Party's clear policy. Some mysterious, and as usual secret, bargaining took place behind the scene, presumably in the hope of avoiding a public battle at Conference; a composite motion was made up from among those broadly favourable, but this upset the supporters; Hendon North complained that their strong support for the *Charter* had been watered down in the compositing process, so that they were listed as proposing a motion which merely noted the *Charter* as a basis for further discussion.[19]

Macmillan and Maudling were among those who wrote to Butler to protest that this was the worst of all worlds for, as Maudling put it, 'either way the Charter will be killed; openly if the resolution is defeated; quietly if the resolution is passed. This is clearly what Herbert Williams and friends desire.' The *Charter*'s supporters were not content to gain so little from their work, and were well placed to extract more. Macmillan was National Union President that year, and Butler, appointed to reply to the debate, knew in advance what tactics the *Charter*'s supporters would pursue. Early in Conference week, the

---

[19] Guildford CA minutes, 26 Sept. 1947; Birmingham UA minutes, 26 Sept. 1947; Sheffield Central Women's Advisory Committee minutes, 4 July 1947; Denbigh CA minutes, 3 June 1947; South East Area Council, 31 May 1947; Northern Area Council, 21 June and 13 Dec. 1947; Conference Agenda, 1947, NUA 2/2/13, CPA; NUEC, 16 Oct. and 11 Dec. 1947, 9 Jan. 1948; LCC, 17 Mar. 1948; Headlam diary, 4 Oct. 1948.

progressives scored a victory by adding to the annual report a reference to a full pledge of support for the Party's 'Industrial, Domestic and Foreign Policy laid down by the Leader of the Conservative Party since the last conference'; this was given extra significance by Thorneycroft's statement in debate that that policy included the *Industrial Charter*, which 'was launched by Mr. Churchill and . . . has been defended on countless platforms by Mr. Anthony Eden'. This, like Macmillan's earlier claim that the *Charter* was Party policy whether opponents liked it or not, was a classic example of Harvey Glickman's famous dictum that in persuading Conservatives to accept change, the best tactic is to tell them that it has already happened and might just as well be defended. In the main debate Ian Orr-Ewing, proposing the Hendon motion, spoke strongly in favour of the original and not the watered-down version, and speakers chosen from the floor were mainly in favour. Reginald Maudling, present as candidate for Barnet, was called to put an amendment which, instead of just noting the *Charter*, committed the Conference to accepting it as 'a clear statement of the general principles of Conservative economic policy'. Herbert Williams desperately argued that 'there can be no compromise with Socialism or Communism' and called on the Conference to 'save the Conservative Party and England' but, when put to the vote, the Maudling amendment was passed with only three dissentients in an attendance of several thousands; it no doubt took considerable courage to be a dissenter in a Conference in such a mood, and, recognising the inevitability of their defeat, many opponents cannot have bothered to vote. Headlam noted in his diary the feebleness of resistance, but in relaxed terms that are a useful corrective to most accounts; it is sometimes a mistake to assume that even MPs were really committed to – or even understood – a policy just because they had voted for it:

> The Party Conference . . . has adopted the 'Industrial Charter' almost unanimously, only poor old Waldron Smithers seems to have spoken against it. He considers it to be milk and water socialism which perhaps it is, but, so far as I have studied it – and that is not a great deal – it seems to lay down as an 'industrial policy' the practices that exist today between employers and employees in the best managed firms – there does not seem to me much harm in this.[20]

Butler was summoned to Churchill's hotel and greeted with the words, 'Well, old cock, you have definitely won through. I wish now to toast your victory.' But, although Churchill then claimed to have read and agreed the *Charter* when first published in the Spring, it was clear when Maudling came to help him draft his own speech for the Conference rally that the Leader had little idea what it contained. When Maudling offered him a short paragraph summarising the *Charter*, he 'read it with care, and then said, "But I do not agree with a word of this." "Well, sir," [Maudling] said, "this is what the

---

20 Macmillan to Butler, 22 Sept. 1947 and Maudling to Butler, 22 Sept. 1947, Butler MSS, H92; Harvey Glickman, 'The Toryness of British Conservatism', in the *Journal of British Studies* (1961), 119; Hoffman, *Conservative Party*, 163, 165.

Conference has adopted." "Oh well," he said, "leave it in", and he duly read it out in the course of his speech.' This conversation was surely a typical piece of self-parody on Churchill's part, but the important thing was that he did read out the paragraph, which explicitly referred to the *Charter* as 'the official policy of the Party' – something only he could say, whatever Conference had resolved. Waldron Smithers wrote to Butler to regret the fact that he now found himself 'in advance of ' the Party Conference! When the National Union formally submitted all the resolutions passed at Brighton to the Leader, now an annual process, it was reported back that he 'approved of all the resolutions and had asked that they should be published as the policy of the Party advocated by the rank and file, with a foreword by himself '. The importance of this solemn ratification was considerable, for few would now rock the boat with disloyal opposition. In January 1948, through seniority, it was Herbert Williams' turn to be chairman of the National Union for the year, usually an election by acclamation to a formal position of dignity, though since Woolton took the question to the shadow cabinet it was clearly felt that in Williams' case the usual processes might lead to embarrassment. Williams was challenged at the Executive by Orr-Ewing, who demanded an assurance that if elected he would 'not speak against the *Industrial Charter* during his year of office'. Williams was deeply upset by this 'heresy-hunting'; he 'denied that he had ever opposed the *Industrial Charter* on a public platform', presumably thinking only of the period since Conference, but refused to give any assurance for the future, as 'it implied he did not know how to behave himself '. After discussion, Orr-Ewing withdrew his point and Williams was elected *nem. con.*, but the warning shot had been effective, for his grumbling ceased – on this issue. October 1947 may be thought of as terminating the five years of tactical uncertainty on fundamental policy that had existed ever since the publication of the Beveridge Report. It was though still a halfway house for, as Woolton pointed out in 1949, the *Charter* had been 'designed to teach the teachers of party doctrine, to provide data for speakers', and was a long way from being a manifesto. Nevertheless, having demanded a policy statement the year before, the Workington Conservatives at least made use of it now that it was available, ordering 65,000 copies of the *Industrial Charter* so as to deliver one to every household in the constituency.[21]

## After 1947

The later stages of formal policy-making were more straightforward, once the *Industrial Charter* had set the framework and satisfied the urgent demands

---

[21] Butler, *Art of the Possible*, 147–8; Maudling, *Memoirs*, 45–6; Smithers to Butler, 21 Oct. 1947, Butler MSS, H92; *NCP*, 27 Oct. 1947; Michael Kandiah, 'Lord Woolton's Chairmanship of the Conservative Party', unpublished PhD thesis, University of Exeter, 1992, 139; Workington CA minutes, 5 Nov. 1947.

that something should be seen to be done. More charters were prepared, on women's issues, on Scotland and on imperial policy, mainly in the same 'impressionistic' tone as the original; when told that he would be secretary of the committee charged with drawing up an agricultural charter, Fraser protested that he knew nothing much about agriculture: Butler replied, 'No, but you know a lot about charters, and the committee will know about agriculture,' a comment that says much about the relationship between the policy professionals and the specialists in this whole exercise. The charters extended the combination of continuity and change that had characterised the 1947 document; the *Agricultural Charter* accepted much of what the Labour Government was doing, but also indicated areas beyond which the Conservatives would not go in collective marketing arrangements; the *Imperial Charter*, if the least forward-looking of the series, could still persuade the Liberal *News Chronicle* that it bore 'the marks of the "new liberalism"' or at least that 'the roll of Imperial drums [was] notably absent'. There could be sharp little contests about detailed content. In May 1948, members of the shadow cabinet angrily complained about a sentence on employment policy in the *Workers' Charter*: 'it was stated that no one reviews pamphlets before they are issued; propaganda is bad and the machinery for dealing with it slow and creaking'; a committee of five frontbenchers under Eden was set up to review the forthcoming *Agricultural Charter* and all later publications. Butler, clearly miffed by this assumption that he needed supervision, told Buchan-Hepburn that the new arrangement was 'more revolutionary (i.e. changing) than was at all necessary'.[22]

Churchill had not modified his basic stance on policy tactics; in December 1947, Moran noted that 'when it is argued that the Conservatives ought to have a policy he grows impatient. The job of the leader of the Opposition, he says, is to attack the Government – that and no more.' In 1948 though, demands for detailed policies again welled up; this time the shadow cabinet remained united behind the idea that a full programme should not be launched until nearer the General Election. Butler was in any case not convinced of his team's fitness to produce these electioneering documents: he told Woolton that 'I think you must have "thoughtful" documents in the first place for intelligent reading. Then I think you want a different brain to transform them.' In April 1948, the National Union learned that the shadow cabinet had turned down its request to set up a committee on banking and trade policy; at the same meeting it considered how to react to a resolution passed at the Central Council calling for a proper definition of what was meant by the 'property-owning democracy' concept, and a further resolution from the

---

22  Hoffman, *Conservative Party*, 175, 182; Lord Fraser of Kilmorack to the author, 30 June 1994; LCC, 12 May, 26 May, and 2 June 1947; Butler to Buchan-Hepburn, 1 June 1948, Hailes MSS, 4/12.

Welsh Area asking for a comprehensive policy document for Wales, to be launched at a mass meeting which one of the Party's leaders would address, 'preferably Mr. R.A. Butler'. Two months later the West Midlands Area was calling for a policy document to be ready for the Autumn Conference, 'that has as its basis the widespread distribution of property and power'. The Eastern Area were delighted to learn that there would now be an *Agricultural Charter* to provide for their own major industry. When the 1948 Conference passed without a detailed policy being published, such demands increased. At the Executive in November, members spoke of 'the necessity of now making clear the position of nationalised industries when the Conservatives regain power'. The same month, Iain Macleod thought that the lack of policy detail had held back the Conservative campaign in the Edmonton by-election, near his own Enfield constituency; in December, Michael Fraser wrote to Butler to support the case for policy work, now needed urgently if votes were to be won back in industrial areas; Central Office surveys of opinion showed that such voters did not trust the Conservatives' sincerity in the *Industrial Charter*. In response, Butler said that it was too late for interim policy statements and still too early for an election programme. There were then greater rumblings of discontent after the Party's failure to win the South Hammersmith by-election in February 1949: the *Telegraph* concluded that 'the party has not succeeded in translating its policy and intentions into terms which are acceptable or even intelligible to large numbers of the electorate', and Selwyn Lloyd's Wirral association deplored 'the intellectual way in which the present policy of the Conservative Party is being presented to the Nation'. Central Council passed a motion proposed by Ian Harvey and Edward Heath, calling for a policy statement, 'in simple, clear-cut terms'. By then though, with the Parliament nearly four years old, the Party leaders were prepared to accede to the demands anyway. Butler, having loyally backed Churchill's instruction not to publish policy in detail, now found a Conservative Research Department draft on unemployment policy referred back to be redrafted 'in more precise terms' and 'giving where possible concrete instances'. He was understandably irritated by this rapid reversal of front. At shadow cabinet on 1 April 1949, the CRD was unleashed on a full, detailed policy exercise and given just seven weeks in which to produce what was later to be called, in the jargon of Old Queen Street, a 'white fish document', since it would cover each and every policy area, including the future of the fishing fleet; it could not be done in the time, taking almost four months. Eden chaired the committee that guided the work, assisted by Butler, Macmillan, Maxwell Fyfe, Salisbury (as Cranborne became in 1947), and Woolton. There was thus official endorsement for policy-making, and Churchill would take an active part in the drafting and contribute a foreword of his own. Quintin Hogg was brought in at Woolton's suggestion to draft the document, in the hope of giving it both style and the appearance of a single authorship; he was soon distressed when he learned what had been done to his prose in the committee manglings of the subsequent drafts.[23]

This exercise, precisely because it was comprehensive, forced the Party to fill in the gaps in its thinking; Hogg told Butler for example that because there was no economic policy he had invented one; the Party's rhetorical commitment to freedom entered the document almost at proof stage. There was also re-ordering of priorities and bringing up to date of promises; a pledge not to make cuts in the social services was deleted because by 1949 there was concern about the mounting cost of the National Health Service in particular, and doubt whether such a pledge could be honoured without disastrous consequences for taxation (which the Party was anyway committed to reduce). There was also some trade-off between different strands of Conservative thinking as the drafts progressed; Oliver Poole found one draft to be too feeble in its rejection of Labour's collectivist policies and its promotion of individualism, while Macmillan found the same draft to be 'too Manchester School'. By late June though, a consensus had emerged and when the document was approved by the shadow cabinet, it had begun to attract considerable praise; Henry Brooke, who 'knew so well the difficulties (and the tedium!) of producing such a document', concluded that 'there is more substance in this policy document than in any other I can remember', while at Central Office Mark Chapman-Walker regarded it as 'an excellent document . . . If I can't sell it, I will eat my hat.' So far the drafts had had no title; Woolton suggested 'This is what the Conservatives will do', which is exactly what the document intended to show, and Chapman-Walker 'The Right Way Forward'. The eventual decision was for *The Right Road for Britain*, first of a line of policy statements with traffic titles chosen to imply forward momentum, and apparently the first official publication to pun on the word 'right' in this way.[24]

*The Right Road for Britain* was launched with several speeches to large audiences, Churchill at Wolverhampton, Macmillan at Saffron Walden and Eden on the BBC. Over the next three months, more than two million copies of the full and popular editions were sold, and at the Party Conference in London in October it was approved with only eight votes against, as insignificant a show of opposition as that attracted by the *Industrial Charter*. Armed with this battery of detailed proposals, Butler used his Conference speech to issue a clear challenge to a divided Labour Party to fight the coming Election on future policy; only the turnaround since 1945 made this possible.

[23] Butler, *Art of the Possible*, 149; Hoffman, *Conservative Party*, 186–7; Lord Moran, *Winston Churchill, The Struggle for Survival, 1940–1965* (Sphere edn, 1966), 354; NUEC, 8 Apr., 10 June and 11 Nov. 1948; Central Office, Chairman's file, 'Correspondence with R.A. Butler, 1940–1958', CCO 20/1/1, CPA; Eastern Area Council, 4 Oct. 1947; Goodhart, *The 1922*, 148; Macmillan, *Tides of Fortune*, 311; Gilbert, *Never Despair*, 476; Wirral CA minutes, 21 Apr. 1949; Central Council minutes, 18 Mar 1949, NUA 2/1. CPA; Ramsden, *Conservative Party Policy*, 133–40; Patrick Cosgrave, *R.A. Butler, An English Life* (1981), 95.
[24] Ramsden, *Conservative Party Policy*, 138–9.

When the Election was called only four months later, the Party manifesto was based almost entirely on the 1949 document, stressing continuity in the title, *This is the Road*. There was though some difficulty occasioned by Churchill's insistence on choosing the words, now that it was to be a statement on which a mandate might be claimed. Butler recalled that 'a real difficulty about finishing the Manifesto arose from [Churchill's] determination to write the English of it himself', though in most cases these interventions were entirely positive: 'incentive' and 'stimulus' were words given greater prominence, indicating the tone of Churchill's coming campaign, but reflecting too the real content of the document. 'It is our intention to initiate consultations with the Unions' became 'We shall consult with the Unions', reflecting the Leader's determination to achieve conciseness in the prose.[25]

When the Guildford Chairman commended to his association the *Industrial Charter*, 'which all recognised as a most important document', he added that 'it was essential that Conservatives should learn the policy outlined in the *Charter*, so that they might be able to explain it at all times'. The next step was indeed to sell the policy to the public, a very different matter. In July 1948, the South Eastern Area were complaining that too little was being made of the *Industrial Charter*, something that Butler was regularly saying too. The Central Office response was to point out that once you had published a document – and got excellent coverage for it in the press – it was no longer news in subsequent months. Conservatives had to discover the hard truth that all oppositions learn, that only governments easily make news, and that oppositions have a struggle to maintain any momentum in publicity. They thought this to be particularly difficult in the late 1940s, partly because the threatening international and financial situation focused attention on government actions rather than opposition words, and partly because in 1948 there were 1,104 public relations and press officers in government departments, compared to the 207 of 1938 (and there was also the new Central Office of Information, partial inheritor of the wartime role of the Ministry of Information). The Party could rail against all this as a further 'waste' of public money, but they could not prevent it from having an effect on the reporting of British politics. Apart from the CRD's attempts to influence opinion-formers, the publication of the Party's own documents was the only response, and with the money raised by Woolton, these could at least be attractively priced: a weekly newsletter cost 8/6d a year, a full service of the magazine *Onlooker* and all Party pamphlets cost 7/6d, and the substantial briefing *Notes on Current Politics* only 10/6d; a comprehensive package offered all of these for a guinea a year. But in policy content, these could only reflect the core documents that the Party published, and in 1948 this presented difficulties. The 'impressionist' texts were valuable ammunition and education for the Party workers, and might well affect educated opinion too, but because of their deliberately imprecise wording they could not sustain the momentum of a publicity drive over years. This was the source of the running battle between the CRD and Central Office, reinforced by rivalry between Butler and Woolton. Butler blamed Woolton for doing insufficient to publicise agreed policies, while Woolton complained that Butler did not give him anything on which publicity could really be mounted. A re-structuring of policy and publicity organisations in Autumn 1949 tidied up difficult lines of demarcation, but was also a partial victory for Woolton over Butler. Butler retained the chair of the new Advisory Committee on Policy, but it was now a body with representatives directly nominated by the National Union and the 1922 Committee rather than chosen by the Chairman, and only five former ACPPE members attended its first meeting, out of thirteen present. Political education was hived off to a separate committee, so that Butler lost direct influence over the CPC, though since the CPC came under the wing of Oliver Poole there would be no likely conflict. Things had come to a head after the South Hammersmith by-election, discussed in the next chapter. Butler now circulated a memorandum highly critical of Central Office, which prompted support for Butler from Eden, and a truce was then worked out. By then in any case the chief cause of the friction was being removed by the transition to detailed policy-making. With *The Right Road*, a suitable document had been produced; Central Office were able to keep the momentum of publicity going over the few months until the General Election, while the CRD could bask in the general approbation of its work. It also sold a lot of copies: the Burton upon Trent Conservatives initially bought 5,000 copies to send to all new voters on the electoral register's B List, but subsequently delivered a copy to almost all homes in the constituency before the 1950 Election; Nelson and Colne passed a resolution welcoming the document and ordered 25,000 copies for local delivery, with a localised back page to highlight parts of the document that were specially relevant in the constituency. Many other associations must have adopted equally ambitious plans, to explain the two million copies sold.[26]

## Collectivism versus individualism

It was suggested by Nigel Harris that the policy work done after the *Industrial Charter* marked a move away from collectivist partnership, and towards 'neo-liberal' individualism, that the language of liberty that characterised Party rhetoric in 1949–51 was in conflict with what the *Industrial Charter* was about, but there are several problems with this view. In the first place, the individualist rhetoric that Churchill had espoused in 1945 certainly accorded

26 Guildford CA minutes, 26 Sept. 1947; NUEC, 8 July 1948; *NCP*, 23 Sept. 1946; Howard, *RAB*, 159, 161, 163; Burton on Trent CA minutes, 13 Sept. 1949; Nelson and Colne CA minutes, 8 Aug. 1949.

with what the Party then wanted, even if it failed to produce an echo from the wider public, and this did not cease after the 1945 defeat. Experience of a majority Labour Government merely increased the demand. In November 1945 for example, Conservative MPs pointed out that two-thirds of the 690 separate wartime controls on private rights were still in force. They were extremely critical of the wholesale renewal of these wartime restrictions for a further five years, and of the executive authority that the new legislation gave to ministers. Eden described them as 'powers not enjoyed since Charles the First' and, from the backbenches, Sir William Darling observed that 'I have lived as a free citizen and I have, as a soldier, been prompted to fight for this land of liberty. Yet, at the conclusion, I have no hopes that the bonds of serfdom will be lifted from me. Five years is the sentence that will be laid upon me.' Such extravagant claims, the word 'serfdom' again indicating Hayek's influence among even those who had most probably not read his book, articulated an important strand of opinion in the country in the post-war years, and an issue on which the Party was at one. While receiving regular constituency resolutions calling for the policy review that led to the *Industrial Charter*, the National Union was simultaneously receiving resolutions calling for the ending of controls and the return of individual liberties. And the same ambivalence went on throughout. Eden's Conference speech at Brighton, on the very day on which the *Industrial Charter* was approved, stressed the Party's attachment to individual liberty as the fundamental divide between Conservatives and Labour. Alongside the language of collectivist partnership that suffused the *Industrial Charter*, the Party's spokesmen continued to stress liberty and individualism, and the first page of the *Charter* itself argued that 'our abiding objective is to free industry from unnecessary controls and restrictions'. The vehemence with which this rhetoric of liberty was advanced did become less restrained as the opposition period wore on. This reflected both an increasing impatience with the Government and a wider change in national attitudes of which the Conservatives were only a part. By 1949–50, there were more widespread demands for restored freedoms and lower taxes from non-political and semi-political groups right across Britain, and Labour ministers also saw the need to respond, first with a relaxation of physical planning and later with a very public 'bonfire of controls'.[27]

Alongside this domestic shift in the debate, a similar change came in from the outside. An increasing fear of Communism swept the country in 1948, prompted by the subversion of democracy in Czechoslovakia and by the Berlin crisis; the National Union was in 1948 considering a claim that there might be as many as forty secret Communists in the Commons, and Woolton appointed an expert to the Central Office staff to collate the evidence. It was characteristic

27  Nigel Harris, *Competition and the Corporate Society: British Conservatives, The State and Industry, 1945–1964* (1972), 145; *NCP*, Nov. 1945; J.E.D. Hall, *Labour's First Year* (Harmondsworth, 1947), 35; NUEC, 17 Oct. 1946; Central Office file, 'Conference 1950', CCO 4/4/38, CPA; Eden, *Days for Decision*, 120; Clarke, *Conservatism*, 49.

of such scares that they mixed up the real with the surreal: a South Shields Tory wrote in to complain that Blackwell's bookshop in Oxford was subverting the population by packing parcels of books for the post in Communist tracts, and Sir Basil Blackwell himself had to confirm that they were so short of paper that they used anything they could find as packaging; but if such correspondents were to be believed, the Communist Party were rampant in places like Buckinghamshire and Hendon; by 1950 the Central Office list of Communist front organisations included forty-seven bodies, including the National Council for Civil Liberties. Churchill argued that the Tories were ready to strengthen the Government's resolve against 'their extreme Leftists and "cryptos"', because these are matters of life and death of the same order and character as those which developed before the last war'. At the end of 1948, Tory MPs had a field day when Cripps inadvisedly told the Commons that 'if we cannot get nationalisation of steel by legal means, we must resort to violent methods'. Chips Channon reported that 'this ill-timed threat of revolution threw the House into an uproar . . . we cat-called, and redoubled our interjections when he mentioned the Communists and the Communist peril'. Conservatives were outraged by Labour claims, by Morgan Phillips and again by Cripps, that Labour represented the last chance for democracy in Britain, and that Labour's rejection would inevitably lead to totalitarianism. A less–totalitarian–than–thou auction ensued. When Bevan and Shinwell made extravagant claims at Labour's 1949 Conference, threatening that civil war would probably break out if the Conservatives regained office, Churchill called on Attlee to denounce all 'loose talk of revolution and violence' and to disown 'this assault upon democratic government'; he also noted wryly that the *Daily Herald* had excluded these inflammatory remarks from its extensive reports of Labour's Conference, no doubt because they were thought to be harmful to Labour. When he introduced *The Right Road for Britain* on the BBC, Eden linked all these themes together:

> Communism today suppresses all freedom of worship and every other freedom wherever it can seize power. Communism is ruthless in its methods and world-wide in its activities. We in Britain have a special opportunity to guide and keep the world in the true path of freedom . . . The Socialist Party is far too much given to control for the love of control. So in restricting liberty in small matters they are playing into the hands of those who would suppress liberty in the greater things of life.

This shift towards 'freedom' and away from 'controls' in the core political debate was certainly most welcome to the Conservatives, but they had not created that change on their own. Macmillan indeed noted that, while Labour's own increasingly anti-Communist position was good for the national interest, it was probably 'politically unfavourable' to the Conservatives.[28]

---

[28] *NCP*, 8 Mar. 1948; NUEC, 8 July 1948; Gilbert, *Never Despair*, 403; Robert Rhodes James (ed.), *Chips, The Diaries of Sir Henry Channon* (1967), 431; Eden, *Days for Decision*, 126; Alistair Horne, *Macmillan, 1894–1956* (1988), 300.

The tone of Conservative policy argument did shift then, but not much of the content changed with it, not least because both collectivist and individualist strands of thought had been present throughout; J.D. Hoffman fairly concluded that:

> The hot white light that free enterprise burned was present in the *Industrial Charter*, but it was blurred by a reddish filter – a filter which balanced support for free enterprise with the determination to apply strong central guidance over the operation of the economy. In *The Right Road* the white light burned as before, but, to extend the analogy, the reddish filter was replaced with one of a fainter hue.

Such filters had everything to do with presentation – inside the Party as well as to a larger public audience – and little to do with the details of prospective action. Conservatives therefore continued to stress freedom even while adopting the *Industrial Charter*, but found that the libertarian half of the package received a better hearing as fashion changed. Nevertheless, *The Right Road for Britain* has been described by Peter Hennessy as a document of 'long–term significance' since it 'endorsed explicitly the Attleean consensus, that famed "post-war consensus" . . . The Keynesian and Beveridgite essentials would be intact, whatever the outcome' of the next election. David Butler's verdict is only a little more guarded: 'although the document promised to stop, and if possible, reverse the process of nationalisation and to end socialist waste and bureaucracy, it did completely accept the newly enacted welfare state legislation and promised not to end full employment.' These were certainly the impressions that the Party sought to give, and Churchill was always careful not just to accept Labour's welfare reforms but to claim responsibility for them. These welfare provisions 'were actually planned . . . by the National Coalition government of which I was the head and which rested on an overall Conservative majority in the House of 150'. But Government is about administration as well as legislation, and the Conservative commitment to the 'Attleean settlement' was always hedged around with provisos of detail that indicated a different set of priorities from those of Attlee's ministers. In the social policy field, as Harriet Jones has shown, Conservatives always intended to secure a more selective distribution of benefits, partly to reduce the cost to the Exchequer, but partly also because many of them were not ideologically convinced of the desirability of free services to all, irrespective of need. Duties were stressed as much as rights, and the whole policy stopped a long way short of egalitarianism except, in Macleod's phrase, in the belief 'that men had an equal chance to make themselves unequal'. Even an interventionist like Butler was in 1948 talking of the need to avoid 'levelling down' through universal contributions and universal benefits, rather than 'rewarding hard work', for failure to do this would lead to 'a disastrous weakening of the moral fibre of the country'. The increasing budgetary difficulties of 1949–51, when the health estimates seemed to be out of control and the international situation increased the spending on armaments, only strengthened this pre-existing view. When challenged in the House about the cost of introducing equal pay for women, promised in *The Right Road*, Churchill virtually repudiated this policy aim as a pledge on financial grounds: 'I and my colleagues have made it absolutely clear that in present developments we shall not go an inch further than the financial resources of the country warrant and, in view of all that has occurred and is occurring, we shall hold ourselves entirely free to take a new view of the situation should we be granted the opportunity [of office].' In December 1949, Bracken jubilantly reported to Beaverbrook that 'Churchill in a very firm and polite way has washed away all the Butler Charters and now rightly declares that devaluation has created a situation that does not allow us to commit ourselves to any policies that involve a large expenditure of public money'. Bracken was hearing what he wanted to hear; Churchill could not 'wash away the Butler Charters' in that way, since they had never contained spending pledges anyway, and he had no intention of reversing the main thrust of the policy that they embodied, only of keeping options open on timing and priorities. But this was precisely the way in which the Conservatives believed that they could govern differently from Labour.[29]

The Party's pledge broadly to maintain the Keynesian and Beveridgite 'Attleean settlement' did not then conflict with a determination to reduce controls, but it did sit uneasily alongside the Conservative pledge to cut taxes; behind the scenes, Macleod was warning that NHS expenditure would continue to rise, and that the Party should take account of the fact. Here the circle was squared by the conviction that the elimination of waste (itself in part linked with the winding down of controls and of the machinery required to enforce them) would provide a breathing space, Conservatives 'honestly believing', as Hoffman put it, that increased production and careful management of resources would solve the problem. This was a continuous Conservative cry. Only one year after the War, Assheton had claimed that 'the Government is taking a vast part of the people's income and a lot of it is being wasted'. In 1949, Churchill told the Party Conference, that Labour had embarked on 'a Rake's progress of unbridled expenditure'. In Summer 1951, a mass survey of the South Battersea constituency, a critical marginal gained later in the year, found many residents complaining about the cost of living and asking what the Conservatives would do about it; 'the canvassers answered this question by saying a lot can be achieved by cutting Government expenditure to a minimum but this can only be done when the Conservatives have access to the national records'. Telling comparisons were made with 1938; taxes and National Insurance as a share of National Income had risen from 22 per cent to 35 per cent and savings from 6 per cent to 11 per cent

[29] Hoffman, *Conservative Party*, 192, 220; Peter Hennessy, *Never Again, Britain 1945–1951* (1992), 388; D.E. Butler, *British General Elections since 1945* (Oxford, 1989), 10; Paul Addison, 'Churchill and Social Reform' in *Churchill*, eds. Robert Blake and W.R. Louis (Oxford, 1993), 74; Jones, 'Conservative Party' thesis, 16, 41, 331; Addison, *Churchill*, 402; Cockett, *My Dear Max*, 108.

(largely because there was little available to buy), so that the public's own share of total spending had fallen by about a third. The right were particularly keen on this line of argument – Bracken reminded the Commons in 1946 that 'we were sent here to keep the public purse. We were not sent here to turn it into a sieve.' But young reformers like Selwyn Lloyd, regarded as well to the left of the Party, were equally hawkish on the question of public finance and 'waste'. Conservatives were contemptuous of the much-trumpeted Labour claim of 1945 that 'a nation can afford anything it really wants, if it wants it sufficiently'. They were therefore delighted when, in his 1949 Budget, Cripps read a lesson to his own backbenchers on public economy. Oliver Stanley used a broadcast to argue that Cripps' case was

> pretty obvious, but as put by the Chancellor it was more than a re-statement of a simple truth – it is the end of an era, an era of socialist policy and socialist promises that has been going on for twenty years . . . It . . . did much to win for the Socialists the general election of 1945 . . . And now it's over, shattered relentlessly and irrevocably in one afternoon. Never again can the easy doctrine be preached that the elector can have his cake and eat it.

Churchill picked up on the same theme in commenting on the devaluation of the pound later in the year: 'The myth that a completely artificial world can be maintained by controls has been finally exploded.' The battle in the Labour Cabinet in 1951, leading to the breaching of the principle of a completely free NHS and to the resignation of Bevan and Wilson, was a further bonus to the Conservatives; Labour had again been forced to move on to the Conservatives' ground, and could no longer easily argue that selectivity in social policy was in all cases bad. During that crisis, a brief for backbenchers had warned that they should make their support for Labour's proposals 'reluctant and not enthusiastic', but that the Bill should not be obstructed, since 'it was important that [NHS charges] . . . should be put on the Statute Book by the Socialists'.[30]

## Reactive policies: food and housing

This whole debate indicates how far the overall balance of Party policy was shaped not simply by Conservative committees, soberly considering the philosophical basis of a new Tamworth Manifesto, but also in the electoral marketplace and in response to a changing atmosphere, the shape of which could not be controlled or determined by Conservatives. In the two fields of food and housing, Conservative policy was clearly more influenced by the pull

---

[30] Ramsden, *Conservative Party Policy*, 125; Hoffman, *Conservative Party*, 194; Lindsay and Harrington, *Conservative Party*, 156; *NCP*, 27 Apr. 1946, 25 Apr. and 24 Oct. 1949; Central Office file, constituency correspondence, South Battersea, CCO 1/8/2, CPA; Jones, 'Conservative Party' thesis, 160–72; Hall, *Labour's First Year*, 139; D.R. Thorpe, *Selwyn Lloyd* (1989), 108.

of public demand than by the push of Party ideas. Ina Zweiniger-Bargielowska has written of the 1946 debates on bread rationing as 'an initial drawing of battle lines between the Conservatives and Labour on the increasingly important issue of consumption'. Food and housing were both issues in which the Tories re-emerged as the champion of the consumer by 1950. The lowering of rations after the fighting ended came as a shock to most in the country, and provided some targets that any opposition would have relished; burdens acceptable in a war of survival rapidly became irksome in peacetime. In February 1946, Churchill, parodying Labour's 1945 manifesto title, urged Attlee to 'face the present' and do something about food supplies, and Butler showed that the issue could also be used as a lever against Labour's trades union legislation, pointing out that housewives had enough to put up with without strengthening the legal powers of the dockers to hold up food cargoes. In the Summer, the introduction of bread rationing, 'which falls most heavily on the poor', was another easy target; Churchill argued that this was 'using a steamhammer to crack a nut', and claimed that 'the government had made no case which could justify . . . an ill thought out scheme involving a great measure of hardship on the people'. The size of Britain's ration was compared unfavourably with the better position even in devastated countries like France and Belgium.[31]

By Summer 1947, a lengthy summary of 'Two Years of Socialist Government', published by Central Office, highlighted food as one of Labour's greatest failures. By then the British Housewives' League had come into existence to pressurise the Government, with Conservative encouragement perhaps but as an independent body. Tory publications gleefully reported 'socialist abuse of housewives': following demonstrations, Shinwell had derided 'infantile processions' and Shawcross had referred to the League as 'either politically ignorant or politically dishonest'. Bracken noted cynically that 'angry housewives are the most formidable enemy of the socialists so we must do everything in our power to increase their fury', and Headlam found in 1947 that 'I am always getting postcards now from ladies demanding that Strachey and Shinwell should be sacked. There is a body called the League of Housewives (or some such name) which runs all of this, but whether it is or is not a political force I have no idea. It is certainly an active body.' There was a natural convergence of interests between the Party and the League, especially when the chairmanship of the League was taken by Dorothy Crisp, a right-wing Tory journalist who had written a book on Conservative policy in collaboration with Oliver Stanley before the War, but even before this Conservative MPs had helped to highlight the housewives' petitions in the Commons. At the League's 1947 Albert Hall rally the convergence became clear; David Maxwell Fyfe was the main speaker, commiserating with the

---

[31] Ina Zweiniger-Bargielowska, 'Bread Rationing in Britain', in *Twentieth Century British History*, vol. 4, no. 1 (1993), 80, 85; *NCP*, 25 Feb. 1946.

housewives for having 'shivered with Shinwell and starved with Strachey', and outside the hall there were demonstration banners on which the Communist Party claimed 'Never mind the label on the packet – the stuff inside is a Tory racket'. The League was also associated with another Tory ally, for in 1947 it admitted to receiving funds from the Road Haulage Association. The League's organiser in Northamptonshire reported to Woolton that 'although we are strictly non-political and non-sectarian the BHL is doing a grand work for the "right cause"!' Nevertheless, there was always a gap between the Party and the League; the Women's department at Central Office was scathing about the League's amateurism (especially when finding that they could not even run a decent bazaar), and Woolton kept his distance too, stating publicly in June 1947 that he had never even met the League's organisers and was in no way responsible for its activities; he told a Scottish MP in 1948 that 'it has been the policy of this Office to dissociate itself from this organisation'. By then, there had been tricky discussions with Crisp, who in December 1947 asked for a meeting with Woolton; at first he refused, saying that he could not now meet her after saying that they were not in touch, but eventually agreed when she had said that she did not want to discuss the League's business; when she arrived this turned out to be untrue, for she asked for support from Party funds, offering that if the League were later to collapse she would tell all the members to join the Conservative Party. Highly embarrassed, Woolton replied that the Party could not afford to subsidise another women's organisation when they already had the largest one in the country, that they would not provide money for a magazine either, and that if the League were indeed to collapse, 'we will naturally welcome recruits from it', but so no doubt would the other parties. During 1948, the League moved far to the right, branding Conservative as well as Labour policy as 'totalitarian' for refusing to allow individuals to contract out from the NHS, and the convergence of views disappeared, except with the Tory right; Sir Waldron Smithers now took to attending League meetings and saying that all parties were equally bad.[32]

However, with the League's assistance up to 1947, the food issue could be used as a general weapon against Labour's interventionist methods; Walter Elliot led the attack on the bulk purchase schemes that the Government claimed would solve the supply crisis; these could be portrayed as not giving consumers what they wanted since they prevented the markets from working freely, but their failure to deliver the goods was the basis for the really damning indictment; in 1949, Elliot was complaining that 'the individual is fortunate if he gets a piece of meat as big as a post-card for a whole week'. Meat

[32] *NCP*, 15 July, 14 Sept. 1947; P. Philips, 'The New Look', in *The Age of Austerity, 1945–1951*, eds Michael Sissons and Philip French (Harmondsworth, 1964), 137–8; *CAJ*, Aug. 1947; Central Council report for 1947, NUA 2/2/13, CPA; Cockett, *My Dear Max*, 108; Headlam diary, 7 Mar. 1947; Paul Addison, *Now the War is Over* (1985), 38–44; Zweiniger-Bargielowska, 'Bread rationing', 82; William Crofts, *Coercion or Persuasion? Propaganda in Britain after 1945* (1989), 104, 106; Central Office file, 'British Housewives League', CCO 3/1/12, CPA.

came to acquire a special significance in this argument, and when Woolton, a former Food Minister, demanded 'more red meat', it was a powerful call, encapsulating the appeal to the consumer over five years. In 1947, the secretary of the Labour Party felt that council seats had been lost in what 'could be called a food and basic petrol election'; in 1951, Channon reported the lobbies of the House as containing 'hundreds of housewives haranguing, and almost attacking, Labour MPs about meat. It was like the French Revolution – only they were on our side.' This certainly all provided an opportunity to put Labour on to the defensive. When he sought an explanation of the defeat of many Labour MPs in 1950, Hugh Gaitskell believed that Labour's lost supporters included many people who 'had at any rate suffered considerable economic disadvantages by our actions'.[33]

Food shortages also provided an opportunity to deal with 'the lie about Tory misrule' in the 1930s: in November 1947, after a detailed food-by-food comparison of pre-war and post-war consumption patterns, it was pointed out, presumably on Macmillan's calculation, that even the unemployed in Stockton in 1937 had averaged a food consumption of 2,910 calories, compared to the national average of 2,700 for all workers in 1947; it is only fair to add that Tory claims of actual malnutrition were not supported by medical opinion. The statistics were effective enough on their own: a briefing note of September 1949 drew attention to the fact that meat imports were still only at two-thirds of the 1938 level, a useful point for a speech. In 1949, three-quarters of the population believed that their diet was worse than before the War, a consequence both of the facts (in some cases) and of the constant trumpeting of the issue both by the BHL and by the Conservatives. In 1947 there was a big Conservative exhibition in London, 'Trust the People', which showed with elaborate charts and diagrams just how well-off most people had been in the 1930s compared to the present, and purporting to show too that systematic falsehoods about the Slump had been put about. So effective was it thought to be that there were calls for it to be toured round the other big cities when its London showing came to an end. Not everyone was as impressed with its veracity; Rab Butler wanted it clearly understood that Central Office and not the CRD was responsible for any claims the exhibition made, and Quintin Hogg feared that 'everybody to do with the Exhibition will go to gaol for libel'. Significantly, the defence of Thirties Conservatism rested entirely on domestic policy; a substantial Party leaflet about the inter-war years tried hard to defend the means test of the 1930s, but made no mention at all of foreign policy. In 1947–48 on the other hand, the self-justifying first volume of Churchill's *War Memoirs* appeared, setting the seal on his denunciation of the appeasers, and Macmillan of all firms re-published in the same year

---

[33] Coote, *Walter Elliot*, 255; Ina Zweiniger-Bargielowska, 'Rationing, Austerity and the Conservative Party Recovery after 1945', in the *Historical Journal*, vol. 37, no. 1 (1994), 169, 184; Rhodes James, *Chips*, 453; P.M. Williams (ed.), *The Diary of Hugh Gaitskell, 1945–56* (1983), 167.

A.L. Rowse's viciously polemical essay, 'Reflections on Lord Baldwin', even taking space in the Party's Conference handbook to advertise its availability. Pre-war foreign policy remained a difficult issue.[34]

Housing also allowed both a celebration of pre-war Conservatism and a denunciation of Labour failures; the CRD circulated to candidates in 1950 figures for annual house completions under every Government since 1900; only the 1929–31 Labour Government could approach the record of Salisbury and Balfour before 1905 or of Baldwin between the wars. The airy promises given by Labour spokesmen in the 1945 campaign, when polls had shown housing to be the electorate's most pressing concern, came home to roost by 1947: Cripps, for example, had promised that 'if the Labour Party is returned, the housing situation would be clarified in a fortnight'. Such phrases were constantly on the lips of Tory spokesmen, as was the remark of Arthur Greenwood, the Labour Leader of the Opposition in 1944, to the effect that the Churchill Government's housing programme was 'chickenfeed'. After two years in office, Labour's record of housing completions was barely half of what that 'chickenfeed' programme had planned for the same period, and the same comparisons were published at intervals throughout the Parliament; it was, of course, easy to compare what the Government had *planned* in 1944 with what Labour had *achieved*, but Labour had only itself to blame for its over-optimism in 1944–45. In Spring 1948, this whole cycle began again, with Bevan confidently proclaiming that 'by the next general election we will have broken the back of the housing problem', and that 'before the next general election every family in Britain will have a separate house'. Again Conservatives attacked the Government without inhibition, particularly enjoying a policy failure by Bevan, and again they linked the policy failure with Labour's interventionist approach. Their claim was that private builders would produce more houses if only licensing controls were removed. Elliot taunted Bevan with this in January 1949: 'it is now quite a time since Mr. Bevan said that by the next general election there will be no housing problem . . . Until the Minister can produce an adequate supply of houses in this country, the problem will continue. The only remedy is an adequate supply of houses. This intensification of control will do no more than intensify the shortage.' This was more than pragmatism, for it fitted in with the Conservatives' core philosophy and, in their view at least, marked them off from Labour in a political debate that was certainly *not* consensual; they believed that rationing and controls eroded liberty and were inefficient at the same time; the Sheffield Conservative women were upset to find in 1947 that the Board of Trade and the Food Office were both interfering in their affairs by heavy-handedly insisting that only non-rationed goods could be sold at their annual bring and buy sale. Churchill accepted that 'while

---

[34] *NCP*, 10 Nov. 1947 and 26 Sept. 1949; Central Office, Chairman's file, 'Correspondence with R.A. Butler, 1940–1958', CCO 20/1/1, CPA.

shortages persist some controls are inevitable, but . . . wartime controls in time of peace [are] a definite evil in themselves'. This could occasionally cause embarrassment, as when the Conservatives of South Derbyshire rejected the Maxwell Fyfe reforms of 1948 as being a prime example of the centralisation and control that the Party was supposed to be against, and when Birmingham Unionists clashed with their own councillors over their support for municipal trading. But housing offered no such threat, and sensing that housing was a good issue to fight on, Conservative candidates in 1950 gave great prominence to it in their election addresses, and believed that they had won many votes by highlighting the issue; a detailed study of the Election in Greenwich found that housing was also the topic most often raised by the public in questions at public meetings. Encouraging demands for more housing more quickly was one thing, but finding a policy to deliver the goods was quite another. Throughout the opposition period, housing was another area where the free marketeers in the Party clashed with the more cautious interventionists, who were entrenched in the CRD. Before 1950, only the liberal wing of the Party was fully committed to an aggressive building policy that would rely mainly on private enterprise through the loosening of controls.[35]

This is the background to the famous housing debate at the 1950 Conference, when what seemed to be a 'spontaneous' rebellion against the platform was in fact a carefully-prepared ambush that followed years of preparation. The agenda included eighteen motions on housing, most of them calling for a big push to increase completions, and the Clapham motion that was selected for debate was couched in strong language; another motion from East Woolwich called for a specific target of 300,000 houses a year, and as the debate went on this approach was clearly the one that commended itself; speakers like Harmar Nicholls were cheered when they demanded that an even higher number be the Party's pledge. Woolton asked Butler if such an ambitious pledge could be carried out, and after consulting David Clarke for technical advice, Butler replied that it could be, but that it still might not be wise to give the pledge, since such a large programme could well absorb resources needed for industry and other investment; earlier in the year the Advisory Committee on Policy had specifically decided against putting forward a target figure. Swept along though by the rising tide of emotion in the hall, and fearing that an even higher figure might emerge if the auction went on, Woolton stepped forward, told the Conference 'this is magnificent!', and accepted on behalf of the platform an amendment to include a target of 300,000 houses in the resolution – which was then passed by acclamation. After the debate, the Party's leaders discussed

[35] *NCP*, Jan. 1947, 10 Nov. 1947, 16 June 1948, 11 Apr. 1949; Sheffield Central Women's Advisory Committee, 14 Apr. 1947; Central Office constituency file, Derbys. S, CCO 1/7/216; Birmingham UA minutes, 30 Jan. 1948; M. Benney, A.P. Gray and R.H. Pear, *How People Vote, A Study of Electoral Behaviour in Greenwich* (1956), 84; Zweiniger-Bargielowska, 'Rationing, Austerity . . .', 287; H.G. Nicholas, *The British General Election of 1950* (1951), 219; Jones, 'Conservative Party' thesis, 139.

the new situation and some tried unavailingly to get Churchill to withdraw from the pledge when he spoke at the end of the week; he described the figure as a target rather than a minimum, and included it in his general proviso of the need to keep policy within available resources, but the pledge remained and was given even greater prominence: 'I accept it as our first priority in time of peace'. The CRD now set about a detailed examination of the issue and the devising of an action plan that a minister could take with him into office. Macmillan, who was to take the chief responsibility for carrying out this policy, was not present for the debate, had taken no part in agreeing to the pledge, and was sceptical about its practicality. Ernest Marples though, who was to be Macmillan's junior minister, had no doubts; he told the 1922 Committee shortly after the Conference that 'within five years this could be achieved at a reasonable price'. He demanded that the Party initiate a housing debate in the Commons precisely to get Bevan to say that 300,000 would be unachievable, and he explained just how it *would* be achieved, largely by re-creating the circumstances in the industry that had achieved similar results before 1939; the minutes record that 'his views were well received by the meeting'. The debate duly took place, Labour obliged by ridiculing the Conservative housing promise as wildly impractical, and Churchill wound up the Tory case in full flow: 'we shall thrust towards it with all our life, strength and wit, but once the figure gleams upon the horizon – "forward again" must be the policy and the order'. The stakes in this policy field were now very high indeed. When Labour left office in October 1951, the outgoing minister, Hugh Dalton, wrote confidently that Macmillan 'won't be able to build any more, if as many, as I'.[36]

As well as responding to the public's agenda of priorities, Conservative MPs also had to make policy by their reaction to the Labour's Government's tidal wave of legislation. Such reactive policy decisions were also fed into *The Right Road for Britain* and the manifestoes of 1950 and 1951, but they are best analysed in the following chapter as part of the tactics and strategy adopted to win back power. This will not materially alter the conclusion that emerges here, that between 1946 and 1950, the Party repaired the serious damage to its policy image that had cost it so dear in 1945, and that it approached the 1950 and 1951 General Elections with a fully-worked out and *official* body of detailed proposals that Conservatives could take with them into office. The thrust of that policy included the acceptance of large parts of the Attlee Government's programme of social and welfare reforms, and in the economic sphere a clear acquiescence in principle to the extension since 1940 of the public sector and of the state's role in the management of the economy.

[36] Jones, 'Conservative Party' thesis, 143; Central Council report for 1950, NUA 2/2/16; Howard, *RAB*, 172; Nigel Fisher, *Iain Macleod* (1973), 77; Ramsden, *Conservative Party Policy*, 157–9; Henry Pelling, *Winston Churchill* (1974), 587; Macmillan, *Tides of Fortune*, 353; Goodhart, *The 1922*, 151–2; Gilbert, *Never Despair*, 566; Ben Pimlott (ed.), *The Political Diaries of Hugh Dalton, 1918–1940 and 1945–1960* (1986), 565.

Parallel to these 'consensus' policies, the Party had consistently argued both its ability to administer the country more efficiently and therefore to lower taxation, and its determination to reduce government intervention across the board, in the interests of consumer freedom and choice – something it had been saying even in 1944–45, but with less confidence of a favourable hearing; the changed temper of the times by 1951 had placed such Conservative instincts back at the head of the public's own agenda, and Labour as well as Conservatives had had to acknowledge the fact. The 'Butskellite' consensus of the 1950s – if indeed there ever was one – was due as much to Labour moving closer to this second, Conservative political agenda, as it was to moves to the left that Conservatives made in opposition.

The Party had also demonstrated considerable continuities over its policy work, from the fumbling beginning in 1946 to the detailed preparations for a return to power in 1950–51. The core of the policy strategy had been the commitment to widen the basis of property, and the late promise of a house-building target merely completed that long-term stance. As far back as August 1946, Cranborne, one of the Party's most clear-sighted thinkers on policy strategy, had put the whole thing with remarkable lucidity in a letter to Eden:

> You have been thinking in terms of a property-owning democracy. I have been thinking in terms of a spreading of capitalism. Yours is perhaps the more tactful phrase. But we mean the same thing. Today, under an unrestricted capitalist democracy, all the power is in the hands of what it is now fashionable to call 'the small man'. He has got the power. What we have to give him is a sense of responsibility. This, as I see it, can only be done by giving him a stake in the country. He must have something that he himself knows he will lose if, as an elector, he acts irresponsibly. It should be our aim to give him this. Anyone who wants to own a house of his own should be encouraged, and where possible given assistance, to buy one. Anyone who works in industry should be encouraged where possible to become a shareholder in the firm in which his life is invested. As, under the present crushing burden of taxation, big estates are broken up, farmers should be encouraged, & if possible assisted, to buy their own farms. These are only a few examples of the practical application of the broad, general principle which should colour and inform our whole approach to domestic policy. It should be combined with the avowed intention to lower taxation and relax controls, in order to give every incentive to the people of this country, to whatever section of the community they belong, to earn and save money. All this is, of course, the very antithesis of socialism, and, I believe, would have a very good chance of capturing the imagination of an electorate exasperated by practical experience of what socialism really means.

It would be difficult to better this – penned a year before even the *Industrial Charter* debates – as a succinct description of what post-war Tory strategy was to be, and it certainly falls well short of anything deserving of the name 'consensus'.[37]

[37] Cranborne to Eden, 9 Aug. 1946, Avon MSS, 20/14/34.

The Policy Review had one further and more intangible consequence; it established in the minds of Conservatives themselves, and particularly in the minds of thinking men on the Party's moderate wing, the principle that intellectual ideas in Tory politics were respectable, a concept that was for at least a generation closely associated with Butler and his Old Queen Street staff, if not entirely to Butler's advantage or to theirs when it came to leadership contests. Iain Macleod was to be derided as 'too clever by half' by Lord Salisbury in the early 1960s, but his career came nevertheless to symbolise the alliance of modernity and ideas to which the generation younger than Salisbury aspired; Patrick Jenkin was not the only member of Margaret Thatcher's Cabinet whose framed photograph of Macleod moved with him through various ministerial offices in the 1980s; Chris Patten, who had hardly ever met R.A. Butler, had a similar framed photograph of Rab in his own ministerial offices – and even on the wall of the Governor's office in Hong Kong. For a Party whose reading habits, even among its intellectuals, still followed Disraeli's advice to read and learn from biographies, heroes could be as important an influence on their successors as anything that those heroes had actually done.[38]

---

[38]  Chris Patten, 'R.A. Butler – What We Missed', unpublished Inaugural R.A. Butler Lecture, delivered 25 May 1994.

# Chapter 5

# 'The time of reaping' – winning back power

Alongside the domestic business of geeing up the Party machine and the more public policy review, the Conservatives in opposition had to react to political questions arising from the legislation and administration of the Labour Government, and from international developments. Their reputation and their claim to office in 1950 and 1951 was to rest as much on this third leg of recovery as on the other two. With the tactics and strategy of opposition as such, went the elusive question of Party morale and self-confidence. The Party would only campaign unitedly and cohesively, as it had certainly not done in 1945, if it believed in itself and its ability to win. Much of this would depend on the course of events in parliament and on interim indications of public opinion.

## Tactics in parliament

In turn, parliamentary progress would rely heavily on the leadership. In the first year, Churchill was not successful in his new role; when he addressed backbenchers in August 1945, Channon noted that 'he seemed totally unprepared, indifferent and deaf'. When he went to America in 1946, conduct of the Opposition improved but his prolonged absence provoked hostile comment; Lord Derby complained that 'it is quite wrong of Winston to have gone abroad at such a time and for so long. I admit he wanted a holiday. Still, that he could have taken, but to be left as we are now without any controlling power in our Party is to my mind bad statesmanship.' Churchill's official biographer points out that he was in regular touch with London, but telegrams from Miami were no substitute for his presence on the front bench. He continued to be criticised as an absentee leader, and with his *War Memoirs* as his priority he was as likely to be absent when based in London as when he was abroad. (It should though be noted that Churchill was not the only one who took a close interest in his memoirs; Cranborne, Thomas, and Eden all collected documents which would place Eden's 1938 resignation in the most favourable light: Thomas sent these to Eden for Churchill's use, having 'marked especially the paragraphs showing your insistence on re-armament'; it is not therefore surprising that Eden emerged so favourably from Churchill's first volume; when the *Telegraph* serialised the book, with its lyrical reference to Eden in 1938 as 'one strong, young figure, standing up against long, dismal, drawling, tides of drift and surrender' – a devastating comment on Churchill's own Party's policy – Thomas filed a copy with his own papers.) As Paul Addison points out, 'between 1945 and 1947 Churchill took part in none of the debates over nationalisation, social insurance, or the National Health Service'. In April 1946, the Opposition had to have two separate lists of speakers for the Budget debate, so that Churchill could decide at the last minute whether to speak; a year later there was Party pressure to ensure that the first Opposition speaker after the Chancellor should be a Conservative, and not Anderson who was Churchill's usual choice. The Leader's fitful presences in parliament could be as awkward as his absences; in August 1946 he told Moran that 'yesterday, I dined out and sat talking till two o'clock, and on my way home I saw a light in the Commons and found them sitting. I listened for half an hour, and then made a very vigorous speech . . . [about] this bread business . . . A short time ago I was ready to retire and die gracefully. Now I am going to stay and have them out . . . I'll tear their bleeding entrails out of them.' He then went off on another extended holiday and, as Henry Pelling records, 'in the course of the next few months, although he was occasionally available for set-piece orations at Westminster denouncing the Government, Churchill spent much of his time visiting other countries in Western Europe, receiving honorary degrees, honorary citizenships, medals and gifts'. Lord Winterton, whose experience of the Commons was almost as long as Churchill's own, recognised how defective was this discontinuous leadership:

> The quality of Mr. Churchill's speeches was of great benefit to the Conservatives in opposition, but the leader of a party in opposition needs to have other qualities than that of the gift of oratory: he should learn to endure boredom without showing how hard the ordeal is, and he should watch and wait in the chamber itself or be at hand in his room for instant recall by the Chief Whip during dull, ordinary debates. For no one can tell when a situation may arise which he alone, with his authority, can handle satisfactorily . . . For reasons with which one can sympathise, Mr. Churchill, unlike most of his predecessors, was not a regular attendant.

Cranborne also complained continuously about Churchill's leadership, telling Thomas in March 1946 that 'I don't pretend to feel at all happy about the return of our great leader':

> Of course, in ability and prestige he stands head and shoulders above anyone else in the Party. But that in itself constitutes a certain danger. For I do not believe that, for the Conservative Party, this is a time when spectacular leadership is wanted. What we need is quiet hard work & thinking by men who are young enough to look forward and not back. Great dramatic speeches, which would have been very progressive in 1905, are no use to us at all and that, I am afraid, is what we are likely to get, so far as home policy is concerned. Nor do I feel any happier about his attitude to foreign policy . . . All we have to do is to sit back

& support [Bevin] when necessary. By ostentatiously identifying his policy with that of the Conservative Party, we increase his difficulties and make his position impossible . . . The Fulton speech has already done a great deal of harm in this way . . .

Clementine Churchill tried to mitigate the effects of her husband's olympian style by organising lunch parties at which the Leader could meet backbenchers, who might in other circumstances have talked to him casually in the lobbies. John Boyd-Carpenter enjoyed both the 'thrill of being invited to lunch by this great world figure' and 'the gastronomic joy' of such occasions in a time of austerity. More experienced backbenchers were less easily impressed, and at a similar lunch in 1948, Channon found Churchill's reception to be 'tepid, but not in the least unfriendly'.[1]

Churchill himself continued to toy with the idea of retirement, when his morale sank or when he was unwell, but he was tenacious in resisting other people's hints about his future; Eden told Thomas in December 1946 of one such attempt: 'latest developments are that James [Stuart] had an hour with W . . . & tells me he was pretty frank. Reactions (1) Great events are impending, but not immediately; he wanted to handle them, (2) He was getting a bed made to put into his room in H of C! (3) There was no hurry for me; I knew he was devoted to me etc . . . [Lord] Camrose said that W. knew what everyone thought he should do, but like a naughty child was determined not to do it. Said Clemmie had tried, as well as himself and Smuts. W. had maintained leadership of party meant power & he didn't mean to give up power.' There was at least one occasion, in July 1947, on which the shadow cabinet tried to force the issue, using the Chief Whip as a lever. Stuart recalled that

about six or eight of the chief people met at Harry Crookshank's house in Pont Street and discussed this awkward and important subject. In the absence of Anthony Eden, they came to the – for me – not very attractive conclusion that I was the one who should tell Sir Winston Churchill the bad news . . . that . . . the head men of the party thought that the time had come, perhaps owing to his age, etc etc, to make a change. I said to Churchill when I went into his room, 'I'm afraid I've got some rather difficult and awkward news to convey to you and I trust it won't annoy you because, as I've said to you before, you've done more than any for this country, and wouldn't you like to have a rest and be able to devote more time to painting?' At which he proceeded to get annoyed and said, 'Oh, you've

[1] Martin Gilbert, Never Despair, Winston S. Churchill, 1945–1965 (1988), 130, 189–90, 461; Alan Thompson, The Day Before Yesterday (1971), 86; Thomas to Eden, 10 Mar. 1947, Cilcennin MSS; The Daily Telegraph, 4 May 1948; Paul Addison, Churchill on the Home Front, 1900–1955 (1992), 390; John Ramsden, The Making of Conservative Party Policy, The Conservative Research Department since 1929 (1980), 117; Lord Moran, Winston Churchill, The Struggle for Survival, 1940–1965 (Sphere edn., 1966), 339; Henry Pelling, Winston Churchill (1974), 567; Robert Rhodes James, Anthony Eden (1986), 316; Cranborne to Thomas, 27 Mar. 1946, Cilcennin MSS; John Boyd-Carpenter, Way of Life (1980), 86; Robert Rhodes James (ed.), Chips, The Diaries of Sir Henry Channon (1967), 426.

joined those who want to get rid of me, have you?' And, I said, 'I haven't in the least, I'm not instigating any plot, but . . . I suppose there is something to be said for the fact that change will have to take place sometime and you're not quite as young as you were', or words to that effect. At which he banged the floor with his stick and got quite annoyed.

Eden had been tactfully absent from the Pont Street meeting, and Stuart was not an Eden supporter, but even so such a half-hearted approach was unlikely to have removed Churchill unless he wanted to go. At this time he had no such intention, and shortly afterwards he announced in a speech in Woodford that he intended to go on until he had 'turned out the Socialists'; the issue was thereby settled for the rest of the Parliament. Friends like Moran and Bracken tried to console themselves with the reflection that this was simply a temporary problem, that once back in office, patronage would ensure full support in the Party and Churchill's own adrenalin would flow again. When in 1949 Churchill had a stroke, the news was concealed even from colleagues, and the press told only that Churchill had 'caught a chill'. Applying his own famous dictum about Tory Leaders, when he stumbled he had to be supported and when he slept he could not be awakened; the Party could not bring itself to decide that he was no good, or to resolve that he should be 'pole-axed'.[2]

Against all this, there were many advantages to the Party that accrued from having Churchill at the helm. As the War receded into the past, the positive side of his leadership remained in the public mind, and the squabbles about domestic policy assumed a lesser significance. On the day of the 1947 royal wedding, Channon noted with surprise that 'the warmest reception was reserved for Winston, and I hear that in the Abbey when he arrived, a little late, everyone stood up, all the Kings and Queens'. This shift in his reputation was owed in part to his own assiduous cultivation of a personality cult through publications; by the end of the period of opposition in 1951, the Party Conference handbook was advertising no less than fourteen volumes of Churchilliana – four volumes (so far) of *War Memoirs*, seven volumes of wartime speeches (many of which were also available on records), and three volumes of post-war speeches too. His great post-war speeches on international affairs, for example at Fulton and Zürich in 1946 and at Strasbourg in 1949, had the effect of re-establishing him as a major international statesman, in a league higher than any other British politician. There was considerable Party advantage to be reaped from this, quite apart from the speeches' actual content. Finally, there is no doubt that the Tory rank and file came during these years to love Churchill with an adulation entirely devoid of political calculation. This may again have owed

---

[2] Thompson, *Day Before Yesterday*, 87; James Stuart, *Within the Fringe* (1967), 147; Gilbert, *Never Despair*, 341, 486; Moran, *Struggle*, 348.

something to the growing gratitude to him for his war service, but it also derived in part from the great skill with which he played his audience at mass rallies, particularly the one that concluded the annual Conference; for these set-pieces, there was no lack of the preparation and staffwork that was absent from routine parliamentary business. Arthur Booth of the Press Association witnessed the 1949 Conference rally, when Churchill really enjoyed himself in an elaborate comic routine, daring even to send up his own advanced age (did Harold Macmillan use this approach as his model ten years later?) Labour had recently published a policy document called *Labour believes in Britain*, a copy of which was in Churchill's hand.

> He peered in anxious bewilderment at the cover of the printed document, the title of which his large audience could not see. He paused for several, puzzled seconds, and he adjusted his horn-rimmed glasses to get a better view of the words which evidently were beyond his intellectual grasp. There was a mysterious hiatus of several seconds in mid-speech, and many members of his audience no doubt feared that 'the old man' had lost his place in his own manuscript and did not know how to continue. The silence became embarrassing – almost painful to persons not in the secret. At last he spoke again, but he did no more than read aloud, somewhat haltingly, the title of the rival pamphlet. 'Labour believes in Britain', said Mr. Churchill, almost stumbling over the words in his apparent bewilderment. There was a further pause while he continued to concentrate the whole of his mental faculties on the meaning of the rival message. Light dawned on him at last; his face beamed with the reassurance he evidently felt; he read the words once more; and then he rapidly added – as if he were addressing Mr. Attlee personally – 'Thankyou very much'. The audience relief was instantaneous and uproarious, a gigantic guffaw from 7000 throats working in unison.

Booth adds that, after this 'custard-pie routine', Labour changed the document's title. These speeches naturally read quite differently in the minutes, the essence being in the performance. With the man's reputation for serious statesmanship beyond question by 1949, the little-boy-who-never-grew-up aspect of Churchill's personality became all the more appealing.[3]

As the 1947 'conspiracy' indicated, the only alternative leader was seen to be Eden, and it was therefore Eden who found Churchill's leadership the most irritating. Despite the acceptance of a number of directorships, necessary to restore his depleted fortunes, Eden was generally available to the Party and a regular attender during parliamentary business. When Churchill returned from his American trip in April 1946, he wrote to Eden to express his pleasure that they would now be working together again as in wartime, and added that he would rely on Eden's help 'in ever-increasing measure'. Eden's response was to warn Churchill bluntly that 'it is only the Leader of the Opposition who can guide and father the party in the House . . . The

---

[3] Rhodes James, *Chips*, 418; Central Council report for 1951, NUA 2/2/17, CPA; Arthur Booth, *British Hustings, 1924–1950* (1956), 262–3.

position is quite different from when a Leader of the House, with a majority behind him, can act for the Prime Minister. In short, there is, I am sure, no room for anything in the nature of a Deputy Leader of the Opposition in the House of Commons.' Nevertheless, that is exactly what Eden had to be. His frustration was at least rewarded by a considerable degree of exposure and hence of public popularity, exceeding even Churchill's own in a poll in 1951. He was especially popular with Conservative women and with younger voters. Press comment attributed that popularity to his non-partisan approach; he was, said the *Liverpool Post*, 'a born unifier', and in that role he contributed importantly to the Conservative presence in the House. All the same, Eden had his detractors as well as his admirers; Sir Archibald James MP wrote to Woolton in 1946, scornfully dismissing him as 'a political prima donna . . . surrounded . . . with a stage door crowd of admirers'.[4]

Other Tories were also able to enhance their reputations in Churchill's loose-rein Opposition. Harry Crookshank was usually able to generate considerable heat in debate by his provocation of Labour backbenchers, and proved a more valuable asset than he was when in office; he was also the Party's leading expert on the exploitation of the rules of the House. Macmillan was generally felt to have come back from his ministerial war service with a new authority; Robert Bruce-Lockhart felt in 1946 that he 'may even succeed Winston. He has grown in stature during the War more than anyone. . . He was always clever, but was shy and diffident, had a clammy handshake and was more like a wet fish than a man. Now he is full of confidence, and is not only not afraid to speak but jumps in and speaks brilliantly. He has a better mind than Anthony.' In the House though, what Richard Crossman called 'the studied Edwardian elegance of his despatch box manner', and Tom Driberg 'his polished manner, surprised Edwardian look, and clear, throaty, pained voice', were felt by some to be out of place in the 1945 Parliament. Butler and Woolton made their advances in fame predominantly outside parliament, and the figure who really did come on in the Commons was Oliver Stanley, whose wit, lightness of touch and ingenuity was ideally suited to a heavily outnumbered Opposition; Anthony Howard is right to ascribe to him the position of acknowledged third man in the Party by the time of his death in 1950, since he was formally left in charge when both Eden and Churchill were abroad at the same time; he had been chairman of the Party's finance committee, and would surely have gone to the Treasury in 1951 but for his early death.[5]

4  Gilbert, *Never Despair*, 277, 633; Rhodes James, *Eden*, 317, 330; James to Woolton, 6 Sept. 1946, Woolton MSS, box 21.
5  Lord Egremont, *Wyndham and Children First* (1968), 143–5; Philip Goodhart, *The 1922, The Story of the 1922 Committee* (1973), 142; Anthony Sampson, *Macmillan, A Study in Ambiguity* (Harmondsworth, 1968), 77, 81; Alistair Horne, *Macmillan, 1984–1956* (1988), 294; Tom Driberg, *Colonnade* (1949), 307; Anthony Howard, *RAB, The Life of R.A. Butler* (1987), 173; Oliver Lyttelton, Lord Chandos, *The Memoirs of Lord Chandos* (1962), 336–9.

The parliamentary leadership functioned around two regular meetings when parliament was sitting: there was a fortnightly meeting of the Leader's Consultative Committee which usually met at Churchill's 'advance battle headquarters', the Savoy Hotel, for lunches variously described by participants as 'heavy', 'gargantuan', and 'alcoholic', at which the shadow cabinet would discuss in general terms the issues of the day, and spokesmen would be appointed for big speeches (it being Churchill's insistence that there should be no shadow ministers as such, since that might fetter his choice of a real Cabinet after the election); secondly, there were weekly meetings of the Business Committee, usually under Eden or Butler's chairmanship, that discussed imminent parliamentary business, and the line that should be taken in each debate; the second of these made more contribution than the first, of which the hostile Crookshank noted in March 1946, 'Shadow Cabinet with Winston – how he can bore one'. The size of the group increased steadily, which cannot have helped in the execution of business: initially there were just eleven Conservatives on the agreed list, but Churchill then added Woolton, Cherwell and Anderson and decreed that Macmillan, Bracken and Law should all join when returned at by-elections; Assheton stayed in the team when he retired as Party Chairman, as did Stuart when he stood down as Chief Whip, and Swinton and Winterton were both added later, making a 1948 total of twenty-two; between the 1950 and 1951 Elections, the full shadow cabinet met only fortnightly, and an inner group of eleven met in the intervening weeks.[6]

Frontbenchers were also playing an important role outside Westminster in the revival of the constituencies: Maxwell Fyfe recalled that he, Eden, Woolton and Macmillan were expected to make a constituency or Area speech at least weekly; in the first half of 1951 for example, Maxwell Fyfe himself spoke at thirty party meetings outside Westminster, seven of these being in Scotland, three in Wales, and a dozen in Lancashire where he had his own seat. Often these constituency speeches became opportunities for policy statements, as when Eden laid down the policy on denationalisation in 1949 at a mass rally at Dalkeith, or when he spoke on industry to a packed Headingley stadium in 1947. The constituency files indicate just how insistent were these demands, especially from the industrial areas; it became steadily more difficult to find big speakers at regular intervals for the Potteries, while areas like Tyneside that had lost most of their MPs in the 1945 rout were loud in their complaints that top-line speakers did not visit often enough to encourage local activists in their efforts to win back lost ground. There were occasional wounded

---

[6] Thompson, *Day Before Yesterday*, 86; Howard, *RAB*, 150; Stuart, *Within the Fringe*, 139; Richard Cockett (ed.), *My Dear Max: The Letters of Brendan Bracken to Lord Beaverbrook, 1925–1958* (1990), 62; Crookshank diary, 27 Mar. 1946, Crookshank MSS; Earl of Kilmuir, Political Adventure, The Memoirs of the Earl of Kilmuir, *Political Adventure, The Memoirs of the Earl of Kilmuir* (1964), 150.

feelings about the arbitrary choice of parliamentary speakers, and in 1948 Macmillan wrote to Churchill to suggest a new approach: the shadow cabinet should have an agenda, secretary and minutes, and a 'small managing group' to ensure coordination; Woolton and Eden were both supportive of this businesslike approach, but Churchill replied in brutal terms: 'I do not agree with what you propose, and I do not think our colleagues would either. It would be a great mistake to formalise the loose and unsubstantial association which governs the work of an Opposition. I propose to continue with the present system so long as I am in charge. I do not think things are going so badly. Thank you very much for writing.' More detailed proposals from Macmillan hit the same brick wall. When Stuart finally decided to retire from the position of Chief Whip in 1947, after seven years in the post, he could not even attract sufficient of Churchill's attention to get him to name a successor without several reminders, even though there was general agreement that this should be the current deputy, Patrick Buchan-Hepburn. But Stuart's retirement was necessitated in part by an unfortunate personal situation, and Buchan-Hepburn had to be *de facto* Chief Whip for several months before formally assuming the role, so as not to draw attention to the fact; in July 1948, Buchan-Hepburn was asked by Churchill 'to fill James's place (as you have already done so long so well) in a formal manner'; the Leader expressed 'my earnest belief that we may together put in a restoration to power of the Conservative and Tory-progressive forces', a form of words that suggested a rather hazy commitment to the Party as it existed; appropriately, a former MP wrote to the new Chief Whip to express the hope 'that your flock will be docile and well-behaved – likewise Winston!' Much of the management was also conducted in more informal ways, and here Thomas was an important liaison with backbenchers. He reported to Woolton in 1946 that 'the prima donna qualities of MPs fall most heavily on those of us who have to handle them in the Smoking Room where alcohol inflames rather than mellows their feelings towards Central Office, unless it is *your* drink they are swallowing! Every night there is a queue waiting with grievances or for advice and each MP expects to have at least half an hour with one. I fear that patience with these sensitive plants is really the only cure. . .'[7]

## Responding to Labour's legislation

Such problems are of course clearer in hindsight than was apparent at the time, when the pressures of the parliamentary timetable forced the shadow cabinet to

7  Maxwell Fyfe appointment diary for 1951, Kilmuir MSS, 1/1; Anthony Eden, *Days for Decision, Selected Speeches, 1947–1949* (1949), 103; Tynemouth CA minutes, 15 Feb. 1946; Central Office constituency files, CCO 1/3/279 and 1/5/187; Churchill to Buchan-Hepburn, 5 July 1948, Hailes MSS, 4/2; Buchan-Hepburn's file, 'Appointment as Chief Whip', Hailes MSS, 2/6; Central Office, Chairman's file, 'J.P.L. Thomas letters, 1946 to 1951', CCO 20/4/1, CPA.

make decisions each week. The easiest perhaps were those relating to Labour's social policies, for these had largely emerged from the wartime coalition and, while individual Conservatives had hedged around their support for them, there had never been an official line against welfare reform which would now have to be ditched. Since Churchill's formula had usually been that reforms must wait till the end of the War, it was relatively easy to support them when the post-war Parliament began to receive legislative proposals, and only when the Korean crisis developed in 1950–51 did the earlier doubts come back into play. Conservative MPs were not mobilised to vote against the 1946 National Insurance Bill and no guillotine was required to secure its quick passage; in the final debate, Butler accused the Government of breaking pledges given to the friendly societies, but nevertheless announced that 'we have deliberately hastened rather than delayed this measure', and that Conservatives would not divide against the third reading. This softly, softly approach enabled the Party to complain about the procedure adopted for the Trades Disputes Bill, forced through the Commons in five days and without a single amendment accepted; it was pointed out that this repealed a 1927 Act on which the Commons had spent twenty-seven days. Not everyone approved of selective opposition: in December 1947, Herbert Williams complained to the National Union when it was decided not to vote against the National Assistance Bill; when Walter Eliott replied that shadow ministers felt this was 'in the best interests of the party', Williams was 'not very impressed'. Elliott was a forceful influence for moderation, leading for the Party on Bevan's Health Bill as soon as he got back to the Commons. In this case, the policy of the Opposition was to be 'reconnaissance in force', not to vote against the Bill but to propose amendments of detail, and to secure the maximum advantage from Bevan's battle with the industry's vested interests, notably the British Medical Association. In that battle, Dr Charles Hill, secretary of the BMA and, like Woolton, a man whose popular reputation derived from wartime broadcasting, emerged as a forceful presence; he had stood unsuccessfully as an Independent for Cambridge University in 1945, but was in due course adopted as a 'Liberal and Conservative' for the marginal constituency of Luton, won it in 1950 and became a minister in 1951. This can have done no harm to the Party in securing the support of a key group of opinion-formers. It can have been no coincidence that when in 1948 Churchill addressed the biggest of all his outdoor rallies, at Luton Hoo in Hill's constituency, it was social policy that formed the core of his speech. His objective was to claim at least an equal share of whatever credit was going:

> The Socialists dilate upon the National Insurance Scheme, Family Allowances, improved education, welfare foods, food subsidies and so forth . . . All these schemes were devised and set in motion in the days before the Socialists came to office . . . I have worked at national insurance schemes almost all my life and am responsible for several of the largest measures ever passed. The main principles of the new Health Schemes were hammered out in the days of the

Coalition Government, before the party and personal malignancy of Mr. Bevan plunged health policy into its present confusion. The Family Allowance Act was passed by the Conservative [sic] Caretaker Government, School milk was started in 1934 by a Conservative [sic] Parliament. The idea of welfare foods was largely developed by Lord Woolton. The Education Act was the work of Mr. Butler . . . These facts should be repeated on every occasion by those who wish the truth to be known.

Whether these were 'facts' is debatable, but they were certainly repeated on every available occasion. On social policy, despite the differences that separated them from Labour on the administrative issues of policy implementation, and on costs, Conservatives anchored their public position firmly to the middle ground, and sought to portray Labour as the divisive force.[8]

Responses to nationalisation were more complex. There were in any case mixed feelings about the first measure, taking over the Bank of England, since Macmillan at least had long advocated a closer connection between the Bank and government. Opposition therefore concentrated not on the issue of principle, but on detail and timing; there was criticism of the provisions as unnecessarily interventionist, and Stanley argued that 'we object, when there are so many real problems demanding the attention of the Government that the processes of the House and the time of its members should be wasted on a piece of political eyewash'. Only Robert Boothby, an old Macmillanite interventionist, defied the whip and voted for the Bill. Rather than argue out the case, it was much easier to rubbish the Government's motives: in December 1945, Crookshank told the Commons that the Bank had been nationalised 'for one purpose only, and that is to demonstrate to the supporters of the Socialist Party that in the first six months they have carried one of their election promises – just one. Are there more homes? No. Has there been quicker demobilisation? No. Is there more food and are there more clothes?' Once the Bill was passed, it was hardly ever referred to again by Conservatives.[9]

Coal was a different matter, given the bitter inheritance of political squabbling on the subject. The first briefing notes issued merely analysed Labour's Bill, complained that the offered compensation was inadequate, and set the scene for later arguments by detailing the 'failure' of earlier public ownership schemes in Australia and New Zealand. Eden was leading in Churchill's absence, and largely determined the whole Conservative view of nationalisation by the line that he took. In the Commons, he complained about the excessive ministerial powers allowed by the Bill, and again attacked the Government's concentration on 'these secondary problems', before 'the drive for production is under way'. At Hull in March he called on 'the political propagandists of the Left' to 'turn from their imaginary Marxist bogies to the

8  Central Office *Notes on Current Politics*, [hereafter *NCP*], 17 June 1946; National Union Executive minutes [hereafter NUEC], 17 Dec. 1947; Colin Coote, *A Companion of Honour, The Story of Walter Elliott* (1965), 253; Addison, *Churchill*, 399.
9  J.E.D. Hall, *Labour's First Year* (Harmondsworth, 1947), 58; *NCP*, 25 Mar. 1946.

real problem of immediately increasing the production of goods and services'. The nub of the Tory case on coal was that the wartime Reid Committee had shown that the problems of the industry were basically technical ones; it had recommended a rationalisation programme of amalgamated companies to allow greater investment and increased output, and this the owners had in principle accepted; a change of ownership could thus be presented as untimely and irrelevant. The credibility of this tactical stance was enhanced when the responsible minister accepted that Labour had come into office with no plan of its own and had largely accepted the Reid proposals, with a change of ownership tacked on; Charles Reid became one of the first members of the new National Coal Board. The coal debates therefore forced the Conservatives to define their position on the principle of nationalisation in response to Labour questioning. Public ownership could not be opposed root and branch in all circumstances without also disowning the pre-war Conservatives who had set up such bodies as the London Passenger Transport Board, but few Conservatives wanted such opposition anyway. David Eccles, debating the King's Speech in November 1945, accepted that 'no sensible man would oppose the principle of nationalisation or public ownership in all its forms', but was nonplussed when a Labour backbencher immediately asked in what circumstances *would* it be acceptable. Eden, in the first coal debate a few months later, seized on a speech made by Morrison in which he had argued that particular acts of nationalisation were needed 'in the public interest', rather than claiming that there was an ideological case for public ownership as such; Eden now replied 'let the argument be directed to the merits, and let the test be the public interest'. At Walthamstow in August 1946, again quoting Morrison as the justification for his own position, he returned to the same point in a speech on iron and steel: 'the nationalisers must make their case'. He was clear that this would be a stiff test to apply: 'Our approach to these matters is essentially practical. We believe that the manner in which the state should intervene in the development of these industries is a matter that must be decided in each case, on a wholly practical basis free from any doctrinaire considerations. By far the largest category in industry is that in which competition still remains and must be encouraged.' The Party would be open-minded but not empty-minded, for it would assume that competition was preferable to monopoly unless there was proof to the contrary. Thus the Conservatives made a show of opposition to the nationalisation of coal, hoping to delay the Government programme by getting the Coal Bill's committee stage taken on the floor of the House. When this failed the opposition became very limited; for the third reading nearly a third of Tory MPs did not turn up.[10]

10  *NCP* 28 Jan. and 11 Mar. 1946; Anthony Eden, *Freedom and Order, Selected Speeches, 1939–1946* (1947), 371, 381, 394, 397, 408; Thompson, *Day Before Yesterday*, 26; Geoffrey Hodgson, 'The Steel Debates', in *The Age of Austerity, 1945–1951*, eds Michael Sissons and Philip French (Harmondsworth, 1964), 310; J.D. Hoffman, *The Conservative Party in Opposition, 1945–1951* (1964), 233.

The right were far from happy with this approach. Bracken viewed the 1946–47 parliamentary session with gloom: 'we shall have Bills to nationalise the railways and electricity . . . The Tories will fight them. But . . . there is not likely to be much convincing opposition from the most of our front bench. I am told that before the war Macmillan wrote a book in which he approved of . . . state control.' In January, Kings Lynn Tories endorsed a branch resolution calling for a more aggressive spirit in fighting Labour legislation. Nonetheless, the pragmatic position that Eden adopted over coal remained the Party's stance, and occasionally the energies of the right could be harnessed to slow down bills by obstruction, as Bracken himelf was employed over the Gas Bill. The main complaint against nationalisation of the railways was that the 1919 grouping system had already eliminated almost all competition, so that a change of ownership was now unnecessary; it was also pointed out, in the context of the 'property-owning democracy' idea, that there were already about a million owners of the railways, and that about a third of all the shares were in the hands of small owners. This pragmatism freed Tory spokesmen to complain about the detail of bills as they came forward and to use them to hold up Labour's programme – Maxwell Fyfe made 178 speeches on the Transport Bill – and to vote against them, without their leaders' speeches being easily quarried for evidence that they were merely unreconstructed right-wingers who had learned nothing since 1939. Tory complaints about compensation levels were rarely justified, and contained an obvious self-contradiction that they somehow seem to have got away with; on the one hand, they complained that owners of nationalised shares were compensated only with Government stock which could not be sold for several years, rather than with cash, and on the other, they claimed that the creation of this stock was somehow consuming financial resources that would otherwise be available for investment or for public consumption. They were on stronger grounds with the Gas Bill, since the compensation to local authority owners was somewhat under-valued, but in this case it was a transaction almost entirely between public authorities, and there was little prospect of exciting the public at large. Conservative complaints about excessive ministerial powers on the other hand were largely subjective, and could not be directly refuted. But the greatest bonus to accrue from a pragmatic stance was that by 1948 – and for years thereafter – the financial results and other policy outputs of public corporations could be scrutinised for evidence that nationaliation had 'failed': if the criterion for nationalisation was simply 'the public interest', then the output figures, consumer prices, efficiency and profits or losses of the public corporations were all fair game in the search for evidence of where the public interest lay. Coal provided an easy target when, in its first year in public ownership, there was both a difficult strike and the collapse of production in the catastrophic winter of 1947. In July, Eden was complaining to the House about reduced output and higher prices, and when challenged by Labour as to what the Conservatives would themselves do, he replied as always that the first priority would be to stop nationalising *more* industries until there was a longer period to judge the success of schemes already in existence. In June 1948, Sir Charles Reid resigned from the Coal Board, saying in his resignation letter that without a greater emphasis on production 'the nationalisation of the mines will prove a disastrous failure', a useful phrase for Conservative leaflets. But by then Churchill was going much further than Eden's singling out of individual industries and claiming that 'the complete failure of nationalisation is already apparent. The experiment has cost us dear . . . Everywhere we see higher prices and increased costs, and it seems a mad way to govern a country by picking out one-fifth of its industries, nationalising them, destroying their profit-making capacity, charging the loss upon the Exchequer, and at the same time hampering the other 80 per cent with higher charges.' As long as Labour retained future nationalisation plans in its programme, the same response could be adopted, as it was throughout the 1950s. A Tory publicity song of 1964 described a 'nationalisation nightmare', in which, 'Last night I 'ad an 'orrible dream, They'd nationalised my football team'; after detailing the bureaucracy, ineptitude and mismanagement that followed, it concluded,

> They say it's good for the Common Weal.
> I'm sure they mean it, but don't you feel,
> That it's hardly the way to run our Steel,
> Which we sell the whole world over.[11]

The pragmatic approach had the further advantage of enabling the Party's spokesmen to avoid commitments to return to private ownership industries already nationalised. In this case, the policy was made explicit in the *Industrial Charter* and commended by Butler to the 1947 Conference. He claimed for the Party complete freedom to judge the question when back in office but it was easy to see what that judgement would entail.

> I have been asked what our view is about railways. Well, there is nothing to stop any member of our Party, any syndicate, any section of opinion, from collecting the money together if they want to . . . buy back any railway, but I would draw the Party's attention to the advisability at this stage of taking one step at a time. I would solemnly advise that we concentrate on the question of management, particularly the management of, for example, the coal industry, than we do on the question of ownership.

Since this was exactly what they were urging on the Government, the Party could hardly refuse to take its own advice. Conference agendas of 1948

11 Cockett, *My Dear Max*, 60; Kings Lynn CA minutes, 28 Jan. 1947; P.M. Williams (ed.), *The Diary of Hugh Gaitskell, 1945–51* (1983), 59; David Marquand, 'Sir Stafford Cripps', in *The Age of Austerity, 1945–1951*, eds Michael Sissons and Philip French (Harmondsworth, 1964), 189; Peter Jenkins, 'Bevan's Fight with the BMS', in *The Age of Austerity*, as above; Kilmuir, *Memoirs*, 151; *NCP*, 27 Jan. 1947, 22 Mar. and 14 June 1948; Eden, *Days for Decision*, 43, 47; Central Office election record, 'Songs for Swinging Voters', 1964, in possession of the author.

and 1949 contain few constituency resolutions demanding denationalisation schemes, and it was extremely unlikely that either the transport or energy industries would ever be denationalised by spontaneous private initiatives. In 1951, on the other hand, the agenda for the Conference, cancelled because of the Election, did include motions on denationalisation, including one selected for debate which would have sought to commit the Party to 'stop further nationalisation of industry, to denationalise wherever practicable, and to decentralise and humanise those that remain in public hands'. The first and third parts of this motion were unexceptional enough, but the middle went further than usual and its selection for debate at what was expected to be a pre-election Conference indicates some shift of direction. That shift owes almost everything to the changed nature/of the parliamentary debate after 1947, and a change in the character of the industries under consideration. Coal, railways, gas and electricity were industries whose leaders largely accepted, and in some cases welcomed, the logic of their own move into public ownership, in part because they were industries with poor recent records of profitability. It was therefore painless for Conservatives to accept, tacitly, that these could be nationalised, without incurring any charge of desertion from their industrial allies.[12]

The very opposite was true of the road haulage part of the Transport Bill, and of Iron and Steel, since in both cases the industries fought tooth and nail against a state take-over; both industries were profitable, and in both there was competition rather than monopoly. This was at last a real ideological divide, for if these industries were to go down, then there was no logical line beyond which state ownership might not legitimately be extended in years to come; the defence of steel was the defence of capitalist private enterprise. Road hauliers were numerous and sturdily individualist: there were 60,000 firms, mostly with five or less lorries, but they came together to fight for their independence, with Woolton as their Federation President, and with close links between the Federation and the Research Department; the East Midlands Area Council resolved as early as March 1946 to 'congratulate the industry on the splendid fight it is putting up and offers, through constituency associations, all possible assistance by way of propaganda, distribution of literature and speakers'. Two months later the road hauliers were top of the list of allies that Bradford Conservatives drew up, with an instruction to their staff to maintain close contact; the others were the National Conference of Friendly Societies, the BMA and the British Hospitals Association, all interests threatened by Labour's legislative plans, as was the Brewers' Association when Labour introduced a Licensing Bill, and with which Bradford Tories also then set up collaborative links. This situation effectively forced the Conservative leaders to take up the hauliers' case and give a clear pledge that road haulage would

12 NCP, 18 Nov. 1946, 27 Oct. 1947; Central Council report for 1948, NUA 2/2/14, CPA; Paul Addison, Now the War is Over (1985), 193; Hoffman, Conservative Party, 237.

be returned to private ownership. Even then, a circular issued to Tory MPs by Peter Thorneycroft, urging the shadow cabinet to make its decision clear and early, presented as an urgent issue at Easter 1946, was not even discussed until July; Churchill was wary of too unconsidered a commitment, but in the end it could not be avoided. Industry's propaganda complemented the Party's by concentrating on similar arguments: private bus-owners asked in press advertisements in 1947 'where is the evidence? You've had a fair sample of government control during the past seven years and if you like it you'll like the British Transport Commission. Even the leading advocates of State Monopoly admit that it is an experiment. Where is the evidence that the buses under State Monopoly could be run as well as they are now?' These debates in turn fostered a renewed readiness to fight by industry itself; the Federation of British Industries began to take off the gloves in its dealings with the Government, and the front organisation Aims of Industry, which had been set up in 1942, now ran explicitly political campaigns against state intervention. Large sums of money were raised and spent in the anti-nationalisation cause, to the obvious advantage of the anti-nationalisation party, and Aims established a strong rapport with Conservatives; agents were told that the Aims office could provide cartoons, illustrations and copy for local publications, and was worth consulting if it proved difficult to get Conservative MPs to write articles for constituency magazines, since Aims could persuade them, presumably by drafting the articles for them. In 1949, Aims was reported to have spent over a £100,000 on the year's campaigns, including 4,000 free cinema shows attended by nearly half a million people, highly professional products with Richard Dimbleby recording the commentary. In 1950, Central Office supplied Aims with a list of Labour marginals where its campaigning might be most helpful. Labour's extreme anger at this manifestation of the spending power of industry led to threats of prosecutions under election law when Aims intervened in by-elections, as they did at Bradford in 1949, but since Aims publicised a policy rather than promoting a candidate they could not be stopped. When threatened with legal action against their own defence campaign, the insurance companies coolly argued that they were not being party political, for they would have reacted just as strongly if the Conservatives had planned to nationalise them.[13]

This was the background to the Steel debates of 1948 to 1950, in which there was, as Lyttelton recalled, 'a pretty hot parliamentary debate, as hot as you've seen'; from the Labour side, the minister felt that 'some of the

---

[13] Central Council reports for 1949 and 1951, NUA 2/2/15 and 17, CPA; East Midlands Area Council, 16 Mar. 1946; Bradford CA minutes, 20 May 1946 and 31 Jan. 1949; Leader's Consultative Committee [hereafter LCC], 28 June 1946, CPA; Ramsden, *Conservative Party Policy*, 119; Thompson, *Day Before Yesterday*, 58; *Conservative Agents' Journal*, [hereafter *CAJ*] Jan. 1948; Central Office constituency file, Bradford, 1/7/163; NUEC, 13 Dec. 1947; William Crofts, *Coercion or Persuasion? Propaganda in Britain after 1945* (1989), 204, 211, 213; Central Office files, 'Aims of Industry', 3/2/56 and 3/3/43, CPA.

Conservative speeches from the front benches were almost hysterical in their hatred and loathing of the Bill'. Hysterical they may have been in tone, but with the benefit of extensive briefing from the industry, they were extremely well-argued; it is rare for an Opposition, without the civil service at its disposal, to be better briefed than the Government, and this was good for morale. The reason for the new mood was in part the demand out of doors, in part the long pent-up feeling of frustration on the Tory benches, in part the fact that Labour was now seeking to advance from the pragmatic case for nationalisation to the more unlimited ideological one. Eden twitted Morrison with abandoning the position he had taken up in 1946, and with now proposing a Bill that had no justification except a political one. Quoting a Labour pamphlet, Lyttelton described this as a fundamental divide: 'they give the whole thing away . . . they believe in the doctrine of centralisation of power in the hands of the State . . . It has long been our doctrine that, in a democracy, power should be dispersed.' With this conviction behind them, the Conservatives strained every fibre against the Iron and Steel Bill: hundreds of amendments were proposed, but after thirty-six days of passionate debate the guillotine fell with more than 200 still undiscussed. This brought the House of Lords into the fray for the first time on a big issue since 1945. Swinton and Salisbury had restrained the Tory peers to avoid giving the Labour Government any excuse for curbing the Lords' powers; as Tom Driberg pointed out in 1946, they knew that 'in effect, they could only have one showdown, and they had better save it for later on'. Headlam grumbled in July 1947, 'what use there is in a Second Chamber like the H of L nowadays I cannot see, except to improve the grammar of our legislation'. Tory peers were just as aware of this as anyone, and in December 1947, Salisbury tried to persuade the shadow cabinet to agree that if the Lords rejected the Iron and Steel Bill, then the Party should in return promise to reform the House of Lords – that is to restore some of its powers in return for a change of composition – but Churchill refused to countenance the idea, still no doubt feeling some affection for the 1911 Parliament Act he had helped to pass. The Lords nevertheless decided that their moment had come and threw restraint to the winds; led by Swinton, to whom Salisbury deferred in industrial matters, they insisted on wrecking amendments to the Iron and Steel Bill, arguing that as the plan had not been spelled out in Labour's 1945 manifesto, so there was no mandate. This had several consequences. First, the Government introduced a new Parliament Bill to limit the Lords' delaying powers to one year rather than two (but this took two years to enact because the Lords delayed it for two years as a further act of defiance), and second the Iron and Steel Bill was also delayed for two years and had to go through debates in three sessions – much as Home Rule had done in 1912–14. Attempts to strike a compromise between the parties failed, and the bitter argument persisted through to 1950 when the Iron and Steel Bill finally became law. Aims and the steel industry itself were both very active in propaganda; during 1948 Gallup recorded that the proportion of voters opposing nationalisation of the industry rose from 67 per cent to 79 per cent. Behind the scenes though, another consequence was being worked out; the Chairman of the Iron and Steel Federation, Sir Andrew Duncan, was a former Liberal who had served in Churchill's wartime administration, and now took the Conservative whip as MP for the City of London; he made an excellent intermediary. The leaders of the industry secured agreement early on that, if they committed themselves wholeheartedly against nationalisation, then the Conservatives would promise to denationalise the industry when returned to office; the agreement was made, and the pledge duly given; between 1948 and 1951, and especially in the latter part of that period, the Party and the industry worked together on the details of a plan for denationalisation.[14]

When in 1950 Labour published plans to add to the public sector the sugar-refining, cement and insurance industries, the ideological divide deepened. These all reacted as iron and steel had done; when Ian Mikardo made a Labour Conference speech in 1948 listing fifteen more candidates for public ownership, Conservatives had been reminded that he had also proposed the vital nationalisation motion at Labour's 1945 Conference. Now that some of this was official policy, there was again a vigorous campaign fought in collaboration with the threatened industries. Insurance companies provided useable quotations from such friendly names as the Prudential, to the effect that nationalising insurance companies was a backdoor way of taking over everything, since they had a billion pounds invested in other companies. For sugar, the lead was taken by Tate and Lyle, which conducted a spirited advertising campaign of its own, centred on posters illustrating the cartoon character 'Mr. Cube'; there was massive targeted mailing to shareholders, employees in the industry, other manufacturers who bought sugar, even to children as consumers of sweets; Tate and Lyle also helpfully provided evidence for the Party, by conducting surveys to show that opinion in sugar-growing colonies was also against state control. The Party Conference handbook for 1950 had a cover advertisement for Tate and Lyle, with the message, 'Leave it to free enterprise to run our sugar industry'. Eden drew on all this for a speech in April 1949, refuting Labour's claims that suger refiners made too much profit and fleeced their customers: 'apparently they suggest that nationalisation will make sugar cheaper . . . Why should it? The precedents are all against it. Has nationalisation made your coal any cheaper? Has it made electricity, gas, or rail transport any cheaper?' Again, the industry's propaganda complemented the Party's, with Mr. Cube saying of nationalisation, 'Oh dear, oh dear – Dearer!' By this stage, the alleged failure

[14] Thompson, *Day Before Yesterday*, 58; Hodgson, 'Steel Debates', 311, 318, 324, 329; Eden, *Days for Decision*, 79, 89–92; *NCP*, 18 Oct. 1948; J.A. Cross, *Lord Swinton* (Oxford, 1982), 257–60; Driberg, *Colonnade*, 365; Headlam diary, 24 July 1947, Headlam MSS; LCC, 2 Dec. 1947; Salisbury to Swinton, 14 Oct. 1948, Swinton MSS, 174/4/1; Kilmuir, *Memoirs*, 155; Crofts, *Coercion or Persuasion?*, 206; Kathleen Burk, *The First Privatisation: The Politicians, the City and the Denationalisation of Steel* (1988), 13–40.

of earlier schemes had become central to the Conservative case; on cement, Eden pointed out that since 1945 its prices had gone up only a third as fast as 'nationalised coal'. No more Bills came forward before the 1950 General Election, and with Labour's small majority there was no appetite for a re-run of the steel debates; the threatened industries remained in private hands. For the 1952 Conference handbook, Tate and Lyle were again on the cover, with Mr. Cube successfully completing a mountain climb, and saying 'I made it'. The same might be claimed of the Party's gradual evolution of a fighting policy on nationalisation since 1945. Over the steel debates, Duncan wrote to Swinton that 'you have forced the Government to make it very clear that they have absolutely no case, other than the party political one, for the Bill, and I am sure the debates will have made a great impression on the country'.[15]

## Conservatives and foreign policy

In the foreign policy field, it was more a case of awaiting the turn of the wheel until the difficulties of 1945 ceased to count. Over the future of India, a field that had remained relatively uncontentious in war circumstances, things were more difficult in peacetime, but this was an area in which the Opposition was powerless to affect the course of events, and in which Churchill's wish to be responsible conflicted with his deeper instincts; Eden complained that he had to put up with Churchill's public 'lamentations' over India when he had no alternative policy to offer, and the shadow cabinet spent a remarkable amount of its time discussing such details as the future of the state of Hyderabad. (Similarly, in a debate on Palestine, Headlam noted in February 1947, 'Winston mercifully – owing to his brother's death – was absent so we were spared a speech from him which might well have caused trouble in view of his Zionist attitude'.) The National Union Executive witnessed a brief flurry of discontent in 1947 when Herbert Williams complained that the Party would not vote against the Bill giving independence to India; Butler agreed to report to Churchill the views that had been expessed, but told the Executive that the shadow cabinet were unanimous in their view. When he himself spoke in the Commons, he was proud to claim a share of paternity for Indian independence as a ministerial sponsor of the 1935 Government of India Act. It was usually better not to commit the Party to anything so definite; a twenty-six-page brief published in January 1947 was almost entirely devoted to attacks on Labour's mishandling of the sub-continent, with just one page tacked on at the end to explain 'where the Conservative Party stands': this last was derived from one speech by Butler that said only what should *not* be done. When partition produced massive bloodshed, Churchill raged against the

---

15  *NCP*, 17 May 1948 and 23 May 1949; Eden, *Days for Decision*, 108; Crofts, *Coercion or Peruasion?*, 213, 215; Central Council reports for 1950 and 1952, NUA 2/2/16 and 18, CPA; Duncan to Swinton, 21 July 1949, Swinton MSS, 174/4/1.

policy in the Commons, but clearly recognised that it was too late to change it, and meanwhile in the Lords more moderate opinions were voiced by Halifax. Churchill then led the Party to accept the adherence of the new India to the Commonwealth even at the price of recognising its republican constitution; when Salisbury complained, he reminded him that 'the clock cannot now be put back', for the pass had been sold by the appeasers in the early 1930s: 'I could not therefore accept any reproach for the present situation from any Conservative who supported the Baldwin and Chamberlain policies.' It was an issue that kept the legacy of appeasement in the Party mind, and while it seems by 1948 to have had little appeal to the public, in either direction, it clearly still mattered to the Party leaders; it may not have been entirely coincidental that the shadow cabinet's decision to give Baldwin a dinner to mark his eightieth birthday in 1947 was taken at a meeting when Eden was in the chair and Churchill absent.[16]

Of greater significance for the future was the issue of the colonial Empire in Africa and the Far East on the one hand, and of Europe on the other. The first was treated simply as a quarry for evidence of 'socialist mismanagement' and 'drift', but there was once again no very definite Conservative alternative. Birmingham Conservatives resolved in 1950 to call on the Party to do more to prevent the disintegration of the Empire, the single dissentient suggesting that since it was not integrated it could not disintegrate anyway. Europe had a higher profile, because of Churchill's personal involvement in the first moves towards European integration and because the creation of the Council of Europe required an institutional involvement by the Party too. The evolution of a United States of Europe as a bastion of democracy was frequently an inspirational subject for Churchill's speeches delivered to European audiences, but once again the detail of the speeches consisted in attacks on the Government for its shortsightedness and for the lack of clear objectives in its policies. Since Eden was at best lukewarm on greater commitments to Europe, it was never likely that the Conservatives would make up their minds to become resolutely pro-European. While the Party could proudly talk of 'Mr. Churchill's United Europe Movement', there was not much substance in it as a policy, as indeed there could not be while other Conservatives placed the predominant emphasis on Empire or on the American economic connection. Churchill squared the circle of these conflicting priorities with his 'three circles' analysis of world affairs, placing Britain reassuringly at the centre of all three, the Empire, Europe and the Atlantic alliance, but without giving precedence to any one; oppositions can get away with such rhetorical devices but, as Pierre Mendès-France was shortly to say, 'to govern is to choose'. How difficult that choice might be was indicated in Summer 1948;

16  Eden to Thomas, 26 Dec. 1946, Avon MSS, 11/12/46; Headlam diary, 25 Feb. 1947; Gerald Sparrow, *RAB, Study of a Statesman* (1965), 98–100; NUEC, 13 Nov. 1947; *NCP*, 17 Jan. 1947, 31 May 1948, 2 Oct, 1950; LCC, 2 July 1947.

Herbert Williams in a speech at Exeter had denounced his Party's leaders for their pro-European policy, likening them to Colorado beetles pestilentially undermining Britain's future trade, which he saw as lying mainly with the Empire. Since he was at the time National Union Chairman, he was carpeted by the Party Chairman; he apologised for his language but not for his concern about the 'fiscal implications of Western Union'. After the debate that this provoked, Woolton reported to Churchill that

> many members of the Executive . . . are disturbed in their minds as to whether a customs union would imperil our ability to protect our industries and agriculture from undue competition from European sources. They are attracted by the idealism on the one hand, and the military necessity of Western Union on the other. They are concerned as to whether its practical application might interfere with our trade and create unemployment in this country.

Churchill wisely ignored Woolton's advice that 'this is a matter in which it would be well for us to clarify our position as a Party'.[17]

In any case, the predominant foreign issue was none of Churchill's three circles, but Russia, the threat from which was what bound the three circles together anyway. The 1948 Conference speech in which Churchill described the 'three great circles among the free nations and democracies' was also one in which he made his most stinging attack yet on 'Russian imperialism'. This led to another parting of the ways with Beaverbrook, who mourned the deterioration of relations with Russia, just as he had been an advocate of aid to Russia in 1942, but this was not likely to deflect the Party's adoption of a more anti-Russian stance. Churchill indeed used the occasion to offer support if Attlee stood up to Russia and armed Britain more aggressively than he had done so far: 'we must do our best to help these "guilty men", to make them better.' Conservatives even briefly joined a Cabinet committee to develop this defence policy consensus, but this level of agreement was kept rather quiet. When the Minister of Defence offered to brief the Conservative Defence Committee in early 1948, the shadow cabinet turned down the idea, but encouraged Churchill to broadcast for an army recruiting campaign, and authorised private talks between frontbenchers only; these talks took place in Summer 1949, when Churchill wrote to Attlee to say 'how disquieted we all were by the information that was given us', including allegations that there were Russian saboteurs ready in place all over British industry. Churchill decided to break the talks off in October; with an election coming there were advantages in not being taken too closely into the Government's confidence. The turning round of the foreign policy question since 1945 was therefore twofold: Attlee's hope to avoid a clash with Russia was claimed

---

[17]    Birmingham UA minutes, 27 Jan. 1950; Pelling, *Churchill*, 570; Gilbert, *Never Despair*, 283, 473; Rhodes James, *Eden*, 321; Woolton to Churchill [undated but July 1948], Woolton MSS, box 21.

to be either naive or insincere, and his alleged failure to prepare Britain adequately for another war was compared unfavourably even to Asquith's and Chamberlain's records. Electors were reminded that when Churchill had far-sightedly warned of the Russian threat in 1946, a hundred Labour MPs had put down a motion of censure on him for doing so. Macmillan summed up this line in a Commons debate in November 1949: 'It was in prophetic mood that Mr. Churchill delivered his Fulton speech three years ago. He was bitterly attacked by what are called progressive circles. Some Honourable Members wanted him repudiated . . . The Government showed no particular enthusiasm. But they have had to follow his advice.' In saying such things, it was easy to forget that Conservatives as well as Labour MPs did not like Churchill's anti-Russianism in 1946; Eden thought that such inflammatory outbursts as the Fulton speech to be very unhelpful. The onset of the Cold War, combined with the rise of anti-Communism, ensured that Conservative instincts in international affairs were as much in tune with the popular mood by 1950 as they had been adrift of it in 1945.[18]

## The quest for anti-socialist unity

The recovery of a fighting spirit probably owed more to these reactions to the external political agenda than to the Party's more controllable recovery of ground in organisation and policy. Improved morale undoubtedly owed something too to actual campaigning that took place in elections for local government and for parliamentary vacancies. But that campaigning required the settling of fundamental questions about identity first. After defeat in 1945, the shock was so great that the name of the Party – and hence its whole relationship to the Conservative tradition – came up for reconsideration, as did its relationship to the Liberals and to the electoral system. Woolton's *Memoirs* claim that a new Party name was his idea, but Churchill and Macmillan had come to that conclusion before Woolton was involved, and Assheton had anyway already suggested a 'Unionist' party in March 1946; Macmillan's suggestion was to create a 'New Democratic Party'. There was certainly some support for such ideas in the downbeat mood of 1946, particularly in the places where a continuing Liberal presence seemed to pose a threat, as Thomas reported to Eden in May; in July 1946 Bradford Conservatives called for Central Office 'to take early steps' to fuse all anti-socialists into one grouping, and expressed a preference for the title, 'Democratic or National Unionist Party'. Churchill addressed the National Union Executive, also in July, and asked it to consider and report to him on the future of the

---

[18] *NCP*, 1 Nov. and 27 Dec. 1948, 31 Jan. and 5 Dec. 1949; information on the Cabinet talks from Peter Hennessy; LCC, 4 Feb. 1948, 19 Jan., 1 July and 19 Oct. 1949; Churchill to Attlee, 24 July 1949, Avon MSS, 19/1/44; A.J.P. Taylor, *Beaverbrook* (1972), 575; Eden to Thomas, 26 Dec. 1946, Avon MSS, 11/12/46.

Party's name and on 'electoral reform and compulsory voting'; members were warned that they must not say that he had asked them to discuss either issue. The next meeting was the first that Woolton attended; views were expressed on both sides of the argument, but at Woolton's suggestion no vote was taken; he undertook to inform the Leader of the views expressed. Some head of steam did build up over the Summer, and resolutions calling for some new anti-socialist party to be created came in from Smethwick, Camden, Barnet and Norfolk among other places. Churchill told Woolton that he was 'of the opinion that we should go forward with the proposal to make "the Union Party", whose members would be called Unionists, but who might be Conservative Unionists, Liberal Unionists, Trade Unionists or Labour Unionists. I should like to discuss this when the shadows meet on September 23, and if there were general agreement I would myself open the matter at Blackpool on October 5.' Reginald Maudling was scathing about all such ideas, writing to Eden that 'it will be a sad thing for the Conservative Party if a future historian has to write that at a time when they had the chance to turn defeat into victory, at a time when the nation needed leadership, inspiration and faith, the Conservative Party produced not even a new, but a fifty year old name'. Presumably the 'shadows' were not enthusiastic either, for at Conference Churchill broached the issue only in the most general terms. With the rank and file assembled at Conference – always the most hawkish of Conservative gatherings – the surrender of the Party's historic identity did not go down at all well. Bracken reported exultantly, not knowing that it had been his hero Churchill's idea, that 'the neo-socialists were lucky to escape with their scalps. The delegates would have nothing to do with the proposal of changing the Party's name.' Only Macmillan spoke in favour of a new name, and was rebuffed by the Conference, cheered on by Peter Thorneycroft who claimed that he was 'Tory and proud of it'; when Thorneycroft ran out of time he was twice allowed an extension as he had the Conference behind him. Even a year earlier, with the shock of defeat fresher in people's minds, there had been considerable loyalty to the old labels; a motion had been put forward to the Northern Area Council, calling for a new Party name so as to attract Liberals; it was amended beyond recognition at the meeting, and ended up asking only for more vigorous propaganda in favour of the 'principles and policy of modern Conservatism'. At the 1922 Committee, those who wanted a new name were savagely mauled by Quintin Hogg; Tory Reformers knew what they meant by the title they had chosen for themselves. The issue then simply died, and while the Party organisations in Scotland and Northern Ireland continued to call themselves 'Unionist', for reasons that had little to do with Churchill's idea and certainly did not endear them to Liberals, most of their brethren in England and Wales remained 'Conservative'. The consequence was that nine different versions of the Leader's supporting letter to candidates had to be prepared in 1950, each one reflecting a different label under which Conservatives and their allies were still operating. The Party could though agree enthusiastically to a parallel suggestion from Woolton, that they should call their opponents not 'Labour' (a user-friendly word to industrial workers) but 'Socialists' (thought to sound partisan, theoretical and foreign). The discussion of electoral reform also petered out: again the Executive did not reach any conclusion, but in this case Churchill let it drop; when Liberal MPs introduced amendments calling for proportional representation in the 1948 Representation of the People Bill, Conservatives joined Labour to vote them down.[19]

None of this indicated indifference in the Party to the need for anti-socialist unity at the polls, but it did indicate that as in the 1920s the Conservatives would challenge the Liberals to rally around the Tory standard rather than make any real concessions to facilitate unity. In 1947, Butler's local association in Saffron Walden decided not to work for a deal with the local Liberals, a decision that had their MP's full support. In Guildford, the failure of attempts to fuse the Liberal and Tory organisations in 1948 was followed by the collapse of the local Liberal organisation and the absorption of Liberal activists into the Conservative association. Churchill, highly conscious both of his own Liberal past and of the increased freedom of action he would have, if he could claim to head more than a Party government, was naturally not satisfied with this strategy, and remained ready to use his position to facilitate anti-socialist cooperation whenever the chance arose. At the start of the 1950 campaign, he hoped to secure the withdrawal of the candidate in Rugby, writing to the Association President, Viscount Margesson, that 'people ought to make sacrifices and lay aside old prejudices. Only you can put this right. I make you my earnest request.' Since the sitting MP, W.J. Brown, had won Margesson's own seat when Churchill himself dismissed him to the Lords in 1942, the Leader was pushing his luck here; Margesson endorsed the letter 'Winston trying to make me agree to withdraw Conservative candidate at Rugby. I went to see him and convinced him of his folly'; the Conservative candidate came second to Labour with Brown a poor third, and after several close results, a Tory won the seat in 1959. Churchill was not so easily put off, securing West Fulham for Brown, which he contested as an Independent but without a Conservative opponent in 1951, but once again lost.[20]

[19] Earl of Woolton, *The Memoirs of the Rt. Hon. Earl of Woolton* (1959), 334; Central Office file, 'Liberal Nationals', CCO 3/1/63, CPA; John Turner, *Macmillan* (1994), 71; Thomas to Eden, 29 May 1946, Avon MSS, 11/12/38; Bradford CA minutes, 8 June and 18 July 1946; NUEC, 11 and 30 June, 17 Oct. 1946; Gilbert, *Never Despair*, 253; Maudling to Eden, 16 Aug. 1946, Avon MSS, 11/12/13a; Addison, *Churchill*, 392; Central Office file, 'Report on 1950 Election', CCO 500/24/2, CPA; Michael Kandiah, 'Lord Woolton's Chairmanship of the Conservative Party, 1946–1951', unpublished PhD thesis, University of Exeter, 1992, 87; Northern Area Council, 6 Oct. 1945; Goodhart, *The 1922*, 149; Cockett, *My Dear Max*, 58; D.E. Butler, *The Electoral System in Great Britain since 1918* (2nd edn, Oxford, 1963), 125.
[20] Saffron Walden CA minutes, 23 Aug. 1947; Guildford CA AGM minutes, 1951; Churchill to Margesson, and Margesson's note, 8 Feb. 1950, Margesson MSS, 1/4/18.

The first need in the consolidation of the anti-socialist vote was to tidy up the ragged relationship with the National Liberals, who had their own separate office, whips and constituency associations, but who were widely regarded as Conservatives in all but name. They did not regard themselves in that light, being conscious of their Liberal past and of the need to avoid too abrupt a conversion if they were to hang on to the support of Liberal voters. Central Office doubted if they had any such pull anyway, noting that in double-member seats in 1945 they had done no better than their Conservative co-candidates, and thought in April 1946 that pressure should be stepped up; Pierssené believed that if necessary, the National Liberal bluff should be called, for they posed no threat to Conservatives. The discussions between Woolton and Lord Teviot, National Liberal Chairman, were therefore complex, but reached fruition in April 1947 when their 'Woolton–Teviot pact' was approved by the National Union; Woolton 'hoped it would lead the Liberals throughout the country, apart from the Liberal Nationals, to become our allies', and this was clearly his main interest in it; Pierssené, on the other hand, thought that the pact could 'solve the Liberal National problem in the constituencies which are affected by it and . . . split the Liberal vote in the country as effectively as possible'. The pact agreed a formal merger at Westminster (though the National Liberals retained their own whip and room in the Commons until 1966), and a commitment to merge local associations into joint local parties. In Charles Hill's Luton constituency, there was a full merger of the two organisations, and likewise in neighbouring South Bedfordshire, but only after some jockeying for position over the appointment of officers. By June 1948, there were twenty-three constituency associations affiliated to the National Union which included the word 'Liberal' in their title, and this increased further as the Woolton–Teviot reforms were implemented locally; by May 1949, there were twenty-three such constituency associations in the Wessex Area alone; in Bradford, the Conservatives reluctantly came to the conclusion that they could not merge with all Liberals and agreed to fuse with the National Liberals instead, though they called the new organisation Bradford Conservative and Liberal Association. On the eve of the 1950 Election, there had been sixty-one local mergers (about a tenth of all constituencies); as their candidates they chose thirty Conservatives and twenty-nine National Liberals, and in Carmarthen and Greenock they backed ordinary Liberal candidates. This practice was the cause of a furious dispute with independent Liberals who claimed that their title had been stolen from them to delude the voters. There may have been justification for this: when a 'merger' took place in Sheffield Central in 1947, no extra members were added to the existing Conservative organisation when the name was changed, but then in Sheffield cooperation in municipal elections since the 1920s had brought many Liberals into the Tory ranks already. In Dundee the joint association had 7,000 members, only twenty of them recent Liberal converts. Since the exact borderline between National Liberals and other Liberals was not always clear, the National Union decided in 1949 that any Liberal candidate or MP who included 'Conservative' or 'Unionist' in his self-description, and was backed by a Conservative local association, would be treated as a Conservative, and be allowed to attend Party Conferences, receive the Party whip and be afforded organisational support.[21]

Churchill and Woolton tried to take things much further: attempts to point out a policy convergence between Conservatives and Liberals, for example over nationalisation, were usually rebuffed by Liberal MPs, who saw well enough that they could easily be swallowed up altogether. When the 1950 Election produced such a narrow Labour victory, with many Labour seats being held on minority votes, there was a further attempt to define an 'overlap prospectus' as a basis for common anti-socialist electoral action. Butler, in charge of the Conservative team, put much energy into the discussions, but again they fell through because neither side would make sacrifices, and because the Liberal demands were now so unrealistic after their 1950 humiliation at the polls. In July, he sharply reminded Lady Violet Bonham-Carter, who headed the Liberal negotiators, and whose access to Churchill made for awkwardnesses anyway, that 'difficulties arise as much from the varied personalities and difficulties in yr. ranks as from the inability to coerce our people'. By then, even Woolton had lost interest. He told Salisbury in September 1950 that

> I am having a very difficult time with Churchill. He is determined to bring about some arrangement with the Liberals; he sees this as the most likely means whereby we can secure a majority at the next election, and he regards it, from a national point of view, as overriding any narrow party consideration. I have told him that I have for a long time been trying to get the Liberals and Conservatives to join together under the dual title, and that some 63 constituencies are now doing this, but not unnaturally his mind goes to what we have *not* got.

These discussions were stormy: Woolton explained that 'I saw no prospect of the Party finding his views acceptable' and Churchill said that in that case he would resign; Salisbury, knowing that little of this was being reported to the shadow cabinet, decided that 'Winston has not been very frank with his colleagues'. Woolton correctly foresaw that it would be utterly unreal to expect forty or so Conservative candidates to withdraw in favour of Liberals who had come third in 1950, and the National Union backed him in refusing to sanction a deal on such terms. One constituency involved was Newcastle East, which the Conservatives had not contested since 1929, and which was held by a National Liberal from 1931 to 1945; local discussions with the

---

[21] Pierssené to Stuart and Assheton, June 1946, and Stuart to Churchill, 5 Dec. 1946, Whip's papers, 'Relations with Nat. Liberals', CPA; NUEC, 17 Apr. 1947, 9 June 1948 and 14 July 1949; Gilbert, *Never Despair*, 346, 503, 529; Eastern Area Council, 22 Nov. 1948; Wessex Area Council, 16 May 1949; Bradford CA minutes, 29 Feb. 1948; Sheffield Central CA minutes, 10 July 1947.

Liberals foundered and there was a three-cornered contest in 1950 – which the Conservatives professed to regret greatly; but the 1950 contest showed that the Conservatives were close behind Labour, while the Liberals could not save their deposit; the Party now refused all overtures for a pact, the Liberals did not put up candidates, and this marginal seat eventually fell to a Tory in 1959. In Barry the benefit came sooner; attempts to reach an accommodation with local Liberals failed in 1949, but the Conservative candidate in 1950 came a close second to Labour with the Liberal well behind; in 1951, with no Liberal standing, two-thirds of the Liberal vote seems to have gone to the Conservatives, and the seat was won. Only at the margin was cooperation possible in 1951; when the Montgomery Conservatives, following 'a little private advice' from Woolton, decided not to put up a candidate against Clement Davies, who despite being a National Liberal in the 1930s now led the independent Liberals, the National Union Executive reluctantly agreed with Woolton, that 'Liberals would find it much easier to vote for our candidates if we did not oppose the Liberal leader'. Churchill's (rejected) offer of a Cabinet post to Davies when he returned to office shows that he had still not accepted as final his defeat on the issue of a deal with Liberals.[22]

But what could not be achieved nationally could sometimes be brought off in the localities, and here the good offices of Woolton were important, both to keep pacts going where they already existed and to extend them where possible. These activities were heavily concentrated in the area that Professor Northcote Parkinson called 'the Left Riding', the Pennine area of Yorkshire and Lancashire where Liberals were both nonconformist and anti-socialist. When a new constituency of Brighouse and Spenborough was created in 1948, much tact was required: Jim Thomas reported that the new association wanted to 'throw out' the former candidate, a National Liberal, and as a result 'the National Liberal headquarters have gone up in smoke'. A meeting in London settled the problem, along with similar disputes in Swansea and Runcorn, but Central Office then had to sell the deal to the locals; Woolton explained that 'the first and overriding consideration is to prevent this seat going to the Socialists'; he explicitly used Churchill's name in support of his action and kept up the pressure. Local Conservatives, who had not had a sitting Conservative MP in living memory, were loath to give up their rights and complained about 'headquarters waving the big stick' but, eventually and sulkily, they accepted that 'you are the Chairman of the Party' and gave way. Woolton invariably based his local interventions on the national

22  Kandiah, 'Lord Woolton' thesis, 91, 167; Butler to Bonham-Carter, 13 July 1950, Butler MSS, G22; Central Office file, 'National Liberals', CCO 3/1/63, CPA; Howard, *RAB*, 169–71; Central Office constituency file, Newcastle East, CCO 1/7/70, CPA; Barry CA minutes, 15 Sept. 1949; NUEC, 9 Nov. 1950; Woolton to Salisbury, 16 Sept. 1950 and Salisbury to Woolton, 30 Sept. 1950, Woolton MSS, box 21.

perspective; 'Conservatives cannot expect support from Liberals if they are going to insist on fighting every seat'. There was a by-election in May 1950 in this highly marginal seat; the local Tories threatened to back the National Liberal candidate only if he called himself 'National Liberal and Conservative', but had to settle for 'National Liberal with Conservative support'. Relations were also difficult in Walsall, where Conservatives claimed that they had to accept the title 'National Liberal' for a joint candidate, but that no Liberals ever appeared to do any work or pay any bills. In Bristol, things were so bad that Woolton had to intervene directly, but the dispute rumbled on until 1955, and in Denbigh a similar dispute that started in the 1930s was still going on in the early 1960s, as a result of Central Office pressurising the constituency to go on backing a National Liberal who had only recently been a much-disliked Liberal without any prefix. In 1947, Churchill intervened with the Scottish Unionist Association to secure a free run in Caithness and Sutherland for his wartime ministerial colleague, the former Liberal Leader Sir Archibald Sinclair, but the Party would have nothing to do with such manoeuvres in a constituency that it had actually won in 1945; the seat was contested and won by a Conservative in 1950, and Sinclair's parliamentary career came to a premature end.[23]

In Bradford, a 1949 by-election raised different sensitivities. A National Liberal had stood for Bradford South in 1945, but this time a Conservative candidate was jointly selected, backed in his campaign by an array of Conservative speakers, including Macmillan, Maxwell Fyfe and Lyttelton. The difficulty was that Viscount Simon, whose name had once defined National Liberalism and who had sat for the adjoining Spen Valley, offered to come too. Simon was extremely unpopular; according to the Central Office Agent, the locals 'did not love him too dearly', and Eden drily advised that 'Lord Simon's appeal to Liberals to vote for the Conservative candidate does not always have the required effect'. Simon's offer was politely declined, and in his place the Party sent Gwilym Lloyd George, another famous Liberal name and a National Liberal since 1939. In High Peak, the Conservatives refused to allow Leslie Hore-Belisha to address one of their meetings, but in this case anti-semitism may have played a part as well as his 'unpopularity'.[24]

For the Leicester North East by-election in 1950, Anthony Nutting was the candidate's minder, and reported that efforts to bring in Liberal votes in the absence of a Liberal candidate had largely misfired: the Liberal vote from earlier in the year had drifted into abstention, rather than following the advice of local Liberals to back the Conservatives, 'all of which only

[23] Central Office constituency file, Brighouse and Spenborough, CCO 1/7/164, CPA; Walsall CA minutes, 23 Feb. 1946; Central Office constituency files, Bristol, 1/7/479–84; Denbigh CA minutes, various dates; NUEC, 9 Jan. 1947.
[24] Central Office constituency file, Bradford South, CCO 1/7/163, CPA; High Peak CA minutes, 12 Aug. and 23 Sept. 1947.

goes to show that "guidance" to the Liberal vote is useless'. He cheekily asked that this experience should be brought to Churchill's attention. In Shrewsbury, negotiations for a deal with the Liberals in 1950 were fruitless, but in analysing the result the local Conservatives felt that this had done them no harm anyway; the existence of a Liberal candidate had probably helped them and split the anti-*Tory* vote. This clearly varied considerably between different places. In Shoreditch and Finsbury there were the usual disputes, but when there was no Liberal candidate in 1951 and the local Liberals strongly backed the Tory, his vote went up by more than 40 per cent, well above the national average. In Cornwall, Liberal support had been retained in 1945, and the Falmouth Tories were in 1947 anxious not 'to offend our friends the Liberals'.[25]

Against this chequered record can be set two towns where the prospects for cooperation were better, and where formal pacts did emerge, Huddersfield and Bolton. These were until 1948 double-member constituencies with a tradition of party horse-trading, and each was then divided into two separate constituencies. In Huddersfield there was a strong National Liberal presence and there had been no Conservative candidate since 1929; when in 1947 the two Liberal organisations reunited, the Conservatives were put in a weak position, even when a later Liberal meeting also voted to accept the Woolton–Teviot pact. Local Conservatives were reported to be 'willing to extend their title in any way that helps'. The division into two constituencies was thought to offer the ideal way forward, with the Conservatives fighting one seat and the National Liberals the other, but also backing each other. A Halifax businessman was selected for the East Division, but the Tory organisation was at a low ebb after so long without fighting any parliamentary election; there was certainly no capacity to fight two campaigns simultaneously, but two candidates were still chosen by the end of 1949. Since Liberal reunion turned out to be more significant than the dissident National Liberals, a pact had to be done with the official Liberals or not at all, and this was duly arranged in January 1950; a form of words was agreed that enabled Conservatives to back the Liberal candidate in the West division and Liberals to back the Conservative in the East. This pact ran right through to 1960 and though the Conservatives failed to win the East Division, it denied Huddersfield West to Labour.[26]

The relative smoothness of the pact in Huddersfield – which Liberals tried unsuccessfully to extend as 'the Huddersfield formula' to other places, but

---

[25] Central Office constituency file, Leicester North East, CCO 1/7/224; Shrewsbury CA minutes, 20 Jan. and 4 May 1950; Shoreditch and Finsbury CA minutes, 22 Jan. 1949 and 12 Nov. 1951; Penryn and Falmouth CA minutes, 13 Dec. 1947.

[26] Central Office constituency files, Huddersfield, CCO 1/5/182, 1/7/168–9, 1/8/168–9; H.G. Nicholas, *The British General Election of 1950* (1951), 82–3; B.J. Evans and A.J. Taylor, 'The Rise and Fall of Two-Party Electoral Co-operation', in *Political Studies*, vol. 32 (1984), 262–3.

without Central Office backing – contrasts with the friction in Bolton that produced a much better outcome. Here the Conservatives had fought every election except 1918 and had a strong organisation; in 1946 they had already readopted one of their losing candidates from 1945 and were on the lookout for a second. The division into two constituencies produced the same thinking as in Huddersfield, for once again the strongest Conservative wards were in the East and the more Liberal wards in the West. Seeking a second candidate, the local Conservatives specified a businessman with Lancashire connections but who was not a Catholic (since their adopted candidate was one, and in such a staunchly Anglican area 'they think two would be overdoing it'). This proved difficult, for the Party had few suitable names on the list, and by June 1949 there was still only one candidate, adopted for the Eastern division. Attempts were made to move over a National Liberal MP who was proving unpopular in Cheshire, but a local man was selected instead and two candidates ran and lost in 1950. Approaches for a pact were then made by the Liberals. Negotiations almost foundered several times on the question of electoral reform; it was eventually agreed, with Central Office approving the wording, that the Party was 'quite willing to have the whole issue investigated afresh'. Woolton then weighed in with a strong plea for a deal to 'wrest both seats from the Socialists'. Within Central Office the Bolton case occasioned for the first time a clear definition of policy; Woolton minuted that he wanted 'such arrangements [to] occur spontaneously and not appear in any way to be dictated from above' and Thomas added, 'I hate these bargains, but if we must have them this is an obvious place'. There was though a flaming row at the Bolton West Executive (which agreed to the pact only by 168 votes to 137 and with many spoilt ballot papers) and a special General Meeting had to be called to ratify the pact; Woolton summoned the association officers to London to ensure that it went through. The pact was announced in the press at the end of January 1951, but the Central Office Agent reported in May that there was 'still bitter opposition' to the deal. That opposition was partly assuaged, and certainly deprived of real impact, by the defeat of Labour candidates in both seats in the 1951 Election, though in that campaign Conservative activists in Bolton West were offered the option of working for their own Party's candidate in the East Division, and steps were taken to ensure that blue Conservative posters as well as red Liberal ones continued to appear in the West. As in Huddersfield, the pact was in force until after the 1959 election and in Bolton deprived Labour of two seats each time. The failure to produce a working pact in the relatively similar situation of Blackburn shows just how difficult it could be to overcome local opposition, and how limited was Central Office's influence.[27]

27 Central Office constituency files, Bolton, CCO 1/7/100–1, 1/8/100–1, 1/9/100–1; Bolton West CA minutes, 22 Jan. and 28 Sept. 1951; Evans and Taylor, 'Electoral Co-operation', 264–6.

## Local and by-elections

In most parts of the country, therefore, the Party geared up for a straight battle against Labour, with Liberals portrayed as an irrelevance that would let Socialism in. The renewed combativeness that this showed was indicated too in a new view of elections to local authorities. Before 1939, there had been Conservatives who had noted the use that Labour was making of local government as a springboard for national power, Herbert Morrison's leadership of the London County Council being a case in point, and a counter movement was under way, but resistance in the constituencies to the wholesale politicisation of local government had retarded the Conservative response. In 1943, a motion from Ilford calling on the Party to fight all local government elections was not reached on the Conference agenda; the local government sub-committee of the PWPCC discussed it and accepted the idea in principle; it recommended that Central Office should include local government specialists among its staff, that there should be more Conservative MPs with municipal experience, and that there should be a National Local Government Advisory Committee to review the Party's position nationally, with equivalent committees in each Area. These recommendations were accepted, though in practice they had to await the post-war revival of the organisation before much happened. In October 1945, in Sussex, Rear Admiral Tufton Beamish proposed that all elections in Sussex (which was hardly Labour's prime target) should be contested by Conservatives, but several members spoke up for ratepayers' associations and independent councillors. Sometimes, alliances with ratepayers, entered into when the Party was weak in 1945, could be dispensed with by the early 1950s; this happened in Brentford and Chiswick. In February 1946, the National Union considered a motion that would have withdrawn Party support from all Independent candidates, and referred it to its new Advisory Committee before taking a decision. Two months later, it was agreed 'as a general rule' to support only Conservative candidates, justifying this with the assertion that 'the Socialist Party have made it impossible to exclude Party politics from local government'. The implementation of this policy advanced the transition to a fully politicised local government system by 1950 in the conurbations and county boroughs, and in the larger counties. But in rural counties, small boroughs and district councils the change was slower, not least because these were also constituencies in which the organisation was decentralised and a strong political lead was difficult to exert; when in 1951 a new agent tried to persuade Nelson and Colne Conservatives to put up more Party candidates, he met stiff resistance from the Nelson representatives, and the others agreed that the matter should remain for the Nelson branches to decide; in nearby North Fylde, it was agreed in 1949 to contest all the county council seats, but only to oppose socialists and left-leaning independents in Fleetwood borough, and to leave right-leaning independents undisturbed in Thornton. In the North East, where the Party still felt extremely vulnerable, old pacts lingered on; Darlington decided to keep up its anti-socialist front for municipal elections, and a proposal that Middlebrough should abandon its 'Civic Association' candidates in 1948 was defeated by twenty-four votes to one, but in the more prosperous Tynemouth constituency it was decided 'as a matter of principle' to oppose all candidates of the 'Rent and Ratepayers' Association'; in South East Cardiff, even in 1953 ratepayers were being supported; at the other end of the Principality, East Flint was in 1952 contesting fifteen county council seats, providing workers for six Conservatives, eight Independents and a Liberal, but before the next county elections they agreed with the West Flint Tories only to back official candidates of the Party: the association chairman, a future National Union President, Alastair Graesser, noted that 'the committee deplored politics in Local Government, but it was useless to close their eyes to the Socialist tactics and they must be prepared to fight'. In the mid-1950s, 60 per cent of county council seats were still being won without any sort of contest; and as late as in 1971, just before Peter Walker's wholesale reorganisation of local authorities, a third of all county councils, small boroughs and urban districts were still run by 'Independents'. In collecting and publicising election results, the local government section of Central Office evolved a distinction between candidates who were 'Independent with Conservative support', who in practice counted as Conservatives, and real Independents who were not; over time the balance shifted between these groups, so that a net loss of 174 for 'Independents' in 1949 concealed a gain of that size by the Conservatives in disguise and a much bigger loss by truly non-party candidates. One consequence was that the Party often had to find election expenses for local government candidates now that it was claiming them as its own; Eden's constituency of Warwick and Leamington, perennially short of association funds in a very decentralised branch structure, had to vote £350 for this purpose in 1954.[28]

The attack on local government fitted well enough with criticism of Labour's policies of 'centralisation': Douglas Jay had infelicitously explained that 'the gentleman in Whitehall really does know better what is good for people than they know themselves', a pre-war phrase that Conservatives frequently quoted back at the Attlee Government of which Jay was a member, and Woolton came up with the campaign slogan 'Town Hall, not Whitehall'. Special attention was given to the London County Council: for a time Henry Brooke withdrew from Westminster politics to give a higher profile to the Conservative position in London as minority leader on the authority; Iain Macleod was Director in 1950, and John Hare the Chairman, of the London

28 John Ramsden, *The Age of Balfour and Baldwin, 1902–1940* (1978), 259; Sussex Provincial Division minutes, 22 Oct. 1945; Brentford and Chiswick CA minutes, 20 Feb. 1952; NUEC 14 Feb. and 11 Apr. 1946; Nelson and Colne CA minutes, 5 Mar. 1951; North Fylde CA minutes, 11 Mar. 1949; Middlesbrough CA minutes, 8 Dec. 1947; Tynemouth CA minutes, 10 Jan. 1949; South East Cardiff CA minutes, 16 Feb. 1953; East Flint CA minutes, 31 Mar. 1952 and 9 Dec. 1954; Warwick and Leamington CA minutes, 31 Mar. 1954.

Municipal Society which ran the Party's local government efforts in London; the training courses for local candidates that Macleod organised, in which he personally took on the role of Labour spokesman and asked them the trickiest questions that his formidable mind could think of, were not easily forgotten by those who experienced them. The attack on local government was valuable in itself since many seats were won. It also provided the impression of action and success (always a difficult thing for an opposition to achieve), and gave the revived Party machine regular contests that tested out men and structures before the 1950 General Election. In 1951, 38 per cent of Conservative parliamentary candidates had local government experience, twice the proportion in 1935, and this certainly ensured that they were more experienced campaigners. In 1948 there was a net gain of about 800 council seats and twice as many as that in 1949; by then Labour controlled only eleven of the sixty-two counties and less than half of the county boroughs, and controlled London only through Aldermen.[29]

The seats gained in local government contests were the more important because there was no signal by-election triumph to prove that the Party was on the road back to power. Of governments with large majorities, Attlee's was unique in not losing a single seat at a conventional by-election; the Conservatives technically gained Camlachie, and the ILP took another Glasgow seat, but both of these were peculiar contests in which the Labour vote was split. Viewed psephologically, the by-elections of 1945–50 produced an average swing of 5 per cent from Labour to Conservative, which would wipe out Labour's 1945 lead in the popular vote – would indeed produce a result remarkably like those of the General Elections of 1950 and 1951; individual contests at Bexley, Edmonton and Croydon suggested that the Conservatives were doing especially well in the South East – again a good predictor of what would happen in 1950–51. Few drew these comforting conclusions at the time, though there was some local satisfaction from increased majorities in Tory seats, as at Hillhead in 1948, and these contests provided opportunities to try out the organisation. Morale in the Party remained fragile throughout the 1945 Parliament, because the scale of defeat had shaken Conservative confidence to its foundations, and because no parliamentary seats were actually *gained*. In Summer 1947 and again in Spring 1949, the National Union was discussing the causes of the Party's apparently poor performance.[30]

The detailed results of individual by-elections and municipal polling were anxiously scanned for what they could yield as political pointers. At first they did not encourage optimism, for in 1945–46 the results indicated no

---

[29] Nigel Fisher, *Iain Macleod* (1973), 75–6; Woolton, *Memoirs*, 341–2; D.E. Butler, *The British General Election of 1951* (1952), 37; *NCP*, 17 Jan. 1949 and 16 June 1950.

[30] Chris Cook and John Ramsden (eds), *By-Elections in British Politics* (1973), 191–2, 374–7, 387; Glasgow UA minutes, 29 Nov. 1948; NUEC, 10 July 1947 and 28 Apr. 1949.

more than the most basic recovery from the 1945 nadir. The turning of the corner came in 1947, the year in which the Labour Government lost its way in simultaneous crises of fuel shortages, freeze-ups and finance, much of the public lost patience with it, and the Conservatives produced their *Industrial Charter*. In February, Churchill told the shadow cabinet that he was 'terrified of the position of the country on looking at figures supplied to him by the secretariat', but there were undoubted Party opportunities in the crisis. In April, Sheffield Conservatives resolved to campaign mainly on fuel shortages as 'a subject of grievance'; in September they agreed 'that the National Crisis should be the principal method of attack'; in November, they thought that their municipal results were 'disappointing' in view of 'the country's swing to the right'. In each year of the Parliament from 1947, by-elections produced a net swing bigger than was needed to return the Conservatives to office, local government elections produced a crop of gains, and opinion polls placed the Conservatives alongside or ahead of Labour. In November 1947, the Party had a net gain of 600 seats in the borough elections and Bracken exulted that 'the result of the Municipal elections alarmed the Socialists and astonished the Tories. There was a great increase in the Socialist vote. But the enormous increase in the Tory vote was an overwhelming compensation.' He felt that 'the Tories are recovering confidence and are out for blood'. This new optimism encouraged the belief that Gravesend could be captured at an imminent by-election. When Labour held the seat, the National Union held a sombre inquest; Woolton concluded that the swing was good enough to win a general election, but attributed the failure to capture the seat to the loyalty of male voters to Labour – they had not yet suffered the same privations as their wives. Under pressure, he agreed that in future Central Office would give greater priority to by-elections. Headlam found that 'our not winning Gravesend has somewhat dispirited our young men . . . I am sure – as I have always been since the general election – that the comrades will need a deal of getting rid of.' Pierssené's verdict was that 1947 had 'witnessed some turn of the tide in our favour, but it is clear that we still have far to go before we make a deep impression on Labour strongholds'.[31]

The very totality of the 1945 defeat made it difficult to see how and where recovery would come; but gradually, as a result of several years of post-war local elections, some understanding emerged as to different categories of seats, and which would offer the prospects of real success; Holborn and East Islington had both been Tory seats before 1945, but they were now more realistically categorised as 'marginal minus' in 1949: the first was only won once more (in 1959) and the second was never won again. After the 1948 redistribution of boundaries, 120 constituencies were listed as 'marginal

[31] LCC, 2 Feb. 1947; Sheffield CA minutes, 30 Apr., 2 Sept. and 13 Nov. 1947; Cockett, *My Dear Max*, 75, 79–80; Hodgson, 'Steel Debates', 308; Kilmuir, *Memoirs*, 153; NUEC, 11 Dec. 1947; Headlam diary, 4 Dec. 1947; *CAJ*, Jan. 1948.

plus' (eighty-four of which were Tory by 1951, thirteen more by 1959) and 111 as 'marginal minus' (of which only twenty-three were gained by 1951); 'wrong' predictions are almost entirely explained by the regional variations in swings that nobody had foreseen in 1948, but there were also some very odd allocations; Bridgwater and St Albans were seen as 'marginal minus', while Bishop Auckland came out as 'marginal plus', possibly with some wish fulfilment foreseeing the removal of 'the dirty doctor' Hugh Dalton, and so did Penistone where Labour's lowest ever majority was to be over 11,000. The widespread use of the word 'swing' was in itself an indication of a more sophisticated approach that Party professionals were discovering along with other political commentators, in what was the natal period of British psephology. McCallum and Readman's *The British General Election of 1945* was warmly welcomed when it appeared in 1947, and its framework of analysis was adopted for the interpretation of subsequent results; in 1949, for example, William Deedes argued in *The Daily Telegraph* that, in terms of average swings and the McCallum and Readman model of constituency behaviour, by-elections since 1945 had pointed to a Conservative recovery of winning proportions in a general election. In any case, the 1948 results were generally more satisfactory, perhaps because the disappointment at Gravesend discouraged over-optimism. A much-increased majority in Croydon in March gave something to celebrate, particularly after Churchill had staked his prestige on a visit to the campaign – quite a shift since his view in 1943–44. Chips Channon felt that 'the news . . . has sent a thrill through the country: it is an almost unbelievable Conservative victory . . . Is it the turn of the tide?' In November, Edmonton was even better, with a swing of 16.8 per cent; Bracken shrewdly noted that only 250 houses had been built in Edmonton since the end of the War, and several thousand people were still awaiting homes. Pierssené issued a New Year message for 1949 that claimed that Edmonton showed victory to be on the way, and Churchill claimed 'another El Alamein'.[32]

Once again, over-optimism produced a sharp reverse when the next contest was not so successful, at South Hammersmith in February 1949. Bracken was one of the few who realised just how far social change and population movement had undermined the Conservative position in inner London, much as his own North Paddington seat had gone to Labour in 1945, and stayed that way. The South Hammersmith association was not strong, and much of its money had to be raised in the Constitutional Club. The mistake was to pin the Party's hopes on a constituency that was no longer really a marginal seat, despite the small Labour majority of 1945, and then to invest so much capital in the contest, including a much-photographed visit by Churchill to the constituency on polling day. The Party's dilemma was succinctly outlined

[32] Central Office constituency files, Holborn and Islington East, CCO 1/7/17 and 18; CPA; *CAJ*, Jan and Apr. 1949; Central Office file, 'Marginal seats', CCO 4/2/116; Rhodes James, *Chips*, 422; Kilmuir, *Memoirs*, 154; Cockett, *My Dear Max*, 98; Pelling, *Churchill*, 574.

by Chapman-Walker in seeking Woolton's guidance; if Central Office went openly for a win and said so to the press, but then did not win, then 'we shall show that we lost despite a full organisational recovery and the press will blame our policy'. If on the other hand they did not make a pitch to win, then the press would say that the organisational recovery was bogus. Woolton as ever went for the policy of risk, and made a big splash with the extent to which the Conservatives were pouring help into Hammersmith. Encouraged by Woolton's appeals, the help certainly did pour in; there were 300 canvassers a day during the campaign, producing a very accurate final canvass return that enabled Central Office to get the result right (but too late to save the Party's face), teams of MPs were drafted in to address meetings every night, and 1500 workers were in the constituency on polling day. The result was a crushing disappointment when Labour held the seat, even though there was a respectable 5 per cent swing to Conservative. There was a heavy inflow of critical letters to Churchill and Woolton, many of them from Party workers who had helped in the campaign and had their own views on what had gone wrong, and several inquests were held. Central Office passed the responsibility to the policy-makers; Pierssené told Chapman-Walker that the weakness was on the policy side, but he should not say that in press briefings: 'let the suggestion come spontaneously from other sources'. The defeated candidate, Anthony Fell, who had already fought and lost a by-election at Brigg less than a year earlier, was highly critical. The final organisational report noted that 'Mr. Fell was most emphatic that the electorate does not trust the Conservative Party' on policy; vague phrases like 'the property-owning democracy' would not do unless spelled out as a programme, and 'the meeting generally agreed that it was only a long-term policy which would convince the electorate of the futility of Socialist policy'. This report was then given wide circulation around the Party and helped to step up the search for scapegoats; the Area Agent for Yorkshire, for example, wrote that 'from what I have seen here, I have to agree with Mr. Fell's opinion'; Jim Thomas minuted more equivocally that 'people do *not* trust the Tory Party. If we can win back that trust we are home.'[33]

This unleashed the Party crisis of Spring 1949; *The Economist* blamed Churchill's lack of leadership for the Conservatives' failure, while Churchill had to attend a meeting of the 1922 Committee and listen to a solid hour of critical comment, in what Philip Goodhart called 'the most severe crisis of confidence in [his] leadership'; the press release spoke of a 'full and frank discussion, in which Mr. Churchill took part'; Headlam's note of the meeting reported 'people rather critical and disgruntled, and not at all impressed by his optimism. Why should they be? For the time being at any rate, clearly the Socialist State is in the ascendant.' It was this crisis of confidence that

---

[33] Cockett, *My Dear Max*, 105; Central Office constituency file, Hammersmith South, CCO 1/7/15.

shifted the emphasis of policy-making towards detail at last, and produced *The Right Road for Britain*. Things were not as bad as they seemed; from the Labour side on 20 March, Dalton wrote that 'we are children of the instant, and the Tories are in a very low state today. But they will gain seats in the municipal elections and the Budget may be cold comfort for all.' The Conservatives did have good borough results in May, taking control of Birmingham, Leicester, Manchester and Newcastle on very high turnouts. The Labour Government's economic difficulties did deepen and the crisis mood in the Party simmered down; an Organisation Department file entitled 'Defeatism, 1949' only accumulated four pieces of paper. In hindsight, March 1949 seems an extraordinary over-reaction: in 1951, the Conservatives took office for thirteen years, and only once in that time did South Hammersmith elect a Conservative MP (for the more middle-class Baron's Court in 1959), and it has never done so since. A pre-war marginal was now a Labour seat, and more generally in inner London the 1949 local elections were not as good for the Conservatives as cities in the provinces: even after 274 Tory gains in May 1949, the London boroughs still had more Labour councillors than Conservatives, and five boroughs elected no Conservatives at all. But, while it gradually became clear that these areas were never again to be the swing seats that determined which party formed the government, the furore indicates just how frustrating the opposition years had been, how anxious the Party was for real evidence of success, and how it was now desperate to get at Labour in a General Election.[34]

## The 1950 General Election

One final uncertainty contributed to Conservative apprehensions of the coming election, changed electoral rules and new boundaries. The review only partially implemented in 1945 fed through into a major Bill and a large-scale redistribution in 1948. This once again led to bad feeling between the parties. Conservatives, and Churchill in particular, argued that Labour was in 'bad faith' reneging on the all-party agreement of 1943–44 and, instead of seeking all-party agreement on electoral matters as had been traditional, was legislating its own partisan programme. There was some justification for this, but Churchill protested too much in his anxiety to catch Labour out rigging the rules; ironically, Labour did not actually benefit anyway. Some of the individual changes did harm Conservative chances: business votes were finally abolished for parliamentary elections, though they survived in local

[34] Goodhart, *The 1922*, 144–6; Headlam diary, 3 Mar. 1949; Lord Butler of Saffron Walden, *The Art of the Possible, The Memoirs of Lord Butler* (1971), 150; Howard, *RAB*, 163; Ben Pimlott (ed.), *The Political Diaries of Hugh Dalton, 1918–1940 and 1945–1960* (1986), 447; *NCP*, 23 May 1949; A. Sutcliffe and R. Smith, *Birmingham, 1939–1970* (1974), 83; Central Office file, 'Defeatism, 1949', CCO 4/2/33, CPA.

government polls until 1968, a big loss compared to the pre-war position, but a small one compared to what had already gone by 1945; the City of London lost its two members and the universities all twelve of theirs, the large majority of which would have been Conservative again in the 1950s; restrictions were imposed on the use of cars at elections, negating (if they were meticulously observed, which seems unlikely) the advantage accruing in rural areas to the Party that had the wealthier supporters. Churchill promised to restore university constituencies, and resolutions were passed to that effect by the National Union. Against these losses was set one substantial, long-term gain, the creation of postal voting for removals and those travelling for their work. Conservatives gained from this partly because the effort to trace removals had to be done between election campaigns, and so a premium was placed on continuous paid organisation, and partly because middle-class voters who were predominantly Tory were more likely to claim their rights anyway: in 1950 there were on average twice as many postal votes cast in Tory constituencies as in Labour ones. The beauty of the advantage gained through postal votes, compared to such earlier practices as plural voting, was that in theory they applied equally to all, and so could not be denounced as undemocratic. On average in the 1950s, postal votes accounted for only about 2 per cent of votes cast, but the turnout among postal voters was very high, they were concentrated in Tory, Ulster and marginal seats, and the evidence suggests that up to three-quarters of them were Conservative. About half a million extra votes were cast that would previously have been lost, and the *net* Conservative advantage over Labour was something around a quarter of a million votes, but concentrated where they could be most useful; David Butler concluded that 'there can be little doubt that in 1950 the postal vote enabled the Conservatives to win a dozen seats that would otherwise have fallen to Labour'. Changed boundaries made forecasting the 1950 Election particularly difficult, but on balance also helped the Conservatives. For example, in the East End of London, a Labour stronghold, thirteen constituencies were reduced to six, while in the Middlesex suburbs seventeen seats, already raised to twenty-four in 1945, now went up again to twenty-eight. Again, this was easy to justify since the changes produced constituencies of a more equal size, though the 1950s electoral map as a whole contained a small (and entirely accidental) pro-Conservative bias, caused by the piling up of wasted Labour majorities in the safest seats; if the parties got about the same number of votes, the Conservatives would win more seats, as indeed they did in 1951. The contemporary estimate was that the net gain to the Conservatives, aggregating all these changes, was worth about thirty seats – a third of the Party's entire recovery when 1950 is compared to 1945; the Party certainly thought so, for Churchill was in February 1948 urging his colleagues not to vote against the Representation of the People Bill 'which would greatly benefit the Conservative Party', but he was also warning them not to be too enthusiastically favourable to it either, in case they encouraged

Labour and Liberal MPs to delay its passage. The actual net effect is hard to call, and the closeness of the 1950–51 contests allows contradictory claims: if there had been no redistribution and no postal votes, Attlee would in 1950 have achieved a majority sufficient for a full parliament; conversely, had the City and the universities kept their representation, he would have lost office altogether; without postal votes and redistribution, the Conservatives would not have returned to office in 1951 and so had the chance to show what they could do.[35]

That was what they most wanted, for by 1950 they had become steadily more angry about the way in which Labour portrayed them as reactionary and insincere – Attlee dismissed *The Right Road* as 'one of the most dishonest documents' he had ever read. Such charges could never be refuted in words, only by actions in office. In February 1950 the chance at last came: the Election was announced on 11 January, with polling on 23 February. The date ensured that the Election would be on an old register, compiled in June 1949, and this gave the Conservative organisation an extra chance to show its skills. Unlike 1945, this time the Party was ready. A *Campaign Guide* was already published, the manifesto was easily produced from *The Right Road for Britain*, the CRD and Central Office had poster and literature material already in draft, and a speaker campaign already mapped out. A full-scale briefing was held for candidates on 23 January, when Butler reviewed the policy exercise since 1946:

> I have for the past four years been involved in helping to prepare the variety of policy documents which we have brought out. As one who has been primarily responsible, I may perhaps be able to criticise them. They have been produced under the principle of diffused authorship. Now diffused authorship is very difficult to carry out, and as I am the editor I have had a hell of a time! But not such a time as during the last fortnight since Mr. Churchill's return from Madeira. This has been one of the most inspiring experiences of my life. When you read the [manifesto] you cannot fail to see the enormous influence which Mr. Churchill has had upon it himself. When you study the English and compare it with the efforts that have come out before, you will see it is not only crisper and shorter but better and purer prose.

Part of the reason for the sharper edge to Party policy-making at the end of the 1945 Parliament lay simply in Churchill's own greater interest in what was going on. For the rest of the campaign candidates were sent detailed daily briefings on urgent topics of debate, an unprecedented degree of central coordination of the local contests; for example, Daily Note 11 provided material for responding to Labour speeches on tax and on employment. The disappointment at the outset was the large number of Liberal candidates,

35  Butler, *Electoral System*, 103–9, 122–7, 133–9; LCC, 11 Feb. 1948; F.W.S. Craig (ed.), *British Parliamentary Election Statistics, 1918–1970* (Chichester, 1971), 66; Booth, *British Hustings*, 245.

475 in all and in nearly every Conservative or marginal constituency; the anti-Labour vote would thus usually be split; Headlam's 'great fear' was that 'the infernal Liberals are going to queer our pitch all over the country'. But sixty-five Conservative candidates also claimed to stand for Liberalism in some form under Woolton–Teviot arrangements. At Leeds on 4 February, Churchill roundly denounced the Liberals for their refusal to cooperate: 'here and there a sensible arrangement may be made, but in the main the die is cast'. The Conservative revival showed up in a young team of candidates, two-thirds of whom were under fifty; this at least offset the fact that Churchill was now seventy-five. On the other hand, the limits of new, modernised Toryism can be seen in the fact that over a hundred of the Party's candidates were old Etonians (seventy-nine of whom were elected, a quarter of all Conservative MPs in 1950) while H.G. Nicholas concluded that 'of the 621 Conservative candidates, seven could properly be described as manual workers'; more than half of the Party's candidates had stood at least once before, and three-quarters had served in the forces, more pointers to continuity from 1945.[36]

Being extra-careful of election law, Woolton warned off the anti-nationalisation organisations, urging them to suspend their activities during the campaign, and they duly did so; in 1951 though, Mr. Cube and his allies remained on the hoardings, Labour took a test-case to the courts and lost: the anti-nationalisers were thereby freed from restraint for the future. The caution indicated by Woolton's approach in 1950, and the early preparation on both sides, ensured a relatively quiet campaign. Hearing Ed Murrow on the radio praising Britain on the decorum and fairness with which it conducted its electoral affairs made Noël Coward 'feel very proud. As long as we can retain the sense of decency that prevailed all over the country . . . we shall never go far wrong.' Churchill did raise sparks in verbal fencing with Bevan, and he also raised the temperature with a claim that Labour was not pressing ahead quickly enough with the atomic bomb, but the only real 'Limehouse talk' was old material like Bevan's 'vermin' speech, of which the Conservative papers regularly reminded their readers. According to Arthur Booth, 'Mr. Attlee thought it was the quietest election he had ever known, and Mr. Churchill called it "demure"'. It was sometimes more contentious lower down – there was a lively contest in Plymouth, where Randolph Churchill was standing against Michael Foot – and in the last week Attlee was nastily heckled in Leicester. Moran tried to persuade Churchill to save his energies and concentrate on broadcasting rather than stumping the country, but 'I saw he was hardly listening. He isn't going to learn any new techniques; he isn't interested in them.' Churchill's face hardly appeared on Conservative posters and he was careful not to repeat the personal barnstorming of 1945; after

[36] Nicholas, *General Election of 1950*, 42–53, 83–5, 93; Headlam diary, 14 Jan. 1950; Rhodes James, *Eden*, 332; text of Butler address, 23 Jan. 1950, Hailes MSS, 2/8; Central Office *Daily Notes*, 15 Feb. 1950.

lunching with Churchill in the previous November, Headlam had 'gathered rather thankfully that he did not intend to perambulate the country again and realised that he must be careful about his broadcasts'. His colleagues were equally anxious to build up his reputation for calm statesmanship; Eden argued on 13 February that 'there is no figure anywhere who compares in stature and in authority with Mr. Churchill. No one can more forcibly recall to harassed and perplexed humanity the choice that now confronts it, between real collaboration . . . and hatred ending in destruction.' As in 1945, broadcasts were important not only in their direct impact but also for their direction of the debate on the hustings. There was a wider range of Conservative radio speakers than in 1945, Churchill speaking only once in the campaign proper, but with variable results. Eden, Woolton and and Florence Horsbrugh (presumably included to appeal to the housewife vote) were all thought to have done fairly well, and attracted average audiences. Maxwell Fyfe was credited by Nicholas with having made a 'factual, reasoned, sober case' but attracted an audience of only 17 per cent of possible listeners, compared to 51 per cent for Churchill, and Salisbury did even worse than Maxwell Fyfe. The real find of the campaign was Charles Hill, a new politician but a familiar broadcaster, who was the only speaker apart from Churchill and Attlee to attract over 40 per cent of listeners; Nicholas felt that 'even more important than what he said was his manner of saying it. Here was expressed, in popular phraseology, in an occasional pungent phrase, and in a continuously "folksy" delivery, the politics of the unpolitical'; here then was both the ghost of Stanley Baldwin and the shape of things to come.[37]

Five years of Labour government had at least ensured a disciplined and supportive campaign from the Conservative press; the *Telegraph* and *Mail* were staunch but low-key in their devotion to the Conservative cause, *The Times* returned to the fold after its indecision in 1945, and the *Express* began the campaign less excitably than usual though then shifted gear, 'whether by coincidence or contagion', when Beaverbrook returned to Britain. All celebrated Churchill's foreign policy speeches as marking him out as a world statesman, and singled out for particular praise his call for a 'summit' meeting with Stalin to make a settlement with Russia. The Conservative press largely concentrated on the Party's chosen themes. These can perhaps best be isolated by noting the slogans chosen for the ten main posters in the national campaign, which were (this time each of them also saying 'Vote Conservative'):

(1) 'Give him a chance and he will grow you more food' (picture of a farmer)

(2) 'For family, happiness and home' (family picture)

---

[37] Nicholas, *General Election of 1950*, 93–5, 101–7, 127; Butler, *General Election of 1951*, 33; Moran, *Struggle*, 361; Graham Payn and Sheridan Morley (eds), *The Noël Coward Diaries* (1982), 145; Booth, *British Hustings*, 249, 253; Headlam diary, 24 Nov. 1949; Kilmuir, *Memoirs*, 169; Pelling, *Churchill*, 582.

(3)  'Make Britain great again' (bulldog, recalling Churchill)
(4)  'For fair wages, fair prices – and a house to live in' (worker)
(5)  'It's common sense' (naval officer)
(6)  'A vote for the Liberals is a vote wasted'
(7)  'Your future is in your hands'
(8)  'Fight the rising cost of living' (balloon)
(9)  'After four years Labour, £ going down, prices going up' (scales)
(10)  'Socialism leads to Communism'

It may be hard to see where the earnest language of the *Industrial Charter* fitted into all this, for the predominant note now was negative and populist. It did of course fit in, in the sense that knocking the Government and the Liberals would have made little sense unless enough of the electorate already believed that the Conservatives had a sensible alternative to offer; as Butler put it, 'we have already established a favourable comparison between our policy and that of the Socialists'. At the Election itself, that alternative was not much promoted or reported.[38]

Gallup polls had put Labour just in the lead as the campaign started and continued to show only a narrow gap; Central Office had foreseen that a drift back from 'doubtful' to Labour would happen, a view taken after George Gallup had given his personal advice. A private poll run by the *Daily Express* more dubiously claimed a large Conservative lead, very likely from a fictitious sample. The canvass returns telephoned to Central Office told the same story, a recovery but not enough to win with; they were also a surprisingly good basis for making predictions, for of the ten marginals categorised as 'good' on the eve of poll, the Party won nine (and lost the tenth by only 388 votes), while of the eight categorised as 'bad' Labour held all eight. With a full canvass, there would be no shocks like 1945 to fear. At the outset, Chips Channon had foreseen 'a deadlock, perhaps with a small Tory majority', and the expectation of a close result was general. On 23 February, it was clear that gains were being made on a big scale, and for a brief period on the 24th it seemed is if Labour might lose its majority, before late declarations in mining constituencies saw them home. The final results were received with a mixture of pleasure and disappointment: the Liberals had done disastrously, winning only nine seats and losing over 300 deposits, but Labour retained an overall majority of six. New boundaries made direct comparisons difficult on a seat-by-seat basis, but the overall pattern and the regional distribution were clear enough. The Conservative vote had risen by about two and a half million over the 1945 'National' total (and was well above their own 1935 winning vote too), giving 43.3 per cent of the popular vote nationwide, but Labour's vote had also risen by half that much, which

---

[38] Nicholas, *General Election of 1950*, 143–210, 240; Butler address of 23 Jan. 1950, Hailes MSS, 2/8.

had kept them ahead. In seats, of the eighty-five additional Conservative MPs elected, fifty-six came from southern England (where the swing was twice the national average), eighteen from northern England, and only a handful from anywhere else. On the social rather than the geographical spectrum, Conservative candidates improved their position most clearly among middle-class voters, especially in residential suburbs: according to Gallup, the Tory share of the vote in this group rose from 54 per cent in 1945 to 63 per cent in 1950. The Tory recovery of votes was more marked among women than men, perhaps the combined effect of food shortages, continued rationing, the British Housewives' League and Mr. Cube. The areas where recovery had been least marked were those heavy industrial areas where the memory of unemployment in the 1930s was most marked; there at least the Conservative conversion to full employment still seemed to be doubted, and Labour did better even than in 1945 in the coalfields of Durham and South Wales. Since two-thirds of the employed population were manual workers, and two-fifths of the population were in mining or heavy manufacturing, this resistance to Tory recovery was very significant; what Robert Blake called Labour's 'defensive' argument about full employment was one that applied to a lot of voters, and exerted a strong electoral pull. In response to this, Tories once again considered ideas of electoral reform; Macmillan in particular suggested a devious scheme, not unlike one adopted in France at the time, to introduce 'proportional representation, limited to the big cities', while leaving the Tory shires unaffected. 'It could do no harm and might do good. How else are the great Socialist "blocs" to be eaten into?' Herbert Williams more robustly argued that 'all the chat about proportional representation merely encourages the Liberals to go on, and I think we have got to take steps to prevent the present nonsense on the subject in certain high quarters'. It was one of the few Party arguments in which Williams was on the winning side.[39]

## Opposition again, 1950–51

The indecisive result heightened the Party's frustration. There was certainly relief: the lurking fear that an entirely unanticipated rout like 1945 could recur was laid to rest, and it could be assumed that something like normal two-party politics had returned. But there was disappointment that the Party had come so close to winning, without doing so. The consolation was that Labour's massive majority of 1945 had gone; in this context, Woolton spoke

[39] Ramsden, *Conservative Party Policy*, 144–5, 151; Nicholas, *General Election of 1950*, 284–7, 297–8, 307–11; Central Office file, 'Canvass Returns', CCO 4/3/115; Rhodes James, *Chips*, 440; D.E. Butler, *British General Elections since 1945* (Oxford 1989), 59; Robert Blake, *The Conservative Party from Peel to Thatcher* (1985), 266; Harold Macmillan, *Tides of Fortune, 1945–1955* (1969), 318.

of 1950 being 'a moral victory for the Conservatives if there ever was one'. Moreover, the hill to climb to get Labour out was now a small one: as Churchill expressed it in both words and mime at the 1950 Conference, it needed just 'one more heave'; and it was expected that another election could not be long in coming, for a majority of six would not be enough for stable government. Conservatives were fresh for the renewed parliamentary fight, reinforced by the 'class of 1950' which Nye Bevan called 'the finest Tory vintage in history'. There certainly was a high calibre of recruits to the backbenches, returners like Alec Dunglass as well as the newcomers Macleod, Powell, Maudling, Maude, Carr and Heath; of ninety-three new Conservative MPs, forty-one went on to become ministers and twenty-four Privy Councillors. Facing them, Labour's team was tired and even more disappointed by the result than the Conservatives; when parliament met, Headlam was pleased to find 'the comrades more subdued than they were in 1945!'[40]

Despite the setback, and further murmurs from colleagues about his age, Churchill hardly seems to have considered retirement, concluding rather that the prize of a last term of office was now his for the taking. During the 1950–51 Parliament, he was a more regular attender in the Commons, though not much more available to backbenchers. He made effective speeches to cheer up his supporters. Chips Channon noted in March 1950 a confident Churchill speech that lasted an hour and added 'no extinct volcano he'. Macmillan wrote in July 1951 that,

> Conscious that many people feel that he is too old to form a Government and that this will probably be used as a cry against him at the election, he has used these days to give a demonstration of energy and vitality. He has voted in every division; made a series of brilliant little speeches; shown all his qualities of humour and sarcasm; and crowned all by a remarkable breakfast (at 7–30 a.m.) of eggs, bacon, sausages and coffee, followed by a large whisky and soda and a huge cigar. This latter feat commanded general admiration.[41]

Churchill enjoyed the fighting tactics which the Party adopted for this Parliament: pairing with Labour MPs was banned, so that the Government would have to keep its own MPs in the House till all hours, and occasional snap divisions were arranged in the hope of defeating minor measures, on seven occasions with success. At first this was only a shadow-boxing campaign, for the public were not thought likely to welcome another election before Labour had been given a fair chance, and the onset of the Korean War brought a new sense of national crisis in which Churchill committed his Party to support the Government. The King's private secretary reported that

---

40  *CAJ*, May 1950; Fisher, *Macleod*, 72; Headlam diary, 2 Mar. 1950.
41  Gilbert, *Never Despair*, 512; Ina Zweiniger-Bargielowska, 'Rationing, Austerity and Conservative Party Recovery after 1945', in the *Historical Journal*, vol. 37, no. 1 (1994), 183; Rhodes James, *Chips*, 439, 442, 449, 457; Macmillan, *Tides of Fortune*, 320–2.

'the manoeuvres . . . were being conducted, as it were, with blank rounds rather than with live ammunition'. This was only partly true; analysis of 1950's divisions by the whips showed that Labour MPs were absent more often and in larger numbers than Tories, and in July the Party leaders discussed what sanctions to apply to MPs who did not play their full part in the parliamentary offensive; a note in the shadow cabinet files indicates a decision that 'Headlam, Roberts and Kingsmill be invited to retire in October, if unable to guarantee full and regular attendance, including late sittings. The reason to be made known when the writs moved.' In fact Harold Roberts died in September, and the vacancy was filled by the far more active Edward Boyle, elected at the age of twenty-seven; the other two retired before the 1951 General Election. Early in 1951 though, with a year gone, with meat rationing actually tightened again, and with the Conservatives ahead in the polls, the parliamentary offensive was stepped up into an all out war in the lobbies; the 1922 Committee resolved to demand an 'intensification of our attacks'. In a much-reported speech at Banstead, Bob Boothby proclaimed that 'we shall harry the life out of them. We shall keep them up night and day. The only way to get rid of them fairly is to wear them out. We will make them sit day and night and grind away until they get absolutely hysterical and say "We can't stand any more", and this is what we are going to do for the next two or three months.' Enthusiastic supporters reckoned that they could force the necessary six by-elections in a year, and when the Party's barrister MPs complained that the policy of keeping sittings going all night and into the following morning was hard to combine with earning a living in the courts, their views were not sympathetically received. The same fighting spirit was applied in by-elections; at Barnsley in Autumn 1951, Tory slogans accused Labour of 'un-British-like Election methods' and of 'dishonourable election tactics', and another pointed out that 'Socialist and Communist election slogans are the same'; in approving this approach, for which the local association had pressed, Pierssené noted that he did not particularly like such slogans but that there would be 'nothing to lose in Barnsley'. Not everyone was keen on ruthless parliamentary tactics, which were producing disorder in the House and the loss of control by the Speaker. Butler for example preferred to keep good relations between the parties; Maudling and Carr went to the whips and refused to continue obstruction when Attlee was abroad on national business; others like Macleod and Elliott came to realise pragmatically that it did not look good to the public when the press photographed ambulances bringing very sick Labour MPs in to vote night after night. Things gradually settled down as the strain began to tell equally on both sides: Harold Watkinson recalled that 'desperation sometimes drove Members to stand around like harlots in the Lobby, pleading with Members of the other party to pair'. But the pressure was relentless, especially over the 1951 Finance Bill, and it seems clear that this tactic did contribute to Attlee's decision to go to the country in the Autumn of 1951, earlier than Labour's best interest would have suggested.[42]

More positively, the new MPs were also looking outward to the electorate, and seeking to carry forward their earlier policy work into the parliamentary party. Iain Macleod found that few other Tory MPs specialised, or wished to specialise, on health matters; he moved within two years of his election to the House through the positions of secretary, vice chairman and then chairman of the parliamentary Health and Social Security Committee, and was quickly picked out as a key opposition speaker on domestic issues; he continued his CRD double act with Powell in these health debates, one asking an innocent question to set up a deadly supplementary from the other. Macleod also had the rare satisfaction of delivering a speech in the House based on a brief that he had himself written at the CRD. Macleod and Powell were part of the One Nation Group formed by new MPs shortly after the 1950 Election; neither was in the founding group, which included only Angus Maude, Cub Alport and Gilbert Longden, but they were both early recruits, along with Heath and Carr. Macleod was joint editor with Maude of the booklet that they produced for the 1950 Party Conference and which gave them their name, a title suggested by the historically-minded Maude. Although its progressive proposals were not presented as committing the Party in any way, the CPC published it, Butler wrote a complimentary but non-committal foreword and *One Nation* made a considerable impact. Its moderate tone did not indicate any lesser opposition to Labour than that of the old-fashioned right, as Macleod's own chapter on social policy made clear:

> There is a fundamental disagreement between Conservatives and Socialists on the question of social policy. Socialists would give the same benefits to everyone, whether or not the help is needed, and indeed whether or not the country's resources are adequate. We believe that we must first help those in need. Socialists believe that the State should provide an average standard. We believe that it should provide a minimum standard, above which people should be free to rise as far as their industry, their thrift, their ability or their genius may take them.

But if content was clearly Conservative, tone was moderate and the One Nation Group was in that sense carrying forward towards government the impetus of the Party's more official statements. Reconsidering the work of the Group in 1954, when reviewing its book *Change is Our Ally*, the reviewer in *The Economist*, noted that Group members were as often to be found on the right as on the left, but that they were all serious thinkers: 'the

---

42 Hoffman, *Conservative Party*, 251; LCC, July 1950; 1922 Committee minutes, 22 Feb. 1951, CPA; Central Office constituency file, Barnsley, CCO 1/9/158, CPA; Howard, *RAB*, 174; Butler, *General Election of 1951*, 14; Goodhart, *The 1922*, 154; Reginald Maudling, *Memoirs* (1978), 52; Fisher, *Macleod*, 73; T.F. Lindsay and M. Harrington, *The Conservative Party, 1918–1970* (1974), 168; Harold Watkinson, *Turning Points, A Record of Our Times* (Salisbury, 1986), 32; Thompson, *Day Before Yesterday*, 90.

almost traditional anti–intellectualism of the Tory Party has thus been broken';
he also quoted the contributions by Maude, Powell and Arthur Seldon as
demonstrating how free-thinking the Group had become; the combination
of those three thinkers was a remarkable prophecy of ideas to come, even
if they were not to become the Party's mainstream until a generation later.
Churchill's 1951 Election broadcast presented social policy much as Macleod
had described it though: 'The difference between our outlook and the socialist
outlook on life is the diference between the ladder and the queue. We are for
the ladder. Let all try their best to climb. They are for the queue. Let each
wait in his place till his turn comes.' If One Nation seemed, ambiguously, to
demonstrate the Party's moderate stance, in other ways the Party seemed to be
shifting its stance more clearly to the right during the 1950–51 Parliament; this
was the time of the housing pledge, of Richard Law's influential book *Return
from Utopia*, of an increasing anti-communism as the Korean War impinged,
and of a more uninhibited rhetoric of liberty that found its apogee in the
1951 slogan 'Set the People Free'. Gravesend, Truro and Hampstead were
three very different constituencies in which the housing pledge to set private
builders free was now at the centre of local campaigning.[43]

In two areas in particular, detailed spadework laid the ground for tilts of
policy. Once Labour had been re-elected, the chance of preventing the Steel
industry from being nationalised through delaying tactics had gone. The Party
now had to decide whether it really intended an explicitly *reactionary* policy,
to return a publicly-owned industry to the private sector. Encouraged still by
Duncan and the leaders of the industry, the commitment did not waver: in
September 1950 Churchill formally pledged to denationalise the industry, and
detailed discussions continued between the industry, the Party and the City
to prepare a working plan; only Churchill and Butler were fully informed
of the detail, though the ACP was briefed on the direction of the Party's
thinking and the commitment of principle was clear enough. It was also
limited to steel; Swinton chaired a group that considered denationalising gas
and electricity, spurred on by Herbert Williams, but its findings were in favour
of decentralised management rather than a change of ownership; even a strong
denationaliser like Oliver Poole had agreed by 1951 that denationalisation was,
except in limited cases, 'unworkable and unrealistic', and the 1951 manifesto
made no commitment to return any of the energy industries to the private
sector.[44]

There was one other area though, not previously much discussed, in which
an attack on the public sector did appear on the Party's agenda – broadcasting;
its appearance was almost entirely due to Selwyn Lloyd. The 1951 report of

43  Fisher, *Macleod*, 74–9; Egremont, *Wyndham and Children*, 146; Harriet Jones, 'The
    Conservative Party and Social Policy, 1942–1955', unpublished PhD thesis, University
    of London, 1992, 44, 201; *The Economist*, 25 Dec. 1954; Gravesend CA minutes, 29 Mar.
    1951; Truro CA minutes, 30 Oct. 1950; Hampstead CA minutes, 27 July 1951.
44  Burk, *First Privatisation*, 26–37; Ramsden, *Conservative Party Policy*, 154.

the Beveridge Committee on the future of broadcasting came down solidly for continued state monopoly, but Lloyd's minority report quietly argued for advertising and competition. It made little impact at first, not least because establishment-minded Conservatives like Eden were firmly behind the BBC, but when the Party set up a broadcasting committee to consider its policy in February, the choice of the free enterprise-minded Ralph Assheton as chairman and of several 'young turks' among its members opened the way for a change of mind. Lloyd, who had been Butler's deputy in the policy machine for the previous two years, now had good contacts in the Party on whom to press his views, and he gained the backing of Woolton; the shadow cabinet decided on 11 July not to vote for a motion approving the Beveridge report, but to keep options open by voting only to note it. On 22 July and again four days later, John Profumo was asking for a full Party meeting to discuss the issue; he had to ask again on 15 November, by which time there was a Conservative Government. The Party's policy did not change before the 1951 Election, but all the pieces were in place for the Conservatives to discuss introducing commercial broadcasting afterwards.[45]

A minor issue of the same sort was provided by a reconsideration in 1950 of the New Towns; the Party did not oppose the principle of New Towns, despite local opposition from rural interests in the Home Counties, but it did criticise the powers and activities of the New Town Corporations, objecting in particular to their running of pubs and shops as an unwarranted extension of the public sector; promises were given to limit these powers. In the same spirit, East Midlands Conservatives asked what had happened to the pledge to sell council houses to sitting tenants, given in *The Right Road* but not much mentioned by Party spokesmen since; the Local Government Advisory Committee pressed for the same policy, noting that it had been successfully pursued in Cambridge, Wolverhampton, Southend and Birmingham before the Labour Government banned the practice; this policy, it was argued, made 'the property-owning democracy' idea a reality. It continued not to figure much in public declarations of policy, perhaps because it would at least seem to complicate the pledge to build more actual houses. Overall, these policy shifts carried only a little further the trends that had been evident in 1949 and in the 1950 manifesto, and such appearances as One Nation may well have counteracted them in a leftward direction in the public mind. The calling of the Election necessitated the cancellation of the 1951 Conference, which might well have given the Party's profile a sharper edge, one way or the other. One of the fallers was Miss Margaret Roberts, candidate at Dartford, who was down to propose her constituency's motion calling for a return to the fundamental principles of Conservatism to counter the demoralising effects

---

[45] D.R. Thorpe, *Selwyn Lloyd* (1989), 133–7; LCC, 11 July 1951; 1922 Committee minutes, 22 and 26 July, and 15 Nov. 1951, CPA; *NCP*, 16 June 1950.

of six years of socialist government – a significant but entirely unremarked pointer to the future.[46]

Beyond these limited policy tilts, the emphasis of the Party's campaigning was on the areas that had stubbornly resisted Conservatism in 1950. Re-categorising marginals after the 1950 Election, Central Office decided that there were now 158 seats that were 'safe Tory' but 198 that were 'cast-iron Labour'; of the rest, thirty-six were 'reasonably safe Tory' (which still only gave a 'safe' Tory total lower than the number held in 1945), and sixty-two were 'precarious Tory'; the main effort would be directed at fifty-two 'Labour marginals we expect to win'. Clarke and Chapman-Walker agreed in April that the 'paramount objection to the Tory Party, which we have to overcome, is a widespread distrust of our motives – the working man thinks we are competent but selfish and will only vote for us in extremity'. Michael Fraser's later conclusion that the Conservatives were believed to have 'hard heads but hard hearts' and Labour 'soft heads but soft hearts' was a version of the same analysis. The *Conservative Agents' Journal* editorialised in April 1950 that 'we have been impressed by the many favourable comments made on the success of the Conservative electoral machine in the Election, but none of us can be unaware that, in the industrial areas in particular, something more is needed'. Woolton told the National Union in March that he needed half a million pounds in six months to keep up the plans for the next campaign, and to extend the effort in industrial areas; it was agreed not to have an appeal, since it had been promised in 1947 not to make appeals a regular event, but to concentrate on quotas. More work was put into the Conservatives' own trades union organisation; questions were asked in September 1951 about eleven parliamentary candidates who were also Party employees, this being seen as a dangerous precedent; Woolton's reply was that they were trades unionists who were already candidates and who had then been put temporarily on the payroll to allow them to do propaganda work full time. In July 1950, Chapman-Walker reported that 'whereas at the last election the bulk of our propaganda had been aimed at the lower middle classes, and particularly the white-collared workers, it was now being directed to organised labour'. The new magazine, *Popular Pictorial*, was 'our first attempt at a low-brow publication'. Another attempt to break down Labour's monolithic industrial majorities, and to enlist rumour as an ally, was 'conversational propaganda', a series of 'pass it on' points that were circulated to Party members and estimated to generate at least 3,000 conversations a day. The same considerations would have informed the increased attention paid to film propaganda: hirings increased steadily in 1950 and 1951, and Churchill was reported as having 'finally' agreed to make

---

[46] NUEC, 9 Nov. 1950 and 14 June 1951; Central Council report for 1951, NUA 2/2/17, CPA.

a film. However, the attack on industrial seats was not entirely uninhibited; in June 1951, Churchill was shocked to find that most of the electorate at the Westhoughton by-election had not even been canvassed, the local policy being not to stir up the hostile parts of the constituency by appearing there in Tory colours; he denounced this as 'the essence of defeatism'.[47]

Despite Westhoughton, between the 1950 and 1951 Elections, Conservative fortunes seemed to be riding high; there were satisfactory local government results in 1950 and many gains again in 1951 when the Party was anyway defending most of the vacancies; Glasgow, Nottingham, Southampton and Leeds joined the Tory fold, and by the end of 1951, only five of the twenty-three biggest cities had Labour majorities; in opinion polls, Labour and Conservative were neck and neck in 1950, but there was a definite Conservative lead in 1951, a shift that contributed to the enthusiasm for forcing Labour back to the hustings; in by-elections, there was a net overall swing of 4 per cent, again higher in 1951 than in 1950. No seats changed hands, but after Easter 1950 no seat that could be thought of as marginal fell vacant. There was now a much clearer sense of the relative marginality of seats, where redistribution, a hope that 1945 had been a special case, and the long period since the last 'normal' contest in 1935 had combined to make things difficult to predict before 1950; now with only a short time before the next contest, such calculations could be more reliably made. One consequence was that unrealistic expectations were not applied to by-elections: good swings were welcomed, but not much was made of them. The death of Oliver Stanley (and friendship with Jim Thomas) opened the way for Walter Monckton to step straight into the safe seat of Bristol West, which he duly 'stormed' with a 17 per cent swing, making himself a replacement frontbencher for Stanley as well as an MP. The second consequence of a more calculated approach to marginality was that constituency associations could now plan to help each other and concentrate voluntary workers where it mattered; little of this took place in 1950 since neither agents nor candidates in 'safe' seats were inclined to be generous until they had actually seen an election result on the new boundaries. In December 1950 though, the Esher agent read a stern lesson to his colleagues on the theme 'help thy neighbour'.

> I consider that every agent who has a Conservative majority of over 5000 should say to his Member, his Chairman and himself, 'It is our duty to the Party to spare some workers for regular canvassing in the nearest marginal seat now held by the socialists. The next general election will not be won by Members of Parliament with majorities of ten, fifteen and twenty thousand. They have only one vote on the floor of the House of Commons, whatever their majority. It will be won by means of seats we capture from the Socialists'.

47 Central Office file, 'Marginal Seats', CCO 4/3/190, CPA; Kandiah, 'Lord Woolton' thesis, 214; *CAJ*, Apr. 1950; NUEC, 16 Mar. and 13 July 1950, 8 Feb. and 6 Sept. 1951; Central Office file, 'Party films', CCO 4/3/232, CPA; Gilbert, *Never Despair*, 616.

The theme was eagerly taken up, and Area Agents spread the idea whenever they attended agents' meetings over the next year. Thus was born the concept of 'mutual aid'; it was, necessarily, more a one-way trade than the equal partnership that its title suggested. In practice, mutual aid worked best in the conurbations, and especially around London, where a ring of very safe seats could be raided for assistance to the urban marginals, and where distances were relatively short. Guildford set up in 1951 a close link with Clapham, with officers from each association attending each other's meetings to establish a rapport; the Tory commuters of Guildford could easily stop off in Clapham for political work on their way home, and in 1951 many did so; later the link was with Wandsworth where in 1959 over a hundred Guildford Tories put in 300 evenings of work. Surrey was the birthplace of the policy; in 1953, all fourteen Conservative seats were involved in support for the twelve marginals within reach. Other suburbs followed suit; also in 1953, ten constituencies in urban Kent were lined up to help Dartford. Churchill's Woodford constituency set a similar example, and here the enthusiasm was reinforced by the fact that the candidate receiving help in neighbouring Walthamstow was their own former YC Chairman, John Harvey. The Woodford agent's report for 1955, when Harvey won the Walthamstow seat, said that the results showed 'how right we were to give freely of our labour to our neighbours rather than retain it to add another thousand to Sir Winston's majority. It is seats that count, *not* majorities.' Similarly, the arrangement whereby Woking assisted Battersea South was credited with one of the critical Conservative gains of 1951. Guildford, Woking and Woodford were untypical; in the more dispersed East Midlands in 1951, mutual aid 'on a limited scale' was organised to produce help for Nottingham, South East Derbyshire and Lincoln, from Horncastle, Rushcliffe, Harborough and Melton, but many of those involved would have had to travel very long distances to provide assistance. In the West Midlands conurbation there were few safe seats to find helpers from anyway, but Solihull was lined up for Birmingham Yardley and Warwick and Leamington sent help into Coventry South. There were other places where mutual aid hardly got going at all, as in the Northern Area, but its impact in a number of tight contests should not be underestimated.[48]

## The 1951 General Election

These promising omens therefore ensured that the Party embarked on the Election of October 1951 in good spirit. The *Conservative Agents' Journal* told

48  NUEC, 6 Sept. 1951; Cook and Ramsden, *By-Elections*, 193, 387–9; Cockett, *My Dear Max*, 113, 120; Monckton to Thomas, 3 Sept. 1956, Cilcennin MSS; Butler, *General Election of 1951*, 19; *CAJ*, Dec. 1950; Central Office file, 'Mutual Aid', CCO 4/5/251, CPA; Guildford CA minutes, various dates; Woodford CA reports and minutes, various dates; Watkinson, *Turning Points*, 38; East Midlands Area Council, 2 June 1951; Warwick and Leamington CA minutes, 10 Mar. 1952; Northern Area General Purposes Committee, 22 June 1953.

its readers that the 'winter of discontent' was over, and the frustrating work of planting and hoeing had been done: 'it is for us the time of reaping'. Again preparations had been made well ahead of the campaign; a new *Campaign Guide* was out in April, and full electoral plans had been made; Central Office had booked 7,000 poster sites around the country (Labour, 3,000), and was to distribute eighteen million centrally-produced leaflets (Labour, fourteen million); Conservative candidates spent practically up to the legal limit all over the country; 44 per cent of electors were canvassed (compared to 37 per cent by Labour), but far more in Conservative and marginal seats. The manifesto *Britain Strong and Free* contained few surprises, being drawn almost entirely from the 1949 and 1950 documents; Robert Hudson was given the delicate task of drafting a form of words on Resale Price Maintenance, since, as the shadow cabinet noted, 'the party was completely divided on our policy on this matter'. Churchill surprised his colleagues by including at the last moment a proposal for an Excess Profits Tax, intended to deflect claims that industry would do too well out of rearmament for Korea, and by insisting that a shorter, popular version of the manifesto written entirely by himself should also be published; in the event, neither made much difference to the campaign, which was seen by almost all participants as a second round of the 1950 contest; the proposed new tax did though 'infuriate RAB more than anything in the whole of the 18 years that I was closely involved with him' (to quote Michael Fraser), for it was just the sort of off-the-cuff gambit that could make a nonsense of all his methodical work on policy since 1946; as Chancellor he had to introduce the tax in 1952 but then had the pleasure of abolishing it a year later. Three-quarters of the constituencies had the same Tory agent, and again almost every one had a paid agent ready in post; over two-thirds of Tory candidates had also fought in 1950; there was very little fresh that could be said about either party's policy, though three-quarters of Tory candidates did highlight the new housing pledge in their election addresses, for them the biggest single issue. The one significant change in the electoral equation was that instead of the 475 Liberal candidates of 1950 there would be only 109 in 1951; a high proportion of 1950's two and a half million Liberal votes would be open to bids from the other parties, and Churchill set off in hot pursuit of them. He had recently irritated senior colleagues by insisting that the Party circulate a speech by his old friend Violet Bonham-Carter, though she was still a straightforward Liberal. During the campaign, he visited her constituency and even appeared with her on a platform. Having backed Asquith's daughter in the Colne Valley, he went on to Newcastle to speak for Lloyd George's son (Gwylim), who was at least a Tory in name. Despite evidence to the contrary, he was convinced that 'guidance' to the voters from Liberal names was crucial; he was also aware of the importance of the Liberals' own credibility, and angered by a poll in the *News Chronicle* that seemed to show their vote improving. He was correspondingly cheered when the *Manchester Guardian* urged Liberal voters who had no Liberal candidate to back a Churchill government, which effectively meant that most must vote Conservative. The CRD worked out careful advice to candidates as to how they should appeal to Liberal voters in several different types of contest and Megan Lloyd George complained that her Tory opponent was quoting an anti-socialist speech made by her father in 1925, presumably in the hope of persuading Liberals to vote against socialism in 1951. In the event, the ex-Liberal vote did divide in the Conservatives' favour, if only by a small margin and to different extents in different places; David Butler concluded that in most seats the Tories picked up between 55 per cent and 70 per cent of these votes, not many actual votes but 'enough to change the Government and sway the course of history'. Robert Blake wisely comments that, though the fact that there were so few Liberal candidates was entirely fortuitous, their voters' net movement to the Conservative side owed a great deal to what the Conservatives had said and done since 1945.[49]

Churchill again broadcast only once, leaving the other opportunities to Woolton, Hill, Eden and Pat Hornsby-Smith. He had to be over-ruled though by the shadow cabinet over his wish to give one of the Conservatives' broadcasts to Violet Bonham-Carter. His own broadcast was thought to be exceptionally effective – 'his finest personal effort since the war', thought Macmillan, who had helped to write it. For the first time, television was also used for an address by the Party leaders; it is clear that this owed something to pressure from the Conservatives who alone had urged the acceptance of the BBC's offer of facilities to the parties, and who alone made effective use of them. Eden's TV broadcast was a milestone in electioneering, the first part a contrived interview with the news presenter Leslie Mitchell, a Conservative sympathiser who had advised on Conservative films before the War. This had been exhaustively rehearsed, but the second half was an effective address straight to camera by Eden; David Butler reminded his readers that this made an impact because 'the vast majority of his audience can never have seen Mr. Eden in the flesh'. Tories were still re-learning the lessons of the 1930s. The other feature of the campaign was more negative. Woolton had argued unsuccessfully for an adventurous Conservative campaign that would take a few risks and exploit the freedom theme; Churchill more cautiously described his approach as 'housing, red meat and not getting scuppered'. Even on housing, few spokesmen were explicit about the timing of the pledge to increase completions, or described it as a promise rather than a target; David Butler indeed felt that 'the Conservatives did not make many promises during the election'. The Conservatives had to respond in the campaign to a

---

[49]    *CAJ*, Apr. and Oct. 1951; Gilbert, *Never Despair*, 559, 616, 633, 637; Howard, *RAB*, 176; Butler, *Art of the Possible*, 155; Macmillan, *Tides of Fortune*, 352, 355; Addison, *Churchill*, 404; Moran, *Struggle*, 370; Pelling, *Churchill*, 591; Butler, *General Election of 1951*, 22, 28, 35, 56, 95, 139–43, 270–2; Lord Fraser of Kilmorack to the author, 30 June 1994; LCC, 22 Sept. 1951; CPA; Blake, *Conservative Party*, 268.

barrage of Labour scares, designed to frighten the voters with worries about their jobs, the free health service and other advances made since 1940, and to jolt the Conservatives into making gaffes of their own; the culmination came with the *Daily Mirror*'s 'Whose Finger on the Trigger?' editorial on polling day which sought to exploit any lingering distrust of Churchill as a warmonger and to add a nuclear dimension to the scare. Despite provocation, Churchill remained calm, though he later successfully sued the *Mirror* for libel, and from the Tory side the Election was almost as low-key as 1950 had been. When it was over, Macmillan decided that 'the truth is that the Socialists have fought the election (very astutely) not on Socialism but on fear. Fear of unemployment; fear of reduced wages; fear of reduced social benefits; fear of war. These four fears have been brilliantly, if unscrupulously, exploited.' In Totnes, the local Conservatives, when they met to discuss their comfortable victory in the constituency, recorded their regret at the 'unhappy feelings dividing the political parties at the election', and several times in 1952 considered an approach to the other parties locally in the hope of re-establishing harmonious relations. In Cumberland mining villages, it was noted that Tory posters were torn down almost as soon as they went up, so hostile to the Party were some local Labour supporters. In Hull, the Conservatives bemoaned a quiet whispering campaign that raised scares against them on the council estates – 'the night patrol began its deadly work' – and argued that this had induced the Labour vote to pour out on polling day. The West Midlands Area annual report concluded that 'consistent Labour propaganda representing Conservatives as war-mongers no doubt had some effect in the narrowly-held divisions'. Milne and Mackenzie's study of Bristol North East confirmed this in reporting that 'the Conservatives were in a more favourable position two-and-a-half weeks before the election than on polling day'. However, since the Conservatives actually won against such scares, Macmillan could also detect an opportunity: 'if, before the next election, none of these fears have proved reasonable, we may be able to force [them] to fight on Socialism. Then we can win.' Woolton, reviewing the Election for the National Union in November, reached a similar conclusion: he was 'saddened' by the Labour campaign of 'lie following on lie', but the fact of a Conservative Government devoted to healing wounds and working for 'one nation' would change all that.[50]

Conservatives had expected a good win, and had rather dreaded having

[50] LCC, 22 Sept. 1951, CPA; Addison, *Now the War is Over*, 53; Rhodes James, *Eden*, 338; Pelling, *Churchill*, 590; Butler, *General Elections since 1945*, 13; Macmillan, *Tides of Fortune*, 358; 361; Butler, *General Election of 1951*, 63, 76–7, 102; Michael Cockerell, *Live from Number Ten, The Inside Story of Prime Ministers and Television* (1988), 10–13, CAJ, Dec. 1951; Totnes CA minutes, 1 Dec. 1951 and later dates; Workington CA minutes, 26 Nov. 1951; West Midlands Area annual report, 17 May 1952; R.S. Milne and H.C. Mackenzie, *Straight Fight: A Study of Voting Behaviour in the Constituency of Bristol North East at the General Election of 1951* (1954), 28–9; NUEC, 8 Nov. 1951.

to govern with a small majority, but the opinion polls showed a steady improvement in the Labour position week by week during the campaign. The overall result was closer even than in 1950, with Labour a shade ahead in votes (though not so far as it appeared, for constituencies with unopposed Unionist returns in Ulster would have greatly swelled the Tory figure had there been contests), and the Conservatives just ahead in seats. Labour and Tory candidates shared, almost equally, 97 per cent of the vote on almost the highest turnout ever, the greatest ever extent of electoral polarisation, and something that puts an odd gloss on any idea that the electorate thought there was a post-war consensus, as does the 'fear' campaigning from the left. Only six Liberals were elected, and only one of these had beaten a Conservative opponent. This rough parity had been achieved by another rise of over a million Conservative votes since 1950. Twenty-one seats were gained from Labour and two from Liberals, half of them in the south of England, where Conservatives once again held nearly three-quarters of the seats; there were a few gains in the northern counties, Wales and Scotland; the seats that changed hands between the two knife-edge results of 1950 and 1951 show where the electoral battleground now lay in post-war Britain – such places as Darlington, Doncaster, Reading, Buckingham, Kings Lynn and Yarmouth were a good cross-section of middle England. This pattern conceals the fact that the swing was small, only just over one per cent, but very uniform across the country. Efforts to achieve a dramatic breakthrough in industrial areas had not been successful and the social constituencies of the parties' voting support had scarcely changed. But the overall balance had shifted very slightly the Conservative way, and the winning of Liberal votes had tipped over just enough crucial marginals. The Conservatives had an overall majority of fifteen, and could at last return to office to show what they could do. BBC radio, present when the crucial gain came through, recorded Woolton shouting as he jumped up and down, 'We've won! We've won! We've won! After six years we've beaten the Socialists.'[51]

How though had it happened? Organisation, unity and high morale in the Tories' own camp had certainly in itself brought about the recovery of some of the lost ground, and the 1948 electoral rules and boundaries had contributed to the recovery too. Churchill remained as unconventional a Party leader as ever, if not as negative a factor as in 1945. Labour had certainly returned some supporters to the Tories by its policies in office, as it has done in all five of its periods in office, though an Opposition needs to work hard to reap such benefits. Labour had also, through the exhaustion of a generation of leaders and, just as importantly, the exhaustion by implementation of the programme that that generation had worked on for a political lifetime, presented a less formidable opponent in 1950–51 than in 1943–45. Finally though, it is clear

51  Butler, *General Election of 1951*, 237–9, 241, 251–76; Kandiah, 'Lord Woolton' thesis, 236.

that elements of the Conservatives overall strategy pursued under Baldwin had also been put back into place by 1951 – hardly surprising when the policy review was in the hands of an admirer of Baldwin's such as Butler had been; once again the Party was rhetorically committed to a package that included resistance to socialism at home and abroad, moderate reform at home with the avoidance of anything smacking to confrontation, and the championing of the interests of the direct taxpayer, the householder and the consumer; that stance was essential to the restoration of the Conservatives' informal electoral coalition with other anti-socialists which Baldwin had generally enjoyed between 1924 and 1935 and which had been shattered in and after 1940. No one of these factors can in itself explain the recovery of power in 1951, not least because it was achieved by such a narrow margin, and it remained to be seen how successfully Churchill could pursue in government those goals of policy that he had allowed Butler to commit him to by 1951.

# Part III

# Promise Postponed, 1951–57

The 1950 vintage (and notably its *premier cru*) the 'One Nation' group, has made a unique contribution to the revival of Conservatism after the 1945 disaster . . . Nearly all were, and are, Butler men . . . The reforms of the Maxwell Fyfe Committee . . . and the boundary changes which by 1950 had freed many constituency parties to choose a new candidate, relaxed the grip of wealth on the party . . . The contrast they made with the Tory Party of 1945–50 first startled and then disconcerted Socialist MPs . . . They were a little younger than the Tory average . . . and gave the impression both of maturity and force . . . Only 30 per cent had been both to Public Schools and to Oxford or Cambridge, as against 50 per cent previously . . . There were business men amongst them, but hardly any of the self-made manufacturer type; the 1950 Tory business man was rather the professional manager, often educated at grammar school and provincial university, versed in technology and economics – a man whose ideas of labour relations were precise and sociological, and very different from the 'I know the men, I'm one of them myself' attitude put over in a carefully preserved northern accent by the wallowing business battleships of an earlier era.

(From 'Class of 1950', *The Economist*, 25 December 1954)

Anthony Eden is one of the most delightful chaps you could find & it is impossible not to feel some affection for him but, fit or unfit, he is *not* the right Prime Minister for Great Britain c. 1953–54. Things have always fallen his way, up to his recent illness, but he has never really scored a six off his own bat . . . I am not saying this behind his back. I sat next to him at dinner soon after the war & more or less said it to his face & he has not thought much of me since.

(Ralph Rayner MP to R.A. Butler, July 1953)

# Chapter 6

# Churchill's last term, 1951–55

The return to office in 1951 provided the Conservatives with the needed opportunity, but was also a risk; if they failed, as seemed not impossible when the first year went badly, they could crash to another 1945. Confidence did not return quickly or steadily. Local election defeats in 1952 were a shock to morale; there were good by-election results in 1953–54, but the Party's lead over Labour was never more than marginal; in 1955 there was a new Leader associated with the modern face of Toryism and triumphantly re-elected in his first few weeks in office, but this proved the prelude not to assured government but to a new collapse of confidence in 1956; finally, with another new Leader in January 1957, the most common expectation in the political world was of a Labour victory next time. For the first half of the thirteen years of Conservative rule that began in 1951, there was hardly more than a year in which the overall prospects looked rosy.

## Settling into office

In the first place, there was the problem of settling back into the first overtly Conservative Government since 1929. There was unfinished business and there were debts to be paid from opposition. Woolton in particular was fêted as the organiser of victory; special resolutions of thanks were passed by the National Union, which was anxious to retain him as Party Chairman in the fear that Churchill's small majority would necessitate a third general election: at the Executive, 'Mrs. Emmet brought a message from the Women's Advisory Committee to say "they loved Lord Woolton very much and hoped he would not desert them"'; at Central Council a few weeks later, the resolution not only called for him to continue as Chairman, but 'emphasise[d] the importance which the ordinary housewife attaches to his presence in the Government'. Woolton responded that he was willing to stay on, but that it was a matter for Churchill; he was reappointed, partly at least 'because we shall have a lot of money to raise next year'. But as the Vice Chairman succeeding Thomas, John Hare was considered more as a deputy to share all the political burdens; his appointment involved fighting off Churchill's own preference for Sir John Howard (Chairman of the Eastern Area, but not even an MP). Though the Chairmanship was to be 'of Cabinet rank' when created in 1911, Woolton now became the first Party Chairman actually to combine the job with a Cabinet post when made Lord President of the Council. Churchill may though have been jealous of his popularity; Woolton wrote in his diary that the premier felt 'resentment against the amount of power that had come to me'. When Woolton was taken seriously ill during the 1952 Conference, he was demoted from Lord President to the Duchy of Lancaster while too weak to complain. Though Lady Woolton told Churchill precisely what she thought of all this and prevented a change of Chairman at the same time, when Woolton recovered in early 1953 Churchill suggested that he should no longer be 'burdened' with Central Office duties. He intended to replace Woolton with Malcolm McCorquodale MP; this would have downgraded the Party's top post, for, while McCorquodale had given the Party good service, his highest ministerial position had been as a Parliamentary Secretary and he was not currently in the Government at all; Woolton, perhaps a prejudiced witness, thought him 'a very weak person' who would do Churchill's bidding. After seeing Churchill, Woolton returned to Central Office, where his resignation letter went through many drafts as his advisers sought to put on the record a summary of his achievements since 1946 and to indicate therefore why the Party needed such a senior man in charge; the other Party managers were rallied to point out that members would strongly object to Woolton's removal against his own wishes. He was rescued by the draughtsmanship of Harold Macmillan, who suggested that the opening of the resignation letter be changed from 'In accordance with our conversation on 10th March . . .' to read 'In accordance with your wishes . . .', so making it clear that Woolton had not offered to resign at all, but had been told to. Macmillan advised that 'He *can't* publish that!' – 'even he can't sack you like the proverbial office boy'. (As Prime Minister, Macmillan himself sought to avoid publishing resignation letters at all, successfully in 1958 but not in 1962.) Once Woolton's sacking was delayed in this way, Butler, Eden, Crookshank and the Chief Whip could all be involved to argue against a change of Chairman; it was agreed that Woolton's presence was vital for 'the morale of the members' and 'the goodwill of the business among the customers'. Woolton stayed on, and a few months later demonstrated to Churchill just how effectively a dual position in Government and Party could be used against the Prime Minister over the future of television, but his suggestion in 1954 that he also take over the chairmanship of the Liaison Committee was refused by Churchill with the backing of the whips. Woolton's high spending on the organisation was cut back: the CRD team of research officers was reduced by six to a new peacetime establishment, and the Area offices also lost half a dozen posts.[1]

---

[1] National Union Executive minutes [hereafter NUEC], 8 Nov. 1951 and 14 Feb. 1952, CPA; Central Council minutes, 21 Mar. 1952, CPA; Woolton diary, 25 Mar. 1953, and various letters, April 1953. Woolton MSS, box 22; Churchill to Butler, 4 Dec. 1954, Butler MSS, G46; John Ramsden, *The Making of Conservative Party Policy, The Conservative Research Department since 1929* (1980), 164; Central Office file, 'Area offices', CCO 4/5/3, CPA.

In 1951 thanks went wider: in Churchill's first honours list, for New Year 1952, ten members of the National Union Executive were honoured, re-establishing pre-war custom, and a year later Pierssené was knighted. Continuity was established too in the machinery: despite attempts by Herbert Williams to get Butler's progressive policy organisation wound down, now that policy would be a matter for ministers rather than for the Party, the National Union agreed to keep the Advisory Committee on Policy in existence. After consulting Churchill, Woolton announced that he 'had made arrangements for the Research Department to continue'. Some sniping continued. In May 1953, Butler reported to the Executive on the ACP: 'last year we sent a good document to Mr. Churchill which he returned marked "good". Others have been completely re-written by him . . . Making policy in Government is more difficult than in Opposition. We have got to stand on our record and project it forward.' After some probing questions about the ACP, he explained that 'there is no mystery about it. We do not decide anything, because the Leader decides what is to be published.'[2]

The difficulties of this interface between making and publishing Party policy emerged in 1953. In 1952 there had been a full policy statement for the Conference, entitled *We Shall Win Through*, though this was simply a progress report on a few months in office. It was assumed that one would also be needed for 1953 and it was decided to press ahead with this through Party rather than governmental channels, since material published by ministers tended to be, as Butler put it, 'contradictory, voluminous and not always convincing'. A great deal of work was done through the Summer on a document to be called at first *On With The Job*, later *Onward In Freedom* ('The title is the most sick-making thing I have seen for some time,' was Powell's comment). This time though the press and Party were unlikely to be satisfied with just another progress report, and the Party could not publish in October the forward-looking proposals that would not be in the Queen's Speech till November. Attempts to deal with the dilemma by constructing a more philosophical framework than was usual in Government statements also foundered, and in August the whole project was scrapped. The CRD did though continue to service parliamentary committees of Conservative MPs, as the backbenchers were anyway insistent that it should, so these other parts of the new policy relationships of 1945–51 remained intact.[3]

In every way, relationships between Government and Party had to be worked out afresh. Already in February 1952 there were complaints that senior ministers were no longer making themselves available for Party social and fund-raising events; at the same Executive meeting Henry Brooke urged Woolton to remind his ministerial colleagues that they should avoid making

2  NUEC, 15 Jan. 1953; Woolton to Churchill, 15 Nov. 1951, Woolton MSS, box 21; NUEC, secretary's notes, 14 May 1953, NUA 4/3/1, CPA; Earl of Woolton, *The Memoirs of the Rt. Hon. Earl of Woolton* (1959), 363–4, 394.
3  Ramsden, *Conservative Party Policy*, 164, 170–4.

unpopular announcements just before the local government elections. When things got rough there was always a tendency for the activists to feel that ministers gave the Party too low a priority; when in 1956 Central Office was searching for speakers for a by-election, the Chief Organisation Officer minuted that 'it is a waste of time to ask for Walter Monckton as he always excuses himself on one pretext or another, Iain Macleod has put up a smokescreen now he is Minister of Labour, while Duncan Sandys declines most things we ask him to do'. The campaign in question eventually comprised seventeen speakers including four ministers, but it was hard work getting such a team together, while before 1951 it was relatively straightforward; Eden spoke at every by-election between 1945 and 1951, but hardly ever after he became Foreign Secretary. In view of the small Government majority, Churchill relaxed his traditional rule banning Cabinet ministers from speaking at by-elections, but the rule changed only for certain types of contest, and still provided a smokescreen behind which the reluctant could hide. Something similar occurred over routine radio discussion programmes, from which ministers were also barred lest they demean their national status; the National Union complained that rather 'dim' Tory MPs were now being put up by the BBC against Labour ex-ministers, since the Conservatives' best performers were now in office. They also complained that too much attention was given to mavericks like Bob Boothby whose independence from the Party line was exactly what made him attractive to the BBC and its audience. When he did not join the Government, Walter Elliot became an acceptable compromise, a heavyweight political figure who combined loyalty with personality.[4]

The Party had to be reminded that the Government now represented the whole country and not just its supporters. Churchill declined to take a Party press officer into Downing Street with him; the National Union was unsuccessful in 1953 when it complained that its members had not been given enough seats for the Coronation – it was particularly incensed at the number given to, and enthusiastically accepted by, the TUC; constituency associations were reminded in a circular from the General Director that they must not print pictures of the Queen in their literature, nor adopt any other form of words, decoration or layout 'in such a way as to suggest any special association between Her Majesty and a particular political party', which suggests that constituency parties may have been trying to generate political capital from the new monarch; Pontefract were running a Coronation Ball and East Flint a Coronation draw with a television as prize. A curious exception to this wish to separate off the Party from the state involved the design of a Party membership card, unfinished business from the Maxwell Fyfe Report; the Party Treasurers

---

[4] NUEC, 14 Feb. 1952; Central Office, General Director's file, 'Tonbridge by-election', CCO 120/2/46, CPA; Robert Rhodes James, *Bob Boothby, a Portrait* (1991), 359; Colin Coote, *A Companion of Honour, The Story of Walter Elliot* (1965), 260.

had pressed for this in the hope that part of a national minimum subscription would come direct to them, though in view of constituencies' new obligations under the quota scheme, this was turned down. Central Council though, on a motion proposed by Eden's nephew, decided that a card be prepared, containing, as earlier local versions had done, a statement of the Party's aims. This led to the design of a standard card, the possession of which would define Party membership for the first time, and the question therefore arose as to what the card should say the Party's objectives were. What were members signing up to? A draft was agreed by the National Union in 1952, and passed to ministers for comment; Churchill surprisingly had the Cabinet Secretary circulate this Party document to colleagues (together with his own alternative wording which added a clause committing the Party specifically to the defence of free enterprise); it appears not to have been discussed at Cabinet, but only when officials had left. The decision was hostile to the whole idea: too generalised a statement of objectives would be useless, and too defined a statement could be 'subject to criticism' – as the Conservatives themselves ensured that Labour's 'clause four' was constantly criticised; a safe statement such as a quotation from Disraeli would do instead. The Government therefore advised that the Conservative Party's aims should remain undefined.[5]

Parliamentary relationships also had to be re-learned. The 1922 Committee had included frontbenchers at its meetings for the past decade, but ministers were now again excluded from membership under the rules. The problem was more serious because the new generation of backbenchers felt a considerable gap between themselves and the Cabinet, in Powell's view an unbridgeable gulf between those with and those without pre-war parliamentary experience. To improve communications, the rules of the 1922 Committee were amended to allow all Party whips to attend the meetings as of right (though not to vote, in practice a restriction that applied only to the election of officers and sub-committees, since votes were almost unheard of at meetings); other ministers would continue to be invited to address the meeting as and when suitable opportunities arose; the new chairman, Derek Walker-Smith, also managed with the assistance of James Stuart to establish the practice of regular meetings with the Prime Minister, sometimes just for the chairman but sometimes for the whole 1922 Executive.[6]

Churchill became a steadily more remote figure to young backbenchers as his health declined and his deafness increased. He confidently proclaimed on taking office that a majority of one was quite enough. His own nerve held out remarkably well under the inevitable pressures, for Labour MPs were

5 Woolton, *Memoirs*, 379; NUEC, 10 July and 4 Sept. 1952, 12 Feb. 1953; Wirral CA minutes, 23 Jan. 1953; Pontefract CA minutes, 15 Dec. 1953; East Flint CA minutes, 2 Mar. 1953; Central Council minutes, 20 Mar. 1952; Cabinet information from Peter Hennessy; NUEC, secretary's notes, 12 Feb. 1953, NUA 4/3/1, CPA.
6 Alan Thompson, *The Day Before Yesterday* (1971), 106; Philip Goodhart, *The 1922, The Story of the 1922 Committee* (1973), 159–65; James Stuart, *Within the Fringe* (1967), 162.

determined to repay the Tories for their harassment of the previous year; when the Government suffered a technical defeat on a minor Scottish legislative issue and the Secretary of State offered to resign, Churchill's reply was that 'I do wish you'd stop talking nonsense and leave me alone'; correspondingly, although he had to accept the loss of his Minister of Agriculture over the notorious Crichel Down affair, he would have no truck with the junior ministers' honourable offer to go down with their chief. He remained ever conscious of the narrowness of his Government's margin of authority. When John Boyd-Carpenter became Minister of Transport, the Prime Minister told him to ensure that no more than five Tory MPs ever boarded the same aeroplane, so as not to have 'too many baskets in one egg'. In 1952, the Chief Whip 'was discussing with Mr. Churchill the danger in which the Party stood because of its small majority and said that if the Almighty chose to call to Himself half a dozen people with slight majorities this Parliament would be finished, to which Mr. Churchill replied, "Oh but I am sure He would not do anything of the sort," and then after a pause, "and anyhow, I think he has got his hands petty full at the moment."' After a late-night ambush by Labour MPs in 1953, when twenty-seven Tory MPs had been absent unpaired, the Chief Whip read a lecture to 'the boys' at a meeting of the 1922 Committee; 'all must remember that the Opposition are learning better all the time as an Opposition the methods which we used so successfully in their place'. This one defeat, on a prayer on the scarcely-vital Miscellaneous Controls (Revocation) Order, was far from typical; a Whip's Office report in December 1954 noted with pride that the average majority had been 27.4 even in the difficult 1952–53 session, and over thirty in the other sessions of the Parliament, double the Government's paper lead over all other parties, news received by the Prime Minister with the minute, 'a prodigy!'[7]

Strong nerves were needed, for the Churchill Government did not enjoy the customary honeymoon period after its arrival in office. The first Christmas recess was thought to be excessively long and Harry Crookshank made a faltering start in the key role of Leader of the House. Throughout 1952 the Government was well behind in opinion polls, and local council elections in April and May were a disappointment; one senior member of the National Union complained that the Government 'had been slow in carrying out a Conservative policy' and after a meeting with the 1922 Committee, Churchill had to issue a statement saying that the Government's determination to complete its legislative programme was undiminished. The Government's defenders were able to assert that they were taking unpopular action to deal with the inheritance from Labour, but the Party was restive; some of the council losses arose from the Party's successes of earlier years, so

[7] Stuart, *Within the Fringe*, 166; Lord Carrington, *Reflect on Things Past, The Memoirs of Lord Carrington* (1988), 93; John Boyd-Carpenter, *Way of Life* (1980), 92; Woolton note of discussion with Buchan-Hepburn, 7 Oct. 1952, Woolton MSS, box 22; Buchan-Hepburn note of 12 Sept. 1953, Hailes MSS 2/5; whip's note of 5 Dec. 1954, Hailes MSS, 4/2.

that they were now defending most of the vacant seats, but this could not explain away a crushing defeat in London, where the number of Tory county councillors fell from sixty-four in 1949 to thirty-seven. From the other side, Richard Crossman felt that 'their confidence has certainly been shaken' by these results. Jock Colville recognised that this reverse arose from expectations that Conservatives had themselves raised: 'the country hoped a Tory Government would mean relaxations and more food; in fact it has meant controls as stringent as ever and more rationing'. By the end of May he was despondent: 'the Government is in a bad way . . . Their popularity has fallen owing to bad publicity, rising prices and a silly policy of denationalisation. Winston is, I fear, blamed both in the country and by his own party in the House. Mrs. Churchill does not think he will last long as Prime Minister.'[8]

This malaise should not be exaggerated. Although some constituencies complained about the timing, it was during exactly this period that the Party embarked on a recruiting campaign which aimed to find a quarter of a million new members and exceeded that target by 100,000; over a hundred constituencies found more than a thousand recruits and the national total rose to the highest level ever. In the Wirral, where the membership was already over 8,000, all branches took part and raised the total to 10,323, a third of Selwyn Lloyd's 1951 Tory vote. In Bradford there were almost 4,000 new recruits, with significant gains in all four constituencies. All the constituencies in the industrial Northern Area increased their membership, and even in this difficult area the average constituency now had 3,000 paid up members.[9]

Colville was not alone in blaming 'bad publicity' for this slump in Tory fortunes. Others bemoaned the deluge of untimely government announcements coinciding with the local campaigns, and the 1952 Conference agenda contained twenty-five constituency resolutions complaining about the Government's poor public relations record; Gravesend, Reigate, and Brentford and Chiswick were just a few of those that passed critical motions in Spring 1952; Newark felt in April that 'there could be little doubt that there was at present a measure of apathy amongst Party supporters and some discontent with the Government'. From the first, the Government had been warned that it should pay attention to public relations, a sharp memorandum to that effect having been circulated by John Wyndham just after the election. This was taken up by Michael Fraser, and the result was the formation in December 1951 of a new Liaison Committee under the chairmanship of Lord Swinton, a Party forum at which ministers and Party officials could meet to discuss

8   Anthony Seldon, *Churchill's Indian Summer, The Conservative Government, 1951–1955* (1981), 54; NUEC, 15 May 1952; Central Council report for 1952, NUA 2/2/18, CPA; Henry Pelling, *Winston Churchill* (1974), 598; Janet Morgan (ed.), *The Backbench Diaries of Richard Crossman* (1981), 107; John Colville, *The Fringes of Power, Downing Street Diaries, 1939–1955* (1985), 644, 649.
9   Central Office file, 'Recruiting', CCO 4/5/89; Wirral CA minutes, 28 Mar. and 27 Nov. 1952, 18 Apr. 1953; Bradford CA minutes, 26 Feb. 1953.

imminent issues and the best way in which they could be presented; the Liaison Committee became a pivotal part of the machinery whenever the Conservatives were in office, for years ahead. In the first place though, ministers were slow to learn how to use this Party machinery, and their officials naturally gave it little priority. In March 1952, the National Union's Speakers and Publicity Committee lamented the fact that ministers 'failed to justify what they are doing', and in response Woolton revealed the existence of the Liaison Committee and explained its role; he 'concluded by saying that the best publicity that anybody could have was the propaganda that arises from a job well done'. The council results reopened this continuing argument, but Churchill's reluctance to allow the Party an influence within Whitehall was still an obstacle. Eventually, as John Cross related, 'even Churchill was disturbed when, on one occasion, fourteen White Papers were issued on the same day, and, on another, when the Ministry of Food announced the end of cheese rationing without notifying him (or apparently anyone else) in advance'. Pressure built up from the 1922 Committee and from his ministerial colleagues, and in May Swinton was given the ministerial responsibility and authority to coordinate Government publicity, with an experienced former journalist to assist him. Over the rest of 1952, the parallel systems of Party and Government gradually eased into smooth operation, and in December Churchill agreed to a meeting of ministers without civil servants present to review publicity arrangements in general. In due course, ministers became more adept at getting news from the work of their departments. Indeed some came in for reassuring attacks from Labour for their playing to the gallery, as James Stuart did when he was photographed driving in the first pile for the new Forth road bridge, and Macmillan both when he visited the flooded Devon resort of Lynmouth in 1952, and when he presented the keys to the young couple whose house took the Government over the target figure of 300,000 completions; in February 1953, Churchill circulated a note to colleagues, reminding them of the need to produce favourable news stories just before the local elections, to prevent a repeat of the 1952 defeats. As part of the same review of procedures, the parliamentary lobby system was also re-started, again with some reluctance on Churchill's part, and this provided a forum in which friendly journalists could be briefed off the record; by 1954, a civil service brief for Churchill could note that Swinton was known as 'the Lobby Minister', and that 'since 1952 the general relations between the Lobby and the Government, which in the early stages of its term of office were bad and undoubtedly poisoned reporting and comment, have steadily improved'. In October 1952, the Party Conference passed a congratulatory resolution on the 'action taken by the Prime Minister to coordinate public relations in Government'. But Woolton and Butler were clearly right to argue that the Government's lasting popularity must depend on its actions rather than its words. In the case of the 1951 Government, this was inextricably bound up with Churchill and his relations with his senior colleagues.[10]

## The Churchill team

Churchill's last period of office has not been judged either by contemporaries or by historians against conventional standards. After 1951 he was more than ever a world figure among mere politicians. Roy Jenkins concluded that after 1951 Churchill was 'gloriously unfit for office', and that his selection of ministers was 'at least as much a pageant to commemorate the great days of the first government as it was a realistic preparation for office'. Even when the Government ran into serious difficulty in May 1952, and the Tory poll rating fell to 42 per cent, the same sample found 51 per cent satisfied with Churchill as Prime Minister. When by the end of 1954 almost all of his colleagues were anxious to get him out, *The Times* felt that it would be 'embarrassing' to speculate on such a thing. He was outside and above normal considerations.[11]

He certainly encouraged such views by the way in which ministerial appointments were made, and by the unconventional structures that he decided on. Having accepted the King's commission to form a ministry on Friday 26 October, only nine senior appointments were made before the week-end, and neither press nor Party was told whether this was the whole Cabinet or only part of it; that first group did not include Macmillan who became Prime Minister five years later. Other appointments were made in stages over the following week, sometimes without senior ministers being told who their juniors were to be (and in some cases not liking it much when they found out), and Churchill could hardly be got to devote his mind at all to the appointment of law officers. Casualness and confusion produced some extraordinary consequences; Walter Elliott was not at home when telephoned and thereby missed a Cabinet post, it apparently being decided before a return call could be made that Education should go instead to a token woman; Florence Horsbrugh thus became the first woman to be a Conservative departmental minister (though not at first in Cabinet) but was hardly a successful choice; Selwyn Lloyd suspected that he had been appointed

10  Central Council report for 1952, NUA 2/2/18, CPA; Gravesend CA minutes, 12 June 1952; Reigate CA minutes, 21 Apr. 1952; Brentford and Chiswick CA minutes, 4 July 1952; Newark CA minutes, 24 Apr. 1952; Lord Egremont, *Wyndham and Children First* (1968), 146–9; NUEC, 27 Mar. 1952; J.A. Cross, *Lord Swinton* (Oxford, 1982), 267–71; Harriet Jones, 'The Conservative Party and Social Policy, 1942–1955', unpublished PhD thesis, University of London, 1992, 193; Stuart, *Within the Fringe*, 168; Seldon, *Indian Summer*, 60, 250; Churchill circular, 26 Feb. 1953, Hailes MSS, 4/2; brief for Churchill, 29 Oct. 1954, Butler MSS, G46; Central Office, *Notes on Current Politics* [hereafter *NCP*], 27 Oct. 1952.

11  Roy Jenkins, 'Churchill, the Government of 1951–1955', in *Churchill*, eds Robert Blake and W.R. Louis (Oxford, 1993), 492–3; Paul Addison, *Churchill on the Home Front, 1900–1955* (1992), 412.

to the Foreign Office only because the Prime Minister thought he was *Geoffrey* Lloyd, and Stuart allegedly smuggled Churchill's old adversary Alec Dunglass into the Scottish Office because Churchill seemed not to know that he had just become the Earl of Home and did not recognise the name. The prevalence of such stories, even if mostly apocryphal, says much about the way in which colleagues *perceived* the Prime Minister's grip on affairs in 1951.[12]

Four clear principles underlay the appointments: first, the balancing of youth and experience; secondly the appointment of men to departments for which they had not preparared while in opposition; thirdly Churchill's longing for the glories of 1940–45; and fourthly his desire to provide a non-confrontational, 'national' team. Over many of the younger ministers were placed 'overlords', peers who were experienced former colleagues of Churchill and who were charged with the coordination of the work of departmental ministers in neighbouring fields; Butler at the Treasury was given not only an elderly Minister of State to keep him in order, but a ministerial committee to supervise policy too. These arrangements were universally unsuccessful, for only the departmental ministers could be accountable in the Commons and only they had the civil servants and budgets at their disposal. The deliberate choice of non-specialists originated from Churchill's desire to keep policy options open on entering office, for previous Party spokesmen in the same field might bring with them hostages to fortune from earlier speeches and writings. Selwyn Lloyd protested that he was unsuitable for the Foreign Office because he had never visited a foreign country, spoke no foreign languages and did not like foreigners; Churchill impassively replied, 'Young man, these all seem to me to be positive advantages.' Lloyd was to be a success as Eden's number two, but Churchill's old wartime colleague Alexander, recalled from the Governor Generalship of Canada to be Minister of Defence without any political experience whatsoever, was not. In fact, not all appointments followed the generalist rule; Ernest Marples' appointment to assist Macmillan at Housing, Harold Watkinson at Labour, and Derick Heathcoat Amory at Pensions were all examples of horses for courses, though these were all second-rank positions in which Churchill may not have taken so personal an interest.[13]

Nostalgia for his finest hour certainly did weigh on his mind. As well as Alexander, Churchill recalled to the colours Lords Ismay and Cherwell, tried to persuade Bracken and Anderson to serve, and reappointed Colville as his secretary; the Cabinet Office greeted his return to Number Ten with a pile of his red 'action this day' stickers for Prime Ministerial minutes, hoarded in the

12  Harold Macmillan, *Tides of Fortune, 1945–1955* (1969), 362–6; Coote, *Walter Elliot*, 265; Reginald Maudling, *Memoirs* (1978), 52; D.R. Thorpe, *Selwyn Lloyd* (1989), 153; Stuart, *Within the Fringe*, 162; Boyd-Carpenter, *Way of Life*, 88.
13  T.F. Lindsay and M. Harrington, *The Conservative Party, 1918–1970* (1974), 174; Stuart, *Within the Fringe*, 161; Boyd-Carpenter, *Way of Life*, 96; Thorpe, *Lloyd*, 153; Colville, *Fringes of Power*, 633; Harold Watkinson, *Turning Points, A Record of Our Times* (Salisbury, 1986), 40; W. Gore Allen, *The Reluctant Politician, Derick Heathcoat Amory* (1958), 119.

office since 1945; Churchill initially took the Defence ministry as well as the premiership (until Alexander could be brought back) and tried to make Eden Leader of the House as well as Foreign Secretary, combinations which rapidly proved too much for either; Eden was in any case more anxious to ensure that he was recognised as deputy Prime Minister. As the Cold War deepened, even the Home Guard was revived. It was 1940 come again, and Colville noted that 'Auld Lang Syne was ringing out along the Whitehall corridors'. There was also a family grouping at the heart of the Government; Churchill's son Randolph had again failed to get into parliament, and never stood again after 1951, but both of Winston's sons-in-law were in office, and in 1952 his niece became Eden's second wife. A Tory MP grumbled to Hugh Dalton that 'to be in this Government you must either be a member of the Churchill family or in the House of Lords'. All this lent a different flavour to the Prime Minister's appointment of a Lloyd George (Gwilym) and his unsuccessful attempt to appoint an Asquith (Cyril) to his team. Nostalgia and dynasticism went hand in hand. There were on the other hand, as in 1940–45, very few traditional Tories in the Cabinet, Crookshank and Salisbury being the only obvious examples. Over time, the nostalgic character of the Churchill Government was diluted as the warhorses returned to their stables and the classes of 1945 and 1950 forced their way in, but right to the end of Churchill's tenure of office this was a Government with the handbrake at least halfway on the motor of progress.[14]

Nothing brought this out more clearly than the most symbolic issue of 1950s modernity, television. The decision to introduce commercial television was forced on the Party's old guard by the younger generation, but when it came to using television imaginatively, the old guard hung on; in early 1955, the last bout of pre-election planning for which Churchill was in charge, the Party was represented in discussions with Labour and the BBC by Swinton, Crookshank and Buchan-Hepburn (average age sixty-three), and they happily agreed with Labour to reject any extension of television coverage of politics; a year later, with Eden as Leader, the Party was represented by Butler, Heath and Hill (average age forty-eight), who duly backed the BBC in forcing on a reluctant Labour Party ministerial broadcasts to the nation. Such forward-looking attitudes represented a generational leap that could occur only when Churchill stepped down, and the frustration of his colleagues in 1954–55 indicates an increasing awareness of he fact. The black coats, striped trousers and watch chains, which were ministerial dress in 1952 as they had been since the First World War, were scarcely to be seen at the end of the decade, though still popular with some backbenchers.[15]

---

[14]  Richard Cockett (ed.), *My Dear Max. The Letters of Brendan Bracken to Lord Beaverbrook, 1925–1958* (1990), 127; Robert Rhodes James, *Anthony Eden* (1986), 343; Addison, *Churchill*, 407; Thompson, *Day Before Yesterday*, 92; Colville, *Fringes of Power*, 633–5; Ben Pimlott (ed.), *The Political Diaries of Hugh Dalton, 1918–40 and 1945–60* (1986), 569.

[15]  Central Office, General Director's files, 'Political broadcasting', CCO 120/1/1–3, CPA; T.E.B. Howarth, *Prospect and Reality, Britain, 1945–1955* (1985), 183.

Churchill was also anxious that his Goverment should have 'national' credentials, an inheritance from 1940–45, as well as a reaction to his fragile majority in the House. *The Times* advised that 'precisely because their majority is so small Mr. Churchill and his ministers must see themselves less as a party than as a national Government'. The clearest sign of this was the invitation to the Liberal leader Clement Davies to join the Cabinet; Davies wanted to accept, a decision that could well have brought about the final absorption of the Liberals into the Conservative Party, but other Liberals would not agree without the simultaneous offer of proportional representation, and this Churchill could not deliver; in December 1952 though, the 1922 Committee was still suspiciously asking for information about Churchill's recent talks with the Liberals over electoral reform, suggesting that the premier had still not quite given up hope. Lord Waverley (formerly Anderson) would not join in the post offered, and the non-political Lord Salter did join but did not last long. The Government's centrist character therefore had to be achieved by the selection of appropriate Conservatives for the key domestic portfolios, especially the Exchequer, Labour, and Housing. After Stanley's death, Oliver Lyttelton had become the senior spokesman on finance, and this appeared to give him the first claim on the Exchequer – though earlier specialisation was anyway not a decisive qualification in 1951. Churchill instead turned to Butler and made him Chancellor, recognising that in doing so he would again disappoint his old friend Lyttelton. It may be that all Butler's policy work in the domestic field would have secured him the job in any case, but in 1951 his appointment was seen – and was intended to be seen – as a pledge to the nation that the spirit of the *Industrial Charter* would hold good in office; Butler was only seventh in the overall hierarchy though, a low ranking for the Chancellor. Equally significant was the appointment of Monckton, only in parliament at all since February, rather than the expected Maxwell Fyfe, as Minister of Labour. Monckton, sneeringly dismissed by Margesson as 'that old oil can', was indeed chosen for his skill in lubricating industrial machinery, as well as for his knowledge of industrial relations law. His 'riding orders' from the Prime Minister were that he should keep the industrial temperature as low as was humanly possible. Macmillan on the other hand was given instructions to be a dynamic minister, and to carry out at any cost the Party's pledge to build 300,000 houses a year. Since like most senior Conservatives he doubted that it was even possible, he hesitated for some time before accepting, and thereby won the unqualified backing of Churchill for his programme when he did finally accept; it was the decision that would propel him to the premiership. The character of the ministry had one further structural aspect in the new provision for Scotland and Wales, for Conservatives had begun to worry (if not yet very much) about the growth of nationalism, and had published pre-election plans for devolving government to Edinburgh and Cardiff; Home was appointed Minister of State at the Scottish Office specifically to spend most of his time in Edinburgh rather than London, and thereby raise the political profile of the Government in Scotland; the success of what Churchill described to Stuart as 'your Home, sweet Home' in this all-round job was the re-launching of Alec Home's career towards the premiership as well. Wales was given a less enhanced status, when the Scotsman who became Home Secretary, David Maxwell Fyfe, was also made Minister for Welsh Affairs; in the Principality, where the name Fyffe was synonymous with fruit, he acquired the nickname 'Dai Bananas'; the Welsh Tories enthusiastically welcomed this highlighting of Welsh business in Cabinet, and Barry Conservatives in 1954 directed their demands for a new Severn bridge to Maxwell Fyfe as 'the right quarter' from which 'to bring pressure upon Government'. Looking at the team as a whole, Richard Crossman recognised what Churchill had intended, that 'the real free enterprisers and deflationists seem to have been kept out, and there is a good deal in the view that the general make-up of the Churchill Cabinet means that it will be only very slightly to the right of the recent Attlee Cabinet. Just as Attlee was running what was virtually a coalition policy on a party basis, so Churchill may well do the same.'[16]

The casualness and nostalgia that characterised the Government's initiation remained a part of the story throughout its life. Woolton recalled that 'the Cabinet under Mr. Churchill was often reminiscent of bygone times . . . Not infrequently the entire time of the meeting had gone before he arrived at the first item on the agenda; he had no hesitation in keeping other ministers waiting in the corridor for an hour or more after the time they had been called to attend the Cabinet meeting, whilst he talked to us about things that he thought important for the country, but about which the Cabinet secretariat had been given no notice and about which, of course, there were no papers. All very irritating to busy ministers.' Boyd-Carpenter was one of those often kept waiting: 'he could certainly get decisions when he wanted them, but equally sometimes enjoyed being discursive. He liked to lunch at half past one and saw no reason why cabinets should break up before then.' Early in 1954, Eden was asked to chair a Cabinet at which cuts in the spending programme would be discussed, but with little preparation: his secretary noted that 'Woolton rang A.E. in a great state – "one might just as well not be a member of the Cabinet if one is not allowed to discuss financial matters" . . . The fact of the matter is, there is no PM worth the name and they are all at sixes and sevens.' At the end of the year, Eden

16  Howarth, *Prospect and Reality*, 177; 1922 Committee minutes [hereafter 1922 Cttee.], 11 1952; Addison, *Churchill*, 409; Oliver Lyttelton, Lord Chandos, *The Memoirs of Lord Chandos* (1962), 343; Earl of Kilmuir, *Political Adventure, The Memoirs of the Earl of Kilmuir* (1964), 190, 194, 204; Woolton, *Memoirs*, 363–4; Lord Birkenhead, *Walter Monckton* (1969), 275; Lord Butler of Saffron Walden, *The Art of the Possible, The Memoirs of Lord Butler* (1971), 156; Lord Home, *The Way the Wind Blows* (1976), 102; Kenneth Young, *Sir Alec Douglas-Home* (1970), 80, 85; John Dickie, *The Uncommon Commoner, A Study of Sir Alec Douglas-Home* (1964), 89–90; Seldon, *Indian Summer*, 127; Wales Area Council, 17 May 1952; Barry CA minutes, 10 Mar. 1954; Morgan, *Crossman Diaries*, 30.

himself complained to his diary about 'drawling Cabinets, the failure to take decisions, the general atmosphere of "aprés moi le déluge"'. Anthony Seldon has argued that such views exaggerate the problem since, at least until his last months in office, Churchill was as businesslike as most premiers; in the decision to build a British hydrogen bomb in 1954, taken to full Cabinet by Churchill (unlike similar decisions under most other premiers), there was a wide-ranging philosophical debate. It is clear though that colleagues did resent his methods at the time as well as later. Eden was perhaps the most frustrated of all, for he was conscious that if only Churchill would retire he could get his hands on on the machine and (as he thought) restore order. The lack of trust was mutual, and reinforced by jealousies over the conduct of foreign policy – the special interest of both of them; Eden must have read with some exasperation Churchill's note to him when he was about to go off for an operation in 1953, informing him that 'it will be necessary for me to take over officially from you. Happily we are fully agreed in outlook'; in July 1954 Churchill was gleefully noticing that Eden's return from a diplomatic triumph at Geneva had not produced the popularity in the House that he had expected. From his side, Eden suspected that attacks on his policy in the Beaverbrook press were being orchestrated by Churchill's family and intimates, even perhaps with the Prime Minister's connivance.[17]

## 'The march to freedom'

None of this should give the impression that a strong line of policy could not be followed when Churchill's mind was fully engaged and where a minister had his confidence. In broad economic policy, in housing and in industrial relations this was certainly the case. On coming into office, Churchill had been shocked by the Treasury's initial report on the country's economic prospects; he circulated the threatening memorandum to his new colleagues with an equally gloomy covering note, and was anxious to put on to the public record his inheritance from Attlee (who was sent a copy of the same papers); the rearmament programme brought about by the Korean crisis was having a disastrous effect both on public expenditure and on the balance of payments; in place of 'housing, red meat and not getting scuppered', Churchill's dictum now was 'housing, red meat and not going broke'. Butler rapidly established a rapport and a mutual respect with advisers at the Treasury, much as he had done with the CRD, and with the Prime Minister's backing took drastic action. Overseas purchases of food were slashed to provide a breathing space; ironically it was only the survival of wartime controls that the Conservatives

---

[17] Woolton, *Memoirs*, 377; Boyd-Carpenter, *Way of Life*, 90; John Charmley (ed.), *Descent to Suez, Diaries of Evelyn Shuckburgh, 1951–56* (1986), 46, 135; Seldon, *Indian Summer*, 85; Peter Hennessy, *Whitehall* (Fontana edn, 1990), 138; Rhodes James, *Eden*, 351, 393; Churchill to Eden, 6 Apr. 1953, Avon MSS, 19/1/76; Geoffrey McDermott, *The Eden Legacy and the Decline of British Diplomacy* (1969), 116.

were pledged to abolish (and did abolish not long afterwards) that made this possible; he also proved a more determined cutter of public spending than Gaitskell had been. An astonished Brendan Bracken exulted that 'our Mr. Butler has a stronger digestion than the toughest of ostriches. He has evacuated his charters with no sign of a blockage & is now preparing to slaughter the do-gooders & easy spenders in Government service.' It was these crisis measures that prompted the worsening of the food situation and occasioned the unpopularity of mid-1952, but they also made the room for relaxations and tax cuts later; the Chief Whip, replying to a constituent who was complaining about class sizes in Kentish schools, wrote in February 1952 that 'as soon as the country is solvent again, we can then turn our attention over more to building more schools'; a Party publication in November contrasted 'the situation in 1951' with 'paying our way' under Butler. He had one early setback in which he was unable to get Churchill's support; he became convinced that a bold way out of the country's economic dilemma would be to free the pound from fixed exchange rates, a policy only followed in very different circumstances after 1970. This would have finished once and for all any idea that Conservative and Labour policy converged in the person of the 'Mr. Butskell' that *The Economist* detected, for it would have introduced a strongly deflationist international influence into the heart of British policy, strongly deprecated by Labour. But in any case, in 1952 the old guard in the Government, led by Woolton and Cherwell, were sufficient to persuade a reluctant Churchill that the policy was too risky.[18]

Bracken could scarcely have been more wrong though about Butler's long-term intentions, for which again he had the Prime Minister's backing. As the benefits of the emergency measures of 1951–52 worked through (for which the Government could reasonably claim some credit) and as the terms of international trade moved in Britain's favour (from which they also benefited, but could not claim credit), the strain on both trade and public expenditure lessened. The financial screw could be loosened a little in 1953 when Butler's Budget was the first since the War that neither increased tax rates nor created new taxes; income and purchase tax were each reduced and the excess profits levy abolished. *The Economist* felt that this was 'a turning of the fiscal tide', and approvingly quoted Butler's claim that his measures 'step[ped] out from the confines of restriction to the almost forgotten but beckoning prospects of freer endeavour and greater reward for effort'. The economy entered on a period of sustained growth, slow by international standards but very noticeable in Britain after years of austerity; before the end of the Parliament

---

18    Thompson, *Day Before Yesterday*, 92, 94; Martin Gilbert, *Never Despair, Winston S. Churchill, 1945–1965* (1988), 725; Pelling, *Churchill*, 596–7; Buchan-Hepburn to Mrs Cripps, 6 Feb. 1952, Hailes MSS, 1/15; *NCP*, 4 Feb., 18 Mar., 26 May and 10 Nov. 1952; Butler, *Art of the Possible*, 157, 160; Anthony Howard, *RAB, The Life of R.A. Butler* (1987), 182, 186–7; Howarth, *Prospect and Reality*, 184, 187; Boyd-Carpenter, *Way of Life*, 97–8; Cockett, *My Dear Max*, 129.

Leicester was officially judged to be the most prosperous city in Europe; the value of shares on the stock exchange more than doubled between 1952 and 1955; unemployment remained low, though when it threatened to rise in 1953 the Government prepared some highly interventionist public works schemes to keep it down, so aware were they of the electoral signifiance of the issue – and so far were the younger Conservatives anxious to banish once and for all the memory of the 1930s; Butler advised that those who were talking airily about 'creating pools of unemployment should be thrown into them and made to swim'. But such stern language hardly seemed necessary; in May 1954, Butler looked back on 'a year of full employment without inflation . . . the economists' dream – the desirable country so difficult to enter. Perhaps we have found a way.'[19]

The visible side effects of growth were spectacular: rationing was abolished in stages, sugar in 1953 and both fuel and meat in 1954; consumer goods became more widely available and in particular there was a rapid increase in car-ownership (up by over a million) and televisions (up 300 per cent); public expenditure rose, with increases in the social policy budget as it held its share of an expanded national output, and there were the beginnings of a motorway programme. In May 1954, the first steps were taken towards equal pay for teachers, a symbolic reversal of the contested parliamentary vote of 1944. The end of rationing was part of a more general programme of decontrol that proceeded, first with care, and then with carefree abandon as the economy picked up. Churchill was a powerful force behind this, harrying ministers with minutes about the slowness of their push for freedom: when Gwilym Lloyd George argued for caution on winding down rationing, the Prime Minister countered that, 'We were *elected* for this! We must do it!' He worried though about press speculation that there would be increased prices when eggs were decontrolled, producing from him the cry, 'Oh, my poor people, they can't pay a shilling for eggs'; they did not need to, for decontrol rapidly produced higher production and lower prices; the black market (estimated at nearly half of all eggs consumed) now vanished altogether. Labour claims that food decontrol would only benefit the better-off were easily dismissed: Crookshank pointed out in December 1953 that if the extra food was indeed going entirely to rich families then they must each be consuming an extra hundredweight of meat every week and equally absurd quantities of sugar and bacon. Three months after taking office, the Government abolished identity cards, and almost as quickly the New Town Corporations lost their pubs to private enterprise; wood, metals and other raw materials were decontrolled, and

[19] *NCP*, 16 Mar. 1952, 4 May and 12 Dec. 1953, 7 June 1954; Kilmuir, *Memoirs*, 200–1, 215; Howard, *RAB*, 193, 204, 211; Michael Pinto-Duschinsky, 'Bread and Circuses? The Conservatives in Office, 1951–1964', in *The Age of Affluence*, eds V. Bogdanor and R. Skidelsky (1970), 56–8; Howarth, *Prospect and Reality*, 194, 199–200; Jenkins, 'Churchill, the Government', 501; Chris Patten, 'R.A. Butler – What We Missed', unpublished R.A. Butler Inaugural Lecture, delivered 25 May 1994; Thompson, *Day Before Yesterday*, 94.

much of the bureaucratic machinery dismantled; the London Metal Market and the Liverpool Cotton Exchange both reopened; in 1954 Woolton was appointed Minister of Materials with a brief to close down the Ministry itself within six months; in the same spirit, Maudling refused to become Minister of Supply on the unusual ground that the Ministry should not exist – it was wound up in 1959; from 1953 agriculture, fisheries and food came into one Department, and from 1953 so did transport and civil aviation, and pensions and national insurance. This was not always just an uncontroversial matter of rationalisation; agricultural opinion was not happy for farming to be bracketed with food, lest the new ministry lose sight of the producers' interests in its wish to protect the consumer, and letters of protest were received when it seemed that most of the new Ministry's officials would come from the food side. Ralph Assheton's characteristic backing for an end to the Ministry of Food, and the control policy that it symbolised, shows just how far the return of peacetime conditions had undermined the credibility of rationing; 'it is difficult to justify a system which allows me as many cigars, bottles of wine and television sets as I can afford, but prevents me from buying food for my hens or a leg of mutton for my family'. The policy proceeded, and whereas in 1951 there had been over 20,000 prosecutions for infringements of controls, by 1954 this was down to under a thousand. In 1955, the intake for national service was reduced, a first move back towards professional armed forces and freedom from conscription for civilians. Butler celebrated this thrust of policy in a much-quoted speech at Gloucester in July 1954:

> in the last three years we have burned our identity cards, torn up our ration books, halved the number of snoopers, decimated the number of forms and said good riddance to nearly two-thirds of the remaining wartime regulations. This is the march to freedom on which we are bound. And the pace must quicken as we go forward . . . Our aim is freedom for every man and woman to live their own lives in their own way and not have their lives lived for them by an overweening State.

There were political consequences too: whereas in 1952 Crookshank had been the Government's number three, when both Churchill and Eden were incapacitated in 1953 it was Butler who took charge; in 1954 he had a hero's reception from the Party Conference. This was though perhaps a shade misleading, for Butler's Treasury years were to be a rare moment when his political instincts ran fully alongside those of the Party, as they had not earlier done over India or Munich, and were not to do subsequently at the Home Office and over Africa. 'At the Treasury', on the other hand,' as Chris Patten puts it, 'all were tuned to the same frequency'.[20]

[20] Addison, *Churchill*, 415, 423–4; Carrington, *Reflect on Things Past*, 61; Seldon, *Indian Summer*, 211–13, 262; Boyd-Carpenter, *Way of Life*, 111; Woolton, *Memoirs*, 405–7; Maudling, *Memoirs*, 61; Cleveland Fyfe to Maxwell Fyfe, 11 Jan. 1955, Kilmuir MSS, 6/8; Assheton to Butler, 7 Jan. 1953, Butler MSS, G26; Butler, *Art of the Possible*, 172–3; Patten, 'R.A. Butler'.

In structural terms too, there were moves towards freedom, notably over nationalisation and commercial television. For iron and steel, plans carefully made during 1951 were available, but these fell short of a complete reversal of Labour's Act; the 1951 King's Speech promised only 'the reorganisation of the industry under free enterprise but with an adequate measure of public supervision'. The detailed drafting took several months, during which Tory MPs began to get suspicious of the Government's intentions, but a battle was still going on in Cabinet; the free enterprise hawks, particularly Lyttelton and Woolton, wanted full repeal of Labour's Act, but the responsible Minister, Duncan Sandys, with the backing of Butler, Salisbury and Macmillan, preferred a compromise that would not tempt Labour to attack the industry again. The White Paper of July 1952 was a victory for the compromisers, and this approach remained that of the Bill, introduced in November and enacted in May 1953. Despite earlier worries, the nationalised companies were then easily sold back to private shareholders, with the issue being oversubscribed threefold. This caused real difficulties in the Party. The compromise formula gave the new Iron and Steel Board influence, and in the last resort powers, over a wider range of companies than had been nationalised, and the small firms involved were far from happy about this; when Sheffield's makers of special steels complained to Woolton they were told that this was in principle a reversion to the pre-war pattern, and that the reserve powers were most unlikely to be used. The inclusion of foundries in the Bill provoked even greater hostility, in Wakefield, Wolverhampton and Huddersfield among other places, for this was entirely new. There were several threats to cancel industrial subscriptions to the Party, and the Treasurers became involved. Attempts at a compromise through amendments to the Bill in committee stage did not pacify industrial critics, and Sandys had to offer to meet them. Pierssené noted that the threat of withdrawn subscriptions actually made it more rather than less difficult for the Party to influence the Government, since anyone who had made such a threat could not be allowed to meet the Minister. Michael Fraser's drafts for Woolton's replies to these representations made a non-ideological case; he stated defiantly that 'appeasement is not the keynote of our denationalisation policy', but went on to argue that 'the only practicable safeguard against nationalisation is to take steel out of politics by a sensible industrial structure which both sides of industry will eventually accept'. This accurately summed up the Government's intentions but, considering that steel was intended to mark the great divide between the parties, both the policy and the way in which it was defended fell well short of a ringing endorsement of capitalism. The same can be said of the lower profile debate about denationalising road haulage; less work had been done to prepare for this, but Churchill decided in 1952 that this legislation should be given priority over steel. The Transport Bill was therefore half-hearted, and its later implementation by the four Ministers of Transport who held office between 1951 and 1955 equally cautious. Only a twentieth of the lorries had been taken over by 1951, and not even all of these were sold off. There was no will to unscramble those parts of the industry that were thought to be working well in public ownership and, though there was ministerial disagreement about this in 1954, the Ministry of Transport's pragmatic view prevailed. The CRD's *Notes on Current Politics* declared in June 1953 that 'in formulating its plans the Conservative Government did not ask Parliament systematically to set about dismantling State industry wherever it can be found. The case for legislation in transport and steel rests upon economic grounds.' This was all within the centrist politics of the *Industrial Charter*, and Fraser described the steel policy in just those terms, as 'a middle way'. In case anyone in the Party had a wrong impression, there was no credence given to ideas of denationalising more industries; in the road haulage debate, Churchill declared that 'the railways are and will remain nationalised'. Not all Conservatives were content with this; the One Nation Group called for denationalisation in 1954, and in the same year Enoch Powell tried unsuccessfully, from within the Advisory Committee on Policy, to have more denationalisation proposals prepared in time for the next manifesto; even on road haulage, the Welsh Tories in 1956 formally expressed their regret that so little had been done. And there were regular criticisms in the House of the performance of the public corporations and their consumption of resources. Nevertheless, political capital could still be made out of the difference between the parties and the extent to which the central ground had moved since 1949; when a Labour policy document of 1952 did not repeat the 1951 threat to nationalise chemicals or sugar, the Party could appeal to businessmen to go on paying their 'insurance against socialism' with the claim that it was only the Tory and industrial campaigns that had made Labour give ground. By 1953, the Conservatives had staked out a new *status quo* that should now be conserved, and there was no further attempt to change the balance of ownership between public and private sectors for a generation.[21]

The pragmatic outcome of the anti-nationalisation campaigns ensured that more attention was paid to the one entirely original breach in a long-term state monopoly – broadcasting: Ian Orr-Ewing felt that in the first year of the Government, when other things were going all too slowly, 'here was a field in television where we could go ahead and introduce some competition'. A decision had to be taken in the early days of Churchill's Government because the BBC's charter was coming up for renewal, and because, while Labour had accepted the Beveridge committee's support for state monopoly, it had not

21  Kathleen Burk, *The First Privatisation: The Politicians, the City and the Denationalisation of Steel* (1988), 42, 61, 66–9, 76–139; *NCP*, 15 June 1953; Central Office files, 'CBF', CCO 4/5/16, and 'Denationalisation of Steel', CCO, 4/5/116, CPA; Boyd-Carpenter, *Way of Life*, 115–16; Cockett, *My Dear Max*, 162; Jones, 'Conservative Party' thesis, 194; East Flint CA minutes, 26 Jan. 1956; Gilbert, *Never Despair*, 731; R.J. Jackson, *Rebels and Whips: Dissension, Discipline and Cohesion in British Political Parties since 1945* (1968), 104; Philip Norton, *Dissension in the House of Commons, 1945–1974* (1975), 125.

legislated to that effect. A well-attended meeting of the 1922 Committee on 28 February 1952 decided that 'a very large majority of members were in favour of bringing the BBC monopoly to an end and of there being some form of alternative programme', which in effect supported the stance of Lloyd and Profumo; Lord Salisbury, attending on behalf of the Government, dismissed this vote on the grounds that there was 'no public demand for a change', that public policy should not be made under commercial pressures, and that it would all take a long time to bring about anyway; Woolton, also present at the meeting, urged all concerned to work for a compromise that would retain Party unity. The Cabinet chose to renew the charter for a short time only, while working out its policy, and then announced in May 1952 that there would be *some elements* of competition. This statement begged more issues than it settled and opened the flood gates of a controversial public debate. There was a very definite interaction between Party and Government; Profumo, who chaired the backbench pro-competition group, had been the Party's broadcasting officer before 1950, and Mark Chapman-Walker of Central Office was also actively involved in the debate. The advocates of change were almost bound to win the day if only they could get the issue openly discussed; advocates of the *status quo*, on the other hand, seemed increasingly out of touch with Party opinion as the battle went on; as Quintin Hogg later acknowledged (of himself), they were thought to have badly overstated their case. It was an issue on which right-wing supporters of free enterprise and one-nation progressives could come together. When Profumo addressed a later meeting of backbenchers he was supported by Ralph Assheton, and of a hundred MPs present only two opposed the introduction of competition. Central Office advised the Prime Minister in 1953 that three-quarters of television sets were owned by people earning less than £650 a year, a group that opinion polls showed to favour the introduction of ITV by a large margin.[22]

Churchill himself had no particular love for the BBC monopoly, recalling that in the 1930s 'they prevented me from expressing views that proved to be right. Their behaviour has been tyrannical', and Tory MPs still remembered the BBC's apparent left-wing bias during the War. But much of the Cabinet favoured the safe option of continuing with the BBC alone, and Churchill accepted their collective opinion on a subject in which he had little personal interest. The 1922 Committee would not accept this retreat, pointedly resolving in June 1953 that it was 'still in support of the policy already announced by the Government and approved by Parliament'. Woolton, always instinctively a supporter of competition, now played a key role, authorising a Party leaflet with the provocative title *There's Free Speech – Why Not Free Switch?* Churchill bridled at being described as an opponent of

---

22 Thompson, *Day Before Yesterday*, 101; Woolton, *Memoirs*, 389–92; Kilmuir, *Memoirs* 225–6; 1922 Cttee., 28 Feb. 1952 and 18 June 1953; Goodhart, *The 1922*, 161–4; Lord Hailsham, *A Sparrow's Flight, Memoirs* (1990), 276.

'the principle of freedom' for backing the BBC, and was contemptuous of 'the stupid and interested campaign which has brought [the issue] into undue prominence'; he ordered in August 1953 that the leaflet be recalled. Woolton's reply did not give an inch; first he quoted Churchill back at himself, from his 1952 Commons statement opposing 'the present complete monopoly'; then he reminded his Leader that he had told him that he should 'try to keep the Party together' on the issue, implying that the Leader and a few senior colleagues were the only ones out of line; he told Churchill that the decision to go into the propaganda battle had been agreed by Cabinet while Churchill was off sick and with Butler therefore in the chair, he reminded Churchill that the BBC's campaign to defend its monopoly was also that of an interested party; and finally he explained that 27,000 copies of the leaflet had already been issued and refused to embark on 'the first class row' that would be involved in re-calling them all. Since Churchill had only recently failed in his attempt to sack Woolton, there was little more he could do, and Woolton no doubt helped to place the issue on the agenda for October's Party Conference. At Margate there was a vote by 'a very large majority' for 'competitive television', after a debate that was shrewdly claimed by its advocates to be a symbolic vote for or against private enterprise; the continuation of state monopoly was declared to be 'authoritarian in conception and in direct contradiction to the principles for which the Conservative Party stands'. Having won the battle, Woolton then patched up a compromise, whereby an independent television authority would supervise the overall programming and there would be no programme sponsorship, but both competition and advertising would be introduced. Victory had gone to the advocates of change, and while there were some small Commons majorities in committee, the Bill passed its major votes by majorities of between twenty-seven and forty-two. It also required great efforts by Woolton to get the Bill through the Lords, where 'young turks' were few and far between, and where there was vocal opposition from bishops who were more concerned about the demoralising influence of advertising than about monopoly and competition; in that sense, the television debate was also an important stage in the Party's move towards the stance of giving the consumer what he wanted and not just what was thought to be good for him. The Lords mustered their largest ever attendance for this symbolic vote, but backed competition and advertising nonetheless. Very little was said in all this about the possibility of Party advantage, except in the sense that some Conservatives who were in general hostile to the BBC supported a change because they did not think that they fared well under existing arrangements; but it seems likely that some at least shared Pierssené's view that while commercial television would have to be non-political, it would still 'give a platform to free enterprise, capital and management. Such a "platform" would probably not, to say the least, be inimical to Conservatism.' When Chapman Walker, as managing director of the new programme company TWW, was proposing to bid for the franchise for the Plymouth area in 1958, he asked Central Office to provide him with the names of a few 'prominent citizens' who could be induced to take part, as 'we might as well start off with the right political complexion'; he already had Jim Thomas as one of his directors in TWW for his Welsh connections. It seemed a fair bet that commercial television would behave like commercial newspapers, but the outcome, the campaigning investigations of *World in Action*, the probing interviews of Robin Day, and the iconoclasm of ITN, may well have caused some rapid revision in this opinion.[23]

## Housing and industrial relations

Alongside Butler, the other coming man was certainly Harold Macmillan, whose housing programme was also a combination of decontrol and intervention, and another manifest success. He inherited detailed plans made in the CRD since the 1950 Party Conference, but put his own stamp on them, not least in the machinery he devised and the personnel he appointed. The model was Beaverbrook's tenure of the Ministry of Supply in 1941–42, when Macmillan himself had been Under Secretary; now businessmen were again brought into Government, red tape was cut, political pressure was maintained to bludgeon the Treasury into keeping up the release of resources, and a network of area boards, run by the Ministry and the industry together, identified bottlenecks and ensured that the programme was implemented. He was assisted in the pursuit of large numbers of completions by a change in the recommended size of houses to be built, a change already in the pipeline under Labour but implemented by Macmillan. He also enlisted the cooperation of both builders and building societies, both groups making confident noises in response to ministerial decisions. His own view, often repeated, was that the housing drive was central to the Party's intention to diffuse the ownership of property, was indeed the key component in the 'property-owning democracy' concept. It was therefore with this in mind, as well as in the effort to conserve public funds, that the emphasis was gradually shifted away from local authority construction towards private builders; comparing 1951 with 1955, building of houses for rent increased by only 17 per cent while building for sale rose by 443 per cent. Woolton strongly backed this shift of emphasis, noting in 1952 that it would 'remove in some measure the herding of more people into these huge County Council housing areas, which become predominantly socialist in political outlook'. In

---

[23] Churchill to Woolton, 11 Aug. 1953, and Woolton to Churchill, 13 Aug. 1953, Woolton MSS, box 22; *NCP*, 26 Oct. 1953; Central Office, Chairman's file, 'Correspondence with R.A. Butler', CCP 20/1/1; Central Office, General Director's file, 'Political broadcasting', CCO 120/1/4; *The Daily Telegraph*, obituary of Thomas, 14 July 1960, filed in Cilcennin MSS.

March 1953, a congratulatory resolution at the Central Council was amended to add a proviso that the programme should be kept 'within the public purse', the amendment moved by the same Harmar Nicholls who had spoken so eloquently for the 300,000 pledge at Blackpool, but who now saw a danger that this would become a licence for the municipalisation of housing. In the same spirit Macmillan implemented the pledge to allow sitting tenants to buy their local authority homes, though few local authorities implemented the policy; within Government David Eccles was, as Minister of Works, pressing for the lifting of licensing of private building. On occasion Macmillan clashed with Butler over the allocation of resources, since housing was in 1952–53 absorbing a very large share; Churchill's backing was unwavering, on one occasion minuting, on a suggestion from Cherwell that housing should take its share of the general cut-back in expenditure, '*No.* We are pledged to 300,000.' Benefiting from the general conviction that this was a policy with considerable electoral significance, Macmillan won the day. On one occasion, he wore down Butler's arguments in a late-night private confrontation, a pointer for the future; reporting Macmillan's battle with the Treasury, Hugh Massingham decided that Butler was 'not quite the iron Chancellor'. The drive to build private houses in record numbers was yet another way in which Tory policy replicated that of the 1930s; after the transition period in which local authorities played the key role, the private builder for sale became the main agent for the delivery of government policy and local authorities were relied on mostly for special programmes like slum clearance; in the later 1950s, as Harriet Jones has pointed out, 'the housing programme shared more features with its prewar equivalent than with Bevan's postwar vision of housing as a universal social service'. The outcome was certainly spectacular. Building accelerated sharply even in 1952, and the 300,000 target was not only reached but considerably exceeded by 1955. So successful indeed was the policy that it became a fixed point of Conservative thinking until 1964. During the thirteen years 1951–64, a quarter of the entire population was rehoused in new properties, and the proportion of families owning their own homes doubled to about half of all households. Again the political effects were considerable: the National Union Executive was congratulating Macmillan on his record as early as September 1952; a member remarked darkly that the 'lead' Macmillan was giving contrasted with the drift in other policy areas. In 1953 Central Council passed a resolution of congratulations, and the Conference agenda of that year included thirty-two grateful resolutions from constituencies – many of them explicitly linking his policies to the 'property-owning democracy'. This remained a limited commitment though where the interests of occupiers and owners came into conflict, and in 1953 it was explicitly decided not to go for a policy of leasehold enfranchisement, a Party leaflet arguing that 'more good can be done by protectiing the right of occupation than by giving a new right of ownership'. For most homeowners, it would be a 'property-leasing democracy' so far as the land on which their houses stood was concerned.[24]

Macmillan was seen as one of the Government's stars, much in demand for constituency engagements, and chosen for one of the first ever television Party Political Broadcasts in 1953; his didactic performance indicated that he still had some skills to learn. He mused on his popularity, disbelievingly, in his diary in October 1952: 'it really is rather comic, after all the years of conflict and unpopularity! But it will not last. It is all right to put up the houses. But the next job is to put up the rents.' As after 1918, the problem was that years of controlled rents had reduced the value of rented property to landlords, and removed the incentive to build properties for rent; Churchill insisted that no Bill could be prepared which would make the landlords better off; this vitiated the idea of doing anything at all, and so Macmillan's Bill of 1953 was rather limited. The next stage would have to wait until his successors, including the more libertarian Enoch Powell as Parliamentary Secretary, were in office. In any case, the drive to encourage ownership was gradually reducing the impact of rents as a political issue, and by 1960 only a fifth of households were in the private rented sector. In the meantime, Macmillan's three years at Housing had given him an appetite for power and had shown the Party something of his flair for presentation, hitherto generally unsuspected; from 1954 he moved within two years through the Ministry of Defence, the Foreign Office and the Exchequer, and so developed an all-rounder's claims on the highest post of all.[25]

The domestic policy area that attracted the most direct Prime Ministerial involvement and the greatest undertow of Party discontent, was industrial relations. This had been a constant worry; the historian G.M. Young, at work on his hostile biography *Stanley Baldwin*, had chaffed Fraser in 1950, 'so you think you can get on with the Trade Unions? S.B. used to say that the greatest error his Party ever made was in not redressing the Taff Vale situation . . . I thought in 1927 that his Trades Disputes Act was an equally grave error. And Trades Unionists have long memories. Will they believe you?' Lord Cherwell, also in defeatist mood, told Churchill in the month he took office that 'we must always remember that a coal strike lasting even a week would be disastrous; a fortnight would compel us to surrender'. When appointing Geoffrey Lloyd Minister of Fuel and Power, Churchill told him, 'Geoffrey, remember, no trouble with the miners', and a policy document

[24] Ramsden, *Conservative Party Policy*, 157–9; Cockett, *My Dear Max*, 144; Anthony Sampson, *Macmillan, A Study in Ambiguity* (Harmondsworth, 1968), 97–101; Alistair Horne, *Macmillan, 1895–1956* (1988), 336–8.
[25] Macmillan, *Tides of Fortune*, 404, 406, 413, 439; Thompson, *Day Before Yesterday*, 96; Jones, 'Conservative Party' thesis, 213, 253, 259, 262, 269; Pinto-Duschinsky, 'Bread and Circuses?', 55–6, 61; NUEC, 12 Sept. 1952; Seldon, *Indian Summer*, 255, 258; *NCP*, 23 June 1952, 14 Mar. 1955 and 23 Mar. 1956; Central Council report for 1953, NUA, 2/2/19, CPA; Addison, *Churchill*, 418; Andrew Roth, *Enoch Powell, Tory Tribune* (1970), 128, 148–9.

published in the last weeks before the Election of 1951 promised no trades union legislation without prior TUC agreement.[26]

As in so many areas of policy, only experience would show, but Churchill could at least do his best not to fan the flames; when the Home Guard was reintroduced, it was made very clear that it could not be used to break strikes. He also stamped on any suggestions that the 1927 Trades Disputes Act should be reinstated, and this may be one reason why Maxwell Fyfe did not go to the Ministry of Labour. Churchill argued much as Baldwin had done in 1925 that the case against 'contracting-in' was a just one, but that his Government would not take any action to worsen relations in industry; this was a retreat from a policy demand that the ACP had pressed for as recently as June 1951. Monckton's record in office certainly matched up to Churchill's intentions when he appointed him; he developed a close relationship with leading trades unionists, at that time a pretty moderate group of men; the Transport Workers' leader told his union in 1953 that 'we have been able to do things that were difficult to do when our own people were at the Ministry'. So good were relations that in 1953 the TUC agreed to nominate a member to the new Iron and Steel Board, so, in effect, accepting that denationalisation should be given a chance to work; in December 1952, the TUC chairman went as far as to send a message of goodwill when Churchill left for economic discussions with the American government. Partly by this means, and partly by a generous attitude to the terms of settlements, Monckton managed to avoid for the most part the damaging disputes that would have shown that Conservatives were going back to 1926. The industrial relations resolutions chosen for debate at Party Conferences were studiously non-provocative; when a mildly critical one on closed shops came up in 1954, an amendment moved by Ray Mawby of the Party's Trades Union Advisory Committee, adding the words 'but considers that decisions on these matters can best be achieved by the trades unions themselves as part of their domestic policy', was agreed with only one dissentient. Only 1954 witnessed more than two million man-days lost in strikes, the first year since 1948 to pass that threshold. The price of harmony was paid in generous settlements of wage claims, and it was widely said that Monckton's skill in settling disputes lay simply in splitting the difference between the two sides; there was no wages policy as such, and Butler was not even involved in policy on some important occasions. Randolph Churchill wrote in 1959 that 'in nearly every industrial dispute during his period of office [Monckton] gave in – thus earning himself the reputation of being a successful Minister of Labour'. When Monckton intervened personally in 1953 to settle a railway dispute, he received many congratulations for his efforts; the *Telegraph* suggested that older MPs had to pinch themselves to

---

26  Howarth, *Prospect and Reality*, 181, 195; Ramsden, *Conservative Party Policy*, 141; Addison, *Churchill*, 413; Justin Davis Smith, *The Attlee and Churchill Administrations and Industrial Unrest, 1945–1955* (1990), 112, 115.

ensure that they were awake, for 'was this a *Conservative* minister earning the heartfelt plaudits, without exception, of Socialist ex-Ministers and MPs?' But there was concern on his own side, and *The Economist* wrote that 'the railway rumpus was handled with sympathy, patience and funk . . . As Sir Walter Monckton surveys the wreckage . . . he should not forget the truth behind the applause that his skill in negotiation has earned. His triumph is really one more retreat from reality.' Discontented Conservative MPs referred to the Minister of Labour as 'the architect of slippery slopes'. Monckton was unrepentant and continued to proclaim his support for the pursuit of partnership with the unions and industrial peace; he also continued to enjoy Churchill's support, but the inflationary effects of his policy became increasingly worrying to other ministers; when he moved to the Defence ministry in 1955, his replacement by Macleod was thought to be a response to the need for a Minister with equally moderate credentials but a tougher strategy for carrying them out. Until then though, there *was* what Justin Davis Smith has called an 'industrial Butskellism'.[27]

The concentration of time and effort on individual disputes prevented Monckton from pursuing structural initiatives. Nonetheless, the administration of the office and the decision to retain the National Joint Advisory Council of employers and unions, created by Labour in 1946, marked at least a half step towards the implementation of one of the *Industrial Charter*'s key proposals; Monckton's junior minister Harold Watkinson argued in October 1954 that 'ever since the days when we drew up the *Industrial Charter* . . . we have never lost sight of our objective, that the right way to earn our living as a nation in a tough and competitive world is by getting this problem of human relations and industrial relations right'. With Watkinson's support, Monckton was tireless in his efforts to turn the NJAC talking shop into an effective agency for co-partnership in industry. In May 1952, Butler also attended a meeting of the NJAC, warning its members of the dangers of an unrestricted free-for-all in wage bargaining and inviting them to take some responsibility for the future of the economy. What later became the National Economic Development Council of 1961 could have evolved a decade earlier, but the TUC were not at all happy with Butler's reference to 'a wages policy' and nothing came of the 1952 proposal, while Party men derided any idea of imposed policies on incomes as 'very real dangers to freedom'. Butler's was in any case an appeal for restraint that ran counter to the whole way in which Monckton and Churchill saw the duties of the Minister of Labour at that time. Writing much later, Watkinson felt that 'Winston, Walter and Anthony had failed to take the prize of uniting both sides of industry. I, as a businessman

[27] Seldon, *Indian Summer*, 196; *NCP*, 21 Jan. 1952, 19 Jan. 1953, 18 Oct. 1954; Advisory Committee on Policy minutes [hereafter ACP], 13 June 1951; ACP 2/1, CPA; Pelling, *Churchill*, 127; Howard, *RAB*, 203; Randolph Churchill, *The Rise and Fall of Sir Anthony Eden* (1959), 201; Birkenhead, *Monckton*, 292; Smith, *Industrial Unrest*, 142, 145.

turned Junior Minister, had seen it happen and bear at least some of the responsibility for not trying harder to push my masters into firmer action.' This is unduly self-critical, for it is far from clear that the prize was ever there to be won, but it is certainly true that it was not actively pursued; when it was taken up in the 1960s, the balance in the trades unions had swung to the left and this made success even less likely.[28]

## International policy

The other area in which the Churchill Government has been said to have missed an opportunity was in the first stages of the movement for European integration. Churchill's speeches before 1951 had raised hopes, there were certainly members of his Cabinet such as Macmillan, Maxwell Fyfe and Sandys who were already committed to a European future for Britain as a result of their own war experiences, and American policy was benevolently disposed to such a process. The outcome was a disappointment, for Britain stood aloof from European developments and concentrated most of her diplomatic effort in these years in other directions. The chief stumbling block was Eden at the Foreign Office, instinctively resistant both to interference in his domain and to a pro-European policy; just after he had taken office, he remarked gratuitously in a speech that 'forming a European federation is something that we know in our bones we cannot do', and of the proposed European defence force he wrote to Churchill that 'I have never thought it possible that we could join such an Army'. On the backbenches, a group of Tory MPs that included Robert Boothby and Julian Amery, men who had served in the Council of Europe assembly in Strasbourg, urged a more positive policy; there was a clear divergence between Eden's view and the views publicly expressed at Strasbourg by Maxwell Fyfe. Boothby's group wrote to Churchill to protest, but the Prime Minister sided with Eden – who did not even reply. With biting irony, Boothby was in 1962 to call Eden 'not only the architect but the creator of the Six', because of his negative policy at the Foreign Office, for one consequence of Eden's policy of negation was the withdrawal of Paul-Henri Spaak from the Council of Europe in protest against British lukewarmness; he devoted his efforts henceforth to other means of fostering integration which Britain would not be able to block. In the Cabinet, Churchill did not wish to have any avoidable disagreements with his touchy Foreign Secretary, and on the one occasion on which he did strike out against Eden's policy, when Eden was off ill, he too managed to offend Europeans in the process. Maxwell Fyfe and Macmillan made but the feeblest of protests about the direction of British policy, and were in any case fully occupied with their work at home; Macmillan was, as he wrote, 'entirely

[28] Watkinson, *Turning Points*, 53–4, 66; *NCP*, 7 June and 25 Oct. 1954; Birkenhead, *Monckton*, 284; Howarth, *Prospect and Reality*, 188.

enveloped in clouds of bricks and mortar'; when he did write to Eden in January 1952 to urge on him the danger of leaving Germany in the leading role in Europe if Britain stayed out, a junior staff member replied that the Foreign Secretary was far too busy even to read such notes from colleagues. After further unsatisfactory responses to letters to Churchill, Macmillan even considered resigning over Europe, but was dissuaded by consideration of the effect it could have on a Government with so small a majority, and by the realisation of how little interest there was in Europe in the country at large. With the benefit of hindsight this seems a missed opportunity, but it is clear that even these Tory 'pro-Europeanists' were no more willing than Eden to contemplate anything like a European federation. The most that can be said is that, if they had had their way, Britain might at least have remained part of the dialogue during the crucial formative years of contemporary Europe.[29]

Robert Boothby was convinced that the reason for the feebleness of the Conservative Europeanists in Cabinet was that they were held in pawn by their loyalty to Churchill, who in turn had lost interest in Europe after he returned to office, so as not to prejudice his chances of achieving one last success on the super-power stage by pulling off a settlement with Russia. Russia occupied more of Churchill's attention than western Europe, but the records of debates in constituency associations and in the National Union (where Europe was scarcely even mentioned, but Russia certainly was) suggests that it was Churchill rather than Boothby and Macmillan who was reading the Party's mind correctly. The irony was that whereas Britain was still a power of considerable weight within Europe, and could therefore have had a real influence on developments there, her standing on the world stage was now so far inferior to that of the United States and the Soviet Union, and her connection to American policy so close, that the opportunity of playing the role of an independent broker was non-existent. In Churchill's mind though there was a consistency between his pro-European statements of 1946, when the world needed rallying against Russian expansion, and his attempts at mediation in 1953–54, when Russian expansion had been halted and Stalin had died; it was the same spirit of 'in defeat – defiance' and 'in victory – magnanimity' that formed the theme of his *War Memoirs*. Eden merely felt that generalised offers of talks weakened Moscow's belief in the West's determination; before he went off sick in 1953, he warned Selwyn Lloyd 'Don't appease that Russian bear too much in my absence'. Churchill was still far from pursuing a policy of appeasement, and he revealed in 1954, and mistakenly attributed to his book, that he had in 1945 authorised the collection of captured German

---

[29] Howarth, *Prospect and Reality*, 205; Seldon, *Indian Summer*, 413; J.W. Young, 'Cold War and Détente with Moscow', in *The Foreign Policy of Churchill's Peacetime Administration, 1951–1955*, ed. J.W. Young (Leicester, (1988), 111–112; David Dutton, 'Anticipating Maastricht: the Conservative Party and Britain's First Application to Join the European Community', in *Contemporary Record*, vol. 7 (1993), 530; Rhodes James, *Boothby*, 364; Horne, *Macmillan*, 350–51.

weapons to facilitate the re-arming of Germany if the Russian march west had continued, a revelation that caused real embarrassment. In most areas, in 1951 as in 1945, there was a remarkable continuity of foreign policy across the change of governments; as he continued Labour's anti-communist policy in the Far East, Churchill could be sure to be free of Tory critics, for, as he demanded in January 1952, 'What Conservative in England is in favour of Chinese Communists?' However, Churchill also hankered after a summit conference of heads of state that would thaw out the Cold War and deliver the world from the threat of H-bomb warfare; Eden, at least while he was still Foreign Secretary, distrusted such head-of-government initiatives as much as he had when Chamberlain had indulged in them in 1938. When Churchill made his most public offer to Russia, in 1954, there was a sharp Cabinet crisis in which several ministers threatened to resign, for he had not even warned them before making his statement, and the Government was only saved from serious difficulty by the Russians' rejection of the idea.[30]

However, it was neither Europe nor Russia that attracted the biggest share of Conservative attention in the foreign policy field, but Empire, for the loss of India and Burma had not terminated traditional Conservative attitudes; East Midlands Tories resolved in May 1953 to deplore the lack of emphasis in Government statements on the concept of the Empire, and to urge ministers to use the words 'British' and 'Empire' on all suitable occasions; the Minister of Education should insist that schools continue to celebrate Empire Day. Nevertheless, there was much less attention given to this at Westminster than to domestic policies, and the 1922 Committee spent very little of its time in this period on *any* foreign issue. Colonial matters could still raise the temperature dramatically, and one of them caused in 1953–54 the only dangerous backbench revolt of the whole Parliament. Conservatives simply did not agree after 1951 what the objectives of colonial policy should be. There was, for example, a debate at the National Union Executive in 1952, in which members deplored the lack of grip in British policy in almost all areas except Malaya, where a counter-insurgent campaign had been stepped up by the new Government and was already beginning to go well; but against the members who attacked the weakness of policy, complained of active preparations to leave colonies in the near future, and lamented the lack of a trade deal to unite the Empire, there were others who pointed out that it was too late to go back to a 'Victorian idea of Empire', and argued instead for a flexible readiness to withdraw from colonies as the position became untenable; this was one of many debates at which no vote was taken and the Party Chairman undertook to report to the Government on

---

[30] Thompson, *Day Before Yesterday*, 104, 111; J.W. Young, 'The Schuman Plan and British Association', in *Foreign Policy of Churchill's Peacetime Administration, 1951–1955*, ed. J.W. Young (Leicester, 1988), 57, 72; Callum MacDonald, *Britain and the Korean War* (Oxford, 1990), 61; Rhodes James, *Eden*, 365; Thorpe, *Lloyd*, 171.

the diversity of opinions expressed. Resolutions calling for 'development' in the colonies were usually acceptable because they could mean what each side of the debate wanted them to mean; references to 'education' in the colonies were more divisive, since they implied preparations for a post-colonial world, but references to the 'preservation of the Empire' were also controversial for the opposite reason. Henry Hopkinson, junior minister for Colonies, had to resign in 1955 after a slip of the tongue in which he said that Cyprus would 'never' become independent, but it is not clear what it was that he intended to say. The same confusion of sentiment and policy can be detected in the Party's first open debate on coloured immigration, at the 1955 Central Council; a motion called for a review of all colonial immigration because of the social and economic consequences for Britain, but reaffirmed the right of all 'Commonwealth members' to settle in the UK if they wished, while the Government was urged to take powers to ban 'undesirable immigrants'. This was passed, and a proposed amendment to delete the last part was lost by 170 to 130. To say the least, this indicated some confusion of thought. For the most part, the confusion remained below the surface, because few issues of actual policy necessitated the taking of sides; the creation of the Central African Federation for example, in 1953, was seen as a consolidation of Britain's presence in an area rich in raw materials as well as a device for tying together the developed south of Rhodesia to the undeveloped north, so both delaying Britain's departure and modernising the economies of the more backward territories. This caused few waves in the Party and not many in parliament either, and nor did the anti-terrorist campaigns in Malaya and in Kenya, for all Conservatives could agree to oppose insurgency. Whatever their view of the colonial future; they could also agree to resent the public support given to Mau Mau in Kenya by Prime Minister Nehru of India and other such indications of the changing nature of the Commonwealth.[31]

Problems did arise though when a move away from colonial occupation had to be decided on, to a limited extent over bases in South Africa, and more seriously in the linked cases of Sudan and Egypt. Even over the Simonstown base in South Africa, Churchill was 'reluctant to contemplate any transaction which would be presented as yet another surrender of the political rights and responsibilities of the United Kingdom'. The future of the Suez Canal presented just such an occasion, and the Party rebels specifically based their opposition on the accumulation of grievances; when he resigned the whip, Harry Legge-Bourke MP spoke of a process of 'ignominious withdrawal' in which the Conservatives had at first acquiesced and more recently themselves organised, 'from Palestine, Burma, India, Persia, the Sudan and now Egypt'. He was not alone in that view, for when the Labour Government had first announced the intention to withdraw from Egypt, Salisbury had remarked

31 East Midlands Area Council, 16 May 1953; NUEC, 4 Sept. 1952; Seldon, *Indian Summer*, 350; Central Council minutes, 19 Mar. 1954; Cross, *Swinton*, 276–90.

sarcastically that 'we shall hear next that we are clearing out of the Isle of Wight'. Now in the Cabinet, he knew that it was economically impossible for Britain to maintain her military position in the Middle East without American backing, and that there was American pressure to withdraw. Under that pressure, the Government began in 1952 negotiations to withdraw from the Suez Canal zone, with Churchill growling disconsolately that he had never before realised that Munich was on the Nile; he was eventually persuaded that this made little long-term difference, since under the 1936 treaty with Egypt British troops would anyway have to leave by 1956, and he then helpfully decided that local bases no longer mattered much if the next war was to be atomic. In such debates the vocabulary of appeasement was a constant virility test of all Tory policies at home and abroad, and in 1954 a *Punch* cartoonist even drew Eden returning from a foreign mission with a Chamberlainite umbrella. The discontented formed themselves into a 'Suez Group' under Charles Waterhouse, with Powell, Amery and Assheton among the members; few yet went as far as Powell in voicing strongly anti-American sentiments, but this was to become a steadily more prominent theme. There had already been criticism in February 1953 of the decision to leave the Sudan, but in December forty-one Conservative MPs signed an Early Day Motion rejecting Government policy on Egypt; they developed good relations with the *Daily Express*, which gave them publicity. Richard Crossman could philosophically see how irritated these 'unfortunate Tea Room men' must be by such policies, 'which were considered Bevanite by the right wing of the Labour Party only twelve months ago', but Eden became rattled, suspecting Selwyn Lloyd of plotting against him with the rebels, on the strength of noticing that Assheton had been one of Lloyd's luncheon guests. In the end it was Churchill's reputation derived from 1938–40 that helped to rally the Party at a 1922 Committee meeting; his wife told Moran that 'he gave them a tremendous wigging. They knew that he was not a little Englander, but he told them bluntly we simply could not afford to stay in Egypt . . . They were tremendously impressed. The old lion could still issue from his den and when he did so his growl was as frightening as ever.' He left the meeting to the strains of 'For he's a jolly good fellow' and told Moran that 'I dominated and conquered the committee'. One of the rebels, Fitzroy Maclean, may have been neutralised by appointment to a ministerial post, but there was no widespread attempt to deal with the problem in this way. There was no need to do so, for the rebels represented few but themselves, and were sharply criticised at the 1922 Committee for the waves they were making. When the final treaty was agreed with Egypt, Eden had a personal success in commending it to the House; Labour abstained in order to maximise the Tory dissension, and twenty-eight Conservatives voted against the treaty, but this effectively showed that the Suez Group rebels were by then only a small minority who could not come near to stopping the policy. There was no great echo of this dissension in the Party outside parliament; motions attacking the

Government over Suez were defeated in Hampstead and talked out at the South East Area Council.[32]

## Domestic policies

It was only during the very different Suez Crisis of 1956, when the Suez rebels pointed back to their earlier defiance of the whip and claimed a prescience that had not been shown by ministers, that the debates of 1953–54 seemed significant. They were not much discussed in 1955 when the Party had to seek re-election, and were anyway very untypical of the Parliament of 1951. On the home front, policy differences did arise but in no case did they occasion serious damage to Party cohesion. In the whole Parliament, there were only ten divisions on which any Conservative MPs voted against the whip; most of these were minor 'conscience' matters relating to religious conviction or constituency interest, and only two of the votes involved more than three MPs, Suez in 1954 and the National Health Service in 1952. The vote on the NHS related to a narrow issue, whether free provision should be available to foreign nationals as well as to British citizens who had 'paid for it'; the Government's response was to point to the practical difficulties of enforcing such distinctions, particularly now that identity cards had been abolished, but to avoid further difficulty the whips instructed the Party to abstain on the vote and left it to Labour to vote down the twenty-two Tories who wanted to change the rules. More generally, the Party approached the NHS with great caution, conscious that Labour had claimed that they would do it serious damage. Initially Crookshank went to Health, a downgraded post since housing and local government had been hived off into a separate and high-profile department; his early plans for charging for the 'hotel' services in hospitals were mostly ruled out by the Cabinet, but those that remained were nevertheless subject to a fierce denunciation by Bevan in the House; it was in replying to Bevan that Iain Macleod attracted Churchill's attention, both as a debater and as a future colleague, and he became Minister of Health a few weeks later; Enoch Powell, who had been trying to catch the Speaker's eye when Macleod was called, folded away his own speech and left the chamber, remaining out of office for three more years.

---

[32] G.R. Berridge and J.E. Spence, 'South Africa and the Simonstown Agreements', in *Foreign Policy of Churchill's Peacetime Administration, 1951–1955* ed. J.W. Young (Leicester, 1988), 195; Ronald Hyam, 'Churchill and the British Empire', in *Churchill*, eds Robert Blake and W.R. Louis (Oxford, 1993), 182; Pinto-Duschinsky, 'Bread and Circuses?', 76; Howarth, *Prospect and Reality*, 204, 207; Salisbury to Thomas [n.d.], Cilcennin MSS; Ritchie Ovendale, 'Egypt and the Suez Base Agreement', in *Foreign Policy of Churchill's Peacetime Administration, 1951–1955*, ed. J.W. Young (Leicester, 1988), 138; Roth, *Powell*, 104–5, 117; Morgan, *Crossman Diaries*, 340; Charmley, *Descent to Suez*, 131; Lord Moran, *Winston Churchill, The Struggle for Survival, 1940–1965* (Sphere edn, 1966), 512; 1922 Cttee., 3 Dec. 1953; Pelling, *Churchill*, 608; Rhodes James, *Eden*, 383; Jackson, *Rebels and Whips*, 111–12; Hampstead CA minutes, 23 July 1954; South East Area Council, 30 Jan. 1954.

Macleod's was a shrewd appointment, for he was as well briefed on the issue as any Conservative, was fully behind the NHS in its objectives and would fight its corner within the Government, but would use Commons debates to fight the Opposition and give the Tory troops something to cheer. Earlier in 1952 he had published with Powell a study of the NHS that endorsed the principle of selectivity; in their view the relevant question was 'why should any social service be provided without a means test?' In the event, Macleod's tenure of the office was deliberately unspectacular as to policy, for he both believed and proclaimed that what the NHS needed was a period of consolidation after years of upheaval; he therefore introduced no major legislation and concentrated on getting existing hospitals built up and on providing a role for voluntary organisations. (There was a similar approach in social security policy, where Osbert Peake made no major changes but through administration gradually strengthened the contributory elements in benefits systems.) Even Macleod's limited objective was difficult, for housing was the Government's overriding priority, but in later years the NHS was a beneficiary of increasing public expenditure: both in cash and as a proportion of overall Government expenditure, social spending rose. In 1954, the first new hospital since the War was opened, in Scotland, and the foundation stone laid by Macleod himself for the first one in England and Wales; by then there was a three-year building plan.[33]

Pensions were a further beneficiary of growth. In the last years of opposition, the Party had been careful to avoid pledges to increase payments; at Central Council in 1950, a motion had been proposed which drew attention to rising prices under Labour and called for increased old age pensions to compensate; an amendment in the name of Selwyn Lloyd, then Butler's policy deputy and clearly acting on his instructions, deleted all references to pensions and called instead for cuts in public expenditure as a means of reducing inflation; the amendment was passed without a vote. Back in office the National Union's only forays into this field were resolutions calling for an end to the restriction on what pensioners could earn without losing their pensions (a clear rejection of means-testing), and reiterated demands for better service pensions (which indicates the strength of retired officers in the voluntary side of the party); the Government was deaf to both these pleas. However, as inflation continued and then accelerated, the demand reappeared; in 1954 the Conference agenda contained thirty-two constituency resolutions on pensions, almost all calling for an increase in rates. Pensions and other benefits then rose in value by about a quarter in December. Despite the sensitivity of the issue, the right were not happy with this approach: Assheton told a journalist in 1952, in strikingly modern terminology, that he was 'impatient of the "wets"

---

[33] Norton, *Dissension*, 89–118; Howarth, *Prospect and Reality*, 191; Roth, *Powell*, 90; Nigel Fisher, *Iain Macleod* (1973), 82, 85, 91–3, 101; Seldon, *Indian Summer*, 268; *NCP*, 26 July 1954 and 17 Jan. 1955; Addison, *Churchill*, 417, 419.

in the Party', including Butler and Eden in their number; he felt that he could muster about twenty supporters for an attack on high spending, but 'might even wring out and dry another 50 backbench "wets"' in a campaign to reduce taxes. Such a view also lay behind the regular resolutions against 'waste' that were passed at the National Union, but all these critics were wrong-footed by Butler's ability to produce expenditure increases *as well as* tax reductions in 1954–55. The steady scaling down of the war economy and of defence expenditure allowed this room for manoeuvre, so that Government spending could continue to rise in real terms while falling as a proportion of the Gross National Product; only when this 'peace dividend' was exhausted in the later 1950s did the Conservative Government have to face up to tougher decisions, both about its priorities and about the extent to which it was prepared to tax in order to spend.[34]

A few cases of difficulty arose that were not financial in origin. Calls in the Party to reintroduce corporal punishment attracted support both in the National Union and on the backbenches, but were met with a determined resistance from Maxwell Fyfe at the Home Office. No change in policy was made, but this is perhaps best seen as a prelude to the much greater upheaval over the abolition of the death penalty in 1955–57. Not for the first or last time, there was great agitation in 1954 over proposals to increase the pay of MPs, probably the parliamentary issue that absorbed the greatest amount of Churchill's own time; the annual payment, only £400 until 1937, had been raised from £600 to £1,000 in 1946, but a Select Committee now recommended £1,500. The Government's first instinct was to leave it to a free vote of the House; when MPs voted for the increase but with the majority of Conservatives voting against, there was pressure on Churchill to throw out the proposal with a whipped vote. The Chief Whip advised that there was a danger in the embittered response that was sweeping through the lobbies, 'which may with our small majority endanger the existence of the Government'; he reminded Churchill that they now had 'a new and valuable type of Member in our own Party whose circumstances do not greatly differ from those on the Socialist side of the House', estimating at about forty the number of Tory MPs who actually needed the extra money proposed; 'those who take the view that, if a Member cannot get on under present circumstances, he had better get out, represent, I hope and believe, a minority'. Most constituency associations that discussed the matter came down against an increase of that size, some against any increase at all, as in Cambridgeshire, in Hemel Hempstead and in Lewes; the London Area argued that such generosity to MPs would ruin any chance of wage restraint from trades unionists. Both sides of the argument made sensible points; one side argued that the cumulative increase of 275 per cent over just seventeen

[34] Central Council minutes, 29 Apr. 1950; Central Council report for 1954, NUA 2/2/20, CPA.

years would look unacceptably generous to the electors, and the other that the Maxwell Fyfe reforms made it more necessary than ever to ensure that MPs were properly remunerated, if the parliamentary party was to cease to be a rich man's club. It became extremely heated, and Robert Boothby (who favoured the increase) recalled that this occasioned 'the roughest treatment I ever got from the Tory Party', which is saying a good deal: 'there was a moment when I hardly dared face the party Committee, and addressed it with my hand on the door, in case immediate escape became necessary.' A compromise eventually ensured that MPs would get their increase in the more publicly-defensible form of allowances.[35]

In the longer perspective, because critics of one policy rarely allied with critics of another, these were all storms in the Commons tearoom, given weight only because the Government's small majority allowed even a relatively small number of MPs to threaten its stability. David Butler concluded in 1955 that 'in general the Conservative Party in the House of Commons and in the country enjoyed a harmonious existence'. From the outside, the chronological profile of Government support showed a steady move in the right direction. After being behind in the polls in 1952, the Conservatives drew level with Labour in the Summer of 1953 and remained alongside or ahead for the rest of the Parliament; local government defeats of 1952 were not repeated, and in 1954 and 1955 the Party again did rather well, though less so in the biggest cities, almost all of which were again under Labour control by 1955. In view of the Government's small majority, the greatest attention was focused on parliamentary by-elections, where again the message was positive; no seat was lost over the four years, in most contests there was a swing to Conservative, particularly after 1952, and the Liberals continued to do badly, fighting only eight of the forty-five vacancies and saving only a single deposit. The Conservatives' most noticed result was the rare event of a Government by-election gain from the Opposition, Sunderland South in May 1953. This constituency had had a wafer-thin Labour majority of only 306 votes in 1951, but with memories of Hammersmith in 1949, the contest was approached stealthily; Churchill directed that there must be 'no trumpeting about the National importance of the election, but the utmost silent house to house work'. He did though further relax the rule about Cabinet ministers going to by-elections, and nine ministerial speakers made their way north. After an extensive canvass, Central Office correctly predicted a narrow Conservative win. Attempts to repeat the exercise in North Paddington and in Holborn and St. Pancras South later in the Parliament were not successful. These by-elections marked a further stage in the social polarisation

[35] Jackson, *Rebels and Whips*, 105, 109; Central Council minutes, 20 Mar. 1953; Kilmuir, *Memoirs*, 211; Buchan-Hepburn to Churchill, 5 Mar. 1954, Hailes MSS, 2/5; Cambridgeshire CA minutes, 14 June 1954; Hemel Hempstead CA minutes, 22 June 1954; Lewes CA minutes, 16 June 1954; London Conservative Union minutes, 10 June 1954; Goodhart, *The 1922*, 167–9.

of voting, partly as a result of migration to new suburbs and estates; Labour was improving its position in its inner urban areas, while Airey Neave won Abingdon in 1953 with the largest Conservative majority that the constituency had ever produced; in 1951 Cambridge had had a larger Tory majority than Cambridgeshire, but in the 1960s Labour won the borough constituency while the county had by then a very large Tory majority. Churchill, who had asked to see regular canvass returns from Sunderland, continued to take a close interest, for example demanding to know the reason for an almost invisible swing of 0.27 per cent to Labour at Aldershot in 1954.[36]

The nature of the Tory appeal that produced these favourable omens can be seen in the election address issued at Orpington in January 1955, where (with some irony) the Conservatives had one of their best results. Under the title 'Tories get things done', the candidate listed thirty-seven election promises carried out – the headline successes in bold type being decontrol, tax cuts, pension rises, more savings, housing completions, low unemployment, and world peace. It accumulated to an impressive list, and especially in the context of Labour's dire warnings of 1951. Robert Blake felt in 1968 that 'what one can say without deviating from academic propriety is that in terms of electoral promises Churchill's government delivered the goods'. David Butler's verdict in 1955 was much the same: 'there was some obvious fumbling in the first year . . . but thereafter affairs ran reasonably smoothly' and, more specifically, 'the error of those who feared for the preservation of industrial peace under a Conservative Government was plainly demonstrated in the tributes paid to Sir Walter Monckton's handling of the Ministry of Labour'. Churchill in particular relished such a situation and devoted his considerable rhetorical powers to exploiting it; when Butler's Budget of 1953 began to relax the restrictions, he really enjoyed himself at Labour's expense in a speech at Glasgow:

> No wonder they were upset. But the culminating point, the climax, the top notch, was hit when Mr. Butler perpetrated his most insulting and malevolent deed. He took 6d. off the income tax. I never take pleasure in human woe, and yet I must confess I wish you had been there to see the look of absolute misery and anger which swept across the crowded faces opposite. Sixpence off the income tax! Class favour to over 30 million people. What shocking Tory reaction! Only 9s. in the £ left for the income tax collector. How could anyone tell that in future years more crimes like this might not be committed?

Macmillan, privately congratulating Butler on his Budget, wrote that 'the great thing now about the Government is that people are beginning to feel that we know what we are trying to do'. A few weeks earlier, even before the Budget, Hugh Dalton had admitted in his diary that 'nor is Tory rule so

[36] D.E. Butler, *The British General Election of 1951* (1952), 13; Chris Cook and John Ramsden (eds), *By-Elections in British Politics* (1973), 193–4; Central Office, General Director's by-election files, CCO 120/2/10, 11, 18 and 26, CPA.

bad, or thought to be, as we had prophesied. Unemployment, prices, wages, social services (especially housing), foreign affairs, all better than we expected. And no war!' A leader in *Socialist Commentary* reached the same conclusion, less grudgingly, in January 1955: 'This has been the best Christmas since the war; indeed if the greatest prosperity of the greatest number of people in this country is the measure, probably the best Christmas ever. When before have so many had so much to spend? The shops have been full to bursting and the shoppers have hardly had elbow room along the seductive counters. Everyone has a job; the Scrooges are in eclipse and the Bob Cratchits have all had their Christmas dinners.' The Labour MP John Freeman had in the previous October taken the same argument a little further: 'if capitalism does work in the modern world, our *raison d'être* is gone'. With such electioneering opportunities, and with Labour split as well as demoralised, the Conservatives would find it difficult to lose. But who would fight as Leader? As the Parliament drew to a close, ministers focused back on the Churchill question with which it had begun.[37]

## Getting Churchill out

In the first place, since Churchill was already seventy-seven when he resumed office in 1951, it had been the assumption of his colleagues that he would last only a short while; after a few months at Number 10 had wiped out memories of his 1945 rejection, he would step down gracefully and hand over to Eden, at which time the Government would be properly reconstructed with a more modern feel. It was quickly apparent that Churchill did not share these expectations; several frontbenchers met to discuss the matter, as in 1947 at Crookshank's house in Pont Street, and again failed to dislodge Churchill. There were though rumours that the Party was trying to get rid of Churchill; the Northern Area Conservatives, conscious that either passing or rejecting a motion on the subject would be open to misinterpretation, declined to discuss it at all. When George VI died in February 1952 Churchill decided that he must see the new Queen safely crowned before considering retirement. After a year in office, Eden's principal private secretary noted that he 'is becoming very impatient to get his hands on the control of the Government. He says that the Chief Whip and the previous Chief Whip [James Stuart] have both told Winston to retire, but do not think he will do so.' A few months later he added that the disconsolate Eden 'doesn't think the Old Man will ever go'. After reports in the press about feeling among MPs, Churchill consulted the chairman of the 1922 Committee who unhelpfully told him that only a

37 Central Office, General Director's file, 'Orpington by-election', CCO 120/2/34, CPA; Robert Blake, *The Conservative Party from Peel to Thatcher* (1985), 269; D.E. Butler, *The British General Election of 1955* (1956), 12; Butler, *Art of the Possible*, 168; Macmillan to Butler, 16 Apr. 1954, Butler MSS, G26; Pimlott, *Dalton Diaries*, 604; *NCP*, 31 Jan. 1955.

minority of backbenchers wanted him to retire. Meanwhile his ambitious colleagues waited for their opportunity and sized up their chances. By 1953 the governmental pecking order after Churchill was clearly Eden and then Butler, and this may well have been the public's view too: in Summer 1954, a *Daily Mirror* poll of its readership on the succession showed Eden supported by half the sample, Butler by a third, Maxwell Fyfe by an eighth, and nobody else even in sight, despite Macmillan's housing successes.[38]

In June 1953, Butler noted a meeting with Churchill, and the frustrations this produced; the old man was still in a hurry to achieve a success; 'the most marked impression was his reference to the crowds waiting outside. "I must save them, poor lambs, from the worst excesses. They look to me to let them enjoy their lives in peace." This was apropos of his determination via the Bermuda Conference to ease the tension with the Soviet Union. I remembered almost exactly similar words 14 years ago with Neville Chamberlain.' But Butler noted too the sheer size of the crowds gathered in Downing Street and the fact that 'all the PM had to do was raise his V fingers' to get a roar of cheers. Within days of this, everything was thrown into the melting pot by the fact that, during the lengthy illness of Eden following a botched operation, Churchill had another and more serious stroke. All news about the seriousness of his condition was censored for a year, but rumours percolated out. Butler was put in charge of the Government in the Commons and on the home front, and chaired the Cabinet, while Salisbury ran the Foreign Office. This plan occasioned some jealousy of Butler, and a private arrangement was made, of dubious constitutional validity, that if Churchill did not survive, Salisbury would become a caretaker premier until Eden returned. For a brief period, Macmillan too was in hospital, but promised Butler that he would be back in the Commons soon, 'or perhaps it wd. be more important to be present at a Cabinet in order to help to counterbalance the weight of the peerage?' Hugh Massingham in *The Observer* wrote that Central Office would have to 'produce either Sir Winston or Mr. Eden' by the Party Conference, or face 'a great deal of speculation and uneasiness about the future'. This may have been Butler's one clear chance to 'seize' the premiership, by challenging the fitness of both Eden and Churchill to return and before any other rival had emerged, and there were certainly MPs who were urging him to do so, often on grounds of their hostility to Eden – Ralph Assheton was reported as saying 'he had never yet known Eden fully convinced of anything'. Bill Anstruther-Gray, for example, replying to a note from Butler about the contents of which we can only speculate, asked 'Were Bonar Law or Baldwin "legitimist" successors?' But it was not in character for Butler to push himself forward ahead of two sick colleagues. He could not stoop to conquer, and his

---

[38] Seldon, *Indian Summer*, 38–9; Rhodes James, *Eden*, 345; Northern Area General Purposes Committee minutes, 28 July 1952; Charmley, *Descent to Suez*, 61, 74; Goodhart, *The 1922*, 160; Horne, *Macmillan*, 454; Kilmuir, *Memoirs*, 229.

supporters were anyway warning Butler that his name stirred up hostility as well as warmth; 'a prominent MP of great influence' was reported as saying that in Butler the Party would have 'an appeaser', and Kenneth de Courcy, as a candid friend, urged Butler to use his temporary position as head of the Government to make a bold splash that would still such fears.[39]

When Churchill and Eden returned in the Autumn, speculation about the future resumed. Moran noted a conversation with Colville, who thought that 'Anthony might strike. Somehow it is not a word we associate with Eden, but I am told that he is being pushed from behind. Presently the Party will take charge. It appears that Rab Butler is sitting on the fence with one leg dangling on either side. He likes cricket similes. He is trying to keep a straight bat, he says. He is not trying to make runs.' Churchill, picking up the metaphor, told Eden to play himself in gradually on his return, but reminded him that 'the important thing for you (and me) is to make a good impression on the Margate Conference'. Churchill himself decided to make his speech at Margate the test of his recovered stamina, but colleagues were certainly urging him to go anyway and the Chief Whip predicted trouble if he did not. Churchill tried to placate Eden with the offer of the deputy premiership and Leadership of the Commons. Eden, pointing out 'that it would be asking him to do all the PM's work for him for another six months without any of the credit or the responsibility', was unenthusiastic, but since Churchill's decisions in the Summer had kept the succession open for him, he could hardly now push Churchill out. Colville darkly hinted that if Eden did not do as Churchill wished, then 'the reversion might go elsewhere', but nevertheless the offer was rejected, and relations remained cool. Churchill received an ovation from the Conference, partly because members were relieved to see evidence of his recovery, and he drew the conclusion that the Party was still behind him.[40]

A year later Churchill's 1954 Conference speech was far from successful, and even his family advised him to retire, but he convinced himself that it was his duty to continue, so as not to bequeath the fag end of the Parliament to his successor. A limited reshuffle in Autumn 1954 was also unsuccessful; an offer to Eden to take full control of domestic policy managed to unsettle Butler without tempting Eden to accept; Butler reported, without apparent dissatisfaction, that Eden had come to the conclusion that he could not resign just because Churchill would not let him be Prime Minister, but he also rather patronisingly claimed to favour the idea of Eden taking over the domestic front, for 'the advantage . . . is that he sets his hands on the home affairs, with which he must familiarise himself at some date'; he encouraged the idea of setting up a special secretariat to teach Eden how to do this domestic part of

39  Butler note, 22 June 1953, Macmillan to Butler, 14 July 1953, and various MPs to Butler, July 1953, all in Butler MSS, G26; Howard, *RAB*, 197, 207; Butler, *Art of the Possible*, 170.
40  Moran, *Struggle*, 509–10; Churchill to Eden, 2 Oct. 1953, Avon MSS, 19/1/80; Seldon, *Indian Summer*, 56; Gilbert, *Never Despair*, 889; Charmley, *Descent to Suez*, 98.

the Leader's job. The final decision, not to change existing arrangements, was telegraphed by Butler to the Chief Whip in nicely coded language: 'all went well today in the eyes of uncle, and our younger friend is going to take his time to talk things over with some of us, and I feel despite his great difficulty will do his best'.[41]

Macmillan, moved to Defence, was critical of Churchill's interference in his department and now joined those who urged Churchill to retire. The Government was now running down to a sad conclusion to Churchill's distinguished career, as his most trusted colleagues combined to drive him out. Woolton, for example, in September 1954 forwarded a Central Office report on electoral prospects that predicted that 'an election now, under the present Government, would lead to a disaster, electorally . . . Nothing can avoid this result next year, except a complete change in the structure of the Government and a new PM.' Such arguments were not very effective, for Churchill was wont to reply that he had more experience of electioneering than anyone else and was perfectly capable of making up his own mind; after one such conversation in April 1954, Woolton recorded in his diary that, 'I looked at him very hard, and hoped he knew what I was thinking – that he had lost more elections than any other living politician'. Many no doubt thought that, but nobody said it aloud. The issue was eventually settled early in 1955 because the Parliament was now in its fourth year, and a decision simply could not be postponed; Harold Macmillan courageously took the lead in persuading Churchill that he was unfit to fight another election and must therefore hand over to Eden in time to prepare for one. The handover was finally agreed for April 1955, when Churchill's eightieth birthday celebrations would be well over, and in the meantime the Party joined in; many local associations contributed to the Churchill birthday appeal, though Guildford cannily sent the £443 they had collected to marginal constituencies instead; Bath sent Churchill a box of cigars (occasioning considerable correspondence in their efforts to find out what type he smoked), and many like Lichfield sent telegrams of congratulations. Only at the last minute was it clear that Churchill would this time actually do as he had promised; to Buchan-Hepburn, in a conversation carried on by the exchange of notes across the Cabinet table in March, presumably while Churchill was actually presiding, Butler confided ('Really secret – pl. destroy') that 'things are v. much easier twixt AE and WSC. The latter seems to have come back to being reconciled to the earlier date and sticking to his quasi-undertaking.' At the end of the month, Butler told Woolton that 'we've got the fish on the hook but he hasn't been gaffed yet. Last night I was in a very shallow stream and I got very wet hanging on.' Churchill told those who asked that he would stand for re-election and stay in the House, 'probably as a Conservative'; this was a joke but, within

[41] Moran, *Struggle*, 635; Colville, *Fringes of Power*, 705; Howard, *RAB*, 210; Butler to Buchan-Hepburn, 27 Aug., 30 Aug. and 8 Sept. 1954, Hailes MSS, 4/12.

a few months, with the necessity of keeping up appearances now removed, he was referring to the Conservative Party again as 'they' rather than 'we' in his table talk.[42]

## Eden becomes Prime Minister

There was a suitably long round of dinners and commemorations to mark Churchill's final days in office; he finally stood down on 5 April, and Eden was appointed Prime Minister on the following day. Meeting on 5 April, the 1922 Committee formally decided to take no steps to influence the succession: 'no action was proposed about the election of a Leader in the House of Commons'; on the following day they met again to pass resolutions of loyalty to the new premier. If Eden's succession had been long foreseen, it was not universally welcomed, not least by Churchill himself, for whom Eden's alleged unfitness for the premiership had provided an excellent excuse for his own staying on. But the reservations were genuine. Churchill had some time earlier asked James Stuart why he did not like 'my Anthony', and was told that, while he might do very well at the Foreign Office, he did not have the necessary all-round skills on the home front; Churchill replied thoughtfully 'Well, you'll have to have him'. With his intimates Churchill was less inhibited. Swinton was asked by Churchill early in 1955 if he thought Butler would do better as Prime Minister than Eden, and replied that 'anybody would be better than Anthony . . . [who] would make the worst Prime Minister since Lord North. But you can't think like that now – it's too late. You announced him as your successor more than ten years ago.' Churchill replied 'I think it was a great mistake'. To Jock Colville, on the very eve of his resignation, Churchill confessed that 'I don't believe Anthony can do it'. All this was the talk of disappointed men who by 1955 were not on good terms with Eden anyway but, more chillingly, one of the colleagues on whom Eden would most depend, Macmillan, viewed his accession with similar scepticism: it would be 'interesting to see whether Anthony can stay in the saddle'. Robert Boothby's prediction, delivered to the lobby at large and noted down by Dalton, was that 'the others will be watching Eden and he will be pole-axed in eighteen months time', a prophecy that was only out by three months. Most such thoughts were private, and were strongly contradicted by a very supportive press and by the Party response to Eden's accession. In *The Spectator*, for example, Henry Fairlie drew a distinction between 'the colossal individual genius' like Churchill, and

---

42   Larry Siedentop, 'Mr. Macmillan and the Edwardian Style', in *The Age of Affluence, 1951–1964*, eds V. Bogdanor and R. Skidelsky (1970), 23; Lindsay and Harrington, *Conservative Party*, 182–3; Addison, *Churchill*, 428; Thompson, *Day Before Yesterday*, 115; Gilbert, *Never Despair*, 1037, 1118, 1150; Guildford CA minutes, 9 Dec. 1954; Central Office constituency file, Bath, CCO 1/10/50, CPA; Lichfield CA minutes, 17 Dec. 1954; Butler to Buchan-Hepburn, 7 Mar. 1955, Hailes MSS, 4/12; Woolton diary, 30 Mar. 1955, Woolton MSS.

'the true party Prime Minister whose task is to enable his party to govern as competently as it may', and decided that in this second category Eden would be 'among the greatest of them'. The *Yorkshire Post* actually articulated the doubts about Eden's domestic knowledge, but concluded that 'such questionings are unintelligent . . . He will command respect in the Cabinet room, in the House and in the country.' Fortified by such support, Eden was confirmed as Conservative Leader at a Party meeting on 21 April, attended by about a thousand Party worthies, MPs, adopted candidates, peers taking the Party whip and the Executive Committee of the National Union. This was even more of a formality than usual, for on 15 April, the new Prime Minister already had called a General Election. Eden was determined to be his own man, with his own parliamentary majority – a courageous act, for a failure at the polls would have made his one of the shortest premierships on record. Voting would be on 23 May. His memoirs' account of his instant decision to dissolve parliament for an election was though imaginatively inaccurate; throughout the first half of April he hesitated over the decision while Woolton fumed about him as a man who 'cannot make up his mind, which isn't a very hopeful sign'. Eventually, Woolton ordered an election 'exercise' to get everything on to a war footing by mid-April, and this became the real thing when Eden asked for a dissolution.[43]

## The 1955 General Election

The 1955 campaign was inextricably bound up with the change of premiers and with the Budget, which had been prepared while Churchill was Prime Minister, but not announced or debated until after the Election had been called by Eden; he at least knew that the Budget would contain further tax cuts, including another sixpence off income tax, before he asked for a dissolution. This overlap of events ensured both that the emphasis of the campaign would be on the Tories' highly defendable domestic record, and that when the economy ran into trouble later in the year they would be attacked for producing a Budget motivated by electoral rather than economic considerations. This was not right. Butler's 1955 Budget followed corrective measures taken earlier in the year to deal with inflationary pressures, and it was at least reasonable to hope that enough had been done, and to use part of his projected surplus for tax reductions; that was also the view of his Treasury advisers and of the financial press, all of whom tended in this period to exaggerate the extent to which fine-tuning with Keynesian techniques could produce riskless growth; in April 1957, Butler made similar claims for

---

[43] 1922 Cttee., 5 and 6 Apr. 1955; Stuart, *Within the Fringe*, 178; Cross, *Swinton*, 284; Colville, *Fringes of Power*, 708; Howard, *RAB*, 223; Pimlott, *Dalton Diaries*, 458; Churchill, *Eden*, 195–8; Anthony Eden, *Full Circle, The Eden Memoirs, vol. 3* (1960), 270; Woolton diary, 5 Apr. 1955, Woolton, MSS; Ramsden, *Conservative Party Policy*, 175.

the 1955 manifesto, 'which the Treasury told me was the cheapest Election manifesto, in terms of bribes of the electorate, which in their experience they had read'. There was even some caution in Butler's decisions, for while the Budget was in preparation Churchill had wanted to make even bigger tax cuts; in that sense Butler had gone for the less dangerous alternative. Pressure from the backbenches would in any case not have allowed another 'stand-still' Budget like that of 1954, and there was anyway no avoiding the link between politics and the economic future: one Tory MP asked Norman Macrae 'which sort of Budget would you regard as the more inflationary, a Budget that took sixpence off the income tax and kept us in power, or one that was orthodoxly stern and resulted in Labour getting back into power?' The Budget on 19 April provided a splendid launching-pad for a re-election campaign a fortnight later.[44]

Central Office had been gearing up for a campaign for some time; in December 1954, £159,000 was committed to posters and extra staff in marginals, though only a fraction of this had actually been spent in advance of the Spring dissolution; in the same month, it was decided to prepare the *Campaign Guide* by April so as to keep options open for an early election. Policy work had been proceeding through the ACP, with Butler pointing out in January the electoral importance of agricultural and cotton constituencies, for 'great attention must be paid to our approach to these areas'; resolutions had been passed regularly in the North West, expressing concern about competition in cotton goods from Japan and India under the post-war policy of lowered tariffs. With his strong sense of history, Macmillan joked to Maxwell Fyfe about this, 'How Disraeli would have enjoyed the final result of Peel and Cobden – massive cotton imports into Lancashire!' ACP Members complained that the early manifesto drafts were too vague – too many items began 'we shall consider' – but Fraser reminded them that the Party could not make definite proposals while the Government had still to make up its mind. The eventual Conservative manifesto, in which Eden took a close interest, was published on 30 April; it was a lengthy and unexciting document that attracted little press support for its format, but quite a lot for its content, which was basically a recapitulation of pledges already carried out and rather unspecific promises to keep at the job. The *Manchester Guardian* thought it was like a company chairman asking for a vote of confidence in the board and a free hand to carry on the business. Its original title, 'Together for Peace and Prosperity' was felt by Macmillan to be 'rather banal', and it was decided instead to call it *United for Peace and Progress*. The thrust was in an opening paragraph that stated that 'a Party must not only be judged by what it says. It must be judged even more by what it does.' Voters

---

44 Butler, *Art of the Possible*, 177; Pinto-Duschinsky, 'Bread and Circuses?', 65, 67; Samuel Brittan, *Steering the Economy* (1969), 122–3; Butler note on events since 1951, 18 Apr. 1957, Butler MSS, G31; Seldon, *Indian Summer*, 177–8.

should compare Labour's years in office before 1951 with the Tory years since, and ask themselves 'which were better for themselves, for their families and for their country?' Labour could scarcely complain if Conservatives now adopted the Bevan formula and asked voters to 'read the book' instead of peering into the crystal ball. Candidates' election addresses adopted the same approach; Eden was clearly regarded as a vote-winner, and was mentioned prominently by most Conservatives; the other key issues highlighted were the preservation of peace, housing, the standard of living, the end of rationing and full employment – all areas in which the Conservative record had discredited Labour's 1951 claims.[45]

The Election provided a historic turning point in one sense, for it was the first time ever that no Tory MP was returned unopposed; but this was somewhat misleading, for in other ways it was a far from contentious campaign. The Conservative team of candidates were mainly old hands, especially in the winnable seats; only seventeen of the Conservatives elected in 1955 had not fought at least one previous campaign, and a third had first fought in or before 1935. Among the defeated candidates, there was more sign of change, two-thirds of them fighting for the first time, and the Conservatives continued to have a younger group of candidates than Labour; David Butler also recorded that the Maxwell Fyfe reforms were now producing a visible effect on candidates' backgrounds. The partial success of attempts to pick up the heritage of Liberalism was indicated by seven Tory MPs and six defeated candidates who had earlier stood as Liberals, and two Tory MPs had even switched from Labour. Discussions with the Liberal Party organisation though petered out as before; Eden asked Woolton to try to make a deal, and with Poole and Macleod he met the Liberal organisers; Liberal requests for Tories to stand down for them in seats where Liberals had not even saved their deposit last time rapidly convinced them that no common ground would be found.[46]

There were no significant changes in the electoral battleground. There had been minor boundary changes, but with little net effect. In deference to his own claims that Labour had rigged the system to its own advantage, Churchill had dropped in office proposals made in opposition; there was no revival of university constituencies, and the attempts of the National Union and Central Office to get both an extension of postal votes for holidaymakers, and the removal of the limitation on the use of cars at elections were unsuccessful (though the limit on the use of cars was to be removed by Butler for 1959). With no significant changes in the rules, expectations were almost

---

45  Central Office files, 'General Election', CCO 4/6/120–4, CPA; ACP, 26 Jan. 1955; North West Area Council, 23 Oct. 1954; Manchester CA Executive minutes, 4 Oct. 1954; Macmillan to Kilmuir [n.d. but 1954], Kilmuir MSS, 6/9; Rhodes James, *Eden*, 407; Butler, *General Election of 1955*, 17–18, 29, 33; D.E. Butler, *British General Elections since 1945* (Oxford, 1989), 16.
46  Butler, *General Election of 1955*, 39, 45; Woolton diary, 4 June 1955, Woolton MSS.

universally of a Conservative win: Selwyn Lloyd was as usual beginning the campaign nervously, but Central Office remained confident throughout, and some Labour spokesmen were unable to conceal the fact that they took the same view. The opinion polls, now far more central to the evaluation of public opinion than in 1945, were largely responsible for this; the Conservatives were 4 per cent ahead when Eden called the Election and, although their lead fell and then recovered to about the same level, they were never behind.[47]

In these circumstances, Eden was advised by Woolton not to allow his own campaigning to seem too much like a personal procession to victory, but the Conservative campaign was nevertheless far more leader-orientated than in either 1950 or 1951. Eden's face appeared on many Conservative posters and on quite a few election addresses too, he reserved for himself the key election broadcasts, and he toured the country from end to end as Churchill had done in 1945. Churchill, on the other hand, hurt to be excluded altogether from the Party's national campaign, indulged in some personal mutual aid by making a speech in Walthamstow where his Woodford party workers were committed. Now he was finally at the top, Eden exuded his considerable natural charm, and proved to be a first-rate electioneering asset. His election tour, what the *Daily Mirror* sourly reported as 'miles and miles of the Eden smiles', was seen by the *Coventry Evening Telegraph* more encouragingly as 'taking on the character of a triumphal progress'. He refused any speech draft that included personal attacks on Labour leaders, even when they were merely replies to attacks on him by the likes of Shinwell or Bevan; and whereas Churchill had almost always used the phrase 'the Socialist Party', Eden softened this to 'our Socialist friends', just as he invariably began his national broadcasts with the invocation 'my friends'. He seemed desperate actually to meet the nation and, for his tour, instructed the Party organisers to ensure that rallies were not restricted by ticket but open to the public. In Glasgow, as Maxwell Fyfe noted, 'he not only filled the enormous St Andrew's Hall but two overflow halls for his relay. On the next night Attlee could not get the St Andrew's Hall more than half full.' Likewise the rag market at Birmingham was full for Eden with something approaching 10,000 people, and thinly attended for Attlee. This personal success was carried through to the results when his own constituency of Warwick and Leamington increased his majority with a swing well above the national and regional average. Beneath the confident surface though, there were little pointers to the troubles to come; his staff found him an almost impossible man to write speeches for, and had to get used to his unpredictable moods, occasional rages alternating with devastating charm; at the Party's opening press conference it was noted by Crossman that he was

[47] Butler, *General Election of 1955*, 67, 92, 157; D.E. Butler, *The Electoral System in Great Britain since 1918* (2nd edn, Oxford, 1963), 209–11; Thorpe, *Lloyd*, 184; Cockett, *My Dear Max*, 182.

flanked by Woolton (who remained silent throughout), and by Butler: 'Eden was at ease in foreign affairs, but Butler took over from him on any detail of home affairs.'[48]

There were few stunts or significant events to cause ripples, and only low-key reporting; after it was over, Fraser reported to the ACP that the fact that the Party had held the initiative throughout had 'simplified the conduct of the campaign'. He later recalled that 'as usual I attended the meetings of Swinton's Policy Committee in the morning and there were no disturbances, and Woolton's Tactical Committee in the afternoon just reviewed the campaign, and took no new decisions'. The only major event, the signing of the Austrian State Treaty by Macmillan on 15 May, was generally represented as a foreign policy triumph for the Government and a further lowering of Cold War tension. The campaign began with the national press on strike, but even when Fleet Street re-started work this made no difference, for the Election was rarely even the main news until the last few days of the campaign. Newspapers lined up behind the same parties as in 1951, but made few attempts to shape or change opinions; David Butler attributed this not only to the universal expectation of a Tory victory (which robbed the contest of its usual blood sports appeal), but also to the fact that passions did not run very high anyway:

> While the Conservatives were untroubled by what they might have regarded as the horrors of a Labour victory, because they assumed that it would not occur, on the Labour side, even the minority who thought Labour might win, did not consider that a Conservative triumph would have been an irremediable national disaster. This must have been the first election since the Labour Party achieved full maturity in which its supporters did not believe that their victory was essential to save the country from unemployment, war and misery.

This was an impressive tribute to how far the Conservatives had come since 1945; a 'consensus' is after all not only about the convergence of actual policy but also about how far people think that the remaining differences between the parties matter to them. Polls showed that the electorate in 1955 still thought of the parties and their policies as being far apart, but some at least were less inclined than in 1945–51 to vote along class lines for that reason because the differences of emphasis did not have the same salience as before. A few months earlier, Richard Crossman had written in the *Sunday Pictorial* that 'everything is booming – with two exceptions: unemployment and party politics'. The Government benefited from both of these exceptions.[49]

---

48  Woolton, *Memoirs*, 417–18; Gilbert, *Never Despair*, 1115, 1138; Thompson, *Day Before Yesterday*, 119; Butler, *General Election of 1955*, 103; Kilmuir, *Memoirs*, 246; Central Office file, 'Intelligence summaries', CCO 4/6/126, CPA; Rhodes James, *Eden*, 281; Morgan, *Crossman Diaries*, 419.
49  ACP, 20 July 1955; Lord Fraser of Kilmorack to the author, 30 June 1994; Richard Lamb, *The Failure of the Eden Government* (1987), 12; Butler, *General Election of 1955*, 94, 96; NCP, 20 Sept. 1954.

With the press and the politicians unexcited, the feature of the campaign that attracted the most attention was television, and this was written up as 'the first television election'. In fact 1955 was only the tilt-over point at which radio and television had approximately equal evening audiences, and it was 1959 that was to be the first campaign in which television really dominated the coverage. Nevertheless, Eden's broadcasting triumph in 1951, experiments by the parties between the elections, and Eden's greater receptiveness to television than either Churchill or Attlee, ensured that 1955 would be approached with television as a formative influence for the first time. Commercial broadcasting would not start until some months after the Election, so the BBC was for the last time the only medium. Central Office had prepared itself by sending Profumo to the United States to study technique during the 1952 presidential election, and had allowed cameras in to film the Party Conference in 1954. In addition to taking part in a collective interview by newspaper editors, Eden planned to break new ground by devoting a whole fifteen minute Party broadcast at the end of the campaign to a personal appeal, delivered straight to camera and without notes. How big a step this was may be judged from the view communicated by the Party to the BBC only three years earlier, when the BBC itself had suggested broadcasts by ministers: 'it would be embarrassing and distracting for the speaker, who could hardly be expected to memorise his speech like a paid performer; and, unless the broadcast were tricked out with some adventitious element designed to increase its entertainment value (which would tend to bring it into the "party" category) it would be tedious to the viewer'. Eden did not in fact learn his script 'like a paid performer', but read it from large prompt cards, but his programme was impressive, for he was relaxed in front of the camera and conveyed, in David Butler's words, 'a sense of calmness, optimism, decency and competence'. The BBC's report of viewer reaction, given to the Party after the Election, found that on all five surveys of opinion that had been taken, two by the Corporation, two by newspapers and one by Gallup, Eden's broadcast had scored the highest satisfaction rating; it was though only just ahead of the other Tory broadcasts, all of which were ahead of Labour and the Liberals, which may well indicate that all surveys were skewed by the fact that more Conservative than Labour supporters had televisions at that time. However, the *New Statesman* accepted that 'we were watching the one man among the party leaders who is a television star', and added more equivocally that 'those members of his party who are all for jockeying him out of office, as soon as decency permits, are now thinking again'. Michael Cockerell concluded that through this broadcast 'more of the public had gained a better direct impression of what Sir Anthony Eden looked and sounded like, than it had of any previous prime minister in history'. This is at best only half true, for Baldwin's newsreel audience in 1935 had been much larger than Eden's TV audience in 1955 – for shorter addresses but repeated regularly. Yet the four million or so who saw Eden on television were certainly far more than the number who attended his rallies, and were thought by the BBC to be those who were 'unlikely to think of going to a meeting or reading the party policies'. Since Eden's calm uncomplicated television personality was actually rather similar to that of Baldwin on film, this was another case of old wine in a new bottle.[50]

The results on 26 and 27 May confirmed expectations. Turnout had fallen but there was an improvement in the Conservative position relative to Labour, and the overall majority rose from sixteen to fifty-eight; this was the first time since 1841 that any party had improved its parliamentary position at three successive elections, and Eden was the first incumbent Prime Minister since Palmerston to increase his majority. The reduced turnout reflected the low-key campaign, but while the Tory vote fell by half a million (if some allowance is made for seats not contested in 1951), the Labour vote fell by a million and a half. With the Liberal vote remaining tiny, Eden came within a whisker of getting 50 per cent of the popular vote, nearer than any other post-war premier. The swing to Conservative was under 2 per cent, but evenly distributed around the country, and every region swung by a figure close to the national average. Marginal seats were therefore gained simply where the smallest Labour majorities happened to be, a dozen in southern England, and half a dozen each in the Midlands and the North. The solitary gain north of the border produced the unusual satisfaction of a Conservative majority of Scottish seats – previously a feature only of Tory landslide years like 1924 or 1931 and never subsequently to be approached. The few local variations – a big Tory swing in prosperous Coventry, and the only Tory seat lost being in agriculturally-depressed Norfolk – seemed to confirm that the Government's record had been decisive, if only by encouraging some Labour voters to feel that they could safely stay at home; Dalton found that even in the Durham coalfield 'the plain truth was that people were not much interested in the election. There were no burning issues, no unemployment, and much overtime.' The evidence of the voting figures was that differential abstention had not made much difference, and that the main change of the parties' relative position had come from the small number of genuine conversions.[51]

From the election, Labour drew the conclusions that it could no longer fight campaigns on fear, and should somehow avoid internal divisions, though rather lost sight of those findings in the upheavals of 1956–57. Conservatives for the most part breathed a huge sigh of relief, for 1955 finally laid the ghost of 1945: Rab Butler told his CRD staff that 'by winning the election with an increased majority, the Party has made history, and destroyed for ever the myth that 1945 represented the beginning of some irreversible revolution'. Conservatives were pleased to read that Patrick Gordon Walker had said that

---

[50] Eden, *Full Circle*, 281; Michael Cockerell, *Live From Number Ten: The Inside Story of Prime Ministers and Television* (1988), 15, 21, 36; Central Office, General Director's files, 'Political broadcasting', CCO 120/1/1 and 2, CPA.

[51] Butler, *General Election of 1955*, 154–66; Pimlott, *Dalton Diaries*, 671.

Labour had lost because they seemed old-fashioned, 'while the Conservatives seemed to talk the language of 1955'. Nor would many Tories have quarrelled with the *Daily Mail*'s verdict that 'the result is a vote of confidence in progressive Conservatism. Above all it is a resounding personal triumph for the Prime Minister.' Woolton told Eden that 'we are in no doubt about the inspiration that the campaign derived from your own tremendous efforts in broadcasting and in touring the country'. David Butler concluded a few months later that timing had been crucial, for 'peace and national solvency were outwardly as secure as at any moment in the last few years . . . No untoward events occurred to dim the appeal of a fresh Prime Minister, asking the country for authority to continue to seek "peace and prosperity".' By the time that these last phrases were penned, the adverb 'outwardly' had acquired a special resonance as a result of claims by then that the Conservatives had fought the Election on a false economic prospectus, and within another year the idea that Eden stood for peace and prosperity would have unleashed all the bitter contentiousness so noticeably absent from the 1955 campaign.[52]

---

[52] Butler, *General Election of 1955*, 158, 164; Ramsden, *Conservative Party Policy*, 177; *NCP*, 4 July 1955; Woolton to Eden, 7 June 1955, Avon MSS, 20/19/41a.

**Chapter 7**

# The Eden Government, 1955–57

The Eden Government, like the Churchill Government of 1951, had no honeymoon period after its re-election in May 1955. Within six months the Government was struggling against economic difficulties that enabled Labour to recover its morale and seize the domestic initiative. In February 1956, Noël Coward noted that 'Anthony Eden's popularity has spluttered away like a blob of fat in a frying pan'. Eden's Ministers were an unhappy team, speculating overactively about their future prospects, and their speculations were the stuff of much Fleet Street gossip too; within a year, Eden was driven to issue a personal denial of persistent rumours that he would resign, and in the same period by-elections began to go worse than at any time of Churchill's peacetime premiership. Only a little over a year after his 1955 triumph, Eden was plunged by the nationalisation of the Suez Canal Company into the crisis that would bring about both the collapse of his health and his ignominious early retirement. That crisis materially weakened the Conservatives' hold over the country, led to public divisions among Conservative MPs and resignations by ministers, and – most unusual of all – even to the deselection of sitting Tory MPs by their constituency parties.[1]

Contemporary commentators, who had understood well enough that Churchill had lately been something of a non-playing captain of the Tory team and a source of disaffection in himself, were amazed that his departure had so damaged his Party. In January 1956, Hugh Gaitskell noted in his diary that he had said to Attlee,

> how extraordinary it was that the Government had gone down so much in the last nine months, and added, 'After all, the only important change is the disappearance of Winston. Who would have supposed that he would make so much difference?' Clem said, 'Yep. It's the heavy roller, you know. Doesn't let the grass grow under it' – which I thought was (a) shrewd, and (b) typical, being a cricketing analogy. It is indeed a possible explanation. Clem also talked about Anthony. 'He has never had any experience of running a team.'

Attlee may of course have been giving Gaitskell a coded warning about the possible effect of his own retirement on Labour, but the remark was certainly

---

[1] Graham Payn and Sheridan Morley (eds), *The Noël Coward Diaries* (1982), 308.

shrewd. As long as Churchill remained Leader, with Eden as the ageing dauphin, there was no very lively interest in the subsequent succession; Churchill also had a great tendency to whack on the head any colleague who challenged his own pre-eminence. With Churchill gone and Eden vulnerable, there was now an unseemly jockeying for position among men whose horizons had been limited for fifteen years by the massive Churchillian presence.[2]

## Eden as Prime Minister

None of this would have mattered much if Eden had managed to stamp his own authority on the Party. Instead, he found himself beset in the first year with a succession of problems in the domestic fields that had never been his forte, the result of which was to intensify earlier, subterranean, doubts about his capacity to be Prime Minister; and then in his second year he suffered setbacks even on grounds where he had been thought to be most at home, foreign policy and television. From the start, his leadership style confirmed the worries that even supporters like Woolton had entertained when Eden vacillated about the Election date. Nigel Nicolson concluded in 1970 that,

> Eden was a bad Prime Minister. For one thing, he could never leave his ministers alone. He was always fussing them, ringing them up in the middle of the night to ask them had they done this? Had they seen this in the newspapers? This showed a lack of confidence, and worry, in ministers . . . and from them it trickled down by the natural indiscretions you get in the lobbies and the smoking rooms in the House of Commons to the back-benches.

Nicolson was by then no friend to the reputation of Eden, since his own career had been wrecked over Suez, but his views are borne out by a wide range of other sources. Lord Home, who was not by any means hostile to Eden, told Kenneth Young that Eden 'was a very active Prime Minister and if he had read something in the papers and thought "why haven't you done this, that or the other?", he would be on the telephone early in the morning. Then one had to keep out of his way and get on with one's job!' John Boyd-Carpenter felt that 'Eden worried. He worried at his Ministers, ringing them up with enquiries about matters which either were not ready for submission to him or indeed were not of sufficient importance to bother a Prime Minister. Far worse, he worried himself.' In January 1956, the Foreign Secretary's private secretary noted that the Foreign Secretary had said wearily that he had had 'twenty-four hours "respite" . . . but even as he spoke the PM rang up about something. I hear we now consult No.10 about the appointment of Embassy guards in Amman.' He also noted that Eden's press officer looked 'even more thin and drawn, and is obviously having a terrible time with the PM'. The Prime Minister's conduct clearly occasioned

2 P.M. Williams (ed.), *The Diary of Hugh Gaitskell, 1945–56* (1983), 411.

amusement among colleagues as well as irritation: having left Henry Brooke in charge of the Treasury in his absence abroad, Butler had it reported to him by Brooke himself that 'AE, evidently deciding that I was not likely to be any use to him, has addressed all his Treasury enquiries to [Sir Edward] Bridges and not to me. This has saved me a great deal of wear and tear, but I am afraid it has been a pestilential nuisance to EB. Influenza has now diminished the flow of enquiries.' Eden claimed in his memoirs to have reverted to Baldwin's way of conducting business through bilateral dealings with ministers, and with less reliance on full Cabinet than in Churchill's time – though a less phlegmatically relaxed, less Baldwinian figure than the highly strung, nervously tense Eden would be hard to imagine. In fact, as Robert Rhodes James suggests, Eden, in going for the personal direction of government through bilateral intervention with every minister in turn, was actually over-reacting against Churchill's 'interminable and inconclusive cabinets and substantial paperwork'. As a result of his continual personal interventions, Eden irritated many of his colleagues and exhausted his own reserves of stamina and endurance. This in turn led colleagues increasingly to wonder how long he could last, and to frame their actions accordingly.[3]

These problems were accentuated by the delay in reconstructing the Government, which both increased the Prime Minister's reputation for indecision and made him seem still to be the custodian of Churchill's Government rather than the master of his own. Very few changes were made in April 1955 when Eden succeeded Churchill; Macmillan went to the Foreign Office and Selwyn Lloyd replaced him at Defence; Swinton was unceremoniously dropped from the Commonwealth Relations Office, and Home brought into the Cabinet. The substitution of Lloyd and Home for Churchill and Swinton reduced the average age, but there were no other changes in Cabinet and only two changes of departmental ministers outside. With an election imminent, this was defensible, but the insecure Eden then felt that it would smack of dishonesty to go to the country with one team and replace it with another straight afterwards; Butler, worrying about going abroad in late May, 'at a rather important time', reassured himself with the 'belief that he will not make much reconstruction till the Summer'. He was told by Buchan–Hepburn that Eden did not favour a quick reconstruction because it would be hard to sack ministers, 'after making people fight election', but had 'wondered "if the boys would wait?" I said they would if they knew it was coming.' The decision not to reshuffle after the Election later seemed to Lord Kilmuir (as Maxwell Fyfe had become on appointment as Lord Chancellor in

---

[3] Alan Thompson, *The Day Before Yesterday* (1971), 121; Kenneth Young, *Sir Alec Douglas-Home* (1970), 87; John Boyd-Carpenter, *Way of Life* (1980), 123–4; John Charmley (ed.), *Descent to Suez, Diaries of Evelyn Shuckburgh, 1951–1956* (1986), 324; Brooke to Butler, 16 Sept. 1955, Butler MSS, G28; Robert Rhodes James, *Anthony Eden* (1986), 405–6; Anthony Eden, *Full Circle, The Eden Memoirs vol. 3* (1960), 269.

1954) to be a bad miscalculation, compounded by the 'major lack of judgement' shown by moving Macmillan to the Foreign Office, since he 'was the last person likely to tolerate interference in the conduct of his office'; if Eden interfered everywhere else, he would hardly stop short in his own field. In view of his later distinguished record in international affairs, it is notable that even the appointment of Alec Home to look after the Commonwealth came in for criticism: at the age of fifty-one Home had never set foot in a single Commonwealth territory.[4]

Eden's Cabinet did though perceptibly mark a generational shift, and the Prime Minister himself was more than a little irritated by the press's harping on his own youthfulness – he had after all entered the Commons thirty-one years earlier, joined the Cabinet twenty years ago, and been heir apparent to the premiership for fifteen years. Woolton reminded him that in commenting on his age, journalists were not counting up from zero but down from the age of Sir Winston Churchill. Eden himself in his memoirs noted that 'the long era as crown prince' had been established in 1942, 'a position not necessarily enviable in politics'. There was though a feeling that Eden, who had seemed to personify the younger, modern Toryism of post-1945, had let down such expectations by his appointments, particularly when the 1955 intake of Conservative MPs again broadened the middle-class element in the parliamentary party. Hugh Massingham reported in *The Observer* some such irritations: 'These are the people who . . . rarely get into Parliament and still more rarely are they given the jobs. As one of them sadly remarked to me the other day: "Even at Eton you are only a fag for a limited period." Some of them in fact, think it is high time they were elected to Pop.' For the likes of Enoch Powell, Ernest Marples and Reginald Bevins the advent of Eden was a disappointment, and Henry Fairlie diagnosed many of the Government's problems as stemming from the Prime Minister's reluctance to reflect in his Government the 'social revolution' which (he said) had transferred power from the 'squirearchy' to the 'suburbs' – which only goes to show how successful the Maxwell Fyfe reforms had been in changing the Party's public image, even for a sceptical political journalist. Randolph Churchill, noting that everyone at the Party Conference in October was talking about 'Sir Anthony's long-delayed re-shuffle', brutally reminded his *Evening Standard* readers that 'Mr. Asquith used to say that a Prime Minister must be a good butcher, but as one Minister said to me: "The trouble with Anthony is that politically he is a vegetarian – he can't stand the sight of blood."' Randolph's father had once minuted his Minister of Health to similar effect, saying that he

4 Butler to Buchan-Hepburn, 23 May 1955, and note on Cabinet paper, undated but May 1955, Hailes MSS, 4/12; Earl of Kilmuir, *Political Adventure, The Memoirs of the Earl of Kilmuir* (1964), 243–4; John Dickie, *The Uncommmon Commoner, A Study of Sir Alec Douglas-Home* (1964), 98.

was increasingly worried about myxomatosis: 'do you think Anthony might catch it?'[5]

Behind the scenes there had been discussion of a reshuffle throughout the Summer and Autumn, first centring on Eden's belief that Butler must be moved from the Treasury, and increasingly on the feeling that he must get himself a more compliant Foreign Secretary than Macmillan. Butler had suffered a serious personal setback late in 1954 with the early death of his first wife after a long illness, and was subsequently laid low with a recurrent viral illness that sapped his energy. Those in the Party who worked closely with him over a long period tended to see these two events as a watershed in his career; his edge had gone and Butler was never the same man. Such views are easily exaggerated, for Butler remained, at least until 1963, an acute, intellectually-challenging, central figure in the Party, still with both a colossal capacity for work and a gift for public administration. True or not, there is no doubt that during 1955 the view gained ground, both at Westminster and in the Prime Minister's mind, that Butler had 'lost his grip'. Butler hovered between a wish to be relieved of the pressures of the Treasury, where he had been for four years, and a recognition that, if he stepped down in 1955 when the economy was running into trouble, he would seem like a scapegoat for those difficulties, which would prejudice his leadership hopes. Macmillan, whose move to the Treasury would put a senior minister with a good understanding of economics and a reputation for problem-solving into a key post, insisted that the move should be regarded as a step towards rather than away from the premiership; Butler equally insisted that he would only move voluntarily from the Treasury (and Eden would hardly sack him) if he could become deputy Prime Minister, a post that did not formally exist. In assessing these negotiations, it is worth remembering that Macmillan was three years older than Eden and Butler a mere five years younger, and that Eden had been premier for only a few months. It is striking that in Autumn 1955 Butler and Macmillan were manoeuvring as if either might soon be called on to take over the Government from a Leader of their own generation. It is notable too that there was not much personal warmth between any of the three men involved; as far back as August 1947, Eden had told Cuthbert Headlam 'that O[liver] S[tanley] is alright – plays the game – he is not so happy about H.M. and R.A.B'.[6]

Provided the terms were right, Macmillan was anxious to get away from the Foreign Office where he was at loggerheads with a Prime Minister who had a habit of re-writing Foreign Office telegrams whenever submitted to him for approval – something Eden himself never allowed even Churchill

[5] Earl of Woolton, *The Memoirs of the Rt. Hon. Earl of Woolton* (1959), 417; Anthony Eden, *The Reckoning, The Eden Memoirs, vol.* 2 (1965), 266; Andrew Roth, *Enoch Powell, Tory Tribune* (1970), 121, 124.
[6] Anthony Howard, *RAB, The Life of R.A. Butler* (1987), 213, 215, 217; Headlam diary, 2 Aug. 1947, Headlam MSS.

to do. Nor was Macmillan as discreet as usual about his difficulties, and his unhappiness was discussed on both sides of the Commons. His only real concern was that he should not be replaced at the Foreign Office by 'that bloody Selwyn Lloyd' (as his private secretary noted him saying) and he asked the Chief Whip 'if the Prime Minister's purpose [in suggesting Lloyd for Foreign Secretary] was really to get back control of the Foreign Office'. That is indeed what happened when Lloyd became the first of the class of 1945 to achieve one of the great offices of state. When Macmillan's move to the Exchequer was announced, Hugh Gaitskell noted in his diary the difficulties that the Eden–Butler–Macmillan team had had in working together, and added of Macmillan that 'Tory opinion is now rather veering towards him as the best of the three'. Bracken wrote of the danger to Eden of putting into a key post such a 'dangerous leading colleague' but decided that there was nobody else in Eden's Government 'who would be acclaimed as a daring pilot in our present extremity'. Over two years, Macmillan's successive moves through Housing, Defence, Foreign Office and Treasury had given him a formidable opportunity to advance his claims, much as the fortuitous resignations of colleagues were to do for John Major in 1989–90. Less obviously, Macmillan had sensed both his own opportunity and the potential problem for him if Butler was to succeed Eden; he confessed that he would find it very difficult to serve under Butler. Increasingly, Macmillan was using the public relations skills discovered at Housing to enhance his personal claims. Woolton, a strong supporter of Macmillan who was to help to hoist him into the premiership in 1957, and a man not easily shocked by manipulation of the press, noted with wry amusement Macmillan's habit of loitering on the doorstep of Number 10 after Cabinet, until the photographers had got him in focus, and how he 'posed in the middle of the roadway'.

> I agree that a public man must be something of an actor; I wonder whether it is necessary to be a showman as well. Winston, of course, has always done it; Eden does it in a very gentlemanly way, bringing his hand up to the semi-salute. But there is nothing semi about Harold; he sort of says 'Give me a cheer', and waves to them although they are not waving at him.[7]

## Eden under attack

Talk of a reshuffle continued remorselessly; in June, Butler was informed that Monckton would probably not accept another post, for 'I do not want at my time of life to start being an active party politician' (an interesting commentary on his perception of what was involved in being Churchill's

---

[7] Charmley, *Descent to Suez*, 277, 309, 314; D.R. Thorpe, *Selwyn Lloyd* (1989), 190, 192; Richard Cockett (ed.), *My Dear Max: The Letters of Brendan Bracken to Lord Beaverbrook, 1925–1958* (1990), 186; Williams, *Gaitskell Diary*, 422; Woolton diary, 5 Apr. 1955, Woolton MSS.

Minister of Labour). In July, Macleod urged Butler to use his influence to get Powell a job, not because they were old friends or because they had both worked in Butler's CRD team before 1951, but because 'no one – except yourself – has done as much in the country and the House for the true Tory thinking approach to our problems as he has done'; he conceded that Powell's 'ability of course is not in doubt, only his judgement', but discounted the popular belief that he was not worth appointing because he would resign almost at once on some minor issue. As the Autumn wore on, a reshuffle could not be avoided for the country's economic difficulties could not be denied, and confidence was unlikely to be restored without a new Chancellor; writing about these Summer months in January 1956, Butler noted that 'the PM liked, but most tactfully never mentioned to me, the idea of a change of bowling at the Treasury'. As late as July, Butler had argued that 'there is no question of a crisis', but successive increases in bank rate and tighter hire purchase controls contradicted his optimism. In August, the chairman of the Manchester Conservatives actually resigned his post in protest at the Government's refusal to cut expenditure; he lamented the effects of inflation on industry – and equally on the Manchester Conservatives' own investments, the value of which had dropped considerably because of the economic situation. At the Party Conference in October, Eden was saying that 'our first task at home is to do battle with our economic problems. They are formidable.' A week later a special Autumn Budget, the very fact of which was an admission of economic difficulties, imposed increases in purchase tax and extended its operation to additional classes of household goods. For the Opposition, Gaitskell triumphantly claimed that the Tories were now showing their true colours; 'in a free economy with its unfair shares, there can't be full employment without inflation. Something has to be sacrificed. They are going to sacrifice full employment.' Inevitably, the trade press for the newly-taxed items was also hostile, as a telegram warned Butler: 'In the name of God as Billy Graham would say, why put a 30 per cent tax on babies baths? Herbert Sinclair, Editor, Perambulator Gazette'. This 'pots and pans' budget was not even the bottom of the trough, for further action on hire purchase and interest rates had to be taken in 1956. It was possible to deal with the Labour parliamentary attack by asking why, if the April Budget had been over-optimistic, they had not themselves voted against it, but this debating point was unlikely to impress the country. It was also the case that Gaitskell's assertion that the Conservatives had abandoned full employment would make useful political ammunition in the future, when it had been proved to be untrue, but this could not help Butler in 1955. The Autumn Budget seemed a signal political setback to Butler, who had so recently urged the country to 'invest in success' and had foreseen the doubling of the standard of living in a generation (a good prophecy as it turned out, but this also did not assist him in 1955), and who had spoken so confidently of the economy in the Election campaign. When at the Party Conference he foreshadowed the stern tone of the Budget he was to open in the following week, he was not well received; a few months later he felt that he should have resigned in September when Eden would not support the full economic package that he had then wanted to introduce, and that 'the disillusionment which I felt was reflected in my performance at the Party Conference'. A Central Office opinion survey on the Budget was uniformly negative: it had caused 'dismay and discomfort' among Party workers; all Area Agents reported cancelled subscriptions, and one reported that 'I have not met a single Conservative who has a good word to say about it'; the Yorkshire Area instructed its chairman to make critical representations to Central Office. Butler struggled against the reshuffle that could not now be avoided; he argued that any move had to be made to 'look like promotion', for the sake of Britain's economic prospects (or 'on behalf of credit as well as Butler', as Buchan-Hepburn put it) and tried to avoid being moved into a minor post in which he would be 'a "cockleshell" bouncing about in a great sea without a "great" office'; he even tried to retain Number Eleven Downing Street, so as to be placed geographically between the Chief Whip and the Prime Minister; the premier's own press secretary helpfully recalled that Robert Blake's recent biography of Bonar Law had proved that Law had established just such a precedent as Leader of the House in 1919. On 20 December though, Macmillan replaced Butler at the Treasury *and* at Number Eleven, Butler being made Lord Privy Seal. Bracken's view was that 'Eden, without any great knowledge of financial problems, had the wisdom to see that when Butler's luck had turned he was not the sort of man who could ride the storms that loom ahead'. But Butler remained deputy Prime Minister, Macmillan having accepted that this meant no more than it had done for several years past, that Butler would preside when Eden was away.[8]

The December 1955 reshuffle finally introduced new blood into both higher and lower ranks, and began the 'social revolution' that Henry Fairlie had sought. Edward Heath, who became Chief Whip after only five years in the Commons, had risen most rapidly, but since that rise had taken place entirely as a whip it was easy to overlook; he had actually been Deputy Chief Whip by Autumn 1952, only thirty months after he was first elected. Crookshank and Woolton left the Cabinet, and Macleod and Buchan-Hepburn joined it. The average age now only fifty-five, compared to sixty when Churchill formed his Government in 1951, but the majority of the Cabinet had served

---

[8]  Monckton to Butler, 30 June 1955, Macleod to Butler, 26 July 1955, Butler note, Jan. 1956, and Sinclair to Butler, 1 Nov. 1955, all Butler MSS, G28; Central Office, *Notes on Current Politics* [hereafter *NCP*], 1 Aug., 24 Oct., 14 Nov. and 28 Nov. 1955; Central Office constituency file, Manchester CA, CCO 1/11/116; Gerald Sparrow, *Rab, Study of a Statesman* (1965), 120; Yorkshire Area Finance and General Purposes Committee, 18 Nov. 1955; Buchan-Hepburn note, 10 Dec. 1955, Hailes MSS, 4/12; Buchan-Hepburn to Eden, 5 Dec. 1955, Hailes MSS, 4/1; Clark to Butler, [undated but Nov. 1955], Butler MSS, G28/63; Cockett, *My Dear Max*, 185; Howard, *RAB*, 220–1; Central Office file, 'Public Opinion', CCO 4/6/336, CPA.

since 1951 and only four had been appointed to it by Eden. Lower down there was more room for manouevre: Enoch Powell, Robert Carr, John Hare and Christopher Soames all received their first posts.[9]

In the reshuffle Butler was also made Leader of the Commons and, in partnership with Heath, took much of the Party management off Eden's shoulders. Woolton had finally retired from the Party Chairmanship at the October Conference; just before his retirement he completed the organisational recovery by commissioning (and apparently raising the money for) a new office building in Smith Square, across from Labour's then headquarters in Transport House, into which Central Office and the three London and Home Counties Areas finally moved in June 1958. Woolton had wanted James Stuart, already Scottish Chairman, to take over a merged organisation for the whole of the United Kingdom; Eden felt though that the state of Scottish organisation was not exactly an advertisement for Stuart's talents in this field, did not get on with Stuart, and may also have thought that a former Chief Whip at Central Office would concentrate too much influence in one pair of hands. Malcolm McCorquodale was again considered, and the chosen successor, Oliver Poole, was not an attempt to fill the great salesman's oversized shoes. Poole had been a Conservative MP between 1945 and 1950, undertaking various organisational and policy tasks for Butler in this period, but returned to the City rather than seeking re-election in 1950. He was joint Party Treasurer from 1952 and probably owed his elevation to Chairman to the belief that it was vital to have a Chairman who could at least match Woolton's fundraising skills. Poole became a very important Party figure indeed, serving at Central Office in various senior capacities from 1952 to 1959 and again in 1963–64, but was in 1955–57 the only Chairman ever to serve without sitting in either House, an appointment that went flat against Woolton's considered advice to Eden that his successor should be a Cabinet minister. This necessarily made Poole more of a backroom Chairman than either his predecessor or any of his successors, which again placed emphasis on Butler's partnership with Heath in the management of Party business.[10]

Butler was efficient in this role if lacking in the inspirational qualities needed in a Party manager, and was in any case feeling wounded about his own recent treatment at Eden's hands. The management of the parliamentary party improved, but the impression given to the country at large did not. In any case, Butler was himself guilty of the greatest of all indiscretions. The press had responded negatively to the December reshuffle, and a Party opinion survey reported that 'the ministerial changes do not appear to have increased

[9] John Campbell, *Edward Heath* (1993), 89; Roth, *Powell*, 126.
[10] Woolton diary, 24 June 1955, Woolton MSS; Stuart Ball, 'The National and Regional Party Structure', in *Conservative Century: The Conservative Party Since 1900*, eds. A. Seldon and S. Ball (Oxford, 1995), 193; Roth, *Powell*, 144; Lord Butler of Saffron Walden, *The Art of the Possible, The Memoirs of Lord Butler* (1971), 184; Campbell, *Heath*, 91.

the Government's stock, and have aroused some bewilderment'. Some papers were already calling baldly for Eden to step down; interviewed at the airport on the way to a holiday, Butler was caught off guard and agreed that Eden was 'the best Prime Minister we have', and promised 'my support to the Prime Minister in all his difficulties'. This was not a firm endorsement of the Leader by his deputy and reinforced the press view that Eden was not fully in control. Eden certainly suffered from virulent and unfair personal attacks, even from the Berry family newspapers that could normally be relied on, but other papers also gave him short shrift; Bernard Levin, Malcolm Muggeridge in *Punch* (who famously concluded that Eden was not only a bore but one of international standard who 'bored for Britain') and Randolph Churchill (now freed from paternal control) in the *Evening Standard*, were only the most hostile of a host of critics. Eden was deeply hurt by these attacks, and above all by the virulence of the normally-loyal *Daily Telegraph*, hence his ill-judged denial of an impending resignation. What riled him most was a *Telegraph* article that parodied his public-speaking style. To emphasise oratorical points he was wont to punch one fist into the other (open) hand, but stopping short of an audible impact; now, said the *Telegraph*, 'most Conservatives, and almost certainly some of the wiser Trade Union leaders, are waiting to feel the smack of firm government', an article that Eden was said to have read with 'a pained and pungent oath'. Other papers picked up and quoted the *Telegraph*, the *Daily Mirror* giving it a whole half page; the *Daily Mail* added that 'the Government's trouble seems to be not paralysis so much as lack of will'. When his ministerial protégé Anthony Nutting, who later remembered that the *Telegraph* article 'really hurt him, hit him between the eyes', advised that Eden should on no account reply to press calls for his resignation, since that would only add to the rumours, Eden replied 'Oh, you don't understand anything about politics, you're just a Foreign Office official.' In response to the denial of his intention to resign and Butler's gaffe at the airport, the press were even more outspoken. Randolph Churchill wrote that 'I was told that the Prime Minister was doing his best. I do not doubt it, and that is why I am sure that there has got to be, and quickly, a change at 10 Downing Street.' Ian Waller, in a column syndicated for provincial newspapers, prophetically wrote early in 1956 that 'if the year goes on as it has begun it will not be Sir Anthony Eden but Harold Macmillan who reigns in Downing Street in 1957'. The Labour Opposition had a field day with a Prime Minister who was both on the ropes and easy to provoke, as Ian Trethowan reported in the *News Chronicle*.

> Towards the end of last week's debate Mr. Robens suggested Sir Anthony might be frightened of the Churchill pen. 'Frightened? Frightened?' Sir Anthony's voice shot through octaves of indignation. His flushed face showed that Mr. Robens had brought the Eden temperature to the boil. Angry with Mr. Robens, angry with the Americans, tired from days of non-stop negotiation, . . . his nerves taut as a banjo string, Sir Anthony was then ripe for fiasco.

It is hardly surprising then that Eden's personal approval rating in the opinion polls declined steadily, from 70 per cent in Autumn 1955 to about 40 per cent in Spring 1956 – and all this *before* Suez. The Party's private opinion surveys made equally gloomy reading; in July 1956 Eden ordered them to be discontinued, and they were not resumed until he had gone. His own morale was certainly battered by all this; writing to Churchill in March, he said that 'it is tough going here but we are surviving'.[11]

A minor suit in the battle with the media was the increasing unhappiness of the broadcasters with the 'fourteen day rule' which forbade them from discussing – or even acknowledging the existence of – controversial political events. The Prime Minister's press secretary had to pass on the press's accumulating grievance against this curtailment of the political debate, but acknowledged that the Chief Whip had no alternative but to defer to the weight of parliamentary opinion which still favoured the restriction. Only in the midst of the Suez crisis was the rule tacitly abandoned. In the meantime it contributed to the Government's poor relations with the media.[12]

Eden was an unlucky Leader, in the timing of his accession to office, in the major issues that first confronted him, and indeed in the run of trivial events that so affected the way in which political life was reported; the junior minister who represented Guildford told his constituents in a commendable understatement at the start of 1956 that 'things have not run our way in recent months'. Within weeks of his re-election, Eden was confronted by a three-week railway strike and six weeks of strikes in the docks. When he unwisely announced at Bradford that he would not be resigning, even this speech was upstaged by a young demonstrator who seized his microphone and said insolent things about him on behalf of the League of Empire Loyalists before she could be bundled from the platform by the Party's Vice Chairman. But his unluckiest stroke of all was to be the first Conservative Prime Minister to have to face a House of Commons ready to abolish capital punishment. This arose largely from the poor judgement of the Home Secretary, Gwilym Lloyd George, and of Stuart and Buchan-Hepburn, who advised Eden that they could judge the temper of the Commons better than Heath. A 1954 Royal Commission report had recommended changes that stopped short of abolition, but even this was rejected by the Churchill Cabinet and confirmed by the Eden Cabinet in 1955. Prompted by the Chief Whip, the Cabinet did wonder whether there was still a parliamentary majority for capital

---

11  Howard, *RAB*, 222; Rhodes James, *Eden*, 412, 425; Kilmuir, *Memoirs*, 257; Thompson, *Day Before Yesterday*, 122–3; Central Office file, 'Public Opinion', CCO 4/6/336, CPA; Geoffrey McDermott, *The Eden Legacy and the Decline of British Diplomacy* (1969), 128; Malcolm Muggeridge, *Tread Softly, For You Tread on My Jokes* (Fontana edn, 1968), 135; Randolph Churchill, *The Rise and Fall of Sir Anthony Eden* (1959), 227–8; John Ramsden, 'Churchill to Heath', in *The Conservatives, A History from their Origins to 1965*, ed. Lord Butler (1977), 439; Central Office file, 'Public Opinion', CCO 4/7/375, CPA; Eden to Churchill, 11 Mar. 1956, Avon MSS, 19/1/91.
12  Clark to Buchan-Hepburn, 30 Sept. 1955, Hailes MSS, 2/5.

punishment, but resolved to table a motion for its retention in February 1956 and to allow a free vote. In that debate, enough younger Conservative MPs backed Labour's abolitionist amendment, or abstained (as did three Cabinet ministers – Macleod, Heathcoat Amory and Lloyd) to allow the abolitionists to win by 293 to 262. Foreseeing no such outcome, the Cabinet had authorised Butler to say in advance that the Government would accept the views of the House: they could hardly now expect the House to reverse its view, but meanwhile the Party outside parliament was on the warpath. For the 1956 Party Conference, there were thirty-three constituency resolutions calling for the death penalty to be retained, and one of these was carried after a debate in which the only speaker against the motion was scarcely allowed even to finish his speech. For the time being the Lords saved the Government's face by rejecting an abolitionist private member's bill, but now the Government had to evolve a compromise which they could carry through both Houses, or face a vote in each succeeding session while having no Commons majority for its policy. Kilmuir's compromise proposal, to retain the death penalty only for particular types of murder, was duly carried in 1957 on a whipped vote, but still against strong Party feeling outside.[13]

## The middle class revolt

Constituency associations were restive. Accrington nervously noted the severe problems for the textile trade arising from the Government's failure to get a grip on the economy. High Peak resolved in January to deplore 'the present drift', noting a year later that it had cost them money in lost subscriptions, and Burton decided in March that they could not usefully start any recruiting 'since the electorate was disgruntled with the Government'. In South Walsall there was a strong plea for loyalty to the Government in March, but the association then passed its own critical resolution in July. The Area Agent reported in May that Solihull had lost about 600 members 'due to the difficulty in collecting subscriptions', a loss of about 12 per cent of the membership. Next-door Warwick and Leamington, the Prime Minister's constituency, was attributing its loss of income to the difficulty of getting members to come to its social events in the prevailing atmosphere. North Cornwall continued to complain about the Government's poor public relations, and West Dorset blamed the poor turnout at their AGM on disaffection with the Government. In early Autumn, a series of eight conferences of constituency officers in the East and West Ridings of Yorkshire found that discontent centred on the Government's failure to take a strong line against trades unions and

---

13  Guildford CA minutes, 5 Mar. 1956; T.F. Lindsay and M. Harrington, *The Conservative Party, 1918–1970*, (1974), 186; Churchill, *Eden*, 208; Richard Lamb, *The Failure of the Eden Government* (1987), 34–9; Conference Agenda for 1956, NUA 2/2/22, CPA; Campbell, *Heath*, 92; Kilmuir, *Memoirs*, 264–6.

on the financial burdens falling on the middle class (though, significantly, Conservative trades unionists were noticed to be the only group praising the Government's domestic policy, because it had *not* initiated trades union legislation). It had been widely said that the Eden Government had not produced 'recognisable Conservative policies', and that there had been a 'lack of coherence and positive leadership'; in these circumstances, mobilising the organisation was difficult, for 'whilst Party workers appeared generally to support the Government, this seemed to be more from a sense of loyalty than from conviction'. Buchan-Hepburn had found as early as 1953 that rising prices had turned housewives into just as stern critics of the Churchill Government as they had been of Attlee, for he received a constant battering of correspondence from a constituency group that he privately christened 'the wild women of Anerley'; in October 1955, a supporter told him pointedly that 'middle class people are being hit enough without a Conservative Government hitting us too'. The easy hits against Labour before 1951 were now pointing the other way.[14]

Before the 1955 Election, efforts had been made to target some policies towards middle-class voters, what Macleod with his proverbial nose for the 'E[lection] factor' called 'the £500 to £1,000 group', but budgetary contraints now made such concessions impossible. With these difficulties, and a hostile press to publicise them, by-elections were dangerous events. The first feature was the entirely unexpected reappearance of a Liberal challenge. At Torquay in December 1955 the Liberal candidate took 23.8 per cent of the vote, and on a single day in February 1956 Liberals scored 36.4 per cent in Hereford and 21.4 per cent in Gainsborough (where there had not even been a Liberal candidate in 1955, and where the intervention now nearly gave Labour the seat). That early Liberal challenge faded away, largely because seats did not fall vacant where the Liberals had any organisation, but this only meant that public disaffection moved voters towards Labour instead. Edward du Cann held Taunton by only 657 votes in a straight fight with Labour in February and the Conservatives came almost as close to losing in the Kent stockbroker-belt seat of Tonbridge in June. What made things worse was that the Party organisation could pick up neither the scale nor the location of the problem, for, while voters deserted in droves, the canvass could not find who were the deserters: the 'worst case' Central Office prediction for Torquay was of a Tory share of 56 per cent, whereas it was actually down to 50 per cent. Likewise, the General Director felt that the Hereford result was 'a bit of a shock', and after the event attributed the near defeat to 'the

14  Accrington CA minutes, 20 Mar. 1956; High Peak CA minutes, 27 Jan. 1956 and 1 Mar. 1957; Burton CA minutes, 21 Mar. 1956; Walsall South CA minutes, 19 Mar. and 16 July 1956; Central Office constituency file, Solihull, CCO 1/11/303, CPA; Warwick and Leamington CA minutes, 13 Feb. 1956; North Cornwall CA minutes, 14 Apr. 1956; West Dorset CA minutes, 15 June 1956; Central Office file, Area correspondence, CCO 2/4/4; Isaacs to Buchan-Hepburn, 27 Oct. 1955 and various letters of 1953, Hailes MSS 1/15.

present loss of confidence in the Government and our very bad Press'. West Walthamstow polled in March, after Attlee's elevation to the Lords, and the Conservatives found themselves facing heavy barracking on the issue of rising prices. Eden took a close interest even in this hopeless contest: his secretary responded to the Central Office final prediction with the news that 'Sir Anthony commented that he would be surprised and depressed if the Liberals poll so many votes as is estimated'. In the event the prediction proved insufficiently gloomy, and Pierssené wrote to Eden on the day after the declaration to explain the result. 'The alarmingly low Conservative poll is mainly accounted for by the general attitude of resentment and discontent that pervades the middle class'; they had estimated a Tory poll of 5,500 (compared to 10,037 votes only nine months earlier), but got only 4,184, 'and the error in the forecast is a measure of the deterioration that has set in'. The point was rammed home in some unusually frank advice to a Prime Minister who did not like criticism: 'the middle classes feel that thay have not had a square deal and are looking for somewhere else to go˙ . . . Canvassers yesterday were frequently greeted with such remarks as "We shan't trouble this time" and "What does it matter who's in?" '[15]

The contest in Tonbridge was not therefore looked forward to with enthusiasm: Pierssené told Heath in April that 'with Liberal intervention we are not likely to put up a very convincing performance', though the Area Agent, after visiting the unhappy and divided local association, concluded nervously that 'something catastrophic would have to happen for us to lose the seat'; Poole advised Eden that 'no good can come of this by-election' but added that 'I am confident that we shall hold the seat with, I am afraid, a very much reduced majority'. Efforts were made to draft in the scale of outside help that would normally have attended only a campaign in a marginal – which was what Tonbridge now was. Canvassers reported that 'many supporters are in a critical mood, particularly in regard to the importation of foreign produce and the continued acceptance of wage demands', while the Tory-owned *Kent and Sussex Courier* vied with its Fleet Street counterparts in attacking the Party. The final canvass looked ominous and the eve of poll prediction was of a 10,196 majority down to 3,600 or less, because 'Conservatives are disgruntled about the cost of living and the rates and are still critical of the Government'. The seat was held but the majority fell to 1,602, entirely because of the fall in the Conservative vote since Labour's vote remained almost exactly as in 1955. Central Office reported and endorsed the local view that 'the adverse result is due to the abstention of the middle class vote'; even many Party members had refused to come out on the day, and it was felt that only the outside teams

---

[15] Harriet Jones, 'The Conservative Party and Social Policy, 1942–1955', unpublished PhD thesis, University of London, 1992, 194; Chris Cook and John Ramsden (eds), *By-Elections in British Politics* (1973), 194, 378–9; Central Office, General Director's file, by-elections, CCO 120/2/41–5, CPA.

of speakers and agents, and a mass of mutual aid from other constituencies, had saved the seat from being lost. *The Times* gave considerable attention to a correspondent who applauded the Tory middle classes of Tonbridge for refusing to vote, and who expressed a common theme:

> For – and let the Conservative headquarters be under no apprehension about this – if we refuse to vote and thereby admit the Socialists to power, we allow a period of Socialist legislation which can later be revoked. If we permit the Conservatives to frame Socialist measures in their ill-considered bid for left-wing support, we are saddled with such measures for ever. Which is the greater evil?

The point then was that some middle-class voters had now lost that terror of perpetual Labour Government that had rallied them loyally to the Tory cause after 1945 and kept them loyal when there was only a tiny parliamentary majority before 1955. Now they were resentful of an appeasing policy towards the trades unions which had the effect of putting up prices. As Macmillan wrote in 1957, 'while the great mass of the working population and the majority of the entrepreneurial class have gained from inflation, those who have been injured by it are disproportionately represented in the party organisation in the constituencies'. There was as yet no concept of annual reviews of salaries to compensate for inflationary pressures on household budgets, no awareness that inflation had become a regular part of the political scenery, for older voters well remembered falling prices between 1921 and 1935. But this in turn produced a new political problem for Conservative governments: as a result of the two housing booms since 1935, there were now some two million more homeowners buying on mortgages, and for the first time in peacetime interest rates seemed to be out of control: bank rate, which had been only 2 per cent from 1931 to 1951 and had risen only to 4 per cent while Churchill was Prime Minister, was now 5.5 per cent and would be 7 per cent by early 1957. It is not surprising that the (mainly middle-class) mortgage payers were bitter when they read in the press that (their) Government was conceding pay rises to manual workers – and apparently without a fight. As the Summer break approached, Chief Whip Heath was urging backbenchers to spend as much time as possible in their constituencies to put the Government's case across to the electors.[16]

Faced with this disaffected middle class 'looking for somewhere else to go', at a time when the Liberals could not even manage to put up candidates in many places, there were worries that the Conservatives could now be outflanked on the right. The League of Empire Loyalists, which had embarrassed Eden at Bradford, was one such worry, articulating a white supremacist view of Empire that was directly at odds with the thrust of

---

[16] Central Office, General Director's file, Tonbridge by-election, CCO 120/2/46, CPA; Rhodes James, *Eden*, 439; John Turner, *Macmillan* (1994), 233; Central Office file, '1922 Committee', CCO 4/7/64, CPA.

Government colonial policy and backed by the weekly magazine *Time and Tide*, but the League seems not to have made any numerically significant impact in the suburbs and the shires that were the Tory heartlands. Much more worrying were two mushroom organisations that sprang up to articulate concerns on the home front, the Middle Class Alliance and the People's League for the Defence of Freedom. A Central Office investigating committee set up in Summer 1956 drew a clear distinction between these two challengers. The MCA had largely the same objectives as the Conservative Party since, while the Party was 'not the mouthpiece of any one class or section', it had 'always recognised the key position the middle class occupy in our national life'. Plenty of Tory MPs turned up for the MCA's formal launch meeting at the Commons in May 1956, when, as a whip noted laconically, there was 'plenty of drink on the middle class', but it was recognised that a body with 50,000 members who were 'mainly good Tories' would need careful handling. The MCA's chairman was a Conservative MP, Henry Price, who sat for West Lewisham; he was the son of a builder's labourer and had received only an elementary education, a classic 'Maxwell Fyfe man'. The Central Office view was that the MCA should not be encouraged, since any effort or money that went into it was likely to be diverted from the Party, but that its members should not be antagonised. Poole met Price to discuss the situation from time to time and Central Office discouraged retaliatory action or expulsions when local members joined the MCA. The MCA constituted no long-term threat, since it would wither away as the economy recovered, much as the Anti-Waste League had flourished in 1921 and died in 1922. The MCA remained a pressure group mainly within the Party; in October 1956, there were complaints from Party members that Price had not been called to speak at the Party Conference, and in the following January Price wrote to Macmillan to congratulate him on becoming Prime Minister and to remind him of his earlier speeches about the interests of middle-class voters. This was in fact the parting of the ways between Price, who after Suez and the change of Party Leader had no further wish to rock the boat, and other MCA organisers who wished to go the whole way to the formation of a new centre party: Price then resigned the chairmanship, but total membership was by then already down to 4,000 and in March 1957 the organisation was wound up. Price was reported in the *Kentish Mercury* as saying that 'the Middle Class Alliance is dead (so's my political future)'. [17]

The People's League for the Defence of Freedom was something altogether different, as its populist title suggested. Briefing Eden, Poole noted that whereas the MCA was basically 'a Conservative front', the PLDF was 'a

---

[17] Rhodes James, *Eden*, 439; Central Office, General Director's files, 120/2/1–5, 'Special Committee on MCA and PLDF', CCO 120/3/1–5, CPA; Central Office file, 'MCA', CCO 3/5/99, CPA; M. Stenton and S. Lees, *Who's Who of British Members of Parliament, 1945–79*, vol. 4 (1981), 301.

Liberal front' that should not be touched. It was Liberal in the sense that its leaders had been Liberal candidates and officeholders, but it was manoeuvring at the extreme rightward end of the political spectrum, where most western European 'Liberals' now operated, rather than in the political left-of-centre where the British Liberal Party was beginning to regroup. Like European Liberals of the right, it combined a libertarian philosophy in economic matters with a readiness to countenance extreme interventionism in policies designed to weaken organised labour. This philosophical stance gave it some natural appeal to Conservative voters, but the real danger lay less in its philosophy than in its leadership. The PLDF was run by Edward Martell, a supremely successful self-publicist with his own newspaper and with great organisational flair. In 1954, when Woolton had decided that the Party should stand aside from the organisation of Churchill's eightieth birthday presentation, so as to allow it to be truly national rather than a party activity, Martell seized the initiative and, when that appeal was a big success and attracted millions of subscribers, Martell gained great kudos. The PLDF was founded as an offshoot of another Martell organisation, the Free Press Society, created after he had used non-union labour on his paper the *Recorder*. Concern with the trades unions remained central to the PLDF's activities and goes some way to explain its success in attracting middle-class support in 1956; in September it was reported to have a London office with twenty-two staff and more than a hundred constituency organisers, chiefly concentrated in Tory seats in the South East and in Lancashire; the PLDF's October claim to have recruited a million members was surely a fantasy, but its undeniable growth prompted Central Office to instruct Area Agents to submit all the information they could on its activities. This intelligence suggested that it had made little impact on leading Conservatives, for few branch or constituency officers had joined; apart from Martell, its national leaders were Lord Moynihan (former Liberal Party chairman), W.J. Brown (Independent MP during the war years and a former associate of Oswald Mosley), and H.E. Crawford and Air Vice Marshall Donald Bennett (both former Liberal candidates); of its eleven-member national committee only three were Tories and the most senior of these was a former councillor who had been rejected in 1952 for the parliamentary candidates' list. On the other hand, the impact on Tory voters was considerable. In July 1956, when Poole made a highly-publicised speech attacking fringe organisations in general and the PLDF by name, more than 400 letters of protest were received, mostly from typical rank-and-file Conservative members – 'solid, reasonable folk' (as a Central Office analysis of this hate mail concluded). At a meeting at Ditchingham Hall, Poole had outlined the case against the PLDF as being that it confused the fight between the major parties and would thus help socialism to triumph. This was no statement of a post-war consensus against extremism, for the interventionism of the PLDF on trades union reform was linked to Labour's statism too:

Some people seem to think that there really isn't much to choose between the parties – that they are going very much along the same road, and that the only real difference is the speed at which they want to travel . . . Not only do I not want to arrive at the planned and regimented socialist, equalitarian State, but, believe me, I would not waste my time in a Party that was merely taking me there by a slow train instead of a faster one. No. The Conservative Party and the Socialist Party are divided by a sharp, unbridgeable gulf. We are travelling entirely different roads.

Some of the many who wrote in to complain about this speech made eloquent sense. The chairman of Shrewsbury Conservatvies, for example, wanted it understood *why* people were going over to the PLDF: 'Clearly a state of affairs has been reached where words alone are insufficient' and where the 'passive resistance' of refusing subscriptions was also regarded as no longer enough. If the case for repressive trades union legislation was to be the key issue that divided the Party from the PLDF, then this was a difficult argument to take to the disaffected middle-class voter in 1956, for the Research Department as well as the Ministry of Labour continued to advise that the strike problem was exaggerated, that such policies as compulsory strike ballots would do more harm than good, and that they would undermine the moderate leaders that currently ran most unions. The CRD argued that 'our conception of freedom . . . leads us to look to reform voluntarily brought about inside the unions themselves'. Attempts to press for a more positive policy had been discouraged by Harold Watkinson: he told a CRD officer committee that 'the policy of the Ministry of Labour was to "divide and rule". [The Ministry of Labour] only had clashes of opinion with one Union, not with the TUC'; he opposed the setting up of a Royal Commission, since that would be filled with lawyers and would antagonise the TUC; most discouragingly of all, he 'felt that it would be impossible for any Conservative Government to introduce legal enforcement unless there were an approach from the TUC'. At the 1957 Conference, Macleod proclaimed his continued faith in the partnership approach of the *Industrial Charter*, and warned Conservatives that just because Labour thought the unions were always right, Tories must not fall for the opposite fallacy. The CRD continued its work, but in 1956 there was no question of changing the Party's basic approach. Throughout Summer and Autumn 1956 the PLDF continued to attract attention, with big meetings at Liverpool and Edinburgh, and with the launch of a new paper *The People's Guardian*. Its impact was then actually blunted by the Suez crisis, for the PLDF's members clearly expected it to back the Government in a foreign crisis and the League anyway had no alternative view to propound; when there were ministerial resignations, the PLDF's vice chairman said at a meeting that he was 'ashamed to be standing on the same platform as Sir Edward Boyle' had done, for Boyle was 'a man who had stabbed the Government in the back'. Such remarks only linked the PLDF even more closely to the Government's position, and its fortunes seem to have gone into a nosedive over the Winter as a result of Suez.[18]

In February 1957, a different sort of attack from the right came when the Empire Loyalist who had disrupted Eden's Bradford meeting stood at Lewisham North, and got more votes than the Labour majority when Labour captured the seat; Central Office by this time saw the League as the successor of earlier fascist groups and was seeking to ensure that its anti-semitism was exposed in the press. There was a final brief flurry in May and June 1957, when Martell tried to revive the flagging fortunes of the People's League with a direct challenge to the Government. He decided to stand himself in the by-election in the safe Labour seat of East Ham North and cheekily invited the Conservatives to stand down and give him a free run against Labour. Forewarned by a friend within the PLDF (the mole being a right-wing Conservative candidate) that this request would be forthcoming, Central Office prepared not only to reject Martell's suggestion but to put in an intensive effort for the East Ham contest. Labour would anyway hold the seat, but the contest for second place would be more important, since it would be a chance to call Martell's bluff. Equally, if Martell were to come second, he would again become a threat. Things were not assisted when YCs from the local branch defected to Martell, and when the Empire Loyalists unexpectedly backed his campaign; this had now become a trial of strength with the entire right, in most unpromising territory. The Conservative candidate was advised that he should on no account debate with Martell, and canvassers were told to stress Martell's Liberal past for all it was worth in an area where Tory voters were not notably liberal. Attempts were made to get Churchill to take part in the campaign, to neutralise Martell's claim to association with him through the Churchill Birthday Appeal, but he felt that this would be too embarrassing and stood aside. Other Conservatives were less inhibited: when it became clear that Martell's main policy plank would again be a call for repressive trades union legislation, the Minister of Labour, Iain Macleod, volunteered to go down to East Ham personally to brief Conservative canvassers on the Government's reasons for not legislating; this proved to be impracticable, but a detailed written brief was produced for the same purpose, and Robert Carr, Macleod's junior, was lined up to issue a statement about the Government's ongoing review of trades union restrictive practices, to give the impression that action was in contemplation. Worryingly, the canvass, done almost entirely by workers from outside the constituency, found only seventy-three people who said they would vote for Martell, whereas he actually got 2,730 votes; the agent's final report concluded that many people must have lied, as they were

---

[18] Central Office, General Director's file, 'Special Committee on MCA and PLDF', CCO 120/3/1–5, CPA; Central Office file, 'Public Opinion', CCO 4/7/374, CPA; John Ramsden, *The Making of Conservative Party Policy, The Conservative Research Department since 1929* (1980), 182–3; *NCP*, 28 Oct. 1957.

usually to do when candidates of the extreme right stood for election in the years ahead. But the Conservative got 6,567 votes and easily retained second place, while Martell lost his deposit. Since the swing to Labour was below the average for the period, Martell's candidacy may well have harmed the Labour candidate (Reginald Prentice, of all people) more than the Conservative. But, whatever the statistical details, the main result demonstrated that for the time being the Party had beaten off the challenge from the right. The Party's mole had reported Martell as saying in advance that 'if he came a bad third the game was up with the League', and the PLDF was now wound down, its national organisers sacked and its publications discontinued. Martell bided his time, renamed his party and his newspaper, and awaited another opportunity – which duly came when the economy next ran into deep trouble in 1961.[19]

It is hardly surprising that MPs and constituency parties found the first part of 1956 a trying time, and passed on their worries to the Government. Buchan-Hepburn had foreseen this as soon as the Election result was clear in 1955; he wrote to James Stuart that he had been 'saved by the swing, but thank God no need to worry about that for a few more years . . . I wish the papers would stop calling 60 a comfortable majority. I think that it will be the reverse when the boys get tired.' One of his juniors, Martin Redmayne, took the same view, noting that the different type of Tory MP now being selected meant that 'from the whip's eye view we now have an interesting pudding to mix'. In June, Eden had to meet the 1922 Committee several times, and a note on one of the meetings records some unusually plain speaking: 'Sir Ian Fraser asked whether Ministers really believed that we should win through? . . . Major Legge-Bourke asked what the real aim of Conservative trade policy is.' The 1956 Conference agenda included seventeen critical resolutions on Government public relations, blaming the messenger for the quality of the news. There were also fifty-nine resolutions on economic policy, the majority of them calling for cuts in public expenditure, and thirty more calling for lower taxes. Similar feelings led to the only serious parliamentary rebellion of the session, when in May twenty-two Conservatives defied the whip to oppose the extension of the National Coal Board's borrowing powers, which, as Gerald Nabarro remarked in moving the rejection, 'permits a large increase in public expenditure upon an undertaking that has made continual losses'. Again the rhetoric deployed against Labour before 1951 was now turned on its originators. Some of the discontent was articulated in an insulting manner: one resolution, passed by the Purley YCs and leaked to the press by a member, produced a heated debate at the National Union Executive. Sir Nigel Colman, a former chairman, argued that 'I cannot look upon this resolution in any other way than as a vote of no confidence in the Government. This has

---

[19] Central Office, General Director's files, 'Revived Special Committee', CCO 120/3/6, and East Ham and North Lewisham by-elections, CCO 120/2/61 and 63, CPA.

been done in a seat which is so safe that you could not lose it if you tried . . . I cannot think of a resolution that would be more unfortunate. I hope you will wish to express to these people . . . our stern displeasure.' Others, and particularly the YCs and former YCs present, tried to defuse the situation but were slapped down by another member: 'The point remains that the time to criticise the Government is when it is doing well, and there are times to stand fast . . . I do think we should do all what we can to support the Government.' Nevertheless, perhaps because the Executive meeting had to discuss a leak from its own previous meeting to the *Daily Express*, it was decided that it was better to provoke no further comment, for 'it would be a pity to place in the hands of the enemy any propaganda'. If Conservatives assembled in meetings up and down the country were determined to attack the Government, there was little to be done to stifle these expressions of discontent. Eden was not always so philosophical. When Evelyn Emmet MP completed her year as National Union Chairman in March 1956, she asked for a meeting to give Eden her trenchant views on the state of the Party 'if you can spare me half an hour of your valuable time'. Eden's secretary asked the advice of the Chief Whip, noting that 'the Prime Minister cannot see Mrs. Emmet in the near future and does not particularly want to do so at all'. Heath advised Eden to make time, which with a bad grace he had to do, but only fifteen minutes and after a long delay. As Robert Rhodes James concluded, 'it was all understandable, but in political terms very unwise'. Despite the rallying effect of Suez, disaffection remained at the start of 1957; Butler's Saffron Walden constituency decided that it would be pointless to try to recruit new members in view of the middle-class hostility to the Party, and Ruislip noted sadly that the Government's economic policy had cost them a lot of members. Battersea South noted 'with alarm' the Government's 'attitude to the middle classes'.[20]

## Macmillan at the Treasury

Party management could do little to offset the problems of Government unpopularity until the economic news improved, and such a policy success for the Chancellor would be a mixed blessing for the Prime Minister anyway. After the 1956 Budget, Macmillan noted in his diary 'the best press I ever had'. During 1956, irrespective of Suez, the balance of political clout between Eden and Macmillan tilted in Macmillan's favour; as Larry Siedentop put it, Macmillan was increasingly seen 'as the sort of man who was at his

---

[20] Buchan-Hepburn to Stuart, 25 May 1955, Hailes MSS, 2/5; Redmayne to Butler, 25 May 1955, Butler MSS, G28; Note of meeting with 1922 Committee, and Correspondence with Mrs Emmet, Avon MSS, 20/19/60 and 85; Conference agenda for 1956, NUA 2/2/22, CPA; National Union Executive minutes [hereafter NUEC], secretary's notes, 12 Apr. 1956, NUA 4/3/1, CPA; Philip Norton, *Dissension in the House of Commons, 1945–1974* (1975), 124–5; Rhodes James, *Eden*, 413; Saffron Walden CA minutes, 19 Feb. 1957; Ruislip CA minutes, 29 Jan. 1957; Battersea South CA minutes, 29 Mar. 1957.

best only when he commanded or dominated; while Eden was at his best when he served as a deputy'. Macmillan was initially not pleased with his move to the Treasury, and continued to hanker after international aspects of policy even before Suez placed these at the centre of all the Government's efforts. However, he soon found the job absorbing and in intellectual alliance with Edward Boyle, Economic Secretary since April 1955, began to explore unorthodox policies. Bank rate was further raised and credit restricted to combat continuing inflation, but Macmillan's only Budget also levied taxes on profits and introduced premium bonds. In private Macmillan was to be heard questioning the cost of the defence forces and speculating on the merits of a more interventionist economic policy; the economist Andrew Shonfield noted that Boyle and Macmillan were also considering the reimposition of building licensing and the need for higher income tax; all these things demonstrated 'a lack of doctrinal inhibitions'. It took the first of Macmillan's many hints at resignation in 1956 to get some of the budgetary policies past Eden, but the Prime Minister did succeed in vetoing increases in income tax. In presentation, Macmillan was now a master: his speech was unusually witty, but with some of its humour, according to Hugh Massingham, 'in slightly bad taste. It was a typically Macmillan speech.' The introduction of premium bonds, and the fierce debate occasioned by Harold Wilson's dismissal of the innovation as 'a squalid raffle', gave Macmillan another chance to develop the new populist, materialist line that had originated from his period at housing and would lead on to 'never had it so good' in 1957. Indeed he was already telling the Commons in July 1956 that 'the general position of the mass of the British people – and they know it – has been better almost 'than ever within living memory'. It is fair to say then that the most striking phrase of his 1957 speech at Bedford has generally been taken entirely out of its context (which was a warning note rather than one of complacency), but the gist of it had been in his speeches for some time. In November 1956, Macmillan launched his premium bond scheme at a public shindig in Trafalgar Square that also featured the Dagenham Girl Pipers, a diversion from the Suez demonstrations that more often occupied the Square in that month. The public proved supportive of premium bonds, both as opinion polls recorded their views, and as customers, while Macmillan had some harmless fun at Labour's expense by asking what was wrong with the ethics of the new scheme compared with the previous Labour decision to tax football pools. Economic indicators did gradually improve; 1955 turned out to be the only year in this period with a balance of payments deficit and by Summer 1956 the Government had a surplus on it own account too; inflation remained a problem. Macmillan's short time at the Treasury did not allow for structural reforms in the system and methods of economic policy, though these were certainly under consideration. In view of his pro-European position before and after 1956, the surprising omission of Macmillan's Chancellorship was his refusal, or inability, to shift trading policy towards the emerging EEC in its critical year. But Macmillan, for all his pro-European sympathies, was no more ready to contemplate British adherence to an emerging supra-national European entity than Churchill or Eden. Instead he pursued the chimera of a free trade association with the Common Market countries, which would give Britain the same economic benefits but without political commitments. This plan never captured the attention even of the Cabinet, and by the time it came before Parliament in November, Suez dominated all thoughts and, as Macmillan himself wrote, 'there was a certain unreality about the discussions'. These were though precisely the months in which an EEC without Britain became a virtual certainty, something that Macmillan deeply regretted but did little to prevent.[21]

## Suez – the crisis

All issues were anyway subordinated in the second half of 1956 to the difficulties arising from Suez. President Nasser of Egypt had already been singled out by Britain and France as a threat to their interests in the Middle East, before he announced the nationalisation of the Suez Canal in July. Summer and early Autumn were taken up with attempts to secure the reversal of this decision by international pressure on Egypt. Britain and France, though determined to use force if no other means would secure their objectives, became entangled in a secret plot of 'collusion' with Israel. In November their air forces bombed Egypt and their forces landed in the attempt to occupy the Canal Zone before international opinion could become sufficiently aroused to stop them. In the event military action had to be halted just short of its immediate objective and, when the troops were then withdrawn under international pressure, the whole military and political operation came to be seen as a fiasco, and a setback to Britain's position in the world community. Ironically, the failure of Britain's most extensive post-war military action to preserve the imperial heritage may have had a considerable – if unacknowledged – influence on Conservative opinion about the subsequent speed of decolonisation. After 1956, there were few Tories who wanted to stand and fight for the preservation of the colonies.

The weakness of Eden's overall political position may well have contributed to his risky over-reaction against Egypt, and his increasing sense of being beleaguered certainly encouraged the indirect way in which policy was developed on a 'need to know' basis. Nevertheless, there is no doubt that the bulk of the Party agreed with the strong line that the Eden

[21] Alistair Horne, *Macmillan, 1894–1956* (1988), 383, 385–7; Lamb, *Failure*, 55–8, 77–9, 101; NCP, 7 May 1956; Rhodes James, *Eden*, 423; Larry Siedentop, 'Mr. Macmillan and the Edwardian Style', in *The Age of Affluence, 1951–1964*, eds V. Bogdanor and R. Skidelsky (1970), 24; Anthony Sampson, *Macmillan, A Study in Ambiguity* (Harmondsworth, 1968), 113, 115, 118.

Cabinet took in reaction to Egypt's unilateral seizure of the Canal, shared his frustration at delays imposed by American policy procrastination, and backed his readiness to use force when other alternatives seemed to have failed. Inside the Government and within parliament, Eden had to step carefully in order to carry with him those he was to call in his memoirs 'the weak sisters'; those memoirs signally failed to acknowledge that the eventual opposition of these Conservatives arose mainly from their extreme distaste for the ethics of his policy, rather than from any inherent weakness or lack of consistency on their part, but then his memoirs still refused to acknowledge the secret 'collusion' with Israel that was the chief ground of their dissent. For the bulk of the parliamentary party and practically the whole Party outside, there was loyal support for the decision to invade, outrage that others should condemn it while British troops were under fire, and a refusal to believe in charges of duplicity once Eden had denied them. For this overwhelming majority of the Party, the problem was not the bombing and invasion of Egypt but the British capitulation to American and United Nations pressure shortly afterwards, and the abandonment of the plan when it seemed so near to success. Opinion polls give an equivocal view of the British public's overall view of the crisis, but there is no doubt that the Conservative-voting section of it backed the Government at least until after its policy had failed. At that time, a by-election at Chester produced a fairly good result for the Government and certainly disproved any theory that its policy in Egypt had been repudiated by the electorate. After the handover of the Canal Zone to United Nations troops though, Party and public support seeped away as it was increasingly understood that the affair had been a major British humiliation. To misquote Lady Macbeth, it was the failed attempt that confounded Eden, not the deed. Once diplomatic solutions were failing to deliver a triumph, not to have tried a more risky option would have sealed his fate just as surely. Nor was there any doubt that it was Eden who was in charge of foreign policy, a point not very subtly made by the 1922 Committee's minute for a meeting on 13 September: 'The Prime Minister replied to the more important points, before leaving the Foreign Secretary to reply to the remaining matters.'[22]

Loyalties were seriously strained in the highly charged atmosphere that prevailed through Autumn 1956. Butler recalled a meeting in the Treasury building, from which he could constantly hear 'the roars of the crowd from Trafalgar Square where Nye Bevan was addressing an anti-Suez demonstration'. A member of the Executive of the 1922, returning to London in November after a period abroad, said that rejoining the Commons 'was rather like going on board a steamer at the end of a very rough crossing. There was a slight smell of sickness in the Smoking Room and everyone looked green'. Peter Rawlinson, newly elected in 1955, found the mood of

[22] Eden, *The Reckoning*, 557; 1922 Committee minutes [hereafter 1922 Cttee.] 13 Sept. 1956.

the Commons quite a baptism of fire, and one that left neither opportunity nor inclination to question Eden's policy:

> In few other national assemblies could the leader of the nation be confronted daily, and for weeks on end, by nearly three hundred shouting and jeering political opponents . . . It is a little macabre to write that one had enjoyed it . . . For a government backbencher it was rather like being a spectator at a particularly bloody prize fight, in which one's own man was often on the ropes, sometimes driven to the floor, but somehow always climbing back on to his feet to carry on the fight . . . To witness at close hand the venom directed at that tall figure standing at the dispatch box, outwardly debonair but inwardly wracked with illness and anxiety, was certainly not an agreeable spectacle. Indeed it was terrible. But it was also very exciting . . . The hooligans . . . had taken over. It was touch and go lest the sitting turned into a major brawl . . . It was impossible for anyone to achieve any sense of detachment or to weigh up arguments in debate. We were all naked partisans.

Willie Whitelaw, also a freshman in this Parliament, recalled not just the brutal mood on the floor of the House, but 'highly charged meetings of the 1922 Committee'.[23]

Almost from the start, the Party debates were hi-jacked by members of the Suez Group with demands for action that limited Eden's room for manoeuvre. Julian Amery, recalling the 1954 decisions as the mistake which had caused the present crisis, nevertheless detected 'a gleaming opportunity . . . to re-establish British influence in the Middle East on a firm and permanent foundation'. At the Party Conference in October, the official resolution calling on the Government to pursue 'a just solution' was regarded by such men as far too feeble; late-night pressure was applied to ensure that a fierce amendment in the names of Charles Waterhouse and Angus Maude was called; it was duly passed with only a single vote against, that of William Yates MP. In the debate, Waterhouse told the Conference that 'at this very moment Britain is at a vital cross-roads in her history', while Amery urged that Britain must be free 'to use any and every measure that is necessary to achieve our ends'; Lord Hinchingbrooke had told his constituents that he favoured 'a little bit of gunboat diplomacy'. Hawks within the Government were hardly less outspoken. Butler's memoirs are at their most felicitous when he records Macmillan returning as Foreign Secretary from Geneva late in 1955 'with the happy comment: "There ain't gonna be no war." This did not turn out to be an entirely accurate prophecy nor, in his own political deportment, a lasting mood.' Although Macmillan had better contacts within the American Government than anyone else in Eden's Cabinet and ought therefore to have been the most aware of the perils of ignoring warnings from Washington, to which the Chancellor should anyway have been the most sensitive, given

---

[23]  Butler, *Art of the Possible*, 193; Philip Goodhart, *The 1922, The Story of the 1922 Committee* (1973), 175; Peter Rawlinson, *A Price Too High, An Autobiography* (1989), 68–70; William Whitelaw, *The Whitelaw Memoirs* (1989), 42.

the vulnerability of sterling, he talked in the most apocalyptic way of the need to take action to arrest the terminal decline of British power and threatened to resign if strong action was not taken. In a generation imbued with the absolute conviction that the Second World War, which had blighted so many lives, had been caused by the refusal of the appeasers to take firm action early enough, such a stance as Macmillan's could only enhance his prestige in the Party – whatever the outcome.[24]

By comparison, although his private views were as outspoken as Macmillan's and for much the same reason, Eden was bound to appear indecisive until the final invasion took place, for he could neither dissociate himself from diplomatic efforts while they were being followed nor draw attention to secret military preparations. So secret were these that when Lord Hailsham took over as First Lord of the Admiralty in September he did not know that the Navy was planning a war against Egypt. When his insistent demands for information ensured that he was finally briefed by a planning officer on his own staff, he was aghast; 'I heard him out and then asked one question. "What do you think of it?", I said. "I think it is madness," was his reply. "So," said I, "do I," and I took steps to see my view was passed on to the right quarters.' Shortly afterwards Hailsham found himself in charge of the Navy at war and having to work to prevent the First Sea Lord, Mountbatten, from resigning. The Minister of Defence, Monckton, also had grave doubts, and was permitted to leave his post and become Paymaster General, so as not to have to take political charge of the War he disapproved of, but confining disagreement to the privacy of the Cabinet. Monckton's own record of events suggests that he was the only Cabinet minister who advised formally against the invasion, 'though it was plain that Mr. Butler had doubts and I knew that Mr. Heathcoat Amory was troubled about it'. Buchan-Hepburn's note on the Cabinet of 23 October, a few days before the vital vote to commit troops, lists Stuart, Heathcoat Amory, Butler, Monckton and himself as all being against using force while negotiation was still possible, with Lloyd, Macleod and Selkirk all in a middle position; only eleven out of eighteen present were unequivocally with Eden, while Buchan-Hepburn recorded that his own remarks compared the possible position of Britain in Egypt with Japan before Pearl Harbor, risking an 'immense moral disadvantage' by making an unnecessary attack. On these debates, the recollections of those involved have differed. Heathcoat Amory, for example, quoted by others as well as by Monckton and Buchan-Hepburn as a doubter, actually telegraphed his constituency association to tell them to disbelieve such rumours, for he both supported the invasion of Egypt and accepted full collective responsibility for it, a deliberate statement of loyalty when the troops went in. On the other side, there are those who after the event claimed, or had claimed for them,

[24] Lindsay and Harrington, *Conservative Party*, 189; Churchill, *Eden*, 260–1; Butler, *Art of the Possible*, 184; Sampson, *Macmillan*, 119–22.

that they opposed the invasion though they gave no contemporary sign of dissent. Boyd-Carpenter and Watkinson were both talked out of resignation by Monckton, but held posts in which they were not involved in the War. Despite rumours to the contrary and definite reservations about the policy, Macleod seems not to have seriously considered resigning, though his biographer speculated that he might have done so if there had been a lead given by Butler. All this suggests that there was a bigger reservoir of dissent in the Government than was indicated by Monckton's covert resignation or by the two junior ministers who actually left the Government, Anthony Nutting and Edward Boyle. Nutting's departure was especially resented by Eden, for he had been hand-picked by Eden himself to occupy the second position at the Foreign Office, from which his resignation was anyway particularly damaging. As Nutting had been one of the first leaders of the YC movement and had gone on to chair the National Union Executive, he also had quite a standing in the Party. Nutting's original resignation letter would have made collusion public in 1956; he was sent for by Macmillan and persuaded not to issue it, since it 'could easily bring down the Government. You have been proved right and we have been proved wrong.' He hinted that a sensible attitude by Nutting now would allow him to return to office later. In the published letter, Nutting was more circumspect, stopping short of revealing undesirable secrets about Government policy until his memoirs came out in 1967; Boyle on the other hand wrote with care, but indicated that he 'felt bound to associate myself with that body of opinion which deeply deplores what has been done'. An ex-Minister who could have caused acute embarrassment was the former Attorney-General, Sir Lionel Heald, who was contemplating putting down an explosive motion 'relating to the position of the Law Officers in the Government's Egyptian policy', but seems to have been persuaded not to do so by Kilmuir.[25]

On the backbenches, the breadth of dissent over the Suez invasion was rather greater, but was limited by the refusal of Butler to give the dissenters a clear lead and by the effective whipping organised by Heath. Nigel Nicolson believed that there were between thirty and forty Tory MPs who like him opposed the invasion of Egypt, but rather fewer ever came out into the open, mainly because their constituencies did not just back Eden but supported him very strongly indeed; twenty-four Conservative MPs on this wing of the Party did denounce the invasion policy by signing an Early Day Motion on 28 November, but few of these took any other action, and by then the real crisis was over anyway. The eight who went as far as abstaining on a

---

[25] Lord Hailsham, *A Sparrow's Flight, Memoirs* (1990), 285, 288, 290; Lord Birkenhead, *Walter Monckton* (1969), 308; Buchan-Hepburn note, 23 Oct. 1956, Hailes MSS 4/1; W. Gore Allen, *The Reluctant Politician, Derick Heathcoat Amory* (1958), 167; Boyd-Carpenter, *Way of Life*, 127; Harold Watkinson, *Turning Points, A Record of Our Times* (Salisbury, 1986), 63; Nigel Fisher, *Iain Macleod* (1973), 116–7; Churchill, *Eden*, 306; Lamb, *Failure*, 279; Lord Chancellor's office to Kilmuir, Nov. 1956, Kilmuir MSS, 6/9.

whipped vote – on 8 November, the day after the ceasefire, for there were no rebels against the whip until the fighting was over – were Nicolson, Nutting, Boyle, Boothby, Yates, J.J. Astor, Sir Frank Medlicott, and Cyril Banks, but these were never an organised group, and were not even those most urgently trying to change Government policy before 7 November (these were Heald and Sir Alexander Spearman). William Yates went so far as to raise in the House the rumours of collusion with Israel, and asked the Speaker if it would be proper to bring the Government down on these grounds, but his views tended to be undercut by his well-known pro-Arab sympathies. Macmillan, in his diary, was contemptuous of these anti-invasion rebels, noting in September that they were 'mostly sons of "Municheers" – like Richard Wood' (whose father Halifax added some credence to this view by expressing his own guarded dissent in the Lords); Heald, Elliot and Boothby, Macmillan regarded as 'the waverers'. Heath also seems to have been 'profoundly troubled' by the Government's policy, to quote Rhodes James; part of his success as Chief Whip lay in not hiding those views when talking to anti-invasion dissidents, but at the same time appealing to their loyalties to the Government and the army in an extreme crisis. He also cannily reminded dissenters like Keith Joseph and Peter Kirk that if they went too far and got themselves deselected by their constituencies, they would simply leave the right in charge of the Party, something that he wanted as little as they did. Lord Kilmuir felt that 'it was the sort of situation where only the most tender handling was possible; any attempt to dictate to Members, as some Chief Whips of my experience would have done, would have been absolutely disastrous. While never showing weakness or forgetting his responsibilities to the Government, Heath calmly and gently shepherded the Party through a crisis that might have broken it.' However, the position of the rebels was really wrecked from outside when, in a television address on Suez on 4 November, Hugh Gaitskell made a public appeal to them to join forces with Labour and bring Eden down. Richard Crossman at once saw that 'if any Tory MP had ever dreamt of abstaining on the vote on Monday [5 November], Hugh's appeal would have finally dissuaded him'. Spearman then rang Crossman to ask him to persuade his leader to lay off: 'It's Country before Party, Dick. I beg you to stop the "Eden must go" campaign, since this will make it impossible to get rid of him.' On the same day, Harrow Conservatives passed a motion that was as bitterly hostile to Gaitskell as it was supportive of Eden, and the Monmouth Tories deplored 'the attitude of the Socialist Party in placing party before country' (though putting on record too their 'admiration of the whole-hearted cooperation of our French allies'); St Marylebone was just one of many that did the same over the next few days, while Hampstead Tories convened a special meeting to deplore the 'objectionable broadcast' of the area's most famous political resident. Crossman and Spearman agreed to keep in touch and act as liaison between the anti-invasion forces in both parties, but the decision to stop the fighting was taken on the following day anyway. The anti-invasion rebels now became valuable supporters of the Government's new policy, but that did not help them in their constituencies, where those whose rebellion had come into the open came under heavy pressure.[26]

These anti-invasion rebels mattered so much only because they were numerically sufficient to bring down the Government, had they been prepared to do so, and because of the theoretical possibility that Butler's resignation would both increase their determination and add significantly to their numbers. Butler's exact views on Suez were not easy to define at the time and have not become much clearer since; Randolph Churchill both recorded his own hostile view that 'the state of Mr. Butler's conscience is hard to fathom' and cited the remarkable fact that Butler asked a couple of complete strangers at a dinner party shortly after the cease-fire, 'Do you think I ought to have resigned over Suez?' Eden, perhaps suspecting that Butler would be hard to keep on board if force became the preferred policy, had not placed him on the Cabinet's Egypt Committee, and Butler had no departmental responsibility that required that he be kept informed; Butler therefore had an opportunity to keep his hands clean and avoid direct responsibility, but as deputy Prime Minister he insisted on being kept up to date, sometimes attended the Egypt Committee anyway and was certainly well enough informed by the crucial time for making decisions. He seems to have felt that he could act as a restraining opinion against the use of force, as on occasion he did, but the momentum of planning (which he had known about, and could not now denounce), and the escalation of events, then placed him in a tricky position. At the end of October he could only resign, and probably bring down the Government, or go along with the majority view that an invasion should now go ahead. He did though continue to express his doubts in some unlikely and unsuitable quarters, as he did, for example, by speculating on his possible resignation to the surprised visiting Prime Minister of Norway; it was on Butler that Gaitskell's hopes of bringing down the Government were really pinned. Nigel Nicolson thought that Butler 'played a double game, which lost him a lot of backing. He would speak up for the Government in the House, and then go into the Smoking Room and say how terrible it was. He thought it would get him support; in fact it did the reverse.' Eden's press secretary, who *did* resign over Suez, exclaimed to his diary at the end of the crisis, 'The way Rab has trimmed and turned!' Such statements were perhaps only unfair in underestimating the tremendous conflict of loyalties that Butler had to resolve in October and November 1956. As a former

26 Thompson, *Day Before Yesterday*, 141; Rhodes James, *Eden*, 553, 558; Lindsay and Harrington, *Conservative Party*, 191; R.J. Jackson, *Rebels and Whips: Dissension, Discipline and Cohesion in British Political Parties since 1945* (1968), 146–8; Kilmuir, *Memoirs*, 281; Campbell, *Heath*, 94; Janet Morgan (ed.), *The Backbench Diaries of Richard Crossman* (1981), 542–3; Harrow West CA minutes, 5 Nov. 1956; Monmouth CA minutes, 5 Nov. 1956; St Marylebone CA minutes, 9 Nov. 1956; Hampstead CA minutes, 9 Nov. 1956.

'appeaser', he was suspect to many in the Party: any opposition to the use of force from him would be dismissed simply as a reversion to type, rather than as a matter of ethics or judgement. He had both a deep loyalty to the Party, which seemed to be breaking up before his eyes, and a reasonable ambition to lead it when Eden's apparently catastrophic period came to an end, probably soon. It was hard to see where loyalty should lead, and harder still to reconcile it with conscience; for Butler, as for the backbench rebels, Gaitskell's television appeal finally removed any room for manoeuvre, though persistent rumours did speak of Butler eventually threatening to resign so as to ensure that the UN ceasefire was accepted; by then such threats would not need to have been openly articulated, but nor were they particularly needed to change the Cabinet's mind. The ambivalence of Butler's position – formally supporting Eden while indiscreetly denouncing his policy in the semi-public, and letting the world know that he was thinking of quitting but not actually doing so – did him great harm. It was interpreted not as the consequence of a tortured conscience but as the indecision of a man who could not make up his mind, and as disloyalty to a leader when he most needed support. Reginald Maudling, a long-term supporter of Butler in Conservative politics, concluded sadly that,

> Suez destroyed Rab's chances of ever becoming Prime Minister. At the time he gave the impression that he was lifting his skirt to avoid the dirt. The feeling in the party was that if he would not take responsibility we could not have him as leader. Afterwards Rab was hounded for that very reason, by what I call the 'blue blood and thunder' group, and one or two of them did their best to stop Rab becoming Eden's successor.

Chris Patten, another admirer of Butler, recently concluded that Butler's political weakness (purely from the viewpoint of getting to be Leader) was that 'Rab, to his credit, lacked the effrontery so attractive to partisans, especially when it is drenched from time to time in a shower of gravitas. And – fatal flaws – he possessed both a sense of humour and a sense of the ridiculous.' In an approaching contest with Macmillan, the lack of the 'effrontery' to be uninhibitedly partisan, and the ability to see both sides of any question, was indeed to be a fatal flaw.[27]

The blue blood and thunder Tories were indeed in their element during the Suez invasion, sensing that for once the Party was with them, and that the public was behind them too. The invasion produced an avalanche of letters and telegrams pledging support for the Government and its policy. Those received at Central and Area Offices, reinforced by the Party correspondence sent over from Number Ten, required large secretarial efforts to send even

[27] Churchill, Eden, 306–7; Thompson, Day Before Yesterday, 127; Howard, RAB, 233, 237; Sparrow, Rab, 132; Horne, Macmillan, 457; Reginald Maudling, Memoirs (1978), 54; Chris Patten, 'R.A. Butler – What We Missed', unpublished Inaugural R.A. Butler Lecture, delivered 25 May 1994.

standard replies. Already by 5 November, the Prime Minister's office had more than 200 telegrams of support from the Party. By the end of the crisis, support had been pledged by all fourteen Area organisations, 467 constituency associations, almost a thousand main and YC branches, 141 Conservative clubs, and nearly a hundred miscellaneous Party groups; North Cornwall's congratulations to the Prime Minister for his 'courageous and far-sighted action in the Middle East' was a typical form of words. Bath considered a motion which welcomed Eden's courage and 'congratulate[d] the Prime Minister on his determination to uphold the rule of law'; an alternative motion calling for the UN to be more involved was defeated, and the original proposal then carried with only one dissentient, but with the reference to the 'rule of law' replaced by a vaguer claim to have 'prevent[ed] the spread of war'; two guineas were voted to cable this resolution to Eden, any unspent balance to go to the Hungarian refugee fund – a very rare reference in Conservative debates to the fact that a second, quite separate, international crisis was raging alongside Suez. The South East Area Council passed a resolution backing Eden and deploring the 'anti-British attitude of the socialists' but, after the intervention of Tufton Beamish MP, it was decided to delete a reference to 'the complete lack of understanding of our position displayed by the government of the United States' as being unhelpful to the Government; Selwyn Lloyd's own constituency supporters in the Wirral contented themselves with expressing their 'disappointment' at American policy, but backed Eden and Lloyd to the hilt. There is no evidence whatsoever of resolutions critical of Eden or his policy from any Party organisation, while local records frequently indicate that supportive resolutions were unanimous and that they were carried with acclamation. The letters and telegrams from individuals were more mixed, since only eighty-eight were in support of Government policy out of 177 received; but not much should be read into this, for the mass of Conservative activists, having had their views passed on in official resolutions, would have seen no need to write personally. The official resolutions were as likely to denounce those who opposed Eden's policy – by implication, Conservative as well as Labour opponents – as they were to support the invasion. Likewise, even if there were as many as forty dissenters on the backbenches and half a dozen dissenting ministers, that still meant that nearly 300 Conservative MPs were supportive of Eden, and the tone of many of their speeches was as outspoken as their constituents' resolutions. This was the mood put to the test in the Chester by-election on 15 November, where, as the National Union's General Purposes Committee concluded, 'Suez greatly overshadowed all other issues'. Back in July, Poole had suggested that a November poll would be best, but added that he could not foresee the effect on the result of 'recent events in Egypt'. In August–September, Central Office asked Selwyn Lloyd to speak in the campaign since he was a neigbouring MP, but he refused to go. When canvassing began, it was reported that one issue alone was on the voters' minds, but reported too that the invasion had hardened the Tory vote. The Central Office final prediction was a majority of about 4,000, and Eden was advised that anything above or below that would demonstrate the effect of the international crisis; in the event the pro-invasion Tory candidate won by 6,348 votes and announced that 'this is a great victory for our Prime Minister, Sir Anthony Eden, and I am proud to be the recipient of such a vote of confidence in his action over Suez'. This was pardonably exaggerated, for there had been a swing to Labour of 4.8 per cent, but that was low for 1956; in fact the share of the vote for all three parties candidates was almost exactly what it had been in the same constituency back in 1950, suggesting a far better result than those at Taunton or Tonbridge, but something short of a full endorsement of the Government. Crucially though, the Tory vote had remained loyal; it was the large Tory vote and high turnout at Chester that demonstrated that there had been less middle-class abstention than earlier in the year – and less than there was to be in 1957. The Central Office general survey of public opinion reached similar conclusions.[28]

The depth of feeling over Suez caused strains in normal political mechanisms too. Convinced that the press were inveterately hostile, Eden determined to plead his case before the public on television where he was a master of the medium. His Suez broadcast though, prepared in a hurry and with the solo performer nervous and irritable, was not a success. He became convinced that 'those Communists' at the BBC had deliberately shone lights in his eyes to put him off. When the BBC allowed Gaitskell the right of reply to one of his broadcasts, Eden and many Conservative MPs reacted with outrage, especially when Gaitskell used his air time to undermine the Government during a war. Finally, the sheer urgency and extremity of the crisis persuaded the BBC and the new ITN to disregard the fourteen-day rule. The Attorney-General had recently given a weighty legal opinion in favour of the fourteen-day rule, but the Government's bluff was now called, and television would never again be excluded from contemporary politics. Since the BBC reported Labour attacks on the Suez policy, such as Jim Callaghan's description of the Government as 'a menace to the British people and the peace of the world', and Egyptian radio then cited these statements to show that Britain was not united, Conservatives became very angry indeed. The Party mechanisms were also strained. The speed with which events developed made it difficult to issue briefs that were up to date, and the secrecy with which the Government conducted policy ensured that those writing the briefs were not in the know anyway. The CRD's *Notes on Current Politics* covered Suez in great detail in four issues,

28  Central Office file, 'Summary of letters on Suez', CCO 4/7/131, CPA; National Union General Purposes Committee papers, NUA 5/2/1/32, CPA; Central Office, General Director's file, Chester by-election, CCO 120/2/51, CPA; Central Office file, 'Public opinion', CCO 4/7/375, CPA; North Cornwall CA minutes, 6 Nov. 1956; Bath CA minutes, 7 Nov. 1956; South East Area Council, 1 Dec. 1956; Wirral CA minutes, 6 Dec. 1956.

between 17 September and 28 November but there was no issue while the fighting was on. The result was that explanation of the policy had to be left mainly to Government rather than Party machinery; how badly this worked may be seen in the fact that Eden's press secretary resigned in the middle of the crisis because of the strain of being an intermediary between an increasingly suspicious press and a jealously secretive master, and because he knew enough of the truth strongly to disapprove of Eden's policy. None of this seemed to make much difference, for the tribal feelings that Peter Rawlinson described above produced an impressive rallying of support; the first opinion poll after the military action began found that 68 per cent of Conservatives backed Eden's policy, but only 16 per cent of Labour voters; by mid–November, this had hardened even further to 89 per cent of Conservatives backing the Government and only 2 per cent against; for the first time in twelve months a poll showed the Conservatives ahead of Labour.[29]

## Suez – the aftermath

Overwhelming Tory support therefore remained a constant in the crisis, but this in itself caused a new problem when Government policy had to be reversed and military action discontinued: James Stuart's autobiography tells us that 'I did not object to our going IN: what I did object to was our coming OUT. I had to tell the PM of this privately and I did so in vigorous terms.' Political pressure at the United Nations and through the Commonwealth demonstrated the isolation of Britain and France even from regular friends and allies, but it was America's refusal to help prop up sterling internationally and the threat of a UN oil embargo that really put the Cabinet under strain. Macmillan now had to advise acceptance of the UN ceasefire, and to threaten that he would resign if the Cabinet did not agree; this provided the basis for Wilson's jibe that Macmillan had been 'first in and first out' over Suez. A defence of Macmillan's actions could be made, based in part on the official advice he was receiving, but as Alistair Horne put it, whatever the Treasury advice, 'ultimately, it was he who was the Minister and he was responsible'. In reaching its decision, the Cabinet was aware that it would be difficult to sustain its position in the Commons if it refused to stop the fighting when the original objective had ostensibly been achieved, but also knew that many Conservative MPs would be deeply suspicious of handing the Suez Canal over to the United Nations. Initially, the Government sought to hail the ceasefire as a success for its policy, and the 1922 Committee gave Lloyd an ovation. For about a fortnight relative calm prevailed and the more sensible members of the 1922 rediscovered their appetite for moderation. Walter Elliot helped

---

[29] Michael Cockerell, *Live from Number Ten, The Inside Story of Prime Ministers and Television* (1988), 45–50; *NCP*, 22 Oct. 1956; Ramsden, *Conservative Party Policy*, 185; Rhodes James, *Eden*, 556–7.

to argue the case that once negotiations had re-started, it would be foolish to take further unilateral action; among younger Members, Peter Rawlinson issued an appeal for loyalty to the leadership now that the Party had pulled back from the very brink of self-destruction: 'these platitudes caused a few grey heads to nod and the Whip to make a note'. In the Commons on 12 November, Macmillan issued an uncompromising defence of the invasion policy: 'All my [Treasury] interests would have been to follow what we used to call appeasement . . . Why have I not followed that? I tell the House frankly and sincerely. It is because I have seen it all happen before.' It is not perhaps entirely fanciful to think that Macmillan's readiness to use this argument even after he at least knew that the policy had failed was a deliberate attempt to keep Butler on the defensive.[30]

The ceasefire was only the beginning of the withdrawal process, each step of which had to be painfully defended to the Party, but this task did not fall to the Prime Minister. Eden's already precarious health had given way under the strain of recent events and on 19 October his doctors finally insisted that he must take a complete rest in a warmer climate; on 23 November, he flew to the West Indies, leaving Butler in charge of the Government as acting Prime Minister (though this had to be deduced, since there was no official announcement of the fact). Butler's memoirs list his melancholy inheritance as 'withdrawing the troops, re-establishing the pound, salvaging our relations with the US and the UN, and bearing the brunt of the criticism from private members, constituency parties and the general public'. Macmillan, like Eden worked up to a high pitch of nervous strain, exploded with anger when told that Eden would be abroad for a prolonged period, leaving others to sort out the problems of the Middle East. The Party reacted with incomprehension and the press was again hostile; Randolph Churchill went so far as to say that the only historical parallel for the British troops now abandoned in Egypt was the German army at Stalingrad, 'but even Hitler did not winter in Jamaica'. Such polemics did terminal damage to Eden's reputation. An association officer from Maidstone wrote in to ask for advice on how to justify 'the Prime Minister's "holiday" in Jamaica at the height of the crisis . . . On all sides one hears it said "Churchill would never have done such a thing".' Staunch Conservatives in the constituencies were said to be extremely upset by Eden's apparent abandonment of the helm at the height of the storm. It was hard to persuade such critics that Eden really was ill – unless he were to prove it by resigning.[31]

Over the next three weeks, a triumvirate of Butler, Macmillan and Heath effectively kept the show on the road, but the public responsibility for its

---

30  James Stuart, *Within the Fringe* (1967), 176; Horne, *Macmillan*, 443; Rhodes James, *Eden*, 573–4; Goodhart, *The 1922*, 173–4; Whitelaw, *Memoirs*, 42–3; Colin Coote, *A Companion of Honour, The Story of Walter Elliot* (1965), 168; Rawlinson, *Price Too High*, 71.

31  Rhodes James, *Eden*, 582–3; Sampson, *Macmillan*, 125; Butler, *Art of the Possible*, 194; Central Office file, 'Criticism of Leaders', CCO 4/7/179, CPA.

actions had to be taken by Butler; in addition to other burdens he had to persuade colleagues not to quit, notably James Stuart whose hostility to Eden was now unlimited; he wrote to Butler on 13 December, after several meetings and exchanges of letters, that 'my confidence and respect for the man have evaporated totally . . . I couldn't shake hands with him and don't want to be in the same room with him'; engagements in Scotland provided a legitimate reason for Stuart's absence from London when Eden returned, but he still intended to resign after a decent interval. Butler, Heath and Macmillan all showed political skills of a high order, but the Government was on a tightrope; writing to Eden on 28 November, Butler predicted that anywhere up to 150 MPs might sign an anti-American motion; 'we think we can hold the Party up to the debate to be held next week . . . It would be an unwise man who said more yet. The colleagues are united and Ted and the whips in good heart.'[32]

Butler continued though to mix deftness with lack of judgement in off-the-record conversations; the worst of these was a dinner with the right-wing Progress Trust, at which he revealed far too much of the Cabinet's inner secrets of the past few weeks, and hinted at an unconditional withdrawal from the Canal Zone, before any announcement had been made. In his memoirs he wrote that 'wherever I moved in the weeks that followed, I felt the Party knives sticking into my innocent back'. Butler could reasonably claim that in this period there was progress in restoring the political situation, and that his own contacts in the US Treasury were as valuable as Macmillan's in repairing recent damage to relations, but nothing could disguise the basic facts: once negotiations started, it became clear that Britain's bargaining strength was non-existent, that America was insisting on terms that would be humiliating, and that the Cabinet would have to swallow its pride and agree. British isolation was made very clear when on 23 November the UN General Assembly voted by sixty-three votes to five to condemn the Anglo–French action at Suez. The key figure in securing the withdrawal from Suez that the UN was demanding was Macmillan, now concerned about the deteriorating position of British trade and the value of sterling if the UN should impose oil sanctions as threatened. The Cabinet accepted the Chancellor's third ultimatum, and Butler skilfully manoeuvred the decision past Eden, who was still trying to control policy from Jamaica but who had lost touch with the realities of the situation since his withdrawal from London. It was probably also Macmillan who persuaded the Foreign Secretary Lloyd not to resign now that his policy lay in ruins, a resignation that would have done serious damage to the attempt to restore credibility. Nevertheless, the 1922 Committee cut up very rough when the direction of policy became clear and there were threats of a major rebellion from the right. When Lloyd announced the unconditional

[32]  Stuart to Butler, various dates in Nov. and Dec. 1956, and Butler to Eden, 28 Nov. 1956, Butler MSS, G46.

withdrawal of British troops to the Commons on 7 December, he was coldly received from his own side, and there seemed again to be the prospect of a rebellion big enough to bring down the Government. Brendan Bracken, who had been amazed by the vitality of Eden's policy during the invasion, reported on 22 November that between thirty and fifty MPs said they would refuse to back 'a scurry from Suez', but he added that 'my experience of the Tories leads me to believe that they are inclined to talk a lot of hot air in committee rooms upstairs, and to obey the whips when they are shepherded into the lobbies. I shall be surprised if more than 10 or 15 Tories abstain, and the figure may be less'. The damage was again limited by shrewd work in the Chief Whip's office; this time Heath apparently indulged in more traditional strong-arm tactics than he had used on the left-wingers a few weeks earlier. He was assisted in this by the fact that it was now too late to change Government policy; and after Gaitskell's behaviour over Suez, few Tory MPs wanted to risk changing the Government. At first eighty-six MPs had signed a letter of protest, but these were whittled down by Heath to the point where the number of abstentions would make the strength of their feelings clear, but without either bringing down the Government or doing further damage to the pound. The final number of abstentions was fifteen, and again no Tory MPs voted against the Government; with an overall majority of fifty-two in the vote, the parliamentary crisis had been weathered.[33]

The subsequent fates of the Suez rebels clearly indicates on which side of the divide the Party activists came down. All eight anti-invasion rebels came under pressure from their local parties and four were deselected, never to be Conservative candidates again. Central Office applied mild pressure against these witch hunts, and came near to saving at least Nigel Nicolson who, with the support of the Party Chairman, persuaded his local party at Bournemouth to put the issue to the whole membership in a referendum, only to lose the vote in 1958 by a mere ninety-one out of 7,433 votes cast. After this he gave up the fight, but Nicolson had antagonised his local supporters over a whole range of issues, including his opposition to capital punishment, and his Suez abstention was the pretext rather than the sole cause of his removal. Anthony Nutting was dropped by the Melton Conservatives rather more unceremoniously, with the chairman and president both threatening to resign (in support of the Government) if Nutting did not stand down; they were backed by the association at a general meeting in which there was 'not one single word of support for Mr. Nutting nor one single regret expressed at his departure' (to quote the Area Agent); personal issues now became entangled with the policy dispute, and he resigned from the House at once to limit the damage; the Party narrowly held the seat at the by-election. Banks and Medlicott also had wider grounds of disagreement with their local

33  Campbell, *Heath*, 95–6; Lamb, *Failure*, 285, 293; Howard, *RAB*, 238; Rhodes James, *Eden*, 584, 587–90; Cockett, *My Dear Max*, 197–9.

associations, and neither stood for re-election in 1959. On the other hand, four of the rebels did survive, if sometimes with great difficulties – and Yates was to be dropped as candidate for The Wrekin after disagreements over the 1967 Arab–Israeli War that must have re-awakened memories of 1956. Robert Boothby, who had represented East Aberdeenshire since 1924, was almost ousted in the battle that followed his Suez abstention, and was saved only by the staunch support of his association's chairman. Boyle, alone of the eight, went on to a successful political career, and only because the patronage of Macmillan was behind him; he rejoined the Government only nine weeks after he had left it, went back to the Treasury in 1959 and joined the Cabinet in 1962. Survival, but not prosperity, was the fate the rebels on the other side. Although several maintained their public opposition to the further stages of withdrawal from Suez throughout the first half of 1957, and eight resigned the whip in May to indicate their deep objection to Government policy, few got into serious trouble with their constituencies and none were deselected; but only Maude reached the top, and that by a circuitious route that took twenty years and wasted the best years of his political life. Maude told his South Ealing supporters that 'if Nasser is allowed to triumph on the Canal while we go crawling to the Americans for oil, then the Conservative Party under its present leadership is no place for me or for some of my colleagues'; he received a vote of confidence from his constituency executive by thirty-six votes to two. The constituency chairman in Liverpool Garston thought that Victor Raikes was backed by 95 per cent of the local members. Although only five of the eight stood as Conservative candidates in 1959, this owed more to the others' disappointment with the Party than vice versa; three of the eight served as chairmen of the Monday Club when it emerged in the 1960s, which shows a continuation of oppositional politics rather than a return to the Party fold. Angus Maude even survived a rash decision to resign his seat and take up a job in Australia in 1958, being successively adopted for two good Tory constituencies after he returned. In Monmouth, where the sitting Member was Peter Thorneycroft, an association that had been strongly supportive of Eden in September, was critical of the policy pursued after the end of the fighting; in July 1957, the association resolved that, 'having regard to the strong feeling of dissatisfaction and humiliation which persists concerning Suez, and to the failure to explain the causes for our withdrawal, and furthermore our failure to support the French Government at the United Nations General Assembly, suggests that H.M. Government should issue a full explanation of the course being pursued without delay'.[34]

---

[34] Peter Paterson, *The Selectorate* (1967), 130; Central Office, Chairman's file, Chief Whip, CCO 20/1/5, CPA; Jackson, *Rebels and Whips*, 149–51, 281–9; Lindsay and Harrington, *Conservative Party*, 190; Central Office, General Director's file, Melton by-election, CCO 120/2/53; Robert Rhodes James, *Bob Boothby, A Portrait* (1991), 384; Morgan, *Crossman Diaries*, 551; Stenton and Lees, *Who's Who of MPs*, 251; Central Office, General Director's file, Garston by-election, CCO 120/2/65, CPA; Monmouth CA minutes, 27 July 1957.

Many Conservatives may well have shared such feelings, but few expressed them, and apart from the sixteen rebel MPs, the Suez crisis left remarkably few scars on the Party, largely because of the way in which it was handled tactically when the dust began to settle. When Selwyn Lloyd claimed in the Commons on 7 December that, despite Britain's withdrawal of troops, it had all been a great success, Nye Bevan ironically sympathised with him for 'having to sound the bugle of advance to cover his retreat', but this was to be precisely the tactic that limited the damage. Just before he left for Jamaica, Eden had addressed a YC rally and had not been at all well received in the part of his speech in which he attempted a detailed justification of his recent actions, but he then received an ovation that took him by surprise when he asserted that, 'we make no apology and shall make no apology for the action that we and our French Allies took together'. Despite his earlier hesitations, Butler also now adopted a defiant tone on public occasions, and as Prime Minister Macmillan was to do so to such effect that Harold Wilson was forced to remark admiringly of him, that 'the man's a genius. He's holding up the banner of Suez for the Party to follow, and he's leading the Party away from Suez.' Apart from Nutting, none of the ministers closely involved was to publish memoirs that made damaging admissions until at least twenty years after the event, even though French and Israeli sources had revealed the damaging truth much earlier; most of them took a dignified silence with them to the grave. The 1959 Party manifesto did not mention Suez and there was no attempt to justify the invasion during the campaign either, but by then it could be made to seem like old news, and there was no sign that the public wanted to hear about it. David Astor's advice to Macleod, that the Tories could only avoid national disgrace by baring their souls and telling the whole truth to the public, whatever that meant in consequent resignations, was perhaps true enough for liberal intellectuals and readers of *The Observer*, many of whom never did forgive the Conservatives for Suez, but it was completely off the beam as far as the general public were concerned; they may indeed have welcomed the reassurance allowed by *not* investigating Suez too closely. It was a classic exemplification of Disraeli's dictum that in politics the best advice after a setback is 'Never complain. Never explain.'[35]

## Macmillan succeeds Eden

It did not fall to Eden to conduct this political rearguard, and perhaps it needed a new man in charge for the tactic to be successfully pursued anyway. He had fretted during his absence from London and was burning to take up the reins again; others were not so sure. One of Butler's letters to Eden in Jamaica contained the classic 'Butlerism': 'There are many who would like

---

[35] Rhodes James, *Eden*, 585; Ramsden, 'Churchill to Heath', 441, 477; Sparrow, *Rab*, 135–6; Paul Foot, *The Politics of Harold Wilson* (Harmondsworth, 1968), 127; Lamb, *Failure*, 300.

to see you back, including members of the Cabinet.' But the relative shift in the balance of power was made clear by the re-writing by the Cabinet of the statement Eden proposed to make at the airport on arrival on 14 December; he had to deliver the amended text. Lady Eden remembered that they 'returned to find everyone looking at us with thoughtful eyes'. There were abundant rumours that he would soon announce his resignation, and also that the Cabinet would remove him in favour of Macmillan. He may or may not have had forceful advice to go from Cabinet colleagues, but there was certainly a collective embarrassment in the air at meetings, and ministers were discussing the question with each other, more in terms of 'when' than 'if '; Macmillan's diary indicated that he had realised as soon as Eden broke down in November that he 'could never return and remain PM for long', and he had told Butler that this was his view in mid-December. At Cabinet on 17 December, Buchan-Hepburn made a forceful plea to Eden to stay and fight, backing Salisbury's earlier urgings to the same effect; he also noted that Thorneycroft, Stuart, Lloyd and Eccles were now 'anti-PM', which is paradoxical in view of the fact that most of these men had supported the invasion, while Buchan-Hepburn had opposed it. When Eden entered the Commons, a backbencher's loyal attempt to start an ovation by leaping to his feet and waving his order paper turned into humiliation when no other MP joined in; observing this as a Clerk of the House, Robert Rhodes James felt that 'at that moment one knew that it was all over'. From the Labour side, Crossman was convinced by 19 December that 'since Eden has been back it's pretty clear he isn't going to regain ascendancy'. The premier faced forty-five minutes of tough questioning from the 1922 Committee two days later, though at the end he was 'warmly applauded by the Committee'. Over Christmas, Eden consulted Kilmuir, asking whether he should resign, whether in fact the loss of his authority had left him any choice, but the Lord Chancellor advised him to carry on. Buchan-Hepburn sent him a forceful letter on 27 December to the same effect: he thought the Party might break up, that a resignation would tacitly admit to a policy failure, and 'it that would be a grievous blow to us in every particular if it was thought that the US could influence the tenure of office of the British Prime Minister'; but even such a keen supporter also accepted that Eden might well want to stand down after an interval, in 'circumstances that would be much more dignified and appropriate for yourself, the Party & the country than could possibly be the case at this moment'. Others were more tough-minded: when Woolton volunteered to see Eden to stiffen his resolve, the Party Chairman asked him not to, 'on the grounds that he thought it might be better if he went'. It seems inconceivable that Eden's retirement could have been delayed for much longer, but on 7 January it was settled by his health. Other ministers, notably Salisbury and Butler, were involved in the consultations with the Prime Minister's doctors, and it may be that considerations other than the purely medical played a part in the final decision. What is clear is that Eden's health was sufficiently bad to make a resignation on that ground both plausible and convenient, and that this news was received with relief all round. He saw the Queen on 8 January and told her he would resign. It was a wretched way to end a career of unstinting service to Party and country, and Eden left office with a great resentment, much of it directed against recent colleagues. Noël Coward's verdict on the sadness of unfulfilled promise in his friend Eden was typical: 'poor Anthony has resigned, given up, and is on his way to New Zealand, a tragic figure who had been cast in a star part well above his capabilities'.[36]

There were only two possible successors, Butler and Macmillan, though the Communist *Daily Worker* showed its deep understanding of the governing class by headlining its story on the day Macmillan went to Number 10, 'Eden quits – new Premier today: Selwyn Lloyd the hottest tip.' Randolph Churchill asked his readers rhetorically whether the choice would make any difference, between Butler who over Suez had urged the Cabinet not to go in, and Macmillan who had made the Cabinet pull out. It was a characteristically wicked way of framing the question, for this distinction was exactly what did matter to a Tory Party whose post-Suez collective belief was that it was better to have tried and failed than never to have tried at all. Peter Rawlinson recalled that,

> Rab Butler, it was generally felt, had had his head well down during the parliamentary crisis when the shot and shell were at their fiercest, as, many believed, was his wont . . . Harold Macmillan, it was felt, had like the Grand Old Duke of York marched his men to the top of the hill and then very smartly turned about and marched them down again. But it was also felt that he had at least been in action.

Butler's damaged right arm, which would have prevented him taking part in the War whatever his age, his involvement over appeasement, his primary concern with home policy even between 1940 and 1945, and what his critics saw as his vegetarian political manner (Churchill sometimes turned 'Rab' into 'rabbit' in conversation), all contributed to the reputation that a wobbly final few months as Chancellor and an extended period of equivocation in 1956 amply confirmed; that reputation was in many ways most unfair, but it was widely believed all the same. In this sense it was exceptionally damaging to Butler that the Leadership contest happened so soon, before emotions settled and judgements cooled. The head-to-head contrast when Butler and Macmillan jointly addressed a meeting of the 1922 Committee on 29 November 1956 did not help him either, since Macmillan used the occasion

36    Butler letter in PREM 11/1548 file at Public Record Office, drawn to my attention by Peter Hennessy; Rhodes James, *Eden*, 391–5; Buchan-Hepburn note, 17 Dec. 1956, Hailes MSS, 4/1; Cockett, *My Dear Max*, 199; Morgan, *Crossman Diaries*, 557; Howard, *RAB*, 242–4; Thompson, *Day Before Yesterday*, 145; Horne, *Macmillan*, 453; 1922 Cttee., 21 Dec. 1956; Kilmuir, *Memoirs*, 281–3; Buchan-Hepburn to Eden, 27 Dec. 1956, Hailes MSS, 4/1; Woolton diary, 12 Jan. 1957, Woolton MSS; Payn and Morley, *Coward Diaries*, 349.

to turn in one of his virtuoso, knockabout performances (literally almost knocking Butler off his chair with one expansive sweep of the arm); Enoch Powell, later recalled it as 'one of the most horrible things that I remember in politics . . . the way in which Harold Macmillan, with the skill of the old actor–manager, succeeded in false-footing Rab. The sheer devilry of it verged upon the disgusting.' As well as the actual performance, the tactics to which Butler had agreed disfavoured him too: Macmillan would concentrate on the centre and left, which had the effect of disarming critics who saw him as too hawkish, while Butler was supposed to answer critics of Government policy from the right – which he could never do convincingly. As he left the meeting, Macmillan remarked disarmingly to Nigel Fisher, 'I held the Tory Party for the week-end. That was all I intended to do.' Over the next few weeks Macmillan's tactics and his feel for the rapid shifts of mood remained excellent; regular meetings of his ministerial supporters were convened and the maximum was made out of his public appearances; when he went to Woolton's flat to seek the elder statesman's advice on the succession, he walked the length of Whitehall with an admiring entourage of photographers. He may also have been utilising his transatlantic contacts to seek Eisenhower's backing for his candidacy, and putting about the idea that he was better able than Butler to re-build relations with the United States; but that is highly speculative, and in the anti-American mood of January 1957 would hardly have won him Conservative support anyway. The American Government was quite ready to acknowledge that it did not want to deal with Eden, but would not express a view between the alternatives. While Macmillan prepared with his supporters at Number 11, Downing Street, Butler seems to have felt that Eden could at least get through to the Summer recess, which would give him time to prepare for a contest on more favourable grounds; when he lost the January contest, Bracken applied to him Coleridge's line, 'I lost the race I never ran'. Liverpool Tories, who had on 6 November congratulated Eden on doing at Suez 'what we had been hoping a Prime Minister would do', wrote to the Party Chairman on 11 December to urge that Eden remain in office, and to complain about the manoeuvring for the succession by his colleagues, 'particularly the names of Messrs. Butler, Macmillan and Head were voiced unfavourably and antagonistically'. On 10 January, they decided they would like a 'young, energetic and healthy man', and opted for Hailsham, but on the same day Macmillan was chosen. Butler seems to have shared the disadvantage of being discussed as an over ambitious contender without actually running a campaign.[37]

---

[37] Thorpe, *Lloyd*, 269; Rawlinson, *Price Too High*, 71; Goodhart, *The 1922*, 274; Howard, *RAB*, 241–4; Fisher, *Macleod*, 116; Woolton diary, 12 Jan. 1957, Woolton MSS; Horne, *Macmillan*, 452; Cockett, *My Dear Max*, 203; Max Beloff, 'The Crisis and its Consequences for the British Conservative Party', in *Suez, 1956*, eds Roger Louis and Roger Owen (Oxford, 1989), 333; Liverpool CA minutes, 10 Jan. 1957.

It is unlikely that any of this made any difference to the outcome. Neither backbenchers nor the officers of the 1922 Committee had any direct involvement in the decisions made on 9 and 10 January, and Party members and the public at large, who might have been affected by Macmillan's playing to the press gallery, were even further from the centre of events; the succession was played out as a strictly constitutional matter in which advice from a limited circle would be given to the Queen concerning the choice of her Prime Minister; the fact that the Party Leader was being chosen at the same time was treated almost as an incidental consequence. Indirectly though, ministers were subjected to the same lobby conversations as other MPs, and the whips certainly made them aware of the overwhelming preponderance of support for Macmillan over Butler. Also, they can have hardly been unaware that the depth of hostility to Butler on the right was infinitely deeper than any resistance to Macmillan on the left. (Given Macmillan's antecedent opinions and basic political philosophy it seems extraordinary that he could have made himself appear to be on the Party's right wing at all, but that is how it was seen after Suez, at least in comparison with Butler.) The choice of Butler would have been deeply divisive as well as against most MPs' wishes, quite apart from the fact that Macmillan himself said that he 'did not find it easy to contemplate serving under Butler'; the choice of Macmillan presented no such risks, as well as giving the majority what they wanted. The greatest surprise is that lobby correspondents failed to pick up the tide of opinion that was sweeping Macmillan along, though with a longer hindsight we can see that the press was equally misinformed in 1963, 1965 and 1975 too. Nearly all the newspapers predicted that Butler, the deputy now for four years, would become Prime Minister, which only increased his disappointment in the outcome. Talking to one of his few supporters, Buchan-Hepburn, on the day Macmillan became Prime Minister, Butler was 'very calm and sensible', according to Buchan-Hepburn's note: 'He said he had not got it because, (a) Cabinet were against, (b) There had not been time to master H of C & talk to Members, (c) Society and press network. He said he would carry on & make a success of the "middle thing".' Nevertheless, his disappointment was deep, and Buchan-Hepburn found their conversation 'awkward, as the gentlemanly touch did not quite seem to work'.[38]

Eden told Butler, Macmillan and Salisbury about his resignation on the morning of 9 January; since the other two were candidates, and since Eden did not wish to offer his own advice to the Queen, it largely fell to Salisbury to stage-manage the process, though Eden did tell the Palace how well he thought Butler had done in his absence. Salisbury consulted the Lord Chancellor, who confirmed his own view that this was a matter in which the Queen – as in 1923

---

[38] Sampson, *Macmillan*, 126; Campbell, *Heath*, 97; Butler, *Art of the Possible*, 195; Howard, *RAB*, 248; Woolton diary, 12 Jan. 1957, Woolton, MSS; Lord Egremont, *Wyndham and Children First* (1968), 158; note by Buchan-Hepburn, 10 Jan. 1957, Hailes MSS, 4/12.

– must not be fettered by any Party election machinery, but that the views of Cabinet ministers should be ascertained for the Palace. Later on the 9th, Eden announced his resignation to the Cabinet; as ministers left they were called into Salisbury's office one by one and asked bluntly by the Lord President, 'Well, which is it? Wab or Hawold?' Almost all opted for Macmillan, with only one clear 'vote' for Butler (Buchan-Hepburn) and one clear abstention (Lloyd). Heath, Poole, and the chairman of the 1922 Committee all gave the same advice, and it was to that effect that Salisbury advised the Queen; consulted separately, Churchill also recommended Macmillan. Having spent the morning of the 10th reading *Pride and Prejudice*, Macmillan was summoned to the Palace and appointed Prime Minister.[39]

Butler was deeply shocked, particularly after having read a *Times* editorial that picked him as being easily the best choice for Prime Minister. Setting down his views in February, he decided that there were three reasons that explained Macmillan's success. First, there was the experience of MPs in their constituencies over the Christmas recess, when they had first realised how deeply the Party faithful resented the Suez withdrawal that Butler had had to supervise in Eden's absence; second, there was 'the view of younger members of Cabinet', including Sandys, Eccles, Lennox-Boyd, Thorneycroft and Macleod ('those since elevated') who had, he said, seen Eden in early January and helped to force him out quickly in order to make Macmillan Prime Minister; finally, there was 'the "ambiance" & connections of the present incumbent of the post at No. 10'. There was a big inflow of sympathetic letters to the Butler household, many of them from complete strangers (which casts some doubt on the common assumption that Butler could not inspire the ordinary voter); many of these correspondents expressed admiration for the stoical way in which Butler had accepted his defeat. The diplomat Gladwyn Jebb wrote on 29 January that 'everybody is saying how perfectly you have conducted yourself since AE's departure & the enormous bulk of the Tory Party has no doubt at all, I am sure, that you will one day be their leader'.[40]    It remained to change the Leader of the Party and to complete the closing of ranks that had begun in the second week of November. No Minister refused to serve under Macmillan; Butler and Macmillan had agreed in advance to serve under the other if chosen (though Macmillan's support for Butler would have been less than wholehearted), and Butler now redeemed his pledge by remaining deputy Prime Minister. At the Party meeting to enthrone Macmillan on 22 January, Salisbury's first motion, proposed from the chair, expressed regret that Eden had had to retire, and this was seconded by Walter Elliot; Salisbury's second motion, to elect Macmillan

---

[39] Rhodes James, *Eden*, 595–600; Kilmuir, *Memoirs*, 285; Howard, *RAB*, 246–7; Thorpe, *Lloyd*, 270; Horne, *Macmillan*, 460.

[40] Butler notes, [one undated but Feb. 1957] and 21 Feb. 1957, and many letters from friends and from the public, Jan. to Mar. 1957, Butler MSS, G31.

as Leader, was proposed in a gloomy speech that stressed how difficult the task would be; this was seconded by Butler in nicely ambiguous terms: 'I find it particularly appropriate to support this motion when I think of the effort and sacrifice which must be involved for every citizen of this country if we are to surmount our present difficulties.' He was though careful to point out to his recent critics that 'I support the election of our new Leader in the belief that our views are the same'. Both motions were passed by acclamation. The Party was on its very best public behaviour and Butler was behaving true to ambiguous type. Macmillan's speech of acceptance contained a passage that was a strong hint that he would seek national as well as Party unity after a trying time:

> It is nearly 34 years since I first stood as a candidate for Parliament . . . The chief thing I have learned is what I would call the warmth and friendliness of our Party. You know it is not those who are always addressing each other as comrade who necessarily show the most brotherly feelings . . . .
>
> I hear a lot of talk about the Left and the Right. To the broad stream of our philosophy there are many tributaries. Indeed we are always adding to this flow as the parties of the Left break up into a kind of delta of confusion. And so our great river flows on triumphantly to the sea. We do not believe much in expelling people. I think that is a good thing, because I, no doubt, would have been a candidate for expulsion many years ago. It is this tolerance which makes us not only a national Party but a Party at the roots of whose philosophy lies the conviction that we are all in the same boat, with common problems to solve and a common destiny before us.

Nonetheless, this unity was for the time being rather brittle. Macmillan told the Queen on appointment that, in the shaken condition of his Party, he thought it unlikely that his Government would last for more than six weeks. If that sounded melodramatic – for in modern times Governments with majorities of over fifty simply have not disintegrated in peacetime, and even the Middle East was now at peace – it was in the mood of the time, and one officer of the 1922 Committee was more downbeat even than the new Prime Minister: 'I doubted whether the Government would survive for three weeks.' Meeting the National Union Executive at its next meeting, Macmillan appealed for loyalty and support, 'from the team spirit we have always had'. He also indicated the tactical lines that he was to follow to generate a revival. First, it was vital for the Party to recover its self-confidence after the buffets of the past year: 'we must not allow ourselves to be knocked about, and we must not allow ourselves to be rattled or flustered.' Second, confidence had to be applied to the nation as well as to the Party, despite the sweeping changes that had come in since 1945: 'we do not like to be told we are, and we are determined not to be, a second rate power.' Finally, he had a stern lesson for those Tories who had flirted with anti-American feelings during 1956; there had, for example, been 120 signatories for an Early Day Motion attacking American policy over Suez, while a rival motion supporting the

Americans attracted only twenty-six. 'When I was having lunch with the greatest living Englishman today, he said to me that we have got to face the years ahead with our American friends – as friends and not become satellites or subservient to them. We are to be good partners . . . Since we are the older and more experienced, we must have patience with them.' This was a version of Macmillan's favourite analogy of America as the modern Romans, powerful militarily and economically but influenced by the older civilisation of the (British) Greeks; this analysis neatly side-stepped the realities of great power status that had been humiliatingly revealed in the previous November. On this basis, Britain's – and the Party's – pride could be restored. If that could be done, then gloomy expectations about the Government might well be unjustified.[41]

There remained though one loose end from the change of Leaders. Since the press had almost universally picked the wrong winner, the result tended to be reported as one taken by secret processes, and against the wishes of the Party at large; if Butler in part blamed 'Society and press network', the press tended to blame Society, Salisbury and Churchill. Beaverbrook, who really should have known better, reassured Butler that 'you have been deprived of your estate', telling him that both the Commons and constituencies had been all for Butler but that 'Churchill is all powerful at Buckingham Palace'. From the Fleet Street left, Hugh Cudlipp sent Butler the cartoon that the *Daily Mirror* had had all ready to print, showing Butler wielding the axe over his former colleagues. Misinformed by the press, how would the Party react? This was after all only the third visible contest for the Party's Leadership, and 1911 and 1923 might reasonably be seen as precedents invalidated by post-war changes in the Party towards a more democratic spirit; it is notable though that Maxwell Fyfe (Kilmuir) who had allegedly done so much to introduce such a spirit into the Party in 1948, was a staunch upholder of the Queen's Prerogative over the Party's rights in 1957. Even in the Government there were a few who did not like the process, though they were happy to accept the result it produced; one of Selwyn Lloyd's reasons for refusing to express a preference was that he disapproved of the way in which opinions were being sought. Just after the change of Prime Minister, Central Office had its Area Agents in England and Wales quickly test opinion both on the change of leader and on the system. They found a general regret in the Party at Eden's departure but (now at last) an acceptance that his health had made it necessary. There was broad approval in all Areas for the choice of Macmillan, 'and almost complete absence of comment regarding Mr. Butler's position', though the Northern Area reported that 'a minority openly expressed their fear that Mr. Butler might be appointed'. There was though

[41] Boyd-Carpenter, *Way of Life*, 151; Goodhart, *The 1922*, 176; *NCP*, 21 Jan. 1957; NUEC, secretary's notes, 14 Feb. 1957, NUA 4/3/1; Beloff, 'Crisis and the Conservative Party', 328.

a feeling, particularly in the Eastern and Welsh Areas, that the system itself should be reviewed. 'The balance of power in giving advice lay in the hands of "the old guard". There were fears that a selection might be made at some time which did not accord with the wishes of the Party, and that the "Old School Tie" might carry too much weight.' This feeling was ignored, and no review took place. When the General Director was asked in a radio interview in 1960 how he could defend the Party's undemocratic system of choosing leaders, he was unrepentant: 1957 had shown that the Party respected the Queen's Prerogative, and 'a real election would do more harm than good' since anyone elected needed the support of the whole Party, not just a bare majority. This confidence in the traditional system was to be seen to be seriously misplaced only three years later.[42]

January 1957 was the last occasion on which the 'customary processes' were able to select a new Leader to general approval, but the fact that even this success for traditional forms occasioned some criticism from below shows that more democratic ideas were now stirring beneath the surface. If in policy terms, the main legacy of Churchill and Eden to their successors was that it still remained to settle Britain's place in post-war Europe and to keep up the provision of economic benefits to the Party's voting clients in increasingly competitive circumstances, in Party management, the main problem would be to reconcile a more broadly-based Party with inherited structures that placed little premium on the mobilisation of consent. These issues would between them dominate the generation ahead, in which the key Party figures would be Macmillan and Heath, who as Leader and Chief Whip dined together on champagne and oysters on 10 January 1957 to celebrate Macmillan's elevation to Number Ten. They would lead a very different Party from the one that Churchill had taken over from Neville Chamberlain, and one that was much more difficult to steer. As Patrick Buchan-Hepburn told James Stuart during the Suez debates, noting the changing character of the parliamentary party, it was 'not so easy to deal with a Party of Backroom Boys as with a Party of Backwoods Boys. (Not so "naice").'[43]

[42] Beaverbrook to Butler, 23 Jan. 1957, and Cudlipp to Butler, 14 Jan. 1957, Butler MSS, G31; Thorpe, *Lloyd*, 270; Central Office file, 'Public opinion', CCO 4/7/374, CPA; Central Office, General Director's file, 'Broadcasting', CCO 120/1/5, CPA.
[43] Sampson, *Macmillan*, 127; Buchan-Hepburn to Stuart, 22 Nov. 1956, Hailes MSS, 2/5.

# Bibliography

## Primary sources (private papers)

Avon MSS: diaries and papers of Sir Anthony Eden, Earl of Avon, Library of Birmingham University.

Butler MSS: papers of R.A. Butler, Lord Butler of Saffron Walden, Trinity College, Cambridge.

Cilcennin MSS: papers of J.P.L. Thomas, Viscount Cilcennin, Dyfed County Record Office, Carmarthen.

Crookshank MSS: diary of Harry Crookshank, Viscount Crookshank, Bodleian Library, Oxford.

Hailes MSS: papers of Patrick Buchan-Hepburn, Lord Hailes, Churchill College, Cambridge.

Harvie-Watt MSS: reports to Churchill on parliamentary business by George Harvie-Watt MP, Churchill College, Cambridge.

Headlam MSS: diaries of Cuthbert Headlam MP, Durham County Record Office.

Kilmuir MSS: papers of David Maxwell Fyfe, Earl of Kilmuir, Churchill College, Cambridge.

Margesson MSS: papers of David Margesson, Viscount Margesson, Churchill College, Cambridge.

Swinton MSS: papers of Philip Cunliffe-Lister, Earl of Swinton, Churchill College, Cambridge.

Willink MSS: unpublished autobiography and papers of Henry Willink, Churchill College, Cambridge.

Woolton MSS: diary and papers of Frederick Marquis, Earl of Woolton, Bodleian Library, Oxford.

## Conservative Party papers (parliamentary)

Minute Books of the 1922 Committee, 1940–43 and 1950–57, Bodleian Library, Oxford.

Minutes of the Leader's Consultative Committee, 1945–51, Bodleian Library, Oxford.

Whips Office papers, Bodleian Library, Oxford.

## Conservative Party papers (National Union)

Party Conference agendas, minutes, and reports of meetings with Leaders to discuss resolutions, Bodleian Library, Oxford.

Central Council agendas and minutes, Bodleian Library, Oxford.

Executive Committee minutes and secretary's notes, Bodleian Library, Oxford.

General Purposes Committee, secretary's notes and committee papers, Bodleian Library, Oxford.

Minutes of ad hoc National Union Committees, Bodleian Library, Oxford.

Advisory Committee on Policy and Political Education (to 1949) and Advisory Committee on Policy (from 1950), minutes and papers, Bodleian Library, Oxford.

## Conservative Party minutes (Area Organisations, seen in Area Offices)

London Conservative Union and sub-committees.

Home Counties South East Area Council and sub-committees.

Eastern Area Council and sub-committees.

East Midlands Area Council and sub-committees.

West Midlands Area Council and sub-committees.

North West Area Council and sub-committees.

Yorkshire Area Council and sub-committees.

Northern Area Council and sub-committees.

Wessex Area Council and sub-committees [in the Bodleian Library].

Western Area Council and sub-committees.

Wales and Monmouthshire Area Council and sub-committees.

## Conservative Party minutes (Local Organisations, seen in constituency offices unless otherwise indicated)
listed by Conservative Party Areas:

Battersea South CA; Brentford and Chiswick CA; Dulwich CA; Hampstead CA; Harrow West CA; Holborn and St Pancras South CA; Ilford CA; Islington East CA; Islington South West CA; North Camberwell [subsequently Peckham] CA; Ruislip CA; St Marylebone CA; Shoreditch and Finsbury CA; Twickenham CA; Uxbridge CA; Woodford CA [in the Essex County Record Office].

Ashford CA; Brighton Kemptown CA; Gravesend CA; Lewes CA; Maidstone CA; Guildford CA [in the Surrey County Record Office]; Reigate CA [in the Surrey County Record Office].

Bury St. Edmunds CA; Cambridgeshire CA; Bedfordshire South CA; Hemel Hempstead CA; Kings Lynn CA; Saffron Walden CA.

Derby CA; West Derbyshire CA [in Derbyshire County Record Office]; High Peak CA; Horncastle CA; Kettering CA; Newark CA.

Birmingham UA [in Birmingham Central Library]; Birmingham West UA [in Birmingham Central Library]; Burton upon Trent CA; Coventry CA; Rugby CA; Lichfield CA; Shrewsbury CA; Solihull CA; Walsall South CA; Warwick and Leamington CA [in Warwickshire County Record Office].

Accrington CA; Bolton CA; Bolton West CA; Liverpool CA; Manchester CA; Manchester Ardwick CA; Manchester Cheetham CA; Manchester Exchange CA; Manchester Wythenshawe CA; Nelson and Colne CA; North Fylde CA; Southport CA; Wirral CA.

Barkston Ash CA; Bradford CA; Bradford West CA; Bradford National Liberals [at Bradford Central Library]; Leeds CA; Leeds North West CA; Pontefract CA; Ripon CA; Sheffield CA; Sheffield Central CA; Sheffield Ecclesall CA.

Darlington CA; Hexham CA; Middlesbrough CA; Newcastle CA; Tynemouth CA; Workington CA.

Aylesbury CA; Basingstoke CA; Newbury CA [at the Berkshire County Record Office]; Oxford CA; Swindon CA.

Bath CA; Bristol CA; Bristol West CA; Cirencester and Tewkesbury CA; Cornwall North CA; Dorset West CA; Penryn and Falmouth CA; Truro CA; Totnes CA.

Barry CA; Cardiff South East CA; Denbigh CA [in the Clwyd County Record Office]; Flintshire East CA; Monmouth CA.

Aberdeen South UA; Angus South UA; Dunbartonshire West UA; Edinburgh East UA; Edinburgh North UA; Galloway UA; Glasgow UA; Glasgow Bridgeton UA; Glasgow Craigton UA; Glasgow Pollok UA; Glasgow Scotstoun UA; Kirkcaldy Burghs UA.

## Conservative Party papers (Central Office, all at Bodleian Library, Oxford)

CCO 1 series (constituency correspondence).
CCO 2 series (Area correspondence).
CCO 3 series (correspondence with outside organisations).
CCO 4 series (subject files).
CCO 20 series (Chairman's files).
CCO 120 series (General Director's files).
*Conservative Agents' Journal*
*Notes on Current Politics*
*Notes for Speakers*
*Interim and Final Reports of the Committee on Party Organisation*, (1949)

## Secondary sources: books, theses and articles

All books cited were published in London unless stated otherwise.

Paul Addison, 'By-Elections of the Second World War' in *By-Elections in British Politics*, eds Chris Cook and John Ramsden, Macmillan (1973)

Paul Addison, *The Road to 1945: British Politics and the Second World War*, Cape (1975)

Paul Addison, *Now the War is Over*, Cape/BBC (1985)

Paul Addison, *Churchill on the Home Front, 1900–1955*, Cape (1992)

Paul Addison, 'Churchill and Social Reform' in *Churchill*, eds Robert Blake and W.R. Louis, Oxford, OUP (1993)

Julian Amery, 'A Conservative view of the Commonwealth', in the *Political Quarterly*, vol. 24 (1953), 167

Julian Amery, *Approach March*, Hutchinson (1973)

Stuart Ball, 'The National and Regional Party Structure', in *Conservative Century: The Conservative Party since 1900*, eds A. Seldon and S. Ball, Oxford, OUP (1995)

Stuart Ball, 'Local Conservatism and the Evolution of Party Organization', in *Conservative Century: The Conservative Party since 1900*, eds A. Seldon and S. Ball, Oxford, OUP (1995)

John Barnes and David Nicholson, eds *The Empire at Bay: The Leo Amery Diaries, 1929–1945*, Hutchinson (1988)

George Beardmore, *Civilians at War: Journals, 1938–1946*, Oxford, OUP (1984)

Alan Beattie, *English Party Politics, Vol. II, 1906–1970*, Weidenfield and Nicolson (1970)

Max Beloff, 'The Crisis and its Consequences for the British Conservative Party', in *Suez, 1956*, eds Roger Louis and Roger Owen, Oxford, OUP (1989)

M. Benney, A.P. Gray and R.H. Pear, *How People Vote, A Study of Electoral Behaviour in Greenwich*, Routledge and Kegan Paul (1956)

G.R. Berridge and J.E. Spence, 'South Africa and the Simonstown Agreements', in *The Foreign Policy of Churchill's Peacetime Administration, 1951–1955*, ed. J.W. Young, Leicester, Leicester UP (1988)

Hugh Berrington, 'The Conservative Party: Revolts and Pressures, 1955–1961', in the *Political Quarterly*, vol. 32 (1961), 363

John Biffen, 'Party Conference and Party Policy', in the *Political Quarterly*, vol. 32 (1961), 257

Lord Birkenhead, *The Prof in Two Worlds, A Life of Lord Cherwell*, Collins (1961)

Lord Birkenhead, *Walter Monckton*, Weidenfield and Nicolson (1969)

Robert Blake, *The Conservative Party from Peel to Thatcher*, Faber (1985)

A.H. Booth, *British Hustings, 1924–1950*, Mueller (1956)

Robert Boothby, 'The economic policy of the Conservative Party', in the *Political Quarterly*, vol. 24 (1953), 148

John Boyd-Carpenter, *Way of Life*, Sidgwick and Jackson (1980)

Samuel Brittan, *Steering the Economy*, Secker and Warburg (1969)

Henry Brooke, 'Conservatives and Local Government', in the *Political Quarterly*, vol. 24 (1953), 181

Stephen Brooke, *Labour's War: The Labour Party during the Second World War*, Oxford, OUP (1992)

Ivor Bulmer-Thomas, 'How Conservative Policy is Formed', in the *Political Quarterly*, vol. 24 (1953), 190

Kathleen Burk, *The First Privatisation: The Politicians, the City and the Denationalisation of Steel*, The Historians' Press (1988)

D.E. Butler, *The British General Election of 1951*, Macmillan (1952)

D.E. Butler, *The British General Election of 1955*, Macmillan (1956)

D.E. Butler, *The Electoral System in Great Britain since 1918*, 2nd edn, Oxford, OUP (1963)

D.E. Butler, *British General Elections since 1945*, Oxford, Blackwell (1989)

D.E. Butler and G. Butler, *British Political Facts, 1900–1986*, Macmillan (1986)

D.E. Butler and Michael Pinto-Duschinsky, 'The Conservative élite, 1918–1970. Does unrepresentativeness matter?' in *Conservative Party Politics*, ed. Z. Layton-Henry, Macmillan (1980)

Lord Butler of Saffron Walden, *The Art of the Possible, The Memoirs of Lord Butler*, Hamish Hamilton (1971)

Angus Calder, *The People's War, Britain 1939–1945*, Cape (1969)

Angus Calder, *The Myth of the Blitz*, Cape (1991)

John Campbell, *Edward Heath*, Cape (1993)

'Candidus', *Labour's Great Lie*, Hutchinson (1945)

Lord Carrington, *Reflect on Things Past: The Memoirs of Lord Carrington*, Collins (1988)

'Cato', *Guilty Men*, Gollancz (1940)

'Celticus', *Why Not Trust the Tories?*, Gollancz (1944)

Oliver Lyttelton, Viscount Chandos, *The Memoirs of Lord Chandos*, Bodley Head (1962)

R.A. Chapman, *Leadership in the British Civil Service*, Croom Helm (1984)

John Charmley (ed.), *Descent to Suez, Diaries of Evelyn Shuckburgh, 1951–56*, Weidenfield and Nicolson (1986)

Randolph Churchill, *The Rise and Fall of Sir Anthony Eden*, MacGibbon and Kee (1959)

William Clark, *From Three Worlds*, Sidgwick and Jackson (1985)

David Clarke (ed.), *Conservatism, 1945–50*, CPC (1950)

David Clarke, 'The Organisation of Political Parties', in the *Political Quarterly*, vol. 21 (1950), 79

Michael Cockerell, *Live from Number Ten, The Inside Story of Prime Ministers and Television*, Faber (1988)

Richard Cockett, *Twilight of Truth: Chamberlain, Appeasement and the Manipulation of the Press*, Weidenfield and Nicolson (1989)

Richard Cockett (ed.), *My Dear Max: The Letters of Brendan Bracken to Lord Beaverbrook, 1925–1958*, The Historians' Press (1990)

Richard Cockett, *Thinking the Unthinkable, Think-Tanks and the Economic Counter-Revolution, 1931–1983*, Harper Collins (1994)

John Colville, *Footprints in Time*, Collins (1976)

John Colville, *The Fringes of Power, Downing Street Diaries, 1939–1955*, Hodder and Stoughton (1985)

Chris Cook and John Ramsden (eds), *By-Elections in British Politics*, Macmillan (1973)

Colin Coote, 'Conservatism and Liberalism', in the *Political Quarterly*, vol. 24 (1953), 204

Colin Coote, *A Companion of Honour, the Story of Walter Elliot*, Collins (1965)

Patrick Cosgrave, *R.A. Butler, An English Life*, Quartet (1981)

F.W.S. Craig (ed.), *British General Election Manifestoes, 1918–1966*, Chichester, Political Reference Publications (1970)

F.W.S. Craig (ed.), *British Parliamentary Election Statistics, 1918–1970*, Chichester, Political Reference Publications (1971)

F.W.S. Craig (ed.), *British Parliamentary Election Results, 1950–1970*, Chichester, Political Reference Publications (1971)

F.W.S. Craig (ed.), *The Boundaries of Parliamentary Constituencies, 1885–1972*, Chichester, Political Reference Publications (1972)

F.W.S. Craig (ed.), *British Parliamentary Election Results 1918–1949*, rev. edn, Macmillan (1977)

Dorothy Crisp and Oliver Stanley, *The Rebirth of Conservatism*, Methuen (1931)

William Crofts, *Coercion or Persuasion? Propaganda in Britain after 1945*, Routledge (1989)

J.A. Cross, *Lord Swinton*, Oxford, OUP (1982)

Gerard de Groot, *Sir Archibald Sinclair*, Hurst (1993)

John Dickie, *The Uncommon Commoner, A Study of Sir Alec Douglas-Home*, Pall Mall Press (1964)

Piers Dixon, 'Eden after Suez', in *Contemporary Record*, vol. 6 (1992), 178

Michael Dockrill, *British Defence since 1945*, Oxford, Blackwell (1988)

Gerald Dorfman, *Wage Politics in Britain, 1945–1967*, Charles Knight (1974)

Tom Driberg, *Colonnade*, The Pilot Press (1949)

Tom Driberg, *Beaverbrook*, Weidenfield and Nicolson (1956)

David Dutton, 'Living with Collusion: Anthony Eden and the Later History of the Suez Affair', in *Contemporary Record*, vol. 5 (1991), 201

David Dutton, 'Anticipating Maastricht: the Conservative Party and Britain's First Application to Join the European Community', in *Contemporary Record*, vol. 7, (1993), 522

Robert Eccleshall, *English Conservatism since the Restoration*, Unwin Hyman (1990)

Anthony Eden, *Freedom and Order, Selected Speeches, 1939–1946*, Faber (1947)

Anthony Eden, *Days for Decision, Selected Speeches, 1947–1949*, Faber (1949)

Anthony Eden, *Full Circle, The Eden Memoirs, vol. 3*, Cassell (1960)

Anthony Eden, *The Reckoning, The Eden Memoirs, vol. 2*, Cassell (1965)

Lord Egremont, *Wyndham and Children First*, Macmillan (1968)

B.J. Evans and A.J. Taylor, 'The Rise and Fall of Two-Party Electoral Co-operation', in *Political Studies*, vol. 32 (1984), 257

Arthur Fawcett, *Conservative Agent: A Study of the National Society of Conservative Agents*, Driffield, Yorkshire, NSA (1967)

Keith Feiling, 'Principles of Conservatism', in the *Political Quarterly*, vol. 24 (1953), 129

Nigel Fisher, *Iain Macleod*, Purnell (1973)

Paul Foot, *The Politics of Harold Wilson*, Harmondsworth, Penguin (1968)

G.K. Fry, 'A Reconsideration of the British General Election of 1935 and the Electoral Revolution of 1945', in *History*, vol. 76 (1991), 43

Andrew Gamble, *The Conservative Nation*, Routledge and Kegan Paul (1974)

Brian Gardner, *Churchill in his Time, a Study in a Reputation, 1939–1945*, Methuen (1968)

Martin Gilbert, *Finest Hour, Winston S. Churchill, 1939–1941*, Heinemann (1983)

Martin Gilbert, *Road to Victory, Winston S. Churchill, 1941–1945*, Heinemann (1986)

Martin Gilbert, *Never Despair, Winston S. Churchill, 1945–1965*, Heinemann (1988)

Harvey Glickman, 'The Toryness of British Conservatism', in the *Journal of British Studies* (1961)

Philip Goodhart, *The 1922, the Story of the 1922 Committee*, Macmillan (1973)

W. Gore Allen, *The Reluctant Politician, Derick Heathcoat Amory*, Christopher Johnson (1958)

'Gracchus', *Your MP*, Gollancz (1944)

Lord Hailsham, *The Door Wherein I Went*, Collins (1975)

Lord Hailsham, *A Sparrow's Flight, Memoirs*, Collins (1990)

J.E.D. Hall, *Labour's First Year*, Harmondsworth, Penguin (1947)

Nigel Harris, *Competition and the Corporate Society: British Conservatives, the State and Industry, 1945–1964*, Methuen (1972)

Tom Harrisson, 'Who'll win?' in the *Political Quarterly*, vol. 15 (1944), 21

Tom Harrisson, *Living Through the Blitz*, Collins (1976)

Ian Harvey, *To Fall Like Lucifer*, Sidgwick and Jackson (1971)

John Harvey (ed.), *The Diplomatic Diaries of Oliver Harvey 1941–1945*, Collins (1978)

Peter Hennessy, *Cabinet*, Oxford, Blackwell (1986)

Peter Hennessy, *Whitehall*, Fontana (1990)

Peter Hennessy, *Never Again, Britain 1945–1951*, Cape (1992)

Charles Hill, *Both Sides of the Hill*, Heinemann (1964)

G. Hodgson, 'The Steel Debates', in *The Age of Austerity, 1945–1951*, eds Michael Sissons and Philip French, Harmondsworth, Penguin (1964)

J.D. Hoffman, *The Conservative Party in Opposition, 1945–1951*, Macgibbon and Kee (1964)

Quintin Hogg, *One Year's Work*, Hutchinson (1944)

Quintin Hogg, *The Left Were Never Right*, Faber (1945)

Christopher Hollis, 'The Conservative Party in History' in the *Political Quarterly*, vol. 32 (1961), 214

Lord Home, *The Way the Wind Blows*, Collins (1976)

Tom Hopkinson (ed.), *Picture Post 1938–1950*, Chatto and Windus (1990)

Alistair Horne, *Macmillan, 1894–1956*, Macmillan (1988)

Anthony Howard, 'We are the masters now', in *The Age of Austerity, 1945–1951*, eds Michael Sissons and Philip French, Harmondsworth, Penguin (1964)

Anthony Howard, *RAB, The Life of R.A. Butler*, Cape (1987)

T.E.B. Howarth, *Prospect and Reality, Britain 1945–1955*, Collins (1985)

Ronald Hyam, 'Churchill and the British Empire', in *Churchill*, eds Robert Blake and W.R. Louis, Oxford, OUP (1993)

R.J. Jackson, *Rebels and Whips: Dissension, Discipline and Cohesion in British Political Parties since 1945*, Macmillan (1968)

Kevin Jefferys (ed.), *Labour and the Wartime Coalition, from the Diaries of James Chuter Ede, 1941–1945*, The Historians' Press (1987)

Kevin Jefferys, *The Churchill Coalition and Wartime Politics, 1940–1945*, Manchester, Manchester UP (1991)

Peter Jenkins, 'Bevan's Fight with the B.M.A.' in *The Age of Austerity, 1945–1951*, eds Michael Sissons and Philip French, Harmondsworth, Penguin (1964)

Roy Jenkins, 'Churchill, the Government of 1951–1955' in *Churchill*, eds Rober Blake and W.R. Louis, Oxford, OUP (1993)

Harriet Jones, 'The Conservative Party and the Social Policy, 1942–1955', University of London PhD thesis, 1992

Michael Kandiah, 'Lord Woolton's Chairmanship of the Conservative Party, 1945–1951', unpublished PhD thesis, University of Exeter, 1992

Earl of Kilmuir, *Political Adventure, The Memoirs of the Earl of Kilmuir*, Weidenfield and Nicolson (1964)

Richard Lamb, *The Failure of the Eden Government*, Sidgwick and Jackson (1987)

Zig Layton-Henry, 'The Young Conservatives', in the *Journal of Contemporary History*, vol. 8 (1973), 143

J.M. Lee, *The Churchill Coalition, 1940–1945*, Batsford (1980)

Roy Lewis and Angus Maude, *The English Middle Classes*, Harmondsworth, Penguin (1953)

T.F. Lindsay and M. Harrington, *The Conservative Party, 1918–1970*, Macmillan (1974)

W.R. Louis, 'Churchill and Egypt', in *Churchill*, eds Robert Blake and W.R. Louis, Oxford, OUP (1993)

C.E. Lysaght, *Brendan Bracken*, Allen Lane (1979)

Callum MacDonald, *Britain and the Korean War*, Oxford, Blackwell (1990)

Harold Macmillan, *Blast of War, 1939–1945*, Macmillan (1967)

Harold Macmillan, *Tides of Fortune, 1945–1955*, Macmillan (1969)

Geoffrey Mander, *We were Not All Wrong*, Gollancz (1944)

David Marquand, 'Sir Stafford Cripps' in *The Age of Austerity, 1945–1951*, eds Michael Sissons and Philip French, Harmondsworth, Penguin (1964)

Angus Maude, 'The Conservative Party and the Changing Class Structure', in the *Political Quarterly*, vol. 24 (1953), 139

Reginald Maudling, *Memoirs*, Sidgwick and Jackson (1978)

R.B. McCallum and Alison Readman, *The British General Election of 1945*, Oxford, OUP (1947)

Geoffrey McDermott, *The Eden Legacy and the Decline of British Diplomacy*, Frewen (1969)

Ross McKibbin, *Ideologies of Class*, Oxford, OUP (1990)

Donald McLachlan, *Barrington-Ward of The Times, 1927–1948*, Weidenfield and Nicolson (1971)

R.S. Milne and H.C. Mackenzie, *Straight Fight: A Study of Voting Behaviour in the Constituency of Bristol North East at the General Election of 1951*, The Hansard Society (1954)

Lord Moran, *Winston Churchill, The Struggle for Survival, 1940–1965*, Sphere edn (1966)

Janet Morgan (ed.), *The Backbench Diaries of Richard Crossman*, Hamish Hamilton/Jonathan Cape (1981)

Malcolm Muggeridge, *Tread Softly, For You Treat on My Jokes*, Fontana (1968)

Sir Gerald Nabarro, *Nab 1, Portrait of a Politician*, Maxwell (1969)

H.G. Nicholas, *The British General Election of 1950*, Macmillan (1951)

Nigel Nicolson (ed.), *The War Years, The Diaries and Letters of Harold Nicolson, 1939–1945*, Collins (1967)

Philip Norton, *Dissension in the House of Commons, 1945–1974*, Macmillan (1975)

Ritchie Ovendale, 'Egypt and the Suez Base Agreement' in *The Foreign Policy of Churchill's Peacetime Administration, 1951–1955*, ed. J.W. Young, Leicester, Leicester UP (1988)

Peter Paterson, *The Selectorate*, MacGibbon and Kee (1967)

Chris Patten, 'R.A. Butler – What We Missed', unpublished Inaugural R.A. Butler Lecture, delivered 25 May 1994

Graham Payn and Sheridan Morley (eds), *The Noël Coward Diaries*, Macmillan (1982)

Henry Pelling, *Winston Churchill*, Macmillan (1974)

P. Phillips, 'The New Look' in *The Age of Austerity, 1945–1951*, eds Michael Sissons and Philip French, Harmondsworth, Penguin (1964)

Ben Pimlott (ed.), *The Political Diaries of Hugh Dalton, 1918–1940 and 1945–1960*, Cape (1986)

Ben Pimlott (ed.), *The Second World War Diary of Hugh Dalton, 1940–1945*, Cape (1986)

Michael Pinto-Duschinsky, 'Bread and Circuses? The Conservatives in Office, 1951–1964', in *The Age of Affluence, 1951–1964*, eds V. Bogdanor and R. Skidelsky, Macmillan (1970)

Michael Pinto-Duschinsky, *British Political Finance, 1830–1980*, American Enterprise Institute (1981)

Enoch Powell, 'Conservatives and the Social Services' in the *Political Quarterly*, vol. 24 (1953), 156

John Ramsden, 'From Churchill to Heath' in *The Conservatives, A History from their Origins to 1965*, ed. Lord Butler, Allen and Unwin (1977)

John Ramsden, *The Age of Balfour and Baldwin, 1902–1940*, Longman History of the Conservative Party (1978)

John Ramsden, *The Making of Conservative Party Policy, The Conservative Research Department since 1929*, Longman (1980)

John Ramsden, 'A Party for Owners or a Party for Earners? How Far Did the Conservative Party Really Change after 1945?' in *Transactions of the Royal Historical Society*, 5th series, vol. 37 (1987) 49–63

John Ramsden, 'The Conservative Party since 1945' in *UK Political Parties since 1945*, ed. Anthony Seldon, Hemel Hempstead, Philip Allan (1990)

Peter Rawlinson, *A Price Too High, An Autobiography*, Weidenfield and Nicolson (1989)

Robert Rhodes James (ed.), *Chips, the Diaries of Sir Henry Channon*, Weidenfield and Nicolson (1967)

Robert Rhodes James, *Anthony Eden*, Weidenfield and Nicolson (1986)

Robert Rhodes James, *Bob Boothby, a Portrait*, Headline (1991)

P.G. Richards, 'The General Election' in the *Political Quarterly*, vol. 21 (1950), 114

N. Rose, 'The Resignation of Sir Anthony Eden', in the *Historical Journal*, vol. 25 (1982), 911

J.F.S. Ross, *Parliamentary Representation*, Eyre and Spottiswoode (1943)

Andrew Roth, *Enoch Powell, Tory Tribune*, Macdonald (1970)

Michael Rush, *The Selection of Parliamentary Candidates*, Nelson (1969)

Anthony Sampson, *Macmillan, A Study in Ambiguity*, Harmondsworth, Penguin (1968)

Anthony Seldon, *Churchill's Indian Summer, the Conservative Government, 1951–1955*, Hodder and Stoughton (1981)

Larry Siedentop, 'Mr. Macmillan and the Edwardian Style', in *The Age of Affluence, 1951–1964*, eds V. Bogdanor and R. Skidelsky, Macmillan (1970)

Justin Davis Smith, *The Attlee and Churchill Administrations and Industrial Unrest, 1945–1955*, Pinter (1990)

William P. Snyder, *The Politics of British Defense Policy, 1945–1961*, Columbus, Ohio State UP (1964)

Gerald Sparrow, *Rab, Study of a Statesman*, Odhams (1965)

M. Stenton and S. Lees, *Who's Who of British Members of Parliament, 1945–1979*, vol. 4, Hassocks, Harvester (1981)

James Stuart, *Within the Fringe*, Bodley Head (1967)

A Sutcliffe and R. Smith, *Birmingham, 1939–1970*, Oxford, OUP (1974)

A.J. Taylor, 'Conservatives and Trade Unions since 1945' in *Contemporary Record*, vol. 4 (1990), 15

A.J.P. Taylor, *Beaverbrook*, Hamish Hamilton (1972)

A.J.P. Taylor, '1932–45' in *Coalitions in British Politics*, ed. D.E. Butler, Macmillan (1978)

Robert Taylor, *The Trade Union Question in British Politics: Government and Unions since 1945*, Oxford, Blackwell (1993)

Norman Tebbit, *Upwardly Mobile*, Futura (1989)

William Teeling, *Corridors of Frustration*, Johnson (1970)

Alan Thompson, *The Day Before Yesterday*, Panther (1971)

D.R. Thorpe, *Selwyn Lloyd*, Cape (1989)

John Turner, *Macmillan*, Longman (1994)

D.W. Urwin, 'Scottish Conservatism, a Party Organisation in Transition', in *Political Studies*, vol. 14 (1966), 145

J.T. Ward, *The First Century, A History of Scottish Tory Organisation*, Edinburgh, Scottish Conservative and Unionist Association (1982)

Harold Watkinson, *Turning Points, a Record of Our Times*, Salisbury, Russell (1986)

William Whitelaw, *The Whitelaw Memoirs*, Aurum Press (1989)

P.M. Williams (ed.) *The Diary of Hugh Gaitskell, 1945–56*, Cape (1983)

Earl of Woolton, *The Memoirs of the Rt. Hon. Earl of Woolton*, Cassell (1959)

Kenneth Young, *Sir Alec Douglas-Home*, Dent (1970)

J.W. Young, 'Cold War and Détente with Moscow' in *The Foreign Policy of Churchill's Peacetime Administration, 1951–1955*, ed. J.W. Young, Leicester, Leicester UP (1988)

J.W. Young, 'The Schuman Plan and British Association', in *The Foreign Policy of Churchill's Peacetime Administration, 1951–1955*, ed. J.W. Young, Leicester, Leicester UP (1988)

Ina Zweiniger-Bargielowska, 'Bread Rationing in Britain', in *Twentieth Century British History*, vol. 4, no. 1 (1993), 57

Ina Zweiniger-Bargielowska, 'Rationing, Austerity and the Conservative Party Recovery after 1945', in the *Historical Journal*, vol. 37, no.1 (1994), 173

# Index

Aberdeen South, 122
Abingdon, 269
Acland, Sir Richard, 65
Accrington, 70, 126, 294
Addison, Paul, 21, 39, 63, 65, 178
Agents, 49–51, 69–71, 95, 103–6, 136,
    225, 227; *CAJ*, 49, 62–3, 96, 103,
    105–9, 148, 224, 226; NSA, 63, 71,
    95, 104–8
*Agricultural Charter*, 159–60
Aims of Industry, 191
Alamein, battle of, 32
Alexander of Tunis, Earl, 243–4
Alport, Cuthbert ('Cub'), 12, 93, 117,
    144, 147–8, 150, 221
Amery, Julian, 42, 244, 260, 264, 307
Amery, Leo, 15, 19, 23, 30, 31, 35, 42,
    46, 83, 86–7, 140
Anderson, Sir John, 15, 21, 46, 178,
    183, 243, 245
Anstruther-Gray, William, 66, 271
anti-Communism, 81, 164–5, 197, 262
areas, Eastern, 34, 36, 45, 51, 122–3,
    139, 156, 160, 328; East Midlands, 35,
    86, 111, 129–30, 136, 190, 223, 226;
    Home Counties South East, 33, 35,
    86, 121, 139, 154, 162, 313; London,
    156, 267; Northern, 34, 51, 78, 108,
    116, 119, 155–6, 198, 226, 240, 270,
    327; North West, 51, 115, 140, 276;
    Scotland, 140; Wales, 155, 160, 252,
    328; Wessex, 43, 70, 130, 140, 200;
    West Midlands, 58, 63, 68, 85, 99,
    130, 156, 160, 226, 229; Yorkshire,
    45, 56, 106, 156, 211, 290, 294
Army Bureau of Current Affairs, 59,
    63, 90
Asquith, Cyril, 244
Assheton, Ralph, in wartime, 22, 25,
    35, 42, 44–5, 47, 54, 58, 60, 62, 69,
    73–5, 78–9, 87, 91; post-war, 95–6,

98, 100, 141, 144–5, 150, 167, 183,
197, 223, 250, 264, 266
Ashton-under-Lyne, 100
Astor, David, 320
Astor, John Jacob, 310
Astor, Nancy, 50
Astor, Waldorf, 41
Attlee, Clement, 15, 20, 37–8, 61, 63,
    65, 82–3, 87, 127, 165, 169, 181,
    196–7, 214–16, 220, 278, 283
Attlee Government, 9, 138, 147, 166,
    174, 177, 186, 190, 246–7, 195
Australia, 4
Aylesbury, 49

Baldwin, Stanley, Earl Baldwin of
    Bewdley, 1–3, 8, 12, 14, 16, 25, 64,
    80, 87, 89, 102, 152, 172, 195, 216,
    231, 257–8, 271, 280–1, 285
Balfour, Arthur James, 3, 172
Ball, Sir Joseph, 73, 96, 144
Bank of England, 141, 186
Banks, Cyril, 310, 318
Barnet, 156–7, 198
Barnsley, 65, 220
Barry, 112, 115, 134, 202, 246
Bath, 70, 126, 274, 313
Battersea South, 167, 303
Beamish, Tufton, 206, 313
Beardmore, George, 81
Beaverbrook, 1st Lord, in wartime, 14,
    17–20, 22–3, 27, 31, 35, 60, 255; in
    1945 General Election, 75–7, 79, 82–3,
    86, 89, 91; post-war, 99, 155, 167,
    196, 216, 247, 327
Beckenham, 125
Bedford, 304
Bedfordshire South, 200
Beeching Plan, 9
Belper, 106, 110
Bennett, Air Vice Marshal Donald, 299

Bennett, Peter, 149

Bevan, Aneurin, 9, 39, 61, 127, 165, 168, 172, 174, 185, 215, 219, 256, 265, 278, 306, 320

Beveridge, Sir William, 87, 153, 223, 252

Beveridge Report, 2, 32, 42, 45–6, 49, 61, 158

Bevin, Ernest, 8, 15–17, 27, 46, 59, 63

Bevins, Reginald, 154, 286

Bewdley, 64

Bexley, 125, 208

Biffen, John, 120

Birkenhead, 107

Birmingham, 58, 62, 66, 86, 90, 105, 119, 121, 123, 126, 136, 149, 151, 156, 195, 212, 223, 278

Birmingham Sparkbrook, 78

Birmingham Yardley, 226

Birmingham, Bishop of, 64–5

Bishop Auckland, 210

Blackwell's bookshop, 165

Blain, Sir Herbert, 95

Blair, Colonel Patrick, 55, 75, 86

Blake, Robert, 218, 228, 269, 290

Bonham-Carter, Lady Violet, 201, 227–8

Booth, Arthur, 76–7, 81, 181, 215

Boothby, Robert, 89, 99, 186, 220, 237, 260–1, 268, 274, 310, 318

Bosworth, 106

Bournemouth, 100, 111, 318

Boyd-Carpenter, John, 77, 97, 155, 179, 239, 246, 284, 309

Boyle, Sir Edward, 220, 300, 304, 309–10, 318

Bracken, Brendan, in wartime, 6, 15, 19–20, 22, 29, 74–7, 79, 83, 87, 89, 91; post-war, 100–1, 111, 139, 149–50, 167–9, 180, 183, 188, 198, 210; 1951–57, 243, 248, 288, 290, 318

Bradford, 56, 62, 70, 72, 77, 110–12, 190, 197, 200, 240, 293, 298

Bradford South, 122, 191, 203

Brentford and Chiswick, 122, 124

Brewers, 190

Bridges, Sir Edward, 285

Bridgwater, 210

Brigg, 140, 211

Brighouse and Spenborough, 202–3

Brighton, 67–8, 73, 120

Bristol, 104, 121, 203

Bristol North East, 229

Bristol West, 225

British Broadcasting Corporation, 3, 36, 59, 63, 161, 165, 228, 230, 237, 244, 253–4, 280, 314

British Housewives' League, 169–71, 218

British Medical Association, 185, 190

British United Industrialists, 114

Broadcasting policy, 9–10, 222–3, 244, 252–4

Brogan, Denis, 64

Brooke, Henry, 23, 41, 125, 127–8, 133, 152, 160, 207, 236, 285

Brown, Ernest, 21, 53

Brown, W.J., 199, 299

Bruce-Lockhart, Robert, 182

Buchan-Hepburn, Patrick, 6, 98, 125, 184, 235, 239, 244, 248, 267, 270, 273, 285, 288, 290, 293–4, 302, 308, 321, 323–5, 328

Buckingham, 230

Buckinghamshire, 87, 165

Burn, W.L., 88

Burton upon Trent, 130, 163, 204

Bury St Edmunds, 42, 50, 63

business votes, 72

Butler, David, 136, 166, 213, 228, 268–9, 277, 279–80, 282

Butler, Richard Austen (Rab), pre-war, 1–2; in wartime, 5, 15–16, 18, 26–8, 34, 39–41, 44–5, 48, 53, 74; in 1945 General Election, 73, 75, 83, 87, 90; in opposition, 6, 93–4, 97, 101–2, 109, 117–18, 121, 160, 169–71, 182–3, 201; and Party policy-making, 139, 143–6, 148–55, 157, 159–63, 166, 173, 176, 189, 194–5, 214, 233, 236, 266, 276, 281, 291; in 1950–51, 217, 220–3, 228, 231; in the Churchill Government, 235, 241, 251, 253, 271–3; as Chancellor of the Exchequer, 243–5, 247–50, 256, 259, 266, 269, 275–6, 285, 287–90; in the Eden Government, 274, 279, 288–92, 308, 311–12, 316–17, 320; in the Leadership crisis of 1957 and after, 129, 321–8

'Butskellism', 8–9, 175, 248, 259

by-elections, wartime, 56–7, 66–9; 1945–50, 208–12; 1950–51, 225, 268–9; 1951–55, 234; 1955–57, 295, 313–14

Caithness and Sutherland, 203
Calder, Angus, 19
Callaghan, James, 314
Camberwell North, 50
Cambridge, 131, 156, 223, 269
Cambridge University, 147, 185, 233
Cambridgeshire, 70, 114, 269
Camrose, Lord, 179
Canada, 4
Cannock, 148
capital punishment, 293–4
Cardiff, 56, 118, 149, 155, 245
Cardiff North, 126
Cardiff South East, 114, 207
Carlton Club, 86
Carmarthen, 200
Carr, Robert, 126, 156, 219–21, 301
Cartland, Ronald, 66
Catering Wages Bill, 46
Central Office of Information, 162
Challen, Charles, 125
Chamberlain, Neville, 1–2, 8, 14–17, 19,
    25, 28–9, 37, 57, 102, 144, 152, 195–7,
    271, 328
Channon, Sir Henry ('Chips'), 20–1,
    28–30, 48, 68–70, 87, 165, 171, 177,
    179–80, 210, 217, 219
Chapman-Walker, Mark, 116, 160, 211,
    224, 253–5
Chatham, 77
Chelmsford, 67, 73
Cherwell, 1st Lord, 20, 91, 183, 243,
    248, 257
Chester, 305, 313–14
Chippenham, 67
Churchill, Clementine, 18, 179, 240, 264
Churchill, Randolph, 19, 215, 244, 258,
    286, 292, 311, 316, 322
Churchill, Winston S., as wartime
    Leader, 3–6, 12, 14–48, 59–65; and
    1945 General Election, 68, 72, 73–7,
    79–89, 91, 163; as Opposition Leader,
    6–8, 93, 96, 98–103, 110, 116, 118,
    125, 127, 135, 165, 169, 177–84, 186,
    194–9, 201–3, 209–12; and Party
    policy-making, 138–44, 150, 157–8,
    161–2, 166–7, 172–4, 189, 191, 195,
    214; in 1950–51, 215–16, 219, 222,
    224–5, 227–31; as Prime Minister
    in 1951–55, 10, 234, 237–9, 241–7,
    250–4, 257, 259, 263, 267, 269–74,
    277, 283, 285–7, 290, 295, 328; after

retirement, 274, 278, 293, 301, 325,
    327; *War Memoirs*, 3, 102, 118, 139,
    171, 177–8, 180, 261–2
Chuter-Ede, James, 47, 73
Clapham, 173, 226
Clarke, David, 145–6, 148–50, 173, 224
'Class of 1950', 11, 219
Clay Cross, 111
Clitheroe, 156
coal, 186–7, 189, 302
Cockerell, Michael, 280
Cole, Margaret, 84
Colegate, Arthur, 133
Colman, Sir Nigel, 302–3
Colonial policy, 195, 262–3, 305
Colville, John ('Jock'), 18, 58, 65, 75,
    77, 83–4, 240, 243, 272, 274
Combined English Universities, 147
Common Wealth Party, 67–8
Commonwealth, 35, 263
conscription, 250
Conservative Party, ACP, 135, 163,
    173, 222, 236, 252, 258, 276; ACPPE,
    117, 144–5, 155; Ashridge College,
    116; bookshops, 118; CBF, 113–15,
    123, 128–9; Central Office, 24, 96,
    104–5, 107, 109–10, 122, 131–2, 136,
    145, 163, 165, 169–71, 173, 184, 200,
    206–7, 211, 227, 237, 253, 276, 291;
    CPC, 117–18, 146, 155, 163; CRD,
    73, 96, 117, 136, 144–7, 160, 162–3,
    171–2, 174, 176, 190, 214, 221, 228,
    235–6, 247, 281, 289, 300; clubs, 112,
    114, 124; finance, 73, 90, 106, 110,
    113–15, 128–32, 224, 276; Liaison
    Committee, 235, 240–1; membership,
    110–12, 238, 240; missioners, 111,
    121–2; name, 197; *NCP*, 34, 62, 151,
    162, 252, 314; Party Chairmanship,
    22, 129, 135, 235, 291; Party
    Treasurers, 113, 129, 237–8, 251;
    party organisation, 4, 69–73, 90,
    94–137, 276; policy-making, 5–8,
    38–49, 128–76, 184–97, 221–4, 236–7,
    275–6; shadow cabinet, 91, 96, 141,
    143–4, 150, 155, 159, 179, 183–4,
    191, 195, 220, 223; SACC, 131;
    Swinton College, 116; trade union
    organisation, 117; Young Britons,
    113; YCs, 118–19, 135, 302–3; *see also*
    agents, areas, 'Class of 1950', films,
    National Union, 1922 Committee,
    PWPCC, TRG

Cooper, Duff, 15
Coote, Colin, 88
Cornwall North, 51, 90, 124, 294, 313
Courtauld, Samuel, 149
Courthorpe, George, 26
Coventry South, 226
Coward, Noel, 29, 76, 91–2, 215, 283, 322
Cranborne, Viscount, 5th Marquess of Salisbury, 7, 16, 36, 93, 102, 141–2, 160, 175–8, 192, 195, 201, 216, 244, 251, 253, 264, 271, 321
Crawford, H.E., 299
Crete, 28, 34
Crichel Down, 25, 239
Cripps, Sir Stafford, 15, 23, 26, 31–3, 165, 168, 172
Crisp, Dorothy, 169–70
Croft, Sir Henry Page, 152
Crookshank, Harry, 18–19, 30, 83, 86, 97–8, 100, 102, 113, 143, 150, 155, 179, 182–3, 186, 235, 239, 244, 249, 265, 270, 290
Crosland, Anthony, 43
Cross, John, 241
Crossman, Richard, 182, 240, 246, 264, 278–9, 310, 321
Croydon, 78, 110–11, 208, 210
Cudlipp, Hugh, 327
Czechoslovakia, 164

*Daily Express*, 59–60, 76–7, 82, 86, 99, 153, 216–17, 264, 303
*Daily Herald*, 33, 41, 82, 155, 162
*Daily Mail*, 216, 281
*Daily Mirror*, 3, 59, 65–7, 82, 228, 271, 278, 292, 327
*Daily Telegraph*, 74, 82, 88, 155, 160, 178, 216, 258–9, 292
*Daily Worker*, 322
Dalkeith, 183
Dalton, Hugh, 20, 26, 33, 35, 58, 85, 174, 210–11, 269, 274, 281
Darling, Sir William, 98, 164
Darlington, 51, 112, 206, 230
Dartford, 223
Davidson, J.C.C., 95, 123, 136
Davidson, Lady, 123, 133
Davies, Clement, 202, 245
Day, Robin, 255
Deedes, William, 210
Defence policy, 196, 247, 262, 264

de Courcy, Kenneth, 272
de Gaulle, Charles, 18,
Denbigh, 50, 70, 156, 203
Derby, 110, 114
Derby, 17th Earl of, 177
Derbyshire South, 173, 226
Derbyshire West, 56, 67–8, 123, 130
Devonshire, 10th Duke of, 68
Digby, Simon Wingfield, 43
Dimbleby, Richard, 191
Doncaster, 230
Dorking, 126
Dorset West, 43, 67, 121, 130, 294
Dover, 87
Driberg, Tom, 77, 79, 182, 192
du Cann, Edward, 295
Dugdale, Sir Thomas, 18, 22, 25, 107
Dulwich, 56
Dumfries, 77
Duncan, Sir Andrew, 193–4, 222
Dundee, 200
Dunglass, Lord, *see* Home, Earl of
Durham, Bishop of, 64
*Durham City Advertiser*, 51

Ealing South, 318
Easington, 112
East Grinstead, 126
East Ham North, 301
Eccles, Sir David, 67, 149, 187, 256, 321, 325
Eccleshall, Robert, 150
*The Economist*, 8, 48, 88, 211, 221, 233, 248, 259
Eddisbury, 67
Eden, Sir Anthony, 16, 177; in wartime, 3, 14–15, 19, 26–30, 35–7, 46, 48–9, 52, 63; and 1945 General Election, 75, 78–81, 83, 89–90; in opposition, 6, 8, 95–8, 100–3, 111, 132, 134, 148, 153, 165, 179–84, 192, 194–5, 197, 203, 216, 223, 228, 237; and policy-making, 140–3, 145, 154–5, 157, 159, 161, 163, 175, 186–9, 195, 197; in Churchill Government, 235, 244, 246–7, 250, 259, 266, 270–3; Foreign Secretary, 237, 243–4, 260–5; Prime Minister, 10, 233, 244, 274–82, 283–8, 290–4, 296, 298, 302–4, 305–9, 311–16, 320–2, 325, 328
Eden, John, 238
Eden, Lady, 321

Edinburgh, 78, 149, 245, 300
Edinburgh East, 50, 86, 122
Edinburgh North, 37, 70
Edmonton, 160, 208, 210
Education policy, 39–40, 48, 186
Edwards, Capt. R.H., 105
Eisenhower, President, 323
elections, *see* by-elections, General
  Elections, local elections
electoral law, 71–2, 132–3, 199, 212–15,
  218
electricity, 44, 185, 193
Eliot, Walter, 27, 97, 100, 120, 147, 170,
  172, 185, 220, 237, 242, 310, 325
Elliot, Katharine, 133
Ellis, Vivian, 117
Emmet, Evelyn, 234, 303
Enfield, 87, 157, 160
Epping, 72
Epsom, 99
equal pay, 48, 151, 249
Errol, Frederick, 97
Esher, 225
Erskine-Hill, Sir Alec, 28, 30
European integration, 195–6, 260–2,
  304–5
*Evening Standard*, 74, 286, 292
Exeter, 196

*Fabian Journal*, 134
Fairlie, Henry, 274–5, 286, 290
Falmouth, 204
Farnham, 113
Federation of British Industries, 191
Fell, Anthony, 211
Fenby, Charles, 82
Fields, Gracie, 117
Films, Party, 94, 116, 224, 228
Fisher, Nigel, 323
Flintshire, 207, 237
food policy, 168–72, 247–9
Foot, Michael, 60, 74, 215
Forfar, 122
'Fourth Party', 43
Fox, Marcus, 116
Fraser, Ian, 302
Fraser, Michael, 98, 145–6, 148–9, 155,
  159–60, 227, 240, 251–2, 257, 276
freedom rhetoric, 10, 164, 222, 247–9,
  253–4
Freeman, John, 270
Fulham West, 199
Fulton, Missouri, 197

Gainsborough, 295
Gaitskell, Hugh, 8, 171, 283, 288–9,
  310–12, 314
Galloway, 50
Gallup polls, *see* opinion polls
gas, 188, 193
Gates, Ernest, 43
Gateshead, 56
General Elections, 1945, 4–7, 12, 57, 61,
  72–3, 75–92, 103, 125; 1950, 162, 194,
  201, 208, 215–18; 1951, 116, 226–31;
  1955, 10, 275–82, 284
Getty, Paul, 124
Gilbert, Martin, 22, 47, 177
Glasgow, 51, 72, 84, 88, 97, 149, 208,
  225, 269, 278
*Glasgow Herald*, 84
Glasgow Pollok, 51
Glasgow Scotstoun, 122
Glasgow University, 147
Gloucester, 250
Goldman, Peter, 145–6
Gollancz, Victor, 3, 61
Goodhart, Philip, 211
Gordon Walker, Patrick, 281–2
Graesser, Alastair, 207
Grantham, 67, 106
Grattan-Doyle, Sir Nicholas, 66
Gravesend, 57, 121, 123, 209, 222, 240
Greece, 28, 49
Greenock, 200
Greenwich, 173
Greenwood, Arthur, 172
Grigg, Sir James, 22, 56, 87
Gubbins, Nat, 60
Guildford, 50, 56, 122, 130, 139, 156,
  162, 199, 226, 273, 293
*Guilty Men*, 14, 60, 118

Hacking, Sir Douglas, 22, 24–5, 46, 53
Hailsham, *see* Hogg
Haining, General, 124
Halifax, 1st Earl of, 14, 17, 26, 195, 210
Halliley, Elton, 63, 69, 90, 105, 107, 110
Hammersmith South, 160, 163, 210–12,
  268
Hampshire North, 51
Hampstead, 66, 122, 125, 222, 310
Harborough, 111, 226
Hardman, Fred, 148
Hare, John, 139, 207, 234
Harris, Nigel, 163
Harrisson, Tom, 13, 43, 74

Harrow, 68, 81, 310
Harrow School, 64
Harrow West, 110, 121, 123
Hartlepool, 110
Harvey, Ian, 2, 160
Harvey, John, 226
Harvey, Oliver, 28
Harvie-Watt, Sir George, 17, 22, 27,
    31–2, 37, 53, 67, 73, 75, 80
Hay, John, 119, 143
Hayek, Friedrich von, 62, 74, 83, 164
Headlam, Cuthbert, in wartime, 22,
    25, 29–32, 38, 45–6, 67, 74, 78, 86–7;
    post-war, 95, 97, 102, 106, 113, 125,
    138, 146, 157, 169, 192, 194, 209, 211,
    215, 219–20, 287
Heald, Sir Lionel, 309
Heath, Edward, 125–6, 160, 219, 221,
    244, 290–1, 293, 296–7, 303, 310,
    316–18, 325, 328
Heathcoat Amory, Derick, 97, 149, 151,
    243, 294, 308
Hemel Hempstead, 70, 123, 267
Hendon North, 156–7, 165
Henley, 87
Hennessy, Peter, 166
Hereford, 295
Heston and Isleworth, 78, 121
Hexham, 50, 114
High Peak, 43, 119, 130, 157, 203, 294
Hill, Dr. Charles, 185, 200, 216, 228,
    244
Hinchingbrooke, Viscount, 42, 307
Hinsley, Cardinal, 27
Hitchin, 87, 115
Hoare, Sir Samuel, Viscount
    Templewood, 14, 27, 100
Hoffman, J.D., 166–7
Hogg, Quintin, 2nd Viscount Hailsham,
    42–4, 61–2, 101, 131, 139, 143, 146,
    148, 160–1, 171, 253, 308, 323
Holborn and St.Pancras South, 209, 268
Home, 14th Earl of, 37, 77, 100, 219,
    243, 245–6, 284–6
Home Guard, 50, 244
Honiton, 110
Hopkinson, Henry, 263
Hore-Belisha, Leslie, 203
Horncastle, 34, 226
Horne, Alistair, 315
Hornsby-Smith, Patricia, 228
Horsbrugh, Florence, 216, 242

Houghton-le-Spring, 110
housing policy, 20, 80, 168–9, 172–4,
    245, 247, 255–7
Howard, Anthony, 149, 182
Howard, Sir John, 234
Huddersfield, 110, 204–5, 251
Hudson, Robert, 15, 108, 227
Hull, 141, 186
Hutchinson, James, 149

Ilford, 51, 121
immigration, 262
Imperial Airways, 9
*Imperial Charter*, 159
Imperial Group, 5
*The Independent*, 130
India, 35, 194, 262
*The Industrial Charter*, 7, 8, 146–8,
    150–3, 155–8, 160–4, 175, 189, 209,
    245
Industrial Policy Committee, 143,
    148–50, 153
iron and steel, *see* steel
inflation, 297
Islington East, 50, 139, 209
Ismay, 1st Lord, 243

James, Sir Archibald, 182
Jarrow, 84, 124
Jay, Douglas, 207
Jebb, Gladwyn, 325
Jenkin, Patrick, 176
Jenkins, Roy, 242
Jones, Aubrey, 143
Jones, Harriet, 9, 32, 62, 166, 256
Joseph, Sir Keith, 310
Junior Imperial League, 118

Kandiah, Michael, 98–9
Keir, Thelma Cazalet, 43, 50
Kennedy, Captain, 49
Kettering, 51, 109, 113
Keynes, John Maynard, 80, 153
Kilmuir, *see* Maxwell Fyfe
King-Hall, Sir Stephen, 76
Kings Lynn, 42, 50, 64, 122, 188, 230
Kingsmill, William Henry, 220
Kingston-upon-Thames, 78
Kirk, Peter, 310
Korean War, 10, 185, 219, 227, 247

*Labour's Great Lie*, 62

Ladies' Carlton Club, 114
Lanark, 100
Lane, Allen, 3
Laski, Harold, 83
Law, Andrew Bonar, 1, 16, 25, 271, 290
Law, Richard, 16, 26, 100, 183, 222
League of Empire Loyalists, 297–8, 301
Leeds, 45, 118, 121, 149, 183, 225
*The Left Were Never Right*, 61
Legge-Bourke, Harry, 263, 302
Leicester, 127, 149, 212
Leicester North East, 203, 248–9
Lennox-Boyd, Alan, 325
Levin, Bernard, 292
Lewes, 50, 267
Lewisham, 301
Liberal Party, 197–8, 200, 202–5,
    214–15, 227, 230, 245, 277, 299; *see
    also* National Liberals
Lichfield, 68, 91, 223
Lincoln, 226
Liverpool, 115, 149, 300, 323
Liverpool Garston, 125, 319
*Liverpool Post*, 182
Llandudno, 120
Lloyd, Geoffrey, 243, 257
Lloyd, Selwyn, 97, 129, 160, 168,
    222–3, 240, 242–3, 261, 265–6, 278,
    285, 288, 294, 313–15, 317–18, 320–2,
    325, 327
Lloyd George, Gwylim, 203, 227, 244,
    249, 293
Lloyd George, Lady Megan, 228
local elections, 1945–50, 103, 208–9,
    212; 1950–1, 225; 1951–5, 234, 239,
    268
London, City of, 72, 193, 213
London County Council, 1, 206, 240
London Municipal Society, 207–8
London Passenger Transport Board, 187
Longden, Gilbert, 221
Lords, House of, 92, 254, 293
Loughborough, 106
Low, David, 60, 82
Low, Sir Francis, 124
Luton, 122, 185, 200
Lyttelton, Oliver, 6, 15–16, 21, 44, 96,
    100, 148–50, 191–2, 203, 245, 251

McCallum, R.B., and Readman, Alison,
    55, 76, 80, 84, 87, 92, 209
McCorquodale, Malcolm, 235, 291

Maclean, Fitzroy, 264
Macleod, Iain, 72–3, 94, 133, 145–6,
    156, 160, 166–7, 176, 207–8, 219–22,
    237, 259, 265–6, 277, 289–90, 294–5,
    300–1, 325
Macmillan, Harold, 16, 181; pre-war, 2,
    117, 141, 152, 186, 188; in wartime,
    15–16, 65, 78, 86–7, 89; in opposition,
    6, 96, 100, 102, 109, 113, 165, 171,
    182–3, 197–8, 203, 218–19, 228–9; and
    Party policy-making, 139, 146, 148–9,
    153–7, 160–1, 174; in Churchill
    Government, 235, 242, 251, 257,
    260–1, 269, 271, 273; as Minister of
    Housing, 10, 241, 245, 255–7; in Eden
    Government, 274, 276, 279, 285–8,
    303, 307, 310, 316–18; as Chancellor
    of the Exchequer, 290, 303–5, 308,
    315–16; becomes Leader, 312, 321–8;
    later, 235, 297, 318, 320
Macrae, Norman, 276
Maidstone, 316
Major, John, 288
Maldon, 67
Manchester, 111, 149, 212, 289
*Manchester Guardian*, 74, 76, 82, 227, 276
Mander, Geoffrey, 60
Margesson, David, 1st Viscount
    Margesson, 15, 21–2, 30, 199
Marples, Ernest, 97, 174, 243, 286
Martell, Edward, 299–302
Massingham, Hugh, 256, 271, 286
Mass Observation, 64, 69, 74, 89, 91
Maude, Angus, 219, 221–2, 307, 318
Maudling, Reginald, 116, 126, 133, 142,
    145–6, 148–9, 156–8, 198, 219–20,
    250, 312
Mawby, Ray, 258
Maxwell, Robert, 134
Maxwell Fyfe, Sir David, 1st Earl
    of Kilmuir, 40, 100, 115, 133, 142,
    148–9, 160, 169, 183, 188, 216, 245–6,
    258, 260, 267, 271, 276, 278, 285–6,
    294, 309–10, 321, 324–5, 327
Maxwell Fyfe Report, 11, 94, 127–35,
    173, 233, 237, 268, 277, 286, 298
Medlicott, Sir Frank, 310, 318
Melton, 226, 318
MPs' salaries, 267–8
Mendés-France, Pierre, 195
Menzies, Sir Robert, 101
Middle Class Alliance, 298

Middlesbrough, 72, 207
Middleton and Prestwich, 43
*The Middle Way*, 152–3, 188
Mikardo, Ian, 193
Milne, R.S., and Mackenzie, H.C., 229
'Mr. Cube', 193–4, 218
Mitcham, 156
Mitchell, Leslie, 228
Molson, Hugh, 42–3, 144, 157
Monckton, Sir Walter, 225, 237, 245, 257–60, 269, 288, 308–9
Monday Club, 319
Monmouth, 122, 310, 319
Monsell, 1st Viscount, 40
Montgomery, 202
Moran, 1st Lord, 76, 83–4, 99, 101, 178, 180, 215, 264, 272
Morrison, Herbert, 8, 15–16, 58, 98, 187, 192, 206
Morrison, W.S., 27
Mortimer, Raymond, 76
Mountbatten, Lord, 308
Muggeridge, Malcolm, 282
Munro, Patrick, 50

Nabarro, Gerald, 302
Nasser, President, 305, 318
National Farmers' Union, 34
National Health Service, 9, 44, 52, 70, 79–80, 161, 166–8, 170, 178, 185–6, 265–6
National Insurance, 185–6, *see also* Beveridge Report
nationalisation, 43–4, 151–2, 183, 186–94, 201, 222, 251
National Labour Party, 53, 77
National Liberal Party, 53, 67, 77, 87, 200–5
*National Review*, 43, 45
National Society for Freedom, 43
National Union of Conservative and Unionist Associations, Central Council, 35, 38, 58, 101, 128–9, 131, 144, 159–60, 234, 238, 256, 263; conferences: 1943 (London), 56, 69; 1945 (London), 39, 52, 54, 56, 69, 75; 1946 (Blackpool), 7, 109, 120, 141, 143, 154; 1947 (Brighton), 113, 115–16, 120, 127, 132, 153, 156–8, 164, 189, 198; 1948 (Llandudno), 112, 128–9, 160, 189, 196; 1949 (London), 120, 161, 181,

190; 1950 (Blackpool), 120, 173–4, 193, 219; 1952 (Scarborough), 235–6, 240; 1953 (Margate) 250, 254, 256; 1954 (Blackpool), 272, 284; 1955 (Bournemouth), 289–90; 1956 (Llandudno), 293, 298, 302, 307; Executive Committee, wartime: 32, 36, 44, 57, 59, 70, 105–6, 131; in 1945–51, 95, 108, 110, 113, 115, 119–20, 127–9, 133, 135, 140, 143, 148, 154, 158–60, 185, 194, 197–9, 201–3; in 1951–57, 236–7, 239, 256, 262, 275, 326; General Purposes Committee, 313; Local Government Advisory Committee, 206, 223; Speakers and Publicity Committee, 241; Trade Union Advisory Committee, 258; Women's Advisory Committee, 234
Nelson and Colne, 163, 206
Newark, 114, 240
Newbury, 124
Newcastle-under-Lyme, 63
Newcastle-upon-Tyne, 108, 149
Newcastle-upon-Tyne East, 201–2
Newcastle-upon-Tyne North, 66–7, 227
Newport, Monmouthshire, 73, 122
*News Chronicle*, 69, 159, 227, 292
Newton-le-Willows, 121
New Towns, 223, 249
Nicholas, H.G., 136, 215–16
Nicholls, Harmar, 173, 256
Nicolson, Sir Harold, 18, 26, 38, 42, 45, 64, 83
Nicolson, Nigel, 284, 309–11, 318
1922 Committee, in wartime, 15, 17, 20, 24, 28–33, 35, 37, 59, 66, 131; post-war, 98, 102, 129, 135, 154, 163, 198, 211, 220; 1951–55, 238–9, 241, 245, 253, 262, 264; 1955–57, 274, 306, 315, 321–4, 326
Niven, David, 65
Norfolk, 87, 188, 281
North Fylde, 206
Norwich, 212
Nottingham, 104, 225–6
Nuneaton, 85
Nutting, Anthony, 203, 292, 309–10, 328, 320

The *Observer*, 153, 271, 286, 320
One Nation Group, 11, 221, 223, 233, 252

opinion polls, 57, 69, 85, 192–3, 216, 225, 239, 242, 268, 278–9, 292, 314–15
Ormskirk, 108
Orpington, 269
Orr-Ewing, Ian, 126, 157–8, 252
Oxford, 131
Oxford University, 147, 233

Paddington North, 157, 210, 268
Parkinson, Cecil, 123
Party truce, 55–8, 66
Patten, Chris, 40, 176, 250, 312
Peake, Osbert, 266
Pelling, Henry, 178
Penistone, 210
Penryn and Falmouth, 56
People's League for the Defence of Freedom, 298–302
Petersfield, 56
Phillips, Morgan, 165
*Picture Post*, 48, 60
Pierssené, Sir Stephen, 96, 103, 105, 107, 110, 128, 132, 135, 200, 209–11, 220, 251, 254, 296
Pinto-Duschinsky, Michael, 129
Plymouth, 50, 215
Poland, 37
Pontefract, 112, 237
Pontypool, 122
Poole, Oliver, 25, 155, 160, 163, 222, 277, 191, 198–9, 313, 321, 325
Portal, 1st Viscount, 20
postal votes, 213, 277
Post War Problems Central Committee, 5, 40–1, 45, 54, 57, 144, 152, 206
Powell, Enoch, 126, 141, 145–6, 219, 221–2, 236, 238, 252, 257, 264–6, 286, 289
Premium Bonds, 304
Prentice, Reginald, 302
Price, Henry, 298
Priestley, J.B., 59–60, 65
Profumo, John, 116, 223, 253, 280
Progress Trust, 5, 43, 317
'Property-Owning Democracy', 141, 159, 175, 188, 211, 223, 255–6
*Punch*, 292

Raikes, Victor, 319
railways, 9, 188–9, 193
Ramsden, Sir Eugene, 26
Rawlinson, Peter, 306–7, 315–16, 322

Reading, 230
recruiting, *see* Conservative Party, membership
redistribution of seats, 4, 71–2, 213, 277
Redmayne, Martin, 302
Reid, Sir Charles, 187, 189
Reigate, 240
Resale Price Maintenance, 227
Rhodes James, Robert, 285, 303, 310, 321
*The Right Road for Britain*, 160, 163, 165 167, 174, 212, 214, 223
Ripon, 43, 134
Rippon, Geoffrey, 78, 143
road haulage, 170, 190–1, 251–2
Roberts, Harold, 220
Roberts, Margaret, later Margaret Thatcher, 223
'Robot' scheme, 8, 248
Robson Brown, William, 127, 133, 154
Roosevelt, President F.D., 30
Rosebery, 6th Earl of, 16
Ross, J.F.S., 131
Rowse, A.L., 172
Rugby, 67–8, 90, 199
Ruislip, 124
Runcorn, 202
Rush, Michael, 134
Rushcliffe, 78, 154, 226
Russia, 8, 12, 20, 27–9, 35–9, 81–2, 196–7, 216, 261–2
Rutland and Stamford, 104

Saffron Walden, 34, 121, 130, 161, 199, 303
St. Albans, 210
St. Marylebone, 124, 310
Salisbury, 4th Marquess of, 40
Salisbury, 5th Marquess of, *see* Cranborne
Salter, 1st Lord, 245
Sandys, Duncan, 6, 15, 144, 237, 244, 251, 260, 325
Sargent, Malcolm, 117
Scarborough, 120
Scotland, 55, 86, 146, 183, 245
The *Scotsman*, 140
Scottish Universities, 147
Selborne, 3rd Earl of, 21, 47
Seldon, Anthony, 247
Seldon, Arthur, 222
Selkirk, 10th Earl of, 308

Sevenoaks, 44
Shawcross, Sir Hartley, 169
Sheffield, 109, 120, 123, 156, 172, 209, 251
Sheffield Central, 51, 90, 200
Shinwell, Emmanuel, 34, 39, 165, 169, 278
Shonfield, Andrew, 304
Shoreditch and Finsbury. 204
Shrewsbury, 70, 121, 204, 300
Siedentop, Larry, 303–4
Simon, 1st Viscount, 14, 53, 203
Sinclair, Sir Archibald, 53, 203
Singapore, fall of, 31
Skelton, Noel, 141
Skipton, 67–8
Slim, General Sir William, 90
Smethwick, 85, 198
Smith, Justin Davis, 259
Smithers, Sir Waldron, 139, 154–5, 158, 170
Smuts, J.C., 179
*Socialist Commentary*, 270
Solihull, 294
Somervell, Sir Donald, 87
Southampton, 156, 225
Southby, Sir Archibald, 27
Southend, 21, 87, 223
South Shields, 165
Speaker's Conference, 71–2, 212
Spearman, Sir Alexander, 310
The *Spectator*, 3, 74, 131, 153, 274
Stanley, Oliver, 16, 24, 27, 40, 97, 99, 148, 153, 168–9, 182, 186, 225, 245, 287
steel industry, 9, 190–3, 222, 251
Stockton on Tees, 78, 86, 171
Stokes, Richard, 39
Strachey, John, 169
Stuart, James, in wartime, 6, 16, 19, 22–3, 26–7, 35, 47, 55–7; and 1945 General Election, 75, 83, 86; post-war, 98, 102, 112, 141, 148, 179, 183–4; in Churchill Government, 238, 241, 243, 270; in Eden Government, 274, 293, 302, 308, 315, 317, 321, 328
Suez Canal, 10–11, 263–5, 283–4, 300, 303, 305–18
sugar industry, 193
Summers, Sir Spencer, 43
Sunderland South, 268–9
*Sunday Times*, 33

Sussex, 206
Swansea, 202
Swindon, 130, 132
Swinton, 1st Earl of, 14, 40, 77, 116, 147, 183, 192, 194, 240–1, 244, 274, 279, 285

Tamworth Manifesto, 148, 165
Tate, Mavis Constance, 36
Tate and Lyle, 193–4
Taunton, 295, 314
taxation, 50, 151, 164, 175, 227, 248, 275
Taylor, A.J.P., 15, 82
Tebbit, Norman, 87, 123
Teeling, William, 67, 97, 130
Temple, William, Archbishop of Canterbury, 64
Teviot, 1st Lord, 200
*This is the Road*, 162
Thomas, J.P.L. ('Jim'), 17, 45, 96, 102, 124–5, 132, 142, 177–8, 184, 197, 202, 205–11, 225, 234, 255
Thorneycroft, Peter, 42, 44, 100, 148, 150, 157, 191, 198, 319, 321, 325
Thurtle, Ernest, 15
*The Times*, 82, 88, 216, 297, 325
Tonbridge, 295–6, 314
Topping, Sir Robert, 36, 54, 56–7, 68, 71–2, 96, 105–6
Torquay, 295
Tory Reform Group. 5, 41–5, 48–9, 152
Totnes, 51, 77, 124
Town and Country Planning, 47
trade unions, 162, 185, 257–60
Trethowan, Ian, 292
Truro, 130, 222
Twickenham, 122
Tynemouth, 50, 206

unemployment, 47–8, 151, 229, 249, 289
United Industrialists' Association, *see* British United Industrialists
United States of America, 34, 102, 139, 195, 261, 305, 313, 317, 323, 326–7
Urton, William, 328
Uthwatt Report, 47
Uxbridge, 103, 111, 124

Wakefield, 251
Wales, 85, 119, 146, 183
Walker, Fred, 105–6

Walker, Peter, 207
Walker Smith, Derek, 238, 270–1
Wallasey, 67, 73, 156
Waller, Ian, 292
Walsall, 51, 124, 139, 203, 245
Walthamstow, 84, 187, 226, 278, 296
Wandsworth, 226
Wardlaw-Milne, Sir John, 31
Warwick and Leamington, 51, 134, 207, 226, 278, 294
Waterhouse, Capt. Charles, 27, 133, 264, 307
Watkinson, Harold, 65, 123–4, 126, 220, 243, 259–60, 300, 309
Wembley North, 111
Western Isles, 72
Westhoughton, 225
*We were not all wrong*, 60
White, Charles, 56
Whitelaw, William, 307
*Why not trust the Tories?*, 61
Wigg, Col. George, 59
Williams, Sir Herbert, 45–7, 75, 133, 154–8, 185, 194, 196, 218, 222, 236
Willink, Henry, 29, 46, 78–9
Wilson, Harold, 168, 304, 320
Wimbledon, 87
Winchester, 87
Winterton, 6th Earl, 30, 178, 183
Wirral, 160, 240, 313
Woking, 124, 226
Wolmer, *see* Selborne
Wolverhampton, 161, 223, 251
Wood, Sir Kingsley, 14–15, 19–20, 27, 31, 35, 46–7
Wood, Richard, 310

Woodford, 121, 189, 226, 278
Woolton, 1st Earl of, in wartime, 15, 18, 38, 42; Party Chairman in opposition, 6, 94–7, 103–5, 107, 109–21, 125, 132–3, 135–7, 182–5, 190, 196–205, 209, 211, 216, 218–19, 228–30; and Party policy-making, 143, 145, 147, 150, 158–63, 165, 170–1, 173; and Churchill Government, 234–7, 241, 246, 248, 250–1, 253–5, 273; and Eden Government, 275–7, 279, 282, 284, 288, 290–1, 299, 321, 323
Woolton, Lady, 235
Woolwich East, 173
Woolwich West, 111
Worcestershire, 80
*Workers' Charter*, 159
Workers' Educational Association, 59, 63
Workington, 109, 140, 158
Worthing, 147
Wrekin, 318
Wyndham, John, 146, 240

Yarmouth, 140, 230
Yates, William, 307, 310, 319
York, Christopher, 43
*Yorkshire Post*, 45, 83, 109, 275
Young, G.M., 257
Young, Kenneth, 284
'Young England', 43
*Your MP*, 60

Zweiniger-Bargielowska, Ina, 169